Pottery in the Making

Pottery in the Making

World Ceramic Traditions

Edited by
Ian Freestone and David Gaimster

Published for the Trustees of the British Museum by
British Museum Press

This book is published in conjunction with the exhibition *Pottery in the Making: World Ceramic Traditions*, supported by the British Museum Society and mounted by the British Museum at the Museum of Mankind, 6 Burlington Gardens, London W1, from 3 July to 31 December 1997. Related events include a conference on Ceramic Technology and Production organised by the Department of Scientific Research, a Crafts Council funded Potters in Residence programme and a public lecture series, organised by the Education Service. An associated exhibition entitled *Touching the Past: Evidence of Tradition*, mounted by the Craft Potters Association to show the work of potters mentioned in the final chapter of this book, runs from 5 to 20 September 1997 at Contemporary Ceramics, 7 Marshall Street, London W1.

Front cover: Detail of a Predynastic Egyptian Black-topped pottery vessel, *c.* 4500 BC (see ch. 5, p. 46). Photo by Anthony J. Milton ARPS, BM Photographic Service (BM EA 27753)

Frontispiece: Female potter, from a pack of playing cards presented to the imperial Habsburg court, mid-15th century (see ch. 18, fig. 2, p. 123). Courtesy of the Kunstkammer, Kunsthistorisches Museum, Vienna (KK 5105)

Back cover: Wood-burning stoneware kiln, photographed through the spy-hole by the potter. Courtesy of Nic Collins, Powdermills Pottery, Dartmoor, Devon

© 1997 The Trustees of the British Museum
Published by British Museum Press
A division of The British Museum Company Ltd
46 Bloomsbury Street, London WC1B 3QQ

ISBN 0-7141-1782-X

A catalogue record for this book is available from the British Library

Designed in Photina by James Shurmer

Photography by British Museum Photographic Service

Origination by Jade Reprographics Ltd, London

Printed in the UK by Jarrold Book Printing, Norfolk

Contributors

Donald M. Bailey (*Greek & Roman Antiquities*)

Nigel Barley (*Ethnography*)

T. Richard Blurton (*Oriental Antiquities*)

Sheila R. Canby (*Oriental Antiquities*)

Emmanuel Cooper (*Ceramic Review*)

Aileen Dawson (*Medieval & Later Antiquities*)

Ian Freestone (*Scientific Research*)

David Gaimster (*Medieval & Later Antiquities*)

Cathy Haith (*Medieval & Later Antiquities*)

Victor Harris (*Japanese Antiquities*)

Jessica Harrison-Hall (*Oriental Antiquities*)

Julie Hudson (*Ethnography*)

Pamela Magrill (*Western Asiatic Antiquities*)

Colin McEwan (*Ethnography*)

Andrew Middleton (*Scientific Research*)

Beverley Nenk (*Medieval & Later Antiquities*)

Jane Portal (*Oriental Antiquities*)

Val Rigby (*Prehistoric & Romano-British Antiquities*)

Paul Roberts (*Greek & Roman Antiquities*)

Louise Schofield (*Greek & Roman Antiquities*)

St John Simpson (*Western Asiatic Antiquities*)

A. J. Spencer (*Egyptian Antiquities*)

Dora Thornton (*Medieval & Later Antiquities*)

Gillian Varndell (*Prehistoric and Romano-British Antiquities*)

Derek Welsby (*Egyptian Antiquities*)

Dyfri Williams (*Greek & Roman Antiquities*)

Contents

Director's Foreword

The British Museum has long prided itself as being a universal museum of archaeology and antiquities. From time to time, this view has been publicly expressed: giving evidence to the Royal Commission on National Museums and Galleries in October 1928, the Keeper of Ceramics and Ethnography offered his view that the collection was 'designed to illustrate the whole history of pottery all over the world'.

In fact, the pottery collection has always been scattered amongst many departments in the Museum and has never been brought together for public exhibition. *Pottery in the Making* takes up the challenge. The boundaries which are introduced by treating cultural groups separately can in some ways be practical and useful but in others can be detrimental to more complete understanding. The focus in both exhibition and book is on the working methods of the potters themselves, their raw materials and production techniques, whether within the family, workshop or factory. We know that this approach will have wide appeal, and it is gratifying that the British Museum Society, strong supporters of innovation in the Museum, have provided a substantial sum of money to enable the exhibition to take place. Similarly, through their generous grant, the Crafts Council has funded the Potters in Residence programme, providing an added dynamic to the whole event.

The British Museum is uniquely placed to put on an exhibition of this kind, with its remarkable breadth and depth of collections. The work is a joint effort, involving nine departments and twenty-five curators. Nevertheless, I would like to express my special thanks to Ian Freestone, Head of Ceramics in the Department of Scientific Research, and David Gaimster, curator in the Department of Medieval and Later Antiquities. *Pottery in the Making* is their concept and they have co-ordinated a remarkable collaborative project in the British Museum.

R G W ANDERSON

Editors' Acknowledgements

Over the course of a four-year gestation period the organisers of this exhibition and editors of this book have accumulated many debts. Much of that indebtedness stems from the enthusiasm and encouragement of a group of like-minded colleagues without whose support this project would never have been realised: most notably Dr Robert Anderson, Director, British Museum; Dr Sheridan Bowman, Keeper, Scientific Research; Neil Stratford, Keeper, and John Cherry, Deputy Keeper, Medieval and Later Antiquities; Dr Dyfri Williams, Keeper, Greek and Roman Antiquities; Lawrence Smith, Keeper, Japanese Antiquities; Dr John Mack, Keeper of Ethnography; Dr Nigel Barley, Ethnography; Dr St John Simpson, Western Asiatic Antiquities; Dr Andrew Middleton, Scientific Research; Margaret Hall, Head of Design; Sarah Carthew, Head of the British Museum Society; Chris Jones, Head of Administration; and Nigel Wood, Ceramics Department, University of Westminster. Equally, we are grateful to our twenty-five curatorial colleagues who have contributed lucid and informative texts and display material on their own subject areas, to our team of 'potters in residence' who have brought such a welcome dynamic element to the exhibition, and to Emmanuel Cooper, co-editor of *Ceramic Review*, who has written the final chapter.

Such a large number of contributors, however, require careful organisation, and we reserve our greatest appreciation for Nina Shandloff, Senior Editor at British Museum Press, who, virtually single-handedly, has steered this not insubstantial volume through to final publication. The editors owe her much, particularly for her infinite patience (with us), good humour and fortitude throughout the long process of turning what seemed like a good idea at the time into a real book. In turn, Nina wishes to thank James Shurmer, book designer, and his family; Mitzi Bales, editorial reader; Lesley Adkins, indexer; Bob Lockhart of the Smithsonian Institution Press; and her colleagues at British Museum Press, especially Emma Way, Head of the Press; Julie Young, Production Manager, and her deputy Susanna Friedman; the rights and marketing team of Alasdair MacLeod, Katherine West, Liz Edwards, Caroline Sanderson, Salma Blackburn and Jane Hovey; and publishing assistants Catherine Wood and Jemima Scott-Holland. In addition, she would like to acknowledge the support of Gaynor Lindsell, Vice-Chair of the Craft Potters Association, and her fellow potters, especially Emmanuel Cooper, Phil Rogers, Mick Casson and Nic Collins; Patricia Morison, Editor of the BM Magazine; and Fiona Burtt, Events Officer of the British Museum Society.

This project, with its diverse elements of exhibition, publication and educational programme, could not have come about without the support and dedication of a large team of professionals on the staff of the British Museum. For the visual realisation and design of the exhibition we are extremely grateful to Simon Muirhead and his colleagues in the Design Department including Jude Simmons and Paul Goodhead (graphics), Andrea Easey (editorial) and David Williams (finance and production). Tony Milton of the Photographic Service produced the photography for the book's front cover and the poster while Tony Simpson and Mena Williams of Scientific Research supplied additional artwork and vital administrative support, supplementing the efforts of graphic illustrators and photographers throughout the Museum.

Almost one thousand individual pots are represented in this exhibition. All have been assessed, surface-cleaned, and in many cases radically reconstructed by a dedicated team of conservators led by the Acting Head of the Ceramics Conservation Section, Loretta Hogan. She was ably assisted by her colleagues, Fiona Ward, Janet Haynes, Janet Quinton, Sophia Brookes, John Cooper, Lorna Butler and Denise Ling. These thousand pots also had to be transported from their permanent home in the British Museum and its out-stations to the Burlington Gardens site. The move represented a major logistical challenge for each of the Senior Museum Assistants responsible for their departmental contributions. The organisers wish to record their particular thanks to Helen Wolfe (Ethnography) and Ruth Spires (Medieval and Later Antiquities), who co-ordinated the smooth and efficient transfer of objects to the Museum of Mankind.

The organisers also wish to register their gratitude to a number of individuals within the Museum who, by their efforts in the Education Department, the Directorate and the Department of Press and Public Relations, ensured that this exhibition would actually reach the public in the form we envisaged. John Reeve, Head of Education, organised the substantial 'Potters in Residence' programme funded by the Crafts Council alongside his regular series of public lectures and school visits. Lady Harriot Tennant, Special Assistant in the Directorate, worked tirelessly in an attempt to attract corporate sponsorship, while Andrew Hamilton and Jill Ravenscroft of the BM Press Office took responsibility for press and publicity with their customary flair.

Finally, the organisers and editors of this project wish to acknowledge their debt to their respective families and dedicate this book to them.

Introduction

David Gaimster and Ian Freestone

A potter kneading his clay laboriously moulds every vessel for our use, but out of the self-same clay he fashions without distinction the pots that are to serve for honourable uses and the opposite; and what the purpose of each one is to be, the moulder of the clay decides.[1]

Wisdom of Solomon 15:7

Pottery is a truly global medium. Ever since human beings began to move from a nomadic to a fully sedentary way of life, the pottery vessel has been a basic utensil. Mainly confined to the home, ceramics have always played a pivotal role within both family and community. With the proliferation over time of ceramic bodies, forms and decorative styles, pottery has acquired a distinctive duality of function – first and foremost as a utilitarian product, but also as a means of social and cultural expression. This unique set of characteristics invests ceramics, whether recovered from the ground or preserved in museum collections, with enormous potential for the investigation of technological, economic and cultural development within individual societies, past and present.

Ceramics and culture in the British Museum

Today ceramics are the single largest category of material culture held in the seven Antiquities Departments of the British Museum. In many instances they have formed the baseline of our understanding of individual societies. In fact, the importance of the medium for the study of human development can be traced as far back as the foundation of the British Museum in 1753. Among the miscellaneous collections – of books, natural history specimens and antiquities from the ancient world – left to the nation by the physician and collector Sir Hans Sloane (1660–1753), which formed part of the foundation collection of the British Museum, it is possible to identify a number of early specimens of ceramics from classical, medieval, Renaissance, Oriental and contemporary cultures which now occupy a prominent position in the Museum's displays. Among his huge collection, documented in Sloane's own catalogue and in John and Andrew Van Rymsdyk's *Museum Britannicum* of 1778 (fig. 1), are the Museum's first Greek figure vases, Roman terracotta lamps and *terra sigillata*, canopic jars from ancient Egypt, Romano-British and Anglo-Saxon funerary urns, Italian maiolica, medieval floor tiles, Chinese *blanc-de-Chine* figures, Meissen imitations and Chimú pottery from Peru.[2]

The second major phase of acquisition coincided with the heyday of the Grand Tour during the late eighteenth century. One of the most important among contemporary travellers to the Mediterranean was Sir William Hamilton (1730–1803), British Minister Plenipotentiary to the Kingdom of the Two Sicilies, who lived in Naples for thirty-six years and in 1772 donated the first of his extensive collections of Greek figure vases from southern Italy to the British Museum.[3] Hamilton intended that this 'first vase collection' (fig. 2) should not only contribute to the study of Greek culture in the Mediterranean but, more importantly, serve to inspire the potters and artists of his own day. Sir William's stated aim in publishing his vase collection was to revive the principles of Greek vase production and so provide a model for contemporary manufacturers to follow. Chief among these were Josiah Wedgwood and his partner Thomas Bentley at their Staffordshire pottery works, aptly named Etruria (ch. 31).[4] Today the vast ceramic collections of the British Museum remain an invaluable source of technical and artistic inspiration for potters working in a multitude of different ceramic traditions (ch. 32).

Despite this antiquarian interest in artefacts of the classical world, ceramics of other archaeological or ethnographic cultures remained little more than objects of curiosity until the mid-nineteenth century, when they emerged as the focus of legitimate scholarly study in their own right, central to the didactic display of material history. Pivotal to this development in Western Europe was the British Museum's most eminent and influential curator of the last century, Sir Augustus Wollaston Franks (1826–97).[5] His active scholarship and collecting, from his appointment as a young curator in 1851 until his retirement as Keeper of British and Medieval Antiquities and Ethnography in 1896, mark the real foundation of the Museum's holdings of European, Oriental, Islamic and Central and South American ceramics. To mention just two areas of his wide-ranging collecting interests, the British Museum's collections of Oriental pottery and porcelain, deriving from a myriad of cultures in China, Japan, Korea and Thailand, can be traced back directly to Franks' curatorship; and, at the beginning of his career, Franks was responsible for acquiring the nucleus of the Museum's holdings of historic European ceramics, notably the purchase in 1855 of a major part of the medieval to Renaissance collection of Ralph Bernal MP,[6] and in 1856 the purchase of medieval and early modern ceramics collected by the antiquary Charles Roach Smith from building operations in the City of London (fig. 3). Franks'

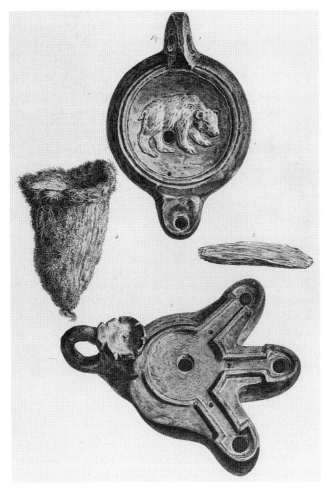

Fig. 1 Top left: Roman terra sigillata bowl (see ch. 29) impressed with the mark 'Primani', found on the Thames foreshore at Chatham (Kent). From the collection of Sir Hans Sloane, which on his death in 1753 formed the foundation collection of the British Museum. Illustrated in John and Andrew Van Rymsdyck's Museum Britannicum of 1778, the first catalogue of the British Museum's holdings. Left: Roman terracotta lamps (see ch. 25) and other 'curiosities' from the collection of Sir Hans Sloane, also illustrated in the Van Rymsdycks' catalogue.

Fig. 2 Above: The 'Hamilton Vase', a red-figure volute-krater (wine-mixing bowl) made in Apulia, southern Italy, about 330–310 BC (see ch. 12). Part of the 'first vase collection' given to the British Museum in 1772 by Sir William Hamilton, British Minister Plenipotentiary to the Kingdom of the Two Sicilies, and illustrated in d'Hancarville's Antiquités Etrusques, Grèques et Romaines, tirées du Cabinet de M. William Hamilton, Envoyé extraordinaire et plénipotentiare de S. M. Britannique en Cour de Naples (AEGER), vol. I, Naples, 1766–7 (actually 1767–76).

various personal gifts of ceramics to the Museum over the course of his long career, culminating in the bequest after his death of his remaining collection, are characterised by a unique catholicity of taste and scholarship.[7] It is this global dimension, introduced and encouraged by Franks, which continues to distinguish the British Museum's current holdings of ceramics and which makes it the only institution capable of hosting such a cross-cultural exhibition on this medium, based entirely upon its own collections.

Ceramic production

I went down to the potter's house and found him working at the wheel. Now and then a vessel he was making out of the clay would be spoilt in his hands, and then he would start again and mould it into another vessel to his liking.[8]

Jeremiah 18:3–4

Production forms a central and universal focus for the study of world ceramic traditions. It not only incorporates technology – that is, how the object was made, including each step in the building or fabrication process, the raw materials and the machinery involved – but includes supply and demand, the organisation of the workforce and the relationships between the producers and other groups in society. It is affected by natural factors such as climate and topography as well as artificial ones such as the proximity of roads and cities. It cannot be isolated from the unseen structures that govern our everyday lives, our laws, our traditions and our beliefs. It provides a framework within which we may compare and contrast across as well as within cultures and, in so doing, reach new understandings about human behaviour.

This collection of case studies is offered in that light. It is neither a comprehensive nor unilinear history of ceramics and could not hope to be, given the number of complex and very diverse societies that have made pottery. Rather than pursue a simple chronological development, therefore, the contributors explore world ceramic traditions according to their respective mode of production, incorporating not only the technology and manufacturing processes involved but also the social and economic organisation and the relationship of pottery-making to the physical environment.[9]

The diversity of individual case studies represented here reflects the geographical and chronological extent of the British Museum's collections. Ceramics from most of the world's continents are represented – from the Far East to India, Africa, Western Asia, Europe and South America – while their cultural focus ranges from hunter-gatherer communities of the Japanese and Nubian mesolithic to the ceramic factories of the Roman Mediterranean and eighteenth-century Staffordshire. Whether acquired by excavation, ethnographic fieldwork or passed from hand to hand through several centuries of recent history, the material represents a rich source of information on the

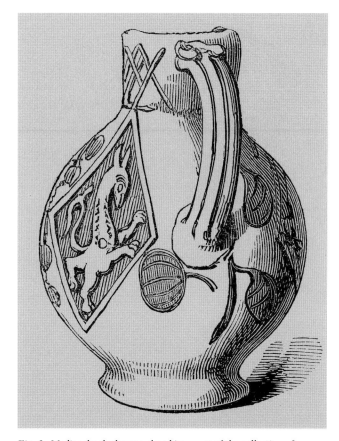

Fig. 3 Medieval polychrome glazed jug, part of the collection of antiquities recovered by Charles Roach Smith from London building sites between 1841 and 1856 and now in the Department of Medieval and Later Antiquities (see ch. 13, fig. 2, right). Illustrated in the Catalogue of London Antiquities collected by, and the property of Charles Roach Smith, London 1854, no. 593.

technological adaptations, environmental and economic conditions of individual communities as well as their social motivations and aspirations. The wide range of disciplines and specialisms of the twenty-six individual contributors and the varying focus of their chapters, from a single workshop to the history of a whole tradition, offer the reader some indication of the great diversity of current approaches to the study of culture through ceramics, which are almost as diverse as the traditions they study.

Sources of evidence

Although essentially one physical medium, ceramics around the globe demonstrate an infinite diversity of material, form and decoration, resulting in the multiplication of literally thousands of individual ceramic traditions. How can we define these products culturally or scientifically, or even trace the development of individual technologies and craft traditions? How can we measure the impact of one tradition on another? To appreciate these questions more fully we must turn to a range of archaeological, ethnographic, scientific and documentary evidence.

In their efforts to understand the economic and social foundations of past societies, archaeologists have since the late 1950s increasingly recognised the need to understand the production process itself. Our ability to understand how pottery was made, distributed and used has improved dramatically as a result of this change in focus, which can be traced back to the work of Anna Shepard.[10] Pottery is no longer considered almost exclusively a tool for dating, in which changes in pottery 'type' are related to chronological periods, but also as a key to social and economic organisation, trade and technical skills. With this change in emphasis has come increased interest in the pot as product and the potter as producer. The excavation of production sites can be invaluable, and this direct evidence of pottery-making activity has been documented increasingly from all over the world. Workshops, kilns and associated areas not only tell us where a particular ware was made, but also something of the scale on which it was made, the technology of production and the standardisation of the products. This evidence from the centres of production is complemented by the measurement of the quantity of pottery of different types found in the excavation of consumer sites – the places where the pottery was used.[11]

Pottery-making is dependent upon a vast range of factors, from the proximity of raw materials such as clay, temper, fuel and water to wind direction, ambient temperature and rainfall. The topography of an area may determine the accessibility of both clays and markets; it is much easier to transport heavy clays and pots by river than across a range of mountains by donkey. The nature of the subsistence economy – the type of crops grown, seasonal changes in activity and the division of work between male and female – affects the types of pots made and their uses as well as when they are made. The population density and distribution of towns and villages will dictate if there is a market for pottery and whether it is worthwhile for the potter to produce more of the product than is needed for self-sufficiency in order to sell it elsewhere. This interaction between the production process and its environment has been termed ceramic ecology by Frederick Matson; the study of the environment in all its aspects is essential evidence for a complete understanding of pottery-making in the past.[12] The profound influence of this approach is felt through many of the case studies included here, even where it is not directly acknowledged.

Besides the need for excavation in the case of ancient, medieval and early modern societies, there is much to be learned from contemporary potters in traditional societies, who may work under environmental and socio-economic circumstances which are comparable to those of archaeological or historic cultures. Ethnoarchaeology uses the techniques of ethnographic investigation to infer the behaviour of people in the past by analogy with those in the present, and much of our current understanding of early pottery-making derives from the observation of the potters of our own time. In what is arguably one of the most expansive and synthetic studies of this type, Arnold[13] has produced an analysis which allows generalisations about the relationship between potter and environment to be extended into the past. Questions such as the distance a potter would have travelled to collect raw materials, the effects of population pressure upon the development of pottery-making as a subsistence strategy, and the factors affecting the introduction of new technologies may all be quite usefully considered using Arnold's model. Peacock[14] has used models based upon ethnographic observations as a framework for the interpretation of Roman pottery production; this extremely helpful approach to the interpretation and conceptualisation of early pottery production is discussed in more detail below. Such ethnographic parallels are drawn upon in a number of our case studies, while our examples from the modern world not only underline the importance of such sources of information, but remind us of those elements of the production process that are very difficult to extract from the archaeological record.

Many societies, from Dynastic Egypt to nineteenth-century China, have documented their working practices in the form of written records or graphical representations. These descriptions or images can help us to interpret what is often a very fragmentary archaeological picture of potting in the past. While such sources can be immensely useful, caution is always required in interpreting them. The modern requirements of accuracy and objectivity were neither an obligation nor an ideal for early recorders. For example, the well-known representations of Qing dynasty potters (fig. 4) give a useful illustration of porcelain production methods and the division of tasks, but these are set in an idyllic rural background rather than the industrial city that we know Jingdezhen to have been (ch. 30). Thus this type of evidence is complementary to but does not supplant other approaches. Where available, ideally it can be tested against independent lines of evidence.

The emphasis on pottery as a product and commodity has led to increasing reliance upon the extraction of the evidence hidden in the pot itself, using a variety of scientific techniques. From influential studies such as those of Anna Shepard[15] in the United States and David Peacock[16] in Europe, the study of the fabric of the ceramic (essentially the physical and chemical characteristics of the fired body) to determine its provenance, the place where it was made, has expanded to incorporate a bewildering array of scientific techniques, from the simple hand-held lens through to gamma ray spectroscopy of samples excited by neutron bombardment. By determining the composition of a pottery fabric, we can identify a 'fingerprint' which may then be compared to those of other pots or to all the

Fig. 4 Chinese watercolour print, showing the application of glaze (see ch. 30), from a series of twenty-four scenes illustrating 'ceramic processes', Canton, 19th century AD. The first such series was painted in the Qing dynasty for the Qianlong emperor (r. 1736–95) and annotated by his supervisor of porcelain production, Tang Ying. Many similar series were produced during the 19th century in the southern port of Canton for sale to foreigners. 39.5 × 51 cm (15.5 × 20 in).

products of a kiln which have been analysed.[17] As well as the place of origin, methods have been developed to investigate how ceramics were made. X-rays may be used to determine the method by which a particular pot was constructed, while microscopy may be used to determine the way the clay was prepared as well as the temperature at which it was fired. Slips, glazes, paints and other surface treatments are receptive to investigation using scanning electron microscopy, as shown in the boxes throughout this book.[18] Such work has undergone a remarkable growth in the last few decades and, where appropriate to an under-

standing of the relevant technology of production, information derived from these scientific approaches is included.

Finally, experiment is crucial to an understanding of past ceramic production. From the skilled modern potter replicating an early masterpiece to the experimental archaeologist carefully reproducing the detailed characteristics resulting from a particular method of building the rim of a cooking pot, our understanding of the behaviour of clay and its response to the hands of the maker and the heat of the kiln can provide insights which are available in no other way. Equally, however, conclusions based upon practical experience of modern materials and methods but not tempered by an understanding of the social and environmental contexts of the ancient potter can be misleading. Many of the contributors have benefited from a two-way interaction with working potters who have taken an interest in the materials in their care, and these invaluable informal discussions underpin much of our understanding of early ceramics.

Pottery in the making: from family to factory

A general model of production is a useful tool, allowing comparisons to be made between different cultures. Such a model has been produced by David Peacock for Roman pottery, based upon archaeological evidence and ethnographic observations of traditional potters around the Mediterranean. Peacock[19] identified six principal modes of production characterised by an increasing level of complexity and scale, from single households making pottery for their own use to complex factories employing workers under a managerial structure. Each mode of production is defined by its own level of organisation and associated technology. Although devised specifically for the Roman world and unlikely to be applicable in detail to all situations, there is a universal element inherent in the model, within the broad terms of scale and technology, which provides a valuable framework in which production across a wide range of societies may be considered.

Peacock's model provides a useful tool for investigating our case studies of ceramic production. However, some of these are too broad to be readily categorised in such a way. Pottery discussed within a single chapter in this book may have been produced within a number of production modes. For many cultures, our understanding of the archaeological record is not yet sufficiently comprehensive to recognise the differences between adjacent production modes for all pottery types, e.g. household production as opposed to household industry. Finally, the modes of production described are based upon modern ethnographic examples; there is a probability that production in some early cultures would be better described by alternative models (see, for example, ch. 14, on Korean celadon production). In view of these points and the great diversity of societies described, we have here grouped the case studies according to a more general approach, acknowledging the wide variations in cultural context and available forms of evidence. Within this framework, the Roman model may be usefully applied as a general tool for the purposes of comparison, while bearing in mind that it is not prescriptive. The framework which follows has been developed, therefore, to take account of the variability in ceramic production across time and space. Both extremes – family and factory – may co-exist within a single culture, and there can be considerable overlap within each mode of production.

Early sedentary communities

The power of fire to transform a soft, malleable clay into a robust and durable material was recognised at least 25,000 years ago by nomadic cave-dwellers in eastern Europe, who have left evidence at a number of locations in the form of numerous small, fragmentary ceramic figurines.[20] However, the first appearance of pottery vessels came

---

Modes of pottery production (Peacock)

Household production For domestic consumption only; a sporadic activity of secondary economic importance.

Household industry The first steps towards craft specialisation; a secondary, part-time (and predominantly female) activity; pottery made for exchange or trade; not an essential means of subsistence; increasingly 'professional' organisation; little investment in equipment; probably a turntable but not a wheel; open firings the rule.

Individual workshops Although mainly seasonal, pottery-making is the main source of subsistence; higher production geared towards wider markets; requires greater investment in technology, including wheel and kiln; increasing involvement of men, reflecting growing economic importance; possible employment of assistants; technological investment and labour required favour sedentary existence.

Nucleated workshops Individual workshops grouped together to form a clustered industrial community; ceramic production the primary source of income; highly professional activity, with standardisation of products across all workshops; advantages of nucleation include mutual co-operation and the benefit of higher sales through a wider distribution network.

Manufactory A group, often specialising in a particular product, working together in a single space or building.

Factory Large-scale production of standardised products for both local and long-distance markets; some mechanisation; employment of workers and specialisation of labour on one site.

---

much later, coinciding with the development of sedentary (settled) ways of life. Pottery is relatively heavy and fragile, and hence not well suited to a permanently nomadic existence. However, while the link between pottery use and sedentism is well established, it would be naive to assume that a fully sedentary existence is a precondition for the use of pottery, as we know that pottery is used by nomadic peoples today.[21] Pottery-making requires periods of sedentism that are sufficiently long to allow the gathering of raw materials and the making, firing and drying of the pot, and these periods must be spent close to appropriate clay resources and under suitable (usually dry) climatic conditions. A survey of the time required to dry traditionally made pottery before firing suggests that this is typically days or even weeks,[22] which would militate against the introduction of pottery by highly mobile societies. Even for cultures that were mobile for part of the year, it would have been possible to make pottery if they remained in a suitable locality for a sufficient period of time. The gradual move to a more sedentary way of life was thus the single most decisive factor – as opposed to the development of agriculture *per se* – in the introduction of pottery production.

The Jomon culture of Japan, essentially a hunter-gatherer society, produced some of the earliest pottery for which we have clear archaeological and scientific evidence (ch. 1). According to radiocarbon dates, the Jomon culture was making pottery over 12,000 years ago. As agriculture determined sedentary living for the farmers of later neolithic societies, so the favourable hunting and fishing conditions of the Holocene fostered a number of semi-permanent settlements for the Jomon. In the mesolithic regime of the early Japanese, pottery was introduced in order to store and cook the diverse animal and vegetal products of their rich habitat. This was no mere accident of technology; rather, pottery was an essential component of their subsistence strategy. In the same way, pottery rapidly became a fundamental part of the material armoury of the first sedentary communities along the Middle Nile Valley during the early to mid Holocene (ch. 2), where radiocarbon dating has pushed the ceramic production back to around 9000 years ago. Here, according to our case study, it is possible that the benefits of pottery may have actually helped stimulate a move towards a more settled lifestyle.

The first farmers needed a means of storing grain and other produce, including liquids. Despite the substantial investment of energy in the collection of raw materials, clay preparation and firing (see ch. 3 on household potters in neolithic and Early Bronze Age Britain), pottery could be made in quantity for a lower investment of labour (and often less skill) than that required for making containers of animal skins, bark, basket or hollowed-out stone or wood. Perhaps the most important advantage of pottery over other materials was its utility for cooking and processing the new range of cultivated foodstuffs being produced. Direct cooking and boiling over a fire was not possible in organic vessels, and heating a pottery vessel was a good deal more efficient than the indirect method of dropping hot stones into a wood or leather vessel of water. Pottery could also be used in the introduction of new methods of food processing, such as baking and brewing.[23] As a malleable medium, pottery also offered enormous scope for elaboration, and the decorative dimension enabled it to become established as an element in social relationships between individuals and communities, and even part of high-prestige 'good culture'.[24] Some early pottery-using societies, such as the European Beaker culture (ch. 3) or the meso-lithic cultures of Predynastic Egypt (ch. 5), developed specialised ceramic vessels for funerary use.

A characteristic of much early pottery is a substantial investment of time and energy in the production of indi-vidual pots, as evidenced by their rich decoration and finely burnished finishes. This often involved specialised tools and techniques, while firing took place in open fires (i.e. bonfires or pits), without enclosing walls or roofs and where the fuel was in contact with the pot. Production, at this early stage, is likely to have been a seasonal activity of secondary economic importance, taking place within the household. The part-time nature of production favoured the role of

women as potters, as the hand-building techniques employed often required interruptions to allow the partially built vessels to dry and strengthen, and these enforced breaks in the process allowed potting to be fitted in around other domestic tasks.

Potters in the early agricultural villages of late neolithic and chalcolithic Mesopotamia (ch. 4) and Predynastic Egypt (ch. 5) were among the first to develop a more profes-sional level of production, with a degree of craft specialisa-tion.[25] The development of specialist groups of potters who produced, at least in part, for profit is demonstrated quite graphically by the production of wares for a regional market by the Halaf culture, between c.6000 and 5000 BC. The Ubaid potters (6000–4000 BC) boosted output and quality by the introduction of rudimentary updraught kilns, allowing more controlled, higher-temperature firings, and of a hand-turned tournette or turntable, which assisted the finishing stages of pottery-forming and decora-tion. These same early cultures traded pottery over long distances, with Southern Ubaid painted wares reaching the length of the Persian Gulf. Similarly, certain types of pottery are found tens or even hundreds of kilometres from their source in neolithic and Bronze Age Britain (ch. 3).

Urbanisation

The growth of population and development of stable clus-tered settlements led directly to new and more professional modes of ceramic production. The adoption of new potting and firing technology represents a response to a larger and more accessible ceramic market with a higher demand. The gradual migration of farmers from isolated settlements to fortified cities forms the backdrop to the professionalisation of potting in Mesopotamia during the fourth to first millennia BC (ch. 6). Communal living stimulated a number of important technological and cultural developments, including the emergence of writing and new craft skills. In ceramic production, a major innovation was the intro-duction of the fast-rotating wheel, which enabled the potter to produce a much wider range of pottery, designed for specific functions, more quickly than had previously been possible. The increase in the scale of production engendered by these social and technological changes eventually resulted in the movement of ceramic production to the edges of towns or to its concentration in specialised settle-ments of multi-kiln 'nucleated workshops' covering several hectares. Textual sources of the Ur III period (2100–2000 BC) refer to potteries of between two and ten people, work-ing on a seasonal basis under a supervisor, the remainder of the year being spent in agricultural work. Despite its seasonality, pottery production in Mesopotamia had by this time become a highly professionalised activity and the principal source of income for its practitioners.

The growth of towns or proto-urban settlements, the

oppida, in pre-Roman Britain saw changes of a similar type, although beginning several thousand years later, in the first century BC (ch. 7). Population changes and contacts with urbanised Roman society stimulated increased production and the adoption of new methods and techniques, not only the potter's wheel but also in other aspects of the production process, such as the permanent kiln and the development of standardised methods of clay preparation. In this case, however, the new techniques were not native innovations but seem to have been introduced from the outside, and several stages of change may be recognised from the archaeological record.

A characteristic of much of this urban production is the plain or relatively simple decorative character of the pottery, particularly in comparison to the intricately decorated nature of some of the wares produced at the household level. This reflects the emphasis on high output to supply the market alongside the need to minimise the amount of effort expended on each pot. Dynastic Egyptian pottery (ch. 8) is very typical of this type of product. Robust and utilitarian, it was produced to satisfy the everyday needs of a complex urban society in which prestige goods for the use of the élites were available in other more valuable materials such as stone, metals, faience and, from around the fourteenth century BC, glass, and it is unlikely that investment in complex ceramic decorative techniques could be justified in terms of increased value of the final product.

The contents of a Late Bronze Age potter's workshop, discovered in a cave at the foot of the large Canaanite town of Lachish (Tell ed-Duweir) in Palestine (ch. 9), reveal something of the organisation and hardware required to operate an urban pottery industry at this time, and the case study shows the nature of some of the detailed evidence and arguments upon which our understanding of the broader picture is based. Even the identification of the use of the wheel is not always straightforward and requires careful analysis.[27]

The increasing demand for quantity, variation and sophistication in the ceramics of a complex, large-scale urban culture is demonstrated by the Partho-Sasanian pottery industry of the second century BC to seventh century AD (ch. 10). The use of alkali silicate glazes, coloured by small amounts of added copper, satisfied the need for a product of improved appearance without substantially reducing the quantity of pottery that could be produced nor adding greatly to the cost. The high level of professional skill accumulated by these potters is illustrated by the spectacular series of glazed coffins made in different sizes for adults and children.

Urbanisation and the development of larger regional markets for pottery in Japan led, in the fifth century AD, to the importation from Korea of the wheel, along with a number of radical innovations in kiln design which enabled

---

The potter's wheel

The potter's wheel is arguably the most significant single innovation in the history of pottery production. The throwing of pottery on the wheel differs dramatically from hand-building methods such as coiling or slab-building. The clay used in wheel-throwing requires a high water content to make it sufficiently plastic. The wheel rotates at a high speed so that centrifugal force tends to push the clay away from the centre of the wheel and against the hands of the potter. Exercising precise hand control, the potter gently squeezes the clay and lifts it, forming a thin-walled vessel in what is essentially a single movement. The vessel can then be cut from the clay adhering to the wheel by passing a fine wire beneath it. Using the wheel, a traditional potter typically can form about ten pots in an hour, as opposed to about one per hour using hand-building techniques.[26]

The tournette or turntable is a simple, slowly rotated aid to hand-building or finishing a pot. It does not exploit centrifugal force to form the pot, nor does it offer the increased output of the potter's wheel. Pressing soft clay into pre-formed moulds is another technique that can be used to increase production, and this was extensively used in the urbanised societies of South America (ch. 27), where the potter's wheel was not developed, as well as in the mass-production of Roman lamps (ch. 25).

---

potters to fire pottery to higher temperatures (ch. 11). The natural ash-glazing process, which was incidental to the high-firing temperatures and fuel used, is a further example of the exploitation of a relatively inexpensive effect to provide considerable added value to the vessel. Such was the success of the resulting ash-glazed stonewares that this firing technology survived unchanged into the sixteenth century.

Professional workshops

[The potter] must vie with goldsmiths and silversmiths and copy the bronze-workers.[28]

Wisdom of Solomon 15:9

The technological and artistic refinement of the ceramics discussed in this group of case studies reflects the highly professionalised mode of their production. Although separated by continents and in some cases by millennia, each example can be characterised by a high degree of technical investment and by the organisation of production into workshops, either discrete or clustered into industrial complexes. In some settlements potting became the main industrial activity. Most workshops were run on a family basis, while others employed workers and apprentices. The training of personnel ensured the manufacture of a standardised range of high-quality products. The mode and scale of production was determined to a large extent by the nature of the society and the wider commercial and cultural networks in which they operated.

In increasingly complex societies the demand for pottery

for different functions and occasions introduced a strong element of competition into the pottery market, not only among potters but between potters and other artisans. The development of increasingly sophisticated forms, surface treatments, glazes and decorative styles increased the status of domestic ceramics and enabled the product to compete with more precious media such as metalware. The use of the potter's wheel and the high-firing kiln enabled potters to exploit markets far beyond their own communities. Mutual co-operation within pottery-making settlements increased total output and resulted in wider sales.

Pottery production in Bronze Age Greece was probably still based on the household and operating on a partly seasonal basis. During the sixth century BC, however, the scattered household workshops of the Attic countryside moved to form a nucleated industry based in Athens (ch. 12). At the same time, in response to changes in demand, a number of workshops began to invest in the manufacture of sophisticated forms and elaborately painted tablewares which involved a high degree of specialist skill and experience. Some activities, particularly painting, were often shared by two workers, the names of whom are recorded for the first time. The personal marking of wares reflects the intensity of inter-artisanal competition within Greek Iron Age society and underlines the highly professionalised approach of pottery workshops to the retailing of their wares.

Korean celadons (ch. 14) were luxury wares, used by the court aristocracy and in Buddhist ritual. They were initially developed in response to the celadon wares of China, which were admired in Korea. Government officials, or *yojik*, oversaw the manufacture of celadons at workshops located far from the court. The rigidly hierarchical nature of Korean society at this time meant that members of a potter's family were confined to making pots and skills were passed down through the children, often the result of inter-marriage between families involved in the same trade. In this way, the maintenance of pottery-making skills and knowledge was assured. The low-caste potters were responsible for a number of innovative developments, such as the new decorative techniques which produced the outstanding inlaid wares of the twelfth century.

Social and cultural pressures are also evident in the development of lustreware in the Islamic world (ch. 16) and polychrome painted maiolica in Renaissance Italy (ch. 17). The production of highly decorated ceramics in these cultures demanded further investment in new raw materials (pigments and glazing materials) as well as refinements in firing technology. As in ancient Greece, the success of lustreware in the Near East and maiolica in Europe depended on the development of professional expertise within the workshop which was then passed down from master-potter to son and apprentice, along with privileged information on clay and glaze compositions. In sixteenth-

century Italy one potter, Cipriano Piccolpasso, even produced a detailed and illustrated treatise on maiolica production, such was its manufacturing complexity. The development of sophisticated painted designs, mostly based on contemporary printed sources, introduced an artistic dimension into Italian maiolica which raised it to the status of a luxury commodity unique in European Renaissance ceramics.

The growth in status of domestic ceramics in the Islamic world and Renaissance Mediterranean is a phenomenon which was paralleled in north-western Europe. During the thirteenth to early fourteenth centuries in England, potters working mostly on the edges of towns or in the countryside began to produce a series of highly elaborate polychrome glazed and slipped jugs for dining and drinking purposes (ch. 13). This development reflects the increased purchasing power and changing attitudes to pottery among a socially aspirant urban community which could not afford more precious metal vessels. With the mid-fourteenth century came economic and demographic decline and a corresponding fall-off in sales. The rapid rise and fall of highly decorated pottery production in medieval England underlines the susceptibility of contemporary potters to changing social and economic circumstances. The same connection can also be observed in the development of the stoneware industry in late medieval to early modern Germany (ch. 18), where the growth in demand for robust, impervious, stain- and odour-free tableware by the mercantile communities of northern Europe led to an expansion in the scale and mode of stoneware production during the fourteenth to fifteenth centuries. In order to produce the quantities of stoneware required for the international export market, firing technology was perfected and production concentrated in nucleated potting villages or urban settlements, where products were sold on a communal basis to middlemen who organised regional and long-distance distribution. The introduction of moulded applied relief ornament, based on contemporary printed designs, reflects the new social role of domestic ceramics in the changing cultural climate of the sixteenth century. With the elevation in status came changes in the organisation of the stoneware workshop. Men took a firm grip on the family business and formed guilds to control access, production levels, prices and distribution networks.

The diversity of surface treatment and ornament to be seen in contemporary North African polychrome glazed ware reflects the complex demands of the urban ceramic market in the region. This elaborately decorated, twice-fired pottery plays a prominent role in social and ritual life in the community, particularly in the celebration of life-cycle events such as births, marriages and deaths (ch. 20). The association of a much earlier ceramic with the spiritual life of the society is demonstrated by faience in the ancient Mediterranean (ch. 15), which is often found in Bronze Age religious deposits in both Egypt and Greece. A non-clay ceramic with a white body and bright blue overlying glaze, faience emulated precious materials such as malachite and turquoise and was probably produced by specialist craftsmen from a very early stage. By the Late Bronze Age, faience production was closely associated with glass-working and pottery-making in special industrial quarters at cities such as Tell el-Amarna, in Egypt. Its religious associations along with its use in jewellery suggest that faience may have been satisfying a niche market, in which its especially pleasing visual properties were particularly valued and its relative fragility was not a disadvantage.

A strong diversity in the decorative repertoire of English post-medieval slipware reflects the strength of regional traditions and the changing character of ceramic consumption in the hundred years leading up to the Industrial Revolution (ch. 19). Based mainly in the countryside, family workshops clustered together to form nucleated potting settlements. With the development of national transport networks, communal production catered for both rural and urban markets, some a considerable distance from the source. A number of different techniques of slip decoration were practised between the early seventeenth and mid-eighteenth centuries; most were determined by regional tradition although others, such as the press-mould, were clearly influenced by new technology. Within a few years many of the same potting families had abandoned their businesses and traditional modes of production to join the emerging factory system as employees (ch. 31).

Rural communities

Production in any society may be a complex process, taking place on a number of different levels. Thus, even where innovations such as the wheel and kiln have been introduced in urban areas, traditional methods of production may continue for a range of reasons. There may be no advantage in change, as the traditional approach, in which pottery-making is interspersed with a range of other tasks, does not disrupt more important agricultural activities. In a sparsely populated area, demand may be insufficient to justify the investment required for more specialised methods. Certain types of pot may be preferred for cooking, eating or ritual use and may not be so easily made using newer techniques. Traditional pottery-making may carry important symbolic and spiritual meanings which are not fulfilled by more intensive processes.

For most communities based in the countryside, potting, at least until relatively recently, has played a fundamental part in the rural subsistence economy and social relations. In areas isolated from centres of population pottery is made, like other craft products, by members of the household or community for local use. In West Africa today, as in many rural societies past and present, groups of women (often from the same extended family) take on the role of community potter, while men monopolise what have sometimes been interpreted as 'higher-status' crafts such as metalworking (ch. 21). Here potting – the creation of objects from clay – is associated with childbirth and is restricted to women.

Facilities and equipment are usually meagre in rural societies and production tends to be part-time and concentrated in the dry season of the year. Potter's wheels and kilns are typically absent in this mode of production, vessels being coil- or slab-built and fired in open bonfires. In rural Iron Age Iran, a fine finish was obtained simply by burnishing (polishing) the surface of the vessel before firing (ch. 23). In West Africa, as in early Anglo-Saxon England (ch. 22), there is little technological investment in pottery manufacture, the only exception being to make stamps and roulette wheels for surface decoration. Plastic ornament invests even the most rudimentary utilitarian product with a strong social and cultural dimension. The contemporary ceramics of the Dowayo in Cameroon and the excavated burial urns of Anglo-Saxon East Anglia illustrate the powerful role of incised or stamped ornament in the articulation of cultural messages both within the community and to those outside.

Notwithstanding the obvious economic and technological benefits, the ethnographic record helps us to appreciate that there was also a strong cultural imperative in the production of pottery in some of the early sedentary and agricultural societies discussed in chapters 1–5. The case studies from the Ancient Near East (chs 6, 10) help to emphasise the strong link between pottery style and tribal identity. Equally, in Iron Age Iran (ch. 23), localised ceramic forms and decorative styles proliferated among the patchwork of cultures occupying the western Zagros mountains during the period c.1400–800 BC.

Specialised products

With the professionalisation of pottery manufacture into single or nucleated workshops and the development of competition between producers for customers within the same market, some industries were stimulated into specialising in a single product which was difficult for others to imitate. In many cases, specialisation would have involved a significant investment in technology and the training of personnel, and limiting production to a single product enabled the workshop or factory to work on an industrial scale. For others, the manufacture of specialised non-utilitarian vessels as a sideline to their usual domestic output offered an additional income. Nevertheless, as for other modes of production, the manufacture of specialised products was determined as much by the availability of suitable raw materials as by specific economic, social and cultural motivations.

A number of craftsmen in the eastern part of the modern state of Gujerat, in north-western India, specialise in the production of complex terracotta figurines for ritual purposes (ch. 26). Although intended for the local market, in fact most figurines are individually commissioned, and production involves highly specialised skills including throwing, forming, modelling, slipping and the assembly of individual elements before firing in permanent brick kilns. Other cultures have produced entirely non-utilitarian ceramic items alongside their general domestic output. This would appear to have been the case with the whistling pots of pre-Hispanic Peru, a tradition which lasted for over two thousand years (ch. 27).

In the Roman world, some industries were established primarily to exploit regional and long-distance markets for individual household products such as lamps (ch. 25). Exotic, elaborately moulded lamps enjoyed a wide popularity over broad stretches of the Roman empire.

In the case of tile-makers in Roman Britain (ch. 24), the fact that some tiles were made from different clays but marked with the same roller-die suggests that several specialised producers worked on an itinerant basis, moving from one building site to another, while others worked in a single location using one type of clay and exported their products over a wide area. The nature of the industry and its orientation towards the mass-production of a single product precluded diversification into domestic ceramic production.

Industrialisation

The growth of empire, whether imperial as in the Roman world or colonial as in the eighteenth century, created a virtually global market for ceramics and other household goods. In response, factories were established to exploit the growing trading networks linking countries and continents.

It is the sheer scale of production which distinguishes the final group of world ceramic traditions. They all involve manufacturing technology and working methods designed to sustain mass-production, both for the home and long-distance markets. In this case, a number of craftsmen were grouped together on a single site in order to maximise the production of a standard range of goods. The factory system also necessitated the division of labour at the production site, with employees or even slaves undertaking single, often repetitive, tasks. In several cases these industries established multi-kiln production sites and perfected mould technology in order to maintain high levels of standardised output.

As early as the first century AD, the sigillata industry of Graufesenque in southern France was engaged in 'industrial' production (ch. 29). Here it has been possible to

estimate from excavations the large number of parallel kiln firings and how many potters were required for each. In northern China, potters at the Ding kilns during the sixth century AD introduced the use of saggars and spacers to protect vessels during firing and thereby ensure a high yield; later they introduced the use of coal as a fuel (ch. 28). Porcelain production was achieved on a truly industrial scale at Jingdezhen, in southern China, during the seventeenth to eighteenth centuries (ch. 30), with workers organised so as to perform specific tasks in a manner similar to other industries such as lacquer-making. Thus tasks such as the mining of clay, its preparation, the making of moulds and saggars, throwing and forming, glazing, firing, packing and distribution were carried out by different teams of craftsmen. The scale of this output can be measured in the millions of vessels exported to Europe via the ships of the European East India companies from the early seventeenth century onwards. In each of these industries, mass-production was heavily dependent on a large and well-organised labour force.

General technological and economic conditions were instrumental in the development of the factory system. In England the first moves towards mass-production, which involved the invention of a series of entirely new ceramic bodies by the potters of North Staffordshire, can be traced in part to the adoption of steam-powered machinery and large multi-flue kilns which were capable of firing tens of thousands of vessels at any one time (ch. 31). In addition, the development of the canal network ensured the rise of Staffordshire to the top of the British ceramic market and had a profound impact on the consumers of Europe and North America. As in China, the division of the labour force into specialist tasks was another contribution to the national and international success of the Staffordshire potting industry. By this stage most potters in Staffordshire had ceased to be independent craftsmen; although they had acquired a new range of industrial skills, they had become little more than wage-earning employees.

The success of the mass-production of standardised ceramic products for a global market is now a fact of the modern world. Factory production on the scale of Jingdezhen or Wedgwood has become the dominant mode. However, perhaps in response to this impersonal efficiency, the West has in the last century seen a revival of interest in craft traditions. This new consumer demand for handmade and artistic ceramic objects has helped to sustain the modern phenomenon of the craft or studio potter (ch. 32). By investigating and reinterpreting ancient processes, they provide a link between potters of the past and the future.

Surely the potter can do what he likes with the clay. Is he not free to make out of the same lump two vessels, one to be treasured, the other for common use?

Romans 9:21

Jomon Pottery in Ancient Japan

Victor Harris

What is presently the earliest well-documented pottery in the world was discovered in south-western Japan in 1960 at a cave in Fukui near Nagasaki, inland on the southern island of Kyushu, and since then at a number of further caves and other sites at widely separated locations. This earliest pottery appears alongside stone tools typical of earlier palaeolithic cultures in Japan. Contrary to conventional assumptions that the introduction of pottery is associated with the development of agriculture, these early pottery-makers were not farmers but hunter-gatherers; they lived on the abundant plants, nuts, birds and mammals of the forest, along with shellfish and fish from the sea.

The Fukui Cave proved to have been occupied for several millennia, and it is particularly important because successive strata show a continuity from the pre-ceramic society to the pottery-users. Fifteen distinct strata were excavated to a depth of 5 m (15.5 ft). Radiocarbon dating of levels containing potsherds by Gakushuin University have given dates of 12,400 ± 350 BP for stratum III and 12,700 ± 500 BP for stratum II.[1] The magnitude of these dates and those of material from other sites have since been confirmed by the complementary dating technique of thermoluminescence. Although pottery of a similar date is reported to have been discovered in Siberia, there is no suggestion of

further pottery industry there until several thousand years later. The earliest pottery finds elsewhere on the Asian mainland include sherds from the Xianrendeng Cave in Jiangxi province in China, which were dated to 10,870 ± 240 BP, a thousand years later than the Fukui material.

There are diverse theories about the origins of the Japanese people, their relationship to the palaeolithic cultures of mainland Asia, and the possibilities of a common origin for the first pottery. A strong body of opinion holds that land access to the mainland existed along the length of Japan before the sea rose after the last Ice Age, while another view supports migration by marine transport. But whatever their origins, it is clear that a small population of hunter-gatherers enjoyed an apparently peaceful sedentary existence

Fig. 1 (Below) Vessel reconstructed from a sherd (fig. 2, lower left) measuring 15 × 22 cm (6 × 8.5 in) and dating to the Middle Jomon phase, from the Kasori E site in Chiba prefecture.

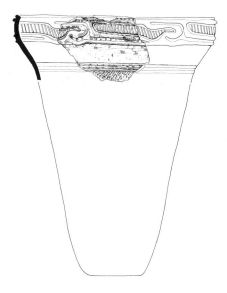

Fig. 2 (Right) Sherds ranging in date from the Initial to the Middle Jomon phase. Top row, left to right: Kayama site, Initial phase; Kurohama site, Early phase; Atamadai site, Early phase. Bottom row: Kasori E site, Middle phase (see fig. 1), 15 × 22 cm (6 × 8.5 in); Katsuzaka site, Middle phase.

Fig. 3 Cord markings on pots dating from the Early and Late Jomon phases. Left: Flat-based conical beaker from north Honshu, Late phase, height 26.5 cm (10.5 in). Right: Flat-bottomed vessel with raised bands and 'fingernail' impressions like those found on Incipient Jomon pottery. It has been lacquered inside in antiquity to adapt it as a water container for the Tea Ceremony. Early phase, height 14.2 cm (5.6 in).

in Japan from around 10,000 BC until the final centuries BC, and that pottery was a universal and important part of their way of life.

The Jomon culture

The fragmentary cooking pots found at Fukui were the forerunners of a pottery culture which continued for well over ten thousand years and has become known as Jomon. The term, which means 'cord pattern', was coined by the American archaeologist Edward S. Morse, who in 1867 discovered pieces of the pottery

decorated with distinctive impressions of twisted cords (fig. 3). Morse excavated sherds of Jomon pottery from a hillock which proved to be an ancient midden of seashells at Omori, in Chiba prefecture, near Tokyo.[2]

Since then many such mounds and other sites have been excavated, yielding great quantities of pottery and other material including stone, bone and wood implements, textile remnants, and traces of foodstuffs such as fish, animal and bird bones, seeds and nuts as well as shells. From these it has been possible to infer the lifestyle of the early Japanese or 'Jomon' people.

Fig. 4 Curved patterns on pots of the Final Jomon phase. Left to right: jar with incised pattern and cord markings from Hokkaido, height 10 cm (4 in); jar with raised curved zones with cord markings from north Honshu, height 6.8 cm (2.6 in); bulbous storage jar with cord markings from north Honshu, height 26 cm (10.2 in); incense burner-type vessel, use unknown, coated overall with a black lacquer or other organic material, height 7.7 cm (3 in); spouted vessel from Hokkaido, with carved cord-marked zones over lower burnished areas and a hole in the base suggesting it was deliberately spoiled, perhaps for funerary use, diameter 17.8 cm (7 in).

The archaeological history of the Jomon is too complex to deal with in detail here except in the broadest terms. But it is convenient to follow the conventional division into six temporal phases, which relate to regional developments in pottery types. Prior to the scientific dating of the Fukui sherds, scholars had already identified five phases in the classification of the many types of Jomon pottery found. The discovery of the earlier pottery necessitated the addition of a sixth 'Incipient' Jomon phase.

The six divisions given below are generally accepted, although the matter is complicated by regional variations, and several alternative groupings have been proposed.[3]

Phases of the Jomon period[4]	
Incipient Jomon	10,000–7000 BC
Initial Jomon	7000–4000 BC
Early Jomon	4000–3000 BC
Middle Jomon	3000–2000 BC
Late Jomon	2000–1000 BC
Final Jomon	1000–400 BC

A further cultural division, called the Yayoi period (400 BC–300 AD) after a site near Tokyo, followed immediately in south-western Japan. During this time Korean and Chinese cultural and technical influences brought about changes in pottery styles, although many pieces retained a vestige of Jomon decoration near the upper rim (fig. 6) and Jomon designs are believed to have persisted for several centuries in the northern island of Hokkaido (fig. 5).

The introduction of pottery in Japan broadly corresponds with the climatic changes which took place at the end of the Ice Age. As the temperatures warmed, deciduous forests expanded northwards and a sedentary life could be maintained, supported by the wildlife of the forested mountains, the warm seas, and the fertile lowlands. The southern forests were predominantly evergreen, and less hospitable to the deer and wild boar which thrived in the deciduous areas of the north, but they abounded in nuts and other fruits of the trees. During the warm months the coastal dwellers ate shellfish and other fish including whales and dolphins, in the autumn they gathered nuts, and in the winter they hunted animals with bow and arrow and caught them in pit-traps with converging walls.

In the earliest (Incipient) Jomon period, a high proportion of sites appear to be inland caves or rock shelters, and the degree of sedentism is impossible to assess precisely, but from the Initial Jomon, small villages of pit-dwellings partially sunk into the ground are known, implying a very settled existence. Pit-dwellings are a characteristic feature throughout the Jomon period. Pillars supported roofs which sloped down to the ground. From the Early period, Jomon houses sometimes had stone floors; the diet included beans, cereal grasses, gourds, roots and other foods which, while not proving deliberate cultivation, at least implies careful management of natural resources. Anthropomorphic pottery figurines, polished stone implements and stone phallic objects associated with the houses indicate a widely practised ritual aspect of Jomon life.

Excavations of a Middle/Late Jomon settlement at Sannai Maruyama, in Aomori prefecture, give a revealing picture of Jomon village structure and raise further questions about the extent of communal activity. At the height of its prosperity the population of the Sannai Maruyama, which proved to have been occupied for some two thousand years, was approximately five hundred, living in about a hundred pit-dwellings. Situated on the edge of Muttsu Bay, the village was divided into separate areas for dwellings, storage-pits, refuse dumps of the usual shell-mound type, and separate graveyards for children and adults. The dwelling houses were situated around the edges of the village, with no surrounding defence structures and no apparent consideration of attack from outside. A road led through the village and down towards the sea. Larger buildings, from 10 up to 30 m (33 to 100 ft) long, are assumed to have been for communal use as factories, stores or meeting-houses. But the most impressive foundations were a set of six post-holes, 2 m (6.5 ft) in diameter and separated by intervals of 4 m (13 ft), situated on a hill at the north-eastern edge of the village. The structure must have been about 20 m (66 ft) high and may have served as a fishery watch-tower, with a clear view of Muttsu Bay at a time when the sea level was several metres higher than it is today. Food was stored in pits, and in one of these a cache of more than a thousand chest-nuts was found.

Shipping must have been a major method of transport for the Jomon people. This is indicated by their fishing activities, the fact that similar pottery is found the length and breadth of Japan from an early period, the presence of stones such as obsidian and jade far from their place of origin, and the fact that Jomon pottery is also found in Ryukyu to the south and on islands distant from the mainland including Tsushima (which is halfway to Korea). A blunt-prowed dugout about 5 m (16.5 ft) long, together with six small paddles and two larger ones, was excavated at Kamo, an Early Jomon site in Chiba prefecture. Such a boat, which has been described as a canoe, could carry a substantial cargo over long distances and could have been used for deep-sea fishing.

The early phases of Jomon pottery

Jomon pottery went through a number of distinctive changes over the 10,000 years that it was produced, although all types are unglazed, low-fired wares. Kilns are unknown throughout the period and the firings are likely to have been in bonfires or in pits, as indicated by the dark surface colours and the presence of carbon-rich cores in the walls (see ch. 22, p. 151). In the early periods, organic fibres are present and were probably added to temper the clay,

Fig. 5 Vessels with cord markings and incised lines from various sites in Hokkaido, Final phase, maximum height 24.4 cm (9.6 in).

while other pots are coarse with a high content of granitic particles such as mica. Little has been published on construction methods. Reconstruction of sherds from Incipient Jomon cave sites has shown the pots to have been made by moulding small flat sections of clay together, and possibly by a form of coiling. From the Initial Jomon onwards, all of the pottery appears to have been made by coiling ropes of clay and smoothing them together by hand into a continuous surface. The coiled structure is sometimes indicated by undulations in the walls of the vessels. 'Paddle and anvil' techniques, using simple tools to beat the coils together (see ch. 5, p. 45), do not appear to have been used, and the potter's wheel was not introduced to Japan until the Yayoi period. Jomon pottery appears to have been made within the household, and the extent of trade or exchange is not yet clear.

The earliest sherds of the Incipient Jomon period have been shown to be mostly of small, deep, pointed- or round-bottomed pots, although some may have had flat bases. They are remarkable for their very thin walls: pots measuring, say, 20 cm (8 in) high had walls only as thick as 0.5 cm (0.2 in) or less. Incipient Jomon pottery was decorated near the rims with circumferential bands moulded in relief, ceramic 'beans' and rows of 'fingernail' impressions, which were more probably made with the end of a split piece of bamboo (fig. 3, right). They have been found distributed over the whole of Japan. Some later pots of this phase have cord impressions. The conical forms of these earliest pots strongly suggest that their purpose was primarily for cooking, as they were suitable for setting into the soft soil and ash in the base of the cooking hearth.

The pottery of the Initial Jomon, characterised by cord patterns on round-bottomed and tapered vessels, lasts until 4000 BC. Cord marks are common, made by rolling cords over the sides of the pot, together with engraved linear patterns and the impressions of seashells. During the Early Jomon phase the culture became well established in the central and northern areas of Japan and Hokkaido, and the pottery has applied and incised

decoration and sculpted rims. Lacquer, used to coat and preserve wooden objects, was sometimes used to decorate the pots and render them impermeable to water. Pots were naturally used for food storage as well as drinking vessels and, possibly, lamps. From the Initial period on, animal and particularly human figurines abound, from simple cruciform anthropomorphs to roundly sculpted figures in the Late and Final Jomon phases.

Middle and later phases

Pottery of the Middle Jomon, between around 3000 and 2000 BC, has complex moulding, with deep whorls (figs 1, 2, bottom left), and sometimes stylised snake-like motifs and human faces moulded in relief. In the later part of this period in central Japan the moulding became extremely complex, with thick-walled vessels having castellated profiles and so-called flame patterns extending upwards from the mouths of the vessels. This thick and highly decorated pottery suggests a ritual use, and at least a highly devel-oped aesthetic sensitivity. An incense burner-like vessel in the British Museum (fig. 4, centre front) appears to have been made with a hole in the base for ritual use, or for an as yet unknown purpose. Earrings and other jewellery bear similar curvilinear designs. At this time the population underwent a marked increase, especially in the central area of the main island, Honshu, and notably in the high volcanic plateau of present-day Nagano prefecture.

The Late Jomon phase, between 2000 and 1000 BC, is characterised by a greater variety of pots, including spouted vessels (fig. 4, right). The exuberant decoration of the Middle phase was replaced by subtler designs, with cord marks within smooth-burnished zones of sophisticated curved pattern. The pottery, generally made with finer clay, became thinner and harder. Much of it is dark in colour, indicating differences in the firing from the pots of the Middle phase.

The Final Jomon phase covers the period from around 1000 until about 400 BC, when wet-rice agriculture and metallurgy became widely practised

along with other technologies and customs introduced by immigrants from the Asian mainland. Final Jomon pottery generally has less exaggerated rim moulding and there was a further increase in the variety of vessels, including shallow bowls and pedestalled vessels, resulting from mainland influences. The curved surface zones became thinner, and towards the end of this period the lower parts of many pots were left undecorated. A close regular 'cloud' pattern of long S-shaped lines might suggest some influence from China in its similarity to bronze motifs. Recent excavations have shown the use of pottery as funerary jars in the later periods. The Chikanainakamura site in Iwate prefecture is that of a typical Late/Final phase Jomon village. The excavation showed the usual round post-holes of the pit-dwelling houses, shell middens and graves. The site has also yielded stone tools, figurines, asphalt, jade and amber ornaments, and ceramic and stone plaques incised with female outlines.

The graves of children are separate from those of adults; the children are interred in jars, often ritually spoiled by breaking a hole in the base or side. At some village sites the children's graves are nearby or even inside the houses. Adult graves were oval in form, typically with the remains curled up into a crescent shape. In some instances the bodies were covered with gravel and stones. Some of the graves contained a surface layer of pots – in one instance, there were ten of assorted types, including spouted vessels. In the Final Jomon phase, hollow figures were made for use as burial urns for children. Some masks, without eye-holes (and therefore of no practical use), are reminiscent of the domestic hearth deities still found in some rural Japanese homes.

Fig. 6 (Opposite) Trumpet-necked storage jar of the Yayoi period, height 44 cm (17.3 in). The cord-pattern relief moulding at the join of the neck and combed wave patterns on the raised band at the neck show the persistence of Jomon forms into the Yayoi period (c. 400 BC–c. 3rd century AD).

Early Pottery in the Middle Nile Valley

Derek Welsby

Detailed archaeological work in the Middle Nile Valley, here defined as the area between the First Cataract – the traditional southern border of Egypt – and the White and Blue Niles for some 300 km (185 miles) upstream, south of Khartoum (fig. 1), was begun in 1907 by George Reisner. As director of the first Archaeological Survey connected with the raising of the Aswan Dam, he not only conducted rescue excavations in the far north of this zone but also formulated a chronology for the different cultural phases he recognised and rapidly published his results.[1] The earliest phase he designated 'group a' (now referred to as the A-Group).

Far to the south, the work of the Wellcome expedition at Jebel Moya was not published for forty years, and it fell to Tony Arkell to reveal, at the Khartoum Hospital site and at Shahainab, the earlier and rather different cultures of central Sudan.[2] With the progressive heightening of the Aswan Dam and with the construction of the Sadd el Ali, extensive rescue survey and excavation was undertaken along the whole valley, from the First to the Dal cataracts. Only in the region upstream of the Dal Cataract is archaeological work in the valley now continuing.

Independent development

The early to mid Holocene, the geological period which followed the last glaciation, was a time when the climate of the Sahara was much more conducive to human and animal life than it is now. Pottery developed independently at that time in the Sahara and in the Middle Nile Valley.

The dotted wavy-line technique of pottery decoration, evolved over a long period in the Central Sahara where it is widely distributed from c.7000 BC, only reached the Nile during the Nilotic mesolithic, about two

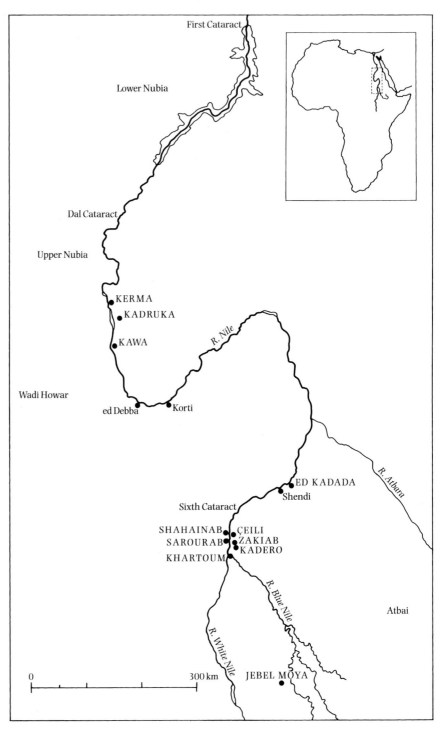

Fig. 1 Map of the Middle Nile Valley upstream of the First Cataract, traditionally the southern border of Egypt (archaeological sites are denoted in upper case).

26

millennia later.[3] By the same token, classic wavy-line pottery, which is very rare in the Sahara, is part of an early mesolithic tradition with a long indigenous development, intimately linked to the cultures of the central Nile Valley and immediately surrounding areas.[4]

The period of close contact which occurred between about 4200 and 3800 BC, at least in as much as it affected the pottery traditions, appears to have been short-lived, and there-after the two areas show largely independent cultural development. The contact was presumably a move-ment of ideas rather than of peoples en masse, as the cultural continuity within the Nile Valley is a striking feature of the periods both before and after the introduction of the new types of pottery decoration.[5] However, not all influences thereafter are related to contacts along the valley itself. Contacts to east and west remained, as can be seen in the pottery recovered from the middle Wadi Howar in western Sudan and in the Atbai, well to the east of the Nile.[6]

There are a number of affinities between later neolithic pottery in the Shendi Reach and pottery of the A-Group and to a lesser extent the C-Group in Lower Nubia.[7] There are also close parallels between A-Group ceramics and those found to the west of the Nile in the Wadi Howar.[8] The calciform beaker, a highly distinctive form with a bulbous base, narrow stem and widely flaring mouth, has an even wider distribution. It is a common type in Sudan, found in late neolithic contexts at sites as far apart as Kadruka and Kadero (figs 2, 4). Very similar vessels are found in the Badarian culture at, for example, Mostagedda,[9] and have been found in small numbers in the intervening area, as at Dakka.[10]

The origins of pottery production

Pottery is one of the most abundant of human artefacts and is of vital importance for the study of ceramic cultures, both from the chronological information that can be derived and for the light it sheds on the way of life of the people using it. The invention of pottery may have had a fundamental effect on early societies. Among the benefits was the use of pottery for cooking, which with the attendant marked increase in efficiency of boiling would have greatly expanded the range of potential foods. The opportunities for storage of foodstuffs over long periods may also have been of considerable importance.

Pottery use goes hand in hand with a sedentary lifestyle, as pottery is generally relatively heavy and fragile. It is thus not ideally suited to people who lead a migratory or nomadic existence – indeed, the nomads of central Sudan continue to eschew its use. It may even be the case that the benefits of the use of pottery stimulated a move towards sedentism in some cultures, rather than the other way round.[11]

On the Middle Nile pottery is first seen, therefore, at the time when the first sedentary settlements have been recognised. At Sarourab, excavations by the University of Khartoum have found pottery sherds associated with material which had been dated by the radiocarbon method to 9330 ± 110 and 9370 ± 110 BP (years ago).[12] At present this appears to be contemporary with the earliest evidence for pottery production elsewhere in Africa.[13]

These people do not appear to have been food producers but to have relied on a hunter-gatherer lifestyle sustained by the rich habitat along the banks of the Nile. There is no evidence to suggest that the domestication of plants and

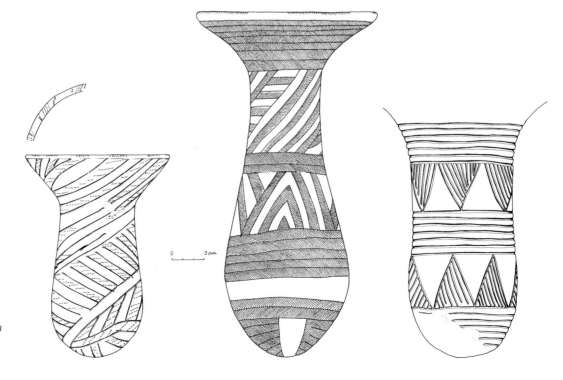

Fig. 2 Three calciform beakers: from site L14 in the northern Dongola Reach, from Kadero, and from Mostagedda.

animals was a prerequisite for pottery production and use. However, as the practice of agriculture and animal husbandry facilitates a sedentary life-style, and as pottery is associated with sedentism, in practice these features are often found together.

Raw materials and firing sites

It may be assumed that pottery production was localised, with raw materials being readily available along almost the whole length of the Nile Valley. Petrographic analysis on material mainly from the area between Khartoum and the Sixth Cataract indicates that clay sources changed over time. The clays used by the east bank potters fall into three well-defined groups: of mesolithic date, of the earlier neolithic and of the late neolithic. This appears to be directly related to the locations of the settlements, and hence of the potters, rather than a deliberate choice of raw material from a given area.[14] On the other bank of the river in the same area, where there was much less

Fig. 3 Neolithic pottery from the area south-east of Kawa.

geomorphological change, mesolithic and neolithic pottery is of similar composition, the potters using the same raw materials in both periods. Localised production is further hinted at by slight variations in form even over relatively short distances, as in the pottery from the region around Kadruka and that from the area immediately to the south around Kawa (fig. 3).

No pottery production sites of this period are known on the Middle Nile, although pottery is abundant. At Kadero 1, however, the concentration of pottery in certain areas of the site has been thought to indicate, on the basis of ethnographic observations elsewhere in Sudan, that those areas were used for the firing of pots.[15] Kilns have not been noted, and it is likely that the pots were either fired in bonfires or in simple pits dug into the ground.

In the Dongola Reach in particular there are very large numbers of what have been termed burnt mounds, piles of very heavily burnt earth overlying a sinuous pit which is also very heavily fire-damaged. A typical example excavated at Kawa was 2.3 m (7 ft) long, 60 cm (2 ft) wide and generally about 20 cm (8 in) deep, with a slightly deeper depression at one end

(fig. 5). A number of these have been excavated, but in no case has any waster material been found associated with them, and their association with pottery production, although possible, is by no means certain. Analysis of pottery from an area slightly north of Khartoum has indicated that mesolithic pottery of the Early Khartoum tradition was fired to a temperature between 800 and 900°C and that the firing time was short.[16]

Construction techniques

Mesolithic pottery tends to be rather coarse and thick, and there is clear evidence that it was made by using coils. The pottery of the neolithic period includes a number of high-quality vessels including the 'fine tablewares' from Kadero[17] and the calciform beakers already mentioned. Vessels, although handmade, are often extremely regular and quite thin-walled. Some may still have been built up from coils: the more skilled the potter, the less obvious the construction technique.[18] X-ray analysis of pottery from Zakiab,

Fig. 4 (Opposite) Calciform beaker from the neolithic cemetery at el Kadada.

however, failed to show any evidence for the coil technique.[19]

Most potters mixed their raw material with temper which fell into one of two main categories. Inorganic temper, usually either fine or at most medium-coarse sand (commonly with grain sizes not larger than 0.4–0.5 mm) was used over a wide area. Chaff-tempered wares are less common but are a particular feature of pottery in the ed Debba to Korti region of the Dongola Reach.[20]

On the basis of ethnographic studies it is assumed that pottery was produced by women.

Form and function

The range of forms is more restricted than in later periods. Globular jars, wide-mouthed bowls, dishes and beakers are the most common, with the addition of a number of special types, among them the calciform beaker, and

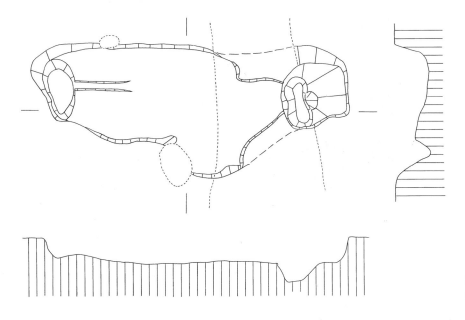

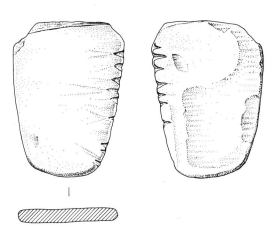

Fig. 5 (Left) Burnt mound at Kawa after excavation: section and plan.

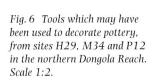

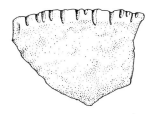

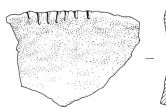

Fig. 6 Tools which may have been used to decorate pottery, from sites H29, M34 and P12 in the northern Dongola Reach. Scale 1:2.

the colander (fig. 7). Most vessels have rounded bases which are ideally suited for placing on the ground. Some, however, have markedly pointed bases, and the very small bases of the calciform beakers would have made it difficult to stand them upright.

A range of forms, including the calciform beaker, appear to have been made specifically for funerary use[21] and need not have been constrained by functionality. Funerary pots are occasionally found nested within one another. A further use for pottery in a funerary context is as containers for the burial of infants, and a number of examples have been found dating to the late neolithic at el Kadada. The pots are usually large, of hemispherical form and decorated, and they sometimes contain grave-goods and multiple interments.[22]

Decorative techniques

A wide range of decorative motifs and techniques were employed, from burnishing to impressed motifs. At Geili it was noted that particular decorative motifs were confined to vessels of specific types.[23] Three broad groups of impressed decoration have been recognised: those formed by using a rocker-stamp, either with a plain evenly or unevenly serrated edge; by using an alternately pivoting stamp with a double-pronged implement; or by making simple impressions using a serrated-edged tool, a stylus or a double-pronged tool. From these a wide range of motifs were created, occasionally with seemingly identical motifs produced by different tools. Other common techniques are rocker-stamp and dotted designs and saw-tooth and dog's-tooth decoration.

A number of experiments have been carried out to try to replicate the designs. Among the tools used have been bivalve shells, the plain-edged tool for zigzag (also termed 'saw-tooth' and 'wolf-tooth') decoration.[24] Serrated-edged tools called 'combs' have been found of bone, potsherds, polished stones and bivalve shells (fig. 6).[25] It has also been suggested that catfish spines were used for this purpose.[26] Dash impressions may have been produced by cord wrapped around a core.

Fig. 7 A nest of three pots in the neolithic cemetery at site L8 in the northern Dongola Reach. The central pot is a colander. Scale 20 cm (8 in).

Changes in form and decoration

Developments in both forms and decorative techniques can be recognised during the neolithic. At Geili there is a move from globular jars to red-slipped bowls and sinuous walled jars, which can be paralleled by the change from traditional rocker-stamped decoration made with the regular serrated-edged tool to the more advanced form made with unevenly serrated-edged combs.[27] The earlier technique is widespread all over the Sahara, the latter type seems to be a local innovation. The later use of the alternately pivoting stamp, however, which rapidly came to the fore not only in the Nile Valley[28] but also in the Sahara, indicates that contacts still existed between the two regions. In the late neolithic, rocker-stamping is almost totally abandoned in favour of incised motifs and impressed dotted lines. Slipping and polishing become common in the later neolithic.

From the early third millennium BC the northern Middle Nile Valley was progressively influenced and sometimes directly controlled by Egypt, although indigenous pottery traditions continued to flourish under the so-called C-Group and Kerma cultures. Meanwhile, to the south a 'neolithic' culture continued for much longer. It was only with the growth of the Kushite state in the earlier first millennium BC that the two areas were united politically and again shared to some extent a common ceramic tradition.

Early Prehistoric Pottery in Britain

Gillian Varndell and Ian Freestone

The earliest use of pottery in Britain is associated with the advent of farming about six thousand years ago. However, hardly any evidence has been recognised for workshops, kilns, claypits or the associated by-products of pottery-making before the Roman conquest, some four millennia later (ch. 7). Occasional deposits of clay, crushed flint or shell may represent supplies of raw material[1] and suitable pebbles or bones could have been used as tools, though interpretation of such material is frequently difficult. A rare example of such evidence is a toothed bone used to stamp impressions into pottery, found at a site of the Beaker culture at Gwithian, Cornwall.[2] We know that prehistoric pottery was made and fired, but we do not know where.

The societies of neolithic and Bronze Age Britain practised agriculture and stock-breeding to varying degrees. That social organisation and power structures altered through time is evidenced by changing modes of settlement and burial practice, although the record may be sketchy and uneven. The scattered farmsteads of the neolithic are far less prominent in the archaeological landscape than are communal tombs and ceremonial sites. Settlements remained small into the Bronze Age, although domestic dwellings began to look more substantial and single burials with valuable grave-goods indicate that some individuals were able to accrue personal wealth and status. The appearance of enclosed settlements of small groups of buildings and of land divisions accompanies a decline in the prominence of burial sites. During the later Bronze Age, larger living sites and defended hill-top settlements testify to social, demographic and economic changes.

Even at this time, when people and their pots are more conspicuous in the archaeological record and the debris of other craft activities such as metal-working abounds, pottery workshops remain elusive. This suggests that the nature of the production process itself must be a significant factor in its low visibility.

In spite of the limitations, some understanding of the methods used can be gleaned from detailed observation of the surviving pots themselves and by analogy with ethnographic observation and experimental replication, which make the absence of direct evidence for ceramic production easier to explain.[3] Unfortunately, we remain in the dark about the locations of production, the immediate social and economic structures in which it occurred and, particularly, the identities and status of the potters.[4] Any spiritual or symbolic significance assigned to the pots by the potter remains obscure or, at best, the subject of much learned speculation.

Open firing and its implications

Although prehistoric pottery may be usefully subdivided into many chronological and regional groups on the basis of its shapes and decoration, the main elements of the underlying technology are continuous. The most apparent evidence for this is the surface colour of the pots – typically browns and buffs through to dull pinks and reds, the surface of a single pot often appearing patchy and uneven (fig. 1). There may be black, sooty marks or scarring where whole areas have spalled off. The rather dull colours suggest low-temperature firing, while surface markings indicate that the pots were not isolated from the fuel and that the fire itself was subject to strong variation. The cores of sherds are commonly black (see ch. 22, p. 151), where the carbon in the clay has not had time to burn out,[5] and they are often soft and friable,[6] indicating a susceptibility to weathering. These characteristics are typical of open firings, where the pottery was placed in a bonfire on the ground or in a pit without any permanent kiln superstructure. Most prehistoric pottery

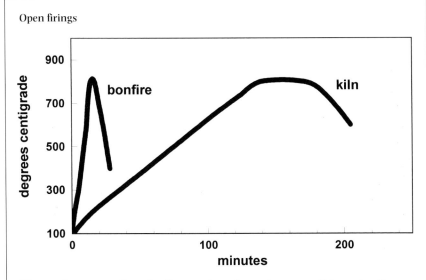

The graph compares the rate of temperature change in an open firing or bonfire with that of a traditional wood-fired updraught kiln. The rapid increase in temperature in the bonfire necessitates the use of a coarse-textured or tempered clay.

Fig. 1 Bronze Age pottery from Britain, showing a wide range of surface colours, dependent upon firing conditions. To the left are two globular urns. One is orange and oxidised, showing a blackened area through contact with the fuel. The other is heavily smudged, due to carbon deposited in reduction. The beakers to the right show a range of incised and impressed decoration; once again, the firing effects are highly variable.

in Britain appears to have been fired in this way, in which the strength and atmosphere of the fire depended upon the prevailing winds and the pottery was in direct contact with the fuel and the flames.[7]

Open firings are well attested ethnographically and have been replicated by archaeologists in many experiments. Temperatures may rise to 800°C within half an hour and the whole firing typically lasts less than an hour (ch. 32).[8] Because there is no kiln superstructure and because firings are short and of relatively low temperature, few traces of this activity are left in the ground. One such firing site, excavated only five years after it had been used, revealed no clues that would suggest it had been anything but a domestic hearth.[9] The reason that prehistoric pottery-making has left so little trace is therefore clear.

Clay and temper

The dependence upon an open-firing technology constrained prehistoric potters in many ways, one of which was in the preparation of the clay. Clay deposits are widely available in Britain, and it is unlikely that the potters were obliged to travel more than a kilometre or so (0.6 mile) to collect their clay, which is the preferred limit suggested by Arnold's survey of traditional potters.[10] A good, plastic clay was often insufficient on its own, however. The water added to make the clay more workable can amount to tens of per cent of the body by weight.[11] In an open firing, where the temperature rises past 100°C very quickly, this water boils with an explosive force. If the clay does not contain pathways which allow the steam to escape, then the pot itself will fail dramatically, due to the build-up of pressure.

This problem was overcome by using clays which were rich in non-plastic (i.e. rigid, non-clay) inclusions which, as the clay dried, opened up small channels in the body which allowed the steam to escape. When a clay was not naturally sufficiently rich in inclusions to allow it to be fired successfully, then the potter would add them as temper. The tempering materials favoured in prehistoric British pottery included flint or other rock types (probably crushed

Fig. 2 Detail of the surface of the orange globular urn in fig. 1, showing particles of crushed flint temper.

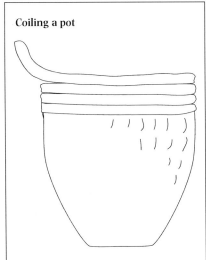

Coiling a pot

Coiling involves building up a pot by applying a series of long rolls of clay. After a few coils have been pressed on top of each other, the surfaces are pressed or scraped smooth to join the coils together. The pot may be left to dry and strengthen between applications of coils. Some potters build pots up using short rings or strips of clay, rather than winding long coils around the pot.

from pebbles), grog (crushed pottery) and shell. Temper may commonly be seen on the surfaces of early pottery as small raised areas of up to a few millimetres across, differing in colour from the clay matrix (fig. 2). The potters appear to have been very conservative in their use of clays and tempers, and the same materials were used over long periods of time and across wide areas. Fabrics tend to reflect local availability of raw materials. For example, in Wessex crushed flint and shell were commonly added to pottery throughout the neolithic, while Beaker wares of the Early Bronze Age showed a marked preference for grog.[12]

The addition of tempering materials modified not only the firing characteristics of the clay but also the working and drying properties and the strength of the pot.[13] Experience and the 'feel' of the clay are likely to have determined the amount of temper that was added. In some cases, coarse temper was preferred for larger, thick-walled pots, to allow a successful firing, but was less favoured for finer, decorated pottery because of its disfiguring effect on surface appearance.[14]

Forming techniques

Pottery was produced using hand-forming techniques. Judging from irregularities in the walls of vessels, the way that much pottery has broken (more or less parallel to the rim) and the distribution of voids in the fabrics, it seems that, in general, vessels were built up using coils, rings, strips or slabs (fig. 4), while smaller vessels may have been pinched or drawn up from lumps of clay. No detailed evidence has been presented to suggest that other techniques, such as 'paddle and anvil' (see ch. 5, p. 45), were used, but until the late neolithic pots were round-based, and such a form could readily have been produced by beating the clay.

Surface finish and decoration

The poorly controlled colours and uneven finishes of many prehistoric ceramics would not have made good grounds for painted decoration and, with the exception of white infilling of the incised decoration on some beakers, pre-Iron Age pottery reveals few signs of original paint or applied pigment.

Fig. 3 Peterborough ware 'Mortlake style' bowl from Hedsor (Buckinghamshire), showing heavy decoration with twisted cord impressions.

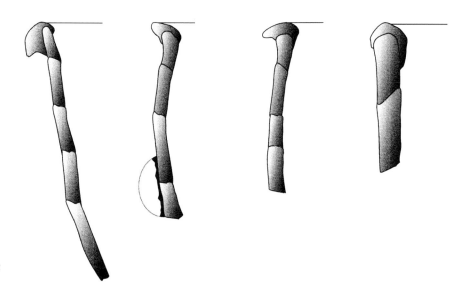

Fig. 4 Fracture patterns and joins of sherds may reveal construction details of pottery, as in these cross-sections of neolithic pottery from Windmill Hill, which reflect the position of the coils used to build up the pot.

The first slips appear in the Late Bronze Age, while the use of hematite (iron oxide), rubbed into the surface of the pot before firing to produce an overall glossy red coloration, was also a Late Bronze Age innovation.[15] For most of the period, decorative methods were very simple.

Temper appears to have been worked into the surfaces of some wares or covered with clay, perhaps by smoothing over the unfired body. Use of a temper such as grog, with a colour and texture similar to the fired pot, allowed the development of a finer finish than did crushed stone or flint, and this is particularly apparent in the finer wares of the later neolithic and Early Bronze Age. The finer Beaker wares commonly contain a very finely crushed (or sieved) temper. The surface was sometimes burnished to produce a smooth glossy finish, by rubbing with a pebble or other smooth tool, before decorating with impressed or incised techniques.

Much of the earliest pottery is plain although decorative elements soon appear, but plainwares continue along-side decorated for some considerable time. During the neolithic a range of techniques became common, such as rows of simple impressions made with improvised tools or fingernails and vertical or oblique incisions. Twisted cord was sometimes pressed into the soft clay (fig. 3). At this time regional differences in style can already be observed. Later in the period pots might be more extensively and elaborately decorated, with impressions of twisted and whipped cord or the ends of bird bones. Another tradition of potting, in which vessels are flat-based, is associated with a rich repertoire of designs including raised ribs and pellets of applied clay; the combination of this and the characteristic grooved decoration is reminiscent of basketwork (fig. 5). It may be that the earliest British pottery copied the leather and basketry containers which they supplemented and replaced, and which do not survive. The use of toothed-comb stamps and cord impressions is demonstrated par excellence in some of the more richly decorated Early Bronze Age forms such as food vessels and beakers. Undecorated pots are present to some

degree throughout the prehistoric period and there is no consistent chronological trend in quality. For example, much of the earlier neolithic pottery is thin-walled, evenly fired and has a smooth burnished finish, in marked contrast to some of the later coarse Early Bronze Age wares. The effort invested in the production of pottery is likely to have been determined by a number of factors, one of which was the intended function of the vessel – whether for cooking, storage or use as a funerary urn. A recent study of Beaker pottery suggests that where the vessels were intended for interment with human remains, the body was less well prepared but the pots were made to look better by careful decoration and surface treatment.[16]

Drying and firing

Activities such as the digging of clay, drying of pots and burning of fuel are dependent on climate and weather, which means pottery-making is a seasonal activity, confined to drier and warmer periods, in most traditional societies.[17] It is likely that this was the case in prehistoric Britain. Ethnographic parallels suggest that a drying time of days or weeks would have been necessary between forming and firing, although this could have been shortened by drying or preheating near the fire.[18]

A more or less uniform surface colour could be achieved by controlling the firing, but this was much more successful in the production of some wares than others. Beaker pottery was quite often fired so that the final stages were fully oxidising and a good overall buff or pink colour was achieved. In contrast, some wares appear to have been covered with fuel or vegetation at the end of the firing, so that they achieved an overall black colour (fig. 1).

Production and exchange

The amount of pottery in prehistoric Britain is small relative to the more urbanised contemporary societies of the Mediterranean and the Near East. Taking into account the absence of wheels, kilns and other specialised equipment, this suggests that potting

Fig. 5 (Opposite) Details showing decorative techniques: (a) whipped cord, made by whipping a fine thread at right angles around a thicker, flexible core; (b) twisted cord, made with a two-strand cord; (c) plaited cord; (d) impressed comb decoration.

a

b

c

d

was essentially a domestic affair, based around the household or homestead. Ethnographically, pottery in such situations is often made by women, for whom the making of pots is but one of a wide range of domestic tasks which make up a complex and seasonally variable routine. It is quite possible, indeed likely, that much earlier prehistoric pottery was made by women, but we have no direct evidence of the gender of the potters.

Modern descriptions of traditional potters whose work is based around the household suggest that this type of activity is typically associated with relatively poor agricultural communities. The cost of producing handmade, openfired pots in such an environment is relatively low. They may be sold or exchanged to supplement the rather uncertain living provided by farming in marginal areas. The scale on which such a 'household industry' is developed can vary greatly, ranging from a single individual to several members of a family, or even more than one family in an area or community. However, it is always subsidiary to the main activity of farming.[19]

Evidence for exchange or trade in pottery comes from the petrological analysis of wares from south-western Britain, which reveals that certain groups were produced from clays which are of very limited occurrence. The pots, however, may be distributed over a very wide area. One such clay is the so-called 'gabbroic' clay, which forms on a rock outcropping over about 7 sq km (2.7 sq miles) on the Lizard peninsula in Cornwall. This clay, which contains naturally included rock fragments as 'temper', appears to have been a very good potting clay, and it was used over a period spanning several thousand years. Pottery from this source was widely traded in the neolithic period.[20] A particular class of Bronze Age pot, the 'Trevisker' urn, was frequently made from this clay, and examples are represented up to 80 km (50 miles) away; one example has even been identified from Hardelot, Pas de Calais, across the Channel in northern France.[21] Substantial quantities of such pottery appear to have been widely distributed. It looks as though one or more communities based on or close to the Lizard was involved in the exploitation of the local clay and traded or exchanged the pots produced over a wide area. Whether these potters lived permanently on the clay outcrop or exploited it on a seasonal basis is unclear. In contrast to the wide distribution of the Trevisker urns, analysis of the more highly decorated Beaker wares suggests that they tended to travel no more than a few kilometres from the place where they were made. The difference may well be one of degree; both types of pot could have been produced by part-time, seasonally active potters, based in or around the home.

Prehistoric Ceramics in Mesopotamia

St John Simpson

Clay was first used in the Ancient Near East during the eighth millennium BC to make sun-dried or lightly baked figurines and 'tokens', as well as architecture. Stone vessels, wooden containers and gypsum or asphalt-coated baskets preceded the earliest ceramic vessels, which appear in the Zagros region. Early plaster and metal industries illustrate familiarity with the potential of fire to transform materials, but it is unclear whether these affected early ceramic production.[1] Within Mesopotamia, different prehistoric cultures developed their own distinctive ceramic traditions. These provide some of the earliest archaeological evidence for kilns, high-quality painted wares and for ceramic trade.

Proto-Hassuna and Hassuna

The earliest known ceramics date to the late seventh millennium BC and are found at small village sites. This pottery is known as Proto-Hassuna ware and consists of handmade low-fired coarse-wares, usually with heavy organic temper and lightly burnished surfaces. Decoration was limited to reddish-brown painted bands on the rim and plastic decoration in the form of small knobs, animals and schematic human figures. Slab-built sagging keel-shaped jars and four-footed vessels were characteristic and large storage jars were sunk into floors as fixed storage containers.[2] Small quantities of thin-walled, shell-tempered, burnished cherry-red (Dark-Faced Burnished)

wares may represent western imports from Syria or Cilicia, suggesting that trade soon followed the appreciation of the economic advantages of ceramics.[3] Unfortunately, the original function of most vessels remains unknown. The extent of inner black cores (see p. 151) suggests that much of this early pottery was fired at temperatures of 600–700°C for about an hour.[4] Early kilns have not been identified and it is likely that the ceramics were fired in bonfires, a practice that survives today in villages of Iraq and Turkey but which is notoriously difficult to recognise as it leaves few archaeological remains.[5]

Hassuna pottery was better fired than earlier ceramics and the earliest identified kilns date from this period. These were discovered at Yarim Tepe I,

Fig. 1 Hassuna coarse incised husking trays (left) and Samarra painted bowls.

a substantial agricultural village, and were circular, measuring 1.2–2 m (3.6–6 ft) across, consisting of a sunken fire-box capped by a permanent clay grate – up to 10 cm (4 in) thick and perforated by up to fifty holes 15 cm (6 in) across – with a sloping stoke-hole at one end.[6] No traces of the actual firing-chamber walls have survived, suggesting that the upper part of the kiln was covered with a temporary dome which could be easily assembled over the loaded kiln yet rapidly dismantled after firing. This feature appears on Near Eastern pottery kilns to the present day.[7] The clustering of kilns within enclosures implies the separation of ceramic production from household activities, although it is unknown who was actually responsible for pottery production. Globular jars and open bowls were decorated with incision, red or black paint or a combination of techniques to form chevron and herringbone patterns, possibly inspired by basketry (fig. 4, top row). Straight-sided oval trays with scored walls and flat corrugated-base interiors are thought to have been used as 'husking trays' (fig. 1) to produce flour, and large jars continued to be used for grain storage.[8]

Samarra

The Samarran culture flourished *c.* 6300–6000 BC, mainly in the Tigris and Euphrates river valleys of central Mesopotamia, although other settlements are known from the Hamrin basin and the Mandali area. The largest known Samarran settlements are Tell es-Sawwan and Choga Mami, each enclosed within a wall and ditch; typical houses include up to fourteen rooms, suggesting extended families. This culture may have developed a relatively elaborate social structure because of the need to co-ordinate labour in the irrigation works which were necessary to sustain settlements in this area of low annual rainfall.[9]

Each settlement was probably largely self-sufficient in ceramics, judging by the number of known kilns and over-fired wasters; the kilns themselves differ little from other early Mesopotamian examples but attained higher temperatures, estimated at between 850 and

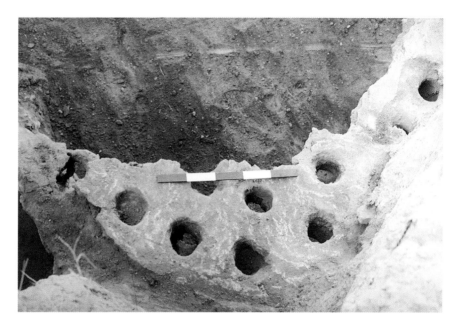

Fig. 2 View from above of the perforated clay grate of an Ubaid updraught pottery kiln at Tell Abu Dhahir, in northern Iraq (50-cm/ 20-in scale). The earliest Mesopotamian pottery was probably fired in bonfires, but circular updraught kilns were developed by 6000 BC. The plans of these were similar in later periods, and different cultures adapted them for firing pottery in different conditions.

1050°C.[10] Bowls and hole-mouth jars were typically painted (fig. 1) with bold geometric reddish-brown designs reminiscent of woven patterns; now and then bichrome designs occur in red and black. Animals (ibexes or goats, deer, birds, fish, crabs, spiders, scorpions), swastikas and human faces occasionally featured, sometimes arranged in a whirling style. Other pots were decorated with fine scratched or rougher deep-slashed incision, presumably executed using a flint blade. A small number of square and oval vessels were also made, perhaps in imitation of baskets or stone vessels.[11]

Painted bowls were sometimes repaired after accidental breakage by drilling holes on either side of the join to enable fastening with gut or fine cord, subsequently plastered over with asphalt (fig. 4, second row); this practice is also attested from Halaf and Ubaid settlements. Despite this reuse they were not as highly valued as stone vessels, which were popular grave-goods at Tell es-Sawwan. Occasional

painted signs on the bases may represent potters' marks, implying manufacture for a market beyond immediate household needs; indeed, sporadic occurrences of Samarran painted wares at sites across Mesopotamia suggest that there was limited trade.[12]

Halaf

Two further cultures, each producing a distinctive range of ceramics, were developing to the north and south of the Samarran homeland, namely the Halaf (*c.* 6000–5000 BC) and the Ubaid. New villages were founded in the dry farming upland plains of northern Mesopotamia, sometimes directly above deserted Hassuna settlements. The economy of these Halaf settlements was similar to that of their Hassuna forebears, yet distinctive new types of pottery (fig. 4, third row), figurines and domestic architecture were introduced.[13]

Painted pottery remains the greatest tangible achievement of the Halaf culture, although plain (fig. 3) and cooking wares form a large proportion of ceramic assemblages.[14] The principle had been grasped that fine clays were desirable for producing thin-walled vessels whereas coarser clays could be used to form jars and cooking wares. One of the longest excavated sequences derives from the site of Arpachiyah:

Fig. 3 Large Halaf plainware jar from Arpachiyah, in northern Iraq. Large handmade jars were one of the earliest categories of vessel produced in the Ancient Near East. Usually undecorated, they were used for storage.

Fig. 4 Selected Hassuna (top), Samarra, Halaf and Ubaid (bottom) sherds. Prehistoric potters in different parts of Mesopotamia produced distinctive local styles of handmade painted wares that help to define these cultures.

early Halaf pottery at this site was decorated with a water-soluble paint but, in later phases, a small number of lustrous bichrome and polychrome painted bowls were also used.[15]

Clays were probably obtained from seasonal watercourses (*wadis*) and river banks. Small lumps of pure clay found in ceramic fabrics suggest that limited soaking was undertaken prior to working the clay. Vessels were normally carefully wet-smoothed, obscuring traces of the forming and leaving a fine self-slip; some vessels were tempered with small quantities of fine sand but others lack visible temper.[16] A common motif was a bull's head (bukranium), popularly interpreted as evidence for stock-rearing or bull cults. Snakes, leopards and human figures were occasionally depicted but chequered, stippled and floral patterns were more popular, prompting comparison with textile designs.[17] Two unique vessels found at Yarim Tepe II were in the forms of a standing naked female figure and an animal.[18] Thin-walled keel-shaped bowls with flaring necks (called cream bowls from their similarity to local milk bowls) were popular, but the primitive level of metalworking at this date excludes the possibility that these were inspired by metalwares.[19] Circular updraught kilns continued to be used, achieving temperatures up to *c.* 950°C, the scarcity of cores implying careful firing.[20]

One building excavated at Arpachiyah contained large amounts of pottery in one room, together with a lump of red ochre, mixing palettes, bone tools, flint and obsidian cores. Some of these had originally been stacked on wooden shelves which had collapsed in situ after the structure was accidentally burnt. This building is usually interpreted as a 'master potter's shop'; based

Trace elements and trade

The analysis of chemical elements present at very low levels in the clay is commonly used to investigate trade in ancient pottery. The assumption underlying the approach is that a group of potters consistently used a single source of clay, which they processed in a consistent manner. The pots produced thus share a trace element 'fingerprint' which is specific to the workshop. This can then be matched to pottery from a wide area, in order to identify other products of the same kilns as well as the movement of pots over long distances. A number of techniques have been used in this type of work, of which NAA or neutron activation analysis (see ch. 24) is the most common.[38]

on both the large amounts of pottery and analogy with recent Iraqi potters, the excavator concluded that the site served as a specialist production centre for the region, possibly trading pottery to a large nearby settlement at Nineveh. This hypothesis is reinforced by trace element analyses of Halaf pottery which suggest that there was a complex pottery trading network, possibly contributing to the uniformity of Halaf painted ceramic styles. Some small settlements must have relied totally upon imported ceramics as they lack evidence for any local production.[21]

Ubaid

This culture developed (c. 6000–4000 BC) in the alluvial plains of lower Mesopotamia, ultimately replacing the Samarra and Halaf to the north.[22] The development of Ubaid culture is currently defined by five stages of painted pottery, referred to as Ubaid 0–4. The earliest of these, Ubaid 0, is known from only one site (Tell el-Oueili) because of the successive burial of early archaeological sites through annual deposits of silt. The pottery of Ubaid 1 and Ubaid 2 are also known respectively as Eridu and Hajji Muhammad wares (after the sites where these styles were first defined), whereas later Ubaid pottery is termed Northern Ubaid when found in northern Mesopotamia. Despite the large region covered during

the late phase, there is a surprisingly high degree of homogeneity of ceramic style; the reason for this is uncertain, yet it does not appear to reflect centralised production. Furthermore, Ubaid pottery is readily distinguishable in form and decoration from contemporaneous Iranian products.[23]

Southern Ubaid settlements depended upon irrigation for the cultivation of date palms and cereals; cattle and other livestock were also reared. Known settlements consist of villages but these include the earliest identifiable Mesopotamian shrines.[24] Despite the unstable nature of natural drainage in southern Iraq, there appears to have been a strong degree of continuity of settlement: Ubaid remains have been discovered underlying most of the later urban centres in southern Mesopotamia.

Despite the use of asphalt-coated baskets (and presumably woodenwares which have not survived), pottery was ubiquitous. As many as 78 ceramic vessels were found within a single house at Tell Madhhur. These included shallow and medium-sized bowls with a capacity of 1 to 3 litres (1 to 3.3 quarts), deep bowls, simple closed forms of 3 to 120 litres (up to 33 gallons), lugged jars of c. 12 to 30 litres (up to 8.25 gallons), ledge-rim jars, storage jars and plain cooking pots with lightly burnished surfaces designed to reduce porosity and facilitate cleaning.[25] Other Ubaid types included spouted vessels with basket handles and thin-walled lentoid 'tortoise' vessels with heavy

trumpet-spouts.[26] The addition of handles, spouts and perforated lugs were innovations in Mesopotamian ceramics.

The popularity and styles of painting varied according to period and site. Hajji Muhammad ware is characterised by heavy use of paint, leaving patterns reserved, whereas more open designs were favoured in later phases. However, there appears to be a decrease in frequency of painted wares in the Hamrin basin by the late Ubaid period.[27] Naturalistic motifs were always rare, but exceptions include birds, felines, human figures, bulls' heads and scorpions.[28] The pigments used consisted of iron and manganese oxides, often applied quite thickly. Variations in paint thickness and stacking position within the kiln contributed to wide variations in the colour of fabrics and paints (fig. 4, bottom row), which is typical of calcareous clays.[29] Ubaid 'sickles' (reaping hooks held in the left hand), pestles, model axe-heads and figurines were also produced in ceramic (fig. 5).[30]

Deliberate temper was used sparingly, probably owing to the natural plasticity of the clay, and consisted of fine sand or occasionally fine organic temper (possibly fluffy bulrush tops or cattail fuzz), although straw temper was heavily used for some late Ubaid wares.[31] Vessels were handmade, although a wheel or hand-turned tournette may have been used in finishing and painting; gypsum discs 10–40 cm (4–16 in) across, found

Mesopotamian pottery pigments

Mesopotamian potters utilised natural iron oxide pigments (ochres) in a skilful and sophisticated manner. They were able to produce black (reduced) paint on a red (oxidised) pottery body, and iron red and iron black paints on the same pot. The technique depended upon the selection or preparation for black pigments of ochres which had high potash contents; potash is a flux and caused the blacks to fuse at high temperatures. This not only ensured a glossy and durable paint but also 'fixed' the black colour, produced in the early reducing stages of firing, by forming a protective glassy coating around the iron oxide

particles. As the fuel burned down the fire became richer in oxygen, which diffused into the open structures of the body and the low-potash paint, turning them red, but which was excluded from the black.[39]

Manganese-rich pigments, which are black in both oxidising and reducing atmospheres, were not often used in Mesopotamia, although Ubaid pottery is sometimes painted with a complex chromium and manganese oxide black; this is likely to have been widely traded.[40] Manganese oxide-based pigments were used to the east, however, in the Indo-Iranian borderlands.[41]

Fig. 5 Ubaid spouted bowl, ceramic pestle, clay sickles and fused sickle wasters from sites in southern Iraq. Most Ubaid pottery was fired in updraught kilns within a temperature range of 1050–1200°C, although coarsewares were fired at lower temperatures. The local clays tended to turn greenish and the iron oxide pigments progressively darkened at higher temperatures. A regular potters' sideline was making hard-fired ceramic tools that were probably fired in the same kilns as the pots.

associated with a possible workshop at Tell Abada, may represent such tournettes.[32] Wet-smoothing during the final stage often left a self-slip, and some vessels may have been lightly polished.[33] The horizontal layout of much decoration may reflect the use of rotary action during painting. Circular or sub-rectangular updraught kilns measuring up to 2 m (6 ft) across have been identified at several sites (fig. 2).[34] Vitrified vessel and sickle wasters found at other sites imply more widespread manufacture (fig. 5).[35] There is evidence for off-site production at Tell Abada and Tell Songor, but this may reflect concern about the risk of fire rather than specialised production. Further-

more, no evidence exists for Ubaid pottery being used by different social groups within Mesopotamia, and pots were interred within graves in standard sets.[36]

Discoveries of Southern Ubaid painted wares at coastal fishing sites along the Persian Gulf provide the earliest evidence for Gulf trade, and further studies suggest the trade of Ubaid pottery within northern Iraq. Finally, there is evidence from Ubaid settlements for the import of Late Halaf pottery and Dalma Impressed ware, a Zagros type which may have been introduced by pastoralists using the natural corridor of the Great Khurasan Road.[37]

Pottery in Predynastic Egypt

A. J. Spencer

The pottery manufactured in ancient Egypt during the Predynastic period, which covers the two millennia between 5000 and 3100 BC, includes some of the most attractive and skilfully made ceramics ever found in the Nile Valley. Well before the unification of the land under the first kings, in about 3100 BC, the Predynastic communities of Upper Egypt attained a widespread distribution of similar styles, as the products of the material culture became increasingly uniform.[1] The Nile Delta region remained culturally different for a time but eventually came to adopt ceramic and other traditions from the south in the late Predynastic period (*c.* 3250 BC).[2]

The bulk of the Predynastic pottery which has found its way into museum collections belongs to the cultures of southern Egypt. In the north, the contemporary settlers of the Egyptian Nile Delta produced ceramics of a different character, chiefly plain and utilitarian, with none of the decorative finishes found in Upper Egypt.[3] The relative scarcity of the northern pottery in museums is due to the fact that early sites in the Delta were not excavated until fairly recently, whereas excavation of the southern Predynastic sites started from 1895.

Unlike much of the pottery from the later stages of ancient Egyptian civilisation, Upper Egyptian Predynastic wares received considerable effort in decoration and surface treatment. The resulting variation in the range of products was of great value in the work of Flinders Petrie, one of the fathers of Egyptology, who in 1898 used the incidence of specific styles in different archaeological strata to suggest a chronological progression for the pottery, creating a framework upon which the basic history of the Egyptian Predynastic cultures as a whole was then built. The vast majority of surviving Predynastic ceramics have been recovered from graves, in which pottery was the largest part of the contents.

Hand-building

The ceramics manufactured throughout the Predynastic period were all made by hand, and several procedures were adopted to facilitate the process.[4] The

Fig. 1 Handmade bowl characteristic of the Badarian culture, c. 4500 BC, manufactured in red-brown silt clay and decorated with combed grooves on the exterior, with the area around the rim and the interior blackened.

44

*Fig. 2   Typical vessels of the Naqada I
Predynastic culture (4000–3600 BC) from
Hu and Mahasna, in the Black-topped and
Red-polished styles of southern Egypt.
All are handmade from silt clay.*

assembly of the body of a vessel could be
achieved by a variety of methods, the
most basic of which was simply to pinch
out the shape of the vessel from a lump
of clay. The shaping could be assisted by
using a flat or rounded tool to support
the inside of the pot while beating the
exterior with a flat implement. This
process has been described as the
'paddle and anvil' technique, and
imprints of the use of the paddle have
been noted on pottery from about
4000 BC.

Slab-building, in which flattened
sheets of clay were joined together to
create the walls of the pot, was also
employed. This technique would have
been particularly suited to the creation
of large open-mouthed vessels, allowing

the hands easy access to the interior as
well as the exterior of the object. It has
been suggested that the use of this
process can be detected through
modern X-ray investigation, which
might reveal the boundaries of the
individual slabs of clay, although the
interpretation of the radiographs has
been questioned.[5] Evidence for the
coiling technique of making a pot is
attested from around 3500 BC
onwards, but it was probably in use
even earlier. This, as the name implies,
involved assembling the vessel wall
using superimposed rolled coils of clay,
which were later pressed together and
smoothed to eliminate the ridges
between the coils.[6]

The advantages of rotating the pot in
the potter's hands on any suitable flat
support in order to ease the work of
slab-building or coiling may well have
been recognised by the middle of the
Predynastic period, although any
rotation would have been too slow to

leave clear evidence. For this, we have
to look at late Predynastic vessels
(*c.* 3250 BC) on which distinct parallel
rilling lines are visible around the
necks, indicating that these were
finished with more rapid rotation and
therefore implying the use of a refined
support, or turning device. These
supports may have been made of wood,
clay or some other material, since all
that was required was something with a
concave depression in the top in which
the base of the pot could rest while
being turned by hand. This method of
production, although still lacking the
centrifugal force of the potter's wheel,
allowed for considerable improvement
in the quality of the finished vessels
and, indeed, continued to be used side
by side with the wheel-thrown pottery
of the Dynastic period (ch. 8).[7]

Firing

Predynastic kilns were little more than simple fires, sometimes enclosed by low walls. The pots were sometimes raised above the fire into the hot gases by supporting them on blocks of fired clay, the so-called 'fire-dogs'. Examples of kilns of this type are recorded from Hierakonpolis, where they have been dated to about 3600 BC.[8] The fire-dogs within one of these kilns were enclosed by a wall of mud bricks some 20 cm (8 in) in height, with an opening at one end to funnel the wind into the fire. The fact that excavated examples of Predynastic kilns are so rare probably indicates that the vast majority of early pottery was fired in the open, by enveloping the pots in the fuel of a fire. This procedure would leave no clear archaeological evidence as to the purpose of the fire, unless such a site happened to be found adjacent to other traces of ceramic production, such as the presence of dumps of spoiled vessels or wasters.

Black-topped wares

Some of the finest vessels come from the very earliest phases of Predynastic settlement in Upper Egypt. The pottery of the Badarian culture of the fifth millennium BC (centred around and named after the type-site of el-Badari) includes a variety of thin-walled bowls made of Nile silt clay and decorated on the exterior with very fine combed grooves, presumably applied with a wooden or bone tool.[9] The surfaces were then burnished; they are usually red or brown with a blackened area around the upper part, and often completely black on the interior (fig. 1). The blackening was achieved by enveloping the pots in a reducing atmosphere during part of the firing process, perhaps by inverting them in the carbon-rich ash of the fire. Alternatively, it has also been suggested that the same effect could have been achieved by burying the pots in the ground up to a level just below the rim and then burning chaff over them in order to blacken the top and interior. This explanation arose from an attempt to explain how the lower portions of the sides might have been protected from the blackening effect.[10]

The use of blackening as a decorative device continued throughout the remainder of the Predynastic period and came to be applied regularly to the upper parts of the exteriors of vessels, creating the so-called 'Black-topped pottery' of the succeeding Naqada culture. Not all of the pottery of the early Badarian people was fine; they also produced a great number of quite rough bowls in very poorly fired Nile silt clay, tempered with sand and chopped straw. The value of pottery at this early stage is shown by the fact that many of the better class of Badarian vessels show evidence of having been repaired after accidental breakage by drilling holes on each side of the break and binding the pieces together, probably with strips of leather.

The Badarian culture was followed by a most important phase of the Predynastic period, which takes its name from the type-site at Naqada and is itself divided into numerous sub-phases on the basis of the evolution of the ceramics and other objects. The most common pottery styles of the earlier stage of the Naqada culture were Black-topped and Red-polished vessels, with the former surviving in decreasing numbers down to the end of the Predynastic period (fig. 2).[11] The shiny red surfaces may have been achieved by the use of a slip of clay containing red ochre, which would then have been polished with a smooth pebble. The fine stripes formed by this method of polishing can be seen on many of the vessels, often aligned in a vertical direction. The Black-topped pottery consisted essentially of the same ware as the Red-polished vessels but with the upper part blackened, as described above. A sub-class of vessels, usually of fairly small sizes, was made with their surfaces entirely blackened and highly burnished.

Red-polished and painted wares

The potters developed the skill to create large vessels entirely by hand, in a whole range of shapes. The Red-polished vases, in particular, were occasionally made in exotic forms such as the double-vase (fig. 3). Less common styles were also manufactured, among which are the first examples of painted

wares. In the first half of the Naqada culture, between 4000 and 3600 BC, white or pale cream paint was applied to Red-polished vessels, usually bowls, after firing to create the so-called 'White cross-line' ware.[12] This appropriate name was adopted by Flinders Petrie to suit the style of the decoration, which consists for the most part of geometric patterns made up of intersecting white lines. A very few vessels in this group bear painted figures of animals.[13]

Painted decoration became much more common during a later stage of the Naqada culture after 3600 BC, when the colour of the decoration was no longer white but a dull purple-red and was applied to the fairly rough beige surfaces of marl clay jars before firing. This class of pottery consists of medium to large jars made in the hard fabrics known in Egyptian ceramic studies as Marl A1 and A4 (see ch. 8). The large jars of this class were sometimes made in two parts by coiling and then joined at the shoulder. The unslipped surfaces are covered with elaborate painted decoration which includes depictions of landscape features and boats with many oars, together with animal and human figures. The most complex versions combine all these elements into elaborate scenes (fig. 5), which may be connected with early religious rites.[14] In the later stages of the Naqada culture, around 3300–3200 BC, the motifs were considerably simplified: the animal and human figures disappear, as do the boats, to be replaced by simple geometric designs or patterns imitating the appearance of hardstone vessels. This imitation may account for the development of a fashion for tubular handles which were modelled separately in the same fabric and attached to the sides of the jars, usually at shoulder level.

Undecorated plainwares

The marl fabrics used for the decorated pottery were also employed to make a form of vessel known as the wavy-handled jar, named for the undulating ledge-handles applied to the sides. This style was copied from pottery of Near Eastern origin and it appears during the Naqada II period (3600–3250 BC).[15]

Fig. 3 An example of the elaborate shapes made in Red-polished ware, modelled by hand, from Mostagedda, c. 3600 BC.

Fig. 4 The probable evolution of the so-called wavy-handled jars: from a broad shape of about 3300 BC, with distinct ledge-handles, to a cylindrical form with vestigial handles some 200 years later; made by coiling and hand-turning, from Hu and Mahasna.

These jars, which begin with a fairly broad shape, gradually evolved to a narrower form, giving rise to a new class of cylindrical jars with debased wavy handles (fig. 4) by the latest stage of the Naqada period, in about 3250 BC. The interiors of the necks of these jars often show rilling marks from hand-turning, whereas the lower parts of the vessels were built up by the coiling technique.[16]

The final stages of the Predynastic period are characterised by the increasing use of plain pottery, particularly of a range of bowls and jars in hard marl fabrics of a pale beige colour (fig. 6). This class was named 'late ware' in Petrie's original typology.[17] A marl bowl in the British Museum shows clear marks of surface scraping to finish the exterior.[18] The drab and utilitarian character of this pottery sets the tone for the majority of the ceramics produced in the Dynastic period (ch. 8), beginning from about 3000 BC.

Fig. 5 (Opposite above) Two decorated vessels of the Naqada II culture (3600–3250 BC), one painted with boats and the other with spiral designs, handmade from hard marl clay (marl fabric A1 or A4).

Fig. 6 (Opposite) Vessels of Predynastic late ware (c. 3200 BC) from Hu, made in characteristic marl clay (marl fabrics A1 and A4). The lower parts of the sides of the bowl have been trimmed by scraping.

Early Urban Ceramic Industries in Mesopotamia

St John Simpson

Mesopotamia, 'the land between the two rivers', is made up of distinct regions comprising lowland alluvium, upland plains, mountains and desert, and the cultural differences between them are reflected in their respective ceramic traditions. The earliest urban centres developed in the lowlands, an area characterised by the secondary clays deposited by annual floods of the Tigris, Euphrates and Diyala rivers. The ubiquity of this natural resource explains both the variety of clay usage, ranging from construction and ceramics to writing materials, and its persistence as a metaphor in ancient Mesopotamian literature.[1]

The local ceramic tradition appears to have evolved gradually, yet certain forms and types of decoration were short-lived and hence are convenient for the purposes of archaeological dating. During the fourth millennium the potter's wheel was developed, leading to mass-production of ceramics in urban and rural industries. Specialised forms of vessels were created for specific functions and local pottery workshops elaborated distinct types of decoration. Experimentation led to improved means of working clays and applying new pigments. An early stoneware was achieved in the third millennium and, in the first millennium, coloured glazes were invented.

The fourth millennium

Known as the Uruk period after the site of the same name, the fourth millennium witnessed dramatic developments in Mesopotamian society, with the appearance of fortified cities, monumental construction, writing, art, long-distance trade and new crafts and industries.[2] These changes also affected ceramic industries (fig. 2). Earlier Ubaid styles were abandoned and Early Uruk pottery was typically red or grey burnished, although a northern variety was painted. Unfortunately, little is known in detail about methods of Early Uruk pottery production, although wasters and pottery kilns have been reported.[3]

During the Late Uruk period there were further changes in ceramic production. Updraught kilns were typical but shallow clamps were also used. Kilns were stacked with mixed loads and fired within a temperature range of 850–1050°C.[4] A potters' quarter excavated at Ur contained circular kilns with shallow firepits 35 cm (14 in) deep by 90 cm (35.5 in) across supporting perforated clay grates 1.3 m (3.9 ft) in diameter; a large ceramic disk-wheel, 75 cm (30 in) across and 5 cm (2 in) thick, was found nearby (fig. 1). This type of wheel has continued to be used, unchanged, up to the present day in Afghanistan.[5]

Time-consuming hand-painted decoration was dropped in favour of rapidly incised designs or simple plainware. Many vessels were sand-tempered and thrown on a slow wheel although others were handmade.[6] Ceramic 'ring scrapers' may have been used to thin

Fig. 1 An early potter's wheel, excavated in a potters' quarter at Ur and dating to around 3000 BC. This weighs about 44 kg (20 lb) and is made of fired clay. It appears to have been turned on a pivot, using a stick inserted into one or more holes near the edge. Similar wheels continue to be used by traditional potters in Afghanistan. The slow rotation of such a wheel explains the appearance of contemporary pottery in Mesopotamia.

Fig. 2 Early urbanised industrial products of the fourth and third millennia BC in Mesopotamia. The invention of the potter's wheel during the fourth millennium led to greater mass-production of pottery, yet some handmade coarsewares were still made. Specialised forms of vessel were also developed, including fruit-stands and hollow 'kernos ring' tubes used for libations, and miniature copies of ordinary vessels were produced as potters' sidelines or toys. In northern Mesopotamia, experimentation in firing fine greywares led to the development of high-quality stonewares.

down vessel walls after throwing.[7] New types included conical beakers, tall jars with short upright spouts, droopy-spouted wine jars, and globular storage jars with perforated vertical lugs, sometimes with burnished red slip or incised decoration; the lugs probably served to secure skin or cloth lids tied down tightly with string through the perforations.[8] Despite the prevalence of wheel-throwing, heavily tempered handmade Bevelled Rim bowls were widely popular from northern Syria to

south-eastern Iran. These were of standard shape yet varying capacity. Their possible function has attracted considerable speculation, ranging from ration bowls, yoghurt containers or bread moulds to vessels for holding religious offerings.[9] Towards the end of this period new regional styles of painted wares became briefly popular. Jemdet Nasr polychrome-painted, burnished, red-slipped jars were produced in central Mesopotamia and traded, perhaps because of their unusual decoration, along the Gulf as far as Oman.[10]

The third millennium

Mesopotamian historical records commence in the Early Dynastic period (3000–2350 BC). During this period the region was a patchwork of independent city-states, each with its own gods and kings. Monumental architecture, the arts, trade and early writing continued to flourish under a high degree of patronage, witnessed by a

spectacularly rich group of 'Royal Tombs' at Ur. Under the subsequent Akkadian (2350–2100 BC) and Ur III (2100–2000 BC) dynasties, Mesopotamia was unified under central administration.[11]

Mesopotamian ceramic production is better documented for these periods (fig. 2). Pottery workshops were sited near the edges of towns, probably owing to a combination of low social status, fire risk and easier access to clay and fuel supplies.[12] At the Early Dynastic city of Lagash, seven separate areas were dedicated to pottery production.[13] Some settlements depended economically on this industry: about 500 Akkadian/Old Babylonian kilns and bread ovens, sometimes associated with soaking pits, were found at the site of Umm al-Hafriyat.[14] Updraught kilns and clamps continued to be used.[15] Trace element analyses suggest that the buff, pink and green colours of sherds were due to accidental variations in firing of a single fabric, a conclusion supported by experimental observations

in Egypt which indicate firing variations of 100–150°C, depending on the exact position within the kiln. Difficulties in maintaining constant firing conditions may explain the high numbers of wasters.

During the late Early Dynastic and Akkadian periods, a more sophisticated ceramic technology was developed in northern Mesopotamia whereby temperatures of 950–1050°C were maintained to produce grey, olive-green or red stoneware jars (often with a reduced core) and thin-walled streaky self-slipped beakers and bowls. These were made from very fine plastic calcareous or non-calcareous clays, thrown on a fast wheel and polished or spiral-burnished in imitation of metal-wares; some were painted.[16]

A small number of Akkadian cylinder seals may represent scenes of pottery-making,[17] but the earliest textual sources for ceramic production date from the Ur III period.[18] These refer to workshops with between two and ten people working part-time under a supervisor, the remainder of the year being spent in agricultural work: part-time ceramic production was the norm, then as now, throughout the Near East owing to the difficulties of drying pots, storing sufficient dry fuel and firing kilns during the winter or spring. Pots were therefore mass-produced during the summer and autumn months, in some instances damaged and crudely repaired by the potter before firing. The huge domestic consumption of pottery is illustrated by the large quantities of ceramics buried in graves, whereas the low frequency of Mesopotamian vessels in Gulf finds suggests that, although they were occasionally used as convenient transport containers, they were not specifically produced for an export market.[19]

Typical Early Dynastic vessels include conical bowls,[20] solid-footed goblets,[21] stemmed dish 'fruit-stands' (also produced in silver),[22] and jars with upright handles decorated with incision and occasional pellets imitating eyes.[23] Small saucers may have been used for

Fig. 3 (Opposite) First-millennium industries in Mesopotamia. A range of fine and plainwares was manufactured in Assyria. Eggshell-thin palace ware beakers were thrown from finely levigated clay, whereas crude copies and plainware jars, bowls and lamps were produced for everyday use. Petrographic analysis of sherds from a work-shop site at Khirbet Qasrij indicates a preferred use of organic temper. Small poly-chrome-glazed bottles were produced from the 9th century into the Neo-Babylonian period, during which time there is evidence for pots inscribed – with the vessel function or place of use – prior to firing.

Fig. 4 (Above) Second-millennium workshop traditions in Mesopotamia. Iron oxides were traditionally used in northern Mesopotamia to produce reddish-brown painted decoration, whereas contemporary pottery further south was decorated with asphalt, probably from a major source near Hit in the Euphrates valley. Pottery animal-shaped toys were wheel-thrown and sold as a sideline. Other specialised products included ceramic pot-stands and perforated lids used in steaming food.

dining, judging by funerary food offerings and representations on seals.[24] Spouted jars served as beer measures: beer and wine were widespread beverages but their consumption required the use of spouted pouring jars or filter-tipped straws because of the coarse sediment.[25] A dairying scene represented on a temple relief at Tell al-Ubaid illustrates the use of churns and funnels.[26] A small number of vessels imitated more costly carved stone containers and miniature copies of wheel-thrown pots were modelled by hand, perhaps as toys.[27] An interesting instance of the reuse of pottery is illustrated by the addition of broken-off jar rims, cemented in place with asphalt, to the upper part of ostrich egg-cups, which were then decorated with shell inlays.[28]

In rural areas of central and northern Mesopotamia, care was taken in decorating certain classes of vessel. In the Hamrin basin, cylinder seals were reused to impress designs on the rims and upper walls of coarse grog-tempered jars. In the Diyala and Hamrin, red- and black-painted Scarlet ware was decorated using hematite or vermilion (cinnabar) and soot. Successive Painted, Incised and/or Excised styles of Ninevite 5 pottery (so called after Level 5 of a deep sounding excavated at Nineveh) distinguished a separate ceramic province in northern Mesopotamia.[29]

During the Akkadian period, new ceramic types emerged.[30] These included basin-shaped pot-stands with three or four strap-handles on the interior, jars with perforated double lug-handles, and troughs decorated in relief on the exterior with snakes and scorpions, presumably with the intention of bestowing apotropaic value. Wavy-combed, comb-stabbed, incised hatched-triangle and relief herringbone decoration were popular. In north-east Syria basalt-tempered cooking pots were used, suggesting both an awareness of and the ability to counteract thermal shock.[31] Cuneiform documents regularly refer to deliveries being measured in litres (*sila*), doubtless facilitated by the use of standardised

Mesopotamian clays and bodies

The alluvial clays of the Tigris and Euphrates rivers are well suited for ceramic production. They are rich in calcium carbonate, $CaCO_3$, which loses carbon dioxide on firing to temperatures above about 750°C and reacts with the clays in the ceramic body to form a range of calcium silicate compounds. These calcareous clays fire to a very stable structure in the temperature range 850–1050°C, which is characteristic of much ancient Mesopotamian pottery. Careful control of temperatures within this range was therefore not necessary.[55] Indeed, observations of traditional potters producing such ceramics have suggested that, in a single firing, a wide range of temperatures up to 1000°C could be attained, depending on the prevalent wind and the position of the pot in the kiln.[56] Pale pinks, yellows, greens and whites are typical of the pots fired from calcareous clays. As the temperature is increased, the iron oxide in the clay is incorporated into the structures of the calcium silicates, and its strong colourant effect is depressed. A wide range of colours could be obtained from a single firing.[57]

Composition of typical Mesopotamian calcareous clay body[58]							
SiO_2	TiO_2	Al_2O_3	Fe_2O_3	MgO	CaO	Na_2O	K_2O
51	0.6	15	6	6	17	2	2

containers: the discovery of identical large jars inscribed on the upper shoulder and interior rim with capacity marks of 167 or 175 *sila* at Ur, Nippur and Bahrain thus may be explained by Ur III trade of sealed commodities.[32] Thereafter, inscribed pots recur in most periods as a minor class of ceramic vessel.

The second millennium

This period was characterised by a complex pattern of shifting alliances and trade networks between different royal dynasties across the Near East. Pottery production remained an essential urban industry in Mesopotamia. However, despite increasingly mass-produced plain and utilitarian wares, distinctive regional styles continued to be developed. These 'ceramic provinces' appear to reflect a combination of the extent of political power, the direction of economic interests and the distribution of different population groups.[33]

One text refers to the teaching of the potters' trade and 'a district of the potters' is attested from Nuzi. Potters are not mentioned in extensive palace archives found at Mari, yet two potters and river transport of large consignments of pots are referred to from Chagar Bazar.[34] By the early second millennium a new type of wheel was introduced from Syro-Palestine.[35] This comprised a pair of close-fitting polished basalt or limestone axle-bearings which, judging by replication experiments, supported a wider – probably wooden – wheelhead that was turned by an assistant while the potter produced slow-thrown pots. The relative scarcity of this primitive type in Mesopotamia is explained by the fact that most Old and Middle Babylonian pots now appear to have been thrown on a fast wheel. Pots were either thrown from the hump (a technique particularly well suited for rapid throwing of small to medium vessels), coiled (large pots) or made from prefabricated cylindrical sections joined together and rethrown (high beakers); the specific technique was dictated by the form and size of the desired vessel. A minor proportion of vessels were made on a tournette or through coiling, pinching, slab construction and scraping. Short but easily workable local iron-rich clays were normally used after brief pre-soaking and heavy tempering with chopped straw, fluff and possibly dung: the vessels were fired in neutral to lightly oxidising conditions at temperatures of 800–1000°C.[36] The preferred fuel was probably agricultural waste and natural vegetation, yet light fractions of crude oil collected from surface seeps may have been used for stoking kilns. Squarish rather than circular updraught kilns were popular throughout the early to mid-second millennium, although other shapes are also attested.[37]

Plain utilitarian ceramic vessels were the norm (fig. 4). Vessels with specialised functions included 'strainers', decorated and fish-shaped pastry moulds, 'pie-crust' and bevelled-rim pot-stands. Rodent traps, animal-shaped wheeled toys and 'pie-crust' rattles were produced sporadically, probably as potters' sidelines inspired by wooden objects.[38] New styles of painted pottery became popular in different regions of Mesopotamia during the nineteenth to eighteenth centuries BC. One class of jar and carinated bowl was decorated with crude but striking geometric and naturalistic designs in a bituminous paint. These may have been distributed from a single centre close to an asphalt source, such as Hit, and are found across Babylonia from Ur to Sippar; asphalt potters' or shippers' marks are common on pottery jars found along the Middle Euphrates.[39] Another distinctive product of an unknown workshop, possibly inspired by Iranian inlaid softstone and incised greyware vessels, consisted of white- and red-filled incised greyware lugged jars decorated with birds, bulls, boats and other designs; coarser plain versions were also used in Mesopotamia and along the Gulf.[40] A third style of painted pottery, called Khabur ware, was popular in northern Mesopotamia: occasional finds in south central Anatolia and north-west Iran reflect Old Assyrian trade networks, whereas it was rare along the Middle Euphrates and absent from southern Iraq.[41] The painted designs on Khabur ware were repetitive but striking and included hatched triangles, horizontal stripes, chequers and concentric circles, the latter copying stamped designs found on bowls and *kraters*.[42]

During the fifteenth to fourteenth centuries BC, another painted fineware known as Nuzi ware was widely used from northern Mesopotamia to the Mediterranean coast, and traded as far south as the Kassite capital of Aqar Quf.[43] Floral, geometric and naturalistic motifs, including birds, fish and goats, were painted in white over reddish-brown or black painted bands on thin-walled stump- or button-footed goblets, beakers and larger jars; the floral patterns show similarities with contemporary Aegean painting, and recent discoveries of Minoan-style frescoes in Egypt and the southern Levant illustrate the popularity of this style. However, Nuzi ware was not simply a luxury or palace ware, as it has been found in domestic as well as palatial contexts. In southern Mesopotamia the local Kassite pottery appears much cruder, although some new forms were developed and traded along the Gulf, including tall chalices with heavy solid feet. Despite the inelegance of their products, Kassite potters successfully counteracted problems of excessive shrinkage through the addition of heavy organic temper to the clay. However, this rendered it more difficult to throw wide forms, hence the prevalence of tall narrow vessels.[44]

The first millennium

The ninth to eighth centuries BC witnessed the growth of Assyrian power, culminating in the unification of

Mesopotamia, the Levant and Egypt under Late Assyrian imperial administration during the seventh century. The sudden collapse of the Assyrian empire was followed in the sixth century by a shift in political power to southern Mesopotamia under Neo-Babylonian kings. Their inheritance was in turn lost, just over a century later, to a new Achaemenid dynasty emerging from southern Iran. Thereafter, the status of Mesopotamia declined to that of an important province within the Persian empire.

Specialised rural – as well as urban – industries are suggested by one Assyrian reference to 'the village of the pots' (*kapru diqarate*).[45] Late Assyrian pottery workshops have been found at several sites, notably Khirbet Qasrij. The kilns (fig. 5) comprised a bathtub-shaped firepit with a sloped stoke-hole at one end and a grate supporting a circular or sub-oval firing-chamber above, measuring about 1.1×1.3 m (3.3×3.9 ft) across.

There is greater evidence for fast-throwing of ceramics at this time, although in Egypt the earliest evidence for the kickwheel dates to the Persian

period.[46] Most Late Assyrian pottery was plain and utilitarian, yet a number of finewares were produced (fig. 3). There was a peak in the production of polychrome blue, yellow and white glazed wares in Babylonia and Assyria during the eighth to seventh centuries BC, using recipes similar to those employed by contemporary Assyrian brick manufacturers.[47] Palace ware was another type of fineware: finely levigated clay was used to throw beakers with lightly dimpled walls, designed to improve one's grasp, whereas shallow carinated flared drinking-bowls imitated Assyrian metalwares.[48] Pottery animal-headed drinking-cups were another type that copied metal prototypes.[49] Reddish-striped painted 'carrot flasks', a distinctive Assyrian product possibly used as perfume bottles, were widely distributed from Ur to Palestine;[50] handmade cooking pots were also traded (although metal cauldrons were probably more widely used) and are shown on Assyrian reliefs.[51]

Monochrome blue glazes were commonly used throughout the Neo-Babylonian and Persian periods.[52] During the Achaemenid period, Ea became the patron deity of potters and other craft workers in Mesopotamia.[53] Persian-period pottery remains a poorly studied subject. However, there appears to be a continuing dichotomy between northern and southern Mesopotamian ceramic traditions, with continuity from the late Achaemenid to early Seleucid periods. Distinctive types include 'husking trays' and flaring carinated bowls inspired by metal drinking-bowls (*phiale*), local versions of which were produced across the Achaemenid empire from the Mediterranean to Central Asia. Special ceramic stamps were used to decorate vessels with pushed-out walls, a type inspired by metal bowls with embossed lobes; fine eggshell-ware bowls were also produced.[54] Many of these types continued to be made after Alexander's overthrow of the Persian empire, when Mesopotamia became a leading province of the Seleucid empire.

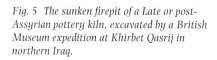
Fig. 5 The sunken firepit of a Late or post-Assyrian pottery kiln, excavated by a British Museum expedition at Khirbet Qasrij in northern Iraq.

Ceramic Changes in Late Iron Age Britain

Val Rigby and Ian Freestone

Iron Age Britain[1] witnessed a movement away from the scattered farming homesteads of earlier periods towards defined settlements or villages, reflecting population growth and increased agricultural activity. Developing regional characteristics of material culture, such as pottery styles, suggest the growth of tribalism. In the south and west large fortified sites or hill forts are thought to have dominated the landscape. With the potential for resident populations of up to several hundred individuals, there is evidence that the hill forts served as grain stores and meeting places as well as important symbols of tribal status.[2] Specialisation of economic activity, whether in salt-making, iron-working or animal husbandry, became more common.[3]

In the period from the second century BC until the Roman conquest of Britain in AD 43–4, extensive contacts were developed with continental Europe, coinage was introduced and south-eastern Britain experienced the rise of oppida – large prosperous settlements, defined by ditches, which were tens of hectares (2.5 acres) in extent. A defining characteristic is considered to be the operation of a coin mint, emphasising their economic and administrative significance and underlining their proto-urban character. Against the background of these broader changes in society occurred marked changes in ceramic technology and production, here discussed based on examples drawn from pottery production in south-eastern Britain (fig. 1).

Native traditions in the Iron Age

Before the first century BC, virtually all pottery produced in Britain was fabricated using hand-building methods such as coil- or slab-building. Firing took place in open fires and pots were commonly made in coarse fabrics, heavily tempered with crushed pebbles such as flint or crushed pottery fragments known as grog. Pot surfaces are generally brown or reduced and sooted from dark grey to black, while the forms are relatively simple, such as open bowls and jars in a wide range of sizes (fig. 2, top, centre). Decoration, where present, took the form of incised or impressed motifs at the rim and shoulder of the pot. Decorative coatings such as hematite are rare.[4] Although these pots are relatively plain, their numbers suggest that they played an important role in everyday life, for example, in the storage and preparation of food. In areas where formal burial took place, pottery was included in the graves, emphasising its symbolic and religious role. Petrographic evidence from the west of Britain, where the geology imposes a significant variability upon the raw materials used for pottery, indicates that pots or their contents were traded or exchanged over distances of tens of kilometres (0.6 mile).[5] It would be much more difficult to identify such movements of wares in the east, as the available clays and tempers are very similar over most of the region and differences between workshops are therefore difficult to recognise. Even so, available evidence from typology and decoration suggests that the movement of pottery beyond a relatively restricted locality was uncommon.[6]

In the second century BC, evidence for external influences is seen in the forms and decoration of the pottery. The shouldered forms of the jars, coupled with the decorative style, reflect those seen on the Continent (fig. 2, bottom).

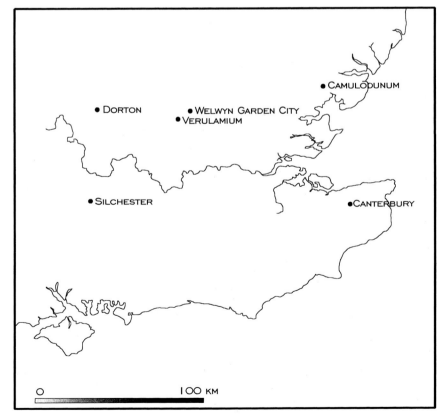

Fig. 1 Map of south-eastern Britain showing sites mentioned in the text.

Imported continental pottery is well known from some sites, such as Hengistbury Head in Dorset,[7] and it appears that this had an influence upon the appearance of the native wares. These imported continental wares were finer and wheel-thrown, sometimes with high-quality graphite coatings. However, the technology used in the production of pottery in Britain continued in the local tradition of hand-building. At this time, the preferred tempering technique across much of the south-east was a combination of grog and vegetable temper (fig. 3, top). The form in which the vegetable tempering was added to the clays is currently unclear; the material is finely divided, and one possibility is that it was added as dung. While the grog would have acted as a conventional opening material, the vegetable temper may have had a number of advantages. For example, it has been found that the addition of dung temper makes a clay easier to form into vessels by improving its workability.[8]

The overall picture for this earlier period is one of primarily local production, perhaps based in or around the household, for local domestic consumption of pottery. Some of it, however, was widely traded, which may imply a degree of specialisation in some areas.

Introduction of the potter's wheel

Native production of wheel-thrown pottery is first seen on any scale in the first century BC. The use of the wheel is indicated by the presence of character-istic spiral ribbing on the interiors of the vessels. A substantial component of pottery assemblages in parts of south-eastern Britain, these wares have horizontal cordons, grooves or combing, produced as the pot was rotated on the wheel (fig. 4, top). In profile, these wheel-thrown wares have a more sinuous form, particularly suitable for a basic wheel-throwing technique. They include the pedestalled urn (fig. 4, top, second from right), a form which had been introduced into northern France with the advent of the wheel some three to four centuries earlier.[9] In spite of the introduction of the new wheel-throwing technique, the production of traditional hand-

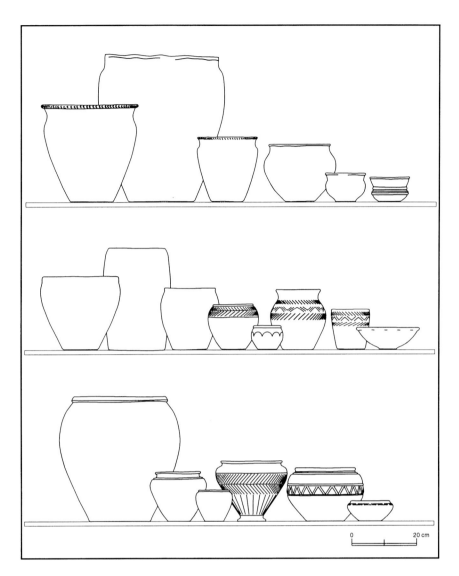

Fig. 2 The changing forms of handmade pottery in southern Britain, 450–50 BC. Simple forms with plain or textured surfaces (top) were gradually replaced by more definite shapes (centre) with incised, stamped and burnished decoration. Some continental influence is shown in the latest group (bottom), dating from after 120 BC, but all were hand-built.

built forms continued. Furthermore, tempering with grog and vegetal matter and open-firing techniques appear similar for both traditional wares and the new wheel-thrown types. No per-manent kiln structures have been found from this period, and the failure of the vegetal temper to fully burn out of the bodies of the pots (fig. 3, top) suggests that firing was short and relatively reducing rather than oxidising.

These first wheel-thrown ceramics are very similar to the pottery being produced at this time in the Belgic areas of Gaul. Although the British pots are made in local fabrics, typologically and technically they are identical to assemblages in northern France. Indeed, if a sherd found in one region was placed in another, it would be almost impossible to recognise it without scientific analysis. While continental pottery had influenced British production in earlier periods, such close copies had not been made. These exceptionally strong parallels seem to imply that the first of these new wheel-thrown wares were produced by immigrant or itinerant potters from Gaul, working in Britain and using local clays.

Late Iron Age imports and their imitations

From about 25 BC a range of very distinctive ceramics appears. Wheel-thrown and oxidised to an even pink colour, sometimes with white clay slips or mica-dusted coatings, or occasionally in white clays, the range of forms greatly expanded to include handled wine-flagons, drinking-beakers, jars with a lid seating inside the rim, platters (plates) and flared bowls or tazzas for serving food (figs 4, centre, 5, 6). This range of tablewares – a series of specialised forms, each with a particular purpose – is characteristically Roman and associated with romanised dining customs. Scientific analysis of the pottery in thin section reveals that these wares were produced outside Britain; for example, a range of exotic volcanic and metamorphic rock fragments in some of the vessels indicates a source in central Gaul.[10] These imported wares are well represented in high-status burials, such as that of a Late Iron Age chieftain from what is now Welwyn Garden City (Hertfordshire),[11] and a burial containing a decorated bronze mirror from Dorton, in Buckinghamshire.[12] They appear to have been associated with the adoption of a more

Cooking pots

Cooking pots must resist thermal stress, caused by uneven heating in a fire, and thermal shock, which can result from rapid changes in temperature. The high temper content and low-fired bodies of pottery produced in open bonfires allow such pots to meet these conditions more consistently than would finer, kiln-fired wares. Wheel-thrown bodies also tend to break more easily than do hand-built ones, because the particles in wheel-thrown vessels are organised into strong alignments along which cracks can more easily develop. Potters working without the kiln and the wheel could therefore find a market niche for their cooking wares, and recent analysis has indicated that coarse cooking wares, although lacking the apparent sophistication of other contemporary pottery, were sometimes more widely traded.[22]

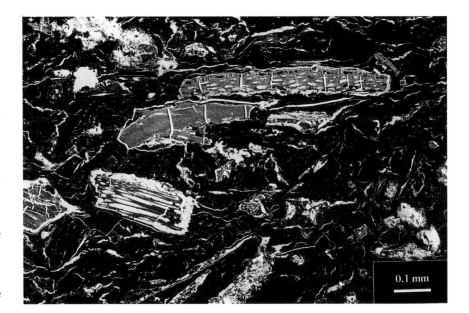

Fig. 3 Micrographs showing (top) vegetable temper in a native fabric, which has not burnt out during firing, and (bottom) numerous grains of very fine sand or silt in romanised ware (seen as smooth in the micrograph). Note the very regular (well sorted) size distribution (scanning electron microscope).

cosmopolitan outlook and customs by the élites of the Late Iron Age.

The mode of production of these imported pots was very different from that used in Britain, even though wheel-thrown pottery had become common. The evenly coloured, oxidised character of these vessels suggests that they were fired in permanent kilns. This is supported by the fine-grained nature of the fabrics – the inclusions are rarely coarser than 0.1–0.2 mm (0.4–0.8 in), which implies that the firing was sufficiently controlled to negate the need for coarse tempering materials. Permanent kiln structures are known from France at this time.[13] Such controlled kiln firings, with a relatively guaranteed product quality, allowed the potters to make use of decorative techniques such as white slips and mica dusting which would have been less advantageous on unevenly fired wares. Copies of these imported wares were soon made by native potters, and the full range of forms seem to have been produced (fig. 4, bottom). However, these were imitations in form only, as the fabrics and finishes of the copies remained those of the native pottery (fig. 5). Both the preparation of the clay and the firing techniques were traditional.[14]

The use of the potter's wheel offers a number of advantages. Symmetrical forms with thin walls and smooth surfaces are much easier to produce than by hand-building methods. A major advantage is in the speed of production: a pot can be produced on a wheel in a fraction of the time that it would take to hand-build the same object. However, in order to take full advantage of the improvements in production capacity offered by the wheel, the throughput at other points of the production process, such as paste preparation and firing, must also be increased. It appears that even those British potters who were using the wheel to copy Roman wares had not at this time reorganised their production methods. The preparation of the clay still involved the time-consuming process of obtaining and crushing grog, then mixing grog and organic temper with the clay. The proportions of grog and organics vary greatly from pot to pot, so that temper would appear to have been mixed with the clay to attain the correct workability on a more or less ad hoc, batch-by-batch basis.[15] In contrast, the fabrics of the imported wares are very standardised and appear to reflect direct use of a clay as it was dug, or with modifications more suited to mass-production such as the addition of fine sand. The kilns used for the imported wares would have been far better suited to frequent, standardised production of large numbers of pots than were the temporary open firings used by the indigenous potters.

Romanisation of the production process

Following the Roman invasion of Britain in AD 43–4, an administrative system was established, initially based upon the need for military control but, with pacification, increasingly oriented towards the civilian population.

Fig. 4   The changing forms of wheel-thrown pots in south-eastern Britain, 80 BC– AD 50. Wheel-throwing favoured the production of sinuous shapes with horizontal grooves and raised cordons. The top group are early wheel-thrown wares in traditional grog-tempered fabrics. Imports from Gaul after c. 25 BC (centre) were copied by British potters in local fabrics and finishes (bottom).

Ceramics have been found in burials predating the Boudiccan rebellion of AD 60–61 which were apparently made using the full Roman mode of production.[16] Flagons, platters and beakers were produced in a fabric characterised by the presence of very regular quantities of fine quartz silt, which can be closely matched in pottery produced later by known Roman kilns in the region (fig. 3, bottom).[17] The surface finishes are evenly oxidised and kiln-fired (fig. 6), and white clay slips were sometimes used. These fully romanised wares were apparently made, in the first instance, to satisfy the requirements of the local population, as suggested by their occurrence in native burials, but other producers soon became established, making flagons, mortaria, jars and bowls typical of those in use at forts all over the north-western frontier of the empire to

fulfil the needs of the new Roman administration. The rather abrupt adoption of Roman methods to produce the same forms immediately after the conquest strongly suggests the involvement of Roman pottery-making expertise.

In the early decades of the Roman period in Britain there was a proliferation of small producers making a wide range of wheel-thrown and kiln-fired wares, and this may reflect the activity of some of the workshops which existed before the conquest. However, these were short-lived and were gradually displaced by the growth of major pottery complexes such as those at Verulamium (St Albans), Camulodunum (Colchester) and Chichester (fig. 1). But traditional methods of pottery production were not lost. In some areas, grog-tempered pottery continued to be made throughout the Roman period.[18] Some types,

including cooking pots, also continued to be handmade and were widely used, even by the Roman military.[19]

Innovation and the potter

Innovation in the ceramic industries of Late-Iron Age Britain was a complex matter, involving a number of stages over more than a century and complicated interactions with the more urbanised societies to the south and east, across the English Channel. The introduction of the wheel, the kiln and more organised production techniques owed much to the importation of expertise from elsewhere, but even so did not completely displace traditional methods of production, which continued alongside the new.

While there is considerable evidence for increasing specialisation of pottery production before the introduction of

the wheel, in the form of trade and exchange, the scale of production was not great. Pottery-making is likely to have been associated with the homestead or family and to have been a seasonal and part-time occupation, probably undertaken by women. In such circumstances, potting could be taken up or left as other more pressing demands, such as those of child-rearing and farming, allowed.[20] Indeed, many hand-building methods require time for the partially formed pot to dry out before the next stage of coils or slabs can be added.

Wheel-throwing techniques did not favour this approach. They were much more intensive, with a high throughput; considerable preparation was required, and pots could not be left but had to be finished while wet, so that pottery-making required substantial continuous periods of time. The neces-

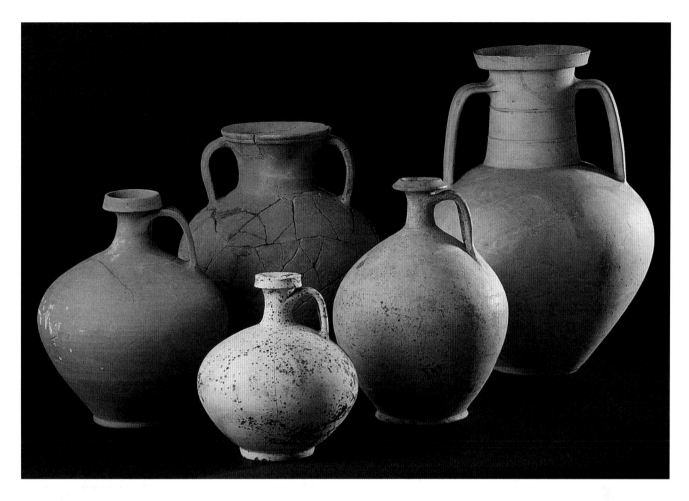

Fig. 5 (Opposite)   Imported butt-beaker in white clay (right), compared with a locally produced version (left) in grog- and organic-tempered fabric, with an unevenly fired finish.

Fig. 6 (Above)   Group of pre-conquest flagons. Back row: imported two-handled flagon (right) in white clay, and native copy (left) in local grog-tempered fabric and poorly oxidised finish (restored from sherds). Front row: single-handled import (right) from central Gaul, with white slip, and British romanised version (left) in silty clay; imported flagon (centre) in white clay.

sary investment in and maintenance of equipment (the wheel) as well as the time and labour needed to become proficient in throwing would have made it less likely that women would adopt the new activity on a part-time basis. To justify the investment, production would have had to be scaled up, more clay dug and prepared, more firings held, etc. With the introduction of the wheel, pottery-making became a task which was much more demanding of labour. At the same time, population growth and the demand for land is likely to have put pressure on small farmers to seek other means of subsistence, while the new oppida provided large markets for commodities such as pottery. This combination of circumstances therefore resulted in the development of the role of the specialist potter, who in general is likely to have been male.[21] In such a situation, women in farming communities would have continued to produce pots in traditional ways, and there was

probably no reason for them to discontinue this activity unless their farming surplus rose sufficiently to enable them to purchase pots made by others, their home-based potting activities no longer making a significant contribution in subsistence terms. Thus the household mode continued alongside the growth of specialised production with its wheels, kilns and, eventually, workshops.

The adoption of the fully romanised mode of production after the conquest, including permanent kilns, standardised bodies and so on, may have required input of technical knowledge from elsewhere. However, once these methods had begun to be adopted, they appear to have spread widely and relatively quickly. The pressures on the 'professional' potters, already using the wheel, were probably those of the market rather than of the farm or the home, and they were in a position to respond much more rapidly to the impact of the new methods.

Dynastic Egyptian Pottery

A. J. Spencer

The pottery of Egypt over almost three millennia of Dynastic civilisation was overwhelmingly utilitarian, competently produced but often lacking in aesthetic appeal. Only at certain specific periods does decorated pottery make a significant appearance, such as during the late Eighteenth Dynasty, when a class of blue-painted pottery was produced.[1] That ancient Egyptian potters possessed considerable skill is without doubt, but they were primarily concerned with the manufacture of robust and functional products.

Tradition was a very important element in Egyptian culture, and the early techniques of hand-forming, including coiling or slow turning (see ch. 5), were never completely abandoned, even after the introduction of the potter's wheel in about 2400 BC.[2] Pots thrown on the wheel exhibit spiral marks (fig. 2), caused by the centrifugal force of faster rotation, which are different from the fine parallel ridges caused by slower hand-turning on a block. Sometimes, the appearance of handmade pottery was reproduced on a wheel-made jar for traditional reasons if, for example, the jar was destined for use as a funerary offering.

Much of the ceramic production of Egypt was destined for funerary purposes and certain types of vessels came to be used almost exclusively in tombs rather than for everyday use, a point which must be borne in mind when considering Nile Valley ceramics (chs 2, 5).

The study of Egyptian pottery has advanced greatly in recent years, with much more attention devoted to materials and techniques of manufacture than was previously the case.[3] It is therefore now possible to give a brief account of significant points of Egyptian pottery manufacture, such as the use of the wheel, the operation of kilns and a summary of some particularly characteristic pottery styles, which offer information on the manufacturing process.

Use of the wheel

The first potter's wheels used in Egypt were a considerable improvement on the older technique of turning the pot on a block, but they were by no means fast and efficient wheels.[4] They were simple turntable devices which the potter had to rotate with one hand while shaping the vessel with the other. This precise action is depicted in a Fifth Dynasty relief from the tomb of Ty at Saqqara (fig. 1), which shows a man working such a wheel. Elsewhere in the same relief are other workers involved in shaping vases by hand and turning the vessels on blocks, showing that both methods coexisted.

Improvements in the wheel down to the Middle Kingdom (*c.* 1985–1795 BC) were essentially a matter of achieving faster rotation, although the force still had to be applied by the potter. That this resulted in rotation fast enough to produce the characteristic spiral marks of wheel-made pottery shows that these simple wheels must have been able to continue spinning for some time after each push.[5] An essential requirement for this would have been smooth surfaces at the pivot, probably combined with some lubricant, such as wet clay, to reduce friction. Pivots for potter's wheels made of paired stones have been found, the upper stone having a smooth projection to engage in a socket in the one beneath.[6] The wide, disk-shaped wheelhead of fired clay or other suitable material would have been attached to the top of the upper stone, with the lower stone of the pivot set into the ground, or attached to the top of the vertical supporting stem

Fig. 1 Pottery workshop of about 2400 BC, as depicted in a relief from the tomb of Ty at Saqqara. Various stages of production are shown, including hand-forming, turning on a block or finishing on a slow turntable, and firing.

Fig. 2 Two wheel-thrown bowls of the early Roman period (1st century AD), from Tanis, showing (left) the characteristic mark of the string-cut base and (right) the spiral rotation marks on the interior.

of the wheel, as is depicted in ancient representations.[7]

The early wheels had a short stem, and variants of this type were still used in the New Kingdom (*c.* 1650–1070 BC), together with an alternative tall-stemmed wheel. The history of the latter begins in the Middle Kingdom and it was used throughout the New Kingdom and Third Intermediate Period (1070–650 BC). Not until the New Kingdom do we see representational evidence for the presence of an assistant to turn the wheel for the potter, allowing him to work with both hands, although it is not impossible that the practice might have occurred earlier.[8]

The sophistication of the kickwheel did not appear in Egypt until around the fifth century BC.[9] The high speed of rotation of this type of wheel is evident in the very distinct angled spiral marks on the pottery of this period and later, as visible on two small bowls of early Roman date (fig. 2). These bowls also illustrate the technique of cutting the base of the vessel off the wheel with a string, in the process creating a characteristic sliced effect in the clay of the

base. This method was already used to remove pots from the slower wheels of earlier times. Vessels with pointed or round bases were often trimmed by hand after removal from the wheel, especially prior to the New Kingdom. This process is clear from the marks of scraping and cutting that are visible on the lower part of the pot.[10] These marks of hand-finishing may obscure the external rotary marks left from throwing on the wheel, although these usually remain clear on the interior.

Kilns

Numerous examples of pottery kilns have been excavated in Egypt, from a wide range of dates.[11] The most basic (see ch. 5) were simple fires enclosed by a limited amount of brickwork to direct the flow of air. More sophisticated Old Kingdom kilns consisted of circular or oval chimney-like structures of mudbrick (fig. 3), with diameters ranging from 1 to 3 m (3–9 ft), and a stoke-hole at one side.[12] The pots to be fired were loaded from the top and stacked above a floor of bricks, made with gaps to allow the hot gases from the firing chamber below to rise through the stack. The bricks of the floor were supported on a central wall or pillar in the middle of the firing chamber.

Similar updraught kilns persisted in use for much of the Dynastic period,

with little evidence for dramatic change in construction until after 600 BC. In certain excavated kilns from around this date, the mudbrick floor was replaced by one formed from a large slab of fired clay, pierced by many circular perforations to allow the flow of heat.[13] Other examples of the same general period, however, were still built according to the older pattern, illustrating the common Egyptian tendency to accept new procedures without discarding old ones. More substantial kilns were introduced with the influx of foreign ideas during the Ptolemaic and Roman periods (after 332 BC), when the production of ceramics in the Nile Valley took on a much more industrial character.

Products and fabrics

Recognisable classes of ceramics can be identified for different periods. In the Old Kingdom, one of the finest groups is the red-slipped ware (fig. 5), used extensively for funerary offerings.[14] This class includes jars, spouted ewers and pot-stands, and a great variety of bowls with carinated rims. The earliest bowls of this type date from about 2600 BC and were found at the site of Meidum, so the type is still sometimes referred to as the 'Meidum bowl'.[15] Derivations of the same general style persisted down to the end of the First Intermediate Period

Egyptian ceramic fabrics

The analysis and classification of Egyptian pottery fabrics has developed relatively recently into a very active branch of study. The distinction between different fabrics is based on the examination of a freshly broken section under low-power magnification (× 30) to study the matrix of the paste and the nature and quantity of the various inclusions within it. This basic identification may be supplemented by chemical testing, petrological analysis of thin sections or by neutron activation analysis (NAA).

Essential to the division of Egyptian clays is the distinction between the fine, ferruginous silt clays and the calcareous marl clays. The pottery fabrics based on these clays have been split into several sub-types, although the criteria for separating individual fabrics are those defined by the modern researchers and include fine distinctions which may have had no significance for the ancient potters. A basic working scheme (known as the 'Vienna System' after a conference in that city) with many useful features distinguishes silt fabrics A-E, of which type B is divided into B1 and B2. The marl fabrics also have five classes A-E, with four sub-types of class A and three of class C. Some recent work has proposed a considerable increase in the number of sub-types, but this process runs the increased risk of making distinctions which would have been unrecognised in antiquity.

progress for some time to establish a classification for the different fabrics used by Egyptian potters, very often the ceramic products are better recognised and dated by an examination of all their features, including fabric, technique, surface treatment and shape, i.e., all those characteristics which might be said to distinguish a ware. The Old Kingdom red-polished vessels mentioned above are a good example of this, in that they are far more easily recognised by their characteristic shapes and surface treatment than by the distinction of their fabrics into classes such as Silt B, Silt C or Marl A1. Indeed, the fact that the same class of pottery has been found to include vessels in all these fabrics suggests that fabric was of less importance to the makers than was the finished appearance.[18]

Much of Egyptian domestic and funerary pottery was composed of Nile silt clay mixed with sand and coarse

chaff, categorised as Silt C. These products were often created over a form, sometimes with the upper portions added by hand-turning. An example is a pointed vase in which the join between the irregular lower part of the body and the turned shoulder and rim is clearly evident. This vessel dates from about 2000–1950 BC and belongs to a type very popular for funerary offerings.[19] Rather better-looking vessels were made in the Silt A and B fabrics, which, lacking such coarse pieces of straw to burn out of the clay in firing, resulted in a less pitted surface. For finer products, marl clays were employed, some of which have an attractive cream or near-white appearance,[20] such as a Middle Kingdom vase of Marl A3 fabric, which is decorated with incised patterns. Painted decoration was relatively rare before the New Kingdom, although decorative patterns might be created in a white wash over the red fabric of the vessel, such as the white

(c. 2000 BC) in all areas from Middle Egypt northwards,[16] while different traditions arose in the south. The fabric of these vessels is most commonly Nile silt, although some marl clay examples have been recorded. Irrespective of the fabric used, however, all surfaces are covered by the polished red slip which is the most recognisable characteristic feature of this pottery. Examination of particular bowls of this class suggests that those from the Fourth and Fifth Dynasties (c. 2600–2350 BC) were made by shaping the lower part over a dome-shaped form and then adding a slow-turned rim, while later versions were thrown on the wheel.[17]

Although work has been in

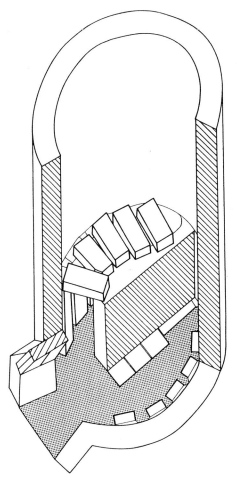

Fig. 3 Reconstruction drawing of a simple updraught kiln of the late Old Kingdom, with a central partition in the firepit to support the floor of the chamber for the pottery. Similar kilns continued to be used in much later periods, alongside more complex types.

Fig. 4 Two decorated vessels of the New Kingdom. Left: marlware jar of about 1350 BC, with complex decoration in blue cobalt-based pigment. Right: tall redware jar from about 1400 BC, decorated with simple black horizontal bands.

spots applied to a handmade square pottery box from Asyut.

One of the most characteristic forms of vessel in the New Kingdom was the drop-shaped vase, which was manufactured in a wide range of sizes. Early examples were often decorated with horizontal bands of black paint (fig. 4, right), as the use of decoration became more popular in the ceramic repertoire. The extent of decoration increased towards the late Eighteenth Dynasty (c. 1370 BC) to include a variety of painted designs, especially floral motifs, executed in blue paint formed from cobalt-based pigments (fig. 4, left).[21] This vogue for decoration is also evident on other kinds of vessels, including squat biconvex vases, amphorae and wine-jars, and it persisted to the end of the New Kingdom.

Regional differences in ceramic production, already mentioned for the First Intermediate Period, are particularly clear during the Third Intermediate Period (c. 1070–650 BC), when the pottery of southern Egypt differs considerably from that being made in the Delta. The chief cause of this variation is the relative absence of marl clay products in the north, since the principal sources of these clays lay in the desert regions between Memphis and Esna.[22] Well-produced wheel-made jars of marl fabrics, chiefly Marl A4, are common from Upper Egyptian sites, and they form some of the most recognisable products in the whole range of Egyptian ceramics (fig. 6). The fabric of these vessels can appear pink, red or even grey in the section, but the surface normally turned greenish-grey on firing. In the Delta, similar jars were manufactured from red silt clay but were often made to resemble the marl fabric of their southern counterparts by the application of a thin cream slip.[23] The technique of using a surface treatment to imitate the appearance of a finer fabric, or of a completely different material, can be traced back to early times, as in the imitation of calcite jars by the smooth polished cream surfaces of marlware cylindrical vessels in the First Dynasty.[24] The production of polished black wares in the Delta during the Ptolemaic period (305–30 BC) may have had a similar motive: to copy the fine black pottery (ch. 12) of the Greek world.

Fig. 5 Two Old Kingdom vessels of red-slipped ware, made by slow turning on a hand-rotated turntable. The vessel on the left belongs to the class known as the 'Meidum bowl', which originated in about 2600 BC.

Egyptian cobalt blue paint

Some two millennia before it was used in the production of Islamic (ch. 16) and Chinese (ch. 30) blue-and-white ceramics, cobalt was used on the blue-painted pottery of New Kingdom Egypt. Furthermore, it was utilised in the form of the compound cobalt aluminate, believed until recently to be a modern pigment (Thenard's Blue) only discovered in AD 1804.[25]

Cobalt deposits are rare in Egypt. However, there are deposits of alum (aluminium sulphate) in the Kharga oasis of the Western Desert, and these were mined extensively in ancient times. Alum was used in tanning leather, as a medicinal astringent and as a mordant in dyeing.[26] Some of these alum deposits contain cobalt and it appears that, in the Eighteenth Dynasty, their potential to yield a ceramic pigment was recognised. This material was also widely used in the production of deep blue faience (ch. 15) and glass.[27]

Fig. 6 Wheel-thrown jar of hard Marl A4 fabric, made in sections. This was a very common ware in southern Egypt during the late Third Intermediate Period (c. 750–650 BC). One of the original pair of applied handles is missing.

A Canaanite Potter's Workshop in Palestine

Pamela Magrill and Andrew Middleton

The Canaanites, known to us from the Bible and other ancient sources as well as through extensive archaeological remains, inhabited much of the southern Levant in the second millennium BC. Alongside their more powerful neighbours, the Egyptians to the south and the Hittites to the north, they played a significant role in the politics and trade of the region.[1]

The discovery of a Canaanite pottery workshop at Lachish (Tell ed-Duweir), a large tell or mound site located about 40 km (25 miles) south-west of Jerusalem, provides a rare opportunity to study in detail the techniques and materials used by these ancient potters. Although large quantities of pottery regularly come to light on excavations throughout the Near East, it is uncommon to find the remains of a workshop where vessels were actually produced.

Major excavations at Lachish were first carried out from 1932 to 1938 by the Wellcome-Marston Archaeological Research Expedition to the Near East, a British team led by J. L. Starkey. During the 1937/8 season a large cave (4034) was discovered, identified by the excavators as the remains of a potter's workshop dating to the end of the Late Bronze Age (1200–1150 BC).

In addition to 'large quantities of unbaked sherds', the excavators described the main contents of the cave (fig. 1) as follows:

We have been fortunate to find scattered about the cavern and especially in the pit, a number of specimens of potter's materials and instruments. Lumps of red and yellow ochre, heaps of prepared clay, crushed stone and shell, represent the potter's raw materials, of his instruments we have found bone points, polishing pebbles and shells, and sherds smoothed down by use in shaping pots.[2]

Also in the above-mentioned rubbish pit (Pit A, fig. 2) were discovered two stone objects, 'one of basalt, the other of the local mizzi limestone, the upper surface of each is highly polished and has a raised knob as a pivot in the centre'[3] (fig. 6a). A second chamber in the cave (Pit B, fig. 2), reached by a flight of rock-cut steps, contained about forty complete fired vessels (figs 3 and 4).

Although the use of the cave had clearly changed over time and the raw materials and tools were not generally found in their original positions, what was recovered provided good evidence that important stages of the pottery-making process had been carried out there. During the excavation much of the material found in the cave was carefully collected, and a brief account of the workshop appeared in the fourth volume of the Lachish report,[4] but no comprehensive scientific study was ever carried out. However, a good selection of raw materials, unfired sherds, tools and some of the finished vessels are now in the collections of the British Museum, and a recent research project has provided many new insights into the activities of the workshop, from raw clay to fired vessel.[5]

Raw materials

Basic questions arise concerning the Lachish potters, such as the kind of raw materials they used; whether the sources of these raw materials were local; and whether the potters prepared specific clay pastes for particular vessel types. Petrographic analysis provided some of the answers. Very thin slices, taken from both fired and unfired sherds and from finished vessels, were prepared as thin sections and examined in the microscope. Two fabric groups were identified. Group 1 consists of a fine brown clay, with numerous small grains of quartz silt (fig. 5a), together

Fig. 1 The Lachish potter's 'toolkit'. A variety of improvised tools was found in the workshop, including polished pebbles and shells apparently used for smoothing and burnishing, shaped ceramic sherds perhaps used for profiling, and a pointed bone tool. Two faceted fragments of ochre, one red and the other yellow, were also found along with sherds used as simple palettes which still retained traces of red pigment. The preserved length of the bone tool is 9.6 cm (3.8 in).

Fig. 2 Plan and section of Cave 4034 at Lachish.

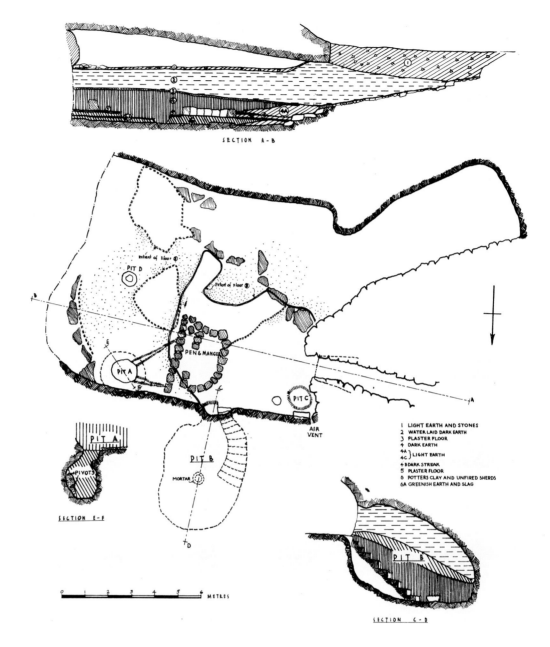

with fewer grains of fine-grained limestone up to about 1.0 mm in diameter, and occasional voids after vegetal material. Group 2 is a similar fabric but, in addition, contains fragments of shell up to about 3 mm in length, often with rounded ends (fig. 5b). Similar fragments of shell can be seen in one of the lumps of raw clay recovered from the excavations (fig. 5c).

The silty clay used to make the pots can be identified as a wind-blown deposit known as loess. Although loess is available in some quantity to the west and south of the Lachish area,[6] studies of wadi deposits immediately adjacent

to the site, carried out by Dr Arlene Rosen, identified a substantial loess deposit within 200–300 m (220–325 yds) of the cave where the workshop was found.[7] There is some evidence that this deposit was exposed during the Late Bronze Age[8] and it may have provided a convenient source of raw material for the potters. The shell in the Group 2 fabric is distinctively rounded and polished, suggesting that it came from a geologically recent, unconsolidated deposit such as a raised beach. Beach deposits dating to the Pliocene period (Pleshet formation) outcrop approximately 10 km (6 miles) to the

west of Lachish and may represent the source of this raw material.[9] Thus the petrographic study indicates that the raw clays were available very close to the workshop, although to collect the shell used for tempering may have involved several hours' walking.

Comparing the fabric groups to the vessel types, we found that Group 1 included several different kinds of bowls and a storage jar. However, all of the Group 2 samples with shell temper were cooking pots (fig. 5d). The shell appears to have been deliberately added in order to produce a specific clay paste for this type of vessel. The use in cooking pots

a

b

of shell and other tempers consisting of calcium carbonate is well known, both ethnographically and archaeologically, and it has been suggested that their use improves thermal shock resistance.[10]

Forming the vessels

Questions concerning how vessels were formed, in particular whether they were thrown on a potter's wheel or hand-built, perhaps by coiling or moulding, were also investigated.[11]

Visual examination provided some evidence. Rilling marks (smooth ridges and grooves parallel to the rim) and the symmetry of the vessels suggest that they may have been thrown on a wheel. The discovery of the two stone objects with central pivots, identified as the upper members of pairs of stones used as bearings for potter's wheels (figs 6a and 6b, lower right), also supports the notion that the Lachish potters threw the vessels. However, it might be argued that these stones were in fact from wheels used as turntables or tournettes,

to assist in the hand-building of pots, and that the rilling arose from the smoothing and finishing of such vessels on a tournette.

To resolve this question, a series of Lachish vessels were radiographed. Features characteristic of wheel-throwing were seen in the majority of the radiographs. As the potter raises the walls of a vessel while forming it on a rapidly rotating wheel, inclusions and voids in the clay are drawn up in a spiral running around the vessel. Well-developed spiral patterns are visible, for example, in the radiograph of the scoop (fig. 6c) and also in the miniature bowl at the centre of fig. 6d. When wheel-thrown vessels are radiographed 'side-on' a cross-hatched pattern appears, as can be seen in the radiographs of the two miniature vessels at either side of fig. 6d.

Thus there is good reason to believe that the Lachish potters used a wheel to throw a range of vessel types. Several possible reconstructions of potter's wheels, using pivots of the type found at Lachish (fig. 6a), have been published, and experiments carried out in their practical use.[12] There seems little doubt that with the addition of a suitable wheel-head, probably of wood or ceramic, such pivots can form the bearings for a wheel on which vessels can be thrown. Whether the Lachish pivots were used in a simple hand-wheel or in a more sophisticated kick-wheel[13] (fig. 6b) is open to conjecture.

In contrast, one group of vessels did not show clearly any of the radio-graphic features characteristic of wheel-throwing. These were the cooking pots (fig. 5d).[14] However, as with most other vessels from the workshop, the rims are well formed and it seems probable that, while the basic vessel was made by a hand-building technique such as moulding, the upper part of the cooking pot was shaped on a wheel from a coil of clay added above the carination. The use of hand-building techniques for the cooking pots would have facilitated the production of round-bottomed vessels, thus increasing

Fig. 4
Group of finished
vessels from the
workshop.
The preserved
height of the
pilgrim flask is
35 cm (14 in).

resistance to thermal shock.[15] Further research, including practical investigation of potential techniques, is underway in an attempt to better understand the methods used to produce the cooking pots.

Tools and decoration

Improvised 'tools' found in the cave (fig. 1) included shaped and smoothed pottery sherds, probably used in the manner of a modern potter's 'rib' to produce particular vessel profiles, and pebbles and shells suitable for burnishing.[16] A bone point may have served as a trimming implement or perhaps as an aid to remove vessels from the wheel-head. Some vessels have painted decoration, probably applied before firing (for example, the pilgrim-flask at the top left of fig. 4). Two deliberately abraded and faceted lumps of ochre[17] and several sherds, each covered on one side with a coating of powdered red pigment and apparently used as palettes (fig. 1), provided some evidence for this stage of the finishing process. Although both red and yellow ochres were recovered, the designs on

the vessels are only in red. It is possible that yellow ochre was used but that it turned red during firing.[18]

Firing

There is no direct evidence as to how the Lachish pottery was fired. No kiln or other suitable fire installation was discovered during the excavations, although investigation of the area adjacent to the cave may reveal one in future. Nevertheless, certain conclusions can be drawn from the nature of the pottery itself.

The predominantly pink/red colour of the fired vessels indicates that the firing was carried out under oxidising conditions, with a plentiful supply of air. Some estimate of the temperature during firing can be made, because the raw clay and unfired sherds contain grains of calcite and shell. In the fired sherds the shell has been transformed from the original aragonite[19] to calcite, indicating a firing temperature greater than about 500°C.[20] Although most of the calcite has been transformed to an apparently amorphous mass, original textures are preserved in the cores of

some sherds. These observations combine to suggest that firing was carried out in an oxidising atmosphere, at a temperature that was only just sufficient to destroy calcite, i.e. about 750°C.[21] This inference was tested by refiring fragments from one of the unfired sherds in a laboratory oven, and observing the textures of the resulting ceramics in a scanning electron microscope. After refiring at 700°C, the texture was very similar to that of the fired sherds from the potter's workshop, but by 800°C the refired ceramic was quite distinct, being significantly more vitrified.[22] This is quite consistent with the interpretation above, that the pottery had been fired originally at about 750°C.

Conclusions

Excavations at Lachish, both in the 1930s and more recently during the 1970s and 1980s, have revealed evidence for a Late Bronze Age city with public buildings and a temple on the summit of the tell.[23] We can probably assume that the Canaanite potters produced their wares for the local

Fig. 5 (a) Photomicrograph of petrographic thin section of a sherd from a bowl, illustrating the abundance of silt (small bright particles) in the fabric; width of field c. 4.5 mm (0.2 in), cross-polarised light; (b) photomicrograph of thin section of a sherd from a cooking pot in a very similar fabric to (a), but with the distinctive addition of shell (the larger particles), often with rounded ends; width of field c. 4.5 mm (0.2 in), cross-polarised light; (c) photo-micrograph showing fragments of polished shell included in a piece of raw clay; width of field c. 3.5 mm (0.14 in); (d) Late Bronze Age Canaanite cooking pot from Lachish. Although rim fragments of cooking pots (both fired and unfired) were recovered from Cave 4034, no complete specimens were found there. This example from Area 100 illustrates the general shape of the vessel.

population, although their products may have gone further afield. However, confirmation of this can only come through future research.

The cave which housed the workshop was located on the lower slopes of the north-east side of the mound, and would have been some distance away from the main public areas of the city.[24] To find pottery-making on the outskirts of a settlement is not unusual: the firing of pottery not only creates a fire hazard but can be unpleasant as well, generating odours and smoke.[25] However, other considerations such as proximity to sources of clay and water may also have played a role in the siting of the Lachish pottery workshop. The particular choice of a cave may well have been deliberate. Because of their low ambient temperature, caves can provide an ideal location for pottery-making in a hot climate, a fact apparently well understood by both

ancient and modern potters in this region. Perhaps the most striking thing to emerge from this study of Lachish Cave 4034 is that, in many respects, the Late Bronze Age potter's workshop was probably little different to one observed in the 1930s in the village of Irtah in Palestine by Dr K. M. E. Murray:[26]

The place they made the pottery in was rather fun – a great big cave. The entrance was below the level of the ground and in a space cleared in front of it, sunk in the ground pots were standing out to dry in the sun ... In the cave against one wall were the pits of clay, brown clay and white clay which they use alone or mixed for different kinds of pots ... Sometimes they dab some reddish brown decoration on ... Against the opposite wall sat two potters ... They sat with their feet down in a hole cut in the rock. They had two wheels both worked by wooden fly wheels in the pit, kicked round. The wooden fly wheel was

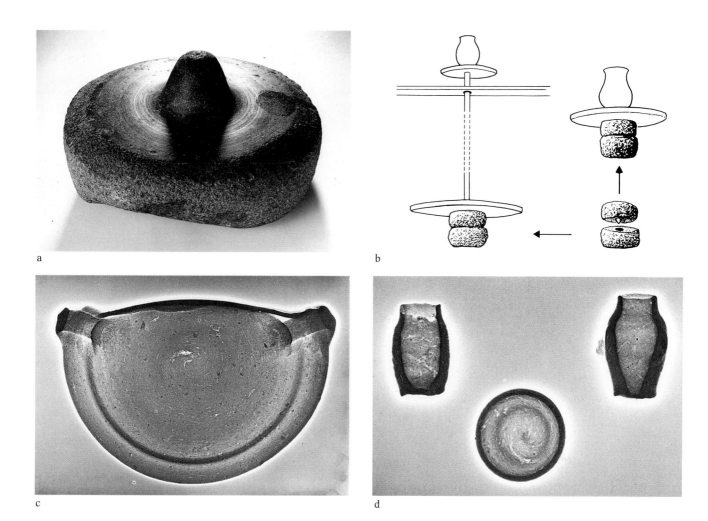

a

b

c

d

connected by a metal rod to the wheel they worked on.

Indeed, from a technological perspective, Dr Murray's description could apply almost as well to the late second millennium BC as to the early twentieth century AD.

Fig. 6 (a) Stone (basalt) pivot, which formed part of the bearing for the potter's wheel. Height 11.8 cm (4.7 in); (b) possible reconstructions of the potter's wheel, using bearings of the type shown in (a); on the right is a simple wheel, and on the left is a composite kickwheel; (c) xeroradiograph of a scoop. Note the well-developed spiral pattern running out from the centre; Exposure conditions: 150 kV, 18 mAs.
(d) Xeroradiograph of three miniature vessels. Note the spiral pattern in the bowl (centre) and the cross-hatching in the walls of the vessels on either side. Exposure conditions: 150 kV, 18 mAs.

Radiography

Radiographic examination is widely used in the study of ceramic technology.[27] The process is precisely analogous to the use of X-rays in hospitals to provide chest 'X-rays' or images of broken bones. Radiography can be used to investigate the texture of the clay body and also the techniques of pottery manufacture. The various methods of forming a vessel from the plastic clay each results in the generation of characteristic orientations of particles and voids within the clay body.[28] Radiography, in particular xeroradiography,[29] is a useful means of revealing these characteristic patterns of voids and inclusions. In this way it may be possible to determine whether a vessel was wheel-thrown or hand-built using a technique such as coiling or slab construction. Radiographic examination also offers the advantage that it is non-destructive, so that it can be used to examine complete or fully restored vessels without inflicting any damage.

Partho-Sasanian Ceramic Industries in Mesopotamia

St John Simpson

Distinct regional traditions typified Partho-Sasanian ceramic production in Mesopotamia, Iran and adjacent regions within the Persian empire. The deliberate foundation of the imperial capital at Ctesiphon, in the heart of Mesopotamia, and its maintenance for over seven centuries emphasise the strong political, strategic and economic importance of this region. Large areas were intensively cultivated with the help of massive canal networks, and this more efficient agricultural base in turn supported a dense rural settlement pattern and a highly developed urban infrastructure. During the Parthian period the ceramic industries adapted classical forms to local tastes, and coloured glazed wares were one particularly distinctive product (fig. 4). Mass-production increased during the Sasanian period, with a large degree of continuity after the Arab conquest.[1]

The Parthian period

The reign of Mithradates I (*c.* 171–138 BC) marked a transformation of the minor province of Parthia, located east of the Caspian Sea, into a powerful kingdom stretching from Bactria to Babylonia. Despite persistent internal political struggles, Parthia became a powerful rival of Rome.[2]

The political fragmentation of the Parthian state is mirrored in the highly regionalised ceramic traditions of Mesopotamia and Iran. Within Mesopotamia, most ceramics were wheel-thrown: a fired clay potter's wheel found at Seleucia may be the remains of 'the upper wheel, and below this connected by a spindle would be the large kick wheel'.[3] Plainwares tended to be more lightly sand-tempered than preceding Seleucid or later Sasanian pottery, and vessels were carefully wet-smoothed at the final stages. Lamps were made by combining wheel-thrown reservoirs with handmade spouts, whereas

storage jars, lids, cosmetic dishes and rat traps were made by hand or in two-part moulds. Other jars were made by combining separate wheel-thrown and handmade sections, finished on the wheel; likewise, pilgrim flasks were thrown in two halves and later joined together.[4]

The versatility of potters is illustrated by the techniques used to decorate amphorae with 'twisted-rope' handles: the bodies were covered with incision and applied pellets, studs and bosses, moulded female heads and horizontal 'pinched-ridge' rope patterns, whereas mould-pressed plaques were added to the neck. These plaques carry a variety of motifs, including grass-hoppers; Eros wrestling with a snake, playing a lyre or holding a bow; seated women; and a figure holding a cornucopia. These amphorae were widespread from Seleucia across to the Euphrates valley but appear to have been rare further north.[5] Other new types of decoration include comb-stabbing and dog's-tooth rocker-

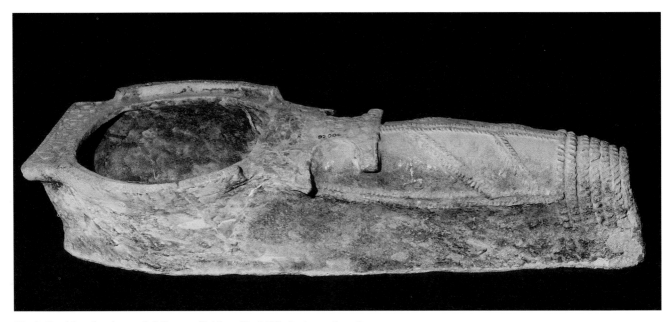

Fig. 1 Parthian glazed ceramic 'slipper coffin' from Uruk/Warka, in southern Iraq.

Fig. 2 Early Sasanian green-glazed rhyton (pourer) from Babylon, in southern Mesopotamia, 3rd century AD. Inspection of xeroradiographs, combined with evidence from the object itself, indicates a possible method by which it was fashioned. The lower part of the vessel was moulded in two parts and subsequently luted together with bands of smoothed clay, whereas the upper part was formed separately, by coiling as a baseless flask, and then inserted into the pre-moulded lower part. The bust on the front of the flask was formed by pressing the wall into a shallow mould but, in the process, the clay was excessively thinned, hence the fine cracks visible on the xeroradiographs. The strap-handle was formed from a strip of clay luted on at the leather-hard stage. When the rhyton is viewed from above, it can be seen that the vessel is slightly distorted, possibly at the drying stage as the object lay on its left side.

Partho-Sasanian glazes

The glazes on Partho-Sasanian pottery form part of a long tradition of alkaline glazing in Mesopotamia which stretches back to the Bronze Age. Glazes were made by mixing the ash produced by burning desert plants with crushed quartz pebbles or quartz sand. This created a glaze rich in soda, lime, potash and magnesia. The blue and green colours of the glazes are due to the presence of minor amounts of iron oxide, with or without copper. Darker browns could be produced by adding manganese; blacks resulted from the development of iron sulphide when fired under reducing conditions.

This type of alkali-rich glaze is not well suited to an earthenware body because it has a much higher coefficient of expansion. As the pot cooled after firing, the glaze contracted at a faster rate than did the body. This often caused shrinkage cracks to open up in the glaze, giving the crazed appearance characteristic of much Partho-Sasanian glazed pottery. There is no evidence for the use of lead glazes in the Partho-Sasanian empire, although they were used to the west, by the Romans, as well as to the east, in China.

Composition of typical Partho-Sasanian glaze[34]							
SiO_2	Al_2O_3	FeO	MgO	CaO	Na_2O	K_2O	CuO
66	2	2	4	8	10	5	2

stamp impressions and, in northern Mesopotamia, diamond-stamped decoration on plainware (and occasional glazed) jars. Eggshell-ware hemispherical bowls and two-handled vases, with walls thinned down after throwing to as little as 1 mm (0.004 in), were typical of the Seleucia area, whereas vertical scored decoration was rare at Seleucia yet common at Nippur and along the Middle Euphrates.[6]

Blue, green and occasionally yellow and brown glazed vessels were a hallmark of Parthian ceramic production in Mesopotamia (fig. 4), although they rarely comprise more than five per cent of a ceramic assemblage.[7] Sodium alkaline glazes were the norm, with copper, manganese and iron oxides used as colourants but no evidence for lead or cobalt. Variations in the colour of green and yellow glazes depended upon bulk chemical composition and firing conditions. More unusual were a series of bowls and bottles covered with a transparent glaze but with the rims dipped into blue glaze; a small number of bowls, jars and pilgrim flasks were covered or partially dipped into brown glaze. Other types, including spouted lamps, appear to have been twice dipped and fired, perhaps to ensure a more durable glaze.[8]

Fig. 3 Sasanian pottery from Mesopotamia. Most Sasanian pottery was sand-tempered and wheel-thrown, and a glazed tradition continued in the Ctesiphon region of central Mesopotamia. Specialised vessel types included glazed fish-shaped pourers and incense burners with basket handles and decoration imitating battlements (merlons and arrow-slits); everyday vessels included storage jars and dipper juglets.

Fig. 4 Parthian glazed wares from Mesopotamia. Coloured alkaline glazes were widely applied by Parthian potters working in or near the capital at Ctesiphon. Blue or green glazes were typical, but transparent yellow or green glazes were also employed.

Eastern Roman ribbed Brittle ware cooking pots produced in Syria were traded as far south as Hatra, whereas local glazed cooking wares were preferred further south; these were glazed on the interior and rim to facilitate cleaning.[9] Within this context it is interesting to note that *De re coquinaria* ('On the Art of Cooking'), a collection of Roman cookery dishes generally attributed to the first-century AD writer M. Gavius Apicius, contains a recipe for *Pullum Parthicum* ('Parthian Chicken'), which specifies cooking the chicken in a

rich wine sauce in 'an earthenware pot'.

Classical forms of vessel that continued to be made by Parthian potters included wheel-thrown fish-plates with central depressions for holding fish sauce, moulded lamps, squat one-handled flasks and ring-footed vessels.[10] Two-handled pilgrim flasks were a distinctive Parthian innovation widely used in Meso-potamia, Iran and the Gulf. These were clearly inspired by water-bottles, and some were even decorated in imitation of embossed or stitched leatherwork.[11]

Pottery kilns have been discovered at sites along the Middle Euphrates, and a kiln with a horseshoe-shaped plan that had possibly been used to fire pilgrim flasks was excavated at Seleucia. Similar updraught kilns were identified in a Parthian potters' quarter at Assur.[12] Most ceramics were fired within a temperature range of 1000–1200°C, whereas contemporary ceramic figurines were normally fired within the lower temperature range of 600–1000°C. The discovery of a kiln at Seleucia used exclusively for firing figurines suggests that different workshops were responsible for producing either pottery or figurines.[13] Archaeo-

logical data throw some light on methods of stacking pottery within the kiln: solidified glaze drips indicate that jars and bowls were stacked upright or upside down, whereas pilgrim flasks were stacked lying flat, one above the other. Glazed wares were separated by tripod stilts or 'occasional chunks of clay…rapidly molded with the fingers into oblongs, triangles, and other suitable shapes to keep the vessels erect and hold them away from the sides of the kiln and one another'. Glazes often crazed, yet excellent fusion of the glaze to the body was consistently achieved.

The confidence and skill of Parthian potters is illustrated further by a spectacular series of glazed 'slipper

coffins' (fig. 1) made in different sizes for adults and children. These were decorated in relief or repeatedly impressed with a rectangular die and covered with a blue or green glaze. At Uruk the most common stamped design showed a male figure with bunched-up hair, trousers, hands on hips and a sword slung at his left side; a ceramic die of this type was found at the site, suggesting that the coffins were made in the vicinity, as might be expected from their enormous weight and size. This is supported by the occurrence of coffins with different designs at other sites, although the kilns used have not yet been identified. The elaborate decoration suggests that they may be skeuomorphs of higher-

Fig. 5 *Detail of a carved wooden stamp impression on a Late Sasanian plainware jar from Nineveh, in northern Iraq. This die measured 8 cm (3 in) across and showed a stag facing left (when impressed); the horizontal grain of the wood of the die can be clearly seen between the tines of the antlers. This style of ceramic decoration was probably inspired by contemporary Sasanian art, particularly metal vases decorated with relief roundels. Different stamps were used to impress consecutive rows around the vessel, and great care was taken to avoid distorting the walls: light finger or cloth impressions visible on the interior reflect support from inside while the die was impressed. Examination of the stamped impressions allows die-linking of ceramics from different sites, suggesting the sale and transport of jars, although the possibility of itinerant potters cannot be firmly excluded.*

value hammered-sheet or cast-bronze coffins – as in earlier periods – although no direct evidence for these survives.[14]

The Sasanian period

In AD 224 Artabanus V (*c.* 213–24), the last Parthian king, was overthrown by a Persian nobleman called Ardashir, who founded a new dynasty which he named after an ancestor called Sasan. Ardashir I (*c.* 224–41) and his son Shapur I (*c.* 241–72) rapidly consolidated their power base and expanded the Sasanian empire until it stretched from northern Mesopotamia to central Asia. Their empire was characterised by a highly developed bureaucracy, army and agricultural infrastructure which exercised strong influence on early Islamic society and culture after the Arab conquest in the seventh century.[15]

Contemporary written sources referring either to pots or potters are rare, yet the Babylonian Talmud refers to drawing water with 'a bucket of clay', religious prohibitions on the use of certain types of glazed ware for liquids, and the purchase of better-quality non-porous pots made by potters in an unidentified town called Be-Mikse.[16] During this period large industrial sites dedicated to pottery and glass manufacture developed next to canals in central and southern Mesopotamia. Excavations have revealed square updraught kilns measuring over 4 m (12 ft) across.[17] Late Sasanian ceramics were sand-tempered and fired in oxidising conditions; the frequency of gritty red-wares at sites in one area prompted comment on the 'reddish color' of the mounds.[18] Glazed wares were mainly produced in the area of the capital at Ctesiphon (fig. 3), reflecting a tradition established in the Parthian period, but they were unusual in other regions.[19] Ordinary potters and glazed-ware specialists are referred to in Pahlavi sources. Alkaline glazes remained the norm, and early reports of Sasanian lead glazes are unsupported by compositional analyses.[20] Despite their utilitarian nature, Sasanian glazed wares were valued in other regions, as they were traded the length of the

Persian Gulf and along the southern coast of Arabia as far as the Horn of Africa.[21] Glazed or coarse grit-tempered globular cooking pots were made, yet the relative scarcity of cooking wares at other sites suggests that iron cauldrons were also widely employed.[22]

During the sixth and seventh centuries, potters across central and northern Mesopotamia produced large or medium-sized jars impressed around the exterior with wooden stamps (fig. 5). Dimpled interiors suggest that paddling was widely employed, possibly to thin the walls, prior to impressing the stamps. Many of the dies were circular and carved from wood, as the grain of the die itself is sometimes visible on impressed surfaces; a small number of square stamps were also used. The designs cut on the dies usually comprised a large central geometric or figural motif framed by a geometric border or a circle of pearl roundels. Rams, ibexes, hump-backed bulls, birds, scorpions, crosses and Catherine-wheel designs were particularly popular, reflecting both widespread Sasanian styles and the important Christian population in this part of the empire.[23]

Another distinctive Late Sasanian type that continued to be used into the early Islamic period comprised large jars with rounded bases and three or four small handles. A particularly rough sandy slip was added to the exterior of these vessels which, at the final stage, were crudely smeared or decorated with finger-trailing or regular honeycomb-like finger impressions. These were probably used to hold drinking water, as the roughened surfaces enhanced porosity and ensured a better grip when transported.[24] Torpedo-shaped jars with pointed bases were designed to be inserted into soft ground and were probably used to transport oil or wine: the deliberate addition of an asphalt lining simultaneously rendered these vessels impermeable and enhanced the flavour of the contents.[25] Hemispherical bowls were thrown from the hump and then shaved down, but other bowls and larger basins retained their flat string-cut bases and were sometimes embellished with 'pie-crust' pinched rims. Other bowls were modified during throwing by the addition of a central

knob on the interior, thus allowing them to be used as lids.[26]

Most of these classes of vessel represent simple shapes developed from earlier local ceramic industries. However, some additional forms are based on new Sasanian types of metal-wares, including one-handled dipper juglets, larger flat-based pitchers with trefoil-mouth pouring spouts, casseroles, and jars with elaborate lid-seatings. Traditional potter's forms of invasive combed or incised decoration were adapted to these skeuomorphs.[27] Blue-glazed jars with graceful pear-shaped bodies, sharply modelled rims and ribs at the shoulder/neck junctions imitated the shape of sixth- to seventh-century silver-gilt vases decorated in *repoussé* with figural scenes.[28]

Three different shapes of animal-headed rhytons were likewise produced by Sasanian potters in imitation of metal examples. The earliest group dates to the third century (fig. 2) and consists of green, blue or brown glazed composite vessels with a portrait or bust at the top, a prominent face in the centre and an animal-head spout.[29] The second variety was somewhat larger in size and characterised by a plain animal-head spout,[30] whereas the third is represented by a single green-glazed deer-headed rhyton excavated at Babylon.[31] A small group of zoomorphic vessels is also known.[32]

Sasanian ceramic traditions did not end abruptly with the Arab conquest of Mesopotamia and Iran in the second quarter of the seventh century. So-called Sasano-Islamic Blue Glazed ware, Brittle ware cooking pots and Honeycomb ware were direct developments from the Sasanian pottery tradition, although new styles of pottery also appeared. Notably, these included greater use of applied barbotine decoration on plainwares and glazed storage jars alike.[33]

Ash-Glazed Stonewares in Japan

Victor Harris

Profound changes occurred in Japanese society between the fourth and seventh centuries AD. The development of centralised government, adoption of the Chinese script and establishment of Buddhism as the official religion were accompanied by extensive contacts with mainland Korea. The first national constitution was drafted in 604, and in 794 Kyoto became the imperial residence and capital, a position which it was to retain, more or less continuously, until the nineteenth century.

Alongside these broader changes came technological developments in particular industries, including the production of ceramics. The adoption and adaptation of new technologies from Korea were to lead to the development of pottery with a 'natural' glaze, resulting in a characteristically Japanese ceramic which is widely admired today and has had a profound influence on modern studio pottery in the West (ch. 32).

New kiln technology

In Japan, pottery had since the tenth millennium BC been fired in low-temperature surface or pit fires, and left unglazed (ch. 1). However, around the fifth century AD, the *ana-gama* or cellular kiln was introduced from Korea. This was a closed kiln built over a channel cut upwards along the slope of a hill to provide a natural chimney and through draught. The new kiln design, with its increased air flow, allowed higher temperatures to be maintained, initially in excess of 1000°C and eventually in excess of 1200°C. These kilns allowed the potters to produce superior hard-bodied stoneware-like pottery with improved strength and reduced permeability to fluids. This period also sees the first Japanese pottery with an accidental or natural glaze (fig. 2).

In wood-fired kilns with a high air flow, ash from the fuel and walls of the kiln can be carried through into the firing chamber, where it settles on the surface of the pottery. Hot ash is a chemically reactive material, rich in lime and alkalis. When ash touches the surface of a pot at high temperature, it fluxes the clay and a surface glaze is formed, which adheres to the body and, if abundant, runs in uneven streaks down the sides of the vessel. Such a glaze is often patchy and uneven, reflecting the areas where the ash was deposited. In addition to the direct settling of the ash on the surface of the pots, it is probable that some of the alkali in the ash enters the kiln vapour, promoting an overall glaze on the

surface (ch. 18). These phenomena are the basis of the 'natural glaze', which can then be enhanced in a number of ways: for example, by packing the spaces between the pottery in the kiln with straw or other organic material, as is practised by some modern potters working in this tradition.

In addition to the high-firing kiln, the fifth century saw the introduction of the potter's wheel. The new methods and equipment imported from Korea by immigrant potters contributed to a significant professionalisation of Japanese pottery-making, with workshop-type production methods becoming widespread.

Since this time, there have been a number of further improvements to the potter's kiln in Japan, nearly all brought from Korea by immigrant potters. The *O-gama* (large kiln) was a version of the simple *ana-gama* but larger, to accommodate a greater number of pots. In the early seventeenth century the *noborigama* or climbing kiln, comprising a series of chambers rising up a hillside, was introduced. This enabled higher temperatures, sometimes in excess of 1300°C, to be maintained. The heat inside the kiln was preserved as each of the linked chambers was fired, one after the other, in ascending order: as each

of the lower chamber firings was completed, the next chamber reached a suitable temperature for combustion. The first Japanese porcelain was produced in kilns of this type.

Sue ware

Although the older low-fired pottery tradition continued for everyday ware even after the introduction of the *ana-gama* kiln and the potter's wheel, the new technology produced superior, harder wares with some natural ash glaze. The first such high-fired pottery in Japan is known as Sue ware (literally, offering) and is found among the ritual grave-goods (fig. 2) of the stone-chambered burial mounds of the regional leaders of Japan during the early Kofun period (*c.* third to seventh century) and in the great tombs of the first emperors.

Sue wares of the Kofun period were made of fine clay fired in a reducing atmosphere at temperatures in excess of 1000°C, which resulted in a grey body, sometimes with patches of green ash glaze. A large number of Sue kilns are known. The ritual Sue-type wares

Fig. 1 (Opposite) Early ash-glazed stonewares from Sanage and nearby Seto. Left to right: Yama-jawan (mountain teabowl), mass-produced for everyday use in Aichi prefecture, Heian period, 11th–12th century AD, diameter 16.5 cm (6.5 in); globular jar with natural ash glaze from Aichi prefecture, 9th century. Such fine-quality white-bodied wares made at Sanage are the precursors of later attempts to make Chinese-style glazed pottery at Seto. This jar has a lacquer repair to the rim, possibly having been deliberately spoiled for use as a burial urn. Height 24.6 cm (9.7 in); sherd from the shoulder of a meiping-type jar with incised floral scrolling, deliberately ash-glazed in an early attempt to reproduce the greatly admired Chinese wares of the Song dynasty. Heian period (11th–12th century), from Aichi prefecture. Length 16 cm (6.3 in).

Fig. 2 (Right) Grey-bodied ritual Sue-ware tomb vessel with applied decoration of boatmen, hunting dogs with a boar and deer at the shoulder, and patches of light natural ash glaze. Kofun period, 5th century AD, height 33 cm (13 in).

Fig. 3 Red-bodied ash-glazed storage jar, with lugs for attaching cords to hold on a lid, from Tamba province (present-day Hyogo prefecture), 15th–16th century, height 49.8 cm (19.6 in).

followed the shapes of Korean originals, and it is generally inferred that Korean craftsmen were working in Japan at this time. The vessels are thin-walled and the forms are generally very uniform, suggesting a high level of specialisation among the potters. Shapes include bottles and various dishes, lidded vessels, and vessels on pedestals with pierced decoration and geometric and combed wave patterns. But the native Japanese sensibility is still evident, even on these revolutionary ceramic types.

The early Sue vessel shown in figure 2 is decorated on the shoulder with applied mouldings depicting scenes of a way of life unchanged from the Jomon period. There is a group of deer sitting, a pack of hunting dogs attacking a wild boar, and a sea-going boat with rowers and a helmsman reminiscent of the excavated dugout 'canoes' of several thousand years before (ch. 1). Small areas of natural glaze adhere around the mouth and shoulder of the vessel.

Fine-quality Sue ware was the dominant form of pottery during the Kofun period, and forms of it remained in use until the end of the Heian period (794–1185), although low-fired pottery for domestic use, known as Haji ware, continued as a universal descendant of Jomon and Yayoi pottery. In the eighth century, a period of extensive intercourse with China, short-lived attempts had been made to imitate the highly admired, technically excellent Chinese *sancai* (three-colour) wares and celadons with the use of lead glazes. But these attempts appear to have been abandoned in favour of utilising ash-glazing in the well-tried Sue tradition.

Developments at Sanage

In the eighth and ninth centuries, in the Sanage mountain area of Owari province (present-day Aichi prefecture), elegant globular and long-necked vessels, some with spouts and handles and with moulded decoration, were made copying Chinese shapes. A kiln improvement was introduced by placing a movable post within the entrance to the kiln to control the air intake and combustion pattern. White-firing kaolinitic clay was obtained from local deposits. High-temperature firings in oxidising conditions were used to produce a fine white body, in place of the grey of the ritual Sue ware of the Kofun period, with a green ash glaze. It appears that the natural glazing effect within the kilns was deliberately enhanced by sprinkling ash over the pottery before firing. Sanage ware has been excavated from temple and palace sites, suggesting that it was used solely by the wealthy, like the Chinese celadon it sought to emulate.

The ninth-century globular jar shown here (fig. 1, centre) has a lacquer repair where a large fragment was missing from the rim, indicating that it was probably deliberately spoiled for use as a burial urn. The ash fell from above and settled around the top of the vessel to form a glaze, which has run down the outside; in addition it has formed a circular patch of glaze on the inside base, directly beneath the mouth. The glaze has broken away from an area on one side, possibly as a result of damage from interment. Faults due to an inclusion which protrudes through the body, and a fragment of the wall of the neighbouring jar in the kiln, were obviously tolerated and not thought to detract from the elegance of the vessel.

The endeavours at Sanage eventually

Fig. 4 Ash-glazed wine bottle with a potter's mark, Bizen ware, from present-day Okayama prefecture, 16th century, height 24 cm (9.5 in).

resulted in the development of deliberately applied mineral glazes in the Chinese style. Cruder white-bodied ash-glazed dishes made at Sanage and elsewhere, known as *yama-jawan* (mountain teabowls) (fig. 1, left), were made in great quantity until the Kamakura period (1185–1333).

Seto and the deliberate glaze

The Sanage potters migrated west around the end of the Heian period (794–1185) to nearby Seto, where white-firing clay was discovered in abundance. During the twelfth to fourteenth centuries the potters at Seto experimented with deliberate glazes. They were the only group in Japan to do so until the sixteenth century, even though the techniques had been perfected and widely used in China for a millennium and in Korea for several centuries. Deliberate ash-glazing involves the mixing of ash with a clay or glaze stone and the application of this mixture to the surface of the pot; hence the development of the glaze does not depend upon the reaction between the ash and the heated body of the vessel. When fully developed, this approach allows a much higher level of control over the appearance of the glaze. Its distribution over the surface can be predetermined; it has a uniform thickness and appearance, and impurities which affect the colour can be controlled.

The Seto potters continued to use the wheel, at first making ash-glazed quasi-celadons in Chinese shapes, particularly the *mei ping*, with Chinese floral scrolling decoration incised under the glaze (fig. 1, right). They eventually developed black, amber and mottled glazes based on Chinese *temmoku*-type wares, to provide tea containers and other vessels for the Tea Ceremony. However, Seto was the only area where the potters used a deliberate glaze. Elsewhere in Japan provincial potters were producing ash-glazed wares in the same *ana-gama* kilns which had been used for Sue ware, often building up

their pots by coiling in the original native Japanese tradition of the Jomon and Yayoi periods (ch. 1).

Natural glaze pottery

With the exception of the developments at Seto, by the thirteenth century unglazed or naturally ash-glazed stonewares had become established as the mainstay of the ceramic industry throughout Japan. A wide range of clays suitable for the manufacture of fine-bodied stonewares and porcelains

were available, as well as grittier clays derived from eroding granite and deposited in river valleys (the names of many kiln groups contain the character *tani*, meaning valley). Many hundreds of workshops are known from this time. The similarity of many of the clays and firing methods produced similar wares, and it is not always possible to distinguish between them.

The gritty clays were used in several regions to produce coarse ash-glazed wares which were valued for their rustic appearance. Iron-bearing clays turned black or grey when fired in a reducing environment in the old Sue style and red in an oxidising environment, which by this time had been adopted almost everywhere. Exceptions were specialist kilns such as those at Mino in Owari province, which continued to produce grey Sue-type roof tiles and other simple ceramic articles. Pots were made for ritual, household, storage and funerary uses. Large storage jars sometimes had 'ears': four lugs arranged at the shoulder so that a lid could be tied down (fig. 3). The shapes were simple and functional, possessing the dignity inherent in those properties. Their sombre rusticity was in keeping with the concept of *wabi* in the Tea Ceremony, in which a simple storage jar might be the primary focus of attention.

During the latter part of the sixteenth century, with the popularisation of the Tea Ceremony and exuberant new

fashions in society, the potteries contrived interesting and exotic new shapes while still relying on nature to produce the beauty in the glazed surface. At the same time, the potters of Seto and their derivatives began to introduce natural-looking effects created by random and haphazard application of the glazing fluid. Despite regional and temporal variations in fashion, storage jars and other vessels made for everyday use continued to be produced without much change.

Two widely differing and striking styles which have preserved their identities since the thirteenth century are the wares known as Bizen and Shigaraki. The pottery of Bizen province (present-day Okayama prefecture) was well known in Japan from at least the thirteenth century. The earlier pots were grey-bodied, part of the Sue firing tradition, but both grey and red-bodied wares were made thereafter (fig. 4). The

Bizen potters chose a fine clay to obtain a smooth and compact body. The pots sometimes have little or no ash glaze, and occasionally splashes of green or yellow. Yellow *hidasuki* (scorch marks) result from the burning of bundles of straw, which were used to pack between the pots when the kiln was charged. Slight irregularities in shape are caused by both movement within the kiln, due to the violence of the fire, and the economic necessity of packing large numbers of pots in together. In recent centuries the irregularities, scorch marks, body colours and ash glazes have been deliberately contrived by the potters. Many Bizen pots bear simple potter's marks, reflecting the probable communal use of the kiln by a number of potters.

Quite different in appearance from Bizen ware are the swelling-shouldered small-mouthed storage jars of Shiga prefecture known as Shigaraki ware (fig. 6). Coarse white particles of feldspar or quartz obtruding through violent rivulets of ash glaze produce their characteristic effect. The coarse nature of the clay and the lack of control over the glaze make Shigaraki ware one of the most representative of the ash-glaze traditions.

The persistence of coil-building, open firing and natural ash glazing stems from the respect for tradition and awe of the forces of nature inherent in the naturalistic Shinto religion, which also recognises a similar holy nature in things non-Japanese. Thus, while some old traditions endure unchanged in Japan (fig. 5), others willingly absorb and adapt themselves to foreign technological innovations. It may be no exaggeration to say that Shinto is the essence of Japan's genius for industry, and that ash-glazed pottery is an embodiment of its art.[1]

Fig. 5 (Left) Ornamental jar, contemporary Bizen ware, from Okayama prefecture, made in 1991 by Fujiwara Yu, a potter registered as a 'Living National Treasure'. Height 34.7 cm (13.7 in).

Fig. 6 (Opposite) Natural ash-glazed storage jar with felspathic particles on the surface and within the glaze. Shigaraki ware (from Shiga prefecture), Muromachi period (16th century), height 34.5 cm (13.5 in).

Ancient Greek Pottery

Dyfri Williams

Pottery is known on the Greek peninsula at the eastern end of the Mediterranean from as early as the second half of the seventh millennium BC, during the neolithic period. At this time all pottery was handmade, built up from coils and slabs of clay; the exact form was achieved by cutting and scraping the interior and exterior.[1] The surface was regularly slipped and burnished or polished, while decoration took the form of designs made either with incised markings or with added slips or pigments. Firing was probably done in bonfires, rather than in kilns.

The shapes of the vessels indicate that pottery was used for storage, cooking, eating and drinking. It seems likely that each household generally produced for its own use. Although pottery has been associated with permanent habitation and so is often used as a means of identifying the settlements of early food-producing communities, some pots were soon carried considerable distances, not only as food containers but also as objects of intrinsic value.

With the onset of the Bronze Age in the late fourth millennium BC, the range of shapes increased, and the appearance of luxury vessels, such as those that held precious trinkets (*pyxides*), reinforces the idea that pottery was already being produced for sale rather than simply for essential home use.[2] At Myrtos on Crete, the discovery of nearly thirty potters' 'mats' (disks of fired clay on which the potters built up their vessels – the slightly convex underside may have aided in turning during the finishing process) is the earliest preserved evidence for the beginnings of technological sophistication in the production of handmade wares and points to a communal potting area.[3]

An interesting Early Minoan handmade fabric, known as Vasiliki ware (2500–2300 BC) after a settlement in eastern Crete, where it was first discovered, but found over much of eastern Crete including Myrtos, suggests both experimentation with firing techniques, including the control of oxidising and reducing atmospheres, and the use of reliable kilns. The surface has a lustrous reddish-brown wash mottled surface with large darker patches (fig. 1). This effect was perhaps intended to imitate the variegated stone vases fashionable at the time.

Wheel and workshop

Only in about 2000 BC, early in the Middle Bronze Age, did Greek potters first regularly use a fast-rotating wheel, a radical advance in technology which

Fig. 1 Early Minoan Vasiliki ware 'teapot', handmade with mottled decoration on Crete, 2500–2300 BC, from Ierapetra; height of body 12.1 cm (4.75 in). The shape of the vessel is of eastern origin. The two tiny pellets of clay added near the rim of the spout give the whole vessel an amusing, bird-like appearance.

enabled them to articulate the clay in a much more sophisticated manner. On Crete the potters produced an eggshell-thin ware with vivid red and white decoration on a dark glossy ground, while on the mainland the elaborately turned profiles of the plain burnished wares were given added crispness. The employment of the fast wheel coincides with the development of a palace-based society, especially on Crete where the earliest preserved wheels have been found, and it is therefore plausible to assume that palace patronage stimulated this technological advance. Nevertheless, the making of pottery was not completely under palace control, for there were also many rural centres of production.

The normal production unit may have consisted of several members of one family: the man perhaps potting, the woman decorating and the children providing the unskilled labour, such as turning the wheel and stoking the kiln. According to documents written in Linear B which have been found in the palaces, the craft workers were usually male, but in one case a woman is named as potter, *ke-ra-me-ja* (Ap 639). A greater commitment of wealth and time is, however, implied in the acquisition of specialised equipment such as a wheel and the construction of kilns, which must have been offset by profit from sales. Nonetheless, it seems unlikely that potters were yet totally specialised artisans: they probably

Greek slips

The high-gloss slips characteristic of Attic pottery were produced by dispersing a clay in water and allowing the suspension to stand. The coarser particles settled more quickly and the overlying suspension, which contained the finest particles, was used as the slip. Analysis of the slip and the results of experiments suggest that, for the best results, the clay used was rich in particles of the mineral illite, which has a sheet-like structure. The fine, plate-like illite particles lay flat against the surface of the pot when applied and dried to form a smooth, thin layer which was densely packed, with few irregularities. On firing, the slip vitrified to form a hard shiny black surface. The glassy characteristics of the slips have led to the use of the term 'black glaze' to describe them. The slip layers are extraordinarily thin.[18]

combined potting with other seasonal activities such as farming and trade.

The Middle Bronze Age saw the establishment of some trading posts abroad. It is clear that potters occasionally accompanied such groups, as is demonstrated, for example, by the discovery on the island of Aegina close to Athens of pottery made in Cretan style but of local clay, as well as potter's wheels of Cretan clay.

The Late Bronze Age, from about 1500 BC, was a time of great prosperity both on Crete and the mainland, but after a series of disasters hit the southern Aegean the centre of political power began to shift to the mainland, especially Mycenae. The quality of potting was very high and the decora-

Fig. 2 Late Geometric pitcher, made in Athens, 730–720 BC; height 44.3 cm (17.5 in). The figured frieze shows women mourning at funeral biers with their hands to their heads in the ritual gesture of mourning, common to many societies; each of the deceased is laid out on a bier and covered with a shroud. On the neck is a very elaborate 'stepped' meander motif, so called after the slow winding river Maiandros in western Turkey, which is the Geometric pattern par excellence. On the front of the vase are two clay nipples, done in relief: these are presumably intended to evoke the long-held idea of a woman as a vessel.

Fig. 3 Head kantharos, made in Athens about 490 BC, said to be from Capua in Italy; height 13 cm (5 in). Only the upper bowl of this drinking vessel was made on a wheel: the double female heads below were made in a mould. The painting has been attributed to the so-called Foundry Painter, who worked for a potter called Brygos. A number of such 'plastic' vases are associated with Brygos' workshop, and he may well have potted this example. The figures on the rim depict participants at a symposium or drinking party. The youth has just finished plucking a note on his lyre, while his elder companion sings on, large skyphos in hand.

tion applied as a fine lustrous slip. The widespread standardised forms and decoration must have originated in the major centres and been disseminated from there to the provinces.

There is an important series of large *kraters* (mixing bowls), however, some of which show figures in chariots. This is the first sustained use of human figures as decoration on the pottery of Greece, although there is little finesse to the painting. In this case the inspiration probably came from wall-painting, but the idea would reappear, without such an impetus, on decorated pottery produced more than five centuries later.

The development of figured narratives

The collapse of the palaces on the Greek mainland around 1200 BC led to cultural fragmentation. As a result, there was a loss of technical quality in the production of the pottery, a reduction in the range of shapes produced and, eventually, greater regional variety. This regional variety persisted into the succeeding centuries, as a slow cultural reawakening began.

Pottery was produced in many of the independent Greek cities that emerged at this time, but the high point in technical achievement was to be reached at Athens.[4] Kritias, the fifth-century BC poet and politician, claimed that Athens 'invented the potter's wheel and the offspring of clay and kiln, pottery so famous and useful about the house', and indeed if this were to reflect a historical moment, then it would probably be the beginning of the tenth century BC, when potting and firing skills suddenly blossomed again at Athens.[5]

Around 770 BC there was a further artistic revolution at Athens – the development of ambitious figured scenes. This was to lead in the end to the truly remarkable feature that marks Greek pottery as different from almost every other pottery produced anywhere: the use of the human form as the major decorative motif. In the Geometric period (named after the strictly rectilinear, geometric decoration that dominates most vases of the time), the images of animals and humans were essentially conceptual, in that the artists drew what they knew to be there rather than what they could actually see. Chests are represented as triangles, with a breast protruding either side, and heads, hips, legs and feet are all shown in profile. The subjects they chose were scenes of mourning around the bier and funerary processions (fig. 2), parades of warriors and chariots, and fight scenes, both on land and sea.[6]

Following on from such narrative scenes drawn from the reality of funerals and battles, attempts at mythological narrative were also to develop during the second half of the eighth century BC. Soon other new ideas and motifs, some drawn from the East, began to loosen the rigidity of the old geometric patternwork as well. In the end the dominance of the Attic school gave way to a flood of independent local centres. Among these, Corinth soon came to the fore.[7] Not only were the city's extremely well-potted products exported over much of the Mediterranean throughout the seventh century BC, but the works of émigré Corinthian potters may be discerned in Italy, where the use of the local clay was masked by a slip of pale clay much like that used at home – thus creating the earliest known 'fake' Greek pottery.[8]

The end of anonymity

Around 700 BC we find the earliest potter's signature, on a fragment of a *krater* from the Italian island of Ischia. Four other such signatures using the word *epoiesen* (made) survive from the seventh century, on a variety of fabrics, and one that uses the word *egraphsen* (painted).[9] These signatures chart not only the rise of writing in the Greek world but also the increase in self-importance of pottery-makers. Indeed, the skills of potting and painting were already recognised as of independent importance.

The sixth and fifth centuries, however, again belonged to Athens, as her craftsmen's skill blossomed. Potters created a huge range of forms that encompassed not only delicately shaped cups and tall, elegant wine-jars, but also more humble objects such as potties for babies or thigh-guards for women carding wool.[10] The painters now employed the so-called black-figure

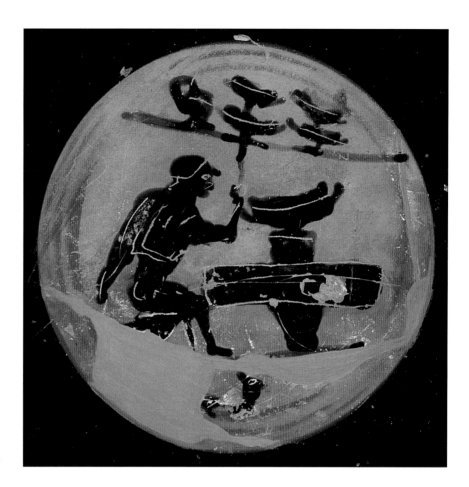

Fig. 4 Black-figure cup, made in Athens about 490 BC; said to have been found at Sakkara, in Egypt; diameter of tondo 6.3 cm (2.5 in). The scene on the tondo of this late, rather rough black-figure cup shows a potter at work. He is seated on a low stool as he fixes a handle to the cup which stands, virtually complete, on his wheel. Above him, a shelf is filled with other recent products, perhaps drying before being decorated, while below his feet a dog waits patiently.

technique, which combines black silhouettes with incisions for interior markings and areas of added purplish red and yellowish white. They not only represented elaborate stories, but at their best could even suggest a certain inner psychological tension.[11]

With the aid of signatures and the recognition of personal stylistic traits, it becomes possible to piece together a more detailed picture of the pottery craft during this period. In the first quarter of the sixth century there were scattered workshops in the Attic countryside, but by the second quarter

Red and black

Close control of both materials and firing conditions was needed to achieve the striking contrasts between paint and body on ancient Greek pottery.

The slips owe their intense black colours to the presence of iron oxide, although the iron oxide contents of the bodies are themselves quite high, as shown in the table.[19]

	Body	Slip	
SiO_2	54	46	silica
Al_2O_3	21	29	alumina
FeO	9	15	iron oxide
MgO	5	2	magnesia
CaO	4	1	lime
K_2O	5	6	potash

The pottery is considered to have been fired once. In an initial oxidising atmosphere, body and slip fired red, due to the formation of hematite, ferric oxide. A reducing atmosphere was then induced by closing the vents of the kiln and adding wood to the fire, which converted the iron oxide of the slip to magnetite, which is black. At the peak of the firing, in the range 850–1000°C, the potash content of the slip, coupled with its very fine grain size, caused it to fuse into a dense black glossy layer which was essentially impervious to oxygen. As the wood burnt down, the vents were opened and the kiln atmosphere became oxidising once more.

Due to its dense, fused condition, the slip remained black. However, the coarse clay of the body retained an open, porous structure throughout the firing, which allowed oxygen to diffuse in, converting the reduced iron oxide to the oxidised form, hematite. Depending upon the precise composition of the clay and the firing temperature, the body then gave a red or buff background to the black slip.[20]

they had disappeared, no doubt drawn into the great urban centre that Athens was fast becoming. The result is that we can now identify about double the number of painters at work in Athens and the appearance of some large specialist workshops. This was also the time of the first Panathenaic prize-amphorae, which were made to hold the oil that served as the prize for the victors in the quadrennial games, when more than 1400 (and perhaps as many as 2000) amphorae were required. There is evidence that the city awarded contracts to secure such large numbers of vases. The production of these prize-amphorae continued well into the Hellenistic period.

Around the middle of the sixth century we find the first occurrence of a clearly foreign name, that of Lydos, who signed himself 'the Lydian'. It is likely, therefore, that he was a slave, for the Greeks regularly called foreign slaves by their ethnic names. One signature of the late sixth century, by another Lydian, actually names him as a slave (*doulos on*). Further signatures on a series of delicate drinking-cups, some twenty-eight those of potters but only four of painters, combine with other factors to suggest what one might have expected, namely that the potters were the dominant financial figures. What is also immediately clear is that the craft of potting was being passed on from father to son: for example, Eucheiros, son of Ergotimos, and even a son of Eucheiros – seemingly a third-generation potter – are named. Furthermore, the mention of the father's name also indicates free-born status, so that we know potters could be free-born citizens as well as foreigners or slaves.[12] No women are named.

New techniques: red-figure and white-ground

Around 530–520 BC a new decorative scheme was invented that eventually supplanted that of black-figure. This was the red-figure technique, in which the figures were left reserved in the red clay while the background was given a slip that fired the new regular glossy black.[13] This new system permitted a much freer rendering of details with a brush, and the painters became very

interested in showing the three-dimensionality of the human figure.

From this time both the amount of activity and the numbers of personnel mushroomed immensely, which is reflected in the sheer number of identifiable pottery work-groups. There is also evidence for the sharing of the decorating of a particular vase between two painters: a sure sign of increased demand, since painting would clearly be slower than potting, as well as an

indication of the increased physical size of some workshops. There are also clear examples of craftsmen moving from being painters to potters and thence, presumably, to becoming the owners of whole workshops. In the last decade of the sixth century and the early decades of the fifth, we find a number of representations of potters and painters at work (fig. 3).

Some potters specialised in the production of particular shapes aimed

Fig. 5
White-ground alabastron, made in Athens about 490 BC; height 16 cm (6.3 in). The shape of the vase imitates Egyptian alabaster scent-jars. Such pottery versions were used exclusively by women in Athens. The scene is taken from the palaistra: a youth wearing a cloak snaps his fingers at a small dog, while on the other side an athlete rests on one of his akontia (javelins). The inscription in the field names the young Chairippos as beautiful.

at the overseas market, which included Cyprus, Thrace and South Italy but most especially Etruria, where there seems to have been a deep interest in Athenian pottery. Other potters occasionally combined thrown parts of vessels with mould-made sections, usually to produce a special drinking or libation vessel (fig. 4), in imitation of a metal form. These mould-made parts were of very high quality, well beyond the usual level of mould-made terracotta figurines.

A further technique was also developed at the end of the sixth century BC. This employed the use of a white slip on which the vase-painters, unfettered by the strict red and black environment, were able to draw or paint in a manner much more akin to the lost free-painting of the time (fig. 5). The white slip, however, not being resistant to wear, was never widely used, and most often for funerary or ritual vessels.[14]

From Athens to South Italy

By the middle of the fifth century BC something of a decline in the quality of the drawing had already begun. In part, this may have been caused by the rise in importance of free-painting, for we begin to find strong echoes of such wall- and panel-paintings, both in theme and technique. In the second half of the fifth century, however, an important red-figure school developed in South Italy, no doubt as a result of the emigration of a number of potters from Athens. Furthermore, it seems likely that the number of workshops in Athens soon began to shrink, this craft-drain reaching a peak at the end of the fifth century BC following Athens' defeat in the Peloponnesian War.[15]

By the fourth century the prolific South Italian workshops dominated the Italian markets, but Athens was to produce one final phase of ambitious red-figure pottery, the so-called Kertch vases that began to appear in the second quarter of the fourth century BC. These richly decorated vases were admired by the wealthy peoples of the northern Black Sea, the Bosporan kingdom, and no doubt their presence is connected with the vital corn trade between Athens and that region.

Fig. 6 Mould-made bowl, made in Athens about 200 BC; height 8.3 cm (3.3 in). This Megarian bowl was made by centring a hemispherical mould on a wheel and then throwing the bowl inside it. The join between the mould and free-thrown rim is quite clear on this example. The figured scenes show Greeks fighting Amazons. On the basis of the stamps used to create the designs in the clay moulds, there is evidence for some eight such workshops in Athens at the end of the third century BC, but signatures are far from common.

Beyond painted figures

From the sixth century BC, Athens and other Greek cities also produced plain, black-slipped pottery. This was an everyday ware: sets have been found in the ruins of public buildings in Athens, specially scratched with a monogram to indicate public ownership, while large quantities have been found in private houses and sanctuaries. The forms of such black-slipped pottery also reveal interesting links with cooking wares and vessels in other materials, such as bronze and silver.[16]

During the fourth century BC, Athenian black-slipped vessels began to receive more elaborate decoration in raised clay, at first gilded and then, at the beginning of the Hellenistic period, simply painted a yellowish brown. This style developed into what is now called

the West Slope style, named after the material found on the west slope of the Acropolis at Athens, although it was produced in a number of Greek cities around the Mediterranean during the third and second centuries BC.

A number of other regional fabrics were also developed in Hellenistic centres, including those that employed a light-on-dark scheme of decoration, such as the red-ware jars from Egypt with their erotic scenes; the Hadra vases, many made on Crete but often used as burial urns for travelling Greeks who died in Egypt; and the white-ground *lagynoi* of Asia Minor.[17] One final black-slipped ware, however, was developed at Athens about 220 BC. This is the so-called Megarian bowl (fig. 6): a mould-made hemispherical bowl with relief decoration, created perhaps in response to silver vessels of a similar shape that arrived from the Ptolemaic court in Alexandria. Although this type of pottery was soon imitated in both the Peloponnese and the Attalid East Greek cities, its real future lay in Italy (ch. 29), where potters who had already begun to follow the new, eastern Mediterranean idea of red-slipped wares (the red slip was actually easier to produce than the black) eventually developed the famous Arretine ware of the late first century BC.

Highly Decorated Pottery in Medieval England

Beverley Nenk

During the thirteenth and first half of the fourteenth centuries, potters in England produced some of the most elaborately decorated ceramics in medieval Europe. Vessels decorated with coloured slips and glazes, often embellished with figures of humans and animals and a wide range of ornamental designs and motifs, are characteristic of this period (fig. 2). The production of these fine glazed wares was made possible by improvements in ceramic technology which had a significant impact on the manufacture, decoration and firing of pottery. The elaborate decoration was stimulated by contemporary styles of ornament, competition from vessels made in metal, and pottery imported from abroad. An increase in the potters' repertoire of vessel shapes at this period reflects an increasingly prosperous market and a growing demand for pottery to fulfil specific functions. The increasingly widespread emulation of the social and culinary habits of the wealthier classes by growing urban communities and poorer members of society created a demand for new forms made in pottery, based on the shapes of costlier metal vessels, and on the forms and decoration of imported ceramics.[1]

Medieval potters

At this period the majority of potters were relatively poor members of society.[2] In the countryside, potting was often a small-scale seasonal activity, combined with agriculture to supplement the livelihood of peasant farmers, many of whom were sub-tenants. Most were either untaxed or assessed at the lowest rate paid by the peasantry, and they are therefore seldom mentioned in documentary records. There seems to have been little difference between the status of rural potters and their counterparts in urban areas. The fact that no potters' guild existed at this period reflects the low status of the industry. Such limited evidence as there is for the organisation of potters suggests production was carried out mainly by family members, probably with the assistance of hired labour.[3] Nevertheless, an increase in the scale of the industry seems to have occurred during this period, probably stimulated by a general rise in population and prosperity and in the number of markets and fairs at which potters sold their products. Correspondingly, the number of production sites, both rural and urban, also appears to have increased. More groups of potters seem

Fig. 1 (Left) Aquamaniles demonstrate the influence of metal forms on pottery vessels. The bronze aquamanile (far left) in the form of a knight on horseback was found in the river Tyne at Hexham (Northumberland), and the pottery aquamanile, also in the form of a knight on horseback, was found at Ditchingham (Norfolk).

Fig. 2 (Opposite above) Group of slip-decorated and polychrome jugs from southeast England. Left to right: 13th-century slip-decorated Rouen jug, found at Sutton Courtenay Abbey; early 13th-century slip-decorated London jug, found at Mark Lane, City of London; late 12th-century slip-decorated London tripod pitcher, found in London; mid-13th-century Kingston zoomorphic polychrome decorated jug, found at Cannon Street, City of London.

to have worked together, demonstrated in many rural areas, for example, by the existence of production centres consisting of many kilns[4] and by the addition of the prefix 'Potter' to existing village names.[5] By the thirteenth century most towns possessed at least one pottery production centre, usually situated either just within or immediately outside the town walls.[6]

Vessel forms and decorative themes

Most pottery produced during the medieval period was plain and undecorated, made largely for domestic use, for the cooking and storing of food.[7] Highly decorated vessels, however, were probably designed mainly as tablewares, and some of the most ornate seem to have been intended to amuse or entertain at mealtimes.[8] Aquamaniles, elaborately decorated water containers used for washing the hands at table, often took the shape of either knights on horseback or animals. This demon-

strates the influence of metal forms on pottery (fig. 1). The puzzle-jug, another elaborately constructed vessel, incorporated a hollow handle connected to a concealed section in the base which held liquid, with a drinking spout on the side of the jug. It presented a challenge, or puzzle, to the user to drink from it without spilling the contents of either the upper or the lower section.[9] Large lobed drinking-cups were decorated inside the base with free-standing modelled figures of humans, animals or birds, which would have been gradually revealed as the level of liquid decreased.[10] The majority of decorated vessels, however, were jugs of various shapes, ranging in size from small to large (fig. 3).

Human and animal figures were among the most popular and frequently produced subjects portrayed on decorated pottery. The face-jug was particularly characteristic of this period: a human face, often that of a bearded man, was depicted either on the front or the side of the rim (fig. 3), or formed the

spout of the jug (fig. 4).[11] The shape of the whole jug could evoke the form of a human figure by the addition of arms and hands to the shoulder or girth (fig. 3, left and centre), or by the depiction of details of clothing such as brooches[12] or buttons.[13] The faces of women with elaborate hair-styles and head-dresses were represented on jugs and ceramic figures.[14] One of the most elaborately decorated types of vessel which portrayed both humans and animals was the knight-jug, consisting of several modelled figures of knights on horseback holding shields which were applied to the neck of the jug. They were often accompanied by scenes of stag-hunts on the body of the jug.[15] Aquamaniles were often made in the form of animals, usually rams.[16] Other animals portrayed included lions or dragons such as those on a jug found at Cannon Street, City of London (fig. 2, right),[17] a stag on a puzzle-jug from Oxford,[18] birds on jugs from London,[19] and apes on a group of vessels from Bristol.[20] Other designs found on pottery include heraldic motifs,[21] seals,[22] and a wide range of geometric patterns (fig. 2, second and third from left) and floral motifs.[23] Religious subjects or symbols are also occasionally found on pottery.[24] At Rye (East Sussex), vessels were decorated with a range of unusual subjects including a jousting scene, a figure of Christ, ships, fish and an elephant with a howdah.[25]

Inspiration for this wide range of subjects was probably derived from the common repertoire of medieval ornament employed by craftsmen working in other materials. Comparative motifs have been noted, for example, on the decorated pavements made by tilers, on ornamental ironwork produced by

Medieval lead glaze

According to the medieval writer Eraclius, lead glaze was prepared by sprinkling lead filings or lead oxide on to the surface of an unfired pot, which had previously been coated with a paste of flour and water to bind the powder to the surface. Modern experiments have shown that, after firing to temperatures of 900–1000°C, a good glaze may be formed by reaction between the glazing powder and the pottery body.[71] Underfired sherds coated with lead oxide have been found in excavation, and analysis has shown that the lead-rich glazes on medieval pottery were formed as a reaction between lead oxide and the body clay (glazes typically contain around 60% PbO, 25% SiO_2 and 7% Al_2O_3).[72] Medieval potters may have used galena, a naturally occurring lead sulphide.

A yellow or colourless glaze could be obtained in oxidation firings, while in reduction firings the iron oxide incorporated from the pottery body could give an olive-green colour. Alternatively, a richer green could be produced by adding copper or brass filings to the glaze powder, and browns could be obtained by adding iron oxides. A glaze paste could be brushed on, rather than sprinkled, to give fields of colour. The difficulties of applying an even coat, the uneven reaction of coarser glaze particles and over-reduction of the lead meant that skill was required to control the quality of the glaze.[73]

Fig. 3 A group of face-jugs. Left to right: late 13th-century face-jug from Faccombe Netherton (Hampshire), miniature 13th-century Kingston bearded face-jug found in London, and a 13th- or early 14th-century Grimston Norfolk bearded face-jug, found in Cambridge.

blacksmiths, and in the figural and abstract sculpture created by masons and carpenters.[26]

The development of the decorated style

The trend towards more ornate forms and decoration gradually developed during the second half of the twelfth and early thirteenth century, notably at a number of urban production centres. The pottery industry established in the vicinity of London was one of the earliest to introduce new techniques of slip decoration and polychrome glazes during the twelfth century, as well as an increased range of specialised forms.[27] In the second half of the twelfth century, potters at Stamford (Lincolnshire) produced a number of highly decorated vessels with modelled zoomorphic ornament in the form of applied birds;[28] at Doncaster (West Yorkshire), elaborate face-mask jugs and aquamaniles were made during the later twelfth century.[29]

The widespread production of elaborately decorated pottery in England occurred principally during the thirteenth and early fourteenth century. Varying proportions of decorated wares were made at most kiln sites during this period. Certain large industries concentrated on the production of fine decorated tablewares, and their products were widely distributed. At the kilns at Scarborough (North Yorkshire), for example, all products were high-quality glazed tablewares such as knight-jugs, bearded face-jugs, zoomorphic aquamaniles and jugs decorated with a range of motifs.[30] The products of these kilns were widely exported along the eastern coast of England and Scotland, and overseas to Norway and the Low Countries.[31]

The influence of continental pottery

Pottery imported from the Continent stimulated the production of new vessel forms and certain styles of decoration in England. Polychrome slip-decorated pottery was produced in northern France, notably at Rouen (Seine-Maritime), during the late twelfth and thirteenth centuries.[32] Imported into coastal ports such as London[33] and Southampton,[34] it influenced the products of a number of contemporary English pottery industries, both in form and decoration.[35] A large tripod pitcher of late twelfth-century form, found in London, is decorated with red and white slip similar to the decoration on vessels from Normandy (fig. 2, second from right),[36] and close similarities between the early thirteenth-century decorated jugs of London and Rouen are evident. A Rouen jug found at Sutton Courtenay Abbey, Abingdon (Oxon), is made in the characteristic off-white clay and decorated with zones of painted red slip and rows of applied white pellets, bordered by rouletted strips of clay which form contrasting bands and triangles on the neck and girth (fig. 2, left). The London products, made in the local red-firing clay, are decorated with applied red and white slip in decorative schemes derived from those on the Rouen jugs, as on an early thirteenth-century jug found at Mark Lane, City of London (fig. 2, second from left), which also demonstrates the similarities in vessel shape between the products of London and Rouen.

It is uncertain whether such similarities were simply due to the influence of imported pottery on English potters, who were fulfilling a demand for jugs decorated in a similar style, or to the presence of potters who had been trained abroad.[37] A twelfth-century kiln in Canterbury (Kent) is thought to have been established by a continental potter, possibly from Normandy,[38] and it is possible that other immigrant potters may have worked elsewhere in England. Nevertheless, the excavation of kiln sites has shown that potters copied the products of other English industries,[39] and pottery produced elsewhere in south-eastern England demonstrates the transference of the Rouen style of decoration indirectly, through the London products.[40]

Other types of continental pottery may also have stimulated the use of new production and decorative techniques in England.[41] Pottery imported from the Low Countries through ports on the east coast of England is thought to have inspired the use of decorative rouletting on pottery produced at kilns at Winksley (West Yorkshire) during the mid-thirteenth century.[42]

An increasing demand for fine whiteware pottery such as that made in France is thought to have been the reason for the establishment of a major industry at Kingston-upon-Thames (Surrey) during the first half of the thirteenth century.[43] Pottery produced at Kingston is characterised by rich green and yellow glazes, and many vessels are decorated with anthropomorphic and zoomorphic elements, elaborate applied strips of clay in complex patterns, stamped ornament and polychrome slips and glazes.

The jug from Cannon Street, London, which was made at Kingston (fig. 2, right), is decorated with lozenge-shaped panels, each containing an applied yellow-glazed animal against a red-slipped background, with additional relief and stamped decoration highlighted in green glaze and red slip. The inspiration for this decorative scheme is thought to have been derived from a type of northern French jug, an example of which has been found in Surrey, also decorated with panels containing applied animals.[44]

The potter's wheel

The manufacture of well-produced, elaborately decorated pottery was made possible by several technological advances during the twelfth and thirteenth centuries, one of which was the potter's wheel. Handmade pottery continued in production at various centres during the thirteenth century, for example at Ham Green (Somerset)[45] and at Lyveden (Northamptonshire),[46] but the adoption of the wheel became gradually more widespread, notably among urban industries producing pottery on a large scale.[47]

The precise form of the medieval potter's wheel is uncertain, as none is known to survive. Manuscript illustrations and other pictorial sources suggest that two types of wheel may have been in use.[48] The cartwheel type, depicted in French manuscripts of the thirteenth century, consisted of a horizontal spoked wheel fixed to a vertical pivot which was rotated by the potter, either with a stick or by hand, until sufficient momentum was achieved to enable the pot to be thrown on the area in the centre of the wheel.[49] The kickwheel type consisted of a solid wheel on which the pot was thrown, connected to a lower wheel at foot level by vertical struts. The lower wheel was propelled by the potter's foot, leaving both hands free for potting, and would probably have been easier to stop and start than the cartwheel type.[50] The kickwheel is depicted in illustrations of the fifteenth century (ch. 18, fig. 2).

Fig. 4 Pouring spout in the form of a monk's head, from a 13th- or 14th-century face-jug found at the Pithay, Bristol. The eyes are stamped with a ring-and-dot stamp; the hair is formed from applied and incised strips of clay, and the eyebrows are incised.

Fig. 5 Three pottery stamps and a fragment of decorated pottery, found in Lincoln.

Techniques of decoration

After the main body of the pot had been formed, additional features such as handles, spouts and tripod feet were applied and the pot decorated. Most of the tools used by the potter to produce and decorate vessels were probably adapted from common domestic objects, such as knives, or were made from widely available material such as wood or bone. Pieces of worked bone found on a kiln site at Ashton (Cheshire) are thought to have been used to produce incised decoration.[51] Roller stamps or roulette wheels for impressing designs on the surface of the pot and combs for incised decoration were probably made of wood or bone.

Medieval potters used a range of techniques to achieve elaborate decoration. Free-standing figures modelled in high relief were applied to vessels such as aquamaniles (fig. 1, right) and knight-jugs. Modelled heads were applied to face-jugs (fig. 3), and details such as eyes, beards and hands were emphasised by incising and stamping the clay; the characteristic round eyes

of face-jugs (fig. 4) were often produced with a ring-and-dot stamp. Some potters used clays of contrasting colours to highlight facial details.[52]

Motifs such as anthropomorphic and zoomorphic figures were applied in clay to the side of the vessel to form decoration in low relief (fig. 2, right). Strips of clay applied to the surface of a vessel formed ornate patterns such as scroll and floral motifs, or human figures.[53] These motifs were often further embellished with impressions formed by a stamp or roulette, or with finger impressions, or were emphasised with coloured slips or glazes. Small pellets or scales of clay in a contrasting colour to that of the vessel could be pressed on to the body (fig. 2, second and third from left) or applied in panels of alternating colour, as on the face-jug made at Grimston (fig. 3, right).

Developments in the use of slip during this period allowed a high standard of surface decoration. Many potters exercised a considerable degree of proficiency and control in the application of liquid slip, enabling them to produce precise decorative patterns (fig. 2, second from left). It is possible that in some industries this may have been achieved by the introduction of

the slip-trailing technique, in which liquid slip is trailed on to the surface of the vessel through an implement such as a cow-horn (ch. 19, fig. 1). The technique of *sgraffito*, in which a fine coating of slip in a contrasting colour to the body is carved away to reveal the clay beneath, was employed by potters at various industries including London (fig. 2, second from right) and Rye (East Sussex).[54] At other industries such as Mill Green (Essex), potters painted designs on to the surface of vessels in slip.[55]

Carved stamps were used to decorate the surface of vessels and numerous stamped designs have been found on pottery, including human heads, animal and bird designs, fleur-de-lis, scallop shells, seals, heraldic shields, and geometric and floral motifs.[56] The stamps were either pressed directly against the side of the pot, the potter pushing the wall of the vessel into the stamp from inside the pot to produce an embossed design on the surface,[57] or on to a pad or disk of clay applied to the side of the vessel,[58] as on a fragment of a jug found with three ceramic stamps (fig. 5) at St Mary le Wigford, Lincoln (Lincolnshire).[59] The Lincoln stamps are made of fired clay. One depicts the bearded face of a man; two, which show the head of a woman in an elaborate head-dress, are identical, and must therefore have been made from a common (positive) mould. Other stamps were made individually: a stamp found on the floor of one of the pottery workshops at Lyveden (Northamptonshire) has a geometric motif formed from the end of a sheep bone,[60] and a stamp made of oolite, incised with the design of an animal on both sides, was found at the kilns at Rye.[61]

Glazing

The elaborate effect of many highly decorated jugs was enhanced by the use of glossy coloured lead glazes (fig. 2, right). Clear lead glaze fires to a red or orange colour over a clay with a high iron content, yellow over a clay with a low iron content, and olive-green when fired in a reducing atmosphere. Copper oxide added to the glaze gave a rich green colour, while the addition of iron oxide produced a deeper orange or brown colour. Glaze could either be sprinkled over the vessel in powdered form, or applied as a liquid by dipping the pot into the glaze or brushing the glaze on to the surface of the pot. This technique gave the potter control over the application of the glaze and enabled detailed polychrome decoration to be achieved (fig. 2, right).[62]

Stacking and firing the kiln

Developments in the design and construction of semi-permanent kilns during this period gave the potter greater control over the firing of pottery, notably in the duration of the firing and the regulation of the temperature of the kiln. The ability to control the amount of oxygen inside the kiln gave the potter control over the colour of the fabric and glaze on the finished vessels. The separation of the pottery from the burning fuel was an important factor which made the firing of elaborate glazed wares possible. Previously, most pottery had been fired in clamp or bonfire kilns, in which the fuel was packed around and over the vessels (ch. 22). During the thirteenth and fourteenth centuries most pottery kilns consisted of a central oven in which the vessels were fired, with two or more stoke-pit arches or flues in which the fuel was burnt and through which the heat was drawn up through the kiln; these kilns are known as updraught kilns (fig. 6).[63] The superstructures or roofs of excavated kilns rarely survive sufficiently to suggest the original form. Some may have been open-topped and covered with a temporary capping which could be removed after each firing, while others may have had a domed structure.[64] They were usually made from clay, or a combination of stone, clay or turves. Variations have been found in shape, structure and in the number and position of flues. Most kilns had a central pedestal; raised floors or platforms in the form of supports or kiln-bars have been identified at some kilns. Elsewhere hollow cylindrical vessels were used as props on which to stand the pottery.[65] At other kilns, vessels are thought to have been stacked on the floor of the firing chamber.[66] Figure 6 illustrates a reconstruction of a double-flued kiln. The flues and pedestal are based on an early fourteenth-century kiln excavated at Eden Street, Kingston-upon-Thames.[67]

Pottery was usually stacked upside-down in the kiln, as is often indicated by the direction of drips and runs of glaze on the body of the vessel. This was partly to aid firing by trapping the heat inside each pot and partly to prevent pieces of any pots which shattered during the firing from falling inside those beneath and spoiling them. The largest and heaviest vessels would have been stacked at the base of the kiln with the smaller and lighter pots near the top. Smaller or elaborately decorated vessels such as aquamaniles may have been placed inside larger pots for protection. Stacking scars are commonly found on medieval pots, caused by contact between vessels during firing; the impressions or outlines of rims are often found on the bases of vessels.[68]

Large quantities of fuel were required for firing the kiln. Wood was commonly used, and many potters obtained brushwood from nearby forests or woodland. Coal may have been used in kilns situated near available deposits, and written evidence demonstrates that peat was used at a number of kilns in eastern England.[69] The assessment by the potter of the correct length of time and amount of fuel needed to fire the kiln to the correct temperature was crucial to a successful firing. The temperature had to be raised slowly to avoid the water in the clay body turning to steam and shattering the pots. If the final temperature was too low, the pots would be underfired, soft and porous and the glaze would not vitrify, whereas if the temperature was raised too high, the clay would melt and the pots collapse.[70]

The production of highly decorated pottery decreased during the later fourteenth century, a period of general economic depression and demographic decline, and was superseded by the production of plainer vessels with simpler forms of decoration. During the thirteenth century no major change seems to have occurred in the organisation or economic circumstances of most potters, whether in town or country. Nevertheless, potters had adapted to an increased demand for a wider range of elaborate vessels, reflecting the prosperity of the period. Technological developments made possible the manufacture of large and complex vessels with elaborate polychrome decoration, and the skill of the potters in forming, decorating and firing these products were significant achievements.

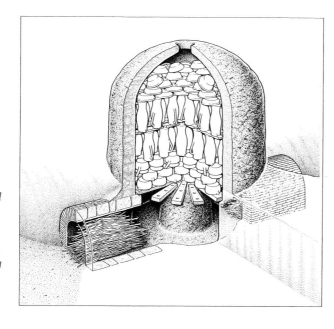

Fig. 6
Medieval updraught kiln, with two flues or stoke-holes, containing fuel, and pottery stacked on kiln-bars supported by the central pedestal. The flues and pedestal are based on an excavated early 14th-century kiln; the domed superstructure, stacking arrangements and vessels are suggested reconstructions.

Korean Celadons of the Koryo Dynasty

Jane Portal

The history and culture of the Korean peninsula, which lies between China, Russia and Japan, have been greatly affected by its geographical position. Divided into several states or kingdoms from early times, it suffered invasion and occupation from China, Manchuria, Mongolia and Japan but remained a unified country from the seventh to the twentieth century.

Korean celadons or greenwares were made during the Koryo dynasty (918–1392), reaching a high point of technical perfection in the twelfth century. The Koryo was a period of great importance for the Buddhist church in Korea and most works of art, including paintings, sculpture, sutras, bronzes, lacquer and celadons, were produced in its honour. This devotion to Buddhism was seen in the carving (twice) of the entire Buddhist scriptures on 81,137 woodblocks, in order to pray for the Buddha's protection against first the Khitan and later the Mongol invasions. The second set of thirteenth-century wooden printing blocks still exists and is stored in Hae'in-sa temple.[1]

Chinese influence

The early Koryo was a period of peaceful economic and cultural exchange with Song dynasty China (960–1279). Chinese influence could be seen in painting, literature, the examination system and the writing of history as well as in ceramics. Korea exported to China local products such as paper, ginseng, gold and silver and in turn imported silk, medicines, books and ceramics.[2] Due to unfriendly relations with both the Khitan and the Jurchen to the north, the land route to Korea from China was blocked and trade and diplomacy were consequently carried out by sea. The most convenient sea route was from south-east China to south-west Korea. The use of this sea route greatly affected the development of celadons in Korea.

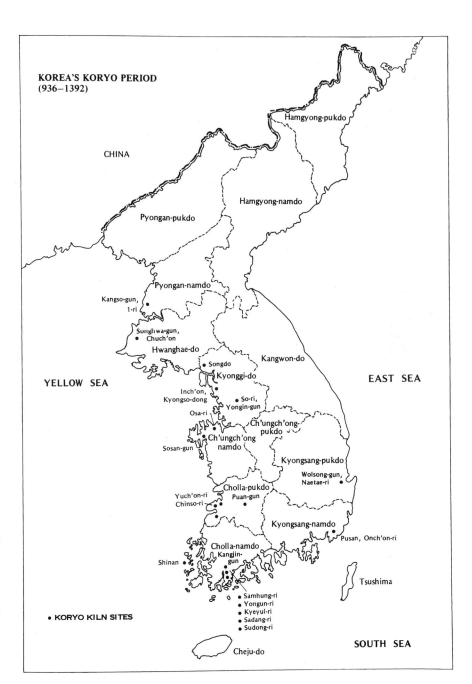

Fig. 1 Map of Korea showing the main celadon kiln sites.

98

Fig. 2 Lidded spouted ewer in the shape of a melon, with sanggam inlay decoration under a celadon glaze, Koryo dynasty, 12th century. Vegetable- and fruit-shaped celadons are typically Korean, as are naturalistic details such as the stalk forming the knob on the lid.

Chinese Yue ware celadons were very influential in the early development of Koryo celadons in the tenth century.[3] It is thought that southern Chinese Yue type techniques were introduced to Korea by sea, and the majority of celadon kilns were located in south-west coastal Korea, in the areas of Kangjin and Puan (fig. 1). Both the shapes and the wide, flat foot-rings of celadons produced, for example, at Yongun-ri in Kangjin are similar to Chinese Yue wares. Scientific analysis of the clays and glazes used in both Chinese Yue wares and Korean celadons also reveals similarities.[4] Whether or not Chinese potters actually migrated to south-western Korea is unknown, but it is a possibility.[5]

However, some Korean scholars, such as Choi Sunu, point out that Chinese techniques must also have been introduced via the northern land route. There is clear influence in shape, decorative techniques and glaze from such northern Chinese wares as Cizhou, Ru, Ding (ch. 28) and northern celadons from Yaozhou.[6] For example, early incised and moulded Koryo celadons are very similar to Yaozhou wares, underglaze iron-painted celadons recall Chinese Cizhou and the vessel shapes of some Koryo celadons are almost identical to Ru and Ding wares. It is perhaps in the bluish colour of some of the finest Koryo celadons that the influence of high-quality Ru wares can best be seen.[7] White porcelain of the (Khitan) Liao dynasty (907–1125), situated between Korea and China, also had some effect on the shapes of Koryo celadons. For example, the 'dished mouth' shape appears in both Liao porcelain and Koryo celadons.[8]

Despite the many influences from Chinese wares, Koryo celadons developed in their own unique way. At first the shapes and decoration were more Chinese. For example, the *maebyong* vase had straight sides in the twelfth century but later developed a more distinctly Korean profile, with a bulbous shoulder and narrow waist curving out again towards the bottom. Characteristically Korean shapes were soon developed, showing the Korean fondness for naturalistic animal and vegetable shapes. Vessels in the shape of gourds, melons, ducks, monkeys, turtles and flowers or with applied figures of lions, dragons, rabbits and fish could not be mistaken for products of Chinese kilns (fig. 2).

Koryo porcelain was probably produced from a single raw material known today as 'Tanmi', meaning 'single taste'. The crushed, wetted porcelain stone could be thrown, moulded or worked into a wide variety of forms. The glaze was probably applied to the leather-hard vessel by dipping and the ceramic fired only once, in common with most Oriental stonewares.

Innovations in decoration

Early decoration on vessels was incised or carved (fig. 4). The most important Korean innovation took place in the second half of the twelfth century, in the form of inlaid decoration (*sanggam*).[9] Inlay had been a feature of Korean art from early times, when bronzes were inlaid with gold and silver and lacquer with mother-of-pearl. This predilection for inlay manifested itself in the beautiful and intricate creations of Korean potters in the late twelfth and thirteenth centuries. Designs of clouds, cranes, flowers or grapevines were incised on the leather-hard body of the vessel. Then the inlay material was painted into the incised designs and the excess wiped off. The vessel was then glazed and fired. The inlays of Korean celadons have been examined by Vandiver, who found that they were not composed of black- and white-firing clays as had been supposed. The white inlays are composed predominantly of crushed quartz, while the black inlays appear to represent a mixture of an

iron-rich material with a glaze which, on firing, produced magnetite (Fe_3O_4), a black oxide of iron.[10] Other decorative features of Korean celadons are open-work designs and carving, for example lotus flowers, in high relief.

Painting in iron brown (fig. 5) or copper red under the celadon glaze and in gold over the celadon glaze were also Korean innovations. Surviving vessels painted in red or gold are extremely rare, but the British Museum is fortunate in having one of the best examples of the very difficult underglaze copper-red technique (fig. 3).[11] Although underglaze copper red was used on Chinese porcelain in the fourteenth century, it was never used on celadons in China and was never very successful on porcelain because it was difficult to ensure a good red.

Kilns and firing

The kilns were of the Chinese sloping 'dragon kiln' type, which had been used in Korea for high-fired stoneware since the Three Kingdoms period (57 BC– AD 668). There were about 270 kilns in existence in the Koryo period, of which about 240 were concentrated in the south-west, in Cholla province (fig. 1). The two kilns at Sadang-ri in

Kangjin district and at Yuch'on-ri in Puan district were, to some extent, regarded as official factories. Excavations at Sadang-ri have shown that the kiln was built on a natural slope, rising at an angle of 5–6 degrees, and has a number of chambers, each with two or three openings. Its length is 7 m (21 ft) and the original width is judged to have been 1.43–1.51 m (4.6–5 ft).[12]

The celadons were fired in a reducing atmosphere at a temperature of 1100– 1200°C. As with Chinese celadons, it was the small amount of iron oxide in the glaze which, combined with a reducing atmosphere, produced the celadon green colour. Some of the very earliest Koryo celadons were sometimes yellow, due to an inability to control the reducing atmosphere.

Court and Buddhist ritual use

Many Koryo celadons were produced for the use of aristocratic ladies in the form of cosmetic sets, including round boxes for rouge or face powder and small bottles for hair oil. Elegant drinking-cups and cup-stands, wine ewers, spittoons, tea bowls and pillows all demonstrate the refined lifestyle of the Koryo court. In fact, celadons became so popular that they were even

---

Koryo celadon bodies

Unlike Ding and other northern Chinese stonewares (ch. 28), which were made from alumina-rich secondary clays, the bodies of Korean celadon are rich in quartz (silica), in common with southern Chinese Yue celadon wares.

	Ding[17]	Yue[18]	Koryo[19]	
SiO_2	63.8	76.3	74.6	silica
Al_2O_3	29.7	16.4	18.1	alumina
K_2O	1.7	2.7	3.2	potash
Fe_2O_3	0.8	2.1	2.2	iron oxide

The celadon bodies fire to a grey colour due to their iron oxide content and mature at lower temperatures than do the northern wares. They were made from pulverised, altered igneous rock, known as porcelain stone. These contain some clay but are also rich in fine-grained mica (sericite), which not only (like clay) imparts plasticity to the body, but also acts as a flux due to its high potash content.

The similarity between Yue and Koryo bodies reflects the geologies of the ceramic-producing areas of southern China and southern Korea, which are part of the same tectonic unit. Thus the porcelain stone characteristic of south China is also found in what is now South Korea, where the kilns are located.

*Fig. 3 (Above)
Bowl decorated in
underglaze copper red
under a celadon glaze,
Koryo dynasty, 12th
century. This is a very
rare example of the
difficult underglaze
copper-red technique.
It can be dated by
comparing the
decoration with that on
inlaid celadons. Under-
glaze copper red was
usually limited to small
details of the decoration
but was sometimes
painted over the entire
vessel.*

*Fig. 4 Cup and cup-
stand with incised and
carved floral decoration
under a celadon glaze,
Koryo dynasty,
12th century. The shape
of this vessel is based on
silver as well as Chinese
ceramic wares such
as Ding, Ru, Yue and
Qingbai.*

used for roof tiles on the summer palace built by the profligate King Uijong (r. 1147–70). The moralising *Koryo-sa* (History of Koryo) records that, in 1157:

More than fifty sections of the people's houses were destroyed and the Taep' yong-jong building constructed. The Crown Prince was ordered to inscribe a tablet; famous plants and flowers were installed; rare and precious articles were displayed on all sides. To the south of this building a lake was made and the Kwallan-jong pavilion built. To the north, the Yang-i-jong pavilion was constructed and roofed with celadon tiles.[13]

This represents the zenith of the high life of the Koryo court at the capital, before it was interrupted by invasions from the Khitans and Mongols.

Celadons were also made in large numbers for use in Buddhist rituals. Special shapes, often influenced by and paralleled in silver and bronze, were produced for specific Buddhist purposes. Examples include the *kundika*, a Buddhist water sprinkler whose shape originated in India and which came to China and Korea with Buddhism, along the Silk Route (fig. 6). Other shapes are spouted bowls, single-handled spouted ewer-and-bowl sets for hand-washing, alms bowls and many different varieties of incense burner, some heavily influenced by archaistic Chinese bronzes of the Song dynasty. These incense burners, often with applied animals, were particularly ingenious. They evoked comment from a Chinese envoy, Xu Jing, who visited Korea in 1123 and said, 'A lion emits incense and is likewise kingfisher-coloured. The beast crouches on the top, supported by a lotus. This is the most distinguished of all their wares...'[14]

Most Koryo celadons were produced in the south-west of Korea and then transported by boat up the west coast to the Koryo capital at Songdo, which is situated at present-day Kaesong, just north of the border with North Korea. A recently excavated shipwreck off the island of Wando, in south-west Korea, attests to the large number of celadons in each shipment.

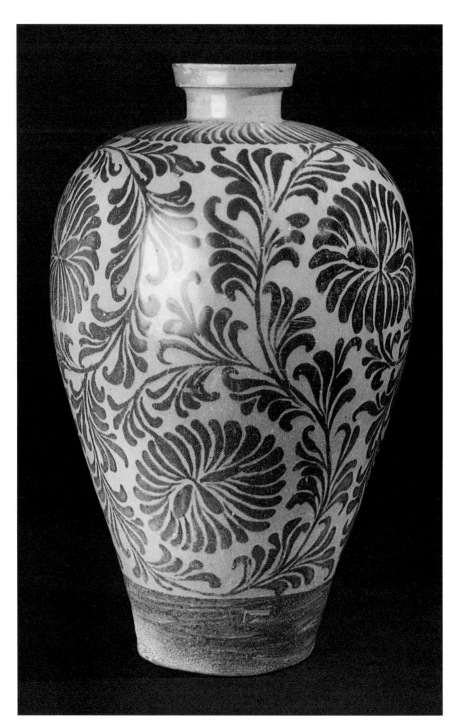

Fig. 5 Maebyong vase with iron-brown decoration of chrysanthemums under a celadon glaze, Koryo dynasty, 12th century. The straight sides of this vessel are similar to Chinese vases of the same shape, suggesting a fairly early date. The iron-brown decoration recalls that on Chinese Cizhou wares of northern China.

Artisan potters

Very little information is recorded about artisans from the Koryo period, so it is difficult to say much about the potters who made the celadons. The Korean social order was highly stratified at this time, with aristocrats at the top, commoners in the middle and 'base people' at the bottom. Artisans such as potters were classed as base people (as were slaves) and grouped into tightly controlled settlements which functioned as administrative units. The inhabitants were regarded as inferior to the commoners who farmed the fields. They had to intermarry and the children carried on their parents' trade, whether the production of metal, paper or textiles. It seems that the artisans were

---

Koryo celadon glazes

The characteristic green of celadon glaze is due to the presence of 1–2% iron oxide. Like the glazes of Chinese Yue ware, Koryo glazes are rich in lime (calcium oxide) and approach the ideal low-temperature melting composition in the lime-alumina-silica system.

Average Koryo glaze[20]			
SiO_2	60	FeO	1.0
Al_2O_3	12	TiO_2	0.1
CaO	19	MnO	0.5
K_2O	2.5	P_2O_5	0.8

These glazes seem to have been produced by grinding lime-rich wood-ash with porcelain stone.

The green colour of celadon is due to the firing of the ceramics in reduction, so that the iron in the glaze is mainly in the reduced, ferrous state. The bluish-greens of the most admired Koryo wares differ markedly in tone from the more yellow-green colour of Yue wares. This difference has been attributed to differences in the contents of minor components such as manganese and titanium oxides.[21] In addition, in Yue ware the underlying grey body is screened from the glaze by an intervening layer of white anorthite crystals, which are less developed in Koryo glazes.[22]

Fig. 6 Two kundika, water sprinklers used in Buddhist rituals, Koryo dynasty, 12th century. The shape originated in Indian metalwork but was reproduced in Korea in both bronze and ceramic. The celadon example here is decorated with inlaid stylised flower roundels similar to those used to decorate silks of the same period, which can be seen in Koryo Buddhist paintings.

exempt from tax and corvée labour. Two such artisans' settlements for the production of celadons were established in Kangjin in south-western Cholla province, where over a hundred kiln sites have been discovered. Celadons were thus produced in isolated and strictly controlled areas, far away from the aristocrats for whom they were

made. One link may have been the kiln attendants (*yojik*), of whom there were six at the beginning of the twelfth century.[15]

Towards the end of the Koryo, the celadons again became yellowish or greyish in colour and the designs either schematic or over-complicated. The complexity of the designs has been suggested as one reason for the decline in the quality of the glaze, which came to assume secondary importance.[16] The greyish, coarser body was a precursor of the *punch'ong*, slip-decorated stone-wares, into which Koryo celadons were to develop in the early Choson dynasty during the fifteenth and sixteenth centuries.

Faience in the Ancient Mediterranean World

A. J. Spencer and Louise Schofield

Faience, a fine ceramic consisting of a crushed quartz body covered with a glaze, was manufactured in the ancient Mediterranean and Near East for over five thousand years. It is not possible at present to be certain whether it was first made in Egypt or in Mesopotamia,[1] but by about 4000 BC faience beads are found in both regions. The development of the technology appears to be related to methods for working soft stone, and to have evolved independently of clay-based pottery.[2] The first glazes on clay-based ceramics did not appear until the Late Bronze Age, in around 1600 BC, some two to three thousand years after those on faience. The quartz-rich bodies of faience, lacking the plastic properties of clay, could not easily be built up in coils or slabs nor thrown on the wheel; they were more readily modelled or moulded. Faience beads were still being produced at Qom, in Iran, as recently as thirty years ago, apparently in a continuation of the ancient tradition.[3]

The white quartz body of faience formed a good ground for its transparent glaze, which was typically coloured blue or green by a few per cent of copper oxide. The blue colour and translucent appearance of the faience glaze emulate semiprecious stones such as turquoise, lapis lazuli and azurite, and its use in religious contexts may be

a reflection of this. Glazes in other colours were developed in the second millennium BC.[4]

Faience glazes are alkali silicates, consisting predominantly of silica and soda with variable amounts of potash, lime and copper oxide. Two principal sources of alkali were available to the ancient artisans; studies of ancient glass suggest that, up to about 600 BC, the ash produced by burning saline plants from the desert or brackish coastal waters was used, while after this time natron, a naturally occurring sodium bicarbonate from surface deposits on dried-out salt lakes, such as those in the Wadi Natrun (in the south-western Nile Delta), was exploited.[5] The limited available analyses of unweathered faience glazes suggest that plant-ash was the principal source of alkali in faience-making, at least up to the Late Bronze Age.[6]

Faience in Egypt

Faience was one of the most popular materials used in Egypt for the manufacture of a whole range of objects, including vessels, statuettes, amulets, beads and decorative inlays. Objects were hand-modelled from the faience paste and the shape could then be adjusted by grinding when dry, prior

to firing. Alternative techniques, such as pressing over a form, moulding or forming over a core, were also utilised at different periods. In the Late Period (650–332 BC), faience could be thrown on the wheel for the manufacture of vessels, copying the techniques of pottery production. This may reflect the addition of a little clay to the quartz-rich body, thereby imparting sufficient plasticity to enable it to be thrown.[7] Many different colours of glaze were produced, but the most common colours were varying shades of green and blue, created through the use of copper. There were three methods for the production of the glaze: efflorescence, application and cementation. The copper colourant was added to the glazing mixture.

Faience was first manufactured in the Predynastic period (ch. 5) for the production of beads, but its uses diversified rapidly during the early dynasties to include tiles, figurines and vessels. From early times, a considerable proportion of faience manufacture seems to have been devoted to the production of votive gifts for religious centres, and many faience objects have been recovered from caches of redundant temple gifts. Among these are the deposit in the temple of Hierakonpolis, caches in the early sanctuary of Osiris at Abydos, and in

---

Faience

Objects from ancient Egypt and the Near East with white quartz bodies and a transparent glaze were initially confused with European earthenwares which had an opaque white tin glaze, so both were called faience. Although it has been known for many years that the two materials are very different in composition and manufacture, the name has continued to be used. Analysis of Egyptian faience[35] reveals that usually it contained no deliberately added clay; the body was composed almost entirely of particles of crushed quartz, as shown in the micrograph, with a small amount of glass which bonded the quartz grains together. In addition, there is a continuous glassy or glaze layer at the surface. The body is very porous; holes appear black in the micrograph. In addition to its important visual attributes, the surface glaze makes an important contribution to the strength and durability of faience.

Fig. 1 Part of a large faience figure of the Egyptian god Bes, with the typical brilliant blue glaze of the Ptolemaic period (332–30 BC). Large figures like this were made in sections and fused together.

the temple of Satet at Elephantine.[8] The faience products in these caches, which display considerable uniformity, are characteristic of the Early Dynastic to early Old Kingdom period (3100–

2400 BC). Prominent are small human or animal figurines, particularly baboons.[9] Also common are small models of vases and rectangular tiles for inlaying into wood or stone. Smaller faience tiles were found in the excavation of the First Dynasty royal tombs at Abydos and in the tombs of high officials at Saqqara.[10] The most extensive early example of their use, however, is found in the Third Dynasty

step-pyramid of Djoser at Saqqara (*c*.2680 BC), the passages below which were embellished with thousands of small blue-green rectangular tiles, aligned on copper wires and plastered into channels in the limestone walls.[11] A development from simple tiles, attested later in the Old Kingdom (*c*.2400 BC), was the creation of inlays in the form of particular motifs or hieroglyphic signs.

Tombs of the Middle Kingdom (2125–1795 BC) have produced numerous examples of finely made faience objects, including a variety of animal figures such as a small jerboa, a desert rodent. Fine details are often indicated in black paint, based on the use of manganese or iron oxides. An example of the striking contrast between the black decoration and the blue-glazed surface is provided by a figure of a woman from a Middle Kingdom tomb.

The use of these dark pigments remained popular at all periods, and they were used extensively for floral decoration on bowls and for adding

Making faience

Evidence for three ways of making faience has been found through examination of the bodies and glazes, coupled with experimental replication,[36] and these are illustrated in the diagram.[37] The body material was prepared by crushing quartz pebbles or milling sand. In the first method the quartz body was mixed with water and a sodium-rich salt and then moulded or modelled into the desired form. As the body dried, the salts migrated to the surface, or effloresced. When fired, the layer of salts at the surface reacted with the body to form a glaze.

The second approach was to prepare the body from quartz as above but to apply a pre-melted glass to the surface, by painting or by dipping the object into a slurry. This is the conventional method for applying a ceramic glaze and is sometimes referred to as the application method.

The final method, cementation, was recorded as still in use in Iran in recent times.[38] The object to be glazed is embedded in a special glaze mixture, which when fired reacts with the quartz of the body to form a glaze.

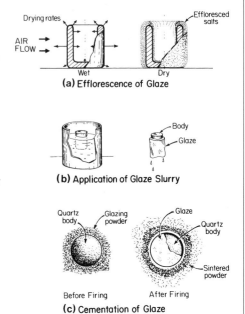

inscriptions. By the New Kingdom (c.1400 BC), there was considerable experimentation with different colours of glaze to produce polychrome decorated tiles which could be inlaid into items of furniture or the walls of buildings. The additional colours were based on the use of compounds of antimony (opaque white), lead plus antimony (opaque yellow, combined with copper for green) and cobalt (deep blue).[12] These colourants were also introduced into glass-making at about this time; at Tell el-Amarna, faience and glass workshops were closely associated in a special industrial area.[13] Designs could be built up by inlaying pieces of faience of different colours into a larger tile of the same material to produce what were, in effect, ceramic pictures.[14] These were then set into the walls of temples and palaces, and often included complex inlays of hieroglyphic inscriptions (fig. 2). The size of individual pieces manufactured in faience increased considerably, particu-

Fig. 2 Polychrome Egyptian faience tile inscribed with the name of King Sety II, c.1200 BC.

larly for items of temple equipment: an exceptional faience sceptre found at Naqada and now in the Victoria and Albert Museum, London, is 2.15 metres (6.5 ft) in length.[15]

Faience vessels were common in the New Kingdom (1550–1070 BC), especially bowls with black manganese-based decoration. The most frequent motifs consist of plant designs, with the petals of the lotus-flower shown on the exterior of the bowl and marsh scenes on the inside.[16] Many of these vessels were made as votive offerings to the goddess Hathor, and large quantities of fragments have been found at sites associated with the cult of the goddess.[17] The lotus motif was also reproduced in the form of chalice-shaped cups, with the body of the vessel created in the shape of the flower and the resemblance heightened by the addition of relief decoration showing the petals on the exterior (fig. 3). The stems of the chalices were made separately and attached to the base of the cup.[18] The type became increasingly popular during the Third Intermediate Period (c.1050–650 BC), when the surface pattern of the lotus-

Fig. 3 Examples of Egyptian faience products. Left to right: a fine shabti-figure of King Sety I; inscribed vase of Amenhotep II; chalice-cup in the form of the lotus. New Kingdom to Third Intermediate period, 1400–850 BC.

flower was sometimes replaced by intricate scenes in relief.[19] The lotus also appears as a motif at this period in examples of tall lamps made of faience, which have been found in both religious and secular contexts. These lamps consisted of three elements: a lotiform cup at the top to hold the burning oil, a tall cylindrical supporting stem, and a flat base into which the stem was set.[20] The production and joining of these separate pieces required considerable technical competence in the working of the material.

Most smaller objects of faience were produced in pottery moulds which were open at the back, so that only the front appearance of the object was moulded. Many thousands of these moulds have been found, and their range illustrates the ubiquitous use of faience.[21] Items moulded included amulets, beads, small inlays, figurines and ring-bezels with designs or hieroglyphic inscriptions. The moulds were used repeatedly, allowing the rapid production of these common types. Many thousands of small amuletic objects were produced in

faience at all periods, but particularly from the New Kingdom and later. Simple amulets of sacred emblems such as the eye of Horus, the *djed*-pillar or the papyrus-sceptre are found in addition to more complex amuletic figures of deities. Although almost all of these were made in basic pottery moulds, the degree of detail achieved on some of the pieces is very fine. The usual glaze colours are blue or green, both of which can decay to a dull grey-white during long periods of burial in archaeological deposits. The finest appearance is generally found on objects recovered from tombs, such as some of the excellent faience *shabti*-figures (funeral servant statuettes) from the period 1050–350 BC. Faience continued to be used extensively in Egypt through to Ptolemaic and Roman times, when some very fine large vessels and figures were produced, many of which exhibit a characteristic deep blue glaze (fig. 1).[22] New techniques were borrowed from glass-making to create the so-called 'glassy faience', which has a marbled appearance, caused by the addition of glass to the faience paste.

Greek faience

The production of faience in Greece was concentrated during three main phases, each apparently stimulated by the

strength of Aegean links with Egypt and the East: the Bronze Age, the Archaic period and the time of the Ptolemies.

The earliest faience known from Aegean contexts consists of Early Bronze Age beads from *tholos* tombs in the Mesara Plain, from Mochlos and from the Trapeza Cave on Crete, probably imported from Egypt or North Syria.[23] The formation of the Minoan palaces (*c*.1900 BC) stimulated a demand for luxury products and the Minoan faience industry flourished, the earliest products dating to *c*.1900 BC, from the Vat Room Deposit at Knossos.[24] Only slightly later in date is a gold and faience vase from the loom-weight deposit at the palace of Knossos.[25] From the Temple Repositories at Knossos comes the finest cache of faience vessels, figures and inlays from Minoan Crete, vividly illustrating the variety and sophistication achieved by Minoan craftsmen working in faience.[26] These included three female figures, the best preserved of which are two 'snake goddesses', beautifully modelled and brightly coloured, one with snakes winding around her arms and her tall head-dress, the other gripping a snake in each upraised hand and with a cat seated on her head-dress. Faience shells and relief plaques, including flowers, flying fish and goats and cows suckling their young, were probably once inlays for furniture or wooden chests. Several small faience vessels were also found, including tall slim cups with one handle and a plant design in relief on the rim.

Expertise in the working of faience spread from the Minoans on Crete to the Mycenaeans of mainland Greece in the Late Bronze Age (1600–1100 BC). The Shaft Graves of Circle A at Mycenae, of the sixteenth and early fifteenth centuries, contained a number of faience vessels as well as faience fittings for ostrich-egg rhyta (ritual pouring vessels). It would appear on stylistic grounds that the Shaft Grave faience comprised both imports from Minoan Crete and products of mainland workshops.[27] Direct evidence for the manufacture of faience on the mainland comes in the form of moulds for the making of faience and glass-paste jewellery.[28]

On the island of Cyprus an eclectic faience industry developed in the Late

humans, animals and fish (fig. 4). The Greek entrepôt at Naucratis in Egypt produced a similar range of artefacts, and excavations by Petrie uncovered a rare example of a faience workshop at the site. In what he called a 'faience factory', Petrie found moulds for scarabs, beads, discs and amulets as well as objects made of faience, including inlay tiles, amulets, parts of vessels and a chariot group with four horses.[30]

Greek interest in faience production waned after the sixth century BC, and it was not until the Hellenistic era (323–31 BC), during which a Greek dynasty, the Ptolemies, was ruling Egypt, that a new phase of faience production began, exhibiting an interesting fusion of the Greek and Egyptian artistic traditions. From Alexandria, the greatest of the Hellenistic Greek cities in Egypt, come numerous vessels, many decorated in relief with a fairly limited iconographic repertoire,[31] and a wide range of figurines.[32] Outstanding products from Ptolemaic Alexandria include a series of wine jugs, decorated in relief with portraits of the Ptolemaic queens, used for the pouring of libations in their honour, and a jug in the shape of a goose with Eros clinging to its back (fig. 5). Until very recently, no faience workshop of the Ptolemaic period had been excavated, a situation remedied by exploration of the city of Athribis, 50 km (30 miles) north of Memphis, where a workshop of the reign of Ptolemy IV has been uncovered, the western sector of which was dedicated to the making of faience vessels. Many fragments of faience vessels were found there as well as cones used to support the vessels during firing.[33]

When the Hellenistic kingdom of the Ptolemies of Egypt fell to Rome in 31 BC, traditions of working in faience continued to flourish in Roman Egypt. Fine vessels in a wide variety of shapes and in plain and highly decorative relief wares were produced. Clear evidence of this industry comes from the city of Memphis, where a total of six kilns of the 1st to 2nd centuries AD were excavated by Petrie in 1907/8 in the southern sector of the city at Kom Halal. All six kilns were square constructions, sunk half into the ground. Although, sadly, the kilns had been robbed between the time of their

Fig. 4 Archaic Greek faience from Kameiros on the island of Rhodes, dating to the 6th century BC. Left: small vase in the form of a kneeling man holding a jar with a frog on its lid. Right: Egyptianising ointment spoon in the form of a swimming girl.

Bronze Age, exhibiting a striking combination of Egyptian, Western Asiatic and Aegean styles. While some of its products were clearly derivative, for instance imitations of Egyptian plates with Nilotic scenes, others were of fine quality and were valued as trade items, such as goblets in the form of a female head wearing jewellery and a high head-dress and cups in the shape of animal heads.

Although the production of luxury items in Greece appears to have all but vanished after the destruction of the Mycenaean palaces in 1200 BC, faience has been found at a couple of sites in Greece dating to the centuries that followed, notably at Lefkandi on Euboea and the Idaean Cave on Crete. However, the next main phase of faience production in Greece belongs to the Archaic period, the seventh and sixth centuries BC,[29] reflecting the influences of both Egypt and the East. A flourishing faience industry was established on the East Greek island of Rhodes, with workshops which produced a variety of figurines, amulets and small vessels, some of the latter in the form of

Fig. 5 Ptolemaic faience, made in Egypt in the 3rd century BC. Left: jug in the form of Eros riding on a goose, dating to 300–250 BC, from Tanagra, Boeotia. Right: wine-jug used in the cult of the Hellenistic Greek Queen Arsinoe III of Egypt (221–203 BC), said to be from Canosa, in Italy.

Fig. 6 Stacks of faience vessels, collapsed and fused during the firing process, from kilns of the 1st–2nd centuries AD at Memphis in Egypt.

first discovery and when Petrie was able to excavate them, enough remained to demonstrate both the range of faience objects produced and the techniques by which they were fired in the kilns.

Dishes, bowls and trays were carefully stacked, one on top of the other, and held in place at each level by three or four small clay cones, placed so as to hold each vessel separate from the others during the firing process. These stacks were then placed inside large pottery cylinders within the kiln and packed around with straw, the fuel used for the firing. Stacks of vessels collapsed and fused together (fig. 6) and piles of sherds of broken vessels all testify to the high quality of faience vessels produced in Roman Egypt, with their brilliant colours, wide range of shapes and relief decoration of plants, animals and humans. In addition, the debris from the kiln area yielded pottery moulds for such items as Horus-eye amulets and *shabti* and plaster moulds for lamps.[34]

Islamic Lustreware

Sheila R. Canby

The advent of Islam in the seventh century AD and the subsequent Arab conquest, from Spain to central Asia, opened borders and lines of communication from the Atlantic Ocean to the Aral Sea. Outstanding ceramics, characterised by the use of opaque, coloured and painted glazes, are among the most visible of the evidence that differentiates Islamic cultures from their predecessors. However, ceramic glaze as such was not a seventh-century innovation. Rather, Islamic potters introduced a marked increase in glaze types, colour combinations and shapes. Certain types of glazed pottery of the Umayyad dynasty (AD 661–750), such as Egyptian lamps with relief decoration, continued a tradition that had begun in the Roman period and persisted under the Byzantines. Similarly, to the east, Iranian potters carried on the production of turquoise-glazed storage jars from the Sasanian into the Islamic period. Only with the advent of the Abbasid dynasty in 750 does a distinct class of Islamic ceramics arise.

The founding of the Abbasid capital at Baghdad in 762 not only inspired the architects, who planned the round city and built its palaces and mosques, and the poets, who wrote about the luxurious life of the caliphs and their subjects. Techniques of ceramic glazing and decoration new to the Middle East led to the creation of at least three classes of pottery: blue-and-white, splashwares and lustrewares. Of these only lustreware, a ceramic decorated with a lustrous metallic coating, can be counted as a wholly Islamic invention, for the former two appear to owe either their shapes or their ornament to Chinese inspiration.

Islamic lustrewares have generated numerous publications which discuss their origins, technique and spread from Egypt and Iraq into Spain and Iran. It appears that lustrewares were produced in a limited number of centres where the skills and knowledge required for this demanding ceramic technique could be found. Some of these centres may have provided a local market to support the production, and all were on trade routes that allowed access to the rest of the Islamic world. Recently scholars have focused on sites such as Basra in Iraq,[1] Kashan in Iran[2] and Raqqa in Syria[3] as centres of lustreware production, but the question of where lustre-painted pottery originated has not yet been resolved.

Origins of the lustreware technique

A plausible theory does exist, however, regarding the origin of the technique. According to C. J. Lamm,[4] Egyptian glassworkers were, by the fourth or fifth century AD, employing copper and silver both to apply decoration to clear glass and to produce coloured glass mosaic. In the former technique, silver and copper compounds were painted on to the cold surface of the glass, which was then heated sufficiently to fuse the colours to the glass. The flames of the furnace consumed the oxygen, thereby causing the silver and copper to change colour and take on a gold, red or olive sheen. The glass mosaic technique consisted of colouring molten glass with metallic oxides of copper, cobalt, iron or manganese and forming multi-coloured rods. These were fused together, resulting in complex designs of circles, rosettes, squares and stripes.[5] Blocks of this *millefiori* glass were found at the ninth-century Abbasid capital of Samarra, confirming their continued production into the Islamic period.[6] Although the two glass techniques would have involved very different methods, Lamm theorised that lustre-ware pottery came about as a result of

Fig. 1 Polychrome lustre-painted bowl with opaque cream glaze and a stylised Kufic inscription on the inner rim, from Iraq, Abbasid dynasty, 9th century AD, diameter 18.3 cm (7.2 in). The 'peacock's eye' decoration is thought to derive from millefiori glass designs. This bowl is said to have been found at Nishapur in north-eastern Iran, attesting to the wide export of Abbasid lustrewares.

Fig. 2 Fragment of lustre-painted fritware, inscribed 'Sa'd' on the exterior, from Egypt, Fatimid dynasty, 11th–12th century AD, 7 cm (2.75 in) high, 9 cm (3.5 in) wide. The large number of fragments found at Fustat (Old Cairo) in Egypt inscribed with this word has led to a discussion of whether one potter or a whole workshop used this signature, or indeed whether the word is simply a benediction, meaning happiness. This extremely thin, hard fragment demonstrates the early use of fritware in Fatimid Egypt.

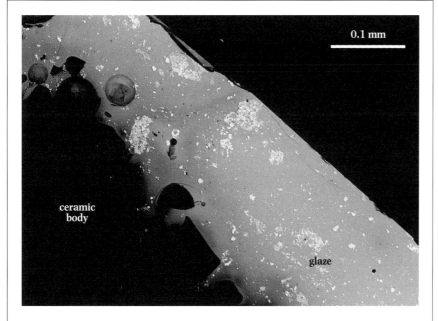

Tin-opacified glazes

So-called 'tin' glazes were first developed by Islamic potters in Iraq in the eighth century AD.[12] The presence of tin in the glaze caused it to be white and opaque, producing an excellent ground for painted decoration. The first step in the production of a tin-opacified glaze was to fire together a mixture of tin and lead to produce the oxides. This lead-tin oxide mixture was then added to an alkali-silicate glaze mixture (similar to that used on Partho-Sasanian pottery – see ch. 10). When the molten glaze cooled, particles of tin oxide crystallised, rendering it white and opaque. A typical Islamic lustre-ware glaze contains around 60% SiO_2, 20% PbO, 10% Na_2O and 5% SnO_2. The micrograph shows a cross-section through such a glaze, with numerous fine white tin oxide particles.

borrowing and combining the technique of the lustre-painted glass with the designs of glass mosaic. The result was the earliest group of lustre-ware ceramics, which were painted in polychrome lustre (fig. 1).

While the earliest dated Islamic lustre-painted glass objects, from AD 772 and 779, come from Egypt, ninth-century examples were made in Basra. Thus the opportunity would have existed in both Egypt and Iraq for potters to adopt the lustre-glassmaker's technique. Many of the same essential raw materials are employed by glass-makers and potters alike, and their furnaces and kilns are usually located on the outskirts of towns to avoid inundating the urban population with smoke. For these reasons, associations between potters and glassmakers could be expected, including the cross-fertilisation of technical and artistic ideas.

Alan Caiger-Smith, a modern potter who has reconstructed the medieval Islamic lustreware technique (see ch. 32), has noted that whereas 'reduction occurs as a matter of course' in glass furnaces, the firing that melts the lead-rich glaze on earthenware ceramics requires 'a clear, oxidising atmosphere.'[7] To fix the lustre pigments on to the glazed ceramic required a second firing in a different (reduction) kiln, in which the temperature could be closely controlled. Here the pots were heated just enough for the glaze to soften and not so fast that they would crack due to the different rates of expansion of body and glaze. The limitation of air and the correct flow of gases in the reduction kiln ensure the extraction of oxygen from the metallic compounds, resulting in an even lustre glaze which, according to the fourteenth-century chronicler Abu'l Qasim, 'reflects like red gold and shines like the light of the sun'.[8]

Developments in lustreware production

For perhaps as long as a century, Iraqi potters experimented with polychrome lustre glazes. Eventually, in the tenth century, monochrome lustrewares replaced those with polychrome lustre glazes. It is not certain whether this represents merely a change in fashion or a conscious desire to imitate precious metal vessels. However, Abbasid lustre-wares, while luxurious by ceramic standards, are unlikely to have competed in price or use with the gold and silver tablewares of kings, although no written documentation confirms this supposition. By the tenth century Iraqi lustrewares were exported to Iran, Egypt, North Africa and Spain, suggesting that there was a strong

demand for these wares. As the power of the Abbasid caliphate declined in the late tenth century, a new centre of lustreware production developed in Cairo under the Fatimid dynasty (969–1171), a breakaway caliphate founded by Isma'ili Shiites. Although the Fatimid lustre-potters did not experiment with ceramic shapes, their wares – decorated with painted designs and depictions of human and animal figures – are considered among the finest of Islamic ceramics.

Although at least six potters' names are known from the Fatimid period (fig. 2), contemporary written sources unfortunately do not shed light on the organisation of their workshops. The

Fig. 3 Lustreware bottle, fritware body, with a poetic inscription, from Kashan, dated Muharram AH 575 / June AD 1179, 14.3 cm (5.6 in) high. This bottle, decorated with a frieze of seated figures, a Persian inscription, two friezes of chasing animals and bands of arabesque, is the earliest known dated Iranian lustreware vessel. Its date, within eight years of the fall of the Fatimid dynasty, supports the theory that Egyptian potters brought the lustre technique to Iran.

uniformity in shape of the bowls which bear lustre decoration may indicate that one set of potters produced the bowls with opaque white glaze to which another group, the lustre-painters, applied decoration before refiring. The decline of the Fatimid dynasty in the

The application of lustre

The production of lustre depended on the grinding of salts of silver or copper with an inert carrier material, which in the case of Persian lustre-ware was fired clay, according to Abu'l Qasim.[13] This mixture was painted on to the surface of the cold glazed vessel. The second firing, in a reducing atmosphere, caused the breakdown of the metallic salts, their diffusion into the surface of the glaze and their reduction to metal. This formed a very thin metallic coating. Careful control of the firing was essential to ensure that the temperature was high enough to allow reduction to metal. However, if it was too high, the glaze would become so soft that the carrier material stuck to the surface and the lustre was spoiled.[14]

twelfth century and the destruction of the Cairo potters' quarter in 1169[9] coincided with the appearance of lustreware in Syria at Raqqa and in Iran at Kashan.

Presumably Egyptian lustreware potters emigrated to Syria and Iran, taking their technical secrets with them. In any event, the earliest Syrian and Iranian lustrewares exhibit a reliance on the pictorial conventions of Fatimid prototypes. The earliest Syrian lustrewares of the 'Tell Minis' type (fig. 5) borrow split-palmette and arabesque forms from Fatimid lustrewares, whereas in the first style of Iranian lustrewares the predominant style is one of large-scale motifs reserved on a lustre ground.

Additionally, in Egypt, Syria and Iran a new ceramic body comes into use in the eleventh century. Akin to European soft-paste porcelain, this material, known as fritware or stone-paste, is described in the fourteenth-century treatise of Abu'l Qasim as consisting of ten parts ground quartz, one part ground glass and one part fine white clay, which produced a harder, thinner fabric than the reddish or buff earthenware bodies of earlier Egyptian and Iranian pottery.[10] Because of the lack of plasticity (stiffness) of the fritware body, it was difficult to throw on the wheel and therefore particularly well suited to vessels produced in moulds. However, thrown vessels were also made with great skill by medieval potters. Furthermore, the compatibility of the body with alkaline glazes contributed to the greatly expanded range of colours and shapes of Iranian ceramics from the eleventh century onwards.

The thinness and whiteness of the fritware body may have been the original source of its appeal, because

Fig. 4 Bottle with lustreware decoration on opaque white and cobalt-blue glazed ground, second half of the 17th century, from Iran, 26.1 cm (10.3 in) high. The vegetal and animal designs on Safavid lustreware closely resemble the gold and silver decoration of manuscript margins and have little in common with the ornament on other types of Safavid ceramics. It seems likely that these wares were produced for clients in Isfahan, the capital, since there is no archaeological evidence of these wares in other parts of Iran.

Fig. 5 Lustreware bowl, fritware body, from Syria, Tell Minis type, mid-12th century, 21.4 cm (8.4 in) diameter, 6.5 cm (2.5 in) high. The earliest lustrewares produced in Syria show a strong reliance on Fatimid models, as exemplified here by the cleanly drawn split-leaf palmette arabesque. 'Tell Minis' wares were found at a site in central Syria but may have been made at Raqqa in the north.

these were qualities prized in Chinese ceramics. However, other advantageous aspects of this ware soon became evident. The white body obviated the need for opacified white glaze, since transparent colourless glaze could still produce a white ground for decoration. While the coarser body of ceramic tiles still required opaque white glaze as a ground for lustre-painting, bowls and other vessels could have either transparent or opaque glaze. Whereas Fatimid potters had occasionally decorated turquoise-glazed pieces with lustre designs, the Syrians and Iranians highlighted areas of their lustre designs with cobalt-blue and turquoise glazes applied at the stage of the first firing of the glazed ground. These variations greatly broadened the decorative repertoire of lustreware vessels and tiles, perhaps ensuring the continuation of the technique after the Mongol invasions of the thirteenth century.

Production in Iran

The documentary evidence for Persian lustreware production derives from numerous inscriptions on tiles and vessels (fig. 6) and a treatise by Abu'l Qasim 'Abdullah of Kashan. Dated AH 700 / AD 1300/1, Abu'l Qasim's treatise is entitled *'Ara'is al-jawahir wa nafa'is al-ata'ib* ('The Virtues of Jewels and the Delicacies of Perfumes') and includes a chapter on *kashi-gari*

0.1 mm

Stone-paste or fritware bodies

The micrograph shows a cross-section, in which the stone-paste ceramic body is seen to consist of numerous particles of crushed quartz. Naturally occurring white quartz pebbles are low in iron and so make a good raw material for a white-firing ceramic. The quartz particles are held together by a glass formed from the fusion of the clay with the glass or frit mixed into the body by the potters. The bodies are often quite porous (the black areas in the micrograph are holes) and this means they can be relatively weak.

Islamic stone-paste is quite similar to the earlier 'faience' bodies of Egypt and the Near East (ch. 15) but differs in that a small amount of clay was added, which meant it could be thrown on the wheel. When fired, the added clay and glass melted and produced a body that was less friable. Recent work has suggested that the stone-paste body may have developed from the Egyptian practice of adding quartz and glass to clay-rich bodies in the tenth to eleventh centuries AD.[15]

Fig. 6 Three moulded lustre tiles with cobalt and turquoise stain and an inscription from the Qur'an (sura XLVIII, 4–5), one tile dated Sha'ban AH 709/January AD 1310, from Kashan, 39 cm (15.3 in) high. These tiles are associated with a group dated AH 710/ AD 1310/11 and signed by Yusuf b. 'Ali b. Muhammad b. Abi Tahir. It has been suggested that they were made for the Mongol restoration of the Great Mosque of Isfahan.

(pottery-making) in a text that also covers minerals, gems and perfumes. The 1300/1 manuscript contains two prefaces, one dedicated to the Il-Khanid vizier and historian Rashid al-Din and the second to his rival and successor Taj al-Din 'Alishah. Abu'l Qasim's genealogy is also mentioned, shedding a glimmer of light on the social standing of lustre-potters and their families in thirteenth-century Iran. The author's name appears as 'Abdullah b. 'Ali b. Muhammad b. Abi Tahir al-Qashani al Muwarrik al-Hasib. While the last two terms, meaning 'the chronicler, the mathematician', refer to Abu'l Qasim's occupations, the *nisbah* 'al-Qashani' attaches to the name of Abu Tahir, Abu'l Qasim's great-grandfather and the scion of Kashan's leading family of lustre-potters. The Abu Tahir family was spared by the Mongol devastation of the thirteenth century, presumably because of their status as master craftsmen and practitioners of a ceramic technique unknown even in China.

Signed and dated lustre tiles by Abu'l Qasim's grandfather, father and brother Yusuf are known from the late twelfth century to *c.*1327 (fig. 6), as well as one overglaze enamel or *minai* ware piece

attributed to his great-grandfather. There is no mention of a family link with Egypt or Syria, which might have explained how the lustreware technique came to Iran. However, the majority of lustreware tiles by the potters of this family were produced for Shiite shrines and tombs in Iran,[11] suggesting that the technique may have been privileged information shared with their spiritual brethren in Iran by the Shiite émigré potters of Fatimid Egypt. While Abu'l Qasim's treatise predates Yusuf's earliest dated tile panel by four years, the other works – tiles and writings – by the brothers are roughly of the same date. It is therefore impossible to determine which brother was the elder. As Oliver Watson has mentioned, the generations in the Abu Tahir family appear widely spread over the years, so it is possible that the sons were not directly apprenticed to their fathers but rather to other Kashan lustre-potters who may have been closer to them in age. This theory is borne out in part by evidence of collaboration on major tile assemblages by several pairs of lustre-potters from different families.

Although Abu'l Qasim's knowledge of ceramic production is amply demonstrated in his treatise, he provides no insight into how he came to be employed as a chronicler for the Mongols. Apparently Abu'l Qasim lived not in Kashan but in Tabriz, the Mongol capital, where he wrote the history of the reign of Uljaitu (d. 1316). According to Watson, this mobility did not extend to the potters in Abu'l Qasim's family. Although large lustreware *mihrabs* (prayer niches) and tombstone panels by members of the Abu Tahir family

were produced for the shrines at Qum, Mashhad, Veramin, Gunbad-e Qabus and Najaf, the technical complexity involved in lustreware production increases the likelihood that the tiles were transported from one central production point, the kilns of Kashan.

Following the Mongol invasion of Iran in the 1220s, lustreware production declined markedly for about twenty-five years. However, as the work of the Abu Tahir family shows, lustreware hardly ceased to be made. Within a generation of conquering Iran, the Mongols themselves were decorating their tombs and palaces with lustre tiles. In the fourteenth century, lustreware tiles were more or less superseded by the new polychrome techniques of tile mosaic and *cuerda seca* and by overglaze enamelware called *lajvardina*. Yet somehow the technique of lustreware was not entirely lost. A few examples are known from the fifteenth and sixteenth centuries and finally, in the seventeenth century, the technique was revived (fig. 4). Numerous vessels and a handful of tiles were produced, perhaps for the burgeoning class of well-to-do Isfahanis. Even in the eighteenth and nineteenth centuries lustreware continued to be made on a small scale in Iran. Possibly, as Watson has suggested, the intense interest of nineteenth-century European collectors in medieval and seventeenth-century Persian lustreware encouraged its continuation in the nineteenth century by potters more accustomed to producing polychrome underglazed tiles in the Qajar style than lustrewares reminiscent of Iran's past ceramic glory.

115

Maiolica Production in Renaissance Italy

Dora Thornton

The movement known as the Renaissance or 'rebirth' had its origins in Italy in the fourteenth century and involved a re-evaluation of the classical cultural inheritance to form distinctly modern social values. Based on financial and trading power, the political and demographic growth of various Italian cities, and a self-conscious civic culture, the Renaissance involved a transformation not just of Italian but of European ways of life, as growing consumer demand fuelled technological and artistic development.

The technical finesse and artistic refinement of Italian Renaissance maiolica (tin-glazed earthenware) elevated the social status of pottery, shaping European taste for over a century.[1] The etymology of the word maiolica reveals much about this development: until the sixteenth century, it was used exclusively to denote lustred pottery imported from southern Spain, and not Italian products.[2] Commercial competition with Spanish imports spurred Italian potters first to imitation and then to rivalry, and with such success that, having pushed Spanish imports out of their local markets by about 1500, they then captured the entire European market, exporting both their wares and their craftsmen.[3]

Evidence for the increased production, diversification and technological advance of maiolica is provided by surviving pieces which, for the first time in post-classical Europe, bear potters' marks, dates and other written information about their manufacture.[4] From about 1500 it is possible to trace the fortunes of workshops and individual artisans as well as the migration of potters.[5] A wide range of documents demonstrate the growth of the maiolica industry, including notarial acts, contracts, tax returns, guild records, business agreements, account books and protective legislation.[6] Technical details of manufacture are provided by an illustrated treatise written around 1557 by an amateur potter, Cipriano Piccolpasso, and called *The Three Books of the Potter's Art*, which is the principal source for this account, given that the economic history of maiolica has yet to be written.

Clays and raw materials

Piccolpasso was a native of one of the many production centres of fine maiolica, Castel Durante (Urbania), a natural pottery area because of the clays deposited there by the river Metauro. He describes how chalky clays silted 'to a depth of a foot or two' above the banks. The clay was checked for inclusions of chalk which, in firing, would turn to quicklime and eventually spall off, damaging the glaze in finished wares. Chalky clay was also dug in sloping ground, in pits with channels between them for rainwater. Clays were flung into heaps to be weathered and broken down, then processed by sieving and straining through cloth, beating to break down impurities, and kneading until smooth.[7]

Not all pottery centres used local clays: Piccolpasso explains that Venetian potters (many of whom were migrants from other pottery towns) used clays from Ravenna, Rimini, Pesaro and Ferrara, as well as Padua.[8]

The principal ingredients of the tin-opacified lead glaze used for fine maiolica included both local and expensive imported elements, the most important of which was tin. Particles of tin oxide, suspended in the glaze layer, produced the characteristic whiteness of the ground for the painted decoration on maiolica.[9] The tin used by Italian potters travelled considerable distances in what must have been a profitable and highly organised trade.[10] In his treatise of 1540, *Pirotechnica*, Vannuccio Biringuccio noted:

Fig. 1
Plate from Cafaggiolo, about 1525, showing a pottery painter and his clients. His dress is not noticeably inferior to theirs and his manner is practical rather than subservient. Note the pigment pots and the finished plate.

This represented considerable capital investment and, not surprisingly, the Macci had the highest tax assessment.[16] Some pottery painters, working in a succession of partnerships with other potters, never achieved such independence; one diversified his activity, painting not only maiolica but also religious images and dowry chests used at weddings.[17] There was thus a huge gap between entrepreneurial family dynasties, such as the Macci of Deruta, Andreoli of Gubbio, Fontana of Urbino and Calamelli of Faenza, and the dependent workers, many of them painters, who relied on piece-work and sub-contracts.[18]

Throwing, forming, moulding and relief decoration

Piccolpasso describes the construction of a foot-driven wheel with heavy flywheel, as painted on a Deruta maiolica plate of about 1525.[19] An inverted wooden bowl fixed on to the wheel-head with clay made it easier to work the undersides of bowls and dishes, using up to five distinct iron tools to finish foot-rims.[20] The

Fig. 2 Dramatic scene from Piccolpasso's treatise, The Three Books of the Potter's Art, around 1557, showing kiln firing.

I have heard from people who know that the largest quantities and best tin found in Europe is what is mined in England [presumably he meant Devon and Cornwall]; I have heard that it is also found in parts of Flanders, and in Bohemia and the Duchy of Bavaria, but the bizarre place-names are too difficult for me.[11]

Ground tin and lead oxides were mixed in water with a flux or silicate of potash (*marzacotto*) to make the tin-glaze suspension.[12] The potash, derived from burning the lees on the insides of wine barrels, was combined with white quartz sand.[13]

Dried wood was required for firing; a fifteenth-century potter's account book records payments for transport by the cartload from up to 8 km (5 miles) away.[14] Brushwood and broom were also used in specialist workshops for the third, low-temperature firing needed to produce lustred pottery. An edict of 1465, prohibiting bringing these materials into Deruta, a maiolica town, except on the day preceding kiln firings, may therefore document an early date for lustre production in the town.[15]

The most successful workshops were those which controlled the entire process of production: for example, the 1489 tax returns for Deruta reveal that the Macci family of potters owned three workshops, a kiln, clay pits and woods.

Maiolica bodies and glazes

The bodies and glazes of Italian maiolica are in the same tradition as those of Islamic lustrewares (ch. 16) and their predecessors. Bodies were of calcareous clays, containing 15–25% lime, which, in spite of about 5% iron oxide, fired to pale colours. These were relatively easy to mask with a white, tin-opacified glaze. As the expansion coefficients of calcareous bodies are relatively close to those of glazes, there was a reasonable fit between glaze and body, so the glaze was less likely to craze.[59] Maiolica glazes contain similar amounts of lead and tin oxides to those of Islamic ceramics, but differ in having high potassium rather than sodium (potassium is the main component of the wine lees used by the maiolica potters). They may also contain crushed sand (quartz and feldspar) to increase the opacity.[60] The use of sand would have been a cheaper option than adding more tin oxide, which was an expensive imported material.

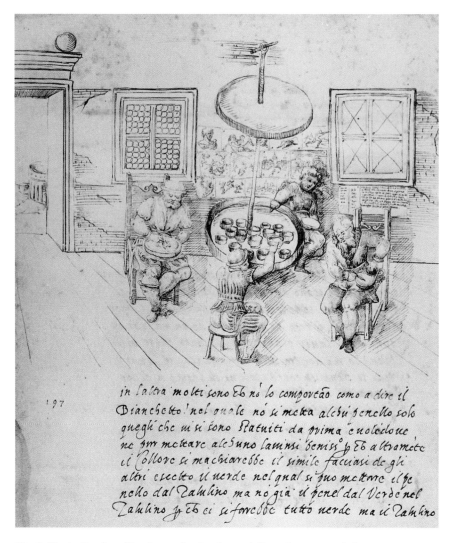

Fig. 3 Illustration from Piccolpasso showing four maiolica painters at work (in contrast to two potters in another of his illustrations), with design sources tacked on to the wall behind them. He says nothing, however, about how such designs were transferred on to pottery for painting.

Fig. 4 Right: 'Coriolanus and the Women', signed, inscribed and dated by Francesco Durantino, Urbino, 1544. A business agreement of 1543 records him working in Guido di Merlino's workshop, one of the largest in Urbino. Far right: Durantino's poorly fired 'Flaying of Marsyas', painted at his own kiln at Montebagnolo in 1547.

introduction of moulding diversified maiolica forms as well as increasing the volume and speed of production while reducing costs.[21] Half-moulds of plaster were used in the sixteenth century for open forms: convex for basket-type wares, concave for pieces with relief decoration imitating embossed metalwork.[22] Complex closed forms, imitating sculptural table silver, were piece-moulded, with cast handles applied with slip.[23] Applied relief ornament, such as floral scrolls on the undersides of flasks and basins, and serpent handles were also moulded: Piccolpasso's illustration of four types of handle current in the 1550s is precisely matched by the remains of plaster moulds excavated at a pottery in Rome, documented as that of a potter originally from Piccolpasso's home-town, Castel Durante.[24]

Saggars were used to protect the biscuit ware and enable it to be stacked in the kiln, where it was given a first firing at about 1000°C.[25] Given that firing temperatures were uneven in the updraught kiln which Piccolpasso illustrates (fig. 2), painted wares were given pride of place.[26]

Suspension glazes, pigments and firing techniques

Wares were then dipped in tin glaze which, when dry, provided a powdery white absorbent surface for painting but could also be tinted by adding cobalt or manganese.[27] From the mid-fifteenth century, a wide range of pigments were developed: blue from cobalt, used for outlining figurative designs; green from copper; tin for white highlights; yellow from antimony and orange from blending this with iron; and purple-brown from manganese.[28] Piccolpasso added, concerning the difficulties of obtaining red, that 'as yet this art has no colour that comes out red', but mentions a recipe of Virgiliotto Calamelli of Faenza, using Armenian bole; his comments on its unreliability are borne out by the way small areas of red have fired as raised grainy patches on surviving pieces from Faenza and Tuscany.[29] The technology of preparing pigments, including recipes, local variations in their preparation and methods of grinding, takes up the entire second book of Piccolpasso's treatise. After painting, some wares were sprinkled with a clear finishing glaze to give surface gloss and saturate the colours.[30] Given the time and labour spent on painting fine wares, it seems surprising that they were laid face down on pointed spurs or pegs within saggars for firing: the marks of these may be clearly seen on finished pieces, while surviving kiln failures show them stuck to the surface of the wares (fig. 5).[31] Piccolpasso's illustrations of pierced saggars are matched by excavated examples.[32] The kiln had to be swept to prevent dust particles adhering to painted surfaces, then carefully set so that the wares did not touch one another and so fuse in the firing (fig. 5) or block the fire vents.[33] Finally the kiln was sealed with mortar: fragments, bearing potters' fingerprints, have been found in potters' waste-heaps in Montelupo.[34] A second firing at about 950°C completed the ware unless metallic lustre was to be applied, in which case a third firing was required to reduce the metal oxide pigments, leaving a metallic coating on the surface.[35]

Lustre techniques were jealously guarded by the potters who knew them,[36] but since there was a commercial incentive to rival imported lustrewares from Spain, fifteenth-century potters can be shown (from local finds and analyses of potters' waste-heaps) to have made their own short-lived experiments in Faenza,

Maiolica pigments

The importance of pigment technology in the development of maiolica painting technique has been emphasised by Kingery.[61] Before the fifteenth century, the ceramic pigments in use were those such as copper green and manganese purple which tended to dissolve in the glaze, resulting in diffuse, blurred boundaries to the painted areas. However, Piccolpasso describes the preparation of pigments such as lead antimonate yellow and tin oxide white, which did not dissolve but were insoluble and remained particulate. These pigments allowed the maiolica painters to paint more precisely, to produce sharp lines and to use effects such as shading. Orange could be produced by adding iron oxide to the lead antimonate, while green was produced by mixing lead antimonate yellow with copper. The red, produced from Armenian bole, a ferruginous earth, was no doubt unreliable because of the tendency of the red oxidised form of iron oxide to reduce and darken, as well as to dissolve. The preparation of the pigments required considerable care, involving careful firing, milling and settling in water to obtain the desired particle size. A transparent glaze layer (*coperta*), which was commonly applied over the pigment particles, has a similar composition to the underlying opaque glaze but lacks tin. The micrograph shows particles of lead antimonate pigment, sandwiched between the tin-opacified white ground and the overlying transparent *coperta*.

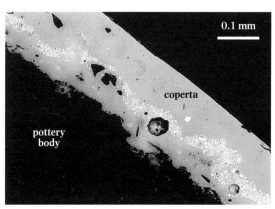

Pesaro, Montelupo and Cafaggiolo.[37] Lustre production was expensive in materials and had a high failure rate (Piccolpasso estimated that only six in every hundred pieces was successful).[38] Perhaps unsurprisingly, therefore, it only came to be practised on a large, almost industrial scale in Gubbio (fig. 7) and Deruta by specialised workshops in the sixteenth century.[39]

Painters and workshop organisation

The combination of technical and pictorial qualities characterised up-market maiolica production, a combination which Giorgio Vasari considered distinctly modern. 'As far as we know', he wrote, 'the [ancient] Romans were not aware of this type of painting on pottery. The vessels from those days . . . are covered with figures incised and washed in with one colour . . . but never with the brilliance of glaze nor the charm and variety of painting which has been seen in our

day'.[40] Biringuccio mentions the same blend of qualities: 'The principal basis [of pottery] is derived from two things – the art of drawing and various secrets and alchemical mixtures'.[41]

Maiolica came to be regarded as a branch of painting, and some of the painters who signed, inscribed and dated their work considered themselves artists rather than artisans.[42] 'History-painted' maiolica depended on new technologies of printing such as woodcut and engraving for its sources; much of the literature on maiolica concentrates on identifying these and analysing the ways in which they were used.[43] Some known painters had favourite sources which reveal that they were literate and had access to certain printed books: Francesco Durantino, for instance, refers to the 1493 Italian edition of Livy as a source of both subjects and decoration,[44] while Nicola da Urbino used the 1497 Italian edition of Ovid on his pieces.[45] Both painters were using these books between twenty and forty years after

Fig. 5 (Above)
Kiln furniture and
failures: two spurs
used to support
painted pieces in
saggars during
firing, a plate with
spurs attached,
a bowl with
visible spur
marks at
centre and
maiolica dishes
fused in the
firing.

Fig. 6 Two dishes painted and signed by Francesco
Xanto Avelli, Urbino. Left: 'Lion Hunt', c. 1530,
both subject and Latin inscription on reverse from
an engraving of a famous Roman sarcophagus.
Above: 'Mars, Venus and Cupid', taken from his
poem in praise of his patron, with figures from
Raimondi engravings, dated 1532 on reverse.

Fig. 7   Above left: Lustred bowl with grotesque decoration and central unidentified badge, Gubbio, dated 1518 on reverse; marked 'Azuro' (blue) on the rim.
Right: Plate finished in lustre at the workshop of Maestro Giorgio of Gubbio, date corrected in lustre from 1530 to 1531 on rim. Grotesques and woman's head, inscribed 'Divine Ippolita'.

they were printed. Xanto did a cut-and-paste job on prints by Marcantonio Raimondi, copying both a print and its inscription, or invented his own poetry as subject matter (fig. 6).[46] The work of other maiolica painters testifies to the diffusion in Italy of prints by Schongauer and Dürer, to the direct and mediated impact of Raphael and Michelangelo, and to the production of drawings and designs made specifically for use in maiolica workshops.[47]

Different evidence points to the rise in status and artistic pretension of maiolica painters, not least a famous plate (fig. 1).[48] Xanto signed his pieces not only by name, but described himself as 'painter' or 'poet'; the fact that those who applied lustre to his pieces tried at one point to obliterate his inscriptions indicates irritation as well as competition.[49] He was one of several

client painters named in a 'lock-out' agreement by five Urbino pottery bosses in 1530 in an effort to resist claims for higher wages.[50]

Figure 3 suggests a degree of collaboration between painters, who may have had specialised functions and worked according to series production methods. On one dish, the complex design has been laid out by a specialist, who left an instruction to a lesser painter to fill in the ground of his design in blue at the 2 o'clock position on the dish (fig. 7).[51] Many other pieces document workshop collaboration, making it difficult to interpret inscriptions on the reverse of a given piece as the signature of an individual artist or the imprimatur of a workshop. Some pieces produced in larger workshops are inscribed in more than one hand.[52] Until we know more about workshop organisation it will be difficult to generalise about typical working practice, since all the evidence – both archival and archaeological – points to a huge variety in the nature, size and organisation of maiolica workshops.[53] What is certain is that the prestige pieces were produced in the largest ateliers, employing specialist painters on contract and highly skilled

kiln operators to ensure maximum success in firing finished pieces so as to lose or damage as few as possible.

Documentary evidence of the scale of production points to impressive – and ever increasing – levels of output. A contract of 1430/31 records an order for about a thousand pharmacy jars placed by a Florentine hospital with Giunta di Tugio.[54] One Faenza pottery painter was painting an average of 669 pieces a month over five months in 1465.[55] Two mid-sixteenth-century contracts in Faenza record orders for 3500 items in two months and 7000 in four, while a workshop inventory of 1556 records 20,000 pieces in over sixty categories.[56]

Such a scale of production created hazards for workers and for those living near pottery workshops. A seventeenth-century treatise on occupational diseases mentions lead-poisoning as characteristic of potters,[57] while Piccolpasso stipulated that wine lees used to make potash should be burnt out of town, 'to a distance of about a mile, because of the bad smell . . . , which . . . is apt to make pregnant women miscarry'.[58]

Stoneware Production in Medieval and Early Modern Germany

David Gaimster

Fully fused stoneware, first developed in the Rhineland by the beginning of the fourteenth century, is a hard, non-porous ceramic ideal for domestic use. Impervious to liquids, the stoneware body was designed for drinking, decanting, transport and general storage purposes. Workshops across Germany, from the Rhine to the Oder (fig. 1), increased production over the course of the late medieval and early modern period, not only in response to local markets but also in order to meet the growing demand of communities, both urban and rural, across the continent of Europe. For the pre-industrial period German stonewares are key artefacts for the study of

chronology, trade and social status on sites across the globe, from early colonial settlements in North America to shipwrecked trading ships in the South China Sea.[1]

The study of stoneware production in medieval and later Germany, its technology and 'ecology', includes the excavation of production sites, macro-scopic and petrological analyses of vessels and wasters, and the examination of archival evidence such as guild records, contemporary graphical sources and ethnographic data for information on workshop organisation and working practices.[2]

Clays and raw materials

Pre-industrial stoneware industries in Germany were generally located close to clay deposits suitable for firing to high temperatures. Stoneware potters also required access to plentiful wood supplies for firing and, from the sixteenth century, salt for glazing and cobalt and manganese for colouring. Our knowledge of the means of extraction and processing of raw materials relies on a combination of historical and ethnographic evidence.[3]

Subject to local geological circum-stances, stoneware clays could be extracted either from the surface or by mining. At Siegburg, in the Rhineland,

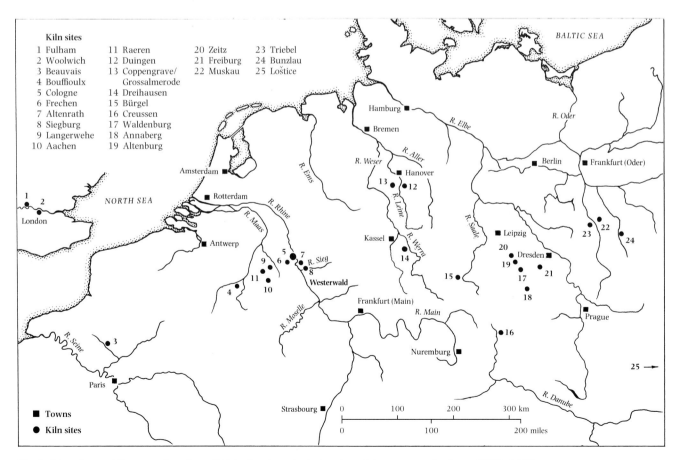

Kiln sites

1 Fulham	11 Raeren	20 Zeitz	23 Triebel
2 Woolwich	12 Duingen	21 Freiburg	24 Bunzlau
3 Beauvais	13 Coppengrave/	22 Muskau	25 Loštice
4 Bouffioulx	Grossalmerode		
5 Cologne	14 Dreihausen		
6 Frechen	15 Bürgel		
7 Altenrath	16 Creussen		
8 Siegburg	17 Waldenburg		
9 Langerwehe	18 Annaberg		
10 Aachen	19 Altenburg		

Fig. 1 Map of central Europe and southern Britain showing principal centres of stoneware production, c.1300–1800.

The stoneware body

Stoneware is an opaque vitreous or glassy ceramic fired at very high temperatures, typically greater than around 1150°C. The body has a very low porosity and high density and is noted for its relatively high strength. Stoneware bodies are traditionally produced from clays rich in alumina and low in fluxes such as alkali, calcium and iron oxides. The high firing temperatures required promote the formation of the aluminium silicate compound mullite, which is responsible for the strength of the stoneware.

Archaeologists have identified a number of stages in the development of the German stoneware body, which became more refined over time. At Siegburg in the Rhineland, proto-stonewares of the mid-12th to late 13th centuries have relatively high porosities of about 5% and coarse sand inclusions visible to the naked eye. Firing temperatures were 1000–1100°C. The near or early stoneware of the late 13th to early 14th centuries has a low porosity (about 1.5%) but relatively coarse sand inclusions – temperatures of 1100–1200°C were typical. True stoneware, with a fine, highly vitrified body (porosity about 0.4%) produced by firing temperatures of 1300–1400°C, became predominant by the second quarter of the 14th century, and this body remained essentially unchanged for the next three centuries.

clays were dug from shallow pits near the town, whereas at Langerwehe, Raeren and in the Westerwald potters were forced to sink vertical shafts with horizontal or bell-shaped galleries.[4] In the Rhineland it was common practice for the raw clays to be left in shallow pits during the winter to break down through frost action. Prior to use the clay was further refined by soaking in troughs and kneading in order to remove air and larger impurities.[5] At this stage sand filler was introduced to the raw clay in order to facilitate drying and counteract excessive shrinkage during firing.[6]

Stoneware production required large quantities of wood for high-temperature firings over several days.[7] In the Westerwald, beechwood was cut and stacked close to the kilns for up to six months to dry it out thoroughly prior to use.[8] With the introduction of salt-glazing during the sixteenth century (see below), large and regular quantities of salt were required.[9] In the Rhineland, the proximity of stoneware producers to the riverine trade network was critical. During the medieval and later period Cologne was the hub of the regional salt trade, importing sea-salt from the North Sea and the Baltic.[10]

Development of the stoneware body

Technically stoneware is a fully fused ceramic body impervious to water. It appears glassy in the break, the temper inclusions fully fused into the fabric. It is so hard that it is resistant to steel. To produce a stoneware body it is necessary to achieve kiln temperatures of between 1200° and 1400°C. A wood-ash or vaporised salt deposit forms the standard glaze. After a long period of experimentation and refinement in kiln technology, a consistently fully fused and impervious stoneware body was achieved in the Rhineland during the final decades of the thirteenth century. The stages in this development are represented by a sequence of stoneware bodies defined by their degree of vitrification. Bernhard Beckmann's 1960s excavations in the Siegburg Aulgasse identified six major periods of manufacture, of which the first four are now published (*c*.1150–1350).[11] These four stages represent the progression from high-fired earthenwares through proto- and near-stoneware stages to fully fused real-stoneware fabrics *c*.1290–1325, although not exclusively until after *c*.1335.[12]

Throwing and forming

German stoneware of the late Middle Ages and early modern period was made on a fast wheel, usually in one action, with handles, spouts and other features added at the leather-hard stage. The characteristic 'frilled' base of the later Middle Ages and early Renaissance was formed by leaving a residue of clay around the base of the vessel, which was then thumbed to produce the characteristic foot-ring[13]

String- or wire-marks on the undersides of flat bases, which were introduced at the beginning of the sixteenth century, demonstrate that the pots were removed from the wheel while it was still moving, suggesting a degree of mass-production whereby it was uneconomic to slow the wheel down in order to remove a vessel and replace it with a fresh ball of clay.

The crisp profiles of German stoneware, which became increasingly complex over the course of the sixteenth and seventeenth centuries, were achieved with the use of wooden templates (*Stege*).[14] The fact that no such tools have survived on production sites confirms that inexpensive and replaceable organic materials were used. The horizontal rilling so characteristic of late medieval stonewares was probably also produced mechanically. A rare representation of a female stoneware potter, on an early fifteenth-century playing card made for the imperial Habsburg court, shows the use of the articular end of a long bone (probably a cow metapodial) to form the corrugated surface of a Siegburg-type funnel-necked jug (fig. 2).[15]

The most important tool of the

Fig. 2 Representation of a female potter (Hefneryn) in a pack of playing cards presented to the imperial Habsburg court, mid-15th century. The card shows the potter using a long bone (probably a cow metapodial) to form the corrugated surface of a funnel-necked stoneware jug of the period.

123

stoneware potter was the throwing-wheel, for which there is both graphical and ethnographic evidence – and now, for the first time, clear archaeological traces.[16] Excavations in 1989/90 on the site of the Knütgen family pottery at Aulgasse 8 in Siegburg revealed the remains of an extensive workshop, yard, drying rooms, storage areas and living quarters which were burnt down by imperial troops during an attack on the town in April 1588.[17] The workshop area was identified by three settings for kickwheels sunk into the tiled floor of the building.[18] The evidence confirms the use of a strutted kickwheel consistent with both the early fifteenth-century representation (fig. 2) and Jost Amman's woodcut of the potter published in his *Book of Trades* of 1568. The kickwheel could be interrupted easily, enabling the potter to move efficiently from fast throwing to turning and other tasks, whereas the cartwheel, the other principal throwing-wheel documented in medieval and early modern Europe, was cumbersome to stop and start again once momentum had been achieved.[19]

Plastic decoration and surface treatment

A defining characteristic of Renaissance and later German stoneware is the use of mould technology in the application of relief ornament. In contrast to painted ceramics, which required the same investment of effort and skills for each vessel, this 'revolution' in ceramic technology required investment of resources only in the initial creation of a mould. Thereafter vessels could be mass-produced to the same standard at no extra cost.

The emergence of the Cologne stoneware industry during the early sixteenth century coincided with the introduction of woodblock printing technology and the increasing accessibility of single-sheet designs and book illustrations.[20] Taken directly from contemporary pattern-books, designs included figurative and botanical friezes and portrait roundels in addition to oak-leaf and rose-plant ornament, which was applied naturalistically over the entire surface of the stoneware vessel.[21] Throughout the second half of the sixteenth century, the Rhenish stoneware industries of Siegburg and Raeren employed engravings by the German *Kleinmeister* artists such as Heinrich Aldegrever (1502–55), Sebald Beham (1500–50) and Virgil Solis (1514–62) (fig. 3).[22] During the seventeenth century the use of armorials and pattern-books replaced individual sheet engravings.

Excavations of production sites have confirmed the sequence of stages in the manufacture of moulds for applied relief ornament on stoneware.[23] The first stage required the cutting of the design in stone (mostly fine sandstone) to create the original negative mould (*Urmatrize*), which was in turn pressed with clay to produce one or a series of positive die impressions (*Patrizen*) (fig. 4). The die(s) were lightly fired in the kiln to harden before being pressed into another strip of clay or fine pipe-clay to produce a final negative matrix (*Matrize*) used in the forming of the applied relief. Clay blanks were pressed into the fired negative matrix and the resulting relief friezes or medallions applied to the body of the vessel while at the leather-hard stage. The mould containing the clay was pressed on to the surface of the vessel and agitated slightly in order to release the relief design. The body was probably wiped with a little liquid slip in order to fix the applied relief into position.[24] At Siegburg, for instance, positive impressions of the original negative, which were frequently made by outside specialist mould-cutters (*Formenschneider*), provided insurance against loss or damage to the original design.[25] The April 1588 fire horizon in the Siegburg Aulgasse provides a datum-point for moulds in use at the time of destruction and also an indication of the lifespan of moulds for relief ornament. Almost three hundred fragments and moulds of the *Schnelle* (tall tankards) were dated to the 1570s and about fifty to the 1560s (the earliest 1567), suggesting that moulds circulated in the workshops for up to twenty years.[26]

The blue decoration on stoneware, which was introduced at the Rhenish centres of Siegburg, Raeren and Frechen and at Waldenburg in Saxony during the second half of the sixteenth century, was produced by cobalt. The most extensive sources in Germany, which are known to have been worked since the 1530s, lie in the Harz mountains of Saxony.[27] In the Rhine-

Salt-glazing

The method of salt-glazing differs radically from all other glazing techniques. Instead of applying a raw glaze to the surface of the pot, which would then melt and form a glaze during a subsequent firing, in salt-glazing the glazing agent is deposited on to the vessel during the firing process. At the height of the firing, salt (sodium chloride) is thrown into the kiln and, at temperatures above 1100°C or so, it decomposes to form sodium oxide and hydrogen chloride vapour.

The sodium oxide reacts with the alumina and silica of the ceramic to form a thin glaze layer. This is a very efficient approach to the glazing of high-fired ceramics, although the glazes so formed are rather rough to the touch due to the presence of numerous small flaws.

The micrograph shows a very thin salt glaze, less than 0.1 mm (0.004 in) thick, on a 16th-century stoneware vessel excavated at Frechen.

land, the cobalt on stoneware was applied sparingly but directly in the form of *smalt* or in a powdered glass form produced by fusing the ore with an alkali such as potash and sand. In contrast, the Waldenburg potters of Saxony could afford to be more generous with their cobalt and by the end of the century had developed the technique of *Smaltebewurf*, by which the pigment was mixed with the salt and thrown into the kiln at the end of the firing process, the fine powder coating the wares as the vaporised salt formed the overall blue glaze.[28]

Firing and glazing

Our knowledge of firing stoneware in medieval and early modern Germany comes primarily from the excavation of production sites and the recording of traditional wood-firing practices.[29] It is evident from the study of wasters from excavated kilns that refinement in stoneware bodies and the introduction of salt-glazing were dependent on developments in kiln technology. During the course of the thirteenth and fourteenth centuries, kiln-builders in the Rhineland made improvements to the firing potential of their kilns by lowering the level of the stoking area.[30] The new type of horizontal kiln was ideally suited to producing high-temperature firing conditions. Excavations at Langerwehe have revealed a kiln producing fully developed stonewares dated to *c.*1400 (fig. 5).[31] The firing chamber of the Haupstrasse kiln resembled a long shoe-sole in plan, its floor rising at a gradient of 20 degrees. It was separated from the stoking area by a central chamber which, when closed, ensured protection

Fig. 3 Salt-glazed Rhenish stonewares of the second half of the 16th century with applied relief ornament (applied dates in brackets). Top row: Raeren baluster jug (1598); Raeren Schnelle tankard (1583); Westerwald baluster jug with cobalt blue (1589). Bottom row: Raeren drug jar with cobalt blue (1591); Siegburg jug (c. 1560–85); Siegburg Schnelle tankard (1591); Cologne jug (c.1520–45); Frechen jug (c.1580–90).

against the flames and escaping gases. The floor of the firing chamber was constructed with three canals for efficient heat transfer. Parallel dimensions among post-medieval Raeren kilns suggest a height of 2 m (6 ft) for the walls of the firing chamber.[32] Excavations in the Siegburg Aulgasse district and at Frechen have revealed evidence for the increasing

sophistication of horizontal stoneware kilns over the fifteenth to seventeenth centuries. Here kilns were built with additional flues or chimneys at the rear of the firing chamber which enabled fumes and gases to escape.[33] In the case of an early seventeenth-century Frechen kiln, firing control was improved with the introduction of vaulting over the stoke-hole, which allowed increased temperature regulation and prevented flames from coming into contact with the pots.[34] The length of the firing floor and the firing capacity of the kiln were also augmented. The seventeenth to eighteenth centuries marked the final stage of kiln development in the Rhineland. Characteristic were the rectangular plan and elevation, the entirely separate and enclosed stoke-

Fig. 4 Negative ceramic mould for a frieze of applied relief decoration from Raeren, in the Rhineland, c.1590. The mould is cut with male and female portraits in Renaissance dress set within an arcade.

hole, rear flues, sloping firing floor with draught openings, and the apertures in the now permanent roof through which the salt was added for glazing.[35]

Excavations in the mid-1970s at Woolwich, on the south bank of the Thames to the east of the City of London, revealed the remains of the first stoneware kiln to have been built in Britain.[36] The suggestion that the kiln was built by Rhenish potters during the 1640s–1650s is supported by its form, which bears a striking resemblance to contemporary Frechen kilns. In contrast, John Dwight, the first man to be granted an official patent for the manufacture of stoneware in Britain, broke with the continental tradition and developed his own bottle kiln in the early 1670s.[37]

Stacking the stoneware kiln was a time-consuming and highly specialised task, the trick being to ensure that all the wares in the kiln received equal exposure to the heat. During the fourteenth to fifteenth centuries potters in the industries of south Limburg, Langerwehe and Siegburg stacked beakers, bowls and jugs inside one another, as stacking scars indicate.[38] At Siegburg and south Limburg, and later in the Westerwald and Eifel, circular discs were used to cover the openings of stoneware vessels.[39] Stacking scars on the body are a common feature of German medieval and later stoneware and do not seem to have affected their final retail value, as scarred vessels travelled widely.[40]

According to the Westerwald and Eifel folk tradition of the mid-twentieth century, furnaces of 30 m³ (36 yd³) required a total firing time ranging from 45–50 hours to three days. Towards the end of this process, when the temperature had reached a sufficient intensity (1150–1200°C) to enable fusion of the stoneware body, salt was introduced into the atmosphere of the kiln, generally after about 40–45 hours. In all, about two to three hundredweight (100–150 kg / 45–68 lb) of salt was introduced by shovel through the side and roof openings.[41] On entry the salt immediately vaporised and reacted with the surface of the stoneware to form the glassy salt glaze, while the gases escaped from the kiln in great white acid clouds (fig. 6). Sealing the vents with clay after the salting process created a reducing atmosphere which ensured the grey body so typical of Westerwald stoneware. The kiln was then allowed to cool down for up to a week before it could be opened and the first stonewares removed.

The practice of salt-glazing, first developed in the Rhineland during the fifteenth century, caused enormous pollution problems, particularly in densely populated areas such as Cologne, where the stoneware potters were situated in the centre of the city. Civic archives of the mid-sixteenth century record the popular opposition to salt-glaze firings within the city walls, and legal proceedings were taken against the Cologne potters by the civic authorities during the late 1540s which culminated in a total ban by 1556, along with the destruction of kilns and imprisonment of recalcitrant potters.[42]

Workshop organisation and working practices

The surviving guild records of the Siegburg stoneware industry document the organisation and working practices of its members over the sixteenth and early seventeenth centuries.[43] The German stoneware industries of the late medieval to early modern period were organised around the family unit, with the main production centres comprising a number of competing families, each with several master-potters operating their own kilns. In the case of Siegburg, records of kiln firings over the period 1572–8 list twenty-five separate masters from four families working simultaneously.[44]

The Rhenish stoneware potters' guilds were governed by members of a few leading families who controlled standards of manufacture, levels of productivity and trading rights. From 1522 the executive council of the Siegburg guild was made up of four

Fig. 5 Plan of a horizontal kiln, c.1400, excavated on the Haupstrasse, Langerwehe, in the Rhineland.

annually elected master-potters (the *vier Gekorenen*) who, among other tasks, refereed local disputes and kept an eye on quality control and the regulation of prices.[45] There were three classes of craftsmen: masters, workmen (*Gesellen*) and apprentices (*Lehrlinge*). A seven-year apprenticeship was required in order to become a workman in the guild.[46] Only legitimate or adoptive sons of masters, who had to be natives of Siegburg, were entitled to become apprentices. It was expressly forbidden for masters to employ foreign crafts-men, lest the secrets of their craft be copied outside the region. The professional exclusivity of the guild system maintained the high demand for Siegburg stoneware from a small fixed workforce.[47]

Recent identification of children's fingerprints on the surface of Siegburg stoneware vessels of the thirteenth to fifteenth centuries has confirmed the employment of children (probably

*Fig. 6
The salting process, Niersback, south-west Eifel, c.1955.*

family members) in the unskilled task of transporting freshly thrown vessels from the wheel to the drying area.[48] Uniquely, guild records from 1516 and 1531 also provide a picture of the status and role of women in the stoneware industry. They reveal that if a master fell ill or died, his spouse would be permitted to continue running the workshop with assistance from the workmen and apprentices for the duration of the indisposition or widow-hood. On remarriage, however, the woman had to relinquish the ownership of the workshop to her new husband.[49]

Finally, the Siegburg archives provide precise figures for the total number of firings carried out by individual masters in seven separate years between 1572 and 1585.[50] The number of firings carried out by the industry as a whole decreased during the second half of the sixteenth century, a trend which suggests concentration on quality rather than quantity in output.[51] The records indicate that during the 1570s the Siegburg potting families fired an average of three to four times a year. In order to prevent unfair competition the firing season tended to be restricted to the period between June and November, thereby forcing potters to fire their kilns every six to seven weeks.[52]

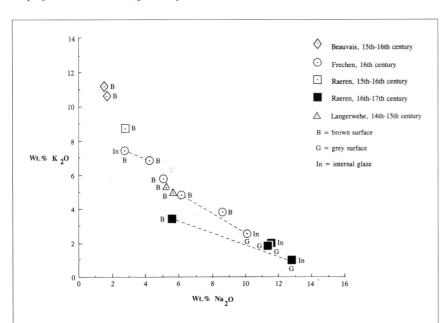

Evolution of salt-glazing

The first true glazes on stoneware appear in the Rhineland during the 15th century. They are thought to have developed from the observation that, under certain conditions, the potassium-rich vapour from the wood-ash used to fuel the kilns reacted with the surfaces of the pots and formed a glaze. The above diagram shows the compositions of glazes from the 15th through to the 17th centuries.

A change from potash-rich (K_2O) to soda-rich (Na_2O) composition is observed, reflecting a move from pure wood-ash glazes towards pure salt glazes. The gradual nature of this change probably reflects increasingly effective ways of introducing the salt into the kiln as well as the development of the kiln itself, which meant that the pots were progressively better isolated from the ash-rich fumes of the fire.

Regional Decorative Traditions in English Post-Medieval Slipware

David Gaimster

A defining characteristic of domestic material culture in early modern England was its increasing multiplicity, diversity and sophistication. This trend can be seen most clearly in the archaeological record of the sixteenth to eighteenth centuries with the introduction of a variety of new wares on to the household pottery market. New forms fulfilled an ever-expanding set of functions and specialised uses, and new bodies and styles of ornament were developed in response to the growing demand for decorative tableware designed both for use and for show. Technical, typological and decorative refinement enabled pottery to move physically from the kitchen and the cellar to the table, thereby competing with other more expensive materials. On both sides of the Channel this post-medieval 'revolution' in ceramic design, technology and status coincided with the emergence of a new mercantile and artisan class with a far greater degree of disposable income for household goods.[1]

Earthenware potters working in southern England, the Midlands and the north during the late fifteenth to mid-sixteenth centuries produced a new range of ceramic tableware at the expense of the humble cooking pot,[2] characterised by the introduction of ornament. The development of applied-slip technology reflected the increasingly sophisticated taste of the new consumer classes. Slip-trailing and incising designs into a slipped surface gave potters an extremely rapid, simple and versatile decorative technique, enabling them to produce more attractive and marketable wares than before. Immigrant communities of merchants and craftsmen from the Low Countries, northern France and Germany, who settled in the south-east of England during the fifteenth and sixteenth centuries, brought not only their own familiar domestic wares but also the social customs in which they were used. Increasing cross-Channel contact helped to consolidate the market for more individual and decorative tableware and to precipitate profound changes in the domestic ceramic repertoire.[3]

Since the Middle Ages lead-glazed earthenware, fired up to a temperature of 1100°C, had been the most widespread ceramic product in England, requiring relatively little in the way of major expense during its single firing. Raw materials for potting and firing tended to be local and readily available. In order to improve the imperviousness of the body, the surfaces of earthenware vessels were usually sealed with a transparent lead glaze. The most common decorative technique involved applying a liquid slip in a contrasting colour to the dry unfired body of the vessel. Trailing the slip in controlled lines or zones was done by using a cow-horn or pottery vessel, the end of which was fitted with a quill or reed through which the liquid slip was piped on to the surface of the vessel, rather like icing on a cake (fig. 1a–b). The design could be embellished by incising a pattern into the dry slip to reveal the body beneath (*sgraffito*) (fig. 1c) or by employing multiple slips of different colours and combing them together to create a 'feathered' effect (fig. 1d). Both slip and glaze were applied at the leather-hard stage before the vessel was fired.

The use of slip for ornament can be traced as far back in the earthenware tradition of south-east England as the late twelfth to late thirteenth century (ch. 13). Potters in the London area employed trailed and applied slip in contrasting colours to the body in imitation of imported polychrome jugs from Rouen in France. During the late fifteenth to early sixteenth centuries, in the north and Midlands, local industries introduced a range of fine-bodied drinking-cups with a dark lead glaze and applied pads or strips of white clay.

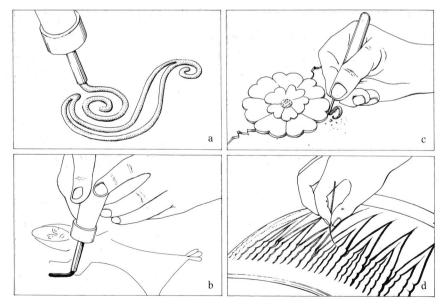

Fig. 1 Slip techniques: (a) trailing with a cow-horn or pottery vessel fitted with a quill or reed; (b) trailing into linear relief on a press-moulded dish; (c) incising patterns through a dried slip ground to expose the contrasting body beneath (sgraffito); (d) combing multiple slip-trailed lines to form a 'feathered' effect.

Fig. 2 Tablewares made by potters of the Metropolitan slipware industry in the Harlow area, Essex, 17th century. Left: sucking cup. Centre: cup with the inscription 'Obeay the King'. Right: plate trailed with a four-pointed star.

Cistercian ware, so called after its discovery on excavations of Cistercian monasteries, enjoyed a widespread distribution across England.[4] Although white slip was applied in zones or as a coating to the surface of red earthenware pottery made in the London area during the sixteenth century,[5] and despite the survival of a series of vessels in this tradition with an elaborate combination of trailed, applied and modelled slip,[6] it was not until the beginning of the seventeenth century that slip-trailing with the aid of a cow-horn and quill became a standard feature of earthenware production in the region.

The emergence of an indigenous slipware industry in England around 1600 follows the spread of slipware production across the Continent and can be seen as part of the development of a pan-European fashion for decorative earthenware designed for table use.[7] It is significant that in southern England, as in several areas of

north-western Europe, the formative stages in this particular ceramic tradition coincided with the permanent establishment of the painted tin-glazed earthenware industry (ch. 17).[8] Influenced by the chinoiserie designs of contemporary blue-and-white Oriental porcelain (ch. 30), which first appeared on the European market during the 1610s and 1620s, London tin-glazed earthenware set the fashion in decorative ceramic tableware for much of the seventeenth century. This radical innovation in technology and design transformed the nature of the English pottery market.[9] Painted tin-glazed earthenware (delftware) was ideally suited to the role of status possession, as the means of decoration could be rapidly adapted to meet new fashions in ornament without the need for a reinvestment of capital.[10]

The rising demand for more sophisticated ceramic tableware in early post-medieval England is also reflected in the widespread archaeological distribution of continental slipwares, principally from the Netherlands, Beauvais in northern France and around the Werra and Weser rivers of central Germany. These imports are characterised by a range of elaborate polychrome painted, slip-trailed and incised *sgraffito*

designs.[11] This combination of factors, both internal and external, led during the early to mid-seventeenth century to the emergence of a number of strong regional traditions in slipware production across the south-east, south-west and the north Midlands of England. The archaeological evidence suggests that slipware was largely confined to the lower end of the social spectrum, its lively ornament and relatively low price ensuring its place in most homes of the lower and middle classes for the next two hundred years.

Metropolitan slipware

Changes in taste within the southern English ceramic market of the early seventeenth century were immediately exploited by potters working on the fringes of the metropolis. In Essex (fig. 2), during the opening decades of the century, the Harlow redware industry introduced the trailing of cream-coloured slip on to an orange-red body, employing a wide range of geometric, botanical and figurative designs and even inscriptions.[12] Waste material from the production sites excavated in Harlow show the years *c.*1635–70 to be the principal period of output.[13] The recovery of these wares

Fig. 3 Large slipware cup with four double looped handles, made at Wrotham, Kent, mid-17th century. Trailed in white slip on a red ground with the inscription 'N...M... Wroth...' and applied around the body with badges and medallions moulded from reliefs on contemporary Rhenish stoneware.

handles being the most common survivals. In addition to slip-trailing with geometric motifs, the local products were also applied with circular, oval or rectangular pads of white clay, which were then impressed with negative moulds or stamps of fired clay or wood to produce positive relief ornament. Apart from potters' initials and dates, the majority of relief-moulded designs have a heraldic flavour. These sub-armorial devices include shields-of-arms, fleurs-de-lis, rosettes and rampant lions. Several applied designs, such as the arms of Amsterdam, oval rosettes and bearded face-masks, were moulded directly from contemporary imported Rhenish stoneware *Bartmann* bottles of the mid-to late seventeenth century (fig. 3). Negative moulds must have been made by applying pads of clay to the relief ornament on the stoneware bottles and firing the resulting negative matrices to produce positive reliefs on the earthenware body.[19]

in central London indicates the degree to which the Essex potters were producing for the urban as well as the local market. The London finds led to the term Metropolitan slipware coming into common usage.[14] Many of the trailed-slip motifs, particularly those of a botanical and geometric nature, can be detected on the products of the contemporary North Holland and Werra slipware industries mentioned above.

One characteristic of the Essex products, unparalleled in European slipware of the period, was the use of the trailed-slip technique to introduce texts to the surface of the ware. These messages were trailed in block capitals, usually in the form of popular aphorisms advocating humility before God, the importance of charity to others and fealty to the crown. Although no connection can be demonstrated, pious phrases were first introduced on to utilitarian ceramics in the Rhineland a century earlier, where stoneware potters at Frechen applied bands of text to the waists of their jugs.[15] The most common inscriptions on the Metropolitan slipwares, such as 'Feare God', 'Fast and pray' and 'Be not hy minded but feare God', underline the strong Puritan atmosphere of the period and the penetration of Protestant values into everyday life.[16] Pious inscriptions appear to have declined after the restoration of the monarchy in 1660 in favour of geometric motifs and secular messages including the royalist slogan 'Obeay the King' (fig. 2).[17]

Wrotham slipware

During the middle of the seventeenth century earthenware potters working in Wrotham, Kent, about 40 km (25 miles) south-east of London, chose to emulate their Essex counterparts by introducing ornate slip decoration to their plain red earthenware bodies.[18] This industry, which continued in production until the early eighteenth century, concentrated on hollow wares for drinking, with straight-sided mugs (*tygs*) with four double- or triple-looped

The sgraffito tradition

In the south-west of England, notably in the areas around Barnstaple and Bideford in North Devon and Donyatt in Somerset, a distinctive local slipware tradition was established among local potters by the beginning of the seventeenth century.[20] Pottery production flourished as these ports became the focus of trade across the Irish Sea and Atlantic Ocean during the seventeenth and eighteenth centuries.[21] Characteristic of the tradition was the use of the *sgraffito* technique, which involved incising the design through a surface covering of slip when it was almost dry, revealing the reddish-buff clay body of the vessel beneath (fig. 1c). Imports of Beauvais *sgraffito* slipware excavated both at local markets and on production sites confirm the strong continental influence in ornamental repertoire and technology. Both the French prototypes and the local products were fired twice, a practice rare among contemporary slipware producers; the Werra industry in central Germany and its northern Dutch satellite workshop at Enkhuizen are further exceptions on the Continent.[22] Incised ornament on the

Fig. 4 A North Devon harvest jug dated 1780, trailed in white slip and incised on the front with a double-headed eagle, the sides with flowers in bloom and the reverse with a crowned heart, containing an inscription with the name of the potter and a description of the manufacture of the vessel and its function. John Phillips worked at Bideford, in North Devon, probably during the 1770s to 1780s.

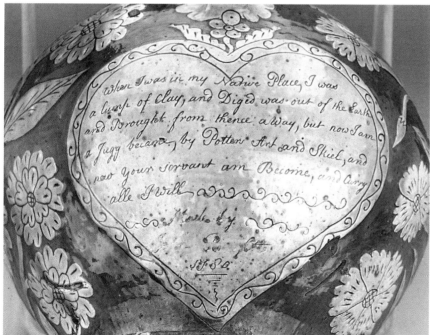

'When I was in my Native Place I was / a lump of Clay, and Diged was out of the Earth / and Bought from thence a Way, but now I am / a Jugg became by Potters Art and Skill, and / now your Servant am Become and carry / Alle I will. / John Ph[illips] Pott. / 1780'.

North Devon and Somerset slipwares took the form of a range of symbolic and popular motifs, including tulips, trefoil-shaped flowers, hearts, sunbursts with face-masks and stylised birds. During the late seventeenth and eighteenth centuries the tradition of *sgraffito*-decorated slipware spread to neighbouring centres such as Bristol and Wales.

South-west *sgraffito* 'harvest jugs', so called because of their association with carrying beer to harvesters working in the fields, were frequently incised with drinking rhymes, dates and names of makers.[23] One such dated example of 1780, signed by the potter John Phillips of Bideford, is now in the British Museum (fig. 4). It is decorated on the front with a double-headed eagle, on the sides with flowers in full bloom and on the reverse with a crowned heart, which contains a rhyme describing the origin of the vessel as a lump of clay in the ground and its prime function as a carrier of ale.

North Staffordshire slipware

Although clear archaeological evidence exists for pottery production in Burslem from the thirteenth century, it was not until the second quarter of the seventeenth century that the local industry embarked on full-scale manufacture of slipware.[24] Robert Plot, in his *Natural History of Staffordshire* of 1686, identified Burslem as the centre of a regional slipware industry spread out among the local villages of Stoke-on-Trent, Hanley, Fenton, Longton and Tunstall. By this date the ready availability of coal and clays had given North Staffordshire the greatest concentration of pottery kilns in the country. With the poor quality of agriculture in the region, the pottery industry became increasingly attractive during the second half of the seventeenth century as a means of alternative employment for small-scale farmers.[25]

The collective archaeological evidence seems to suggest that slip-trailing was well established in North Staffordshire by the middle of the seventeenth century at the latest. The earliest Staffordshire earthenware with trailed-slip decoration has been

Fig. 5 Two slipware dishes trailed in light and dark brown by members of the Toft family, Burslem, Stoke-on-Trent, Staffordshire. Left: dish signed by Ralph Toft with a cavalier, head of King Charles I and the date 1677. Right: dish by Thomas Toft trailed with a portrait bust of King Charles I, final quarter 17th century.

excavated at Eccleshall Castle in a Civil War demolition context of 1646–50. The site produced porringers and cups trailed in two different slip colours.[26] At Woodbank, Burslem, fragments of porringers and cups were found in a context dating to around 1640, trailed with rudimentary interlace and rosette motifs in pale brown slip.[27] Other finds, which can be linked on technological and stylistic grounds to this early phase of production, include a closed group of small hollow-ware wasters in buff- and red-firing bodies with trailed designs in cream and dark and light brown slip, some with gritted surfaces, which were excavated at Newcastle Street, Burslem.[28] In the case of the north Midlands it is not possible to identify a specific trigger for the beginnings of the industry at this time. The argument for any influence from the Continent remains unproven. However, in view of the close technical and stylistic relationship, it is very likely that the Essex Metropolitan slipware industry exerted considerable influence on potters in North Staffordshire, at least by the middle of the seventeenth century. The geometric and botanical designs of slip-trailed dishes of the second half of the century excavated at the Hill Top site, Burslem, and at the Sadler Manufactory site, Stoke-on-Trent, are

perhaps most representative of this connection.[29]

The elaborately decorated trailed-slip dishes produced between the years 1670 and 1730 represent the apex of the Staffordshire industry. The coating of the interior of the vessel with a ground of pale slip and the trailing of slip designs in up to three different colours, often with additional 'jewelling' of tiny dots of cream-coloured slip on to the trailed brown outlines, was a time-consuming exercise and added considerably to the value of the product. The development of multi-coloured slip ornament in addition to press-moulding techniques (see below) was a significant factor in enabling Staffordshire potters to dominate both the regional and national earthenware market for the remainder of the seventeenth and eighteenth centuries. Among the best slip-trailed products are a series of dishes bearing the names of the Tofts, Taylors, Simpsons, Wrights and other local manufacturers. The dated dishes of the Burslem potter Thomas Toft cover the period from 1671 to 1689, with designs including portraits of Charles II, both as monarch and as prince in the oak tree, his queen Catherine of Braganza, cavaliers, Adam and Eve, mermaids, pelicans, eagles, unicorns,

the royal arms and fleurs-de-lis (fig. 5). Further research needs to be done on the relationship between the Staffordshire design repertoire and the painted motifs on contemporary delftware and wriggle-worked images on pewter chargers, as several motifs are duplicated, notably royal portraits and the royal arms.

Close physical analysis of these flanged dishes can reveal details of the manufacturing process and technology. The distortion of the edge and flange profile, the emergency repairs of clay to these weak points and the direction of glaze running across the interior surface indicate conclusively that these dishes were stacked and fired on edge. Perhaps this was thought less risky than stacking the dishes horizontally on top of each other in the kiln. As with the dishes, the seventeenth-century hollow wares were more elaborate in their ornament than later in the eighteenth century. Posset pots and cylindrical handled cups of the final decades of the seventeenth century were often decorated with complex trailed and 'jewelled' slip ornament, rosettes and tulip designs predominating alongside lengthy inscriptions.[30]

From the end of the seventeenth century the quality of trailed-slip decoration declined in favour of zones of 'combed' or 'feathered' slip decoration. This technique involved trailing one or more coloured slips on to a contrasting slip ground and, while the slip was still in a semi-liquid state, drawing a pointed tool across the trailed lines, distorting the pattern into a series of peaks and troughs (fig. 1d).[31] Combing was utilised on a range of hollow and flatware in Staffordshire, including owl-jugs on which the technique was designed to imitate feathers in a naturalistic way. Marbled or 'joggled' ware of the early to mid-eighteenth century, distinguished by marbled zones of contrasting slips across the body, represents a further development of this particular poly-chrome slip technique.[32]

By the late seventeenth century the Staffordshire industry had also introduced a series of press-moulded relief dishes.[33] A small number of domed press-moulds survive, their incised negative designs forming the outlines of the positive relief impression on the finished dish. One such mould, incised on the reverse with the full-length portrait of a man with the initials 'RG', is preserved in the British Museum. The interior side is inscribed 'William Bird made this mould In the year of Our Lord 1751' (fig. 6).[34] These linear relief patterns were usually trailed with slips of a contrasting colour (fig. 1b). A wide range of designs were reproduced in this way; stylised figures, animals and flowers were the most popular subjects. An example in the British Museum, moulded with a version of the royal arms of England, is inscribed on the reverse with the signature of the potter, Stephen Shaw, and the date 1725.[35] Potters such as Samuel Malkin of Burslem (1668?–1741) were responsible for a series of dishes with both popular and religious designs including St George and the dragon, the sun tree, Lot's wife and the 'wee three Logerheads'.[36] The British Museum also possesses a clock-face dish which incorporates in its dial the inscription 'Samuel Malkin/The maker/in bursl/m' and is dated 1722.

Progressively, from the 1720s onwards, the Staffordshire pottery industry converted to the mass-production of fine-bodied wares for a more affluent market (ch. 31). Where slipware was still produced, increasingly simplified combed and slip-trailed designs and moulded techniques predominated. Evidence for the conversion to mass-production for the national pottery market can be traced in the frequency of Staffordshire ceramics found in London contexts from the first quarter of the eighteenth century.[37] However, the continuing demand for traditional slipware products was met by the numerous small-scale industries operating across England by the early eighteenth century. Some, such as the Pennine workshops operating at Burton-in-Lonsdale and Halifax in West Yorkshire, continued in production until the late nineteenth century, servicing rural and industrial town-based populations alike.[38] Irrespective of economic context, slip-decorated earthenware remained in demand long after the Industrial Revolution, particularly where there was strong continuity in the local folk culture.

Fig. 6 Domed ceramic press-mould for a dish, Staffordshire, dated 1751. Carved on the reverse with the full-length portrait of a man and the initials 'RG' (above), and on the interior (right) with the inscription 'William Bird made this mould In the year of Our Lord 1751'.

Urban Pottery Workshops in North Africa

Julie Hudson

In North Africa, a term used here to refer to Egypt, Tunisia and Morocco in particular, two principal pottery-making techniques are employed: coiling and throwing on the wheel.[1] The former is almost invariably practised in rural areas by women, the latter often in urban centres by men and boys employed in workshops. Female potters primarily produce a range of utilitarian wares for their own domestic use, any surplus being sold in the local market.[2] The rural pots are unglazed, porous and decorated with geometric patterns, often recalling those employed on textiles, human bodies or the walls of houses.[3] In contrast, urban ceramics, produced for a wider commercial market, are frequently glazed, kiln-fired and decorated with a range of motifs which combine indigenous designs with those stimulated by external influences. Unglazed vessels are also produced for a local clientele, individual workshops specialising in particular forms.

For centuries writers and travellers have included in their accounts descriptions of the domestic pottery used in towns and have recorded details of the local ceramic industry. In the eleventh century, the geographer and theologian al-Bakri wrote enthusiastic-ally about the ceramics of Tunis, describing 'vases of clay . . . which are used to hold water; they are of a brilliant whiteness and thin to the point of being almost diaphanous. One never finds anything comparable in any other town or region of the country'.[4] The use and display of glazed ceramic tableware became appreciated as a sign of prestige in well-to-do urban dining rooms. During the sixteenth century these vessels were greatly favoured by foreign ambassadors, who took them home as gifts.[5] As recently as the 1930s, the practice of renting glazed plates for special occasions such as marriage, circumcision or religious festivals was popular, indicating the value such vessels were accorded.[6]

Pottery guilds (*ḥanṭa*) flourished in North Africa from the medieval period until the beginning of the twentieth century. The guilds were based on a hierarchical system and governed by strictly enforced rules and codes of professional conduct. The potters' guild became one of the most important in Fes, with members from the same family passing techniques and styles of production down the generations. Today these guilds have been replaced by modern co-operatives or large workshops with paid employees.[7]

Extraction and preparation of clay

The major pottery production sites in North Africa such as Old Cairo (Fustat) in Egypt, Nabeul in Tunisia and Fes in Morocco all exploit local sources of clay. These clay quarries, located on the outskirts of the towns, may be open to anyone or may be privately owned and therefore subject to rent. Casual workers dig out the clay which is then loaded on to flat wooden carts or into panniers carried by donkeys.

Once the rough clay has been deposited on to the courtyard floor, stones and other impurities are removed and the clay lumps are left to dry. The clay is then crushed and emptied into pits filled with water. In Fustat temper is added to this mixture, in the form of Nile silt and pulverised potsherds, to further improve the composition.[8] The clay soaks for several hours or days, after which it is mixed or kneaded and the water allowed to evaporate. The resulting paste is stacked in piles on the workshop floor to dry. On large-scale production sites sophisticated refinement techniques are employed to ensure fine-quality clay. The strenuous physical activity continues: apprentices

Fig. 1 An Egyptian potter in a small family-run workshop in Old Cairo (Fustat) making pots using a foot-operated kickwheel. The potter is throwing 'from the hump', producing a succession of similar vessels from the top of a single cylinder of clay. Further clay cylinders can be seen on the bench in front of him. The neck will be applied once the body of the pot is leather-hard; the foot will be turned on the wheel.

or daily workers knead the clay by hand or tread the clay by foot, repeating the process to eliminate air pockets and distribute the moisture uniformly, thereby increasing the workability of the clay. A period of 'souring' helps to increase the clay's plasticity prior to its use by the potters.

Throwing and forming

Although use of the potter's wheel is prevalent in urban North Africa, the precise form varies widely and is associated with the sophistication of local kiln technology. The foot-operated kickwheel still seen in many traditional workshops (fig. 1) is a solid structure, either set into a pit or raised to the level of the workbench. The wheel comprises a vertical wooden axle, pivoted at the base, with a large heavy flywheel and a smaller wheel-head. The flywheel is operated by foot. Vessels are thrown in succession from the top of a large lump of clay. Upon completion the pots are cut from the still-rotating hump of clay.

Depending on the season it may take several days to complete a vessel, as each stage of production is followed by a period of drying. Many vessels are formed in several parts, with secondary additions such as the neck, foot, handles and spout being applied to leather-hard bodies. Each part may be produced in a single large batch. In the final forming process, excess clay is trimmed from the foot of the vessel using an angled metal tool. Once this turning process is completed, the foot is shaped by hand. The degree of repetition involved in forming pots not only leads to increased technical expertise in the creation of certain parts but boosts daily output, suggesting a degree of mass-production. In Old Cairo a skilled worker can produce up to 1500 pipe nozzles in one day.[9]

Kiln type and firing processes

The archaeological evidence points to an extended history of pottery production in North Africa, and many of the ancient sites have contemporary counterparts. In the area of the 'Amr Mosque in Fustat a settlement of about twenty kilns was described by Ali Bahgat Bey, writing in the fourteenth

Fig. 2   A view of the central door of an updraught kiln in Old Cairo (Fustat). The kiln has been loaded with pottery vessels and is in the final stages of preparation before firing begins. The entrance is filled with damaged plant-pots; it will be completely sealed with mortar made from earth, ash and straw in order to prevent heat loss during the firing process.

century.[10] Today in Old Cairo numerous pottery workshops continue to flourish in the area behind the mosque. Nabeul also retains its position as an important centre for pottery production; remains of kilns dating to the Roman period were discovered at the ancient site of Neapolis, located about 4 km (2 miles) from the modern town of Nabeul.[11]

In urban North Africa pots may be fired twice: initially to biscuit-fire the vessels and a second time to fuse the applied glaze. However, there remains a strong local market for single-fired pots, which are used exclusively for domestic purposes, especially the storage and transportation of water. In recent years the range of these vessels has decreased, with several forms replaced by cheap and durable plastic and metal versions.

Throughout urban North Africa wheel-made pottery is fired in updraught kilns (fig. 2) which vary in their degree of sophistication. Most simply they are domed cylindrical structures divided into two main chambers: the firing chamber, built

level with the ground, and the kiln proper, which may have a separate foyer. The roof of either the firing chamber or the foyer is pierced with holes to allow the homo-geneous diffusion of heat to the kiln above.[12] An embankment of earth and stones is constructed against the walls of the kiln to provide insulation, thereby preventing the sudden reduction of heat after firing. The roof of the kiln is ventilated by means of holes or chimneys. Pots are loaded into the kiln via a central door.

The stacking process is a specialised and time-consuming task. Vessels are carefully packed in neat rows to ensure the even distribution of heat and reduce the risk of breakage. Pots of the same form are stacked together in separate parts of the kiln, occasionally divided from other vessels by brick walls. Sometimes very fragile items will be fired inside larger pots.[13] Once the kiln has been loaded, the chamber door is sealed using a mixture of bricks and potsherds secured with mortar. The kiln

135

temperature is controlled by means of the quantity and type of fuel employed and the blocking and unblocking of doors and vents.

The type of fuel used for firing varies enormously throughout North Africa. The use of good-quality but expensive fuels such as maize stalks, sugar cane or wood must be accurately gauged if the maximum benefit is to be obtained from these precious materials.[14] The firing process takes place over several days, during which the vessels undergo successive stages of heating: an initial pre-heating period is followed by the so-called 'small' fire, which allows any remaining excess water to evaporate before the 'big' fire. The kiln operators carry out tests to confirm the state of the firing process at each stage. The temperature is raised for the big fire by burning fuel with a higher calorific value. Once the appropriate maximum temperature has been attained the vessels are cooked until they whiten. At this stage the fire is allowed to burn down and further doors and chimneys are covered or sealed to ensure that the temperature does not drop too rapidly, which would cause the pots to crack. Over a period of four to eight days (depending on vessel size) the kiln cools, after which individual doors and chimneys are successively unblocked in order to avoid abrupt temperature changes. The unloading of the kiln may take several days, and at this stage damaged or broken pots are discarded.

The second firing takes a similar form to the first, although details of timing and use of fuel may vary. Special devices such as trivets or small pieces of terracotta may be employed to prevent pots from fusing together, which can result in small areas of glaze being removed. The firing process is again monitored by a specialist worker.

In Nabeul potters continue to use traditional updraught kilns to biscuit-fire their vessels. Increasingly, however, glazed pots are fired in electric or gas kilns.[15]

Decoration

A limited number of domestic vessels may be decorated immediately after the first firing and remain unglazed (fig. 4). Locally recognised and appreciated factors, such as the enhanced flavour of foodstuffs and liquids when cooked or stored in pottery vessels, encourage the continued production of such items. In Fes today biscuit-fired, lightweight white vessels are decorated with qutrān, the resin of the thuya tree, which is boiled to form a viscous liquid.[16] The potter or vendor dips his finger into this liquid and, rotating the vessel in one hand, dabs the black resin on to the pot to form geometric patterns. The tar imparts a distinctive taste to the stored water, and once the water loses this taste the pot is discarded and replaced by a freshly decorated one. Qutrān is also used for medicinal and protective purposes; belief in its wider beneficial properties may further explain its continued usage in the decoration of domestic pots.[17]

Four main types of glazed decoration are used in Tunisia and Morocco: monochrome, bichrome, blue-and-white and polychrome. Monochrome glazes are frequently applied to traditional forms such as the pitcher (ghorraf). Green, derived from copper oxide, is seen most often; older examples are emerald-green, while more recent vessels take on a bottle-green hue. Bichrome-decorated ware occurs in parts of Tunisia and Morocco. White and green ornamented dishes and plates may be seen in southern parts of Morocco. In Nabeul the half-green, half-yellow forms remain popular and distinctive.[18]

One of the most widely recognised decorative forms associated with ceramic production in Fes is the use of the colour blue (cobalt oxide) on a tin-opacified white glaze (fig. 5). Some of the finest examples date from the seventeenth century. Over a period of three to four centuries the decorative repertoire was expanded and developed, and innovative motifs stimulated by external influences were incorporated into a well-established decorative tradition. Within this rigidly observed system, controlled by the potters' guilds, foreign designs were assimilated but never totally obscured traditional Moroccan ceramic design.

Urban North African pottery is notable for its elaborately decorated polychrome glazed wares. These fall into two categories: those with painted

---

The use of salt in pottery-making

Salt is widely used in North Africa to modify the behaviour of clays with a high calcite (calcium carbonate, $CaCO_3$) content. Calcite decomposes to calcium oxide at temperatures in excess of about 750°C, evolving carbon dioxide gas. After the vessels are cooled, the calcium oxide absorbs moisture from the air, forming calcium hydroxide. This involves an increase in volume which causes the surface of the pot to flake off, a phenomenon known as spalling or 'lime-blowing'. The addition of salt to the clay before firing greatly reduces the spalling effect.[25]

The addition of salt can also cause the migration of calcium to the pot surface, forming a white-firing skin. The body of the pot also fires to a lighter colour, often close to white. This is due to the incorporation of the iron in the clay into calcium silicates when the vessel is fired, rather than allowing it to form red iron oxide. Throughout North Africa there is a strong preference for whitened domestic vessels, especially those used for water storage. It was noted in Fes at the beginning of this century that cooking salt or, in the case of large vessels, salt water, was added to the clay to render it white. The potters believe that whitened clay is more porous than red and thus more suitable for the manufacture of water vessels.[26] Evidence for the use of salt in this way has been reported in North African pottery from the Roman period.[27] In some societies, the salt is added by the use of sea water to work the clay.[28]

Salt is also employed at the glazing stage, either immediately after application of the tin oxide glaze or once the painted decoration has been completed. The fired vessels are then plunged into a bath of salt water.[29]

Fig. 3 (Opposite) An elaborate pottery vessel from the Serghini workshop in Safi, Morocco. This family of master-potters specialises in producing high-quality glazed vessels with an emphasis on the innovative use of colour. Serghini's 'old rose' became his individual trademark. The use of inscriptions on pots remains rare due to the fear of inaccurate copying or inappropriate placement, for many North African potters are illiterate.

Fig. 4 A traditional unglazed, wheel-made water jar from Nabeul, Tunisia. Vessels for the storage or transportation of water are notable for their persistence of form. Their practicality in terms of handling and their inherent refrigeration properties, in addition to their elegant shape, have ensured their continued production throughout North Africa.

Fig. 5 (Below)
A 19th-century glazed plate from Fes, Morocco. The white (tin-opacified) glaze is applied to biscuit-fired vessels and the blue (cobalt oxide) glaze painted on top. The bold central design is a form of the seal of Solomon motif, which is usually in the form of an eight-pointed star; in this example the star has twelve points. The glaze is missing in three places on the surface of the plate, indicating the position of the tripod support in the kiln.

underglaze decoration and the majority which have designs applied over the glaze. In Morocco vessels in the first group are known as *baldi* (local) and their production is now restricted to a couple of forms associated with ritual usage. The *ta'rīja* (drum) is used at the 'Āshurā' festival'; Boukobza describes the drum as 'a symbol of the earth and the river, because it is made of clay; of ritual sacrifice, because it is covered by a membrane of sheep's skin'.[19] Special bowls (*zlāfa*) are produced as the month of Ramadan nears; both forms are decorated with simple geometric and floral designs over which is applied a clear lead glaze.

The second and most diverse category draws on a long history of production, reintroduction, modification and diversification in the Maghreb. From the tenth until the end of the nineteenth century, glazed ceramics were produced in a potters' quarter on the outskirts of Tunis known as al-Qallaline. Modern potters continue to draw inspiration from these long-established forms, producing ceramics decorated in yellow, brown and green, a combination favoured at al-Qallaline.

The influx of Andalusian refugees (many of whom were artisans) to the towns of Morocco and Tunisia during the sixteenth century introduced a range of new decorative motifs and glaze techniques to the Maghreb. The Ottoman Turks introduced their own decorative traditions, notably floral motifs such as the carnation and tulip. Further designs such as the seal of Solomon, paisley patterns and architectural features can be linked in their inspiration to prevailing external influences.

Today polychrome ceramics from both traditionally run workshops and modern co-operatives are marketed throughout the region and exported abroad (fig. 6). Alongside well-established forms, innovations such as plant-pots and egg-cups have been incorporated to accommodate the demands of the tourist trade and foreign export market.

An interesting additional painted embellishment, first noted by writers during the nineteenth century, is still executed by pot vendors in Moroccan towns. Dots of red lead paint are applied

Fig. 6 A technician employed in a government co-operative in Fes, Morocco, using a turntable to support the biscuit-fired vessel he is painting. Unlike traditional methods of applying painted decoration, in which fingerprints are left on the previously applied glaze, this 'scientific' approach avoids such cosmetic 'flaws'.

by finger to polychrome vessels; the possible motivation for this process has generated numerous interpretations. At the end of the nineteenth century a French traveller, Marius Bernard, described pots in Fes with red paint dots which he noted were designed to conceal faults.[20] Another theory suggests that the red dots were applied by wealthy and successful merchants as a prophylactic device to counteract the fear of envy.[21] It is also possible that the dots were designed to protect the contents of the jars (as they usually appear on the exteriors of containers).

The symbolism of pots

Pottery vessels continue to play a prominent role in certain ceremonies in North Africa: significant life-cycle events such as birth, marriage and death may be marked by the creation of ceramic vessels. In Egypt *al-sebū'*, the seventh day following the birth of a child, is celebrated by a birth ritual

involving the use of a gender-specific pottery vessel. A water pot is made for a female child and a pitcher for a boy; both types are supplied with seven spouts for candles. These distinctive vessels are produced in Fustat, but decorated in the Cairo suburb of al-Ghouriyya. They are used in rural and urban homes and by all social classes. The ceremony marks the transition of the new-born infant from a neutral state into the gendered community.[22]

The *methred* (footed plate or dish) is used in both rural and urban homes in the Maghreb to serve couscous or pastries. It has a symbolic role during Tunisian wedding celebrations. The bride is presented with a *methred* filled with food on the first and second days after marriage and greeted with cries of good luck from her friends. On the third day, after the marriage has been con-summated, the bride's mother brings a *methred* piled high with mutton stew and a mixture of dried nuts and fruit to wish her good luck in her new home and to encourage sweetness towards her husband. Finally, on the seventh day, a further *methred* is brought to her home filled with cakes.[23] The concept of gift-giving at marriage is associated with the creation of new bonds of affection and family obligation.

Pottery vessels filled with water are used in parts of Tunisia and Egypt to observe a death in the family. In Egypt, specially made pots are placed on graves and filled with water each week. It is believed that the soul of the deceased in the form of a bird may visit the tomb; the water is provided to quench its thirst.[24]

Sale of pots

Most urban centres have a large market (*sūq*) which was traditionally divided into quarters arranged according to craft specialisation; both Tunis and Cairo retain pottery markets. Domestic vessels are sold in these centres: pots may be traded in exchange for food-stuffs or other domestic necessities. Some of the innovative glazed vessels produced in modern workshops (fig. 3) have attracted a large export market, which has seen a considerable expansion in recent years, and have also found popularity with the burgeoning tourist trade; government co-operatives and shops often display and sell these 'artistic' ceramics.

North African glazes

North African potters use glazes based upon the use of lead as a flux, derived from the same tradition as Islamic lustreware glazes (ch. 16), maiolica (ch. 17) and medieval glazed wares (ch. 13). Clear lead glaze is applied to a range of ceramic vessels and tiles, and metallic oxides such as copper are frequently added as colourants. The raw lead glaze mixture (lead oxide plus silica) may be pulverised and applied directly to the pottery vessels; however, it has long been recognised that this glaze can be toxic in application as well as in use, as the unbound lead is readily absorbed. In Tunisia, a son of the renowned potter Jacob Chemla died as a result of the absorption of lead oxide.[30] Therefore the glazes are fritted (fused) and then ground before application. Opaque white glazes are produced by the addition of up to about 10% of tin oxide to the glaze, in the same way as for maiolica and lustreware. The white tin glaze produces an ideal ground for painted decoration and is used extensively in Tunisia and Morocco.

Traditional Rural Potting in West Africa

Nigel Barley

The Dowayos are a Cameroonian montagnard people, numbering some 15,000, who live in Poli prefecture of the Republic of Cameroon and share many features with other West African potters. The place of pottery in African life is undergoing rapid change. In the 1970s, pottery was universally used, except – ironically – by potters, who alone had enough cash to buy imported Chinese enamelware. Nigerian aluminium and enamel basins have since made great inroads into everyday Dowayo cooking, but the vessels used in rituals must still be made of pottery. This has important symbolic as well as economic and technical repercussions, in that everyday and ceremonial activities have been separated in a new way. Meanwhile, in African cities, imported tableware and electric rice-cookers have reduced the use of traditional pottery except among a

small, self-conscious élite, who have rediscovered it for highly formal occasions when statements of identity may be involved. Also, new forms have had to be invented for new uses – a lively volume could be written simply on the invention of the African ashtray. No single model captures the vacillating situation of contemporary pottery in Africa, where in some cultural and geographical areas its use is advancing, in others retreating.

Division of labour

The making of pots in Africa is an activity structured, above all, by gender. The vast majority of pots are made by the skilled hands of women using only the simplest of tools: pebbles, leaves, shells and corncobs.[1] Often production is by a special group restricted to marrying among them-

selves. In West Africa such a potting group is commonly associated with 'pollution' through food, water and sex. A long-running debate is whether or not it is legitimate to call such African groups 'castes'.[2]

The classic form of the division of labour, as found among many North Cameroonian montagnards, is that the potter is also the midwife and her husband is the blacksmith who is also the undertaker. But the term 'blacksmith', too, is more than a little slippery. Often he is also the tailor and circumciser, hairdresser and car mechanic. The core of his identity is a mastery over metal, its transformation and use, just as the potter's identity centres on the transformation of clay. Such powers of transformation are intimately associated with the ritual importance of the potter/smith.[3] In West Africa it makes no sense to try to

Fig. 1 Pots for sauce.

Fig. 2 Pot-lid.

distinguish symbolism from technology, since what Westerners see as two different forms of knowledge here share a common structure.

In the North Cameroonian Dowayo village in which I worked, potting was carried out by a single family of potter/smiths consisting of blacksmith husband, two wives, a daughter and a son. The son was expected to train as a smith, making and repairing hoes, knives and arrow-heads. During forging, he normally worked the bellows for his father. Smith/potters were expressly forbidden to touch the normal dead, as they were 'unclean', but would be allocated the sex organs and other 'polluted' and inedible parts of dead animals as food. Their compound was separated from that of 'normal' people by a stretch of bush that went uncleared even at the height of the dry season, when other areas were stripped bare to lessen the risk to the village of fire.

The wives, who were married in from nearby potter/smith families, produced, fired and sold pottery together. Among Dowayos, all stages of a pot would usually be made by one woman, though sometimes a young girl would be asked to perform less skilful tasks such as adding handles to pot-lids or burnishing all sun-dried pots by rubbing them with peanut oil before firing.

Production and sale

Pottery was exclusively a dry-season activity, permitted only after the public inauguration of that part of the year by the rain-chief, who fired the grass on the top of his mountain (*Waaduufi*, 'Boy's Head') and so dried the pots and stones that controlled the rain. This was also the day on which boys returned from the bush and their heads were 'fired' by piling branches over them and setting them alight. Previously, they had been 'wet and smelly' boys. Now they were dry, circumcised men. Any potter who ignored this temporal rule risked mixing the wet and dry seasons

together and so causing droughts or floods.

Pots were made from local clay, which was dug and transported by the women and then crushed and mixed with a grog of ground potsherds. Pots were formed by pulling or coiling or a mixture of both (fig. 1). There seemed to be great indifference to the actual techniques used in different potting households, which became mixed by intermarriage. The repertoire of pot types was limited.

Most abundant was a small, semi-spherical bowl (fig. 1) standing on five round ball feet, used to hold sauce which complemented the millet paste served in a calabash at all meals. A variant stood on a single pedestal foot (fig. 2). Two different sizes of bellied cooking vessels were made which could be set directly on the three-stone hearth. A concave lid, with handle, conveniently fitted both sizes. Most expensive, and less in demand, was a version of the classic West African water-jar, a spherical, long-necked vessel with incised and rouletted

Fig. 3 Water-jar.

Fig. 4 Dowayo potter at work.

decoration (fig. 3). All such pots would be made speculatively and sold directly, either in the village or at the nearby market. Occasionally, special pots would be made to order. One was a cooking pot with three in-built legs which must be used by a man when engaged in the (female) task of cooking, since he cannot use a (female) hearth. Such pots were regarded as inherently humorous artefacts with more than a whiff of gender-bending about them. Also made to order were the lumpy pots used to substitute for the skulls of dead rain-chiefs, whose heads (unlike those of ordinary Dowayos) cannot be removed for ancestral rites.

Demand always seemed to exceed supply. While some people paid in cash, within the village this was felt to be a violation of neighbourhood values. Appeal would be made to services performed for the potter/smith in the past by herders or hunters, since the former cannot easily deal with animals because their 'hot hands' would kill off any animal they touched. If all else failed, payment for a pot could usually be agreed by offering the amount of millet that would fill it.

Firing techniques

Firing was by a simple 'bonfire' technique which produced a very quick low-temperature bake and was notably unsuccessful (fig. 5). Shifting evening winds led to sudden rapid heating and cooling of different parts of the firing pots so that they burst. Local explanations centred on the witchcraft of jealous potters in neighbouring villages. Strikingly, potters refused to countenance using the semi-kiln firing techniques they described to me as being used by a neighbouring people, on the grounds that this would be *berge*, 'bad', 'not good'. For Dowayos, firing of pots – like cooking – must be done in the open. It is a hazardous proceeding and results in an ash that constitutes a mortal danger to all but smith/potters.

Pots are normally red but can be transformed by rolling them, while still hot, in leaves, thereby creating a reducing atmosphere and so turning them black. As elsewhere, containers classify relationships, contents and events. For example, widows eat from blackened pots and other people from red; water is drunk only from a calabash; and at death festivals the neck of a water-jar must be wrapped with rope.

Symbolism and representation

It is impossible to understand the technology of Dowayo potting without appreciating the wider framework within which it is set. Fundamental is the opposition between the rain-chief and the smith/potter, who must never meet. Both would die, the rain-chief from a dry cough, the smith/potter from excessive body fluids. Similarly, potters must never drink while their pots are firing. Since the rain-chief needs special pots for control of the rain and ancestral cults, these are prepared in the shelter where dead men's bodies are stored by a very old (female) potter wearing male dress and conveyed up the mountain, on a moonless night, by a ritual clown. Only thus can the two poles of the system be brought together.

The potter herself is mistress of childbirth and – as elsewhere in Africa – potting provides a model by which childbirth can be understood. Children are seen as red, wet and endangered. Little boys, especially, are prone to fevers until circumcised and 'fired' like

pottery as they return to the village. At death, a pot is broken over the corpse and a woman's spirit takes up residence in her water-jar. Ancestral rites involve dancing with men's skulls and women's jars (fig. 6). Those in mourning are marked by shaving into their heads the patterns ('scars' in Dowayo) that are cut into a water-jar.

The association between childbirth and female potting powers is something of a pan-African theme which appears in a number of different forms. It has been confused by the ways in which European preconceptions have structured the representation of African potters. First, there has been the

assumption, drawing upon Western folklore, that it is the blacksmith who is the ultimate source of ritual power. The potter is mentioned only in a wifely capacity in the footnotes of studies of African metallurgy. This is part of a long-standing tendency of Western archaeology to classify cultural development in terms of heroic metallurgical ages (of bronze, iron, etc) that lead to success through male warfare, while pots are passive, lesser markers of domestic culture – as, indeed, women themselves have been portrayed.

Second, there is a crucial lack of fit between African and Western gender systems at the highest level. A basic

Fig. 5 Firing of pots.

Fig. 6 Women summoning the spirit of a dead woman to her water-jar.

distinction is made in many parts of Africa between reproductive and post-menopausal women, so that older women take on many of the attributes of malehood. So Benin Queen Mothers, the epitome of successful womanhood, are classed as 'male' and are the only royal women who may be touched by male servants. Among potters, this distinction often means that young women must not make human or animal images that would compromise their fertility, but old women – or any man – may do so. In the Dowayo case this is inverted, in that young uncircumcised men are classed with women and the only maker of human images is the – preferably fertile –

blacksmith who carves the wooden dolls that cure female sterility.

In such a situation, the bland assumption of Western archaeology of a universal gender classification based on the 'facts' of biology becomes a hindrance even to the simple matter of correlating forms of funerals with sex. Young men are buried as 'women', old women are buried as 'men', and too many people end up in the wrong columns to make even approximate sense. Finally, both men and women of all ages are associated with broken pottery, since the human life-cycle is equated with that of a pot.

Pottery in Early Anglo-Saxon England

Cathy Haith

Following the withdrawal of the Romans in the early fifth century AD, England was settled by Anglo-Saxons, who were a mixture of Germanic peoples, principally from southern Scandinavia and north-western Germany. Over the next 250 years, from about AD 400 to 650, an essentially rural society developed which was very different from the sophisticated urban economy of Roman Britain. Although they were skilled metalworkers, the Anglo-Saxons did not continue the ceramic traditions of their Roman predecessors, and the production of pottery reverted to locally produced, handmade wares of limited forms and styles.

The pottery of this period can be divided into material from settlement sites, which is usually little more than fragmentary occupation debris,[1] and that found in cemeteries, where complete vessels were used as containers for cremations (fig. 1) or as accessory vessels (fig. 2) accompanying inhumations.[2] The bulk of the material comes from the large burial grounds of eastern England such as the mixed-rite cemetery of Spong Hill in Norfolk (fig. 4), where it is estimated that there were originally over 2700 cremations.[3] Areas such as southern England, where inhumation was preferred, have notably fewer examples.

Cremation urns were first recorded in England in the seventeenth century, but it was not until the late 1930s that any significant advance was made in the study of early Anglo-Saxon ceramics, eventually culminating in the late 1970s in the publication of Myres' *Corpus of Pagan Anglo-Saxon Pottery*,[4] a vast work which catalogues 3470 pots from 341 sites and lists the products of 157 so-called potter's workshops. His aim was to illuminate 'the origin and distribution of the settlers, their relationship to the existing population, their social and economic development, and their notions of religion and of decorative art'.[5]

Viewed in this light, his work might best be described as an heroic failure. It has been extensively criticised on a number of grounds,[6] the major drawback being its inherent bias towards the cemetery material. However, Anglo-Saxon settlements only began to be excavated in any significant numbers in the late 1960s, and there are still disappointingly few examples of sites where both a cemetery and an associated settlement have been located, which would enable us to compare and contrast their ceramic assemblages.[7]

Raw materials: forming

Although it is not uncommon to find a number of different fabrics at a single site, the vast majority of early Anglo-Saxon pots appear to have been manufactured from local clays.[8] Before it can be shaped to make a pot, natural clay often needs to be modified by the addition of temper, which allows it to withstand the stresses of firing, improves its plasticity, reduces shrinkage and increases its porosity. Anglo-Saxon potters employed three types of temper: naturally occurring minerals such as limestone, shell, flint or sandstone; processed mineral temper such as grog or crushed fired clay; and organic ('vegetal') temper such as chopped plant material, chaff or dung.

Fig. 1 Cremation urns. Left to right: biconical urn from North Elmham (Norfolk), with slashed vertical and round bosses and stamped swastika motifs; narrow-mouthed urn from Sandy (Bedfordshire), with raised collars, bosses and arched slashed cables; globular urn from Kempston (Beds), with horizontal bands of stamping including wyrm motifs.

Fig. 2 Accessory vessels. Left to right: from Grave 57, Long Wittenham (Berkshire), with linear, bossed and stamped ornament; from Grave 121, Great Chesterford (Essex), containing eggs; from East Shefford (Berks), with foot-ring base, stamped ornament and slashed chevron bosses; from Grave 11, Howletts (Kent), with a row of stamps on the carination.

The proportion of vegetal-tempered pottery appears to increase during the sixth and seventh centuries,[9] after which organic material is replaced by mineral tempers in the middle Saxon period with the advent of mass-produced wheel-thrown pottery such as Ipswich ware.[10]

All early Anglo-Saxon pots were handmade, either by coiling and drawing or by pinching.[11] Evidence of coiling can be recognised by obliquely streaked lines within the clay matrix. At Spong Hill most of the pots from the cemetery appear to be coiled, while the domestic pottery was slab-built or drawn.[12] After being dried to leather-hardness, the pots were decorated prior to firing. Experimental firing of 'Anglo-Saxon' pottery, based on vessels from the cemetery at Baginton in Warwickshire, involved drying the pots for a period of five days.[13]

Surface treatment and decoration

The surface treatment of early Anglo-Saxon ceramics appears to have been functional as well as decorative. It was limited to smoothing the clay with the fingers; wiping it with a coarse textile or with grass, which results in a scratched surface; combing; or scraping or trimming with a knife. Burnishing –

rubbing with a hard smooth object such as a pebble – added lustre and had the additional advantage of compacting the clay and strengthening the vessel. Pots were often burnished on the inner as well as the outer surface, which would have reduced the loss of fluid through the walls. Deliberate roughening or rustication (pinching the clay between thumb and finger), or adding a slip containing coarse grits (known as *Schlickung*, from the German word for mud), were also employed, especially on the lower portion of larger vessels, which would have facilitated handling and reduced thermal shock.[14]

The decoration on Anglo-Saxon pots can be divided into three main elements: linear, plastic and stamped. These occur separately or combined in various decorative schemes. All three are found throughout the period of settlement, but there is a change of character and emphasis in the use of each as time passes.[15]

In the earlier fifth century, simple linear forms, raised cordons and facetting predominate.[16] Pots tend to be decorated with grooves in horizontal chevron patterns or arches, together with finger-tipping and dots and the restrained use of bosses. Later, bosses become more prominent, culminating in the so-called *Buckelurnen* or bossed

pots of the late fifth century, which also sees the beginnings of stamped ornament, at first combined with the use of shoulder bosses and linear ornament but later becoming more elaborate and the dominant decorative element. Spong Hill has early pots, ornamented with simple linear decoration and bosses, near the centre of the cemetery, and more elaborate stamped vessels dating to the sixth century around the periphery, a chronological shift confirmed by the dating of associated brooches.[17] In contrast, the pottery of the seventh century tends to be plainer and simpler, with the use of such techniques as comb-point impressions.

Linear tooling, such as making grooves around the neck of a vessel, was probably done with a bone point. Plastic ornament involved creating bosses by pushing out the wall of the pot, or applying a separate solid boss and luting it to the surface. Dimples and facets were formed by pushing the clay inwards, the latter most commonly found on sharply carinated bowls.

The stamped ornament on early Anglo-Saxon pottery consists mainly of small geometric motifs such as circles, crosses, rectangles, ovals, chevrons and triangles, diamonds, crescents, horse-shoes, S-shaped or *wyrm* motifs and swastikas, with a wide variety of designs in each category.[18] Up to eleven different stamps have been recorded on a single pot.[19] It has been suggested that the stamps were not merely decorative but had a heraldic or totemic significance and were used to define kinship groups,[20] but this would imply that they were made to order, which does not seem to be the case. Other rarer stamps include animals,[21] motifs such as the *planta pedis* in the form of a human foot, and runic stamps bearing the name of the god TIW. Runes drawn freehand also occasionally occur, as do animals and swastikas, but these form a very specialised group.[22]

Stamped ornament was produced by pressing a carved die into the surface of the clay after the vessel had been dried prior to firing. A number of dies are known from early Anglo-Saxon contexts.[23] None of the dies can be directly linked to stamped pottery found on any of the sites, although generally there are problems in doing so on account of the differential shrinkage of stamped impressions during the drying

and firing process. Antler appears to have been the favoured material; it is particularly suitable for the manufacture of dies, as the design can be cut into the compact tissue at the tip of the tine.[24] Modern experiments have been carried out with various other materials such as bone, wood and chalk, but results were inconclusive as they soon clogged and did not seem capable of producing the number of impressions found on some vessels (often up to 200–300 stamps) without extensive cleaning and/or recutting.[25] It has been suggested that ceramic or metal dies were employed, but the only known Anglo-Saxon examples of metal dies[26] appear far more suitable for decorating leather.

As well as manufactured dies, Anglo-Saxon potters also used a variety of impromptu tools to decorate their pots, including the bones of birds and small mammals. A cremation urn from Lackford in Suffolk bears a row of stamped impressions made by a horse's tooth.[27] Everyday objects were also utilised: some pots are decorated with

comb-teeth impressions, others have stamps created by pressing the feet and knobs or pin-springs of cruciform brooches into the clay.[28]

It is difficult to quantify accurately the percentage of settlement pottery that was decorated, as complete pots rarely survive.[29] In a study of 2440 cremation urns from eighteen different cemeteries,[30] almost 80% were decorated; 75% had some form of incised decoration, 40% had stamped ornament, and 30% had some type of plastic decoration. The incised and plastic decoration showed a high degree of conformity between sites, suggesting that potters were working within similar cultural frameworks, but stamped ornament showed more regional variation.

Firing

Early Anglo-Saxon pots were fired at fairly low temperatures in little more than bonfires over stacks of pots. A shallow hollow would have reduced the amount of fuel required.[31] Examination

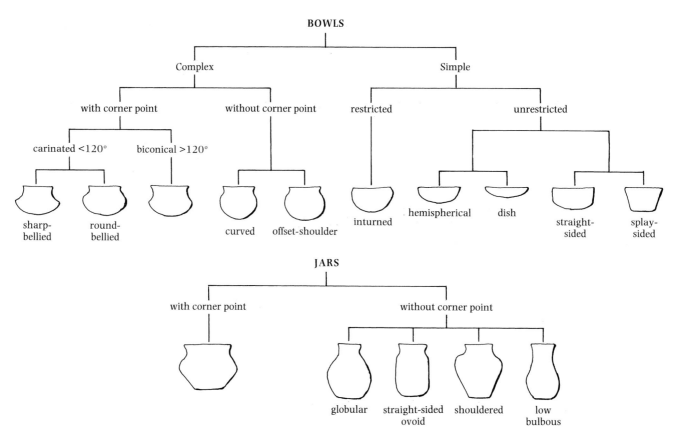

Fig. 3 Dendrogram of basic Anglo-Saxon pottery forms, based on the material from the settlement site at Mucking in Essex.

*Fig. 4
Cremation
urns from the
mixed-rite
cemetery at
Spong Hill in
Norfolk,
during
excavation.*

of thin sections of 471 urns from Spong Hill suggested a firing temperature below 850°C, and possibly well below, i.e. between 500 and 750°C.[32]

Virtually all Anglo-Saxon ceramics have a reduced core and inner surface, as oxidising gases rarely reached the inside of vessels. Their surface colour varies from black (which is most common) through to brown, buff, pink and grey to deep reddish-brown, the differences being mainly due to the initial choice of clay and temper, uneven firing, porosity, the subsequent use of the vessel and post-depositional changes.

Form and function

The range of forms found in early Anglo-Saxon pottery is fairly limited (figs 3, 5). Some pots have pedestal bases or foot-rings and separate lids are also found, although they only survive in relatively limited numbers, being particularly susceptible to plough

damage.[33] Small plates also occur; those found at Mucking ranged in diameter from 18.3 to 21.6 cm (7.2–8.5 in).[34] Richards' study of cremation urns gave an average height of about 19.5 cm (7.75 in), but examples are known as short as 8 cm (3 in), or as tall as 28 cm (11 in). At Spong Hill, the mean volume of vessels was 4430 cm^3 (72,563 in^3); at Mucking the figure was 2557 cm^3 (41,884 in^3).[35]

Little work has been done on the functions of early Anglo-Saxon pottery, apart from the use of cremation urns.[36] Obviously the main uses are likely to have been storage, cooking and food consumption. Some vessels have lugs (fig. 5) for suspension by a cord or thong. There are a few examples of pots intended for specialised use. A mammi-form pot found at Castledyke, South Humberside, has been identified as a feeding bottle,[37] and perforated vessels from a number of sites, previously identified as wool-comb warmers, are now thought more likely to have been

used in food preparation, such as making cheese.[38] Metal mounts and rims, and the small copper-alloy repair-clips found in many Anglo-Saxon graves, are a salutary reminder that many vessels in this period were probably made of wood; the use of other organic materials such as horn is also recorded, so the surviving pottery does not represent the full range of domestic vessels used by the early Anglo-Saxons.

Evidence for pottery manufacture

In striking contrast to the earlier Roman and later Saxon and medieval periods, very little tangible evidence survives for the production of pottery in early Anglo-Saxon England. At Sutton Courtenay in Berkshire, a house was identified as a 'potter's workshop' on the basis of a mass of clay 45 cm (17.7 in) thick, the base of which was confined within a 'rude basket-like pen' which was interpreted as a puddling-hole.[39]

Fig. 5 Rusticated and combed sherds, suspension lugs from cooking vessels, the perforated base from a strainer and a dimpled cooking plate, from the settlement site at Mucking (Essex).

A probable firing area on a settlement site near Pakenham, in Suffolk, was in the form of two circular hearths lined with gravel, and contained partly baked sherds similar to clay deposits found within 100 m (300 ft) of the site.[40]

A clay reserve 5–10 cm (2–4 in) thick, on the eastern edge of the Anglo-Saxon village of West Stow, also in Suffolk, was surrounded by a ditched enclosure measuring 7.6 x 8.5 m (23 x 25.5 ft).[41] As well as pot dies, the

site also produced a pottery trial-piece which suggests that pottery was manufactured there, but there were no kilns, firing-places, or wasters. The distinct absence of such features on early Anglo-Saxon sites would seem to reinforce the hypothesis that most pottery was produced on a domestic scale in simple clamp-kilns, which would leave no discernible trace.

Organisation of production

Archaeologists are divided in their views as to whether there was any kind of specialist pottery production in early Anglo-Saxon England. Although Myres saw it purely as a domestic activity, he

identified individual potters and 'work-shops' (which might include as few as two vessels) on the basis of pots bearing identical stamps. Detailed examination of these workshops has produced varying conclusions. For example, petrological analysis of the pots of the so-called 'Sancton-Baston' potter,[42] which occur over an area from the Yorkshire Wolds south-east to Norfolk, suggests that the clays from which the pots were made were mostly characteristic of and specific to the site. Production by a commercial potter or centralised workshop is unlikely. On the other hand, five out of twenty different clay types attributed to the so-called Illington-Lackford 'workshop' on the

Reduced or black cores

Unprocessed clays commonly contain abundant carbon, derived from plant matter. When first heated in air the organic matter in the clay chars, and the body of the pot will appear black. With time, however, the carbon is burnt out of the clay and the surface of the pot lightens. A core of unburnt carbon remains, which is progressively burnt out as the pot is fired. The diagram shows the effects of heating two clays, one coarse and one fine, at 600°C.[49] The black core is burnt out of the coarse, sandy clay after 20–25 minutes, but remains in the fine body after 30 minutes. The presence of extensive black cores in Anglo-Saxon pottery, which is generally made from well-tempered (coarse) clay, suggests that firings were of a short duration; such firings are likely to have been in open fires rather than kilns.

It might be tempting to see this as a means whereby the duration of firing could be estimated from the thickness of the carbon core remaining in the pottery. However, there is a limitation in that, in order to burn out the carbon, firing conditions must be oxidising. Many pottery firings enter a reducing phase at an early stage, during which the carbon does not burn out. What the size of the carbon core is therefore recording is the relative length of the later, oxidising stage of the firing, when the fuel has burned down. Thus it provides useful supporting evidence for generalisations about firing type, but does not reliably indicate the overall length of firing.

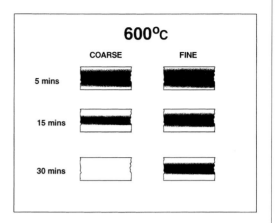

Norfolk-Suffolk border (fig. 6) appear on more than one site and identical stamps appear on widely dispersed vessels, suggesting some form of exchange or small-scale trade.[43]

Analysis of pottery from both settlement and cemetery sites has suggested that there is little intrinsic difference between them, rendering unlikely earlier suggestions that the production of funerary pottery was a more specialised task than the production of domestic wares carried out within the family.[44] A recent model suggests that the majority of both domestic and funerary pottery was produced by individual households for their own consumption. Later, in the sixth century, there is growing evidence for trade or exchange with growing craft specialisation,[45] culminating in the mass-production of pottery by full-time specialists centralised in an urban context – in this case, the production of Ipswich ware in the seventh century.

Further support for the notion that there was some degree of 'traded' pottery in early Anglo-Saxon England comes from recent research into a widely distributed, well-made, coarse domestic ware with a distinct 'granitic' fabric, found mostly in the Midlands but also as far south as London and as far north as Sancton, on Humberside.[46] The source for this distinctively tempered pottery has yet to be closely fixed, although it has been tentatively identified as originating from the Charnwood Forest area of Leicestershire.[47]

The study of early Anglo-Saxon pottery has advanced considerably since the publication of Myres' *Corpus*, but much work remains to be done.[48] Different approaches have stimulated a number of questions but provided few definite answers. Given the nature of early Anglo-Saxon pottery, this is perhaps unsurprising. Close dating remains problematic, and although there is a growing body of fabric analyses from individual sites, detailed regional surveys are still lacking.

Fig. 6 Distribution of pottery from the Illington-Lackford workshop in East Anglia.

Early Iron Age Rural Ceramic Traditions in Iran

St John Simpson

The physical geography of Iran is characterised by a high plateau with inhospitable central salt deserts ringed by mountain chains, valleys and plains. This topography strongly influenced the formation and development of distinct regional cultures from the neolithic onwards (fig. 1). The beginning of the Iron Age in the second millennium BC was marked by the appearance of new styles of architecture, burial customs, metalwork and greyware ceramics. These changes have been assumed to represent the effects of invasions by Indo-European peoples moving westwards from beyond the Caspian Sea, where an Eastern Grey Ware ceramic tradition

existed during the Bronze Age. However, this equation of pots with peoples should be treated with caution, as there was a great variety of different cultures, including non-Indo-Europeans, in the Zagros region, and the problem is compounded by the scarcity of absolute dates or reliable stratigraphic sequences.[1]

Broadly, the Iron Age of Iran can be divided into four phases (Iron I–IV). Within Iron I (*c*.1400/1200–1000 BC) and Iron II (*c*.1000–800 BC), there appears to have been a patchwork of overlapping regional traditions of folk art, suggestive of different tribal groupings. There is, furthermore, a strong impression that the mode of

production was small-scale and centred on individual households and rural village workshops. The subsequent Iron III (800–600 BC) and Iron IV (600–300 BC) phases, broadly corresponding to the Median and Achaemenid periods, are characterised by a greater degree of ceramic homogeneity across western and southern Iran. This is presumed to reflect the gradually increased centralisation of political power and wider diffusion of vessel styles inspired by cheap copies of Achaemenid 'court style' luxury wares.[2]

The Amlash culture

The so-called Amlash culture of Gilan province in north-west Iran was one of the most distinctive of the Iron Age Iranian cultures. This region consists of semi-tropical lowlands bordering the Caspian Sea, rising through densely forested foothills to the Elburz mountains which separate Gilan from the arid plateau to the south. The fertile lowlands were probably intensively cultivated, whereas the upland zone was one of transient herdsmen exploiting the rich summer pastures before moving down to the lowlands in winter; the latter region is where a series of spectacular discoveries have been made, primarily hilltop cemeteries.

The richest of these cemeteries is the site of Marlik Tepe, where fifty-three intact Iron Age tombs were excavated in 1961/2. Grave-goods included gold and silver beakers decorated with animals and human figures framed by registers of guilloche, gold-inlaid silver and plain sheet-bronze spouted jars, mosaic glass and frit vessels, weapons, tools and other metal objects, ingots, gold and silver jewellery, Mesopotamian (Mitannian style) cylinder seals, and a wide variety of grey and red burnished wares.[3] Most of the cemetery dates from the twelfth to the tenth century BC.[4]

Fig. 1 Map of early Iron Age sites in northern and western Iran.

Fig. 2 Burnished greyware spouted jars from northern Iran. One vessel was lightly incised and further modelled in relief to represent a phallic spout. The spouts on the other jars were deliberately modelled to represent stylised bird's heads.

The relatively low number of graves compared to the longevity of the site suggests that, unless many of the earlier objects are heirlooms, this cemetery represented the place of burial of a select social stratum, and less important individuals may have been buried in other cemeteries in the valley below.[5] In the absence of an associated settlement – let alone a potter's workshop – little is known about the people who made or used the objects found in these graves.[6] However, as with other Iron Age Iranian pottery traditions, much can be inferred from the evidence of the ceramics themselves.

Over two hundred ceramic vessels were found at the site of Marlik; some 90% of the tombs contained pots and as many as sixteen were found in one tomb (Tomb 52), which was particularly rich in other grave-goods. The ceramics included trough-spouted bowls, basins or covers, globular flasks with flared necks, double flasks, and jars with long beak-shaped spouts which look like crane profiles. One particularly distinctive group of these, also represented in a cemetery excavated at Ghalekuti, consisted of almost cylindrical hole-mouthed flat-bottomed jars with particularly elegant long beak spouts, counter-weighted by a handle or vertical ridge on the opposite side (fig. 2); the mouldings on the spouts resemble a feature found on bronze beak-spouted jars.[7] The assemblage consisted of completely oxidised reddish-orange as well as reduced grey-brown wares with slipped or self-slipped surfaces; all the vessels were evenly fired, but it is possible that this reflects the deliberate interment of better-fired examples. Very fine grit was evidently used as temper. Burnishing was a standard surface treatment, whereas painted decoration is absent.

The most spectacular group of vessels from Marlik consists of a series of eight burnished redware anthropomorphic vessels. These took the form of squatting bear-like or standing nude female and male figures, often holding a spouted jar and ranging in height from 27 to 46 cm (10.5–18 in). Some of these figures closely resembled smaller cast-bronze statuettes also found at this site.[8] The ceramic figures were heavily stylised with exaggerated physical features, such as prominent buttocks and swollen legs, perhaps designed so that they could stand upright; their pinched ears were pierced for metal earrings. Radiographic analysis of a vessel in the British Museum (fig. 5) suggests that they were made by careful coiling on top of a pair of joined cups.[9] This technique may therefore be related to the local potters' tradition of creating double or composite flasks.[10]

A total of thirty-three burnished zoomorphic vessels was also excavated at Marlik, most in the form of hump-backed bulls but also stags, rams, equids and even a leopard. These are more naturalistically modelled than the anthropomorphic series. The fabrics and surfaces were mainly reddish or reddish-brown and less than a quarter were grey or grey-brown. Some had been pattern-burnished or lightly incised. As many as five identical hump-backed bulls were placed together at one end of one tomb; the similarity of these and of other groups of vessels suggests that they may have been the work of single potters. These containers were clearly intended as pourers, but their exact function remains uncertain. The means of producing them has

Fig. 3 Burnished greywares from northern Iran.

attracted surprisingly little attention,[11] although a replication experiment by one potter suggests that they may have been made in two parts:

... on the one hand the neck (including the hump), on the other hand the hind part of the body and the belly ... The neck, mounted on a lathe, first takes the form of a closed pointed vase. Then the work finished, but still damp, is opened on the side. Care must be taken to bevel the edge of the slit. This opening allows a fragment to be removed, then to curve the point of the hump, in order to close the lips. This movement must be accurate as the effect can never be corrected ... After a day's drying, the belly and hump are added and stuck ... It took M. Clerc three-quarters of an hour's lathe-work to make the two parts, body and hump, then fifteen hours specially devoted to finish the work.[12]

This experiment implied ancient familiarity with wheel-throwing, whereas the available archaeological data suggest a conservative yet highly accomplished hand-building ceramic tradition in Iron I–II. Re-examination of zoomorphic vessels is therefore appropriate. To this end, a similar zoomorphic vessel in the British Museum (fig. 4) was subjected to radiographic analysis. This clearly indicated that an alternative form of construction was employed, combining slabs and coils, followed by careful modelling and burnishing. The results underline the skill of Early Iron Age potters in this region.

Burnished greywares in the Urmia basin

The key sequence for the Iron Age in north-west Iran derives from excavations at the large mound of Hasanlu, located in the Solduz valley south-west of Lake Urmia. Period V at Hasanlu corresponds to Iron I: the pottery tradition consisted of heavily burnished greywares (Early Western Grey Ware). During Period IV (Iron II), these developed into what is known as Late Western Grey Ware. A typical form consists of thick-walled handmade globular or carinated 'teapots' with bridged beak spouts (fig. 6). These were originally placed on top of openwork ceramic tripod supports, with feet ending in cloven hoofs or shoes, that were designed to resemble metal stands. The popularity of beak-spouted jars reflects the wide use of sheet-metal versions during this period in Iran.[13] Likewise, metalwares decorated in *repoussé* inspired potters to decorate greywares with gadroons, flutes, ribs and grooves. Locally produced poly-chrome glazed conical beakers also appear to have been imitated in grey-ware but with the addition of a single loop-handle and characteristic animal-head decoration.[14] The decoration on a small number of pots was modelled in low relief with snakes, ibex, goats or bulls and nude male figures, vaguely reminiscent of relief-decorated metal beakers.[15]

The grey burnished ware vessels, normally sand-tempered with heavily burnished surfaces (fig. 3), were usually burnished all over, but vertical streak and criss-cross pattern burnishing has also been found. This was probably executed while the vessels were leather-hard or completely dry, the main purpose evidently being to create a pseudo-metallic reflective surface. It would also have served to strengthen the walls, reduce porosity and facilitate cleaning. Almost any materials could have been employed as potter's burnishing tools, although ethno-graphic observations across the Near East suggest a preference for pebbles.[16] The relative coarseness of the clays means the procedure may have been slow: in the case of recent Palestinian women potters it has been observed that 'burnishing is a very slow process; to get a really good shine a woman will work at a pot for the best part of a day'.[17] At Hasanlu some 90% of vessels were fired in heavily reducing conditions to produce dark grey or jet-black surfaces. However, other potters appear to have preferred paler effects, as almost a third of Iron I pottery at the

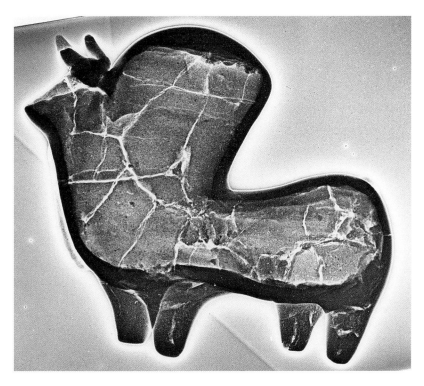

Fig. 4 *Xeroradiograph of an Amlash-type burnished greyware hump-backed bull pourer from northern Iran. It reveals that the vessel has been carefully reconstructed from many fragments but that there is very limited evidence for the use of make-up to fill gaps, for instance on the tip of one of the horns. Further examination suggests that it was handmade: the body was made by coiling around a flat slab of clay that now forms the underside of the belly; the back was probably formed by placing another slab of clay over the top, producing a shoe-like form. Further coils were then added to form the neck, hump and head. The roughly horizontal lines visible in this area may indicate the junctions of successive coils. The top of the head appears to have been closed by a single slab of clay, whereas the muzzle was formed by slitting open the front of the neck. Finally, the horns, tail, dewlap and feet were modelled from added pieces of clay.*

Fig. 5 *Xeroradiograph of an Amlash-type anthropomorphic vase from northern Iran. Examination suggests that the vessel was entirely hand-built. The legs were apparently formed from two small cups joined together, with clay added to smooth the junction. The roughly horizontal (rather than spiralled) alignment of the elongate inclusions in the two cups implies that they were not thrown on a wheel. The remainder of the vessel was probably built up by coiling, although the evidence for this is limited to the horizontal alignment of the elongate inclusions. Xeroradiography also showed that the protruding buttocks were formed by luting on hollow pinched cups rather than solid lumps. The shoulders and facial features were formed through pinching and modelling.*

nearby site of Dinkha Tepe was buff rather than grey, the proportion rising to almost three-quarters in Iron II. The degree of blotching and variation in surface colour from light brown to dark grey suggests relatively poor control over firing conditions, perhaps owing to the use of bonfires rather than constructed kilns.[18]

Local traditions in the Khurvin-Sialk oases

A number of greyware settlements and cemeteries are known from the Tehran area, south of the Elburz mountains, including Qeytariyah, Khurvin and Chandar. These span the Early and Late Western Grey Ware traditions (Iron I–II), suggesting a stable yet conservative period. Thin-walled, highly burnished beak-spouted jars, trough-spouted jars and straight-necked cups from Khurvin were particularly heavily metallic in form, and the quantity of redwares appears to have varied considerably from site to site.

In Cemetery A at Tepe Sialk (Sialk V), 250 km (90 miles) to the south, dark greywares were occasionally embellished with white-filled grooves and pattern burnishing. In contrast, burials in Cemetery B at Sialk (Sialk VI) indicate that these techniques were later dropped in favour of a unique local style of painted decoration and innovative use of imitation rivets and fluting on pottery. The painted vessels were decorated with bold chequered, crossed-square and hatched-diamond patterns, stags, birds and human figures, all painted in a red pigment that was occasionally fired to a pink or purple colour. The geometric designs resemble those found on painted tiles at Baba Jan, perhaps owing to common inspiration by patterned textiles.[19] Many of the shapes from Sialk Cemetery B are also paralleled by Genre Luristan wares further south.

Genre Luristan ware

During Iron II, an equally distinctive local style of handmade pottery developed in the Luristan area of western Iran (fig. 6). This is variously known as Genre Luristan, Kite ware, Baba Jan 'B' ware or Baba Jan III Painted ware. The distribution of this pottery corresponds closely with that of an equally distinctive class of 'lost-wax' cast and hammered sheet-metal objects known as Luristan bronzes, mostly deriving from cemeteries. Archaeological surface surveys and excavations

suggest a fairly dense rural settlement pattern comprising small villages in the fertile highland plains of eastern Luristan, in some cases clustered around a large chieftain's 'manor house' as at Baba Jan Tepe; larger settlements existed in the Hulailan/Tarhan plains to the south and west. Comparison with traditional agricultural practices in this region suggests that during this period certain tribes may have migrated seasonally, spending the summer in the highland pastures and wintering in the lowlands, and using the river valleys as arteries. The ethnic affiliations of the ancient tribes remains unclear, although archaeological and historical research rejects former suggestions that they were Cimmerians.[20]

Genre Luristan ceramics typically have medium to thick walls and were made by hand from sandy clays fired to a warm buff or light brownish colour.[21] Many vessels were simply left plain, whereas others were decorated with a dark brown or reddish-brown paint after the vessels had been lightly burnished. Typical painted designs

consisted of concentric dotted circles, rosettes or wheels, horizontal ladder patterns, hatched pendant triangles, and hatched 'kites' reminiscent of heavily veined leaves. Two-toned effects were sometimes obtained by filling in areas with a more heavily diluted paint. Rosette designs were also popular on painted tiles used to decorate the ceiling or upper floor in one room of the 'manor house' at Baba Jan.[22] A small number of globular hollow anthropomorphic figures ('toby jugs') holding spouted jars, related to the Amlash figures but made locally, were painted with similar kite, dot and stripe patterns.[23]

The propensity of potters to embellish handles and spouts with small horned animal-heads is part of a wider local tradition also seen on Luristan bronzes.[24] Other vessels with beak spouts were decorated with small pellets applied to the walls around the spout junction, imitating contemporary local sheet-bronze vessels with riveted spouts (fig. 6, front row). Plain or twisted basket handles and tubular spouts were commonly added.[25] The addition to

Fig. 6 Iron Age pottery from the Luristan region of western Iran. The tribes in this area produced a highly distinctive class of cast and hammered sheet-bronze objects, including bowls with riveted pouring spouts. Local potters produced a variety of thick-walled vessels with open pouring spouts, bridge-spouted vessels with animal-shaped handles and vessels decorated with reddish-brown painted 'kite' patterns.

Fig. 7 Median plain-wares from Tepe Nush-i Jan in western Iran. The Medes were a powerful force which helped to overwhelm Assyria and Urartu, yet this is one of the few Median settlements to have been excavated. The lightly burnished pottery includes carinated two-handled pots that are probably based on metal vessels.

bowls of single horizontal loop-handles marks a point of similarity with grey-wares from Hasanlu and later Median (Iron III) pottery from western Iran.

The Medes

The end of Genre Luristan in Iron III has been equated with the expansion of Median territorial ambitions during the seventh century BC.[26] The Medes were first mentioned in Assyrian sources in the ninth century (i.e. Iron II) and centred on the city of Hamadan, described in later sources as the Median capital although as many as twenty-seven kings (or chiefs) were mentioned by Shalmaneser III (858–824 BC). Unfortunately, reliable criteria for distinguishing Median objects from those produced by other Iron Age peoples in Iran remain problematic and the religious sanctuary at Nush-i Jan and the fortress at Godin Tepe remain the only extensively excavated Median sites in western Iran.[27] Within Luristan, Baba Jan continues to provide a key sequence, as level II included a number of imported ware vessels that are most closely paralleled from Tepe Nush-i Jan and Godin Tepe.[28]

The Median pottery found at these sites is rather distinctive (fig. 7).[29] Unlike the earlier Iron II Genre Luristan tradition, it is largely wheel-thrown and

contains accidental or deliberate mica tempering. The continuing addition of basket handles, horizontal loop-handles, and occasional animal-head terminals nevertheless represents a link with earlier Iron Age traditions.[30] The use of a single low rib at the shoulder-neck junction of closed forms suggests imitation of metalwares, for which the rib served a practical purpose. Deco-ration was limited to rare use of red slip while the bulk of the pottery was left plain. These Common wares were made from local clays containing mica and shale inclusions and were normally fired to a pinkish colour, either with paler or lightly oxidised surfaces. Small, carefully burnished greyware jars were also wheel-thrown, whereas large bowls and storage jars (*pithoi*) were coil-built. These were prone to breakage along the coil junctions, revealing evidence of regular finger-indenting along the seams prior to the addition of further coils; finger-impressed or incised bands were added to the outsides of *pithoi*, possibly with the intention of adding support to the walls during drying and to facilitate subsequent lifting.

Two other classes of Median pottery were handmade and heavily tempered with mica. These consisted of rounded or carinated cooking pots and Crumbly ware trays. The latter were rectangular in form with rounded corners, low

vertical walls and flat bases, carefully smoothed on the interior but rough on the underside, indicating that they were made on the ground. These handmade wares clearly belong within a domestic tradition of pottery-making, probably by women, that has continued until recent years across much of the Near East. Similar trays were traditionally used in Iraq for cooking, warming food, feeding or watering chickens, and for storing dried food or small objects; the modern Turkish equivalents are used as baking trays.[31]

Epilogue

The final phase of the Iron Age climaxed with the Achaemenid empire. Cyrus the Great (559–530 BC) over-threw the Medes and established an empire that was to envelop the whole of Western Asia   from Egypt and northern Greece to Pakistan and central Asia – and to last for more than two centuries. The wealth of the Persian court, proverbial in classical sources, is aptly illustrated by surviving gold and silver luxury wares. Local ceramic styles did not change overnight but continued to be subtly transformed. As in earlier periods, changing fashions in metalwares exerted a strong influence on these ceramic traditions.[32]

Tiles in Roman Britain

Andrew Middleton

The Romans were not only skilled builders in stone but also made use of artificial products, notably lime-based mortars and concrete, and terracotta (fired clay). Evidence survives in abundance for the quality of both Roman building and the materials they employed. Vast quantities of architectural terracotta were produced – indeed, the predominant building material of imperial Rome was brick.[1] Fired clay products were made in a multitude of shapes and sizes to fulfil a whole range of functions, including bricks for walls and floors, tiles for roofs, and terracotta pipes to carry both clean and foul water.[2] Among the variety of tile designs manufactured were flue-tiles (*tubuli*), which were made in the form of a hollow box and produced especially for use in the hypocaust (underfloor) systems that distributed hot air around private villas and public bath houses.

Considerable insight into the methods of specialist tile production in Roman Britain during the first two centuries AD can be gained by comparing the published archaeological evidence from a kiln-site in south-eastern England with observations of traditional tile-

a

b

c

d

Fig. 1 Sequence of three stages in traditional brick and tile production at the manufactory at Mazzano Romano, to the north of Rome. Collection and preparation of raw materials: (a) clay quarry; (b) preparing the clay in a pug mill; (c) sand is first crudely sieved. Forming and drying: (d) metal moulds are used, with sand as a release agent;

making today at a small manufactory north of Rome. As Potter and Johns have noted, the villa is one of the hallmarks of romanisation, and its overall distribution mirrors closely that of the major and minor towns of the period.[3] They also observe that the number of such buildings in Britain was rather small, about a thousand or so, perhaps implying that the villas were owned by people of relatively high social status. Certainly some, such as the one at Meonstoke, in Hampshire, were fine buildings; the provision of a hypocaust to provide heating (for comfort in the cool, damp British climate) was frequently an integral element in the design of these sophisticated buildings.

Making the tiles

It was usual for box flue-tiles to be combed or scored on the two large faces to provide a key for mortar or plaster. Sometimes, however, the tiles bear more elaborate and decorative patterns. These designs are frequently geometric (fig. 2), but pictorial designs have also been found, including one of a stag confronted by a hound. Despite their decorative nature, these designs were still essentially just an elaborate form of keying. Tiles of this type, with these relief-patterned designs, are common in south-eastern England, and examples come from as far north as

Leicester, about 160 km (100 miles) from London.[4]

A modern analogy illustrating the stages in the manufacture of terracotta bricks and tiles is provided by a traditional family-run brick and tile manufactory near Mazzano Romano, to the north of Rome.[5] The activities on the site include three key stages (fig. 1). The first is the collection and preparation of clay and sand, the locally available raw materials; (wood for fuel and water are transported to the site from elsewhere. Clay is dug from a small quarry (fig. 1a), from a geological deposit of Pleistocene date, and is allowed to weather in situ before being prepared in a pug mill (fig. 1b). The clay

(e) initially the tiles are laid out flat on a layer of sand on the ground (see also fig. 4); (f) once hardened, they are stacked up under 'roofs' of fired tiles. Firing: (g, h) carried out in a brick-built double-flue updraught kiln, fuelled by wood.

Fig. 2 A group of Romano-British tiles. Back row: three relief-patterned box-flue tiles (the one at left is from Reigate, the other two are from Ashtead). Front row: tegula and a flat slab with impressions of two bootprints. The length of the flat slab is c. 41 cm (16 in).

is not sieved, nor is sand or any other material added, apart from water. Sand is obtained from a small quarry (fig. 1c) and is sieved rather crudely to remove larger stones and again through a fine sieve before use (fig. 1f, foreground).

The next stage is the forming and drying of the bricks or tiles. Metal moulds are used (fig. 1d), with sand as a release agent. Initially the tiles are laid out flat on a layer of sand on the ground (fig. 1e; see also fig. 4). Once hardened sufficiently to be moved safely, they are stacked up under 'roofs' of fired tiles (fig. 1f).

The final stage is the firing (fig. 1g–h), which is carried out in a brick-built double-flue updraught kiln, fuelled by wood. The design differs little from the medieval brick kilns described by Biringuccio in the early sixteenth century.[6]

The enterprise is operated on a seasonal (May to September) basis by a workforce of four people. Bricks and tiles are produced side by side, though with separate forming and drying areas. The same raw materials are used for the

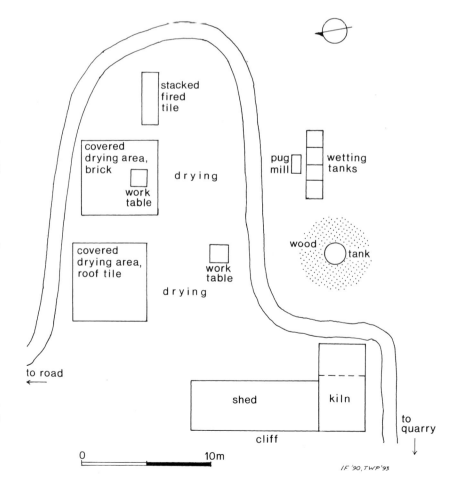

Fig. 3 Plan of the brick and tile manufactory at Mazzano Romano.

160

bricks and the tiles and both products are fired in the same kiln, although again segregated into different areas. The kiln is fired three times each season and about 50–100,000 bricks and/or tiles may be fired in each batch.[7] The layout of the working area is shown as a plan (fig. 3).

These observations can be compared with the very full description of a Romano-British tilery provided by the excavators of a site at Hartfield in East Sussex.[8] In many respects, the techniques used and the layout of the tilery at Hartfield[9] seem to have been similar to the modern manufactory. As at Mazzano Romano, the tiles are thought to have been made with the aid of moulds, although of wood rather than metal, and sand was used as a

release agent to prevent the clay from sticking to the mould. There was evidence at Hartfield for a covered but open-sided shed, within which the excavators suggested the tiles would have been stacked and dried. The area where the tiles are laid out to dry must not only be well ventilated but also covered, so that the unfired 'green' tiles are protected. On the one hand, exposure to full sun may cause them to dry too quickly and crack,[10] while on the other hand, exposure to rain can result in severe damage to the unfired products.[11] Evidence that the newly formed green tiles were laid out flat on the ground, exactly as at Mazzano Romano (fig. 4) and other modern tileries where traditional methods are used, is seen in the presence of animal

imprints (mainly of domestic cats and dogs, but also of young red deer) on some of the tiles from Hartfield.[12]

Firing at Hartfield was carried out in an updraught kiln, similar in principle but different in design to that at Mazzano Romano. The combustion chamber of the Hartfield kiln was rectangular, about 2.4×3 m (7×9 ft) in plan, and the tiles to be fired were placed on a floor of tiles, supported above the burning fuel on a series of cross-walls and pillars made of clay. Fuel was charged into the combustion chamber from a large stoke-hole via a horizontal flue. Analysis of fragments of charcoal showed that the main fuel used was birchwood, together with some oak and lesser quantities of hawthorn, beech and willow.[13]

Analysis of the tiles

Two analytical techniques were used to characterise the clay fabrics. Slices cut from fragments of tile were prepared as thin sections for petrographic examination using a polarising microscope. Additionally, small amounts of powder removed by drilling were analysed chemically using neutron activation analysis (NAA). These two techniques are complementary, with petrography providing mineralogical information mainly on the inclusions present in the clay and NAA providing chemical data relating particularly to the fine clay matrix.

In this way, several different fabrics were recognised.

Petrographically they were characterised mainly on the basis of the amounts and relative proportions of silt and sand inclusions. For instance, tiles from Ashtead contained a high proportion of fine silty inclusions, whereas those from Hartfield had only a small amount of silt. Tiles grouped together as the products of Kiln B were moderately silty but characterised by relatively common flakes of mica, and those attributed to Kiln A contained fine sand in an almost silt-free clay matrix.

Chemically, the various fabrics were distinguished by their respective trace element 'signatures'. Up to nineteen trace elements were analysed for each sample and the results processed using a statistical analysis software package known as CLUSTAN. There was a very distinct chemical separation between tiles from the Ashtead kiln and all other tiles; further analysis, shown in the principal components diagram, revealed less obvious but nevertheless significant differences between tiles attributed to Kilns A and B and those excavated from the kiln at Hartfield.[20]

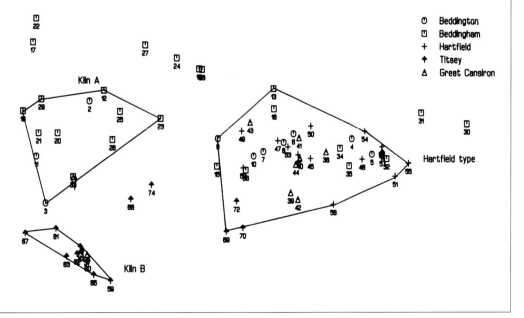

The diagram shows the distinction between three of the kiln sources, revealed by principal components analysis of the chemical data. Tiles from Ashtead are very different in composition and are not included in this diagram.

The tilers: settled or itinerant?

The designs on the relief-patterned tiles provide some clues as to how the supply of tiles, especially of the specialist box flue-tiles, was organised. In a pioneering study published fifty years ago, Lowther recorded a number of distinctive and recognisable relief-patterned designs.[14] Examination of these indicated that they had been impressed into the soft, damp clay before firing, using a roller die, probably made of wood. Tiles with identical patterns, made using the same unique roller die, have been found at widely separated sites, showing that either the tiles were produced centrally at a single tilery and then transported to the places where they were to be used, or that the tile-makers were itinerant, moving about the country (with their own roller dies), making tiles locally wherever they were needed.

Lowther appears to have favoured the concept of itinerant tilers, commenting on the practical difficulties of transporting large but relatively fragile tiles. Nevertheless, others have argued that 'despite their weight, it would not be surprising if tiles travelled distances of forty to fifty miles, for it is known that building-stone was moved a long way on occasions'.[15] A means of resolving this question by scientific analysis was suggested by the observation that there are examples of tiles with the same die-pattern but apparently made from different clays. This would imply that they were made in different places and, if confirmed, would provide strong support for Lowther's concept of itinerant tile-makers.[16]

A programme of investigation was established which included the kiln-site or tilery at Hartfield, a kiln at Ashtead (about 35 km/22 miles away), and several villas or consumer sites which may have been supplied by these tileries. Using petrographical and chemical analyses, it was possible to 'fingerprint' tiles coming from different kilns. Tiles excavated from the two Roman kilns at Hartfield and Ashtead

have distinctive fabrics. The analysis also provides good evidence for the existence of two additional unknown tileries (Kiln A and Kiln B), although the locations of these are not known. The results of assigning the tiles found at the various consumer sites to the different kiln sources are summarised in figure 5.

The results lend support to the notion that the tilemakers were itinerant. For instance, one particular die-pattern (Die 5A/5),[17] found at all but one of the sites included in the study, occurs on tiles identified as coming from three of the four tileries, at Hartfield, Ashtead and also at the unknown Kiln A. The tilemakers who used Die 5A/5 therefore made tiles in at least three different places and, at least to some extent, were itinerant, presumably travelling to particular places to meet local demands for their products. This allowed them to reduce the necessity of transporting heavy loads of tiles. For instance, the iron-working site of Great Cansiron appears to have been supplied mainly with tiles made at the nearby Hartfield kiln.

An important consideration in the location of the Romano-British tileries, just as for the modern manufactory at Mazzano Romano, would presumably have been the accessibility of raw materials. The analysis showed that the kilns at Ashtead and Hartfield were both situated close to suitable clay

sources.[18] As Lowther originally suggested, it seems quite possible that the itinerant artisans who produced the relief-patterned tiles made use of existing manufacturing facilities. Certainly the fabric analysis showed that relief-patterned tiles were made from the same clays as other types of tile, such as *tegulae* and *imbrices*, which would have been used for roofing.[19]

However, the scientific analyses also provide support for the alternative hypothesis, that tiles were transported over significant distances. For instance, tiles in the fabric characteristic of the Hartfield kiln were particularly wide-spread, being found among those from Titsey, Beddington and Ashtead to the north and Beddingham to the south (fig. 5). This is clear evidence that the tiles themselves were transported over significant distances of up to about 35 km (22 miles). The distribution of tiles attributed to the unidentified Kiln A provides further evidence for the transport of tiles, over similar distances. Even so, the rather limited evidence available (the locations of only two of the tileries are currently known) suggests that tileries tended to be major suppliers to those villas which were relatively close to them. A further inference that may be drawn is that most sites seem to have been supplied from several sources. For example, Beddington received tiles thought to have been made at Ashtead, Hartfield

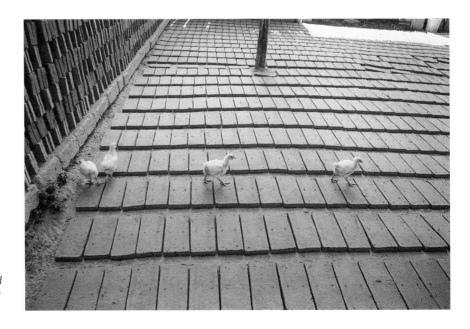

Fig. 4 Tiles laid out on the ground to dry and harden at the Mazzano Romano manufactory (note the chickens).

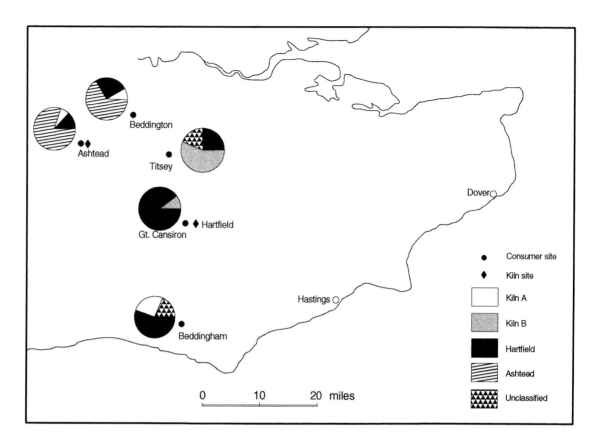

*Fig. 5 Map of south-eastern England,
showing the locations of consumer and kiln-
sites included in the study of tile fabrics.
The circular pie-charts for each consumer site
are subdivided according to the proportions
of tiles identified as originating from the
various kiln sources. The locations of Kilns A
and B are not known.*

and Kiln A. This perhaps suggests the
stocking of tiles made at different
tileries, either by the tile-makers themselves or possibly by middlemen acting
as builders' merchants or suppliers.

Drawing conclusions

The siting of the modern manufactory
close to suitable raw materials seems to
have been paralleled by the Roman
tile-makers. The evidence suggests
further similarities: both the modern
and the Roman tile-makers used the
sand-moulding technique, laid their
tiles out to dry and fired the dried tiles
in a wood-fired updraught kiln. The
levels of productivity attainable using
these traditional methods suggest that
small groups of Romano-British tile-
makers could have manufactured

several hundred thousand bricks in a
single season of operations, even at a
relatively small tilery such as that at
Hartfield.

The programme of scientific analysis
revealed that a relatively complex infrastructure must have lain behind the
supply of tiles, in particular relief-
patterned box-flue tiles, to Roman
builders in south-eastern England. Vital
to this interpretation is the use by the
tile-makers of distinctive roller dies to
impress the relief-patterned designs into
the tiles before they were fired. The fact
that there are tiles made from different
clays (characteristic of different tileries),
but marked with the same roller die, is
strong evidence that the tile-makers
who produced these tiles were itinerant.
They moved between tileries, probably
in response to the demands of local
building works. The makers of the
relief-patterned tiles may have used pre-
existing manufacturing facilities, for the
evidence shows that different types of
tile were manufactured alongside each
other. By contrast, tiles shown to have
been made from the same clay (characteristic of a single tilery) have been
found on different sites, suggesting that

finished tiles were also transported
significant distances between tilery and
building site. These two models (itinerant tilers and transported tiles) may
perhaps be reconciled in a relatively
complex organisation of the production
and distribution of tiles in Roman
Britain. The itinerant tilers moved to
different areas in response to local
demand, but it seems unlikely that they
would have produced just sufficient to
supply a single local building. Rather,
once production had been established at
a tilery, it seems likely that they would
have maintained production, perhaps
throughout a season, and distributed
their surplus to other consumer sites in
the area.

Nevertheless, the limited evidence we
have suggests that the itinerant tilers
travelled greater distances than the
fired tiles, a notion which could be
tested further by extending this study to
include examples of the tiles, impressed
with the same Die 5A/5, which are
known from sites further east and north
of London.

Roman Pottery Lamps

Donald M. Bailey

Pottery oil-lamps served as a cheap and efficient means of supplying illumination in classical lands from the Late Bronze Age, although only those produced during a period of nearly seven hundred years, from the beginning of the Roman empire until the coming of Islam, are discussed here. Fuelled by vegetable oils, they were both easy to use and easily broken, and they survive in huge numbers on archaeological sites throughout the empire. Whether used domestically, dedicated at shrines or placed in tombs, most of the lamps described below were made in moulds, although wheel-made lamps also put in an occasional sporadic appearance in widely separated areas, including second-century Asia Minor and sixth-century Africa among others.[1]

Italy: inventor of shapes

Italy was initially the prime influence on the shape of lamps.[2] Before the time of the very late Republic and early empire, wheel-made and often black-glazed lamps of Greek pattern, as well as Hellenistic-type mould-made lamps with rounded shoulders, were made in Italy, but by the middle of the first century BC, wide dish-topped lamps capable of bearing a decorative scene had been developed. These scenes, designed to appeal to the customer, showed deities and myths, genre subjects, animals and patterns, often floral. By the Augustan period, examples with voluted nozzles (fig. 1, top row, left) were introduced and continued to be made for a century and a half. The most successful shape, however, which persisted to at least the fifth century AD in one form or another in different parts of the empire, was devised in the middle years of the first century AD (fig. 1, top row, centre). This type has a circular oil-chamber and a short rounded nozzle; a handle is normal but not essential. A decade or so later, in the Po valley, another

shape was introduced, the so-called *Firmalampe* (fig. 1, top row, right), which was exported to and copied in huge numbers in the northern and north-western provinces of the empire, but with few going elsewhere; these lamps died out early in the fourth century AD.

Provincial copying and innovation

These three basic lamp-shapes were all exported widely and were all copied and modified in the receiving areas. In some provinces, for example Africa Proconsularis (more or less present-day Tunisia) and Greece, imported Italian lamps were very common for several decades before the local lamp workshops caught up and superseded them with their own versions; in other provinces, such as Britain, Egypt, Cyprus, Cnidus and Ephesus, the lamp-shapes were very quickly reproduced locally.[3] Examples of provincial copying of Italian shapes are shown in figure 1 (bottom row). Some of the finest lamps ever made were produced in second- and third-century Corinth and particularly in third-century Athens, which bore delicately rendered discus-scenes (fig. 2, top row, left and centre). Some of the eastern provinces, such as Egypt and those of the Levant, developed lamp-shapes that were not based upon Italian invention, and everywhere there were lamps of unusual shapes, together with lamps modelled in the form of animals, human heads and objects such as boats. The Egyptian frog-lamp is a shape that owes nothing to outside influence, and this is also true of a splendid series of souvenir lamps bearing the names of saints and holy men made at Aswan in the sixth and seventh centuries.[4] By the fifth century few lamps were being made in the Western Empire other than in Italy, Sicily and North Africa. Also by the fifth century, the elongation of the basic circular-bodied, short-nozzled lamp had

begun, together with the introduction of a shallow channel between the discus and the wick-hole. This development was brought to its finest culmination in Africa Proconsularis (fig. 2, top row, right), and from there the new shape was copied in Rome, Greece, Egypt and elsewhere in the east, as well as at Trier in Germany.[5]

Mass-production and specialisation

Although probably millions were made over the course of seven centuries, it may be inappropriate to use the term mass-production with regard to the Roman lamp industry. The immense time span and vast geographical area must be taken into account when considering the huge numbers fabricated, and the lamps themselves were the products of small workshops. How far these ateliers competed with each other is not known, but many were massed together in comparatively small areas such as those around Rome, in the Po valley and in central Tunisia. Some of these may have shared kiln-space, as did the samian potters of Gaul (ch. 29).

The use of moulds rather than the separate modelling of individual lamps is a potential indication of mass-production; another would be the employment of a production line, whereby separate workers undertake a series of specific tasks towards a combined finished product, but this is not provable. The makers of mould-made lamps did, on the whole, seem to specialise in lamps: only occasionally are their names found on other products, such as money-boxes. This is very different from the practice of Greek potters of earlier centuries (ch. 12), who made both lamps and pots in their workshops, but the Greek products were wheel-made and pre-dated the introduction of mould-made lamps. In Roman times, the main exception to this specialisation were the African Red Slip ware potters of central

Fig. 1 Top row: Italian lamps of the 1st and 2nd centuries AD. Bottom row: provincial versions made in Petra, Cyprus and Britain.

Tunisia, who manufactured both bowls and lamps (wheel-made and mould-made, respectively); their workshops may perhaps be regarded as mass-producers – certainly of pots, and possibly of lamps.

Export, trade and local production

An export trade existed from Greek times onwards, with Athenian lamps found wherever Athenian pottery went, and the situation was no different during the Roman period, when those areas producing the finest lamps were able to send them elsewhere with little difficulty, probably as small items of cargo on merchant vessels shipping large quantities of grain, wine or oil, or as a return cargo on such ships. Italian lamps were likely to have been disseminated by the latter process on ships sent out to bring foodstuffs to Rome, while the African Red Slip ware lamps went out alongside the exported grain or oil sent from Carthage. But the export trade in African Red Slip ware was so large that, although underwater archaeology has not yet demonstrated this, some ships may have set out only with a pottery cargo, including lamps.

The Roman empire was basically a community of cities located on the sea, serviced largely by ships with comparatively cheap cargoes, but it became an area with inland extensions, where road transport and the accompanying extra cost was necessary. This did not prevent the export/import of lamps for long distances overland, as examples found in the Fezzan, the Hoggar, the Eastern Desert of Egypt, and the Negev show.[6] Another means by which lamps from Italy and elsewhere went abroad was through demand from the army (the primary market for lamps in provinces such as Britain and Switzerland, where the use of lamps by civilians was very limited).[7] But the army itself set up workshops to make

its own lamps, often very closely copied from the Italian versions; this occurred, for example, in Vindonissa in Switzerland and at Holt in Denbighshire, in Britain.[8]

Lamps were normally produced in small workshops, the proprietors of which, some of whom were women, occasionally signed their products. Few lamp-kilns have been found: these include one at Weisenau in Germany, making first-century AD volute-lamps; a kiln within the town of Pompeii; and a poor late Roman example at Benghazi.[9] The workshops of the very prolific, mainly second-century lamp industry in the vicinity of Rome, which produced closely similar lamps signed by a large

number of different makers, many probably freedmen (fig. 2, bottom row), have been swallowed up by the modern expansion of the city. The products of these workshops have been found in many places, particularly in Gaul and North Africa. The distribution of these lamps has been much discussed[10] and, although it has been disputed, there is no doubt that most of the lamps are of Italian make and not the products of branch workshops. There are, however, local copies of these lamps, bearing Italian names, particularly in Gaul,[11] but not in North Africa, where various named workshops produced their own versions.[12] Whether the use of Italian names shows the presence of branch

Fig. 2 Top row: lamps made in Corinth, Athens and central Tunisia.
Bottom row: lamps made in the vicinity of Rome, with makers' names.

*Fig. 3 Sprig-mould
made in Cnidus (left)
and lamp-archetype
made in Athens (right).*

*Fig. 4 Plaster moulds
(top halves) from Tunisia
and Egypt.*

Fig. 5 Fired clay moulds (top halves and bottom half) from Ephesus, Egypt and Athens.

Making the archetypes and moulds

The manufacture of lamps was a comparatively simple process.[13] An archetype was modelled by hand (or the plain body made in a mould), incorporating all the details of the desired finished lamp, including the decoration, often added as a sprig (fig. 3, left), and the stamped maker's name, but excluding those features that were later to be applied, for example a separately made handle. Handles were usually moulded with the lamp and thus formed with the archetype but, particularly in some areas of the north-western provinces, lamps copied from handleless Italian volute-lamps had a handle applied after the lamp body left the mould. The archetype illustrated (fig. 3, right) is a Roman-period lamp of Hellenistic shape made in Athens; it has no handle, but the lamps ultimately produced from it had applied handles. This particular archetype, with its applied decoration, was fired. It is possible that many archetypes, few of which have survived, were not fired and after use were simply returned to the clay stock. African Red Slip ware lamp-archetypes were often decorated with a multiplicity of sprigs: a large one on the discus and many smaller ones on the shoulder.

When the archetype was ready, fired or not, a mould was taken. This was normally a two-piece mould, but for complex lamps multiple-piece moulds may have been necessary. Moulds were made either of plaster (much the most common) or of fired clay (figs 4, 5); very occasionally they were carved into soft stone.[14] Plaster was poured so that it surrounded the archetype up to its widest part; this formed the lower half of the mould. When hardened sufficiently, the top half was made by investing the upper part of the archetype in another pouring of plaster. For clay moulds, thick slabs of clay were pressed over the archetype in the same way. After the mould-halves were removed, further moulds could be made as required from the same archetype, which could then be stored for future use (although if unfired it may have been too damaged to keep). It was normal to cut registration notches in the lower mould before making the upper mould: this enabled the correct mould-halves to be matched up within a workshop that may have possessed many moulds made from a single archetype. Other methods of registration included making cuts across both parts of the mould so that they could be identified and lined up.

Occasionally the lamp-maker, especially in first- to third-century AD Cyprus, did not bother to make an archetype but made moulds from an actual lamp. This method is known as *surmoulage*, and it results, because of clay shrinkage, in a smaller lamp than the original; the process can be carried on ad infinitum, using *surmoulage* products as archetypes. Both moulds and lamps that might subsequently be used as archetypes were often touched up, so that the final products in a series

workshops, as is possible, or of itinerant craftsmen, or indicates that a *surmoulage* copy (see below) has been made, or a name has been pirated, is impossible to say at present, and indeed all four are possibilities. The Po valley *Firmalampen* also bear makers' names that are found on provincial products made throughout the northern and north-western provinces, including Britain – again, the mechanism of how they came to incorporate such a name is not yet and may never be understood.

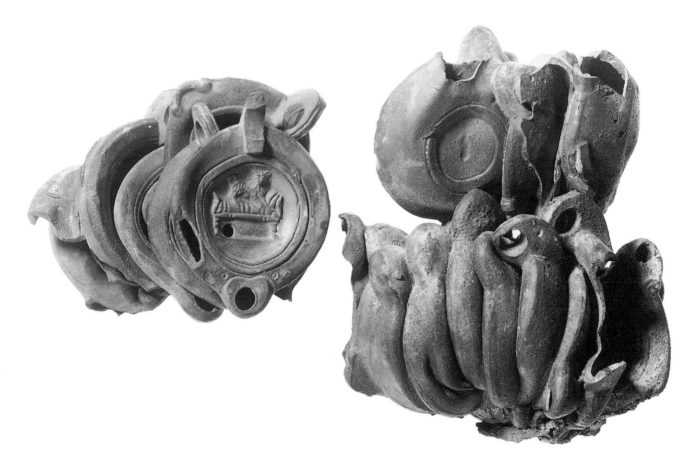

Fig. 6 Fused wasters from Ephesus.

may bear very little relationship in quality, appearance or size to the lamp standing at the head of a genealogy comprising numerous successive generations.[15]

When the plaster mould was dry, or the clay mould fired, it was ready for use. Thin sheets of clay were pressed into both halves, making sure that the handle part was well filled. The sheets were left slightly proud and the two-piece mould was brought together. The excess clay was forced inside to reinforce the join. As soon as possible (plaster takes water from the clay of the lamp more quickly than does fired clay), the halves were separated and the lamp removed. Because this cannot be done immediately (the wet clay would collapse), it was necessary for the lamp-maker to have a large supply of moulds to keep up the momentum of production. On removal, the leather-hard clay lamp was finished, first by trimming off the excess clay on the outside of the join and then by using tubular tools to pierce the wick-hole, the filling-hole and the handle (or an applied handle was added).

When the finished lamp was completely dry it was often dipped into an iron-rich slip, which gave the fired lamp a pleasing colour but, unlike the closely similar Greek black glaze applied inside lamps, did not necessarily stop oil seeping through the clay body. Occasionally, for example in first-century Campania, second-century central Italy and fourth-century Pannonia, the fired lamp was used as the biscuit base for vitreous glazing.[16] It is interesting that lamps made at Cnidus in Turkey were given a vitreous glaze in Campania.[17]

Firing the lamps

The firing was effected in the normal small pottery kiln of the period, usually circular, with the lamps piled one upon the other on the pierced floor of the firing chamber. The fuel chamber below was fed through a flue at one side.[18] The kiln was probably partially buried in the ground, its walls built up with clay that hardened itself during successive firings; in the top was an opening that could be covered as necessary.

Firing was normally carried out in an oxidising atmosphere, in contrast to the reducing atmosphere used to produce greyware products in late Hellenistic times. The normal temperature range was between about 800 and 1000°C, but occasionally the firing was a disaster, the kiln running away with itself and producing lamps melted out of shape and fused together (fig. 6). On the whole, however, the Roman mould-made clay lamp was a supremely successful device, and it was not improved upon as a means for providing light until the invention of the circular wick and glass lamp-chimney in the nineteenth century.

Terracotta Figurines of Eastern Gujarat

T. Richard Blurton

The production of terracotta figurines of both human and animal form has an uninterrupted history in the Indian sub-continent which can be traced back – in the far north-west – to the middle of the sixth millennium BC.[1] This tradition continues in parts of the subcontinent to the present day, thus providing ample opportunity for ethnoarchaeo-logical speculation. Discussed here is the modern-day tradition of terracotta figurine production by caste-potters in the two administrative districts of Baroda and Panch Mahals in the eastern reaches of the state of Gujarat, in western India, where it borders on Madhya Pradesh. What follows is based on fieldwork undertaken in the early 1980s and published in 1985,[2] although the material has been re-examined and new information, both ethnographic and bibliographic, has been added.[3] Before looking at the specific examples from Gujarat, a brief introduction to the ceramics, clay sculpture and position of the potter in India may prove useful.

History of ceramic production

The production of clay vessels in the subcontinent has an ancient but regionally varied history. At Mehrgarh, south-east of Quetta on the western bank of the Indus river, vessels appear at about the same time as figurines in the middle of the sixth millennium BC. In other regions such as the southern Deccan, however, pottery does not make an appearance until *c.* 3000 BC.[4] But irrespective of the date of its first appearance, pottery from most of the Indian subcontinent has traditionally been made of low-fired earthenware. Until the coming of Islam there was no practice, except perhaps in the north-west, of using a foot-wheel[5] or applying glazes, and although the latter technology must have reached at least northern parts of the subcontinent by the Sultanate period in medieval times,[6]

Fig. 1 The Chhota Udaipur potter, Shankarbhai Mangalbhai Prajapati, turns the wheel using a stave set into the outer rim. At the centre of the wheel is the reservoir of clay from which the bodies of the figurines will be made.

170

Fig. 2 Group of terracotta figurines from eastern Gujarat. Left to right: elephant with howdah, decorated with white powder; dome, with splashed white decoration; horse made by the Chhota Udaipur potter.

it has never penetrated beyond the major urban centres, the points of greatest Muslim settlement.

In rural India, ceramics – both vessels and sculpture – have always been and continue to be produced either by hand-building or on low wheels spun on pivots bedded into the ground.[7] The motion required to throw a pot is produced by fitting a stick into a socket in the outer edge of the wheel and thus turning the wheel at ever greater speed. After a number of vigorous turns, the centripetal force thus generated[8] keeps the wheel spinning on the pivot and a lump of clay can then be centred on the wheel and formed (fig. 1). Before the wheel has lost its force, the potter can re-invigorate it by fitting the stick back into the socket and turning it once more. When the throwing is completed, the piece is removed from the wheel and left to dry. Once dry, the vessel (especially the base) can be further

formed with a paddle and dabber. Firing is undertaken at low temperatures and in kilns, often built of brick, which are fed with wood and dung (fig. 6). It has always been (and still remains) a craft whose participants are determined by birth. Potters appear low down in the caste scale, though paradoxically their products are needed by members of every traditional non-Muslim house-hold at some point in their lives, as rites of passage are marked by the use of terracotta vessels and/or figurines.

By far the most numerous ceramics produced in rural India are vessels, and of these the majority are the large round-bellied ones used for carrying water. Brass replaces these in wealthy households, while in recent decades plastic has become a serious contender throughout India, being both lighter and less breakable. The production of figurines and larger sculpture is, necessarily, a secondary and specialised activity for many potters, as it is for the potter Shankarbhai Mangalbhai Prajapati,[9] in Chhota Udaipur (Baroda district), whose production of figurines is discussed below. Because such figurines and sculptures are made of

low-fired material and are produced only for specific events – a festival or presentation to a deity – after which they are abandoned, they tend to survive poorly and thus are rarely represented in museum collections.

Sculpture in clay is, however, a tradition of fundamental importance throughout India. A few of the better-known examples include the production in Bengal (eastern India) of large sculptures of the goddess Durga, which are made at Durga-puja in September/October; in Maharashtra (central India), where processional images of Ganesha are made at the festival of Ganeshchaturthi[10] in August/September; and in Tamil Nadu (south India), where magnificent horse sculptures – sometimes over 4 m (12 ft) in height, fired in situ – are presented to the god Aiyanar.[11] Underlying the connection between terracotta figurines and festivals, religious observance and rites of passage, is the notion of the sacred nature of the earth itself and the understanding throughout India that the earth is synonymous with the Great Goddess, who is fecund, fruitful and the Universal Mother of mankind.

Fig. 3 Forest shrine in eastern Gujarat, with rows of horses and domes lined up at the base of the tree-shrine. Note also the saucer-like lamps in the foreground.

The tribal populations of eastern Gujarat

The population of eastern Gujarat is mixed, with settled Hindu communities (as well as small numbers of Jains, Muslims and Christians) living in close contact with tribal, non-caste communities known generically as Bhil.[12] There are many subdivisions within the Bhils, but they share a lifestyle which has traditionally shunned and despised settled agricultural life in favour of hunting, fishing and forest gathering.

With the clearance of forest tracts for timber and for the provision of land to support the massively increasing population, as well as for the construction of hydro-electric schemes, the habitat of such groups has been seriously threatened. As a result many have now adopted some element of settled agricultural activity. However, there is still a definite distinction between the permanent, caste-divided Hindu townsmen and the forest-dwelling Bhils. In terms of physique, aesthetics, music, belief-systems and lifestyle, they are separate from the urban merchants, shopkeepers and craftsmen. It is the Bhils who in eastern Gujarat[13] are the commissioners of terracotta figurines (there is no tradition of making figurines among the

Bhils), while it is the caste-potters who are the producers. The importance of tribal customers to potters in western India is further demonstrated by the production during the spring months of distinctive vessels for collecting the sap of the toddy palm, which when fermented makes the alcoholic drink consumed in large quantities by Bhils.

Terracotta figurines in eastern Gujarat

Terracotta figurines in this area are of two basic types: animals and 'domes' (fig. 2).[14] By far the majority of the animals are horses, though elephants, tigers (fig. 4) and buffaloes are also made. Terracotta animals are purchased to be deposited as gifts in shrines for the benefit of forest deities. The nature of these forest shrines varies. The most simple are deposits of offerings at the base of a tree or other natural feature where the divine presence is especially felt (fig. 3). Other deposits of figurines are demarcated by standing wooden pillars (*cholia*) up to about 1 m (3 ft) in height. They are often laid out in a grid formation among the trees and are frequently shaped so as to appear (very approximately) as human. A final category of shrine at which terracotta figurines are deposited in Gujarat is the wayside standing-stone slab, which is usually carved with the figure of a horse-riding hero.[15]

Most devotees view the animals – especially the horse – as a means of transport for the gods who, at dead of night, fly through the air riding on their enlivened steeds. In return for the gift, the god is requested to heal a sick family member, ensure that a cow gives milk, or guarantee the birth of a son.[16] The 'domes', referred to by my caste-Hindu informant as *mandir* (Hindi for shrine or temple) but known locally as *dhabu*, are domed terracotta shapes with open bases, small finials and a cut 'doorway' in the wall. These are deposited in shrines, also for the benefit of the deity, as places of habitation.[17] Lamps, incense, alcohol and the offering of chickens (when they can be afforded) may accompany deposits of such terracotta items. Their size varies throughout western India, but the average in the area around Chhota

172

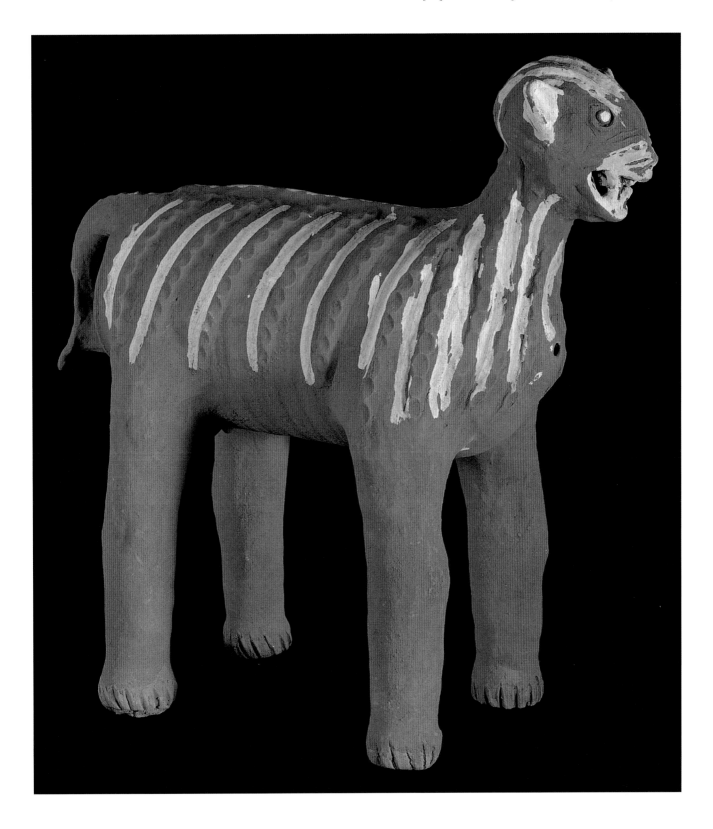

Fig. 4   Terracotta tiger, from eastern Gujarat.

Udaipur is about 30 cm (12 in) for both horses and domes. Domes of a dramatically sculptural style, measuring up to 1.2 m (4 ft) in height, are recorded from Surat district to the south.[18]

The main time of year for the production of figurines in the Bhil area of eastern Baroda district is in the months of November and December.[19] Clay is dug locally and brought to the potter's yard by donkey. All the rest of the production process, including the firing and sale of the finished items, takes place in the yard in front of the potter's house.[20] The work on the wheel is done by the men (fig. 1), though the women of the household engage in some of the subsidiary activities such as cleaning and kneading the clay, adding sand to it, and rolling out hand-fashioned parts or applying slip decoration.

The production of figurines

The animal figurines are made up of different elements which, when luted together, make up the complete animal; this all takes place prior to firing. The various parts are either made on the wheel (and thus hollow) or hand-fashioned (and thus solid).[21] The elements made on the wheel are produced first – these are the cylinders which form the body and the smaller tubes which make the legs (clearly seen in fig. 5). The head and neck of the horse including the bridle (one piece) and the head and trunk of the elephant (two pieces) are also made on the wheel,[22] and these are later bent to accommodate the downward droop of the elephant's trunk and the near 90-degree bend in the horse's neck behind the head. All the other parts – the horse's tail, saddle, reins and bit and the elephant's tusks, howdah and caparison, as well as the ears and eyes of both animals, are hand-fashioned. The luting together of the wheel-made elements does not take place immediately, as allowing the clay to dry to a leather-hard state makes it easier to cut for insertion.

The assembly of the various parts (a process basically identical for both horse and elephant) is as follows: the barrel-shaped body of the animal is held between the potter's feet while four

Fig. 5 Shankarbhai Mangalbhai Prajapati assembles the horse figurine (fig. 2). All elements have been made separately on the wheel, and are thus hollow. He is here luting the legs into the holes cut in the underside of the belly of the horse. He holds the figurine between the soles of his feet, leaving his hands free to assemble the legs.

circular holes are cut in what will be the underside of the figurine; then the ends of the legs and edges of the holes are wetted prior to the two elements being brought together; next they are luted in place both on the outside and inside by thin strips of clay, the former being smoothed with water to form a neat gradation (fig. 5). The hole to receive the neck is then cut at the end of the barrel-shaped body (the equivalent of the lip of a vessel – that is, not the end which is rough from having been cut from the wheel); the edges of the neck and the hole are then wetted and the two are luted together, just as with the legs. The addition of accoutrements (reins, howdah, etc.) is effected through luting in exactly the same way, some being hand-rolled (such as the saddle) and others having been thrown (e.g. the howdah). Finally, decoration is added, which does not replicate any part of the living beast; finger impressions feature especially.

Following assembly, the figurines are left to dry for three days prior to firing. During this time, a vermilion-red slip is painted on to the figurines, followed by the application of a chalky white powder to the finger-impressed areas and other decorated elements. Both the red slip and the chalky white decoration mark these examples as unusually deluxe items. More usual is the plain, undecorated terracotta colour, perhaps relieved only by a splashing of white powder (fig. 2).

The firing of the figurines

In the yard of Shankarbhai Mangalbhai's house, situated on the outskirts of Chhota Udaipur, were two circular brick kilns coated with dung and clay.[23] Slightly tapering and about 70 cm (27.5 in) in height, the kilns had vents at the base (ten in this instance), a design representative of other kilns seen in the region. Elsewhere in Gujarat (though not when these elephant and horse figurines were produced in 1984) the author has seen kilns filled only with horse figurines stacked on their sides, one behind the other, radiating out from the centre (fig. 6).[24] Once all the items to be fired were stacked in the kiln, broken sherds – wasters from previous firings – were placed over the

Fig. 6 Kiln in Chhota Udaipur, stacked with recently fired horse figurines. Note the vents at the base for both introducing the wood and encouraging a draught.

domed top; at the centre a number of complete rim-sherds acted as vents.[25] This layer of sherds around the edges of the kiln was then coated with large dry teak leaves and subsequently a layer of ashy soil, the debris from previous firings.

The fuel used for firing the kiln in Chhota Udaipur was a coniferous wood which had been cut into long strips that could be fed into the kiln through the vents as the wood burned; the fire was begun with kerosene. The kiln was allowed to burn for about forty-five minutes, after which the potter's wife threw large quantities of straw on to the centre of the kiln where there was no layer of ashy earth.[26] This caused a flare-up at the centre of the kiln, with flames blazing upwards, and a great increase in the temperature of the interior of the kiln. This marked the high point in the firing process, as the potter then withdrew from the vents any unburned pieces of wood and doused them with water. Having been set in the late afternoon, the kiln was left overnight and not opened until the next morning when, of all the contents,

only one toddy-collecting vessel was found to be cracked and one small water-vessel chipped.

This completed the production, as witnessed at the workshop of Shankarbhai Mangalbhai Prajapati of Chhota Udaipur in March 1984. However, one further element of decoration should be mentioned, which is the painting with white lime, after firing, of some of the figurines and the *mandir/dhabu*. This takes the form of either a splashed mottling or a complete covering, and both types are represented in the British Museum's collections. This decorative feature is fugitive and, once the figurines have been deposited in the forest shrines, usually lasts no longer than the next monsoon, making it useful for the ethnographer as an indication of the extent to which a shrine is still in use and the divine force still felt to be present. To witness the accumulation of the year's mottled white offerings to the deities of the forest, eerily lined up in front of a massive mound of votive deposits which may reach back decades or even centuries, is a moving testament to the continuance of an ancient Indian tradition.

Whistling Vessels from Pre-Hispanic Peru

Colin McEwan

Some of the most accomplished ancient pottery traditions in the Americas belong to the pre-Hispanic cultures that once peopled the valleys of Peru's arid Pacific coast.[1] Whistling bottle technology features prominently amid the exuberant range of forms and styles created by the Vicús (100 BC–AD 600), Moche (AD 100–700), Lambayeque (AD 800–1350) and Chimú (AD 800–1450) cultures (fig. 1).[2,3] All were settled agrarian societies which depended on a combination of irrigated maize agriculture and maritime resources for subsistence. Artisans worked in stone, wood and metal but were especially renowned for their textiles and pottery. Much of the artistic production was devoted to ritual activity linked to seasonal agricultural festivals, which took place against a backdrop of residential compounds, temples and pyramids.

Whistling vessels are first recorded in Peru towards the end of the first millennium BC, their appearance seemingly inspired, directly or indirectly, by the innovative artistry of the Chorrera culture (1000–300 BC) of neighbouring coastal Ecuador to the north.[4,5] For nearly two thousand years they have appeared in many guises alongside the enormous variety of flutes, pan-pipes, whistles, rattles, bells and trumpets used by native Americans up until the first European contact in the early sixteenth century.[6] The vessels depict a wealth of bird and animal imagery as well as human figures, and they produce a great range of sounds when 'played'.

It is easy to forget that, for much of prehistory, the possibility of listening to the sounds once fashioned by human agency is irretrievably lost, but musical instruments which have survived in archaeological contexts are an important exception. In the case of these whistling vessels we have not only evidence of technical virtuosity: we can also bring back to life the relationship

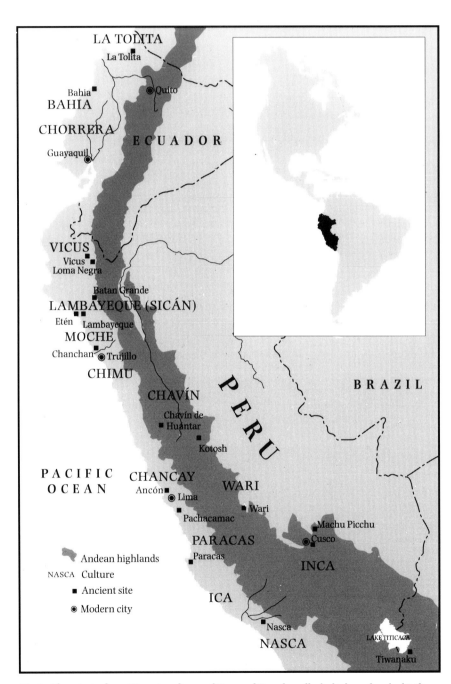

Fig. 1 The principal pre-Hispanic cultures of Peru and Ecuador, all of which produced whistling figurines and vessels.

176

*Fig. 2
Double-chambered
whistling vessel
depicting an owl,
from Peru, south
coast, Early
Middle Horizon
(AD 650–750).*

themes which cut across the different cultures and reflect a common underlying Andean cosmology. Archaeologists and ethnomusicologists have learned much from indigenous informants about the intersection between living musical and pottery traditions in the Andes. In turn, the range of subject matter portrayed on pre-Hispanic whistling vessels offers insights into deep-rooted Andean beliefs and religious practices.

Construction of the whistling mechanism

As far back as the late 1930s, the British Museum was an early leader in the application of the then novel technique of radiographic analysis to penetrate inside intact ceramic vessels.[14] The radiographs accompanying the selection of whistling vessels illustrated here help reveal the hidden ingenuity entailed in their construction. The whistle is first moulded from a small hollow sphere of clay a few centimetres in diameter with an opening on one side. A narrow clay tube or duct is then aligned with this, so that the air flow is directed across the opening.[15] When air is impelled down the tube and against the sharp edge of the opening it resonates (fig. 4), thus producing the characteristic whistling sound.[16]

Certain radiographs clearly show that the clay sphere and duct were pre-

between object, image and sound in the form originally intended by their creators.

The production process

In the earliest Peruvian pottery traditions of the first millennium BC, the way in which a pot was fired would usually determine its colour. Oxidation firing produced a red-to-buff coloured vessel, while firing in a smoke-filled reducing atmosphere turned the object grey or grey-black.[7] Potters created surface designs by incising or texturing the surface prior to firing. Later, post-firing resin paints began to be applied in order to produce colourful polychrome ceramics. Around 100 BC these were replaced by polychrome slip paints, which became the hallmark of the Nasca style. These were also to influence the later Middle Horizon (AD 600–900) styles of the south coast (fig. 2) and adjacent Andean highlands. The ceramic styles of northern Peru, on the other hand, tended to maintain a simple two-colour slip decoration, with Vicús vessels in particular often featuring a post-firing application of organic black pigment (fig. 3).[8]

Very little archaeological evidence has been found for large centres of pottery production or even for potters' 'quarters' within major pre-Hispanic urban settlements in South America.[9] This suggests that most ancient Peruvian ceramics were produced by potters working individually or in

family groups, and that the production may have taken place in a household setting, with both men and women involved.[10] Some fulltime ceramic specialists might have been supported by high-ranking lords, but for the most part potters probably practised their skills on a seasonal basis as agricultural tasks permitted, or during the post-harvest hiatus.[11]

Whistling vessels continued to be produced by native artisans in the centuries following European contact,[12] and simple ceramic whistles and whistle figurines are still made today.[13] Their remarkable continuity enables us to consider the range of iconographic

Fig. 3 Double-chambered whistling vessel with a modelled monkey, from Peru, Vicús (100 BC– AD 600).

fashioned as a single piece and then subsequently incorporated into the vessel, with only the narrow orifice of the sphere being visible from the exterior (fig. 5). Essentially each vessel must have two openings – one for letting air in and one for letting it out. By blowing into the spout the air is forced through the chamber, up into the duct and across the opening of the whistle (fig. 6c). The duct and sphere whistling mechanism is usually placed within the head or body of the modelled figure that forms the main subject of the vessel. This effectively acts as a 'sound box' and is often pierced by holes to let the sound escape. The pitch of the sound emitted differs according to the size, shape and volume of the whistle as well as the characteristics of the sound chamber created by the hollow cavity.

Aural iconography

Nearly all whistling vessels have been found as funerary offerings.[17] Many are in pristine condition, implying minimal use before interment. Although others show signs of wear and tear, we have little direct evidence for their use in specific ritual contexts prior to final deposition in tombs. The modelled subjects encompass a wide range of

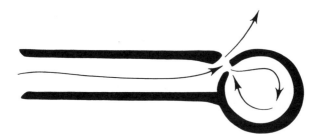

Fig. 4 Cross-section of a duct whistle, showing how air is impelled down the tube and across the opening of the clay sphere.

naturalistically rendered images drawn from nature. Birds (figs. 2, 6, 9), sea mammals and terrestrial fauna (figs. 3, 7) all appear. Certain species recur again and again, and it seems that special attention was paid to creatures that are particularly vocal.

The technology was refined to create a great variety of sounds, ranging from the soft sonorous timbre produced by the owl vessel (fig. 2) to the shrill shriek emitted by the monkey figure (fig. 3). It seems that in some cases the potters sought to emulate the characteristic call of a particular bird or animal. Among the birds depicted, macaws (fig. 6), parrots and parakeets are enduringly popular.[18] Perhaps their ceaseless raucous 'chatter' and the fact that they 'steal' the crops brings them within the compass of everyday human activity. Sea lions also appear frequently, and they too compete aggressively with

humans for fish in times of scarcity. On the other hand, owls, with their distinctive call, are associated with nightfall, darkness and the dead. Other species are rare or appear not to be represented at all, and among these are raptorial birds whose habits take them beyond the human domain. While felines with formidable bared fangs pervade much of Andean iconography, they are less common on whistling vessels, and instead juvenile felines appear to have been selectively emphasised. This seems to reflect an overall trend towards secularisation in ceramic iconography. Frogs are also relatively rare, although they populate Andean symbolism in many other media. The range of subject matter suggests that a fundamental distinction may have been made between the high-pitched cries or shrill whistling sounds characterised by pronounced

Fig. 5 Whistling vessel in the form of a totora reed boat with two paddlers, from Peru, Lambayeque (AD 800–1350), and radiograph showing the whistle embedded within the handle.

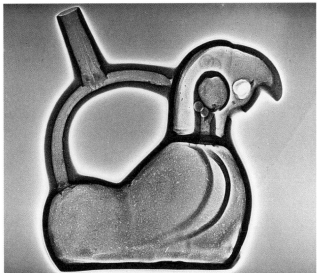

Fig. 6 Whistling vessel in the form of a macaw, from Peru, Moche (AD 100–700), radiograph showing the whistle in the head cavity, and profile drawing showing how air blown down the spout and into the chamber is forced through the duct and past the whistle chamber.

exhalation, and the lower-pitched sounds of croaking, growling and roaring. Among the range of anthropomorphic scenes are figures holding babies, paddling boats (fig. 5), playing instruments and even dancing (fig. 8).

The evolution of production

During the early centuries AD, mould-making technology developed on the north coast of Peru as part of a fundamental shift towards mass-production.[19] In reviewing the evolution of ceramic production in Peru, archaeologist Chris Donnan has noted that whereas polychrome slip designs require a substantial investment of time and skill, much less expertise is needed to produce low relief or sculptural decoration with moulds.[20] With polychrome slip painting, the potter must control the firing process very carefully so as to achieve the precise combination of temperature and oxygen required for optimum colour intensity.[21] This usually means that no more than a few vessels can be fired at one time, and that the kiln must be carefully monitored throughout the process. In contrast, Donnan observed that firing in a smoke-filled reducing atmosphere allows many vessels to be fired at the same time, and the temperature does not require rigorous monitoring.[22] The potter simply adds fuel to the kiln and covers it with soil, allowing the smoke to penetrate and colour the ceramics.

The fact that this kind of pottery became increasingly common on the north coast of Peru demonstrates the concentration on mass-production, which was intensified through the use of more sophisticated and efficient moulds. The widespread use of reduction firing to make the ubiquitous Chimú burnished blackware pottery is almost certainly the result of this emphasis on mass-production (fig. 8).[23]

Symbolism of shapes and sounds

Both double- and multi-chambered vessels are common, although the former are by far the most important category and seem to have been valued for their symbolic significance as much as anything else. Many are unsuited to simple functional requirements as practical containers for storing and pouring. The purpose of successfully fabricating the hidden whistle seems to have been to create a particular effect – to mysteriously animate the figure which conceals it (fig. 7). This provides a clue to understanding why the vessels were created.

Based on his extensive fieldwork among Quechua-speaking groups in highland Bolivia, ethnomusicologist Henry Stobart has found that whistling pots and other forms of whistles using the duct technique form a special category within Andean beliefs. He has observed that many of the various types of duct flutes still played today are considered to have special functions relating to the agricultural year,

Fig. 7
Radiograph showing the unusual 'double' whistle-chamber arrangement within the head and neck of a whistling vessel depicting a llama, from Peru, Vicús (100 BC–AD 600).

Fig. 8 Four-chambered whistling vessel with two figures dancing, from Peru, Chimú (AD 900–1470).

especially the coming of the rains upon which the crops and all human life depend. Consorts of duct flutes are played exclusively during the rainy season by peasant farmers throughout northern Potosí (Bolivia), from shortly before the feast of Todos Santos in November until Carnival in February or March. Their sound is said to attract the rain and to discourage frost and hail, and sometimes in periods of drought they are played throughout the night until dawn.[24] Stobart's informant explained that it was the combination of playing different kinds of high- and low-pitched instruments at the appropriate times of the year which caused the rain to come and plants to grow. High-pitched wailing sounds are particularly associated with critical moments that mark the transition between the dry

and rainy seasons in the Andes, and they are especially associated with the dead, who, as a 'collective' presence, are said to help the crops grow through the rainy season.[25]

Double-bodied vessels[26] are still used for drinking on certain festive occasions among Quechua communities in highland Peru. Various kinds of double cups joined together by a tube at the base are used at wedding feasts to symbolise the union of male and female.[27] Fermented maize beer is poured into one half and alcohol into the other so that, as the newlyweds drink from it, they start by imbibing the beer but finish by drinking the alcohol. The same kinds of paired ritual drinking vessels are used for wedding celebrations in Bolivia. There, too, they symbolise the harmonious and productive bringing together of two

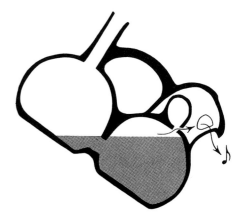

Fig. 9 Diagram showing how the movement of liquid within a double-chambered vessel can make it whistle, drawn from a radiograph of a whistling vessel in the form of a bird, from Peru, Gallinazo (100 BC–AD 100).

separate entities which is at the core of
the marriage ceremony.[28]

There is a similarity in form between
the contemporary double-bodied vessels
and the pre-Hispanic double whistling
pots.[29] In some cases, when the pre-
Hispanic vessels are partially filled with
water or other liquid and then tilted
back and forth, they 'whistle' (fig. 9).
Stobart suggests that the same underlying concept is important to both the
ancient and modern use of this
particular form. The two halves of the
vessel embody the idea of opposed but
complementary principles. Tilting the
vessels creates a condition of disequilibrium, as the liquid passes from one
chamber to the other. Equilibrium is
restored when the vessel is returned
to the horizontal and the liquid is
balanced. This process can be likened
to the disequilibrium created by the
transition between the seasons which
is necessary to sustain life. In the
Andes the intense heat of the dry
season is associated with the shrunken
proportions of the land of the dead, and
the dead themselves are held to be
miniature versions of living people.
Priests are key figures, acting as inter-
mediaries between the living and the
ancestors (fig. 10).[30]

The process of desiccation which
takes place in the world of the dead is
believed to provide the human world
with water. Thus, during the rainy
season, regenerative water flows from
the perpetually green land of the
ancestors via underground conduits to
emerge as springs, streams and rivers in
the world of the living.[31,32] An important
mythical relationship exists between
mountains, as the 'birth-places of life-
giving water', and the ancestors, who
are responsible for the organisation of
irrigation and agriculture. Musical
sounds, including those of whistling
vessels, are said to imitate the water's
song, and this is therefore the language
that is employed to speak to the
ancestors.[33] In turn the whistling
vessels, with their miniature figures and
scenes drawn from everyday life, are left
as offerings to accompany the ancestors
in their tombs, in order to assure the
continued well-being and vitality of the
community.

*Fig. 10 Whistling vessel depicting a priest, wearing a cape knotted at the front, from Peru,
Moche (AD 100–700).*

181

Ding and Other Whitewares of Northern China

Jessica Harrison-Hall

China's potters were producing white-wares early in their exceptionally long and varied ceramic history, millennia before the world-renowned porcelains of southern China (ch. 30). Pure white unglazed earthenwares were first fashioned about 3300 years ago, in the thirteenth to eleventh centuries BC, from secondary kaolin[1] derived from deposits of primary kaolin – a white-firing, iron-poor clay – which lie across the northern plains beneath a layer of loess, the wind-blown ochre-coloured dust known as China's 'yellow earth'.

The vessels are thickly potted from coils of clay and bear designs closely related to bronze wine and food containers. They were made to order for burial in elaborate royal tombs at the late Shang dynasty capital of Anyang, in Henan province, and at other sites along both the Yellow and the Yangtze rivers.

China also has a greenware tradition, but whitewares are technically much more demanding, as they require highly refined clays comparatively free from mineral impurities such as iron, manganese, copper or titanium.[2] Shang white earthenwares were manufactured in small quantities, perhaps in response to ritual rather than domestic needs. Few whole vessels survive today. This experiment in whiteware production appears to have stopped in about 1050 BC and only re-emerges in the sixth century AD.

The earliest porcelain

Excavations at the Gongxian kiln site, in Henan, have unearthed the earliest white porcelains in the world, dated AD 575.[3] Using technology derived from bronze casting, Gongxian ceramics were fired at 1350°C, resulting in dense-bodied, yellow-white glazed wares. Contemporaneous kilns at Mixian, also in Henan, made coarser products often slipped to create a whiter finish,[4] and by the eighth and ninth century whitewares were manufactured in Hebei, Henan, Shanxi and Anhui provinces.[5] The finest of these were made at Xing yao, in Neiqiu and Lincheng counties, Hebei. Unlike earlier whitewares, Xing was praised by contemporary writers in historical texts, style treatises and poetry. In AD 825 Li Zhao, in his widely distributed supplement to the Tang history, describes Xing as used by rich and poor alike. Comparisons with silver and snow made by Lu Yu in the *Chajing* (Tea Classic) emphasise Xing yao's quality and status. Scholars who praised Xing whitewares in poetry include Bai Juyi, the monk Jiaoran and the calligrapher Yan Zhenqing.[6] Xing kilns specialised in whitewares for six hundred years but also manufactured black, brown, *sancai* and greenwares. The popularity

of southern greenwares from Yu yao, in Zhejiang, and northern whitewares from Xing yao gave rise to the Tang idiom *nan qing bei bai* (South green, North white).

Ding ware

Successors to the Xing tradition and the most famous whiteware producers are the neighbouring Ding kilns, located in Jiancicun and eastern and western Yanshancun in Quyang county, Hebei province. Quyang county was regulated by the Dingzhou prefecture from the Tang period, which is why products of Quyang are known as Ding wares.[7] It was well positioned to provide the raw materials necessary for the ceramic industry such as clay and water for forming, wood and coal for firing, and river networks for transporting the finished goods. Plentiful sources of coal and clay were available in the Lingshan area, while the Dasha and Tang rivers are less than 12 km (7.5 miles) to the west and east respectively, connecting with other rivers flowing east into the sea beyond Tianjin and north to Beijing. Benefiting from this advantageous geographical position, the Ding kilns were in more or less constant operation from the early eighth until the mid-fourteenth century.

Early Ding ware was greatly influenced by Xing, and the two can be hard to distinguish. Indeed, until recently, shards from Samarra, Fustat, Japan and Korea were all attributed to Xing kilns (and should now be re-examined).[8] Certain characteristics, however, distinguish Ding ware from Xing. For example, Ding has a scored base whereas Xing is without tool marks; the Xing glaze is more even and less prone to streak than Ding, which

Fig. 1 (Opposite) Two Ding ware moulds, for an open dish and a bowl, both with dated inscriptions and designs of peony scrolls; Song dynasty, late 12th to early 13th century. The inscription incised on the underside of the larger dish translates as: 'Dading, Jiyou year, wuzi month, last week, 5th day, made by Dong Zhang [AD 1189]', and the five characters painted inside the bowl mould mean 'Dish [made in] the third year of Taihe [AD 1203]'. Such moulds significantly speeded up the process of decorating Ding porcelains.

Fig. 2 Porcelain Ding ware bowl with a moulded design of three boys holding fruiting melon tendrils and other plants, bound with a copper rim; Song dynasty, 12th to early 13th century. The addition of a metal rim to a ceramic vessel enhances its status as a precious object. It also has a practical role in hiding the rough mouth caused by firing the vessel upside down in a stepped saggar – a technique invented at the Ding kilns in the 11th century. Such intricate designs are also found in contemporary Song dynasty textiles.

contains a higher proportion of manganese oxide and less aluminium oxide; and only Ding wares have spinning marks under the glaze on the exterior.[9] The earliest Tang Ding wares are covered in a layer of slip. By the tenth century the quality of Xing had declined and Ding had improved, no longer using slip between body and glaze. The quality of production peaked in the Northern Song (960–1127) and Jin (1115–1234) dynasties. After the Yuan epoch, as the popularity of southern porcelains from Jingdezhen grew, Ding production in Quyang declined.

Beautiful porcelains were created using suitable washed and prepared body clay, high standards of forming and decorating, and sophisticated manipulation of glaze and kiln technology. Chemical analysis of Ding ware samples from the late Tang to the Jin dynasty indicate that there was little change in the chemical composition of the bodies. Local clay from Lingshan required little alteration before use and contained 31–35% alumina with 2% lime. Bowls and cups were thrown on a

potter's wheel and the walls shaved down with flat spatulas to create a lighter, finer body reminiscent of silver-ware.[10] Other shapes such as *jingping* were wheel-made in two or three horizontal sections, then luted together. Moulds were used for forming figures for burial and creating angular shapes. During the first half of the tenth century, Ding ceramics were made in the shape of flowers with three, four or five petals and were mostly undecorated. Later, in the tenth and early eleventh century, incised, combed and applied designs were created using iron, bamboo and comb cutters.[11] From the mid-eleventh century, potters used intricately carved intaglio moulds on to which leather-hard clay bowls and dishes were pressed, then peeled off and the mould reused (fig. 1). This technique not only transferred complex decoration and shape but also greatly speeded up the production process, replacing the time-consuming technique of carving and incising individual designs, although exterior patterns such as high-relief lotus petals were still individually etched.

In common with the Gongxian and Xing kilns, Ding potters made other ceramics concurrently – white, black, brown, green and Cizhou types. White monochromes were by far the largest group, covered with a very thin (0.05–0.1 mm) transparent glaze which was applied by dipping and rotating. It had a tendency to streak into *leihen* (tear tracts)[12] because it contained high levels of magnesium oxide (MgO) and low levels of lime (CaO).[13] Rarer black

Ding ware bodies

To produce a fine, white and translucent porcelain, special raw materials are needed. Clays must be low in iron oxides, which can cause a yellow tint, while producing a body which has strength in both the unfired and fired states. The alumina-rich clays which fulfil these requirements are known as kaolins, and are relatively uncommon. They are very refractory, requiring particularly high firing temperatures to make them vitrify. The kaolin deposits in north and south China differ in fundamental respects, and have produced two types of procelain body. The kaolinitic clays of northern China, where Ding ware was produced, are sedimentary deposits, often associated with coal seams. They are rich in alumina and naturally low in the fluxes that promote vitrification, such as potash, lime and soda.[37]

The Ding body therefore has a very high alumina content, of about 30%, which required very high firing temperatures in the range 1250–1320°C. It is hard and dense due to the formation of large amounts of the aluminium silicate, mullite, at high temperatures. However, the proportion of glass in the body is relatively low, so that the property of translucency is not well developed. In addition, the presence of small amounts of iron and titanium oxides has given much Ding ware an ivory, rather than pure white, tone. The Ding body (below) has higher potash, lime and magnesia than the local Lingshan clay,[38] and this has led some researchers to suggest that small amounts of a flux, or second clay, were added.[39]

Composition of a Ding ware body[40]							
SiO_2	TiO_2	Al_2O_3	Fe_2O_3	MgO	CaO	Na_2O	K_2O
63.8	0.7	29.7	0.8	0.9	2.1	0.3	1.7

and brown wares, also called 'purple' Ding, were glazed with solutions containing varying amounts of iron oxide.[14] Green Ding is produced in quite a different way, using a low-fired lead-fluxed solution, following the tradition of Chinese burial wares.[15] Some pillows and jars were painted in caramel-coloured slip on a creamy-white ground and then incised or carved through, resembling Cizhou-type ceramics but with a whiter body. Ding white, brown and blackwares were occasionally further ornamented with gilding,[16] although this method of decoration was not employed for the green and Cizhou types, perhaps indicating the latter's lower status.

Kilns and firing

Ding wares were fired in kilns shaped like *mantou* (steamed bread buns). Initially these were wood-fired and the ceramics fired in a reducing atmosphere which lent them a pale greenish blue-white hue. In the tenth century coal replaced wood and this change in fuel

resulted in an oxidising atmosphere which, together with the sulphur content of the coal, gave the porcelain an ivory tone. Potters created high-firing temperatures in the 1280–1350°C range. Early wares were fired in individual saggars lined with sand, so the unglazed foot-rings often bear traces of sand. Later Ding potters, about AD 1086–1127, revolutionised firing methods, pioneering the *fushao* technique of firing a vessel upside down in a stepped saggar. This reduced fuel consumption and increased potential output dramatically, as up to seven vessels of descending sizes could be placed together in one saggar, saving a substantial amount of space in the kiln for other products. By stacking them on their rims the ceramics were better supported and less likely to warp, yielding less wasted porcelain. For bowls of the same size, L-shaped section ring setters were used alternately in a stack, with the rims of the bowls resting on the horizontal part of the 'L'; to secure the stack for firing the setters were joined using slip before placing the bowls in a fire clay saggar.[17] The major

Fig. 3: Porcelain Ding gourd-shaped ewer with carved lotus petal design; Northern Song dynasty, 11th to early 12th century. Archaeological evidence confirms that Ding kilns supplied northern Buddhist monasteries with white porcelains to supplement the gold and silver vessels used in rituals.

disadvantage of *fushao* was the coarse unglazed mouth-rim, cleaned free of glaze with a sharp tool before firing to avoid the molten glaze sticking to the saggar. Sheet copper (fig. 2) or occasionally gold or silver was cut to fit the rough rims. Fitting such metal mounts increased the status of clay vessels, evidenced by the historical account of the Qian clan of Wuyue in AD 980, who presented two thousand *jinzhuan dingqi* (gold- and silver-bound Ding wares) as tribute to the Northern Song court.[18] Later, in the twelfth century, to increase production further and due to fewer concerns of quality, bowls were wiped free of glaze in the centre and stacked. Black and brownwares were fired on the foot-ring rather than upside down.[19]

The wide range and quality of Ding products reflects the diverse markets supplied by the kilns over six hundred years. Items were made for daily use such as bowls, basins, dishes, cups, cup-stands, spittoons, jars, ewers, bottles, vases, boxes, incense burners, censers, pillows and toys. Other objects were manufactured specifically for burial in tombs: for example, model vessels and figures of monks, entertainers, sleeping children and animals. Ding also made ceramics for use in Buddhist ceremonies, including reliquaries, *kundika*, oil-lamps, alms bowls, incense burners, figurative ewers, conch shells and stem-cups. Dishes, bowls, cups and jars were distributed abroad to customers in south-east Asia, the Near East and Africa.[20] Finely potted jars, bowls and vases were offered as tribute along with other locally made goods to the imperial court; some of these high-quality porcelains were given as presents to important officials and have been discovered buried in their tombs. This range of vessel types developed gradually over time; for example, evidence of ten different variations of food bowls has been excavated from a tenth-century context.[21]

The production process

Kilns at Nanzhen and Beizhen were, by the mid-tenth century, already so productive that a special post had to be established to collect kiln tax revenue for the imperial court. According to the pagoda stele of Wuzishanyuan, this post

Fig. 4 Porcelain Ding ware dish with black spotted glaze; Song dynasty, 11th to early 12th century. Ding potters also manufactured vessels of exquisite quality with coloured glazes. This example is coated in a solution containing varying amounts of iron oxide. Celebrated in contemporary texts, such ceramics are associated with luxurious lacquerwares.

was filled by Feng Ao around AD 957. By the Song dynasty, the kiln site at Jiancicun occupied an area of 1,170,000 sq m (1,404,000 sq yd).[22] Ceramics were not individually crafted but made by production-line processes, with potting, decorating, glazing and firing all carried out by different teams of artisans. Families of potters appear to have specialised in specific areas of production. For example, two extant moulds (in private collections) bear incised inscriptions suggesting that both belonged to the Liu family: one is inscribed *liu jia muzi* (Liu family mould) and the other is marked *liu liu lang* (Liu Liulang) and *Liujia* (Liu family).[23] The social status of these potters was low, and few records pertaining to them survive; presumably they were involved in the agricultural process during part of the year and produced ceramics seasonally for both specific orders and general consumption.

Buddhist and court use

Buddhism flourished in China and its spread meant not only a new philosophy and scriptures but also the need for new paraphernalia for Buddhist ceremonies. These were formed in shapes of Indian origin such as stupa-shaped jars and *kundika* or decorated with Indian motifs including lotus flowers and petals (fig. 3). Archaeological evidence confirms that Ding kilns supplied northern Buddhist monasteries in the Northern Song and Liao dynasties with white porcelains to supplement gold and silver vessels for rituals. A spectacular hoard comprising 160 items of high-quality sacral and secular Ding wares together with items of gold and silver, agate, jade, textiles, pearls and copper coins was excavated in Dingxian, in the crypt of the Jingzhi pagoda, and at the treasury of the Buddhist residential monastery at Jingzhong. The finds are dated at the Jingzhi site from an offering dish with an ink inscription, 'Taiping guangguo ernian' (AD 977), and at Jingzhong as 'zhidao yuannian' (AD 995).[24] Jingguang pagoda, excavated in Shunyi county near Beijing and dated 1013, also contained Ding whitewares: a ewer in human form, four *kundika*, five bowls, a ewer, bottle, three jars and covers and a box, as well as five silver boxes, a crystal pagoda, coins, an ornament and an inscribed stone.[25]

Some of these items were ordered specially and not simply bought. Seventeen of the Ding wares discovered in the Jingzhi and Jingzhong pagoda and monastery sites bore marks – *guan* or *xinguan* – meaning official or new official, suggesting a formal commission. The significance of this mark is the subject of much academic debate[26] and is not unique to Ding but also appears on Yaozhou and Yue greenwares.[27] Nor is it restricted to Buddhist use but also appears on export pieces, found in Egypt at Fustat (Old Cairo)[28] and on wares owned by the court. One of the earliest *guan*-marked pieces is a white petal-shaped Ding dish, excavated in

Mingtangshan, Linan county, Zhejiang province, dated on the basis of coin finds to AD 900.[29] In addition to archaeological evidence, inscriptions on ceramics – poems, workshop marks, hallmarks and the names of offices – can solve questions of patronage. Ding wares ordered for use at court include pieces marked with palace, pavilion or office names which indicate imperial patronage, such as *shang shi ju* (food bureau), *shang yao ju* (medical bureau) or *shang yi ju* (clothing bureau).[30]

Literary evidence suggests that high-ranking officials purchased Ding porcelains. A passage in the *Wenjian Qianlu* (Notes on what has been seen and heard) by Shao Bowen describes a visit of the Renzhong emperor to the

bedroom of Lady Zhang, who was made one of his concubines in 1049 and died in 1054.[31] There the emperor saw a concealed brown-glazed Ding dish, and when he discovered that it was a present from the court official Wang Gongcheng he was so enraged by Lady Zhang's corruption and recklessness in accepting the gift, contrary to his specific advice, that he smashed the precious dish and made the concubine plead for his forgiveness (fig. 4).

The presence of Ding wares in treasuries, palaces and noblemen's tombs testifies to their high status. They were more expensive than any other whiteware produced in northern kilns.[32] By imitating luxury materials, clay Ding wares were elevated to the rank of more

Fig. 5 Porcelain Ding ware bottle; Northern Song dynasty, 11th to early 12th century. Traditionally, Ding wares are regarded by connoisseurs as one of the 'Five Great Wares' of the Song dynasty. The other four are various types of greenware: Ru, Guan, Ge and Jun. Ding wares may first have arrived at court, along with other local products, as part of annual imperial tribute sent from Hebei province.

Fig. 6 Left: Silver dish from the hoard at Beihuangshan, Shaanxi province; Tang dynasty, 9th–10th century. Right: porcelain Ding ware dish incised with a single-horned creature looking at the moon; Jin dynasty, 12th century. The form of the white Ding dish, with a rolled bracketed rim, is copied from silverwork. The similarity of white ceramics to silverware is recorded in Chinese literature from the Tang dynasty (AD 618–906). Silver and ceramic Ding wares have been excavated together from the crypts of several Buddhist temples in recent years. The rare compositional decoration is derived from Southern Song painting.

valuable commodities: shiny, thin white Ding emulates silver (fig. 6), while black- and brown-glazed Ding parallel monochrome lacquers. Unlike celadons, green Ding do not simulate jade, nor are they mentioned in literature, and consequently they can be regarded as less valuable. From the tenth century, Ding white, brown and black ceramics were celebrated in Chinese texts.[33] Descriptions of 'ink-coloured Ding as black as lacquer' and 'purple Ding' are included in the Yuan text *Gegu yaolun* by Cao Zhao. Ding wares were collected as antiques as early as the Yuan dynasty. In 1363, Ding is cited as a collectable in the *Zhizheng youji* by Kong

Qi, who cautions that not all Ding wares are treasures, implying imitations or a later decline in quality.[34] The Ming (AD 1368–1644) text *Bowu yaolan* (A survey of art objects) by Gu Yingtai mentions contemporary imitations of Ding which are difficult to distinguish from genuine Ding, such as King Wen's tripod incense burners and incense burners with handles and an animal face design.[35] Production of

such forgeries confirms the value placed on true Ding wares. Qing dynasty (AD 1644–1911) collectors heralded Ding wares as one of the 'five famous wares of the Song dynasty' (fig. 5), the others being Ru ware from Henan, Guan ware from Zhejiang, Jun ware from Hebei and Ge ware, whose manufacturing site is as yet undiscovered.[36]

Ding glazes

Far Eastern stoneware and porcelain glazes matured at high temperatures of 1150–1350°C, and differed markedly in composition from the low-melting lead- or alkali-rich glazes of Middle Eastern and European traditions. The unfired ceramic was dipped into the suspension of raw glaze, and body and glaze fired together.

Chinese porcelain glazes are rich in

alumina, and fluxed by varying amounts of lime and alkalis. They were typically made by mixing body clay with wood ash, or limestone.[41] Ding glazes appear to have been produced using ash. Like Ding bodies, Ding glazes have unusually high magnesia, a characteristic which has been considered to increase their resistance to crazing.[43]

Composition of Ding ware glaze[43]							
SiO_2	TiO_2	Al_2O_3	Fe_2O_3	MgO	CaO	Na_2O	K_2O
70.60	0.10	18.50	0.97	2.06	3.79	2.43	0.28

Mass-Production of Roman Finewares

Paul Roberts

Roman civilisation dominated the classical world over the course of a millennium. From the sixth century BC, Rome expanded gradually from a small Latin city-state in central Italy into an empire which stretched outwards from the Mediterranean basin to incorporate, at its height in the second century AD, provinces in northern and southern Europe, North Africa and the Near East (fig. 1). Rome tended to absorb and adapt local cultural traditions rather than imposing its own, establishing widespread political and economic stability through trade and conquest.[1]

The first Roman pottery – a term describing ceramics from areas under Roman control or influence[2] – to be exported from Italy in quantity was Campanian ware or Ceramica Campana,[3] so called because Campania, along with Etruria and Rome, was one of the main areas of production. This pottery, part of the Black Gloss fineware tradition of the eastern and central Mediterranean, was produced throughout Italy from the fourth to the later first century BC. Regional productions included polychrome painted Gnathian ware from south-eastern Italy[4] and cups and bowls stamped with small motifs such as palmettes – products of the so-called workshop of the small stamps, *l'atelier des petites estampilles*[5] – and *pocola* (drinking cups) with stamped and/or painted decoration (fig. 3), both from Rome. Others, such as Calenian ware[6] from Cales in Campania, were inspired by metalwork.

Predominant among the Campana wares and exported throughout the Mediterranean from Morocco to the Black Sea[7] was Campana 'A', from Campania.[8] It was mass-produced in huge quantities in a standardised and fairly limited range of easily stackable forms such as cups, bowls and dishes. The finish of the wares, achieved through immersing them in the clay slip rather than by painting it on, facilitated production.

Ceramica Campana, and indeed subsequent productions of fine pottery in the Roman period, constituted essentially a 'piggy-back' or 'parasitic' trade,[9] travelling with agricultural produce such as grain, oil and, particularly for Campania, wine. The main cargo would usually be amphorae,[10] and the availability of this subsidised form of transport enabled Ceramica Campana to travel cheaply and in vast quantities, at least to coastal and hinterland areas, and in some cases allowed the imported fineware completely to supplant the local wares.[11]

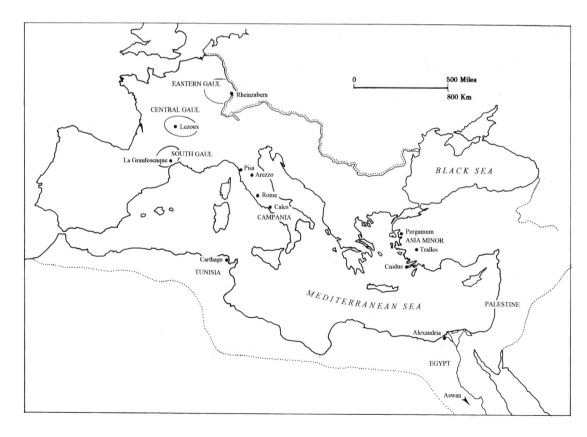

Fig. 1 Map showing centres of fineware mass-production across the Roman empire.

Fig. 2 Early imperial fineware. Left to right: lead-glazed cup (skyphos), made in Tarsus, Asia Minor; Thin-Walled beaker from Italy; mould-made bottle decorated in relief with Bacchic scenes, made in Cnidus, Asia Minor; Thin-Walled cup with barbotine decoration, made in Spain; lead-glazed pourer (askos), made in central Italy.

The emergence of Red Slip ware

In the mid-first century BC, potters at Arretium (Arezzo) began producing standard cup and dish forms drawn from the established Black Gloss tradition, but with a red slip instead of the usual black.[12] The resulting Red Slip ware – a subject of interest and detailed study by scholars for at least the last century[13] – has come to be widely known by the Italian term *sigillata*, which literally means pottery decorated with motifs or scenes. However, sigillata has since come to be used as a generic term for all Red Slip ware production of the Roman period, whether decorated or plain, and indeed it is preferable to terms which are either geographically limiting, such as 'Arretine', or convenient but factually inaccurate and potentially misleading, such as 'samian' (often used in British archaeology as a blanket term for Gaulish sigillata).

It was originally thought that this new development was influenced by the appearance in Italy of Red Slip wares from the eastern Mediterranean, in particular the so-called 'Eastern Sigillata A' wares, perhaps from Palestine,[14] or by an influx of the eastern potters themselves, following Augustus' conquest of Egypt in 30 BC.[15] Recently, however, it has been suggested that the production of red-slipped ware may have been a shrewd marketing move on the part of the potters of Arezzo;[16] it is argued that the forms were already familiar to them and that the new finish, obtained by firing vessels in an oxidised atmosphere – with oxygen, as opposed to the reducing atmosphere, which produced black and grey finishes – posed few technological difficulties.[17]

Certainly the new technique spread rapidly, soon replacing the production of Black Gloss pottery throughout Italy, and by the early first century AD Red Slip ware had become predominant throughout the Roman world. The explosive growth of sigillata production was due in part to the increased markets for all finished goods which were opened up by the establishment of the *Pax Romana* in the early Empire. The combination of the Roman policy of administration through urban centres, the new political and social stability and a mostly unitary economic and fiscal system resulted in a boom in demand for supplies and goods for both the thriving cities and the countryside, a consequent rise in the number of production centres and an increase in the scale and complexity of marketing systems. Reasonable points have been made, for instance, concerning differences in the availability of and access to fine pottery over time[18] as well as the problems of ascertaining the nature of sites through surface finds,[19] yet the abundance of sigillata on a broad range of rural and urban sites[20] suggests that it was widely and, by implication, fairly cheaply available.

Other finewares

In addition to Red Slip wares, many other finewares existed in the early imperial period (fig. 3). So-called Italian Thin-Walled ware was carried through-out the Mediterranean and beyond,[21] and many areas developed their own industries based on its prototypes.[22] From the eastern Mediterranean came mould-made relief-decorated wares from Pergamon, Cnidus[23] and Corinth,[24] and lead-glazed ware from western and southern Asia Minor.[25] In Italy, importedlead-glazed ware inspired productions in Rome and Campania which were widely exported,[26] and these in turn stimulated other production centres beyond the Alps.[27]

Also noteworthy are certain types of mass-produced coarseware, exported all over the empire in large quantities, such as 'Pompeian Red' ware,[28] other Italian cooking wares,[29] and those of North Africa[30] and Asia Minor.[31]

Sigillata in Italy and Gaul

The definitive fineware production of the early Roman imperial period, both in Italy and beyond, was Italian sigillata.[32] Originally the forms comprised cups, bowls and platters, echoing some of the previous Campana productions, but later shapes included mould-made beakers, stemmed cups (fig. 4) and other deep or closed vessels. It seems certain that the elaborate relief decoration often found on these forms was derived from contemporary developments in other fields of art, in particular silverware, sometimes with the use of moulds taken directly from metal vessels.[33] There is abundant evidence for technical aspects of the production of relief-decorated wares, including fired clay moulds which would have been placed on the potter's wheel and stamps used for impressing figures and designs on to the interiors of the moulds (fig. 5). There are also moulds for producing the appliqué motifs used on some forms.

The production of Italian sigillata was widespread, encompassing cities such as Arezzo, Pisa, Luni, Ostia, Pozzuoli, Rome and sites in the Po Plain.[34] The production of Italian sigillata as a whole is often termed Arretine ware, though strictly this term should be used only for the products of Arezzo itself. However, archaeological evidence for production is often limited to stamps or stray finds of wasters or other kiln debris. The excavations in Arezzo, on which so much of our knowledge and assumptions are based, were conducted in less than scientific conditions in the late nineteenth century, while excavations at Pisa in 1965, revealing kiln waste of Cn. Ateius, were unstratigraphic.

Workshop organisation

Production seems to have taken place mainly in workshops, perhaps large enough to warrant Peacock's term of 'manufactory',[35] belonging to individuals such as Perennius or groups (possibly families) such as the Atei and the Rasinii. The large scale of production is certainly suggested by excavations at Arezzo, where the levigation tanks (for settling out impurities in the clay) of M. Perennius, one of the first major manufacturers of Italian sigillata, measured 9 × 4 m (27 × 12 ft)[36] and, it has been estimated, could hold 10,000 gallons of liquid.[37]

Although it is certain that many people would have been involved in the various stages of production, such as the extraction and preparation of clay and the forming and decoration of vases, the exact status of the creators of the vases is difficult to determine. Certainly there appear to have been freedmen (liberti) or perhaps slaves involved in manufacture, as evidenced by the name-stamps impressed into

Terra sigillata bodies and slips

Standardisation of the ceramic was attained in the major *terra sigillata* factories by the use of fine, calcareous clays[74] which fired to bodies of consistent quality over a temperature range of 850–1050°C, corresponding to the temperatures likely to be encountered in a wood-fired updraught kiln of the period. The glossy surfaces are due to the use of a very fine clay slip, similar to those on Greek Attic pottery (ch. 12), but oxidised red rather than reduced black.

The micrograph, of a cross-section of a sherd of Eastern Gaulish sigillata, shows the typical open, partially vitrified structure of the calcareous body and the dense, vitreous nature of the slip. There is a strong adherence between the two, and the resulting tough, impermeable 'non-stick' surface made for a very popular tableware.

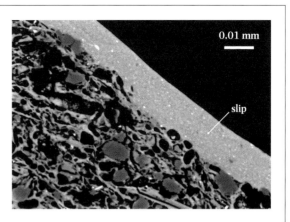

many vessels. These stamps, usually giving one or two names in the genitive case, signified the name of the potter and/or the owner of the workshop. In the absence of reliable archaeological excavations, groups of these stamps, which have been the object of curiosity and study since the seventeenth century,[38] serve as the main basis for our knowledge of the workshops' organisation. Taking into account the stamps recorded to date, only ten workshops seem to have had attached to them twenty or more workers who signed their pieces, while the largest, the workshop(s) of the Rasinii in Arezzo, had approximately sixty who stamped their name.[39]

In spite of the large number of such workshops which must have existed throughout Italy, there is no epigraphic evidence for any formal organisation or guild (*collegium*) of potters, such as are known from Roman Egypt.[40] One of the few pieces of evidence from Italy for a grouping of potters working at exactly the same time (the evidence of groups of potters in particular workshops derived from the evidence of stamps alone can only be relatively precise) is provided by a sherd of an Arretine dish in the British Museum (fig. 5, right).[41] The sherd, inscribed on both sides in Greek cursive script, gives a list of names, and next to one name uses the word *ouerna*, a Greek transliteration of the Latin word *verna* (slave). It is perhaps significant that the name against which this word appears is the only name of all those on the list not to be represented in the corpus of name-stamps from Arezzo, suggesting that only freedmen or freeborn workers could stamp their products. The sherd is not a tally list, as no quantities of vessels are noted, but the way in which the names have been both marked with a point and scored through suggests that it might be a payment document.

With regard to the organisation of the workshops, there were certainly major groupings of workshops in large towns, with some evidence for co-operation between them, such as the joint stamping of vases by the Rasinii and Memmii of Arezzo.[42] There were also clearly sub- and extra-urban 'branches', and the workshop of Umbricius Cordus, at Torrita di Siena,[43] provides a clear example of potters using moulds made in Arezzo to produce vases elsewhere. Other potters seem to have had 'branches' outside Arezzo; the Atei and Rasinii, also manufactured in Pisa.[44]

Although sigillata manufacture could have been achieved without the import of foreign techniques or personnel,[45] certain developments nevertheless seem to be linked almost exclusively to foreign (i.e. Greek) names. This is particularly true of the production of relief-decorated ware, where nearly all the finest pieces are marked with names which appear to have an eastern origin,

Fig. 4 Stemmed cup in Italian sigillata, decorated in relief with figures of the seasons. The cup was made in Arezzo, and is signed by the potter Cn. Ateius.

such as Tigranus and Nicopheros.[46] Such workmen may well have been regarded as the élite in their field; only one in five of the workshops in Arezzo produced relief-decorated ware, and even in these, only one worker in seven made relief-decorated as opposed to plain ware.[47] Many workshops did not produce the ware at all.

Large pottery enterprises clearly had arrangements and dealings of some sort with other workshops and potters throughout Italy, whether through expansion or franchise. The picture of production became international, however, with the establishment of 'branches' beyond Italy. In the eastern Mediterranean, Eastern Sigillata 'B' began to be produced in the early Empire in the area around Tralles in Asia Minor, with forms identical to those in Italian sigillata, sometimes with bilingual stamps in Latin and Greek and some reading Sentius (a potter known from the Augustan period at Arezzo) or even Arretina.[48] The latter could, however, be due to the rise of a generic term for this type of pottery,[49] as with the word 'china' and, as Gatti and Onorati convincingly argue,[50] may be true of the term 'samian' for Black Gloss.

In the early first century AD, at La Muette, near Lyon in southern France, both the Atei and the Rasinii of Arezzo established workshops making sigillata, using moulds (and presumably skilled craftsmen) from their home factories in Italy.[51] It is still uncertain whether this was direct expansion or an example of devolved or franchised production. Further south at La Graufesenque, again perhaps influenced by the Atei,[52] a sigillata industry grew up which, though inspired by the wares of Arezzo, made increasingly distinct forms and decoration, and the manufacture of Gaulish sigillata, often referred to as 'samian' ware, was launched.[53] Produced for over three centuries, Gaulish sigillata originated in many different centres grouped into three main areas: southern Gaul, with sites such as La Graufesenque,[54] central Gaul including Lezoux[55] and eastern Gaul, with centres such as Rheinzabern.[56]

Excavations around La Graufesenque in southern France have revealed an industrial landscape of workshops, kilns and levigation tanks, as well as some of the potters' dwellings and burial grounds.[57] The site has also provided some of the most immediate and dramatic evidence for mass-manufacture of tablewares anywhere in the Roman empire: the size of the kilns and the large number of kiln wasters (misfired vessels) suggest firings on a very large scale (fig. 6). This is confirmed by the evidence of numerous tallies on sherds, giving lists of kiln firings of vessels made by many different workers (or workshops). It is not uncommon to read records on these tallies of firings of between 25,000 and 30,000 vessels, ascribed to between five and ten different potters.[58] Of those potters mentioned on the tallies who are also known from name-stamps, none appear to be of servile status.[59]

It seems likely that the success of the Gaulish sigillatas contributed considerably to the decline of the wares of Arezzo and central Italy. As the market for Italian wares became more restricted – in the north and west by Gaulish sigillata, in the east by Eastern sigillata, and in the south by African sigillata (see below) – the distribution and typological range of Italian sigillata became more limited. The golden age of Italian sigillata production at Arezzo, Pisa and many other sites seems to have come to an end by the mid-first century AD. At Arezzo, the workshops of Perennius and his successors seem to have ceased production abruptly in the late AD 20s.

The rise of African Red Slip ware

In addition to the industries of Gaul and the prolific (though far less widely exported) productions of Spain,[60] Italian sigillata was also the inspiration for a ware which was to outlive virtually all the others, namely African Red Slip (ARS) ware, which became the dominant tableware throughout most of the

Fig. 5 Objects used in the manufacture of Italian sigillata.
Left front: stamp for impressing moulds, showing a figure similar to one on the stemmed cup in fig. 4. Back: part of a mould, with a modern cast, for a cup decorated with a Bacchic scene, signed M. Peren[ni] Tigran[i]. Centre front: plaque, with modern casts, used for making multiple appliqués of theatrical masks. Centre left: fragment of a plate showing a similar appliqué. Far right: sherd from Arezzo, perhaps a payment docket, giving a list of potters' names.

Fig. 6 Left: kiln stack of misfired South Gaulish 'Samian' ware bowls from La Graufesenque in southern Gaul. A kiln spacer is fused to the bowls, which were made by at least five different potters. Centre: South Gaulish 'Samian' ware bowl, made at La Graufesenque. Right: Central Gaulish 'Samian' ware bowl, made at Lezoux.

Fig. 7 African Red Slip ware. Left to right: early to mid-imperial jug, made in northern Tunisia; rouletted bowl, made in northern Tunisia; mid- to later imperial dish with appliqué decoration, from central Tunisia; late imperial dish, made in northern Tunisia.

Mediterranean basin for much of the mid to late Empire (fig. 7).[61] The ware seems to have originated around Carthage in northern Tunisia, in the early to mid first century AD, and began to be exported in quantity in the last quarter of the century.

The production of ARS ware diversified enormously over the seven centuries of its production and, as with the Gaulish wares, the centres of manufacture also shifted, almost certainly in response to changing circumstances in agriculture and the economy.[62]

Sites of ARS ware manufacture have been identified, for example at El Mahrine,[63] which may be connected with rural estates. Very little is known about the potters themselves because, unlike the Arretine or Gaulish makers and workshop owners, they did not name-stamp their pieces. This may re-inforce the idea of estate manufacture,[64] with potters on a particular estate

making pots to be used either on that estate or on other estates belonging to the same owner, or to accompany the produce from the owner's estates on its way to market. This could mean there was no need to stamp pots for tally purposes, as all output would be for the estate for which the potters worked. Many African forms seem to have been made using moulds,[65] which signifi-cantly simplified the process of manu-facture and would have permitted relatively unskilled workers to produce vessels. This perhaps accounts for the vast quantities in which the ware was made and exported throughout the Mediterranean, particularly the large dish forms of the third to fifth centuries AD.

Just as Italian sigillata had inspired imitations in Gaul, Africa and the East, so African Red Slip ware in its turn was the inspiration for other finewares, particularly in the late Empire, such as

Phocaean Red Slip ware from Asia Minor,[66] the so-called 'Cypriot' Red Slip ware[67] and Egyptian Red Slip ware.[68] This last ware, from production sites including those at Aswan in Upper Egypt[69] and Hermopolis Magna in Middle Egypt,[70] was distributed primarily within Egypt itself but was also exported (particularly the products of Aswan) to parts of the eastern Mediterranean.[71] The forms produced were initially close copies of bowls, large dishes and platters from the repertoire of ARS of the fifth and early sixth century, but by the later sixth century a vast array of cups, bowls, dishes and closed forms were produced.[72] Manufacture continued at Aswan until at least the tenth century AD,[73] its potters the final representatives of a tradition which had lasted for over a thousand years.

Chinese Porcelain from Jingdezhen

Jessica Harrison-Hall

Jingdezhen was the most important production centre for pottery and porcelain in the whole of the Chinese empire and one of the earliest industrial towns in the world.[1] In total, the kilns there operated for over a thousand years, employing many hundreds of workers and producing millions of ceramic vessels and sculptures. No other kiln complex in the world can boast such a continuous history.

Pre-modern manufacture at Jingdezhen may be considered in terms of six chronological phases. The first porcelains excavated there were made in the Five Dynasties period (AD 907–60) and imitate the products of successful northern and southern kilns such as Xing white and Yue greenwares. Then, during the Song (960–1279) and first half of the Yuan[2] (1280–*c*.1330) dynasties, *qingbai* porcelains of both high and low quality made at Jingdezhen were sold widely within China and exported all over the globe. During the third phase, from the late Yuan (*c*.1330–68) to the early Ming (1368–*c*.1487) dynasties,[3] *shufu* underglaze blue and underglaze red wares were created, under the patronage of the imperial court. Next, in the late Ming (*c*.1488–1644), a tremendous expansion in the scale of production took place, stimulated both by foreign demand and changes in working practices. Then, in the first half of the Qing (1644–*c*.1795) period,[4] overglaze enamelling was perfected and extended. Finally, from the late Qing to the Republican period (*c*.1796–1911), the failure to develop quality, to innovate new styles of decoration and to modernise, in the face of severe foreign competition and political unrest, led to a decline at the kilns and the loss of Jingdezhen's pre-eminent position.

Fig. 1 Porcelain wine ewer and warming basin, incised beneath a qingbai glaze. Northern Song dynasty, 11th century, from Jingdezhen, Jiangxi province, southern China. Similar sets may be seen in contemporary Song murals and have been excavated in Song tombs such as at Dongshan, Haining county, Zhejiang province. They were used together with fine silver and lacquer tableware in the homes of well-to-do merchants and scholar officials.

Geographical advantages

Jingdezhen is situated in south China, in the hilly north-eastern part of Jiangxi province, along the bank of the Chang river. This flows into Lake Boyang and then enters the Yangzi, giving the town access to a wider river and canal network for transportation of raw materials and finished goods. Land and water trade routes were congested by the scale of mercantile activity, as recorded by a temple stele dated 1487:

The town is producing imperial porcelain for the entire country, couriers are coming and going day and night, officials are arriving from everywhere, merchants doing their business incessantly, the northern route seems to be too narrow for all this traffic.[5]

The kiln complex is located here, in an area rich in the natural assets required for porcelain manufacture. Jingdezhen is skirted by five mountains, where china clay (kaolin or *gaolingtu*) and china stone (petuntse or *baidunzi*) could be collected and quarried to supply the basic ingredients for porcelain. Ample stocks of pine timber for kiln fuel could be gleaned from the surrounding, thickly forested area. In addition to the materials required for forming, firing and transporting porcelain, the region's high population ensured low labour costs. Jiangxi is traditionally noted for its fertile land, agricultural products and tea plantations, making it possible for a substantial workforce to be supplied with rice and pork despite the fact that the craftsmen were not full-time participants in the agricultural process.

Working practices

The potters were organised into groups, each performing specific tasks, as was the practice in other industries such as paper-making or lacquer production. Such a sophisticated system of division of labour was not adopted in Western Europe until the Industrial Revolution in the nineteenth century. Thus the mining of china stone, collection of china clay, grinding of petuntse, washing of clay, preparing glaze, making moulds and saggars, throwing and forming, decorating, glazing, firing, overglazing, refiring, quality control,

Fig. 2 Porcelain serving dish painted under the glaze in blue cobalt oxide with a Mandarin fish swimming among water weeds. Yuan dynasty, first half of the 14th century, from Jingdezhen. Such large, heavily potted serving dishes were supplied to customers in the Middle East and survive from the Ardebil shrine in Iran and the Topkapi Saray, Istanbul. Considered luxuries, these blue-and-white porcelains inspired local copies in inferior materials.

packing and distributing were each carried out by a different team of skilled artisans. These processes are recorded in various works including Song Yingxing's book *Tian gong kai wu* ('Creations of Nature and Man') in 1637, which gives an account of porcelain production at Jingdezhen accompanied by woodblock-print illustrations.[6] Eighteenth- and nineteenth-century watercolour paintings, made for export to Europe (see p. 13), accurately render the techniques involved 'but in a totally unfaithful setting, reducing to gentle cottage crafts what were intensive industries'.[7]

The earliest written Chinese account of manufacture at Jingdezhen is Jiang Qi's notes in the 1270 edition of the *Fuliang xian zhi* ('Annals of Fuliang County'). Père d'Entrecolles (1664–1741), a French Jesuit missionary based in Jiangxi, wrote letters in 1712 and 1722 to Father Orry, treasurer in Paris of the Chinese and Indian missions, vividly describing the scale of porcelain production at Jingdezhen: 'During a night entrance, one thinks that the whole city is on fire, or that it is one large furnace with many vent holes'.[8] Further works in English translations include Zhu Yan's *Tao Shuo* ('Pottery Explanations', 1774),[9] Lan Pu's *Jingdezhen Tao Lu* ('Jingdezhen Pottery Records', 1815)[10] and Chen Liu's *Tao Ya* ('Pottery Refinements', 1906).[11] Tang Ying's *Taocheng Shiyu Gao* ('Instructions on the Making of Pottery', 1740s)[12] records the earliest archaeological investigation of Jingdezhen. Tang Ying collected sherds from Xianghu, a Song kiln site, and made notes on body and glaze. Modern archaeologists regularly publish their Jingdezhen excavations at sites such as Yangmeiting and

Fig. 3 Porcelain jar decorated in doucai style with two single-horned chi-dragons among flowering and fruiting melon plants. Ming dynasty, Chenghua period (AD 1465–87), from Jingdezhen. The base is marked with the character tian (heaven), used to refer to the emperor. Such jars have been excavated with covers from the Chenghua stratum at the Ming Imperial Factory at Jingdezhen.

Shihuwan in the suburbs of Jingdezhen; others in the East River and South River areas of Fuliang county; Hutian, a kiln active from the tenth to early seventeenth century; Ming provincial kilns at Yaoli; and the imperial kilns at Zhushan.[13]

The earliest wares

Over its thousand-year history the manufacturing processes, product range and exact location of the workshops have varied. The earliest wares, dating from the tenth century – mostly dishes and ewers but also jars, shallow basins and water-pots – were excavated from the South River area. Those from the lower levels at Liujiawan, part of the Hutian complex, were made in the early tenth century and imitate southern Yue greenwares, with dark-grey body and green glaze.[14] White-bodied, clear-glazed bowls and dishes with a square-cut foot were found in the upper levels at Liujiawan and possibly imitate northern Xing whitewares (ch. 28). Both of these early types were fired in stacks, without saggars, resting on pure kaolin spurs set on an unglazed ring inside the vessel.[15]

Qingbai porcelains

In the early eleventh century, during the Northern Song dynasty, green and whitewares were gradually superseded by innovative, finely potted, initially plain then carved *qingbai* (bluish-white) porcelains (fig. 1), evidenced by their discovery in tombs dated to 1000 and 1002 at Jiujiang, also in Jiangxi

province.[16] Black-glazed, black-bodied, *temmoku*-type tea bowls, made in imitation of Jian wares, were produced at Hutian at the same time.[17] Early *qingbai* wares were made of pure *cishi* (china stone), mostly modelled with a high foot and thick base, wheel-thrown and pared down to a thin body. They were fired at about 1200°C upright in individual saggars on a clay pad which fitted into the foot-ring. As at the northern Ding kilns in Hebei province (ch. 28), products of the late eleventh and twelfth centuries were fired

Jingdezhen porcelain bodies and glazes

Southern Chinese bodies 36 were produced using primary kaolins, alumina-rich and iron-poor clays produced by the alteration of igneous rocks. At Jingdezhen, these occur in close association with porcelain or china stones, rocks composed of quartz, fine mica (sericite) and feldspar (albite). During the early stages of production a single porcelain stone, which also contained some kaolin (kaolinised porcelain stone), was mined and pulverised to be used as raw material. From the Yuan dynasty, prompted either by a shortage of natural material of the correct composition or by a desire to control the body composition more precisely, the potters changed to a two-component body. This involved mixing kaolin with a kaolin-free porcelain stone.

Southern Chinese glazes[37] were based upon mixtures of lime, or glaze ash, with a porcelain stone known as 'glaze stone'. The lime was produced by burning alternate layers of limestone with brushwood; this caused the limestone to crumble and saved crushing. By varying the ratio of glaze ash to glaze stone, the lime contents of the glazes could be varied. The high lime contents of *qingbai* ware produced fluid and glassy-looking glazes, while the low lime of *shufu* resulted in a failure to dissolve all of the quartz in the raw materials, leading to a more opaque appearance. As they generally contain up to about one per cent iron oxide, Jingdezhen porcelains were generally fired in reduction, to produce a bluish tint due to Fe^{2+} ions rather than a yellow due to Fe^{3+}.

Fig. 4   A pair of porcelain bowls painted over the glaze in famille verte enamels with a bird perched on a fruiting peach branch. Qing dynasty, Kangxi mark and period (1662–1722), from Jingdezhen. Intricate preparation of food is an essential part of Chinese culture. Imperial banquets, such as those celebrating an important birthday, required an extensive range of vessels for hot and cold delicacies. Porcelain, supplementing gold, silver and jade vessels on these occasions, was supplied by the Imperial Factory at Jingdezhen.

upside down on their rims and were decorated with moulded designs, reflecting the desire to produce a greater yield at the expense of quality.[18] Production of *qingbai* continued in the Yuan dynasty, when figures with applied beading or cut-away panels with high-relief decoration were popular. Opaque white ceramics, marked with the characters *shu* and *fu* (privy council), were made for the first time, fired concurrently with *qingbai* wares. However, the bodies, glaze composition, form and functions all differ: clay used for *shufu* is a mixture of kaolin and china stone, unlike *qingbai* which is pure china stone; *shufu* contains 5–6% calcium oxide while *qingbai* contains 12–13%, making *shufu* more opaque. *Shufu* wares also appear in a narrower product range, mostly comprising bowls with everted rims,

saucers and stem-cups, possibly reflecting their use as officially ordered ceremonial wares.

Blue-and-white

From the late Yuan dynasty, *c*.1330, underglaze blue and red porcelains were made at Jingdezhen using a *shufu*-style body mix of kaolin and china stone. Blue-and-white ceramics were first made at Gongxian kilns in northern China in the Tang dynasty (618–906),[19] while underglaze red ceramics had been created in the ninth to tenth century at the Tongguan kiln in Hunan province.[20] The Jingdezhen innovation was not so much the technique but the use of these pigments on a porcelain body to create figural, calligraphic, floral, geometric and abstract designs. Blue pigment used in the Yuan was cobalt with a high iron and low manganese content, imported from Iran. Later, Chinese cobalt, high in manganese and low in iron, was used. The red pigment was a reduction-fired, locally available copper oxide which was much harder to control.[21] This method of decoration was employed with spectacular success on large-scale dishes (fig. 2) as well as jars, stem-cups, bottle vases and pourers.

During the Ming dynasty (1368–1644), private kilns were scattered

around the town and its suburbs, and imperial kilns of the Hongwu reign period (1368–98) were established around Zhushan by 1369. The private kilns manufactured mostly blue-and-white, but also fired monochromes and enamelled wares.[22] During the Hongwu reign, red and white porcelain was favoured at court.[23] By the early fifteenth-century reigns of the Yongle emperor (1403–25) and the Xuande emperor (1426–35), Jingdezhen kilns were producing pieces of extremely fine quality to meet the monarch's demands.[24] The Yongle emperor favoured red-and-white and monochrome whitewares over blue-and-white, and ordered porcelains in Tibetan metalwork forms for Lamaistic Buddhist ceremonies. As well as vessels and sculptures, Jingdezhen also fired construction materials. The Porcelain Pagoda, built in memory of his deceased parents by the Yongle emperor in the grounds of the Bao'en Temple on the outskirts of Nanjing, was faced with white L-shaped bricks, made between 1412 and 1419 at Zhushan, Jingdezhen.[25] This nine-storey building, destroyed in the 1860s during the Taiping rebellion, was also adorned with colourful earthenware tiles.

Jingdezhen recovered and *famille verte*, a new style of enamelling, was introduced. This technique, in which the dominant colour of the palette is green, was either used directly on the fired or unglazed body or painted over a high-fired transparent glaze (fig. 4). In the late Kangxi era, in about 1720, the range of colours in the overglaze enamel palette was extended by the invention of an opaque white enamel and a new pink, and their addition to existing colours produced a whole assortment of pastel hues. In the Yongzheng reign (1723–35), *famille rose* porcelains of the finest quality were achieved (fig. 5). During the Qianlong era (1736–95) the kilns thrived, experimenting with glazes which imitated materials such as lacquer, wood, silver or cloisonné.

The Jiaqing reign period (1796–1820) marked the beginning of a long decline in quality and creativity. Failure to modernise fully during the mid-nineteenth-century reigns of Daoguang (1821–50), Xianfeng (1851–61) and Tongzhi (1862–74) in the face of Japanese, English and German competition contributed to the decline. Before the overthrow of the

Fig. 5 Detail of one of five medallions on the exterior of a porcelain bowl painted in famille rose overglaze enamels with auspicious butterflies among flowers. Qing dynasty, Yongzheng mark and period (1723–35).

Overglaze enamel

Doucai overglaze enamelling, invented in the Xuande emperor's reign (1426–35), was perfected (fig. 3) in the Chenghua period (1465–87).[26] Overglaze enamels had been used in the Yuan but were more extensively employed in the Ming, either to cover an entire vessel or to paint a specific design. Low-fired overglaze enamels are essentially composed of the same material as glass. Ceramics decorated with these enamels were fired for a second time over the glaze in a muffle kiln at a temperature between 700 and 800°C. *Doucai*, meaning interlocking colours, is an overglaze enamelling technique whereby high-fired underglaze blue outlines were coloured in with low-fired red, yellow, green and aubergine enamels. Closely related to this technique are *wucai* (five colours) overglaze enamel wares. A tremendous expansion of the Jingdezhen kilns, stimulated by the demands of the export market, occurred during the reigns of the Jiajing (1522–66), Longqing (1567–72) and Wanli (1573–1620) emperors, when both blue-and-white and *wucai* wares were made in abundance.[27]

Famille verte

After the collapse of the Ming dynasty in 1644, porcelain production was not only affected by the tremendous social upheaval but suffered specifically from the lapse of imperial patronage. Later, in the reign of the Kangxi emperor (1662–1722), the fortunes of

Chinese overglaze enamels

An enamel is a glassy material of low melting temperature which contains a colouring compound, and sometimes a compound to make it opaque. A fired porcelain, sometimes with underglaze blue decoration, was painted when cold with crushed enamels and then refired to fuse them to the glaze. Chinese overglaze porcelain enamels are rich in lead oxide (40–70%), which is a strong flux and caused them to melt at around 700°C. Colourants included copper green, cobalt blue, iron red and manganese aubergine purple. The *famille rose* palette, introduced in the 1720s, included new colours, including pink, based upon colloidal gold, and opaque white, based upon lead arsenate. These colours had recently become common in the European glass industry and it has been suggested that their introduction in Chinese porcelain represents an incorporation of the European colours into the Chinese repertoire 38.

Qing in 1911, joint-venture government and private-sector porcelain enterprises – the Pingxiang, Hunan and Jiangxi Porcelain Companies – were established. The Jiangxi Porcelain Company located its main plant near the former imperial factory at Zhushan, Jingdezhen, and this was still in operation in 1934. *Qianjiang*, an over-glaze enamel technique of painting in black and sepia enamels after the manner of ink painting, was popular in the post-Republican (*c*.1911–49) period (fig. 6). Research institutes and vocational schools were founded in efforts to revitalise the industry, but the Sino-Japanese War and ensuing chaos meant that by 1947 only 76 kilns survived, compared to 150 before the war.[28] Production at Jingdezhen continues still, but mostly comprises reproductions of earlier classic wares, lesser-quality utilitarian wares or overly ornate modern creations which are technically impressive but lack soul.

Administration and organisation

Organisation of the kilns altered over their thousand years of production. Initially the Fuliang Porcelain Office was established in 1278 to supervise the Yuan imperial kilns, according to the 'Account of Court Officials' in section 88 of the *Yuan Shi* ('Official History of the Yuan Dynasty'), 'to manufacture porcelain items and lacquered hats of horsehair, coir and rattan. The Office was headed by one commissioner and one assistant commissioner.'[29] By 1324 this office had been placed under the administration of the local tax bureau and it closed in 1352, eight years before the area fell under Ming control.[30] Production at the imperial kiln was supervised thereafter by an official appointed by the emperor and by a combination of eunuchs and local bureaucrats. The quantity of broken pieces excavated in recent years at Zhushan[31] testifies to the high standards exacted from the potters of the official kilns (*guan yao*), which supplied the court with interior ornaments, utilitarian vessels, presents for important officials and diplomatic gifts. The local kilns (*min yao*) were not producing pieces in response to specific,

Fig. 6 Detail of the cover of a porcelain seal-paste box, painted in qianjiang enamels with a winter landscape and poem in the manner of an ink painting on silk, and dated by inscription Spring of Dingchou year, 1937. Made by Xu Naijing at Jingdezhen. Designed to contain scarlet paste for stamping seal signatures, this box represents some of the fine-quality eggshell porcelains manufactured at Jingdezhen this century. The blue overglaze enamel key-fret border is typical of this type.

officially generated orders, but instead were making everyday wares for local distribution and marketing abroad. Although the kilns were administered by local bureaucrats, the potters had a certain amount of freedom to pursue their own commercial enterprises. Spectacular early collections of Chinese porcelain in the Middle East, such as those of the Topkapi Saray in Istanbul[32] and the Ardebil shrine in Iran,[33] testify to the scale of Ming commerce. Recovered cargoes of shipwrecks plying the routes between Europe and China confirm the continuation of this volume of trade into the Qing.[34]

Today the kilns at Jingdezhen fire reproductions of historical porcelains of all types, including products which were originally made in northern kilns. Some potters create 'art ceramics' such as sculptures or abstract forms, and the kilns also make utilitarian tableware, including much of the crockery used in Chinese restaurants in the West. Technical schools educate potters in ancient practices, and the research institute examines excavated material and sends ceramic exhibitions abroad. Jingdezhen's success as a production centre may be attributed to its geographical position as much as to its technical innovations, organisation and patronage. Jingdezhen's impact on ceramic manufacture has been global, and imitations of its products have been made in areas as far apart as South America, Africa, the Near and Far East and Europe and in countries as diverse as Mexico, Egypt, Holland, Turkey, Iran and Japan.[35]

The Growth of the Staffordshire Ceramic Industry

Aileen Dawson

In the eighteenth century an enormous growth in demand for durable and decorative ceramics accompanied an increase in prosperity and improved living standards all over Europe and beyond.

A good range of clays and easily accessible outcrops of bituminous coal for firing kilns, then known in Staffordshire as pot ovens, ensured the growth of numerous potteries in North Staffordshire (fig. 2). In and around Burslem by the end of the seventeenth century more potteries were making coarse storage wares, milk pans and butter pots, black-glazed, mottled and salt-glazed domestic wares, elaborately decorated slipwares and even unglazed red stonewares than anywhere else in the British Isles.[1] The eighteenth century witnessed a sustained period of technical innovation, led by members of a skilled workforce. Several of the wealthiest potters in the later part of the century, such as Josiah Wedgwood (1730–95) and Enoch Wood (1759–1840), were scions of well-established pottery families already active for several generations and were often interrelated. By the end of the century the potters had adopted at least six new ceramic bodies and new making and decorating methods including printing; a few had even tentatively adopted steam-powered machinery. Ancillary crafts and trades such as flint-milling,[2] lathe-making, lawn-weaving (lawns were fine textiles used to filter liquid clays), engraving, colour-grinding and enamelling were established.

The craft of the Staffordshire potter was on the verge of industrialisation. Staffordshire was poised to become the largest ceramic manufacturing area in Britain, overtaking urban centres such as Nottingham, Bristol, London, Liverpool, Dublin and Glasgow. By the mid-nineteenth century its world pre-eminence was well established.

In the early part of the eighteenth century, crates of ware packed in straw were moved up to 50 km (30 miles) to market on packhorses over appalling unmade roads which were virtually impassable in winter. From the middle of the century, improved roads suited to wheeled traffic, along with the opening of the Trent and Mersey canal begun in 1766,[3] ensured safe and speedy transport to the ports of Liverpool and Hull, and onwards to outlets in London or abroad to Europe and North America. Plastic clays from Devon and Dorset, flints from southern England and, after 1766, Cornish china clay could now be brought more easily to Chester and along the river Weaver to join the canal.[4] The lack of banking facilities and shortage of cash was overcome by the use of exchange or barter, and loans were often made by individuals to finance such building works as new pot ovens, drying kilns and workshops and for the purchase of raw materials. From an estimated total of sixty-seven potters in 1710–19,[5] the number had grown to over three hundred potworks in Burslem by 1800[6] and the industrial population had more than tripled between 1762 and 1801, when it was calculated at 23,626.[7]

Purpose-built potteries, as distinct from those which grew up alongside domestic dwellings, appeared in the middle of the eighteenth century with the construction of Roger Wood's Ash pottery at Lane End in 1756.[8] Josiah Wedgwood I's Etruria pottery was built between 1767 and 1773.[9] However,

Fig. 1 (Left) Staffordshire porcelains (soft-paste porcelain unless otherwise indicated). Left to right: teabowl and saucer, puce print, painted border, attributed to Baddeley-Littler factory, c. 1780; spirally moulded hard-paste teapot and cover, painted, New Hall factory, Shelton, c. 1790; slop bowl with painted scene attributed to F. Duvivier, inscribed on base 'Lane End July 1787', attributed to Turner factory; vase and cover, moulded, applied handmade flowers painted over the glaze, Longton Hall factory, 1751–60, height 25.4 cm (10 in); mug, black print of Society of Bucks signed 'Sadler Liverpool', Longton Hall factory, c. 1760; hand-modelled ewe and lamb, Longton Hall factory, c. 1750; thrown mug (reconstructed), underglaze-blue painted scene, William Steers, Pomona factory, Newcastle-under-Lyme, 1744-7.

Fig. 2 (Opposite) Map A shows the sources of raw materials used in the manufacture of pottery and porcelain in 18th-century Staffordshire. Map B shows the transport system for raw materials and finished products. Map C shows the locations of the main Staffordshire potteries.

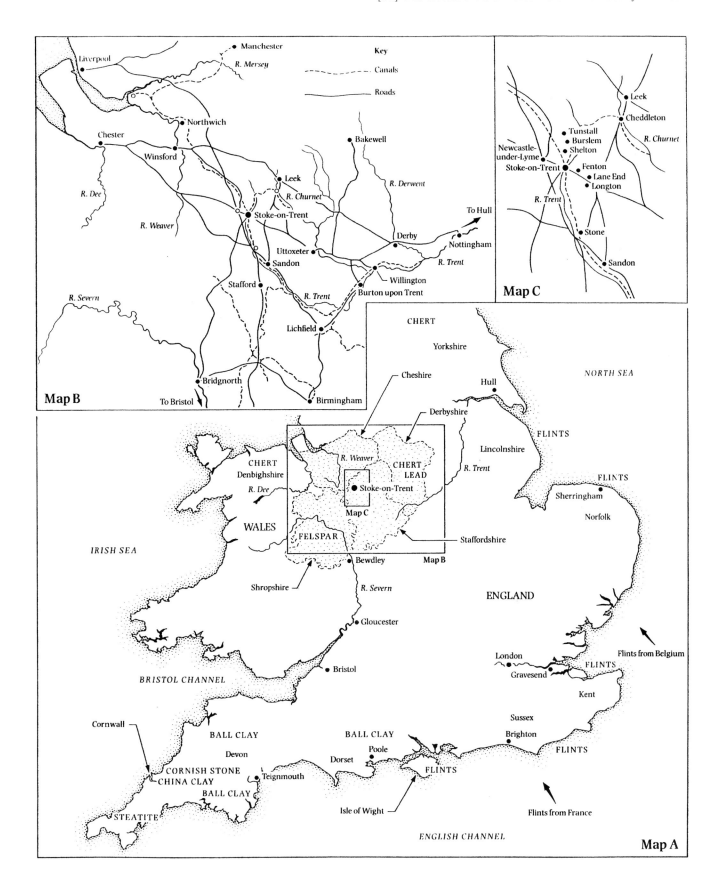

Map B

Key
- - - - -   Canals
————   Roads

Map C

Map A

Fig. 3 Salt-glazed stoneware blocks. Left to right: salt-glazed stoneware kiln support; block for a spittoon, incised on rim 'Aaron Wood', solid, made in a mould; block for a spout, incised 'RW 1748' for Ralph Wood. Height of block 14.7 cm (5.8 in).

many small-scale master potters continued to farm, while larger ones often owned mills or other enterprises. Division of labour, already evident in the 1740s when making handles was mentioned as a special skill in indenture documents, became increasingly common in the later years of the century. Workers were hired annually, with hours governed by the availability of daylight;[10] their wages were higher than those of colliers and rose in proportion to the total costs, including raw materials. Evidence for female and child labour (mainly boys) survives in documentary sources. There were some women painters, as

at Wedgwood, and apprentice children as young as eight might turn the potter's wheel.

New types introduced up to 1760

Unglazed fine red stonewares were made by the Dutchmen John Philip and David Elers at Bradwell, near Newcastle-under-Lyme, around 1693–8 but were apparently abandoned until around 1750, when similar wares became popular. The Elers' redwares, carefully prepared from refined clay, were slip-cast and lathe-turned[11] to a fineness hitherto unknown in English pottery (fig. 6). The red stonewares of the mid-eighteenth century were mainly thrown on the wheel and decorated with applied reliefs. From the 1720s white salt-glazed stonewares, both moulded and thrown and lathe-turned, became a widespread article of commerce, until ousted around 1775 by cream-coloured earthenwares covered with a transparent lead glaze (fig. 7). Creamwares[12] were appearing in the 1750s and later made the fortunes of Josiah Wedgwood I and other potters, as demand grew for dinner-services and utensils for an increasing range of purposes. An unprecedented diversity of

glazes and multi-coloured bodies characterised the 1750s and 1760s: teawares were made in the form of fruit and vegetables and with marbled bodies or glazes imitating hardstones. Marbling was even used to simulate classical marble vases. At the same time, red and black lead-glazed earthenwares (fig. 4) were made in enormous quantities for domestic use, and these were far finer than seventeenth-century types. Twelve different sizes of dish, five sizes of sauceboat and five sizes of stool-pan (chamberpot), both 'best' and second quality, along with butter tubs and stands, cups and saucers, plates, tureens, etc., are listed in the first potters' price-fixing agreement in February 1770.[13]

New types introduced after 1760

Unglazed fine stonewares for domestic and ornamental use were developed by Josiah Wedgwood I in the 1760s and 1770s (fig. 5). These included black basalt (in production by 1769), caneware (perfected a decade later) and, most famous of all, jasperware, an invention of Wedgwood's own which he perfected during the early 1770s.[14] These 'dry bodies' could be thrown,

Ceramic bodies of Josiah Wedgwood

Wedgwood achieved the effects he desired through an extensive and systematic programme of experiment, a scientific approach which led to his election as a Fellow of the Royal Society. In some cases he improved on existing bodies, while in others his results were innovative.

His series of fine-bodied, unglazed ('dry') stonewares included black basalt, produced from ball clay to which slag was added as a flux and black manganese dioxide as a colourant. Caneware, with a fine, hard cream-to-buff body, was initially based on adding alabaster and later Cornish stone as a flux to a refined fire clay. Jasper, so termed because its hardness and fine texture allowed it to be polished on a lapidary's wheel like the semi-precious stone, was a body made mainly of barium sulphate with ball clay, flint and a little gypsum.[33] This barium sulphate-rich body was truly original and could take a colour throughout, for example by adding cobalt blue.

Wedgwood's greatest commercial successes were his cream-coloured earthenware bodies – Queen's ware and later pearlware – based on the use of refined ball clay and calcined flint with, from 1775, the addition of Cornish china clay and china stone. Glazes were soda-lead-silica type.

turned or moulded and were durable and impervious to liquids. Basalt was particularly suited to sculpture, such as library busts, and to vases which could be painted to imitate the Greek originals excavated in Italy from the 1760s.

Adjustments to the creamware formulation allowed the production of whitewares (referred to by Josiah Wedgwood I as 'pearl white' and now often known as pearlwares) for tablewares in the late 1770s. Hand-modelled or moulded figures and animal groups, rustic, topical and mythological subjects were made in salt-glazed stoneware and creamware at many factories. From the 1780s figure production in white earthenware, decorated in

Fig. 4 (Top) Red-glazed earthenwares. Left to right: bowl, thrown and turned, applied cream-coloured reliefs, 1739, diameter 20 cm (7.9 in); tea caddy and cover, press-moulded, black-glazed, gilt, c. 1750–60; teapot and cover, thrown, engine-turned, mark seal and 'IF', attributed to Thomas Barker, Foley Pottery, Fenton, c. 1770.

Fig. 5 (Above) Unglazed stonewares. Left to right: two-handled vase, black basalt, thrown, painted in 'encaustic' enamels, Wedgwood and Bentley, Etruria, c. 1775; teapot and cover, black basalt, thrown, applied reliefs, impressed 'E.Mayer', Hanley, 1790–1800; figure of Voltaire, caneware, moulded, Wedgwood and Bentley, 1775–80, height 31.4 cm (12.4 in); two-handled bowl, cover and stand, jasper, thrown, engine-turned, applied reliefs, impressed 'Turner', Lane End, 1780–90; teapot and cover, jasper, moulded, engine-turned, applied reliefs, impressed 'NEALE & Co', Hanley, c. 1790; teapot and cover, black basalt, moulded, impressed 'ASTBURY', Richard Meir Astbury, Shelton, 1780–90.

English porcelain

Lacking a suitable white-firing kaolin (china clay) and china stone as used in the East (chs 28, 30), some European potters adopted an alternative approach to the production of a white-bodied translucent porcelain. The amount of unwanted iron oxide colourant was kept low by the production of bodies rich in quartz and low in clay, which were vitrified by the addition of a glass frit and lime or gypsum (calcium sulphate). These porcelains are known as 'soft-paste' because of their relatively low firing temperatures (up to perhaps 1150°C). Porcelain of this type was manufactured in France from the late seventeenth century and from the 1740s in Britain.[34] The Longton Hall porcelain was of this type.[35] The Newcastle under-Lyme porcelain was based on a body apparently developed at Limehouse, in London, and was more clay-rich, involving the addition of glass to a ball clay.[36] These bodies tended to slump and fail during firing, leading to high losses which made them uneconomic.

William Cookworthy discovered Cornish sources of kaolin and china stone, taking out a patent in 1768 for the production of 'true' or 'hard-paste' porcelain, using what was essentially the Jingdezhen approach (ch. 30). However, the high firing temperatures required made English hard-paste porcelain expensive to produce, and it could not compete with imported Chinese wares or with Wedgwood's creamwares.

---

high-temperature colours under a transparent glaze, increased dramatically. The first specialist figure-maker, Edward Till of Tunstall, is recorded in 1796.[15] At least twelve potteries are documented in Staffordshire and neighbouring Shropshire in the late eighteenth century making so-called Prattware, named after the Lane Delph/Fenton Pratt family of potters.[16] Among them were James Neale and Enoch Wood, the latter successful enough to build the Fountain Place Works, Burslem, in 1789.[17]

Porcelain in Staffordshire

Attempts were made from 1743 to establish a factory for 'soft-paste' or artificial glassy-type porcelain[18] at Lane Delph by Thomas Briand (d. February 1747), probably without success. However, from 1746 Philip Steers was making domestic wares at the factory at Lower Street, Newcastle-under-Lyme.[19] A partnership including William Littler, the manager, manufactured ornamental and utilitarian porcelains at Longton Hall between 1754 and 1760,[20] when upwards of 90,000 pieces were sold off at Salisbury. Porcelain (fig. 1) containing calcined bone ash may have been made by J. Baddeley in partnership with William Reid at Shelton in the late 1750s.[21] Teawares of 'hard-paste' or true porcelain, containing kaolin, were made by a partnership of ten potters at the New Hall pottery for fifty-four years from 1781.[22]

Technical innovations

New raw materials for the new finer bodies necessitated changes in processes. Paler ceramic bodies needed more efficient purification of the white-firing clays from Devon used by the 1720s.[23] The clays were levigated in water, from the 1730s, in a building called a sliphouse set aside for the purpose. Flint was added to the clay to whiten the body and reduce the risk of warping. Pieces of circular section were still mostly thrown on the wheel, which was hand-operated, but moulding became an increasingly important method of forming. Plaster of Paris

moulds were in use by the early 1740s, probably initially for making salt-glazed stonewares (fig. 6), allowing mass-production of a huge range of shapes.[24] Clay was pressed into the mould or poured as a liquid suspension, known as slip. For technical reasons, porcelain could not be cast until the nineteenth century, but fine salt-glazed stonewares were commonly slip-cast. A series of moulds would be needed for figures and groups; hollow wares, such as teapots, often required separate two-part moulds for handles and spouts. Working moulds lost their sharpness in use and were frequently renewed from the master mould. The initial models (of which few survive) were often made in wood,[25] while solid 'block' moulds, from which master moulds were created, were of salt-glazed stoneware. Blocks, only rarely signed by their specialist cutters or carvers (fig. 3), who sometimes worked on their own account, could be sold, exchanged or even copied.

Lathes, in regular use from the 1720s for both making and decorating pieces, were continually improved. Throughout the century these were foot-operated by a treadle mechanism. Complex 'diced' patterns on Wedgwood's three-colour jasperwares, made on an eccentric lathe (introduced in 1763) in the

1780s, exemplify the ingenuity shown in the desire to produce a fashionable article for a wealthy market.[26]

At the beginning of the century, painting on pottery was unknown in North Staffordshire. Early fine stonewares were occasionally simply decorated in cobalt blue, often in combination with scratched flower motifs (so-called 'scratch blue' wares, made around the 1740s). From the 1760s more sophisticated decoration, whether hand-painted or printed, was frequently done outside Staffordshire, although there is no evidence that Longton Hall porcelains were painted outside the factory. David Rhodes and Jasper Robinson of Leeds are recorded in the 1760s as painters of Staffordshire salt-glaze and creamware, and John Sadler and Guy Green of Liverpool purchased undecorated creamware from Josiah Wedgwood from 1761, reinvoicing it after printing. Wedgwood established a painting studio in London at Chelsea, which was particularly active in 1773–4 during the production of the huge creamware 'Frog' service for Catherine the Great.[27] Painters were, however, enticed to Staffordshire, their work embracing border designs and even figure-painting (fig. 1).

Two methods of printing on ceramics were developed in the 1750s.[28] John

Brooks, a Birmingham engraver, applied for patents between 1751 and 1754. An image created in glutinous enamel inks was transferred from printed tissue to an unglazed pot and then fired on. The so-called 'glue bat' method,[29] known as black printing, was used for printing over the glaze by John Sadler and Guy Green of Liverpool from 1756. This involves the deposition of an image in linseed oil on the surface of the pot on a 'bat' of gelatinous animal glue. The oil left on the surface was dusted with a fusible metal oxide pigment, which was then fired on in a low-temperature enamelling kiln. Little or no

Fig. 6 (Opposite) Salt-glazed stonewares (factories unknown). Left to right: two-handled loving cup, thrown and turned, incised '1744'; (unrelated) unglazed redware mug with silver rim, thrown and turned, applied reliefs, John and Philip Elers, Bradwell Wood, late 17th century; dish, press-moulded, painted over the glaze, c. 1760, length 41.7 cm (16.4 in); teapot and cover, thrown, moulded applied handle and spout, painted over the blue ground, c. 1760; teapot and cover, slip-cast with Mansion House and royal arms, c. 1750; mug with silver rim, press-moulded 'The King and My Master', c. 1740.

printing was done at the Staffordshire factories until the 1780s. It was carried out independently, either by locally based printers or on contract by Sadler and Green.

Kilns and firing

In 1686 Robert Plot described 'pot ovens' 2.5 m (8 ft) high and about 1.8 m (6 ft) wide.[30] Early kilns had two fire-mouths and burned wood or charcoal. Until at least the 1750s, ovens and workshops were generally located at the rear of potters' dwellings, and were often built around a central courtyard. However, purpose-built factories, with offices and warehouses fronting on to the street and an average of four kilns, became common. Large kilns were built with five or more fire-mouths. By the end of the century these were burning 12–15 tons of coal in a typical firing of 1500 pieces.[31] They were enclosed in a distinctive, bottle-shaped encircling chimney, providing both additional draught and a covered area for stoking.

The main change in firing technique was the introduction by the 1720s of a two-stage cycle, the first for unglazed

Fig. 7 Creamwares. Left to right: teapot and cover, moulded, coloured glazes, attributed to Thomas Whieldon, Fenton Vivian, c. 1750–60; plate, moulded, pierced rim, painted flowers and printed scene, Wedgwood, Burslem, c. 1775; bowl, thrown, manganese ground, underglaze-blue painted decoration, 'EB 1743' on base, attributed to Enoch Booth, Tunstall; cup and saucer, thrown, 'marbled' clays, factory unknown, c. 1760; vase, thrown, applied handles, 'granite' (cobalt oxide) ground, Wedgwood and Bentley, Etruria, 1775; ewer, moulded, applied reliefs, gilt unglazed base, marbled clays, Wedgwood and Bentley, c. 1775, height 27.2 cm (10.7 in).

biscuit ware, which was then dipped in lead glaze and refired at a lower temperature.[32] Containers called saggars, which protected the ware from coal by-products in the kiln atmosphere, were made of local clay. These improvements reduced kiln losses, increased the range of possible decorative techniques and improved the appearance of the ware.

Tradition in Studio Pottery

Emmanuel Cooper

Studio pottery, the term used to cover the scope of ceramic activity described in this chapter, can be defined as ceramic objects made largely by hand, by individuals or by small groups of makers working together in a team under studio conditions. One of the major characteristics of studio pottery is a primary concern for the inherent quality of the material and a sound understanding of the techniques and processes required to enable creative ideas to be expressed.

Compared with their illustrious predecessors, studio potters enjoy enormous artistic and technical freedom. Unlike potters of the past, who were producing pots and other ceramic objects to meet specific needs and requirements of the society within which they lived, modern studio potters do not fill any essential role. Their work is not purchased out of necessity but is seen as having 'artistic' value, which gives it a unique status reflecting the individuality of the maker. Without a clearly established market, the demand for studio ceramics must be created through exhibitions in galleries and shops, which seek to persuade people to buy for motives of desire rather than need. This emphasises individuality and uniqueness as opposed to efficient production or economic cost. An equally important difference is that studio potters are not confined by a dominant technology or by prevailing styles, but can use techniques and processes derived from any historical period and virtually all parts of the world.

Within such a free and open structure, studio potters tend to look to the past for much of their inspiration, responding both to particular making techniques, such as hand-building or throwing pots on the wheel, and to firing methods such as salt-glazing, a process now used almost exclusively by studio potters. They also look at specific styles and methods of decoration and adapt these for their own use. Studio potters are not concerned with slavishly reproducing past forms, but prefer to create new work with its own character.

Historically studio potters, sometimes known as artist potters, are a relatively recent phenomenon. Working with clay as a 'medium of artistic expression' began little more than a century ago, and yet within this brief span virtually all ancient processes have been investigated and reinterpreted for a modern audience. Stimulated by wares imported from the Far East (see ch. 30), in the second half of the nineteenth century artists in France, notably August Delaherche, Théodore Deck, Ernest Chaplet and Jean-Charles Cazin, started to experiment with pottery-making. In England the four Martin Brothers produced individual stoneware pottery, much of which was salt-glazed, while William de Morgan made highly coloured earthenwares based on Hispano-Moresque wares and those of the Middle East. At the turn of the century, the hitherto unknown ceramics of the early Chinese potters (see ch. 28), unearthed when the cutting of railways disturbed ancient tombs, stimulated world-wide interest in the craft, and studio potters began

*Fig. 1
Bottle form by Magdalene Anyango N Odundo, black burnished earthenware, early 1990s. Height c. 41 cm (16 in).*

206

working in many parts of the world.
Only in the 1920s did studio potters in
Britain such as Bernard Leach and
Michael Cardew start looking to
indigenous slip-decorated red earthen-
wares (see ch. 19) for inspiration.

Hand-building

One of the oldest and most direct
techniques for making ceramic vessels
is hand-building, a method of joining
together coils or rings of clay. One of
the first processes employed to make
pots, it is still used today in parts of the
world such as Ethiopia[1] and Nicaragua.[2]
When the clay body is leather-hard, the
surface is burnished to make it strong
and smooth and give it a soft shine.
Some potters apply a layer of *terra
sigillata* slip, like that used by potters in
ancient Greece and Rome (see chs 12
and 29), to achieve a semi-glazed
surface. The work is then fired to a low
temperature of around 900°C. This can
be carried out either in a conventional
kiln, which gives a clean, even colour,
or in a smokey atmosphere, which
results in a mottled surface and adds an
element of drama as well as visible
evidence of the firing. Both Gabriele
Koch and Jane Perryman make highly
effective use of this type of firing.

The hand-building method is brought
to perfection in the work of Magdalene
Anyango N Odundo (fig. 1). The forms
she makes recall the vessels of ancient
Egypt and those produced in parts of
Africa, but she gives them an elegant
twist, introducing an intriguing
asymmetrical quality. Her making
process is relatively simple. Clay is
rolled into long coils, laid carefully one
on top of the other to form a wall, then
joined together. The shapes are usually
round and swelling, reflecting the
origins of such pots as containers for
food or water. The surface is smoothed,
first by scratching with a toothed strip
of metal and then by rubbing with a
pebble or something similar, which not
only strengthens the pot but gives it a
dull burnished shine. Decoration tends
to be minimal and limited to smooth-
firing clay slips. Magdalene Odundo's
exact and concise forms, with their
stately necks, reflect on and are part of
a long tradition, but they subvert this
tradition with wit and style.

*Fig. 2 Bottle forms by John Leach,
reduction-fired stoneware, about 1990.
Height of taller pot c. 51 cm (20 in).*

Throwing on the wheel

The development of the potter's wheel
revolutionised production processes,
enabling pots to be made quickly and in
relatively large numbers. As communities developed, so potteries grew up
which produced objects for regional
needs using locally available materials.
Most of the pots were fired to earthenware temperature, and from medieval
times were often decorated with a clay
slip of contrasting colour and finished
with a clear lustrous glaze. Although

rural potteries were eventually superseded by the growth of the ceramic
industry, slip decorated earthenware for
specific local needs continued to be
made in many parts of Britain, Europe
and North America until the end of
the nineteenth and beginning of the
twentieth century.

The Leach legacy

Bernard Leach (1887–1979), often
acknowledged as the father of modern
studio pottery, set up his first English
workshop at St Ives in Cornwall in
1920 after learning how to be a potter
in Japan. He built the first Oriental
climbing kiln in the West and, working

207

Fig. 3 Earthenware bowl with painted decoration by Alan Caiger-Smith, reduction-fired lustre, about 1990. Diameter c. 20 cm (8 in).

and silvers, all enhancing and animating the form. For many years Alan Caiger-Smith ran Aldermaston Pottery in Berkshire, where he developed the processes with potters including Laurence McGowan and inspired others such as Sutton Taylor.

Rural workshops

The concept of the local or artisan potter as an integral part of the local community is implicit in the work of John Leach (fig. 2), one of Bernard Leach's grandsons. Johnny Leach worked for a time at the Leach Pottery in St Ives, where he helped to make a standard range of tablewares fired to stoneware temperatures in a reduction kiln, before setting up his own work-shop. In many ways he follows in his grandfather's footsteps, producing a range of well-designed tableware such as jugs, plates, teapots and casseroles which recall the strength and simplicity of medieval pots (see ch. 13). These are sold at moderate prices alongside inventive individual pieces. All of his work celebrates a sound understanding of the processes of pottery, whether of the flowing thrown forms or the rich toasted effects which result from firing in a reduction kiln.

Porcelain

In addition to working with stoneware, with its robust, wholesome characteristics, Bernard Leach also made pots in porcelain, another material associated with the Far East (see chs 14 and 30). Porcelain was first developed in China some thousand years ago following the discovery of outcrops of loess, a white clay-like substance which, if thinly potted and fired to a high temperature, became bluish-white and translucent. During the firing porcelain becomes glass-like and strong, enabling it to be made with thin walls without loss of strength. Its attributes are associated with refinement and delicacy, and so with objects of significance for special occasions.

Fig. 4 (Opposite) Lidded jar by Clive Bowen, earthenware with trailed slip decoration, 1994. Height c. 31 cm (12 in).

with a small team of potters, produced a range of tablewares and individual pieces. The Leach Pottery and the ideals it expressed were persuasively described in Leach's *A Potter's Book* (1940), regarded as the potter's bible by many post-war potters. Although now best known as a maker of pots in stoneware and porcelain, Leach was also intrigued by traditional slip-decorated ware, conducting experiments to find out how the effects were produced, and he helped to keep the skills alive. Today, Clive Bowen is one of the many potters making red earthenware which takes up this tradition (fig. 4). His work, mostly thrown on the wheel, combines a thrilling sense of form with simplicity of decoration, whether on jugs, dishes and plates intended for use in the home or on large pots for the garden. His

boldly thrown pots burst with life, while the combination of white slip and black trailed decoration, under a rich glossy glaze, unite great sensitivity with strength and conviction.

Tin glaze and lustre

Alan Caiger-Smith takes red earthenware in a different direction, covering his wheel-thrown pots with a white glaze made opaque with tin oxide (fig. 3). This brilliant white glaze, first used in the Middle East as an alternative to the whiteness of Oriental porcelains, was further developed by Italian and Spanish potters (see chs 16 and 17). Such a white surface lends itself to painted decoration, either with brightly coloured pigments or lustres.

Caiger-Smith spent many years investigating traditional Middle Eastern lustre decoration, which is achieved by applying a mixture of clay and metal oxide to the fired glaze and refiring it in a smokey or reducing atmosphere. The result is rich lustrous reds, golds

Fig. 5 Dinner set by Joanna Constantinidis, reduction-fired porcelain, 1996. Diameter of bowl 15.5 cm (6 in), side plate 18.5 cm (7.25 in), dinner plate 24.5 cm (9.5 in).

Joanna Constantinidis is a Western potter who sensitively explores the qualities of this fine material in forms which have classical strength. Among other objects, she produces a range of wheel-thrown tablewares, including tea cups and saucers and bowls and plates (fig. 5), which have a purity of form and definition and bring out the qualities of the porcelain, imbuing what can be a cool material with life and warmth. Other notable potters working with porcelain include David Leach (son of Bernard) and Edmund de Waal.

Salt glaze

Studio potters have often been diligent in pursuing the creative possibilities of techniques and processes which have ceased to be used by the ceramic industry. One such is salt-glazing, first developed in Germany during the fifteenth and early sixteenth centuries (see ch. 18). In this firing process, ordinary salt is introduced into the kiln at high temperature – usually around 1200°C – where it volatilises, part of it reacting with the surface of the clay to form a thin layer of glaze. Unlike most other pottery processes, the pots need not be biscuit-fired first. However, the greatest enticement of salt-glazing is the unique quality of the glaze, which can either be smooth and even or mottled and broken. Unlike conventional glaze,

Fig. 6 Beaky jug by Walter Keeler, thrown and modelled salt-glazed stoneware, 1996. Height c. 40.5 cm (16 in).

which cloaks the object with an obscuring layer, salt glaze is so thin that it becomes part of the surface, thereby enhancing the qualities and bringing out the form of the pot. In Germany, this quality of salt glaze was used to great effect on pots decorated with carefully applied relief designs, the details of which were emphasised by the process, giving the work an almost metallic quality. Jane Hamlyn is a modern potter working with salt glaze who combines inventive relief decoration with a rich range of colours.

Walter Keeler has adapted the salt-glazing process with great skill and invention. The objects he makes, such as jugs, teapots, dishes and mugs, tend to be associated with the table, continuing the association of pottery with domestic use. All of his pieces are thrown and then modelled and assembled. Jugs may be cut away from their original base, gently eased into an oval shape, and then stuck on to a flat base (fig. 6). Minimal decoration, consisting mostly of delicate raised lines of clay running round the pot, gives the pieces a formal but delicate quality. Colour and texture are introduced by the application of different clay slips which react to the salt in various ways. Some have additions of colouring oxides such as cobalt, giving a deep ultramarine blue on a mottled surface, while others containing iron are warm, tan-brown and smooth.

A further aspect of Keeler's work is its subtle references to a number of ceramic traditions. For instance, he uses clay to make vessels which recall the qualities of other materials, including leather, metal and wood. Keeler has examined objects made in metal, such as old-fashioned oil-cans and jugs, and taken these as starting points. Smooth rounded surfaces, neat edges and straight-sided forms are typical, recalling shapes made from tin. This precise quality of Keeler's work was also a vital aspect of pots made in Staffordshire in the eighteenth century (see ch. 31), where thrown shapes were returned to the wheel when leather-hard and turned to give crisp clean outlines. Keeler's varied influences are all beautifully assimilated in his own modern salt-glazed forms.

Fig. 7 Coil pot by David Roberts, hand-built burnished raku, about 1994. Diameter 65 cm (25.5 in).

Raku firing

In contrast to Keeler's finely honed and carefully controlled work, other potters are attracted to the more dramatic, unpredictable and often spectacular effects of raku firing. First used in Japan, raku is a method whereby the pot is covered in glaze, placed in a glowing hot kiln and left until the glaze has matured, then removed and allowed to cool rapidly – the whole firing process taking as little as an hour, rather than the more usual day or so. This process enthralled Bernard Leach when he was introduced to the technique at a raku party in Japan, an experience that was instrumental in his decision to become a potter.

The raku process was further developed following the Second World War by potters such as Paul Soldner in the United States, who invented the idea of post-firing reduction. In this technique the fired pot is buried, while still glowing red-hot, in an enclosed container filled with combustible material such as sawdust or leaves. This causes thick black smoke to be given off, which not only blackens the body of the pot but also affects the glazes. Copper, for instance, is changed from its usual green into a lustrous red or gold. Potters who have made intelligent use of this process include Tim Andrews and David Jones.

For raku potter David Roberts, the post-firing reduction is not so much a method of achieving bright colours as a way of uniting the clay body with the surface decoration. His elegant but assertive shapes, either large flattened dishes or rounded globular bottle forms (fig. 7), are covered with a layer of clay slip which shrinks and crackles during the firing, allowing the smoke to penetrate and leave behind a fine mesh of crackle lines. This decorative surface may be contrasted with an area of glaze or with the smooth body of the pot – successfully echoing many historical processes, but simultaneously and skilfully transforming them into ceramics which could only have been made today.

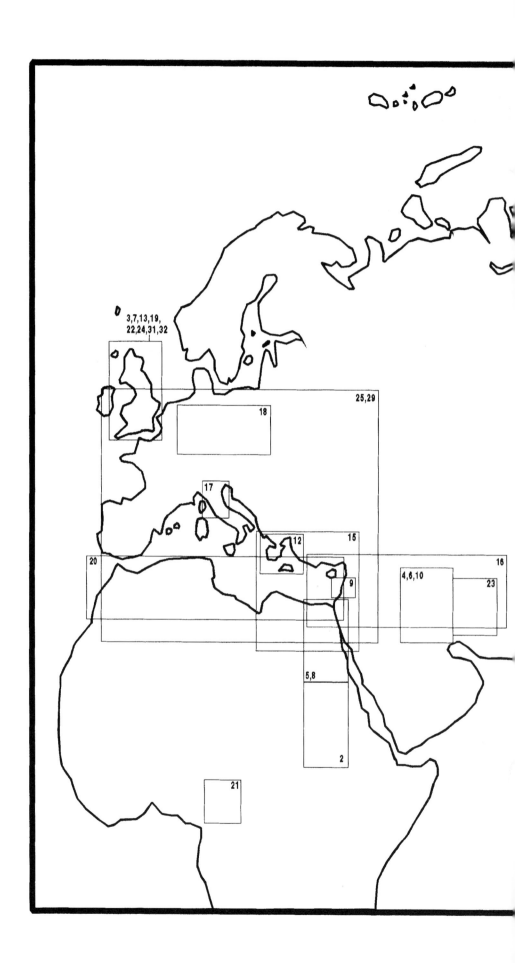

Orientation map showing the approximate locations of the areas discussed in the text, denoted by chapter number (see also ch. 27, fig. 1, p. 176, and various specific regional and site maps in individual chapters).

Glossary of Technical Terms

albite See feldspar.

alkali Here used to mean an oxide of potassium or sodium, which were important fluxes in ceramic glazes and some specialised body types such as porcelain (see below).

alkaline glaze A glaze in which the principal flux is an alkali (see box, p. 75).

alumina Aluminium oxide (Al_2O_3). A major component of pottery clays, present in amounts of c.10–40 weight per cent. The higher the alumina content, the more refractory, or difficult to melt, a clay body tends to be. It can be present in glazes, due to reaction with the body during firing, as well as in raw materials such as clay and feldspar.

antimony A metallic element (Sb), not widely used in early metallurgy but which was used to make opaque and coloured glazes and glasses from the 16th century BC through to the early first millennium AD, when its use in glass began to be supplanted by tin. Fine calcium antimonate particles in a glaze make it opaque white, and lead antimonate is opaque yellow (artists' term 'Naples yellow') (see ch. 15).

applied decoration Addition of clay or components made of clay to the surface of a pot for decorative purposes.

archetype The positive model from which a mould is made (see p. 167, fig. 3).

Armenian bole A fine red iron oxide-rich pigment, originating in the Near East and widely used in painting and pottery decoration from about the 13th or 14th century AD.

ash The material left when wood or other plant matter is burned and all the carbon is lost. Ashing concentrates a range of elements present in only minor quantities in the original plant, particularly lime and the alkalis. In northern Europe, wood ashes are rich in potash, while the plant ashes used in the Mediterranean and Near Eastern regions are rich in soda.

ash glaze A glaze formed by the interaction between the surface of the ceramic and ash, which may be carried over from the fire accidentally with the kiln gases, or deliberately sprinkled on the surface of the pot.

barbotine Decoration formed by piping soft clay through a nozzle, as though icing a cake (see slip-trailing); generally reserved for describing Roman pottery.

basalt A fine-grained, black igneous rock composed of pyroxene and feldspar; a black ceramic body developed in 18th-century Staffordshire (see box, p. 202).

biscuit-fired When glazed ware is fired twice, the initial firing before the application of the raw glaze is known as the biscuit firing. Intentionally unglazed porcelain and stoneware bodies are sometimes termed 'biscuit'.

burnishing Production of a smooth, sometimes glossy surface finish by polishing the leather-hard pot with a smooth hard tool such as a pebble. The burnishing compresses the clay minerals to produce a very dense continuous surface. It can be used to fix pigment particles such as hematite by rubbing them into the surface. Burnishing with a flat or narrow tool can produce a faceted effect (see p. 68, fig. 1).

calcareous clay A clay containing more than about 5% lime, usually in the form of calcite (see below). Clays of this type were widely used in the ancient Mediterranean and Near East and in the manufacture of wares such as *terra sigillata* (see boxes, pp. 54, 117, 136, 151).

calcite Naturally occurring calcium carbonate ($CaCO_3$), the main constituent of limestone and chalk, which is present in calcareous clays.

carbon Element present in most clays which gives a black colour unless it is burnt out during firing

(see box, p. 151). Pottery can be deliberately blackened by firing in a smoky fire, which impregnates the surface with carbon (soot).

celadon A Far Eastern stoneware with a green or green-blue glaze (see ch. 14 and box, p. 103).

cementation See box, p. 106.

china clay See kaolin.

china stone Also known as porcelain stone, a rock composed of quartz and alkali feldspars used as a flux in porcelain. In China and Korea, porcelain stones commonly contain mica as well as feldspar and quartz, and sometimes kaolin; some were used as raw materials without additions of clay (see boxes, pp. 100, 184, 196, 203).

chromium oxide Widely used as the basis of green and yellow pigments in modern glass and glazes, the pure oxide was not isolated until the late 18th century and was first used as a ceramic pigment at Sèvres, the French porcelain manufactory, in the early 1800s. However, the impure naturally occurring mineral, chromite, is quite widely distributed and was utilised as a black pigment in early Mesopotamia (see box, p. 42) and on Islamic pottery. Some Islamic green glazes may owe their colour to chromium, but this effect has not yet been fully investigated.

cinnabar Naturally occurring mercuric sulphide (HgS), basis of the bright red pigment vermilion.

clamp firing An open firing. Usually refers to the firing of bricks, but sometimes used to imply an open firing where blackening of the wares has been achieved by covering with excess fuel or vegetation (see smudging).

clay A fine-grained natural material which, when wet, is characterised by its plasticity, the property which allows it to be deformed by pressure into a desired shape without cracking and to keep this shape when the pressure is removed. In addition to clay minerals (see below), clay typically contains quartz and may contain other minerals such as feldspar, calcite and iron oxide.

clay minerals A group of very fine-grained minerals (alumino-silicates) which are the main constituents of clay (see above). They occur as minute platelets which, when wet, slide across one another, giving the clay its plastic properties.

cobalt oxide (CoO) A blue pigment, used to paint under or over a ceramic glaze or to colour the glaze deep blue throughout (see box, p. 67).

coiling, coil-building Building a pot by rolling out coils or strips of clay which are then wound on top of one another (see box, p. 34).

combing Decoration created by dragging a comb-like tool across the surface of soft clay (see p. 128, fig. 1).

copper oxide Used to colour glazes turquoise or green when fired in oxidation (see below). Also used in reduction (see below) by Chinese and Korean potters to colour glazes red, or as an under-glaze red pigment (see chs 14, 30). Analysis suggests that much of the copper oxide used by early potters was obtained by heating scrap bronze.

crazing Cracking of the glaze (see boxes, pp. 75, 117).

dipping Application of a glaze by immersion of the vessel in the glaze suspension.

dolomite A naturally occurring calcium magnesium carbonate, $CaMg(CO_3)_2$.

earthenware A clay-based ceramic body which is not fully vitrified (see below) and therefore is relatively porous. Earthenware bodies can be quite variable; by definition, earthenware includes the fine white-bodied glazed tablewares of Wedgwood as well as the low-fired common pottery of much of the archaeological record.

efflorescence Migration of water-soluble compounds to the surface of a pot as it dries (see boxes, pp. 106, 136).

enamel A colour consisting of a metal oxide pigment and a glass flux, which is painted over a

pre-fired glaze and then fired on at a low temperature (see box, p. 198).

fabric The combination of clay and inclusions that makes the ceramic. Each pottery-making centre, assuming it uses different clays and inclusions (see below) from others, will produce pots in a characteristic fabric. Potters may use more than one fabric if they produce different types of ware, e.g. cooking pots and tablewares. A fabric may be characterised by its visual appearance, by microscopy, by chemical composition and by physical properties. Fabric analysis is a key element in the investigation of provenance (see boxes, pp. 42, 64).

faience French term for tin-glazed earthenware of post-medieval Europe (i.e. maiolica), derived from the Italian manufacturing centre of Faenza; also a ceramic composed of a body of crushed quartz and an overlying glaze, common in the ancient Near East and Mediterranean. This latter material was initially confused with earthenware which had a white tin-opacified glaze, and the term faience, incorrectly applied, has remained in use (see box, p. 104).

feldspar A group of silicate minerals including albite (sodium feldspar, $NaAlSi_3O_8$), orthoclase (potassium feldspar, $KAlSi_3O_8$) and anorthite (calcium feldspar, $CaAl_2Si_2O_8$). An important constituent of china stone (see above), the combination of alkali, alumina and silica makes feldspars valuable fluxes (see below) for both porcelain and stoneware.

firing The transformation of a soft clay into a hard and durable ceramic by heating to high temperature. Temperatures in the region of 600°C or more are needed to produce a ceramic which will not readily break down in water.

firing temperature In archaeology, this refers to the highest temperature attained by a ceramic during firing, and it can be estimated using a range of analytical techniques.

flint A very fine-grained variety of silica, found as large nodules in chalk and limestone. Commonly crushed for use as a temper (see below) in prehistoric pottery and used as a relatively pure source of silica in post-medieval wares.

flux A substance that lowers the melting point of some other substance. In the formation of glazes, lead or alkalis were important fluxes, causing the glaze to melt and coat the surface of the vessel. In porcelain bodies, a china stone flux was added to make the body vitrify. In bodies made from calcareous clay (see above), the lime (calcium oxide) is an important naturally occurring flux which vitrifies the body.

frit A partially fused glassy material, usually an intermediate stage in the production of a glaze or glass, or an additive for a ceramic body.

fritware Pottery made from a stonepaste (see below) body.

gabbro A coarse-grained igneous rock of pyroxene and feldspar.

glaze A thin glassy layer on the surface of a ceramic (see salt glaze, lead glaze, tin glaze, alkaline glaze, stoneware glaze). Typically applied by dipping the ceramic in a watery suspension of glaze components, but can be brushed on, effloresced from the body, or deposited from a vapour.

granite A coarse-grained igneous rock of quartz and feldspar.

grog Crushed pottery, used to temper (see below) clay.

hand-building To archaeologists, this term implies the fabrication of a vessel without the potter's wheel, using techniques such as coiling, slab-building and pinching. Modern ceramists, however, may include wheel-thrown pots in the 'hand-made' category (i.e. they were produced by the hands of the potter) as opposed to machine-formed, factory-produced wares.

hard-paste porcelain See box, p. 203.

hematite An oxide of iron, ferric oxide (Fe_2O_3) (old spelling: haematite). It is formed from iron compounds in clay when fired in oxidation (see below) and is responsible for the orange-red colouration of many ceramics. Naturally occurring hematite was sometimes crushed and burnished into the surface of pottery to give a shiny red appearance (see boxes, pp. 42, 89).

impressed decoration Decoration achieved by pressing a hard object such as cord, shell, fingertip, etc. into the surface of a soft clay body.

incised decoration Use of a pointed tool to incise lines, usually in an unfired clay body, rarely after firing (see p. 128, fig. 1).

inclusions Coarse, non-plastic particles in a clay body.

iron oxide A component of pottery clay, present in the range 0.5–15 weight per cent. The main oxide responsible for the fired colour of clay (see also carbon, hematite, magnetite, and boxes, pp. 42, 89).

kaolin China clay, rich in the mineral kaolinite ($Al_2O_3.2SiO_2.2H_2O$). Kaolins are white-firing clays low in iron oxides and fluxes such as alkalis and lime. Primary kaolins are found in the position where they were formed from the original igneous rock; the kaolins of both southern China (Jingdezhen) and Cornwall are of this type. Secondary kaolins, including the northern Chinese clays, are sedimentary clays which have been transported over long distances (see boxes, pp. 184, 196, 203).

kickwheel A potter's wheel (see below) which is turned by kicking with the foot (see p. 73, fig. 6; p. 134, fig. 1).

kiln A structure within which pottery is fired. Usually consists of a firebox in which the fire is set, one or more flues carrying the heat into the kiln, a firing chamber in which the pots are stacked, and a vent for the loss of waste gases. Important characteristics include the separation of the pots from direct contact with the fire and the high thermal capacity of the kiln, so that temperature rises much more slowly than in an open firing (see box, p. 32). A kiln is thus more suitable for firing fine-textured clays. In an updraught kiln, the type most frequently used in pre-industrial times, the hot gases pass from the bottom of the chamber and exit at the top (see p. 39, fig. 2; p. 55, fig. 5; p. 64, fig. 3; p. 97, fig. 6; p. 117, fig. 2; p. 135, fig. 2; p. 159, fig. 2; p. 175, fig. 6).

lathe-turned See turning.

lead glaze A glaze in which the main flux is lead oxide (see boxes, pp. 94, 139).

levigation Refining of clay by settling in water, causing a separation of coarse from fine particles.

lime Calcium oxide (CaO). Present in many clays as calcite (see above). Also a major constituent of plant and wood ashes (in some cases 40% or more), in which form it was added to glazes.

lime-blowing See spalling (and box, p. 136).

limestone A rock composed mainly of calcite (see above).

loess A form of wind-blown silt or dust.

lustre A thin coating of metal, giving an iridescent surface on a glazed ceramic (see ch. 16, and box, p. 112).

luting Joining two pieces of clay together, usually by adding a little water or slip to the join (see p. 174, fig. 5).

magnesia Magnesium oxide (MgO). Occurs in the mineral dolomite, in some clay minerals and in plant ash (see above).

magnetite An oxide of iron (Fe_3O_4). Can be formed when clays rich in iron are fired in reduction (see below), e.g. the black slips of ancient Greek pottery (see box, p. 89).

maiolica Italian tin-glazed earthenware (see box, p. 117).

manganese oxide A relatively common metal oxide, used as a black or brown pigment on many earthenwares (see above); can produce a purple or aubergine colour when dissolved in a glaze or enamel.

marl A calcareous clay (see above).

mica A potassium aluminium silicate mineral which occurs in clay, china stone and granite (see above). It has a thin sheet-like form which promotes plasticity.

micrograph An image obtained under the microscope. For this book, the micrographs were obtained using the scanning electron microscope (see below) except where stated otherwise.

modelling Shaping a piece of clay with the fingers or with a tool.

moulding Shaping soft clay by pressing into a mould (p. 152, fig. 8; p. 167, fig. 4; p. 168, fig. 5).

mullite An aluminium silicate mineral that forms at high temperatures when an alumina-rich clay such as stoneware or china clay is fired. Responsible for the high strength of some porcelain and stoneware.

neutron activation analysis (NAA) A method of trace element analysis in which a small powdered sample of ceramic is bombarded with neutrons in a nuclear reactor and the resulting emitted gamma radiation measured to determine the concentrations of a range of elements. Long favoured as a precise, accurate and minimally destructive method of analysis of archaeological materials, the closure of civil nuclear reactors means that there is now a movement towards other techniques (see box, p. 161).

ochre A naturally occurring iron oxide-rich earth, used as a yellow, brown or red pigment (see p. 168, fig. 1).

open firing Firing without a kiln superstructure (see above), in a bonfire or similar device. Open firings are typically short and economical on fuel; they have the disadvantages that the pot is in contact with the fuel and may discolour, they are very vulnerable to the vagaries of the weather, and the type of body that can be successfully fired is limited by the initial very rapid rise in temperature (see box, p. 32; p. 144, fig. 5).

orthoclase See feldspar.

oxidation, oxidising firing Firing in a kiln atmosphere where there is excess oxygen, so that iron oxides tend to form red hematite rather than black magnetite, and carbon is burnt out of the clay body. Typically produces reddish pots in low-temperature earthenware firings.

paddle and anvil Shaping a pot between a hard, smooth 'anvil', which is held against the inside wall of the vessel, and a 'paddle' with which the outside is beaten. Can be used to thin the walls and enlarge a pot formed by some other method, such as coiling (see above).

petrography, petrographic analysis A method of identifying the inclusions (see above) in a ceramic. A thin slice cut from a pot is stuck to a glass slide and ground down until it is a thin section, only 0.03 mm thick. Many minerals are translucent in such a section, and may be examined using a transmitted light microscope in the same way that biologists examine cross-sections of wood or plant material. A technique derived from the discipline of petrology, the study of rocks, petrography may allow the identification of the provenance of a pot from the rock fragments it contains (see box, p. 161; p. 72, fig. 5).

pigment A colourant. Before the modern period, ceramic colours were based mainly upon metallic oxides of copper, iron, cobalt, lead, tin, antimony and manganese (see above; p. 116, fig. 1; p. 139, fig. 6).

pinching Hand-building a pot by opening out a ball of clay between the thumb and fingers.

porcelain A white, vitrified, translucent ceramic which rings when struck. In China, the term is more widely applied to include non-translucent fine stonewares. To see the translucent effect, hold a porcelain cup up to the light and observe the shape of the fingers through the wall (see boxes, pp. 196, 203).

porcelain stone See china stone.

potash Potassium oxide (K_2O). An alkali which is an important flux (see above) in many clays and glazes. Occurs in clay minerals, such as illite, in feldspar and in mica, and is also an important constituent of many plant ashes.

potter's wheel Rapidly rotating device employing centrifugal force for the production of pottery. See also kickwheel (and box, p. 16; p. 50, fig. 1; p. 134, fig. 1; p. 170, fig. 1).

provenance Place where a pot was made.

quartz Mineral of silica (SiO_2), an important constituent of many clays and sands.

radiography See box, p. 73.

reduction, reduction firing Firing in a kiln atmosphere where there is a shortage of oxygen. An excess of fuel and a smoky fire lead to reducing conditions. In high-temperature firings iron oxides may be converted to black magnetite, and in low-temperature firings carbon may not be burnt out of the body. Pottery produced is typically black or grey (see boxes, pp. 42, 89).

rocker-stamp decoration Decoration produced by rocking a stamp on a curved soft clay surface.

roller-die decoration Decoration produced by rolling an engraved cylinder across a soft clay surface.

rouletted decoration Decoration produced by rolling a small toothed wheel across a soft clay surface.

rustication Roughening of the surface of a vessel, for example by pinching the clay or covering with a slurry containing coarse inclusions (see above).

saggar Protective ceramic container in which glazed or decorated pottery is placed during firing, to avoid damage from kiln gases and contact with other pots.

salt Sodium chloride (NaCl). It can be mined, but in traditional societies was usually obtained by evaporation of sea water or saline springs (see boxes, pp. 124, 136).

salt glaze A glaze produced by chemical reaction between the ceramic body and salt vapour in the kiln atmosphere (see boxes, pp. 124, 127).

samian ware See *terra sigillata*.

sand A sediment consisting of particles between 0.06 mm and 2 mm in diameter. Widely used as a temper (see below) in early pottery, sand is usually thought of as consisting mainly of quartz, but its composition is in fact closely related to the regional geology. In volcanic regions, for example, sand consists of particles of volcanic rock.

scanning electron microscope (SEM) A microscope based upon the interaction of a beam of electrons with the surface of a material. Gives a black and white television-type image. Very useful in the examination of ceramics because of its high magnification, the ability to focus on 'hills' and 'valleys' in a sample at the same time, and because it provides information on the chemical elements present. The micrographs illustrating boxes throughout this book were obtained with the SEM.

sgraffito (sgraffiato) decoration Scratching a design through the slip (see below) to reveal the colour of the underlying clay.

silica Silicon dioxide (SiO_2), a major chemical component of clay (see above) and the rocks of the earth's crust. Occurs naturally as quartz, flint, etc.

silt A dust-sized sediment, finer than sand but coarser than clay, with grains between 0.004 mm and 0.06 mm.

slab-building Hand-building a pot using slabs of clay.

slip A fine clay surface coating applied as a suspension of fine clay particles in water. Slips can be prepared by levigating a clay and decanting the solution after the coarse particles have settled. Slips may be applied by dipping the pot into the suspension, by trailing or piping, or by brushing (see boxes, pp. 89, 191).

slip-casting Forming an object by casting liquid slip into a porous mould, usually of plaster.

slip-trailing, slip-decorating Slip decoration applied through a nozzle (see p. 128, fig. 1).

smoke-firing See smudging.

smudging Firing a pot in a smoky, carbon-rich atmosphere so that the surface is impregnated with fine particles of carbon and becomes black. Also known as smoking or smoke-firing.

soda Sodium oxide (Na_2O). An alkali which occurs in the mineral feldspar and in some plant ashes, which were used to make glazes.

soft-paste porcelain See box, p. 203.

spalling Flakes of clay breaking off from the surface of a pot, one cause of which is lime-blowing (see box, p. 136).

sprigging Application of pre-formed decorative elements made of clay to the surface of the vessel before firing. The added pieces may be moulded or modelled and are commonly luted to the surface with slip (see p. 167, fig. 3).

stamped decoration Use of a pre-formed stamp, modelled in wood, bone, etc., to impress a repeated motif into a soft clay surface (see p. 96, fig. 5).

stonepaste A body made chiefly of crushed quartz (see box, p. 114).

stoneware A dense, vitrified ceramic body, typically fired at temperatures in excess of 1100°C. In the European tradition, made from naturally occurring refractory clays, whereas in the Far East, fluxes were commonly added (see boxes, pp. 100, 123, 184).

stoneware glaze A glaze which is suitable for stoneware and porcelain bodies, fired at temperatures between about 1150 and 1350°C. Typically has a high alumina content, and is fluxed by lime with some alkalis (see boxes, pp. 103, 187).

temper Coarse, non-plastic material added to clay to improve working, drying and firing properties. Usually the use of this term implies material deliberately added by the potter, but it is also used to describe any coarse inclusions (see above) in the clay. Performs a range of functions including adding strength to the unfired body, modifying the working properties of the clay, aiding even drying, reducing shrinkage and, in open firings (see above), facilitating the escape of steam and preventing catastrophic failure of the pot.

terra sigillata An orange-red pottery with a glossy red slip surface, made in Italy and Gaul during the Roman period and sometimes termed samian ware (see box, p. 198).

terracotta An unglazed clay-based earthenware body. Typically used to refer to hollow sculpted or moulded ornamental ceramics, but also used for bricks and low-fired unglazed pottery vessels.

thermal shock Abrupt changes in temperature can cause minerals in a pottery body to expand or contract at different rates. This can cause cracks to develop and the pot to break catastrophically.

thermal stress If there is a strong temperature gradient across a ceramic, for example when heated mainly on one side in a cooking fire, then stresses will develop which may cause it to crack and fail.

thermoluminescence dating Determination of the time elapsed since a ceramic (or stone) was fired and its internal 'clock' set to zero. When a sample of the ceramic is heated in the dating laboratory, it emits light, the amount of which is dependent upon the natural radiation to which the pot has been exposed, and thus indicates the time elapsed since firing. Thermoluminescence is a complex and demanding method of dating, which requires the accurate determination of a range of variables such as the environmental radiation dose and the internal radiation emitted by the object itself. It is widely used as an approximate technique for the identification of fakes.

thin section See petrography.

throwing Forming a pot on the wheel (see box, p. 16).

tin glaze More properly, tin-opacified glaze, which is rendered opaque white by the presence of numerous particles of tin oxide. Tin-opacified glazes on traditional ceramics commonly contain substantial amounts of lead, due to the practice of heating a mixture of lead and tin metals to produce the oxide. Tin-opacified glazes do not appear to have been produced before the Islamic period (see boxes, pp. 111, 117, 139).

tournette Slowly rotating turntable device, used to aid the shaping of a pot formed using coiling or slab-building (see p. 139, fig. 6).

trace element analysis Used to 'fingerprint' the clay products from different workshops by measuring the elements present at very low, or trace, concentrations (see boxes, pp. 42, 161).

turning Shaving down a dried, unfired clay body by rotating on a lathe or a wheel and holding against a sharp tool.

turntable See tournette.

umber A naturally occurring earth, rich in manganese and iron oxides, used as a black or brown pigment.

vegetal inclusions Coarse material in a clay which is ultimately derived from plant or vegetable matter. Usually charred or burnt out during firing, and precise identification is not always straightforward. Commonly added as a deliberate temper and may include chopped grass or straw, rice hulls, dung, wheat chaff, etc.

vermilion Bright red pigment based upon mercuric sulphide (see cinnabar).

vitrification When a clay is fired at temperatures of above about 800°C the body begins to melt or fuse. Very small amounts of melt form at first, which increase as the temperature is raised. When the fired pot is cooled, the melt becomes a glass. This process of the conversion of the clay body to glass is known as vitrification. The glass bonds the body together and makes it less porous. Many low-fired pots have undergone very little vitrification: they are soft and porous. Stoneware is highly vitrified and is hard and impervious to fluids. Porcelain is very highly vitrified and its low iron content means that the glassy phase is colourless, producing the characteristic white translucent body. Over-firing can cause too much fusion, so that the body softens and collapses.

waster A vessel or sherd that failed during firing. Commonly found in dumps on ancient pottery-making sites (see p. 109, fig. 6; p. 193, fig. 6).

wood ash See ash.

X-ray See box, p. 73.

xeroradiograph A type of X-ray image, useful in ceramic studies because it emphasises cracks and joins. The radiograph illustrations in this book are xeroradiographs (see box, p. 73).

Endnotes

Introduction

1 *The New English Bible* (1970).
2 See MacGregor (ed., 1994) for various contributions covering collections of ceramics in Sloane's museum, i.e. Jenkins (Greek & Roman), MacGregor (Prehistoric & Romano-British), Cherry (Medieval & Later), Impey (Oriental) and King (Ethnographic). See also Van Rymsdyck (*Museum Britannicum*, London, 1778) for early illustrations of Sloane acquisitions.
3 Jenkins (1996).
4 Jenkins & Sloan (1996, pp. 182–4).
5 Wilson (1984).
6 Both the Victoria and Albert Museum and the British Museum purchased substantial selections of ceramics and glass at the sale of Ralph Bernal's collection in 1855.
7 For a survey of the diverse ceramic collections built up by Sir Augustus Wollaston Franks during the second half of the 19th century, see various chapters in Caygill & Cherry (eds, 1997): Dawson (European ceramics), Harrison-Hall (Oriental pottery and porcelain) & Smith (Japan).
8 *The New English Bible* (1970).
9 Matson (1965).
10 Shepard (1956). For an evaluation of Shepard's work, see Bishop & Lange (1991).
11 For modern approaches to archaeological pottery, see, for example, Rice (1987); Orton et al (1993).
12 Matson (1965). For a collection of papers inspired by Matson's approach, see Kolb & Lackey (1988).
13 Arnold (1985).
14 Peacock (1982).
15 Shepard (1956).
16 See Peacock (1970; 1977), Peacock & Williams (1986).
17 For an overview, see Rice (1987).
18 For approaches to pottery technology, see Rye (1981), Kingery & Vandiver (1986), Rice (1987).
19 Peacock (1982).
20 Vandiver et al (1989; 1990).
21 Arnold (1985, pp. 109–20).
22 Arnold (1985, pp. 66–70).
23 For discussion of these and other advantages of vessels of fired clay over those of other materials, such as flexibility of form, availability of material and durability, see Arnold (1985), Hoopes & Barnett (1995).
24 Hoopes & Barnett (1995) argue for social factors (over entirely functional imperatives) for the adoption of ceramic production in a number of early societies.
25 By craft specialisation, we understand that pottery production may involve concentration on the production of a particular type of pottery, where the potter or potters in a community may devote a large amount of time and resources to pottery-making, or where a potter or group may possess special pottery-making skills which differentiate them from other members of society. See Rice (1981; 1991).
26 Arnold (1985, pp. 202–11).
27 Henrickson (1991).
28 *The New English Bible* (1970).
29 *The New English Bible* (1970).

Chapter 1

1 Radiocarbon dates denoted BP are uncalibrated and refer to dates 'before present' (i.e. the number of years ago) rather than to calibrated calendar dates such as years BC or AD.
2 Morse (1879).
3 For further reading on Jomon pottery and culture, see Kidder (1957); Kidder & Esaka (1968); Higuchi (1968); Yanagi (1972); Egami (1973); Aikens & Higuchi (1982); Pearson, Barnes & Hutterer (eds, 1986); Tsuboi (1987); Kaner (1990); Kenrick (1995); Aikens (1995).
4 Hatsushige & Mitsunori (1996).

Chapter 2

1 Reisner (1908; 1910).
2 Arkell (1949; 1953).
3 Caneva (1991, p. 267; 1993, p. 410).
4 Caneva & Marks (1990, p. 22).
5 Caneva (1993, p. 410).
6 Richter (1989); Fattovich (1996, pp. 71ff).
7 Geus (1984, p. 371).
8 Kuper (1995, p. 133).
9 Brunton (1937, pp. 28–9, pls XII, XIV).
10 Firth (1915, pl. 27f).
11 Haaland (1995, pp. 109–10).
12 Hakem & Khabir (1989).
13 Haaland (1995, p. 109).
14 Francaviglia & Palmieri (1988, p. 356).
15 Haaland (1987, p. 151).
16 Hakem & Khabir (1989, p. 385).
17 Krzyzaniak (1991, p. 520).
18 Caneva (ed., 1988, p. 74).
19 Haaland (1987, p. 146).
20 Nordström (1972, p. 11).
21 Krzyzaniak (1991, p. 522).
22 Geus (1984, p. 364); Reinold (1985, p. 280).
23 Caneva (ed., 1988, p. 76).

24 Ibid. (p. 86).
25 The examples illustrated here were recovered from sites of Kerma date in the northern Dongola Reach. For serrated-edged bone tools of earlier date from Jebel Moya west of Sennar see Addison (1949, pl. LVIIB).
26 Arkell (1949, pp. 81–3).
27 Caneva (ed., 1988, pp. 111–12).
28 Ibid. (p. 112).

Chapter 3

1 Tomalin (1992, p. 72) describes fossil shell apparently stored for use as temper.
2 References to possible pottery-making evidence.
3 See, for example, Gibson & Woods (1990), who relate the various strands of evidence to the production of prehistoric pottery in Britain.
4 Morris (1994) begins to examine these problems for the succeeding Iron Age period.
5 C.f. Matson (1963, pp. 489–98).
6 Allen (1991) discusses the relationship between the hardness of excavated pottery and the burial environment. For further discussion of and references to the weathering of buried pottery, see Freestone (et al, 1985; 1995).
7 Gibson & Woods (op. cit., pp. 44–56).
8 Gibson & Woods (op. cit., pp. 27–30). Woods (1983) provides much information from experimental firings, while Tobert (1984) and Gosselain (1992) present data from ethnographic observations of potters in traditional communities.
9 Gibson (1986).
10 Of 111 cases recorded in the ethnographic literature, Arnold (1985) found that 33% obtained their clays within 1 km (0.6 mile) of the place where pottery was made and 84% within 7 km (4.2 miles).
11 Hand-built pots weighed after forming and later, after firing, were found to have lost typically between 30% and 50% of their weight, the bulk of which was presumably water: Friendship-Taylor (1983/4).
12 Cleal (1995).
13 For discussion of the significance of temper type in low-fired pottery, see Rye (1974), Steponaitis (1983), Kilikoglou (1995). For a cautionary view based upon British prehistoric material, see Woods (1986).
14 Howard (1981) relates the coarser fabrics to their suitability as cooking ware.
15 Middleton (1985; 1995).
16 Boast (1995).
17 Arnold (1985, pp. 71–6, table 3.2) summarises the seasonality of pottery-making, using examples from the ethnographic literature.
18 Ibid. (table 3.1).
19 Peacock (1981; 1982).
20 Peacock (1969).
21 Parker Pearson (1990; 1995).

Chapter 4

1 Mellaart (1975), Vandiver (1987), Yelon et al (1992), Gourdin & Kingery (1975). For the locations of sites mentioned, see Roaf (1990).
2 Braidwood & Howe (1960, p. 38), Matson (1960, p. 64), Kirkbride (1972, pp. 8–10, pls VI–XVI; 1973a, pp. 5–6, pls II–III, X–XI; 1973b, p. 208, pl. LXXXa; 1975, p. 9), Mellaart (1975, pp. 135–41), Bader (1989).
3 Kirkbride (1972, p. 9, pl. XI), Bader (1989, p. 355; 1993, pp. 45–6). The relative scarcity of pottery at Umm Dabaghiyah may have reflected sporadic purchases from travelling potters, and careful repairs of old vessels have been noted elsewhere (Kirkbride, 1973a, p. 5; Akkermans, 1993, pp. 69–70; Le Miere, 1989).
4 Matson (1960, p. 66).
5 Macfadyen (1947, p. 48), Matson (1983). Handmade pots made by villagers at Tell Razuk in the Hamrin basin were 'fired in a pile of dung put into a pit in the ground and covered with mud. The dung is set on fire and left for two days to smoulder. The covering of mud is then broken, and the pit allowed to cool for more than a day' (Thuesen & Heydorn, 1990, p. 100). A pit filled with 'ashes and ceramic dross' at Tell Sotto may have been used as a clamp (Bader, 1989, p. 352), as indeed may have pits with 'fire-hardened walls' found in the earliest levels at Matarrah (Braidwood et al, 1952, pp. 7–8).
6 D. & J. Oates (1976, p. 42), Merpert & Munchaev (1993, pp. 76–7, 84–5).
7 Matson (1995).
8 Lloyd & Safar (1945, pp. 276–81), Mellaart (1975, pp. 147–9).
9 Mellaart (1975, pp. 149–55).
10 Ippolitoni (1970/71, p. 109), Kamada & Ohtsu (1996, pp. 60–63, pls 1, 5–6); cf. Tite & Maniatis (1975).
11 Herzfeld (1930), Ippolitoni (1970/71), Mellaart (1975), D. & J. Oates (1976, p. 43).
12 Herzfeld (1930, pp. 95–9); 'potter's marks' are also found on some Halaf vessels (Hijara 1980). For evidence of trade see Lloyd & Safar (1945, pp. 281–3, figs), Wilkinson & Tucker (1995, pp. 91, 109, fig. 62:16–17).
13 Mellaart (1975, pp. 156–70), Watson (1983).
14 Plainwares comprised up to 40% at Tell Aqab and Banahilk (Davidson & Watkins, 1981, p. 7; Braidwood & Howe, 1960, p. 34), 60% at Kharabeh Shattani (Campbell, 1986, p. 42) and as much as 87% at Girikihaciyan (Watson & Le Blanc, 1990, p. 68). Grey Burnished hole-mouth cooking pots comprised 9% of pottery excavated at Arpachiyah in 1976 (Hijara et al, 1980, p. 143), yet coarsewares were said to be a minority at Damishliyya (Akkermans, 1993, p. 38).
15 Noll (1976), Hijara et al (1980), Davidson & Watkins (1981, pp. 7, 9), Steinberg & Kamilli (1984).
16 Matson (1960, p. 67), Davidson (1981, p. 74), Van As & Jacobs (1992, pp. 533–5), Akkermans (1993, p. 37), Kamada & Ohtsu (1993, p. 190).
17 Mallowan & Rose (1935), Mellaart (1975, pp. 161–2), Frankel (1979, p. 18), Hijara (1980), Hijara et al (1980, p. 148, fig. 10), Akkermans (1993, p. 77, fig. 3.21:40).
18 Merpert, Munchaev & Bader (1981, figs VII–VIII, X–XI).
19 Mallowan & Rose (1935, pp. 107, 131–5).
20 For the kilns see Woolley (1934; cf. Frankel, 1979, pp. 3, 15), Munchaev & Merpert (1971, p. 30), Hijara et al (1980, pp. 133–4), Merpert, Munchaev & Bader (1981, p. 25, figs I–II), Quarentelli (ed., 1985, pp. 32–3). There is some uncertainty as to the precise function of some of these, and 'keyhole-plan' installations at Tell Sabi Abyad may have been drying ovens (Akkermans 1993, pp. 52–4); claypits and another type of sunken installation were excavated at Tell Songor (Kamada & Ohtsu, 1993, p. 187, pl. 4). On firing temperatures see Tobler (1950), Van As & Jacobs (1989, table V.1), Akkermans (1993, p. 7).
21 Mallowan & Rose (1935, pp. 105–6), LeBlanc & Watson (1973), Davidson & McKerrell (1976; 1980), Davidson (1981), Campbell (1986), Akkermans (1993, p. 45).
22 Mellaart (1975), J. Oates (1983).
23 Berman (1994), Hole (1984).
24 Roaf (1984).
25 Roaf (1989), Roaf (ed., 1984, pp. 142–50).
26 Tobler (1950, pl. CXXIII, no. 113), Stronach (1961, pp. 116–17, pl. LVI), Safar, Mustafa & Lloyd (1981, pp. 101, 155).
27 71% of Ubaid 2/3 pottery at Tell Rashid was painted and only 4.5% was undecorated (the remainder being incised or impressed), whereas painted pottery was rare at Ubaid 4 sites (Jasim, 1985, I, pp. 146–7, 159–61, 165–6).
28 Lloyd & Safar (1943, pp. 151–2, pl. XIXa), Parrot (1948, fig. 8), Stronach (1961, p. 120, pls XLV–XLVI), Safar, Mustafa & Lloyd (1981, pp. 156, 188–9, 336–7, fig. 87, pl. 16:2), Jasim (1985, I, p. 146, II, fig. 233), Roaf (1989), Stronach (1961, p. 120, pls XLV–XLVI).
29 Courtois & Velde (1987), Velde & Courtois (1987), Matson (1995, p. 1556). Grinding stones with 'traces of red ochre' found at Tell Abada may have been used in a pottery workshop (Jasim 1985, I, pp. 18, 75, II, fig. 72).
30 Adams & Nissen (1972, pp. 208–10).
31 Thompson (1923, p. 239), Lloyd & Safar (1943, p. 150), Stronach (1961, p. 108), Matson (1974, p. 346), Tusa (1980).
32 Lloyd & Safar (1943, p. 152), Stronach (1961, p. 109), Tusa (1980); cf. Jasim (1985, I, pp. 18, 87, II, fig. 91), Nissen (1988, pp. 46–8), Kamada & Ohtsu (1993, p. 190).
33 Stronach (1961, p. 109).
34 Hall & Woolley et al (1927, p. 165), Tobler (1950), Tite (1969, p. 141), Jasim (1985, I, pp. 17–18, 22–3, II, figs 10–11, 25, 31–40).
35 The over-representation of vitrified sherds among surface collections may reflect their greater resistance to natural erosion, whereas they were extremely rare among excavated assemblages (Matson, 1971, pp. 76–7; Safar, Mustafa & Lloyd, 1981, p. 154).
36 Safar, Mustafa & Lloyd (1981), Berman (1994, p. 29).
37 Davidson & McKerrell (1980, p. 164), Jasim (1985, I, pp. 150, 153, 161, 171, II, figs 217–20), Henrickson (1986), Roaf (1990, p. 53), Roaf & Galbraith (1994). Clay model boats found at Southern Ubaid sites probably represent rivercraft.
38 See also ch. 24 (p. 161).
39 For discussion and details see Kamilli & Steinberg (1985) and Steinberg & Kamilli (1984).
40 Kamilli & Steinberg (1985), Courtois & Velde (1991).
41 Wright (1986).
Acknowledgements: My thanks to John Curtis and Julian Reade for kindly reading and commenting on this and subsequent chapters (6, 10, 23), and to the Photographic Service, especially Lisa Bliss and Barbara Winter, for all their work.

Chapter 5

1 The bibliography for Egyptian Predynastic pottery is too vast to be cited here. Instead a few principal works are noted, in which further references can be found. See particularly the following: Petrie & Quibell (1896, pp. 11–13, pls 18–41; 1921: passim); Baumgartel (1947, pp. 52–102); Needler (1984, pp. 171–237); Payne (1993). The bibliography of early Egypt in Spencer (ed., 1996) may also be found useful.
2 The transition from northern ceramics to those of the Naqada culture is well attested at Buto: Köhler (1992a; 1992b, pp. 7–15; 1989, pp. 289–300). Note the dominance of the southern Naqada culture at Minshat Abu Omar: Kroeper (1986/7).
3 For ceramics of the Lower Egyptian Predynastic cultures see Junker (1930); Eiwanger (1984, pp. 18–39; 1988, pp. 15–31; 1992, pp. 14–42); Rizkhana & Seeher (1987; passim); Köhler (1989, pp. 289–300); Debono & Mortensen (1990, pp. 24–37).
4 Hand-shaping techniques described in Arnold & Bourriau (eds, 1993, pp. 15–41).
5 Vandiver & Lacovara (1985/6); but see Arnold & Bourriau (eds, 1993, pp. 29–33).
6 Arnold & Bourriau (eds, 1993, pp. 33–6).
7 For turning-devices, see Arnold & Bourriau (eds, 1993, pp. 36–41).
8 Hoffman (1982b, p. 12); Harlan (1982, p. 16); see also Arnold & Bourriau (eds, 1993, p. 108).
9 Arnold & Bourriau (eds, 1993, p. 90). For examples of Badarian ceramics see ibid. (p. 174); Bourriau (1981, cat. nos 27, 67–9); Spencer (1993b, p. 26, fig. 11); Brunton & Caton-Thompson (1928, pls 12–20). Many published examples will be found in excavation reports for other Badarian sites, such as Matmar, Mostagedda and Naga ed-Deir.
10 Arnold & Bourriau (eds, 1993, p. 95).
11 Black-topped and Red-polished examples in Bourriau (1981, cat. nos 64–6, 70–73), Petrie (1921, pls 1–14). For the changing fashions in pottery during the Predynastic period see Kaiser (1957) and Hendrickx (1996); also the summary in Spencer (1993b, p. 11).
12 Bourriau (1981, cat. nos 74–7); Petrie & Quibell (1896, pls 28–29; 1921, pls 20–25); Spencer (1993b, p. 30, fig. 14).
13 Bourriau (1981, cat. nos 34–5); Arnold & Bourriau (eds, 1993, p. 96, fig. 104A); Petrie (1921, pl. 25).
14 Petrie & Quibell (1896, pls 33–5; 1921, pls 31–7); Bourriau (1981, cat. nos 30–33); simple later versions: ibid. (cat. nos 78–9); imitation of stone: ibid. (cat. no. 36a–b).
15 Bourriau (1981, cat. nos 257–8); Petrie & Quibell (1896, pls 31–2; 1921, pls 28–30).
16 Arnold & Bourriau (eds, 1993, p. 32, fig. 31C–D); Bourriau (1981, cat. no. 259); Petrie & Quibell (1896, pl. 32).
17 Petrie & Quibell (1896, pls 39–41; 1921, pls 45–51).
18 BM EA 30891.

Chapter 6

1 Foster (1991).
2 Algaze (1993).
3 Lloyd (1940), Tobler (1950), al-Soof (1985, pp. 19–27), Fujii et al (1987, pp. 50–55).
4 Postgate & Moon (1982, p. 105), Killick et al (1988, pp. 18–21), Calvet (1991), Beyer (1993), Tite, Middleton & Postgate (1994/5, p. 49).
5 Woolley (1956, pp. 65–6), Bobrinsky (1993, p. 51, fig. 6:4), Matson (1995, pp. 1561–2). Early Dynastic examples have been reported from other sites (Moorey, 1994, p. 146).
6 Fielden (1981), Wright (1981, p. 304), al-Soof (1985). Fired clay wheels up to about 25 cm (10 in) in diameter and with a central flanged pivot-hole may have been used as tournettes (Matson, 1995, p. 1562).
7 Alden (1988), Ii (1991), Henrickson (1992); for alternative views see Barrelet (1968), Moon (1987, pp. 57, 60).
8 Sürenhagen (1978), Al-Soof (1985), Badler, McGovern & Glusker (1996). An exceptional jar from Habuba Kabira was decorated with repeated impressions of a small lozenge-shaped die (Weiss, ed., 1985, pp. 112–13, pl. 32).
9 Johnson (1973), Millard (1988), Buccellati (1990), Chazan & Lehner (1990), Matson (1995, pp. 1563–4). These were divided by Johnson into three groups (of 0.465, 0.647 and 0.922 litres) yet this division has not been accepted by other scholars (Killick et al, 1988, pp. 39–44), and brimming capacities of British Museum bowls vary between 650 and 870 ml. Replication experiments suggest that they were handmade rather than, as often assumed, pressed into moulds (Kalsbeek, 1980).
10 Mynors (1982), Méry & Schneider (1996).
11 Postgate (1992).
12 Foster (1991, p. 404), Matthews (1995, pp. 460–62); see Matson (1974), Reade (1982, p. 77), Postgate (1990, pp. 103–4), Tite, Middleton & Postgate (1994/5, pp. 49–50).
13 Moorey (1994, p. 144).
14 This site may be identified with ancient Kesh, whose deity was Dingirmah or Nin-bahar ('lady potter') (Foster, 1991).
15 Postgate & Moon (1982, p. 127), Nicholson & Patterson (1989), Tite, Middleton & Postgate (1994/5, pp. 49–50).
16 Reade (1968, p. 251; 1982, pl. 5), Kühne (1976), Fielden (1977), Kelly-Buccellati & Shelby (1977, pp. 11–12), Kühne & Schneider (1988), Schneider (1988; 1989).
17 Frankfort (1939), Porada (1984).
18 Salonen (1966).
19 Martin, Moon & Postgate (1985): Abu Salabikh Grave 80 contained no less than 135 conical bowls, 7 spouted jars and a bottle; Mynors (1982, p. 386), Méry & Schneider (1996).
20 These are often described as 'ration bowls' yet they were probably simply convenient containers (Ellison, 1984a, p. 64).

21 Moon (1987, pp. 17–19): although typical of the Diyala region they are not found in the Hamrin basin (Roaf, 1982, p. 45).
22 The lack of burning excludes their possible use as braziers (Moon, 1987, pp. 46–57). Both these and 'upright handled jars' continued throughout the Akkadian period (Gibson & McMahon, 1995).
23 Moon (1982; 1987, pp. 151–65).
24 Ellison (1986, pp. 157–8).
25 Postgate (1977, p. 293), Moon (1987, pp. 128–50), Gates (1988, pp. 69–71); see Hartman & Oppenheim (1950), McGovern, Fleming & Katz (eds, 1995), Reade (1995).
26 Hall & Woolley et al (1927, pl. XXXI), Ellison (1984a, pp. 64–5).
27 Moon (1987, pp. 34–5, 170–74).
28 Identical examples have been excavated at Ur and Tell Jokha (Woolley, 1982, p. 239; Rumayidh, 1981, p. 128).
29 Ii (1988); Thuesen, Heydorn & Gwozdz (1982), al-Kaissy & Mynors (1987), Makovicky & Thuesen (1990), Thuesen (1990); Roaf & Killick (1988).
30 Reade (1968), Kühne (1976), Adams (1981, pp. 170–71), Wright (1981, pp. 310–11, fig. 7e–f), Moon (1987, pp. 40, 43), Wilkinson & Tucker (1995, pp. 96, 114, fig. 69).
31 Daszkiewicz & Schneider (1996).
32 Adams (1981, p. 171), Højlund & Hellmuth Andersen et al (1994, pp. 103–4, 301–2).
33 Kramer (1977), Mazzoni (1985); see also Parr (1978).
34 Gadd (1940, p. 33), Zaccagnini (1977, p. 174), Senior & Weiss (1992).
35 The Levantine distribution is discussed by Trokay (1989; 1990): Mesopotamian findspots include Tell Yelkhi (Quarentelli, ed., 1985, p. 161); replication experiments are discussed by Amiran & Shenhav (1984), Edwards & Jacobs (1986), Magrill & Middleton (see ch. 9).
36 Van As & Jacobs (1985; 1986; 1991/2; 1992), Jacobs (1991/2).
37 Starr et al (1939, vol. I, pp. 54–5, vol. II, pls 19B, 22B, figs 36, 46), Quarantelli (ed., 1985, p. 167), Fujii (1987, p. 66, fig. 6), al-Najafi (1987/8, p. 87), Yaseen (1995, pp. 39, 79–80, pls 18, 20–21).
38 'Strainers' were developed in the Akkadian period (Reade, 1968, p. 263, pl. LXXXV:16); see Ellison (1984a, pp. 64–6), Moon (1987, pp. 20–23), Yaseen (1995, p. 65, pls 31, 108, 139). Their function as steamer-lids rather than sieves is illustrated by examples with handles on the top (Starr et al, 1939, vol. I, p. 406, vol. II, pl. 95; anon. 1996, p. 9); metal versions also exist (Toker, 1992, pp. 68, 194, no. 47). Moulds: Parrot (1959, pp. 33–57, pls XVI–XXVI), Dalley (1984, p. 88), Ellison (1984a, pp. 66–7; 1984b, p. 91). Pot-stands: Roaf (1983, pp. 75, 77). Traps: Simpson (1993). Toys: Starr et al (1939, vol. II, pl. 103). Rattles: Woolley & Mallowan (1976, p. 182, pl. 92, no. 256).
39 Kelly-Buccellati & Shelby (1977, pp. 7–9, 26–9, 32–3, pls IV, VIII), Gates (1988, p. 72), Minsauer (1991), Yaseen (1995, pp. 75–7). Brush-strokes betray the method of application although Matson (1983, p. 623, fig. 225) illustrates the use of an asphalt crayon to decorate contemporary pots in northern Iraq.
40 Delougaz (1952, pp. 119–20, pls 122–6).
41 Reade (1968, pp. 257–8, pl. LXXXVII), Hamlin (1974), Kelly-Buccellati & Shelby (1977, p. 11), Kramer (1977), Stein (1984).
42 The same motif is found on contemporaneous incised greyware in southern Mesopotamia (Delougaz, 1952, pp. 119–20, pl. 123).
43 This is also known as Hurrian ware, Mittannian ware, Subartu pottery or Atchana ware (Stein, 1984).
44 Adams (1981, pp. 171–4), Lombard & Kervran (eds, 1989, pp. 43–6); for technology see Franken & Kalsbeek (1984), Van As & Jacobs (1987; 1992).
45 Postgate (1987, p. 268), Curtis et al (1989), Simpson (1990, pp. 121–2).
46 Bourriau (1981, p. 16); for typical Late Assyrian pottery see D. & J. Oates (1959), Ellison (1986), Curtis et al (1989), Curtis & Reade (eds, 1995, pp. 152–60).
47 Andrae (1925), D. & J. Oates (1959, p. 138), Simpson (1990, p. 129), Freestone (1991b).
48 Rawson (1954), D. & J. Oates (1959, pp. 133–6, 142–3, pls XXXIV–XXXVII, nos 59–74).
49 Curtis & Reade (eds, 1995, p. 133).
50 Curtis & Green (1987, pp. 75–7), J. Oates (1959, pp. 108, 134, 137, 144, pl. XXXVIII, no. 90).
51 Freestone & Hughes (1989); see J. Oates (1959, pp. 137, 146, pl. XXXIX, no. 108).
52 Hedges (1982); compare glaze composition with glazed bricks, for which there was a well-developed industry at Babylon (Koldewey, 1914; Matson, 1985, pp. 68–9; 1986).
53 Weisberg (1967, p. 96).
54 Gibson (1974), Adams (1981, p. 231), Wright (1981, pp. 319, 322, fig. 16), Fleming (1989), Goodwin (1995), Simpson (1995), Wilkinson & Tucker (1995, pp. 101–2, 215, figs 74:10–17, 81:3, pl. 6b).
55 Maniatis & Tite (1981), Tite et al (1982).
56 Nicholson & Patterson (1989).
57 Ibid.
58 Composite of Matson (1985), Freestone (1991b; unpublished) and Hedges (1982).

Chapter 7

1 Here the British Iron Age is taken to last from about 750 BC until the Roman invasion in AD 43–4.
2 Cunliffe (1984).
3 Cunliffe (1991).
4 Middleton (1987).
5 E.g. Peacock (1968; 1969); see Morris (1994) for an overview.
6 E.g. Hamilton (1985); see Morris (1994) for an overview.
7 Freestone & Rigby (1981); Cunliffe (1987).
8 Skibo et al (1989).
9 Cf. the 'Prunay Group' (Rigby et al, 1989).
10 Rigby & Freestone (1985).
11 Stead (1967).
12 Farley (1983).
13 Sireix (1994).
14 Freestone & Rigby (1988); Stead & Rigby (1989).
15 Freestone & Rigby (1988).
16 Freestone & Rigby (1988, n. 14).
17 Little Hadham, Hertfordshire, unpublished petrological results of the authors.
18 Morris (1994) reviews the evidence.
19 E.g. Black burnished ware (Williams, 1977).
20 Peacock (1982); Arnold (1985).
21 There is evidence for female potters in large-scale Roman production from the stamps on some *terra sigillata*; and also for the use of slaves.
22 See, for example, Peacock (1992, pp. 79–80).

Chapter 8

1 Decoration occurs at other periods, but not to the same extent. See Arnold & Bourriau (eds, 1993, pp. 95–6).
2 Ibid. (pp. 43ff); Bourriau (1981, pp. 15–16); Hope (1987a, pp. 10–17).
3 The principal works are Holthoer (1977); Hope (1987a); Bourriau (1981); Arnold (ed., 1981); Arnold & Bourriau (eds, 1993). These volumes contain extensive bibliographies of the subject, with references far too numerous to cite here.
4 Arnold & Bourriau (1993, pp. 41ff); Hope (1987a, pp. 13–17); Holthoer (1977, pp. 31–4).
5 Arnold & Bourriau (1993, p. 58). Further increase in the speed of rotation was achieved in the late Thirteenth Dynasty (ibid., pp. 61–3).
6 Ibid. (p. 74, fig. 87A); Hope (1981, pp. 127–33; 1982a, pp. 13–14). Experiments have been done to assess the effectiveness of these pivots: see Powell (1995).
7 Arnold & Bourriau (eds, 1993, pp. 44ff, especially p. 50, fig. 53, and p. 60, figs 68–71). For a collection of representational evidence, see Holthoer (1977, pp. 5–26).
8 Arnold & Bourriau (eds, 1993, pp. 75–8, fig. 89).
9 Ibid. (pp. 79–83).
10 Ibid. (pp. 54–6, 63–9).
11 For discussion and bibliography, see Nicholson (1993a); Holthoer (1977, pp. 34–7); Arnold (1976); Bourriau (1981, pp. 15–17); Nicholson (1989).
12 Nicholson (1993a, pp. 108–10); Soukiassian et al (1990, pp. 1–73).
13 Nicholson (1993a, p. 116, fig. 118); Spencer (1993a, p. 19, pl. 15c).
14 Examples in Bourriau (1981, cat. nos 6, 84–8).
15 Arnold & Bourriau (eds, 1993, fig. 44A).
16 See the numerous examples from el-Ashmunein in Spencer (1993a, pls 101–3); also from Dakhla oasis: Ballet & Picon (1987); Soukiassian et al (1990, pp. 96–7, 152–6, pls 40–41).
17 Vandiver & Lacovara (1985/6, pp. 58–9, fig. 18a–b); Arnold & Bourriau (eds, 1993, pp. 22, 24, fig. 21A–B).
18 Extensive discussion of clays and fabrics in Arnold & Bourriau (eds, 1993, pp. 162ff); Arnold (1981); Riederer (1981); Nordström (1986, pp. 629–34); Bourriau & Nicholson (1992).
19 Similar vessels: Arnold & Bourriau (eds, 1993, p. 24, fig. 20); Spencer (1993a, pls 107–9, type 2.4).
20 See Bourriau (1981, cat. nos 99–101); Arnold & Bourriau (eds, 1993, p. 178, fig. 19; p. 179, fig. 21).
21 Hope (1982b; 1987b).
22 Arnold & Bourriau (eds, 1993, p. 160).
23 French (1990, pp. 85–6).
24 Bourriau (1981, cat. no. 19).
25 Noll (1981).
26 Lucas & Harris (1962, pp. 257–9).
27 The source of the cobalt in Egyptian pigments was recognised by Kaczmarczyk (1986).

Chapter 9

1 For further information about the Canaanites see, for example, Millard (1973) and Mazar (1990, chs 6–8).
2 Extract from unpublished Lachish field report, Eighth Report of the Expedition, 31 March 1938 (p. 51).
3 Ibid. (p. 50).
4 See Tufnell (1958, pp. 291–3).
5 The objects from Lachish, along with an archive of documentary material, are held by the Department of Western Asiatic Antiquities.
6 See Porat (1986/7, fig. 1).
7 See Rosen (1986, pp. 58, 129–31, map 3, fig. 17).
8 Ibid. (p. 65).
9 We are grateful to Arlene Rosen for this suggestion, based upon her fieldwork in the area.
10 The use of shell and calcite as tempering materials is discussed by, amongst others, Rye (1976) and Arnold (1985). On heating, calcite expands at a rate similar to that of low-fired clay, a feature which would be expected to improve thermal shock resistance relative to materials such as quartz, which have higher rates of expansion. However, a note of caution against the over-use of such considerations to interpret the behaviour of potters was sounded by Woods (1985), who found that many early cooking pots from Britain were tempered with quartz.
11 For a general discussion of forming techniques in the context of archaeological pottery, see, for example, Rye (1981) and Rice (1987).
12 See, for example, Amiran & Shenhav (1984) and Powell (1995).
13 See, for example, Childe (1954), who refers to the use of a kickwheel at Lachish. Childe also noted that precisely similar stones were still in use in Palestine, as the bearings for kickwheels.
14 These observations are based on a preliminary study of four nearly complete Lachish Late Bronze Age cooking pots from contexts other than Cave 4034. The use of vessels from other contexts was necessary as only rim fragments of cooking pots, both fired and unfired, were collected from the potter's workshop.
15 Rye (1981, p. 27) noted that many cooking pots have round bases, but it should be noted that Woods (1985) found that many cooking pots from Britain have flat bases.
16 The use of shells for burnishing was reported in Palestine during the 1930s by Grace Crowfoot (1932).
17 These samples were identified using X-ray diffraction analysis.
18 Yellow ochre contains hydrated iron oxides, which are converted to anhydrous iron oxide, Fe_2O_3, which is red, on heating.
19 The material of the shell included in the raw clay was identified as aragonite by X-ray diffraction analysis.
20 Aragonite is converted to calcite above about 400–500°C (Deer, Howie & Zussman, 1962).
21 On heating to about 750°C, calcite is destroyed; although calcite is reformed over time the original texture is lost, the original grain being replaced by a mass of very fine crystals.
22 For discussion of the estimation of firing temperatures of ceramics based upon their degree of vitrification see Maniatis & Tite (1981) and Tite et al (1982).
23 The most recent excavations (1973–90) were carried out by a team from Tel Aviv University under the direction of Prof. David Ussishkin. For a discussion of the Late Bronze Age city levels and structures, see Ussishkin (1985).
24 For precise information on the location of Cave 4034 see Tufnell (1958, p. 291; 1953, pls 108, 128).
25 See, for example, Rye (1981, p. 9) and Peacock (1982, p. 38).
26 Described by Dr K. M. E. Murray in a letter to her mother, 28 April 1933. We are grateful to Dr Murray for permission to publish this extract from her personal correspondence.
27 See, for example, Carr (1990), Carr & Riddick (1990), Glanzman (1983), Middleton (forthcoming) and Vandiver (1987), and additional references therein.
28 See Rye (1977; 1981).
29 Xeroradiography is a radiographic technique originally developed for mammography. It is particularly sensitive to small discontinuities and is therefore very useful in the examination of ceramics. See, for example, Middleton et al (1992) and references therein.
Acknowledgements: We are grateful to numerous colleagues for their advice and support. In particular, we thank Lisa Baylis, Andrew Calvert, Tony Milton and Ann Searight for their assistance with the illustrations and Ian Freestone for helpful comments on an earlier draft. Trevor Thomas, a professional potter, provided valuable advice, especially relating to tools and decoration. Sylvia Humphrey carried out much of the scientific examination on which the paper is based and it is a pleasure to acknowledge her contribution to the project.

Chapter 10

1 Haerinck (1983), Simpson (1997a; b).
2 Debevoise (1938), Colledge (1977), Herrmann (1977).
3 Matson (1955, pp. 38–9).
4 Debevoise (1934a, p. 298; 1934b, pp. 12–13), Matson (1939), Fukai (1981).
5 Richter (1938), Debevoise (1934b), Pope (ed., 1938, vol. IV, pls 181–2), Toll (1943), D. & J. Oates (1959, pp. 224–5), Erdmann (1935). The studs, fishtail-like lower handle-junctions and 'bow finials' on the tops of the handles presumably imitate rivets and handle attachments on metalwares (Keall, 1970, pp. 71–2, pl. VII:1–2; Fukai, 1981, nos 96–7); compare Vickers (1986).
6 For Central Mesopotamian glazed wares see Debevoise (1934b), Keall (1970), al-Haditti (1995); for decorated plainwares see D. & J. Oates (1959), Adams (1965, pp. 130–31, fig. 13:11), Keall (1970, pp. 70–71, pls IV, V:2–3); for eggshell wares see Debevoise (1934b), Valtz (1984, pp. 43–4).

7 Debevoise (1934a; b), Richter (1938), Matson (1943), Hauser (1996). Vivid colours remain on a small number of vessels found in less salty or wet ground conditions (Fukai, 1981; Adams, 1981, p. 231; al-Haditti, 1995, p. 228). At Assur, glazed pottery appears to have been increasingly replaced by a hard-fired plainware with red surfaces and a grey core that may have been preferred for economic reasons of cheaper and easier production (Hauser, 1996).
8 Fukai (1981), Keall (1970, pp. 64, 69, pl. II:6).
9 For Brittle wares see D. & J. Oates (1959, pp. 226–7), Northedge (1981), Venco Ricciardi (1982, pp. 63, 75, pl. 8:2), Bartl, Schneider & Böhme (1995); for glazed cooking wares see Keall (1970, p. 68, pl. I:1), Valtz (1991, p. 54).
10 Keall (1970, pp. 68–9), Hannestad (1983), Haerinck (1983), Van Ingen (1939, p. 201, pl. XLVIII, no. 720).
11 Kleiss (1973, p. 185, Abb. 23), Haerinck (1983). Compare Fukai (1981, no. 95) and Fujii (ed., 1976, p. 233, fig. IV–44). Leather containers do not survive under normal archaeological conditions in the Near East but they are attested from Hatrene and talmudic references (Ibrahim, 1986, p. 212; Newman, 1932, p. 97).
12 Debevoise (1934a, p. 299; 1934b, pp. 14, 104, fig. 8), Hauser (1996).
13 Debevoise (1934a, p. 300), Richter (1938), Matson (1955, p. 37), Invernizzi (1977).
14 For early discoveries of Parthian glazed coffins at Uruk/Warka and Nippur see Loftus (1857, pp. 203–20), Peters (1897, II, pp. 214–16, 226–30, 304–5, pls opposite pp. 214, 230), Hilprecht (1903, pp. 422–3, pl. opposite p. 308); later discoveries at Babylon and Seleucia are described by Koldewey (1914, p. 219, fig. 133), Yeivin (1933, p. 36) and Heinrich (1935, p. 32); for a re-evaluation of their dating see Curtis (1979).
15 Christensen (1936), Adams (1981), Howard-Johnston (1995).
16 Neusner (1970, pp. 25, 303, 305), Tafazzoli (1974).
17 Adams (1981, pp. 211–13), Sarfaraz (1969/70, pp. 13, 73), Kawamata (1981, p. 194, fig. 58, pl. 23). A different type of kiln, probably dating to the 3rd or 4th century, was excavated at Tal-i Malyan in Fars: traces of a chimney at one end suggest that it functioned as a cross-draught or downdraught kiln (Alden, 1978).
18 Gibson (1972, pp. 128, 167), Adams (1981, pp. 232–4), Northedge (1988, p. 77), Simpson (1996).
19 Valtz (1984), Venco Ricciardi (1984); see also Debevoise (1934b), Harper et al (1978, p. 160), Adams (1981, p. 211).
20 Tafazzoli (1974, pp. 194–5); see Debevoise (1934a, p. 299), Hedges & Moorey (1975) for glaze analyses.
21 De Cardi et al (1975), Smith & Wright (1988), Munro-Hay (1991, p. 238).
22 Venco Ricciardi (1984, p. 52, fig. 4:5), Herrmann, Kurbansakhatov & Simpson et al (1996, p. 15). Little is known about Sasanian cuisine, yet a number of boiled as well as grilled dishes are attested (Christensen, 1936, pp. 471–3; Ahsan, 1979).
23 Adams (1965, p. 131, fig. 14:12B–D; 1981, p. 234), Curtis (1989a), Peltenburg (1991, p. 86, no. 59), Simpson & Watkins (1995), Simpson (1996), although Sasanian dies do not survive; see Rice (1987, pp. 136–7) for more recent wooden stamps. During the Umayyad period, smaller horseshoe-shaped ceramic stamps were employed. Relief medallions containing similar animal designs occur on Late Sasanian silver-gilt vases (Arnold et al, 1996, pp. 72–5) and Umayyad glasswares (Balog, 1974).
24 Adams (1965, p. 132, fig. 14:12m), Wenke (1975/6), Finster & Schmidt (1976, taf. 52–5, 58–61), Adams (1981, p. 234), Wilkinson & Tucker (1995, pp. 105–6, 121, fig. 77:18–19), Simpson (1996); see Rye & Evans (1976) and Rice (1987, p. 138) for comparable modern pots.
25 This category of vessel was developed from a Parthian type and was occasionally reused to cover the body in graves (Adams, 1965, p. 132; 1981, p. 234; Kawamata, 1981, p. 194, fig. 58:10; Northedge, 1988, p. 82, fig. 38:11–14).
26 Venco Ricciardi (1967; 1970/71; 1984). Hemispherical bowls probably had the dual function of drinking/serving bowls and lids: they were also produced in hammered silver and cut glass, and were depicted in Sasanian art. Bowls and lids were occasionally reused in magical rituals designed to exorcise households of malevolent spirits, as they were well suited to be overturned as 'demon traps'. Bowls with 'pull-knobs' continued to be manufactured as late as the 9th century.
27 Venco Ricciardi (1984). Within Iran, dark burnished ceramic jars with vertical fluted necks appear to have been inspired by a Late Sasanian class of high-tin bronze vessel (compare Harper et al, 1978, pp. 92–4, no. 33c; Whitcomb, 1985, pp. 50–51, fig. 16). Light rippling found on ceramics at Merv, on the eastern Sasanian frontier, again appear to imitate lightly fluted metalwares (Herrmann, Kurbansakhatov & Simpson et al, 1996, p. 13).
28 For a glazed jar found in Khuzestan see Ganjavi (1975); other examples lack excavated provenance (Christie's, 1996, lot 609; same as Sotheby's, 1996, lot 172). See Harper et al (1978, pp. 51–2, 64–7, 71–3) for silver-gilt examples.
29 Ettinghausen (1938, vol. I, pp. 661–2), Pope (ed., 1938, vol. IV, pl. 185A–D), Harper et al (1978, pp. 161–4, nos 83–4), Christie's (1994, lot 195). A Palmyrene sculpture shows a rhyton of this or a closely related type being carried by a male figure (Colledge, 1976, p. 79).
30 Harden (1934, pp. 127–8, fig. 2a, no. 28).
31 Ettinghausen (1938, vol. I, p. 659), Pope (ed., 1938, vol. IV, pl. 184D; misattributed to Berlin as this object is in the Iraq Museum). It is closely paralleled by a silver rhyton and a red-painted coil-built ceramic rhyton, both in the Smithsonian (Harper et al, 1978, pp. 36–8, no. 5), Gunter (1988, pp. 36–7, 39, 47, figs 22, 28), Kawami (1992, p. 222, no. 141). Rhyta of this type are shown being used in a banqueting scene on late 7th- or early 8th-century Sogdian wall-paintings at Penjikent (Marshak & Raspopova, 1990, figs 29–30). Rhyta are also shown on Sasanian seals and silverwares (Harper et al, 1978, pp. 94–6, 148–9, nos 25, 73; Gunter, 1988, pp. 44–6, fig. 27). These pourers contrast with the earlier Seleucid tradition of trumpet- or horn-shaped pourers with, as in the Achaemenid period, animal-head protomes and a spout placed between the forelegs (cf. Gunter, 1988, pp. 37–9, 41, figs 23–5).
32 Harden (1934, pp. 127–8, fig. 2a, no. 29); for earlier evidence see Keall (1970, pp. 72–3, pls VIII:1, IX:2).
33 Pope (ed., 1938, vol. IV, pls 189–90, 193–4), Reitlinger (1951), Adams (1965, p. 132, fig. 14:13A), Fukai (1981, nos 107–8).
34 Composite based on Hedges (1982), Freestone (unpublished), Mason & Tite (1997). Table in weight per cent. Acknowledgements: Thanks are due to Ian Freestone, Colleen Stapleton and Andrew Middleton (Department of Scientific Research) for compositional analyses of glazes, high-magnification photographs of Sasanian stamped sherds and xeroradiographs of vessels in the course of this study.

Chapter 11

1 For further reading on the subject of Japanese stonewares see Miller (1960), Cort (1970), Jenyns (1971), Mikami (1972) and the catalogue of an exhibition at the Birmingham (Alabama) Museum of Art, *Eight Hundred Years of Japanese Stoneware* (Wood, Tanaka & Chance, 1994).

Chapter 12

1 K. Kotsakis et al, in Papathanassopoulos (1996, pp. 107–34, cat. nos 72–168).
2 Hood (1978, pp. 27–46), Dickinson (1994, pp. 101–30).
3 Evely (1988, pp. 88, 96–7).
4 Desborough (1972).
5 Kritias *apud* Athenaeus, *Deipnosophistae* I, 28c.
6 Coldstream (1977; 1991).
7 On Corinthian, see Benson (1989), Amyx (1988), Rasmussen (1991). For descriptions of other Archaic Greek fabrics, see in particular Cook (1997).
8 Williams (1985, pp. 18–20; 1986).
9 On signatures and workshops, see Williams (1995).
10 On shapes, see Sparkes (1991, pp. 60–92).
11 On Athenian black-figure see Beazley (1986), Boardman (1974), Williams (1985, pp. 26–34).
12 Williams (1995).
13 On Athenian red-figure, see Boardman (1975), Williams (1985), Boardman (1989), Robertson (1992). On the invention of the new scheme, see Williams (1991).
14 On white-ground vases, see Kurtz (1975), Wehgartner (1983).
15 On South Italian fabrics, see Trendall (1989).
16 On black-glaze fabrics, see Sparkes (1991, pp. 103–10).
17 On Hellenistic pottery, see Hayes (1991).
18 Jones (1986, pp. 798–809) reviews work on the analysis and composition of the slips on Greek pottery. Noble (1988) provides a general overview of construction and decorative techniques. Kingery (1990) questions the conventional wisdom that the slips on Attic wares were derived from the same clays as the bodies.
19 Tite, Bimson & Freestone (1982). Table in weight per cent.
20 See Jones (1986) for a review of estimated firing conditions.

Chapter 13

1 For surveys of the medieval pottery industry in Britain, see Moorhouse (1981), McCarthy & Brooks (1988), Cherry (1991a). For the influence of metal vessels on pottery forms see Verhaeghe (1991).
2 Le Patourel (1968), McCarthy & Brooks (1988, pp. 54–7).
3 McCarthy & Brooks (1988, p. 79).
4 Ibid. (pp. 70–74).
5 Le Patourel (1968, pp. 108, 124, table IV).
6 For example, Stamford (McCarthy & Brooks, 1988, p. 255), Doncaster (ibid., p. 243), Scarborough (ibid., pp. 227–30), Kingston (ibid., p. 311).
7 For a discussion of the uses of medieval pottery, see Moorhouse (1978; 1981, pp. 114–17).
8 Cherry (1985).
9 See Alexander & Binski (1987, cat. no. 551).
10 For example, see Pearce & Vince (1988, p. 50, fig. 100, no. 388).
11 See, for example, Le Patourel (1966), Ponsford (1979); for the jug from Faccombe Netherton illustrated in fig. 3, see Fairbrother (1990, vol. II, p. 350, fig. 8.55, no. 411).
12 Dunning (1969).
13 Nenk (1992).
14 Thompson (1953), Cherry (1991a, fig. 95; 1991b, fig. 64), Hillewaert (1992).
15 Farmer (1979), Alexander & Binski (1987, cat. no. 180).
16 See, for example, Alexander & Binski (1987, cat. nos 154, 548).
17 Ibid. (1987, cat. no. 184), Pearce & Vince (1988, p. 38, fig. 71, no. 110).
18 Alexander & Binski (1987, cat. no. 551).
19 Pearce et al (1985, fig. 57, nos 227–9).
20 Ponsford (1979).
21 Le Patourel (1986), McCarthy & Brooks (1988, pp. 128–9).
22 Cherry (1992).
23 See, for example, Pearce & Vince (1988, figs 10, 67, no. 87).
24 Cherry (1985, p. 10), Le Patourel (1986, p. 13).
25 Vidler (1933, pp. 53–5, pls VII–VIII), Alexander & Binski (1987, cat. no. 552).
26 Le Patourel (1986).
27 Pearce et al (1985, pp. 127–30).
28 Nenk & Pearce (1994).
29 McCarthy & Brooks (1988, pp. 243–6).
30 Farmer (1979), Farmer & Farmer (1982); see McCarthy & Brooks (1988, pp. 94, 227–30).
31 Reed (1990), Hillewaert (1992).
32 Barton (1965).
33 Pearce et al (1985, pp. 131–2).
34 Platt & Coleman-Smith (1975, pp. 23–7), Dunning (1975, pp. 49–50).
35 McCarthy & Brooks (1988, p. 57).
36 Pearce et al (1985, p. 130, fig. 22, no. 46).
37 Ibid. (p. 132).
38 Cotter (1997).
39 Moorhouse (1981, p. 107).
40 See, for example, Pearce et al (1982, p. 287), Gardiner (1989).
41 See, for example, Pearce et al (1985, p. 128).
42 Bellamy & Le Patourel (1970).
43 Pearce & Vince (1988, p. 82).
44 Dunning (1976).
45 McCarthy & Brooks (1988, pp. 343–5).
46 Moorhouse (1981, p. 106); Nenk & Walker (1991, p. 25, fig. 2).
47 For wheel-thrown pottery in the late Saxon period, see Hurst (1976), Kilmurry (1980).
48 McCarthy & Brooks (1988, pp. 27–31).
49 Ibid. (p. 27, fig. 8, nos 1–2); see Brandt (1927, Abb. 349, 372).
50 McCarthy & Brooks (1988, p. 29, fig. 11, no. 1); see Brandt (1927, Abb. 433), although it is not clear whether this figure represents a potter.
51 Moorhouse (1981, p. 106), Rutter (1977, p. 82, nos 311–12).
52 Pearce et al (1982, pl. IV), Nenk & Walker (1991, p. 25).
53 Alexander & Binski (1987, cat. no. 549), McCarthy & Brooks (1988, fig. 209).
54 Pearce et al (1985, fig. 56, no. 211), Vidler (1933, pp. 53–5, pls VII–VIII), Vidler (1936, pp. 113–14).
55 Pearce et al (1982, p. 285).
56 See, for example, Vidler (1933, p. 49, pl. III), Musty et al (1969, pp. 120–23, 130), Cherry (1992), Turner-Rugg (1995, p. 52, fig. 8, no. 68, col. pl. 2b).
57 See, for example, Pearce & Vince (1988, pp. 42–4).
58 For example, on York glazed ware seal jugs: see Jennings (1992, p. 19).
59 Cherry (1991a, p. 201).
60 Bryant & Steane (1969, p. 36, fig. 15m).
61 Vidler (1936, p. 113, figs 5–6).
62 McCarthy & Brooks (1988, pp. 35–9). See Newell (1995) for a discussion of glazing techniques and the question of 'splashed glazes'.
63 Musty (1974), McCarthy & Brooks (1988, pp. 40–54).
64 See Bryant (1977) and Musty (1984, p. 28).
65 McCarthy & Brooks (1988, p. 45, fig. 18, nos 1–7).
66 Ibid. (p. 368).
67 The kiln was excavated in 1995 by the Museum of London Archaeology Service. For a summary of the site see Nenk et al (1996). I am grateful to Roy Stephenson, Museum of London Archaeology Service, for providing information about the Eden Street kiln in advance of full publication.
68 For example, see Jennings (1992, p. 8); see also Newell (1994).
69 Le Patourel (1968, p. 117).
70 McCarthy & Brooks (1988, pp. 46–54).
71 Newell (1995). For Eraclius, see de Boüard (1974).
72 Hurst & Freestone (1997), Tite et al (1998).
73 Newell (1995).

Acknowledgements: I am grateful to John Cherry, David Gaimster and Barbara Hurman for providing advice and comments on the text; to Peter Stringer (BM Photographic Service) for providing the photographs, and to Jim Farrant for providing the illustration for fig. 6.

Chapter 14

1 See E. McKillop in Zwalf (1985, pp. 235–42).
2 Whitfield (1984, p. 128).
3 See Wood (1994, pp. 39–64).
4 Ibid. (p. 60).
5 See Kim Jaeyeol (1994, pp. 110–17).
6 See Medley (1975, pp. 2–3).
7 See Gompertz (1963, pp. 49–54).
8 Medley (1977).
9 See Gompertz (1963, pp. 59–72). For a technical analysis of the inlay, see Vandiver (1991, pp. 151–8).
10 Vandiver (1991, pp. 151–8).
11 For the development of underglaze red on Koryo celadons, see Ikutaro Itoh (1992, pp. 46–50).
12 Whitfield (1984, p. 136).
13 Gompertz (1963, pp. 55–8).
14 Ibid. (p. 40).
15 Deuchler (forthcoming, pp. 6–8).
16 Gompertz (1963, p. 65).
17 Pollard & Hatcher (1994), mean of ten Ding wares. Table in weight per cent.
18 Pollard & Hatcher (1986), mean of thirty-five Yue wares.
19 Koh Choo (1995), mean of three 12th-century Koryo celadons from the Kangjin kilns.
20 Vandiver (1991).
21 Vandiver et al (1989); Wood et al (1995).
22 Vandiver (1991).

Chapter 15

1 Moorey (1994, p. 168).
2 Vandiver & Kingery (1987b).
3 Wulff et al (1968).
4 See the technical information in Nicholson (1993b, pt I), Kaczmarczyk & Hedges (1983), Lucas & Harris (1962, pp. 156–67), Tite, Freestone & Bimson (1983), Tite (1986), Noble (1969).
5 For a summary of the work on glass, see Freestone (1991a).
6 Early work on the technology of faience (Binns, 1932; Rhodes, 1957; Noble, 1969) emphasised the importance of natron. The analyses of Tite et al (1983) and Vandiver & Kingery (1987b) show a significant potash content, which is characteristic of plant ash; natron contains very low potash. See Freestone (1991a).
7 Vandiver & Kingery (1987b), Vandiver (1983, pp.124–5).
8 Quibell & Green (1902, pp. 30–32, pls XLVIIIa–b), Adams (1974), Petrie (1902, pp. 23–9, pls IV–XI), Dreyer (1986, passim, especially pp. 19–20, 37–52, pls 5d, 6b–c, 7a–c).
9 C.f. Dreyer (1986, pls 24–8), Petrie (1902, p. 25, pls VI, X, XI), Spencer (1980, nos 533–9, pls 58–60), Nicholson (1993b, p. 19, fig. 9).
10 Spencer (1980, nos 503–8).
11 Quibell & Firth (1935, pls 38–9, 43, 45:2), Lauer (1962, pp. 127–31, pl. VIII), Nicholson (1993b, pp. 20–21).
12 Kaczmarczyk & Hedges (1983), Nicholson (1993b, pp. 30–31).
13 Nicholson (1996).
14 Hayes (1937), Hölscher (1951, pp. 37–47, pls 5, 30–38), Riefstahl (1968, nos 27–9, 47–8).
15 Petrie & Quibell (1896, pl. 78).
16 Krönig (1934), Vandiver (1982), Von Bissing (1902), Riefstahl (1968, no. 14), Strauss (1974).
17 Naville (1913, p. 26, pl. 26), Pinch (1993).
18 For a detailed analysis of the construction method of such a cup, see Vandiver & Kingery (1987a), and Kingery & Vandiver (1986, pp. 51–67).
19 Krönig (1934), Brovarski (1982), Tait (1963), Von Bissing (1902, nos 3678, 3692, 3698, 3701, 3703–7, 3712, 3774, 3812, 3848–50, 3851–2), Ricketts (1918), Spencer (1993a, p. 36, nos 95–109, pl. 32), Riefstahl (1968, no. 50), Reeves & Spurr (1995, pp. 20–21, lower illustrations).
20 Spencer (1993a, p. 37, nos 122–4, with refs, pls 33, 35).
21 Nicholson (1993b, pp. 28–30), Petrie (1894, pp. 28–30, pls XIV–XX), Boyce (1989), Herrmann (1985).
22 Nenna & Seif el-Din (1993), Grimm (1972).
23 Polinger Foster (1979, pp. 56–9).
24 Evans (1921, p. 170).
25 Ibid. (p. 252); Polinger Foster (1979, p. 59, pl. 1).
26 Evans (1921, pp. 463–85).
27 Polinger Foster (1979, pp. 118–48).
28 Vermeule (1966, n. 7; p. 145).
29 Webb (1978).
30 Petrie (1886, pp. 36–40).
31 Nenna & Seif el-Din (1993), pp. 567–89).
32 Nenna & Seif el-Din (1994).
33 Mysliwiec (1996).
34 Petrie (1909, pp. 14–15; Knobel et al (1911, pp. 34–7).
35 Vandiver (1983), Tite et al (1983), Vandiver & Kingery (1987a, b).
36 Replication of the various microstructures is given by Tite & Bimson (1986).
37 After Vandiver & Kingery (1987a).
38 Wulff et al (1986).

Chapter 16

1 Mason & Keall (1991), Mason (1994).
2 Watson (1985, pp. 37–44).
3 Porter & Watson (1987).
4 Lamm (1941, pp. 19–31); for lustre-decorated glass see Pinder Wilson in Tait (ed., 1991).
5 Caiger-Smith (1985, p. 24); for the colouration of glass by metallic oxides, see Freestone (1991a).
6 Mosaic or millefiori glass from the Middle East was distributed all over medieval Europe in the form of beads; see Callmer (1995).
7 Caiger-Smith (1985, p. 26).
8 Allan (1973, p. 114).
9 Jomier (1965, p. 959).
10 Allan (1973, pp. 114–19).
11 Watson (1985, p. 154).
12 Mason & Tite (1997).
13 Allan (1973).
14 Kingery & Vandiver (1986, pp. 118–20), Hamer (1985).
15 Mason & Tite (1994).

Chapter 17

1 Wilson (1987b, pp. 10, 148–9, 164–70), Goldthwaite (1989, p. 13).
2 Wilson (1996, pp. 35–7).
3 Caiger-Smith (1985, pp. 103–54), Wilson (1987b, pp. 28–38), Wilson (1996, p. 37), Goldthwaite (1989, pp. 11–13), *Mediterraneum* (1992, pp. 34–8).
4 Goldthwaite (1989, pp. 3–6), Wilson (1987b, p. 32).
5 Wilson (1987b, pp. 39, 65).
6 Goldthwaite (1989, pp. 7–9).
7 Piccolpasso (1980, XVI, sect. 197; pp. 14–16; 16), Norman (1976, p. 4).
8 Piccolpasso (1980, p. 13), Watson (1986, cat. 69), Wilson (1987a, pp. 184–9).
9 Watson (1986, p. 16).
10 Piccolpasso (1980, p. 54).
11 Wilson (1987b, p. 24).
12 Piccolpasso (1980, pp. 56–84).
13 Piccolpasso (1980, pp. 552–3), Watson (1986, p. 21), Norman (1976, p. 7).
14 Lama (1939, p. 36).
15 Wilson (1996, p. 39).
16 Goldthwaite (1989, p. 8, no. 11).
17 Lama (1939, p. 38), Goldthwaite (1989, p. 9), Piccolpasso (1980, XXII).
18 Goldthwaite (1989, p. 9), Wilson (1987b, p. 14), on Macci and Andreoli, see Wilson (1996, pp. 38–9), Fiocco & Gherardi (1994, pp. 45, 46, 50; 23, 24, 46, 55, 68). See Wilson on the Fontana (1987b, pp. 59, 152–3) and on the Calamelli (ibid., pp. 65, 149–150).
19 Rackham (1940, cat. 746), Piccolpasso (1980, p. 33).
20 Piccolpasso (1980, pp. 29, 39, XVII).
21 Watson (1986, cat. 38), Wilson (1987b, cats 172–3).
22 Piccolpasso (1980, pp. 45–6).
23 Examples include pilgrim flasks with moulded screw stoppers (Piccolpasso describes how this is done), made in Urbino in the last two decades of the 16th century: see Wilson (1987b, cat. 242), Piccolpasso (1980, pp. 20–21, 23).
24 Piccolpasso (1980, p. 30), Mazzucato (1986, pp. 131–3).
25 Wilson (1987b, p. 12).
26 Piccolpasso (1980, XIV, p. 69).
27 Wilson (1987b, p. 13).
28 Piccolpasso (1980, pp. 53–6, 61–88), Watson (1986, p. 14).
29 Wilson (1987b, cat. 188), Piccolpasso (1980, p. 104).
30 Piccolpasso (1980, XVII, pp. 105–6).
31 Piccolpasso (1980, p. 40).
32 Mazzucato (1986, p. 137), Piccolpasso (1980, p. 40).
33 Piccolpasso (1980, p. 106).
34 Vannini (ed., 1977, p. 21).
35 Wilson (1987b, pp. 13–14, Caiger-Smith (1985, pp. 129–54), Wilson (1996).
36 Wilson (1996, p. 14).
37 Goldthwaite (1989, p. 12), Vannini (ed., 1977), Blake (1987, p. 15), Wilson (1996, p. 38).
38 Wilson (1996, p. 39), with comments on likely retail prices for lustre.
39 Wilson (1996, pp. 38–41), Fiocco & Gherardi (1994, pp. 214–58).
40 Wilson (1987b, p. 10).
41 Wilson (1996, p. 37).
42 Wilson (1987b, p. 10).
43 Wilson (1987b, pp. 10, 112–30), Collins (1987), Ames-Lewis (1988), Gentilini et al (1993).
44 Wilson (1987b, cat. 83).
45 Watson (1986, cat. 45), Poole (1995, cat. 376), Wilson (1987b, cats 60, 51).
46 Wilson (1987b, pp. 53–8), Mallet (1984), Mallet (1988).
47 Wilson (1987b, cats 40–41, pp. 110–17, cats 203, 186), Wilson (ed., 1991, pp. 157–65), Ames-Lewis (1988), Clifford (1991), Clifford & Mallet (1976).
48 Rackham (1940, cat. 307), Wilson (1987b, p. 10).
49 Wilson (1987b, cat. 75).
50 Goldthwaite (1989, pp. 8–9), Wilson (1987b, p. 52), Negroni (1986, p. 18).
51 Wilson (1993, p. 19), Wilson (1987b, p. 160).
52 Wilson (1987b, pp. 11–12).

53 Piccolpasso (1980, XXII) on 'typical workshop'.
54 Wilson (1987b, p. 32).
55 Piccolpasso (1980, XXII).
56 Goldthwaite (1989, p. 8).
57 Watson (1986, p. 19).
58 Piccolpasso (1980, p. 51).
59 Tite (1991), Ravaglioli et al (1996).
60 Tite (1991), Ravaglioli et al (1996), Kingery & Aronson (1990); compare Mason & Tite (1997) for Islamic glazes.
61 Kingery (1991).

Chapter 18

1 For a full survey of German stonewares of the medieval and early modern period see Gaimster (1997).
2 See Hähnel (1992) for a survey of archaeological and archaeometric approaches.
3 See Schwarz (1937), Kerkhoff-Hader (1980; 1991) and Finke (1983, pp. 7–11) for the recording of traditional practices in the Rhineland and Westerwald.
4 See Päffgen (1995) for the excavation of a clay extraction shaft of 5.5 m (20 ft) in depth at Langerwehe in the Rhineland, containing the contents of several kiln misfirings dating to c. 1450–1500, and Finke (1983, p. 7) for description of clay extraction pits in the Westerwald.
5 Göbels (1985, pp. 44–5).
6 H. L. Janssen & De Paepe (1976, p. 220).
7 See Kerkhoff-Hader (1980) for traditional practices in the Westerwald and south-west Eifel.
8 Finke (1983, p. 19).
9 Ibid. (p. 11).
10 Göbels (1985, p. 58).
11 Beckmann (1975).
12 Gaimster (1997).
13 Reineking-von Bock (1986, p. 34) and Jenner (1985, p. 133).
14 Schwarz (1937, p. 210) and Finke (1983, p. 12, fig. 11).
15 Ragg (ed., 1976).
16 See Finke (1983) for traditional practices in the Westerwald and Kerkhoff-Hader (1980; 1988) for ethnographic studies of stoneware potting techniques in the south-west Eifel district.
17 Ruppel (1991a; 1991b).
18 Ruppel (1991b, p. 26; 1991c).
19 See Kerkhoff-Hader (1980, figs 70–71) for examples of cartwheels, and Jenner (1985, p. 133) for discussion.
20 Von Falke (1899) and Gaimster (1997).
21 Cologne potters drew heavily on Anton Woensam's illustrations in Peter Quentel's pattern-book, published in 1527. See von Falke (1899; 1908, pp. 52–6) and Gaimster (1997, ch. 5).
22 *The Peasant Festival* (1546–7) by Sebald Beham, for example, was applied as a frieze on the body of a baluster jug from Raeren, Rhineland: see Gaimster (1995; 1997, cat. 90).
23 See Dornbusch (1873, pp. 73–82), Krueger (1981), Reineking-von Bock (1986, pp. 35–6) and Ruppel (1991d) for detailed discussion of technique.
24 I am grateful to Nigel Wood for personal discussion of this point.
25 Herborn et al (1987, pp. 89–91) and Treptow (1991).
26 Ruppel (1991b, figs 1–2; 1995, pp. 24–30).
27 Taylor (1977) and Horschik (1978, p. 81).
28 See Horschik (1978, p. 81) for description of technique.
29 See W. Janssen (1987) for survey of archaeological evidence in the Rhineland, and Kerkhoff-Hader (1980; 1991) for ethnographic record.
30 See Jürgens (1985), W. Janssen (1987, fig. 17) and Bruijn (1959, fig. 41) for Brunssum, south Limburg.
31 See Jürgens (1979, fig. 223; 1988, p. 126; 1993) for 1978 Langerwehe-Jüngersdorf Kapellenstrasse kilns demonstrating the development of stoneware firing technology over the 13th to 14th centuries; see Jürgens & Bös (1983) and Jürgens (1988, pp. 134–6; 1993) for 1981 Hauptstrasse kiln dated to c. 1400.
32 Hellebrandt (1977, pp. 16–18).
33 See Rech (1991, figs 5, 7) for an example from the Siegburg Aulgasse district; for Frechen Broichgasse kiln 1, see Jürgens (1988, fig. 7) and Jürgens (1995a, fig. 2).
34 Tzschoppe (1995).
35 See Kerkhoff-Hader (1991, p. 340) and Schmitz (1879, figs I–V) for kiln recorded at Raeren in the 1870s; see e.g. Hellebrandt (1977, pp. 149–53, fig. 134) for drawing of planned kiln at Raeren by Loenard Mennicken in 1877; see Kerkhoff-Hader (1980, p. 322; 1987; 1991, fig. 1) for kiln planned for Binsfeld, south-west Eifel, in 1880.
36 Pryor & Blockley (1978).
37 Bimson (1961, pl. 117b).
38 Bruijn (1962/3, fig. 106).
39 See Bruijn (1962/3, fig. 106) for south Limburg; Rech (1991, figs 6, 8) for Siegburg; Finke (1983, figs 38–9) for Westerwald; and Kerkhoff-Hader (1987, figs 18–19) for Eifel.
40 Falk (1991).
41 Finke (1983, fig. 44) and Kerkhoff-Hader (1987, fig. 21).
42 Von Falke (1899, pp. 22–4) and Gaimster (1997).
43 Dornbusch (1873).
44 Herborn et al (1987, p. 88).
45 Ibid. (pp. 81–5).
46 Ibid. (p. 83).
47 Ibid. (p. 82).

48 Baart (1989, p. 614) and Lima-de-Faria (1995).
49 Herborn et al (1987, p. 85).
50 Ibid. (pp. 88–9).
51 Ibid. (p. 87).
52 Ibid. (p. 89).
Acknowledgements: The author wishes to thank the following specialists in the field of German stoneware who have assisted in the preparation of this summary: Frau Professor Dr Bärbel Kerkhoff-Hader, Lehrstuhl für Heimat- und Volkskunde, University of Bamberg; Robin Hildyard, Victoria and Albert Museum, London; Dr Antonius Jürgens, Amt für Bodendenkmalpflege, Bonn; Dr Thomas Ruppel, Börde Museum, Ummendorf; and Nigel Wood, Department of Ceramics, University of Westminster.

Chapter 19

1 For a review of developments in English material culture (particularly ceramics) of the late medieval to early modern period see Gaimster (1994, pp. 287–94) and Gaimster & Nenk (forthcoming). See Brears (1974, ch. 1), Dawson (1979) and Barton (1992) for discussion of the 'Post-Medieval Ceramic Revolution'.
2 See Barton (1992) and Gaimster (1994, p. 290) for a summary of literature on the subject.
3 See Gaimster (1993; 1994, p. 291) and Gaimster & Nenk (forthcoming).
4 For further descriptions and discussions of Cistercian ware see Brears (1974, pp. 14–15); Barker (1986) and Moorhouse & Roberts (1992) for excavations of a 16th- to 17th-century potting tenement at Wrenthorpe, near Wakefield, West Yorkshire.
5 See Dawson (1979, p. 44) for a description of London-area redwares made during the 16th century.
6 For basins with anthropomorphic lug-handles see Gaimster & Verhaeghe (1992).
7 For a museum and archaeological survey of post-medieval slipware in central Europe see Stephan (1987). For Netherlands slipware see Hurst et al (1986, pp. 154–68); for the archaeology of post-medieval slip-ware in the Lower Rhine see Gaimster (1988; 1991).
8 See Britton (1987) for a survey of the London tin-glazed earthenware industry of the 17th to 18th centuries.
9 See Stephan (1987, pp. 20–35) for a general discussion of the role of tin-glazed earthenware on the formative development of slipware production in Europe; Gaimster (1994, pp. 296–8) for a survey of the excavated evidence for the growing popularity of tin-glazed earthenwares in southern England.
10 Orton (1985); Gaimster (1994, p. 296).
11 For references to North Holland and Beauvais slipware in Britain, see Hurst et al (1986, pp. 154, 112); for a survey of Werra and Weser ware found in the British Isles, see Gaimster & Hurst (forthcoming). For a general discussion of archaeological distributions see Gaimster (1994, pp. 297–8).
12 A date of c. 1615 is suggested for the earliest archaeological fragments of trailed slipware found in the foundations of a kiln on the site of the pottery at Harlow of Emmanuel Emmyng, who died in 1616. Wally Davey (pers. comm.); Dean (forthcoming).
13 See Newton & Bibbings (1960) for excavations on Harlow kiln sites during the late 1950s.
14 Hobson (1903, p. 96); see Orton & Pearce (1984, fig. 18, no. 26; fig. 23, no. 82) for Metropolitan ware excavated at Aldgate, London, in contexts as late as c. 1670–1700 and 1700–1720.
15 See Gaimster (1997, ch. 5.4) for comprehensive list of moulded bands containing pious aphorisms applied to Frechen stoneware of the 1550s and 1560s.
16 For lists of inscriptions see Hobson (1903); Grigsby (1993, p. 20); Dean (forthcoming).
17 Hobson (1903, cat. D26).
18 See Kiddell (1954) and Grigsby (1993, pp. 22–7) for surveys of Wrotham ware.
19 Schnitzer (1977); Gaimster (1997, ch. 3.4).
20 See Grant (1983) for North Devon industry; and Coleman-Smith & Pearson (1988) for full survey of products excavated at Donyatt, Somerset.
21 Grant (1983, p. 114).
22 Twice-firing was also practised by the Werra industry in central Germany and by its north Dutch satellite workshop at Enkhuizen; see Stephan (1987, pp. 85–100 for Werra ware, pp. 200–201 for Enkhuizen).
23 See Brears (1974, ch. 4) for full discussion of 'Harvest wares' from the South-west.
24 Ford (1995).
25 Weatherill (1971, pp. 71–2, 139–40).
26 Excavations by the Mid-Staffordshire Archaeological Society; report by J. Fisher, D. Barker & C. Banks (in progress).
27 Greaves (1976, fig. 9, nos 71–4). The material was dated in the report to c. 1640–70, but on the basis of recent re-analysis by David Barker has been reattributed to c. 1640.
28 Kelly (1975, fig. 2, nos 1–11). Dating of group to c. 1640 by David Barker (pers. comm.).
29 For Hill Top, Burslem, see Kelly (1969, pp. 22–44); for the Sadler Manufactory site, Stoke-on-Trent, see Mountford (1975, figs 3–6).

30 Grigsby (1993, figs 57–9); Barker (1993, p. 17, figs).
31 Grigsby (1993, p. 56).
32 Ibid. (fig. 78).
33 Grigsby (1993, pp. 16, 39–46) for discussion of the technique; David Barker (pers. comm.) for earliest archaeologically recorded contexts for press-moulded vessels made in North Staffordshire.
34 Manchester City Art Gallery (1969, figs 24–5) and Barker (1993, p. 6, fig.) for William Bird mould and dish made from it.
35 BM MLA 1920,3–18,1.
36 Tait (1957); Barker (1993, pp. 17–18); Grigsby (1993, pp. 40–44).
37 Vince (1981, table 1); Gaimster (1994, p. 300).
38 Brears (1974; 1989a; 1989b, pp. 111–33).
Acknowledgements: The author wishes to thank the following specialists in the field of English slipware who have assisted in the preparation of this summary: David Barker, City Museum and Art Gallery, Stoke-on-Trent; Darren Dean, Royal College of Art, London; and Leslie Grigsby, Richmond, Virginia.

Chapter 20

1 It is notable that in Upper Egypt women and men, using different techniques, work on the same pots. Women hand-build the bodies using the paddle-and-anvil technique; after a short drying period, men add the rims or necks on the wheel. The men also make complete pots on the wheel (personal observation).
2 Hélène Balfet (1965, p. 163) distinguishes between these producers and sociological 'specialist' potters, such as widows, who need to supply or supplement the family income by intensive production of utilitarian pottery.
3 Bynon (1982), Van Gennep (1918), Westermarck (1926).
4 Al-Bakri (1965, p. 88).
5 See Al-Manūnī (1979, p. 149).
6 See Loviconi & Belfitah (1991, p. 58).
7 See Golvin, Thiriot & Zakariya (1982, pp. 85–6); Guyot, Paye & Le Tourneau (1952, pp. 268–9).
8 See Golvin, Thiriot & Zakariya (1982, p. 6).
9 Many potters are paid per pot, so production efficiency is a significant motivating force (Golvin, Thiriot & Zakariya, 1982, p. 84; Guyot, Paye & Le Tourneau, 1952, p. 269).
10 Ali Bahgat Bey (1914, p. 234, n. 2).
11 See Couleurs de Tunisie, Institut du Monde Arabe (1994, p. 280).
12 For a detailed description of the large kilns used at Fustat which have a more sophisticated plan and structure, see Golvin, Thiriot & Zakariya (1982, pp. 42–50).
13 See Lisse & Louis (1956, p. 56).
14 See Golvin, Thiriot & Zakariya (1982, p. 54); Lisse & Louis (1956, p. 57).
15 See Couleurs de Tunisie, Institut du Monde Arabe (1994, p. 281).
16 Bel noted that powdered manganese was sometimes added at this stage to give the resin a lustrous finish (1918, p. 112).
17 See Chadli (1982, p. 84, n. 3).
18 In Tunisia bichrome costumes probably dating from the sixteenth century have been recorded. It has been suggested that this technique was brought to Tunisia by immigrants from Andalusia (Sethom, 1969, p. 10).
19 See Boukobza (1974, p. 146). Sheep are sacrificed after Ramadan at the 'Great Sacrifice' ('Eid al-kabir), and their skin is used to make drum membranes.
20 See Loviconi & Belfitah (1991, p. 19).
21 See Loviconi & Belfitah (1991, pp. 19–20). Sijelmassi (1986, p. 219) describes a glazed pitcher, included in the trousseau of a young girl in southern Morocco, which is decorated on the outside with red dots at the time of the marriage ceremony to bring the bride good fortune.
22 See Lobban (1990, pp. 242–3).
23 See Lisse & Louis (1956, p. 197).
24 See Fakhry (1983, pp. 53, 55).
25 This effect was investigated in the late 19th and early 20th centuries by the European brick industry and was extensively discussed in the ceramic literature (Butterworth, 1956).
26 Bel (1918, p. 85). Béart et al (1989) discuss the effects of salt on the colour of archaeological ceramics.
27 Fulford & Peacock (1984, pp. 263–4); also Matson (1974) for a similar effect in Mesopotamian ceramics. The white skin has often been mistaken by archaeologists in the past for a paint or slip.
28 Rye (1976) also graphically illustrates the effect of salt in the reduction of spalling.
29 Boukobza (1974, p. 140) suggests that this process removes glazing flaws and sharpens the brightness of the painted decoration, although it is not entirely clear why this should be so.
30 Loviconi (1994, p. 99).

Chapter 21

1 Barley (1994, p. 21).
2 Vaughan (1970).
3 McNaughton (1988).

Chapter 22

1 For a list of Anglo-Saxon settlement sites see Beresford & Hurst (1971, p. 147); Rahtz (1976); James et al (1984).
2 For cemeteries see Meaney (1964). An updated gazetteer is currently in preparation. Publications dealing with both settlements and cemeteries can be found in the annual bibliography which appears in Anglo-Saxon England; the journal Medieval Ceramics also lists publications of Anglo-Saxon pottery finds by county. Brief details of sites under excavation can be found in 'Medieval Britain', published every year in Medieval Archaeology.
3 Hills (1977; 1980); Hills & Penn (1981); Hills et al (1984; 1987; 1994); McKinley (1994), Rickett (1995). The exact number of cremations and/or pots recovered from the site is problematic, as urns were discovered there as early as the 18th century. This figure is taken from McKinley (1994).
4 Myres (1977), which contains an extensive bibliography.
5 This quote comes from Myres (1969, p. 11), but effectively sums up the aims of the later Corpus.
6 For a critical appraisal of Myres' work see Hawkes (1974); Morris (1974); Kidd (1976); Dickinson (1978); Hills (1979); and Richards (1987, ch. 1), which also includes a more general survey of approaches to the study of Anglo-Saxon ceramics.
7 The best example, with enough pottery from both settlement and cemetery to make statistically viable comparisons, is the site of Mucking in Essex. Pottery from the settlement is discussed in Hamerow (1987; 1993, ch. 3); for cemeteries I and II see Hirst & Clark (forthcoming).
8 Much of the information contained in the following paragraphs has been quite shamelessly plundered (with his permission!) from ch. 12 of Russel's thesis on the early Anglo-Saxon ceramics of East Anglia (Russel, 1984, pp. 532–67).
9 According to Russel it is the commonest form of tempering in East Anglia during the early Anglo-Saxon period, found on 60% of sites in Cambridge and Norfolk, and 76% in Suffolk (Russel, 1984, p. 540). At Mucking, in Essex, 49% of the pottery was vegetal-tempered. Hamerow (1993, ch. 3).
10 Hurst (1959, pp. 14–19); Smedley & Owles (1963); West (1963); Hurst (1976, pp. 299–303); Blinkhorn (1989).
11 Wheel-thrown pottery is found in early Anglo-Saxon contexts, mostly in graves in Kent. It is, however, imported, and therefore beyond the scope of this survey. For a detailed analysis of this material see Evison (1979) and Huggett (1988).
12 Brisbane (1981, p. 234). However, Russel has pointed out that evidence for coiling tends to be more visible on calcareous fabrics than sandy ones, and may be obliterated by subsequent wiping and smoothing (Russel, 1984, p. 550).
13 Stokes (1984).
14 Russel (1984), p. 559.
15 Myres (1969, p. 34). For the complete range of decorative schemes on early Anglo-Saxon pottery see Myres (1977).
16 As shown by the spatial distribution of the Mucking settlement pottery (Hamerow, 1993, p. 34).
17 Welch (1992, p. 82).
18 For Anglo-Saxon pot stamps see Briscoe (1980; 1981; 1982; 1983; 1992). Over one hundred different stamp variants have been recorded in the Archive of Anglo-Saxon Pottery Stamps, which was set up in 1980 to classify and analyse pot stamps from cemeteries and settlements all over the country. By 1995 over 20,000 casts of individual pot stamps had been put on to a database, which is available for consultation by appointment c/o Diana Briscoe, 124 Cholmley Gardens, Fortune Green Road, London NW6 1AA.
19 Russel (1984, p. 557).
20 Arnold (1983a, p. 27).
21 Hills (1983); Capelle (1987).
22 See Myres (1977, pp. 65–7, figs 364–9); Runic inscriptions are discussed by Hills (1974) and Bammesberger (1991); for the use of swastika patterns in the early Anglo-Saxon period see Brown (1981).
23 For pot dies see Stokes (1984); Riddler (1986; 1988).
24 MacGregor (1985, p. 194).
25 Stokes (1984).
26 From Swanley, Kent: see Brown & Bruce-Mitford (1960, pp. 86–7).
27 Myres (1977, fig. 143, no. 986).
28 Briscoe (1985).
29 Russel (1984, p. 553) gives an average of 7.5% for ten settlement sites in East Anglia, but admits that the figure may be seriously skewed. At West Stow in Suffolk only 2% of the ceramic assemblage was decorated, a figure which included the rusticated pottery (West, 1985, p. 128); and at Mucking in Essex the figure was 5% (Hamerow, 1993, p. 51).
30 Richards (1987, p. 194).
31 Stokes (1984).
32 The clay matrices were anisotropic, implying that they had not been fired to sufficiently high temperatures to lose their structurally bound water. Brisbane (1981, p. 234).
33 For a particularly fine example see Hills (1980a).

34 Hamerow (1993, pp. 37–44) gives the average dimensions of each type.
35 Richards (1987, p. 96).
36 For funerary rites in early Anglo-Saxon England see Owen (1981); Welch (1992, ch. 5); McKinley (1994a; 1994b; 1994c).
37 Didsbury (1992).
38 Jones (1975); West (1985, p. 137); Hamerow (1993, p. 44).
39 Leeds (1947, pp. 81–4, figs 2, 3, pl. XXI).
40 For a complete assessment of the material from Grimstone End, see Russel (1984, ch. 9).
41 West (1985, p. 58, fig. 235).
42 Arnold (1983).
43 For the Illington-Lackford workshop see Green et al (1981); Russel (1984, ch. 11); Arnold (1988); Davison et al (1993).
44 Brisbane (1981).
45 Russel (1984, p. v).
46 Timby et al (1993, p. 268).
47 Vince & Young (1991–4); Walker (1978); Williams (1979).
48 For a review of medieval ceramic studies in England including the early Anglo-Saxon period, see Mellor (1994).
49 Based on Matson (1963, pp. 489–98).
Acknowledgements: A cursory overview of this nature inevitably depends heavily on the work of others. I would like to thank all those specialists who took the time and trouble to discuss this essay with me, and who made their own work freely available.

Chapter 23

1 Ghirshman (1964, pp. 72–126), Young (1967). For a revised view see Young (1985).
2 Dandamaev (1989) and Moorey (1980). There is further disagreement over the classification of these periods and the extent to which certain ceramic types can be equated with the movement of ethnic or political groups: see Stronach (1974), Moorey (1985), Levine (1987), Brown (1990), Sumner (1994). The Late Iron Age developments lie beyond the scope of this case study.
3 Negahban (1996).
4 Dyson (1965, p. 211), Moorey (1971, pp. 23–4), Muscarella (1984).
5 A number of cemeteries in this area appear to have been discovered and excavated by local villagers.
6 The site of Kaluraz, in the same region and excavated in 1967, offers a little more information. In addition to stone-lined tombs and circular cut graves, rectilinear stone wall-footings were found that were thought originally to have supported domestic wooden superstructures. The grave-goods included gold vessels, jewellery, weapons and ceramics but, unlike Marlik, the latter included a distinct group of painted greywares. These included well-finished wheel-thrown globular jars with upright trefoil-mouth pouring spouts, burnished brown slipped surfaces and cream-painted geometric decoration (Hakemi, 1968 Matheson, 1976, pp. 74–5).
7 Egami, Fukai & Masuda (1965, pl. XXV:1, LII:17), Negahban (1996, vol. I, p. 242, vol. II, fig. 6, no. 42: bronze; figs 25, 30, nos 572–3, 575, 578, pl. 116: ceramic).
8 Negahban (1996, vol. I, pp. 109–12, vol. II, figs 11, 14, col. pl. XXII, pls 32–3, 41); for bronze examples see Negahban (1996, vol. I, p. 113, vol. II, pl. 34), Gabus & Junod (1967, pl. XVI: right).
9 This vessel has been authenticated by a thermoluminescence test.
10 See Negahban (1996, vol. I, p. 226, vol. II, pl. 105).
11 For the group of zoomorphic vessels found in Tomb 18 see Negahban (1996, vol. II, pl. 6A–B); for individual vessels found at Marlik and elsewhere see, for example, Negahban (1996, vol. II, figs 13–14, col. pls XXIII–XXIV, pls 36–40), Barbier (1962, nos 32, 35, 39, 45), Egami, Fukai & Masuda (1965, p. 58, fig. 8), Buhl (1968, pp. 61, 63, no. 138), Tenri Sankokan Museum (1983, nos 51, 53–4). Gunter (1988, p. 12) has suggested that these may have been used as wine-pourers. Note also that there are a number of modern fakes in circulation.
12 Gabus & Junod (1967, p. 4).
13 For illustrations of jars and tripod supports see Curtis (1989b, p. 20, fig. 21) and Kawami (1992, p. 24, fig. 26). Several glazed faience beak-spouted jars have also been reported (Fukai, 1981, no. 19).
14 Dyson (1989, p. 113).
15 Muscarella (1974, pp. 60–61, fig. 26), Kawami (1992, pp. 114–15, no. 39).
16 Porada (1965, pp. 108–9), Rice (1987, p. 138), Matson (1974, p. 345).
17 Crowfoot (1932, p. 185). In contrast, personal observation of recent pottery production in Northern Cyprus indicates that attractive streak-burnishing can be obtained in a few minutes if the clays are particularly fine.
18 Young (1965), Muscarella (1974).
19 Ghirshman (1938/9), Vanden Berghe (1964), Young (1965), Curtis (1989c); on parallels with Genre Luristan see Goff (1978).
20 See Moorey (1971) for a thorough review of the archaeological evidence, and Reade (1978) for the extension of Kassites into Luristan.
21 Goff (1969; 1970; 1978). Misfired vessels were found at Baba Jan: the painted decoration on these had fired to a pale green.
22 Goff (1970, pp. 151–3, pl. IIIb; 1977, pp. 133–4, 137–40, pls XVI–XIX), Henrickson (1983).
23 Examples are illustrated and discussed by Ghirshman (1964, pp. 83, 320, pls 108, 391) and Goff (1969, pp. 122–3, pl. III).
24 See Kawami (1992, pp. 174–5, 180–81) for other examples of ceramics; Moorey (1971) for the metalwork.
25 Perishable organic materials such as basketry do not survive from archaeological contexts in this region.
26 Moorey (1971, p. 16).
27 For a recent summary of the evidence see Roaf (1995).
28 Goff (1978). A broken Baba Jan III Painted jar was found reused as a lamp during the Median phase at Nush-i Jan (Stronach & Roaf, 1978, p. 9, pl. IVb).
29 Stronach (1978).
30 See Stronach (1969, pp. 16–19).
31 Ochsenschlager (1974, p. 169); Güner's (1988) illustrated survey of modern Turkish ceramic traditions includes a photograph of similar trays being made in the Eskisehir region (p. 42).
32 An ultimate example of this is illustrated by classical Greek pottery copies of Persian silverwares (Miller, 1993).
Acknowledgements: My thanks to Andrew Middleton (Department of Scientific Research) for his xeroradiographic analyses and to Mr T. Ohtsu (Ancient Orient Museum, Tokyo) for his comments on zoomorphic vessels.

Chapter 24

1 See, for example, comments by Adam (1994, pp. 145–50) on the use of brick in Rome.
2 Information on the variety of Roman terracotta building materials may be found in several texts, including Davey (1961), Brodribb (1987) and Adam (1994).
3 Potter & Johns (1992); see especially pp. 84–7.
4 For background information on the use and dating of relief-patterned flue-tiles in Roman Britain, see for example Black (1985), Middleton et al (1992), Betts et al (1997) and references therein.
5 This account is based upon an internal report by Ian Freestone of the Department of Scientific Research, British Museum (RL 6180, 28 July 1992). I am grateful for his permission to use his unpublished observations and photographs by Kate Warren of the manufactory at Mazzano Romano.
6 Biringuccio (Smith & Gnudi, 1943, pp. 400–401) describes a medieval rectangular brick kiln very similar to that observed at Mazzano Romano. He also comments on the use of sand to prevent the soft clay sticking.
7 These levels of productivity are of the same order as those quoted for traditional brick-making in developing countries (Parry, 1979, p. 5) and suggest that a relatively small group of reasonably experienced artisans could have produced large numbers of tiles, perhaps on a seasonal basis.
8 Rudling (1986).
9 This interpretation is derived from an account given by Foster in Rudling (1986, pp. 203–7).
10 See for example Parry (1979, p. 13) and International Labour Office (1984, p. 91). The problem of surface cracking due to bricks being allowed to dry out too quickly was remarked upon by Vitruvius in his commentary on the manufacture of unbaked bricks (see Adam, 1994, p. 61).
11 See Parry (1979, p. 20) and also International Labour Office (1984, p. 91 and fig. VI.6), both of which demonstrate dramatically the destructive effects of rainfall on unfired materials.
12 Foster in Rudling (1986, p. 211).
13 See Cartwright in Rudling (1986, pp. 220–2).
14 Lowther (1948).
15 McWhirr & Viner (1978, p. 371). There is ample evidence from both the archaeological record and ethnographic observations that ceramic products can be transported safely over significant distances: see, for instance, discussion in Peacock (1982) and Arnold (1985).
16 The results of a petrographic study of a selection of relief-patterned tiles from North Oxfordshire were published by Johnston & Williams (1979). Their results were consistent with the suggestion, attributed to Drury, that production was concentrated in four major centres, from which tiles may have been transported quite considerable distances. However, the analyses also provided support for the concept of itinerant tile-makers. Johnston and Williams concluded that there was a need for further petrographic analysis to resolve the question. The analytical work described in this chapter arose from a proposal made by Dr E. Black.
17 Die 5 is a re-cut version of Die 5A, which was produced after the original Die 5A had been damaged. Examples of tiles marked with Die 5A have been found at sites in London and Essex and at St Albans to the north of London, as well as in the present area of south-eastern England. For further discussion see Middleton et al (1992).
18 A sample of clay from Ashtead Common, which had been fired as a briquette, was prepared as a thin section and examined using the petrographic microscope. The fabric was very similar to the Romano-British tiles from the Ashtead kiln. Similarly, the report on the excavations at Hartfield records that the tiles appear to have been made from locally available resources Foster in Rudling (1986, pp. 203–4).
19 A variety of types of tile were recovered from the excavations of the kiln sites at Ashtead and Hartfield, supporting the notion that relief-patterned tiles were produced alongside other types of tile.
20 The results presented here and the methods used to obtain them are described more fully in Middleton et al (1992).
Acknowledgements: I am grateful to several colleagues for their practical support and encouragement at various stages during this study of Roman tile, in particular Ernest Black, Sheridan Bowman, Michael Cowell, Ian Freestone, Catherine Johns, Tony Milton and Tony Simpson.

Chapter 25

1 Asia Minor: Bailey (1988, cat. nos Q 3335–8); North Africa: Sidebotham (1978, pl. 8).
2 Bailey (1980, passim).
3 Bailey (1988, passim).
4 Frog-lamps: Bailey (1988, cat. nos Q 2125–98); Aswan lamps: ibid. (cat. nos Q 2210–38).
5 African Red Slip ware: Ennabli (1976); Bailey (1988, cat. nos Q 1751–1842). Made in Rome: Bailey (1980, cat. nos Q 1429–36); Marconi Cosentino & Ricciardi (1993, passim); Paleani (1993, passim); the two last include some African examples. Made in Greece: Broneer (1930, pls XXI–XXII). Made in Egypt: Spencer (1984, pl. 6, no. 9). Made at Trier: Goethert (1993, pp. 135–248; many moulds included).
6 The Fezzan and the Hoggar: Wheeler (1954, pp. 100, 110, pl. XVIIIb). The Eastern Egyptian Desert and the Red Sea coast: Knowles (1990, pp. 10–11) (Mons Claudianus); Bailey (1995, pp. 16–19) (Mons Porphyrites); Sidebotham (1982, pp. 243–56) (Myos Hormos). The Negev: Negev (1974, pls 15, 61, 63).
7 Leibundgut (1977, pp. 100–129).
8 Vindonissa: Loeschcke (1919, passim). Holt: Grimes (1930, fig. 75).
9 Weisenau: Fremersdorf (1922, pp. 15–25). Pompeii: Cerulli Ireli (1977, pp. 53–72, pls XXVI–XLV). Benghazi: Bailey (1985, pp. 164–6).
10 Harris (1980, pp. 126–45); Bailey (1987, pp. 59–63); Duncan-Jones (1990, pp. 48–58); Harris (1993, pp. 186–9).
11 Martin (1977, pp. 51–78).
12 Deneauve (1969, pp. 87–93) for a table giving both Italian and African makers' names; Bailey (1988, pp. 179–80).
13 Fremersdorf (1922, pp. 30–83); Bailey (1972, pp. 13–16); Bailey (1976, pp. 92–103); Vertet (1983); Bailey (1988, pp. 183–4); Karivieri (1996, ch. II).
14 Bailey (1976, p. 198, fig. 174); Sussman (1982, pp. 8, 15).
15 Bailey (1965, pp. 14–17).
16 Campania and central Italy: Bailey (1980, cat. nos Q 1201, Q 1223, Q 1233–4, Q 1321). Pannonia: Gudea (1987, pp. 409–36); for vitreous glazing of Roman pots in general, see *Rei Cretariae Romanae Fautorum Acta* 34 (1995, passim).
17 Bailey (1988, p. 327, with references).
18 Fremersdorf (1922, figs 22–4 for a kiln, pp. 73–6 for stacking and wasters).

Chapter 26

1 At the site of Mehrgarh, in the Kachi plain on the western bank of the Indus. See Munster (1988, pp. 95–101, 244 ff).
2 Published in Blurton (1985). The fieldwork resulted in a collection of terracotta figurines from eastern Gujarat being deposited in the Museum of Mankind (the Department of Ethnography of the British Museum). The work was commissioned by Dr Brian Durrans, Deputy Keeper of the Department of Ethnography, to whom I am grateful for enabling me to study this material again. Examples from that collection are displayed in the exhibition which this publication accompanies. Within the British Museum, examples of terracotta figurines from other parts of India are also to be found in the collections of the Department of Ethnography as well as in the Department of Oriental Antiquities; the latter are mostly of an archaeological and historical character.
3 Much new work has been done in this field since the present author's article in 1985. The most important publications are Shah (1985) and, most recently, Huyler (1996). The latter deals with contemporary terracotta sculpture throughout India in the most comprehensive way yet attempted. Information from both these books has been included here and is hereby acknowledged.
4 Recorded at 'ash-mound' sites such as Utnur: see Allchin & Allchin (1982, pp. 124–5).

5 For the suggestion that even in the prehistoric period the foot-wheel was known in the north-west, see Allchin & Allchin (1982, p. 108).
6 In the British Museum (Department of Oriental Antiquities) there is a small collection of Indian Islamic glazed tiles from Multan (present-day Pakistan) as well as examples from Bengal and the Deccan, though only one of the distinctive yellow-ground Mughal tiles. All of these examples date to the 15th–17th centuries: see Porter (1995, pp. 86–91). A larger collection of Indian tiles is in the Victoria and Albert Museum (Indian and Southeast Asian Collections): see Victoria and Albert Museum (1982, nos 5–10, p. 26). It is surprising that, despite their substantial dependence on Iranian prototypes in the cultural field, the Mughal court (16th–18th centuries) did not adopt the practice of mass-producing glazed vessels, though they did produce huge quantities of glazed tiles. For high-quality glazed ceramic vessels they were dependent on imported items, especially from China: see Victoria and Albert Museum (1982, nos 401–403, p. 127); vessels of metal had much greater status than those of ceramic or glass and the greatest attention as far as decoration was concerned.
7 Huyler (1996) mentions a variant whereby a pivot is set into the base of the wheel which then spins in a socket set into the ground. The result is the same.
8 In certain parts of India, the motion of the wheel is increased by weighting the outer surface with clay; see Sinopoli & Blurton (1986, p. 444).
9 The family name Prajapati is common among potters and refers to the divine (first) potter, who is thought of as the ancestor of all Indian potters today.
10 For a very useful discussion of this Ganesha festival, see Courtright (1985).
11 See Huyler (1996, pp. 114–41).
12 The description of these groups as 'tribal' is problematic, though it is the most common term used in India. It is understood to refer to groups whose presence apparently predates the incursion of Indo-European speakers into the subcontinent. The term *adivasi* (original inhabitant) also has wide currency, though it is a Hindi word; some scholars speak of 'indigenous peoples' but this is unsatisfactory when dealing with other ancient groups. In eastern Gujarat these groups know themselves by a large number of distinguishing names – Rathva, Chodhri, Dubla – but Bhil has an overall embracing character and seems to be a general term referring to all the tribal groups of this region.
13 The boundaries of the modern state of Gujarat do not coincide precisely with those of where Bhils live. They are also found in the contiguous areas of the neighbouring states of Rajasthan and Madhya Pradesh.
14 These two basic types were recorded by the author in the region of eastern Baroda district and also in Panch Mahals district in the mid-1980s. They are certainly the most common throughout Gujarat. However, Haku Shah, who has written extensively on terracotta figurines in the region, records (1985, pp. 124–5) that at the shrine of Goli Gadh Mata in Surat district 'the votive offerings are terracotta replicas of parts of the human body affected by illness or disease – eyes, ears, navels [sic], hands, feet and chest. But the sanctuary is most famous for curing diseases of the testicles or male genitals, for which purpose terracotta balls are offered. Hence its name – *goli* means ball, *gadh* means castle, and *mata* refers to the Mother Goddess. The name is thus derived from the hundreds of terracotta balls that form a sort of monument to the goddess.'
15 For both these types of sanctuary, see Shah (1985, pp. 95; *cholia* type: 103).
16 For a typically acute description of the transformation of the terracotta offerings into empowered agents, see Kapila Vatsyayan's 'Foreword' in Huyler (1996, p. 11, penultimate paragraph).
17 They are also recorded as being residences for the recently dead. The latter may of course, in time, become the same as the god of the place.
18 See Shah (1985, p. 8).
19 The staple product of most traditional Indian potters is water-pots and these are produced throughout the year with the only exception being the monsoon months. During the rains, the clay will not usually dry sufficiently prior to firing to ensure a well-fired vessel. Other products are seasonal – figurines in the winter, toddy-collecting pots in the spring.
20 This was the situation in Chhota Udaipur at the potter's workshop recorded by the author. However, it is generally the case throughout India – with the exception only of selling at markets – that production, firing and sale of the finished ceramics take place from the yard in front of and around the potter's house.
21 By far the majority of animals have bodies and usually legs made of wheel-thrown elements. However, the smallest animals are entirely hand-fashioned and are thus solid. The domes (*mandir/dhabu*) are wheel-thrown.
22 The trunk of an elephant figurine is sometimes hand-rolled (fig. 2, left) to produce a more expressive result.
23 Potters in India traditionally live on the outskirts of settlements. Both practical and sociological reasons determine this: the need for plenty of space; the need to be close to supplies, all of which come from outside the town; the need to be away from the centre of population when producing large quantities of smoke while firing; and their low-caste status.
24 The author has also recorded an elementary bonfire where both water-vessels and figurines were fired.
25 In Karnataka, where pottery kilns are banked up against a curved wall rather than being free-standing structures, most of the vents are placed closer to the base of the kiln and thus furthest from the permanent wall. See Sinopoli & Blurton (1986).
26 By analogy with the firing of vessels in other parts of India, I suggest that the early, less intense part of the firing dries out the ceramics, and it is only with the sudden increase in temperature brought about by the layering of straw that the actual firing takes place.

Chapter 27

1 For a succinct survey of Peruvian cultures and pottery traditions see Donnan (1992). This supersedes the earlier but still very useful work by Sawyer (1966).
2 Cabello & Martínez (1988) illustrate a range of musical instruments, including many whistling vessels, held in the Museo de las Americas, Madrid. Whistling vessels are also illustrated in Bennett (1946, pl. 60) and Stone-Miller (1995, p. 175, fig. 144) as well as in a number of site reports and monographs.
3 This abbreviated list mentions only the cultures represented by objects shown here. The list could be extended to include many other coastal cultures including Recuay, Gallinazo and Chimú-Inca as well as Chancay and Ica to the south. See e.g. Donnan (1992) for illustrations of a range of whistling vessels from these cultures.
4 Lathrap et al (1975, p. 37, see e.g. figs 7, 8, 35, 40, 44–46, 55, 59, 87, cat. nos 397, 400, 401, 404). Of special interest are fig. 46, which shows a double whistling bottle with a man playing pan-pipes, and fig. 59, a macaw whistling bottle; see also Hickmann (1990, pp. 58, 61, 66); Donnan (1992, p. 23).
5 Chorrera whistling vessels anticipate later developments elsewhere including Peru, Colombia, and Middle and Central America.
6 See e.g. Izikowitz (1935), Hickmann (1990) and Marti (1992) for surveys of both pre-Hispanic and ethnographic musical instruments in South America.
7 Donnan (1992, p. 120).
8 Ibid.
9 Donnan (1997) reports a Chimú-Inca (AD 1470–1530) ceramic manufacturing centre from the north coast of Peru, and references the few other published studies of pre-Hispanic ceramic production. See also e.g. Shimada (1994).
10 Donnan (1992, p. 121; 1997, p. 52).
11 Carmichael (1989, p. 15).
12 Bushnell (1959); Donnan (1992, pp. 116-17, figs 230, 232).
13 Apart from more traditional use, the tourist market offers an obvious incentive for continuing production.
14 Digby (n.d.; 1948; 1951); see Lang & Middleton (forthcoming, 'Ceramics') for a review of the history of the application of radiography to pottery; see also Carmichael (1990) for a later study of the application of radiography in understanding Nasca pottery construction.
15 Izikowitz (1935, p. 331, fig. 190, pp. 369–72).
16 Donnan (1992, p. 23).
17 Unfortunately, many vessels in early museum collections lack further information beyond a general site provenance and the fact that they were found in graves.
18 The distinctive hooked beak of this and other similar birds depicted on whistling vessels has led to their being identified variously as macaws, parrots and parakeets. The fact that native American classificatory systems differ markedly from modern Western taxonomies suggests that each case for identification should be carefully argued on its own merits.
19 Donnan (1997, p. 30). See especially Donnan (1992, pp. 14–17, 60–63) for a concise illustrated introduction to pottery production techniques including the use of moulds. A range of moulds and mould-made pots are illustrated (figs 106–109, 171, 181–182).
20 Donnan (1992, p. 122).
21 Ibid. (p. 123).
22 Ibid.
23 Ibid.
24 Stobart (1996a, p. 68).
25 Harris (1982, p. 58).
26 These are not strictly speaking whistling vessels, since they do not have a whistling mechanism built in.
27 Sillar (1994, pp. 57–8).
28 Stobart (1996b, p. 479).
29 Ibid.
30 Gose (1994, p. 130); see also McEwan & Van de Guchte (1992) for an elaboration of this idea as it applied to Andean concepts of ancestral time and sacred space embodied in the Inca state ritual of *capac hucha*.
31 Gose (1994, p. 129).
32 Stobart (1996b, p. 479).
33 Zuidema (1989, p. 466).

Acknowledgements: I am indebted to Andrew Middleton of the Department of Scientific Research for undertaking the radiography of the whistling vessels for this study. I am also grateful to Henry Stobart and Bill Sillar for generously providing access to both published and unpublished material and for sharing their enthusiasm, insights and observations. Kate Hands contributed diligent archival research into the British Museum's collections and assembled the relevant literature. Thanks also to Clara Bezanilla for vital 'logistical' support, Jude Simmons for drafting the map, Hans Rashbrook for preparing the line drawings and Michael Row for photography. Last, but by no means least, thanks to Norma Rosso for that indefinable *je ne c'est quoi*.

Chapter 28

1 For chemical analysis of Shang whitewares see Wood (1997, forthcoming).
2 Liu Liangyou (1989, p. 164).
3 Li Jiazhi et al, 'A Study of Gongxian White Porcelain of the Sui-Tang period', in Beijing (1986, pp. 129–33); see also Feng Xianming (1959).
4 Feng Xianming (1964).
5 Feng Xianming (1987, pp. 213–16).
6 Hong Kong Museum of Art (1994a, p. 28).
7 Hsieh Ming-liang (1987, p. 35).
8 Ye Zhimin (1995, p. 63).
9 Fan Dongqing (1991).
10 Rawson (1984).
11 Zhang Yizeng et al in Beijing (1986, p. 98).
12 Li Guozhen & Guo Yenyi (1986, pp. 134–40).
13 Ibid. (n. 12).
14 For a black-glazed Jin Ding bowl with moulded floral designs see Hong Kong Museum of Art (1994b, cat. no. 26, pp. 88–9).
15 For a Northern Song green Ding pillow with an incised design of ducks in a lotus pond see Tokyo (1981a, pls 109–110).
16 A brown Ding bottle with gold decoration was excavated at Fei xi county, Anhui province, from a Northern Song tomb. See Yuan Nanzheng (1988); a white Ding conical bowl with gold decoration of the same period is in the Tokyo National Museum.
17 Ibid. (n. 1).
18 Ibid. (n. 15, p. 172).
19 Medley (1980, pp. 2–3).
20 Qiao Wenzheng (1991).
21 Li Huibing (1988, p. 91).
22 Ibid. (n. 15, p. 155, p. 35).
23 Ibid. (n. 15, pls 129, 131, text with pl. 133).
24 Dingxian Museum (1972); see also Xia Nai & Feng Xianming (eds, 1991, pp. 42–3).
25 Beijing shi wenwu gongzuodui (1964).
26 Jing Zhuyou (1996), Li Huibing (1984).
27 Li Huibing (ibid., n. 7, p. 41).
28 Vainker (1991, p. 94).
29 Xia Nai & Feng Xianming (eds, 1991, p. 18, cat. no. 48).
30 Ye Zhimin (1995, p. 68).
31 Ibid. (n. 15, p. 180).
32 Yutaka Mino & Tsiang (1980).
33 Ibid. (n. 2, p. 164).
34 Ibid. (n. 15, p. 180), quoting a Yuan text, the *Zhizheng youji* by Kong Qi, Qing edn, *yueya tang congshu*, vol. 4, section 35.
35 Ibid. (n. 15, p. 181), quoting a Qing text, the *Bowuyaolan* by Guyingtai, *congshu jicheng* edn, vol. 2, section 14.
36 Tregear (1982).
37 Guo Yanyi (1987).
38 Mean of ten Ding wares from Pollard & Hatcher (1994). Lingshan clay from Guo Yanyi (1987).
39 Li Guozhen & Guo Yenyi (1986), Guo Yanyi (1987), Yap & Hua (1994).
40 Pollard & Hatcher (1994). Table in weight per cent.
41 Zhang Fukang (1985), Wood (1997).
42 Wood (1997).
43 Li Guozhen & Guo Yenyi (1986). Table in weight per cent.

Chapter 29

1 Greene (1992, p. 7).
2 Hayes (1997).
3 Morel (1981a).
4 Forti (1965); Morel (1981a, p. 47).
5 Morel (1969; 1981a, pp. 48–9).
6 Pagenstecher (1909); Gilotta (1985).
7 Morel (1981a, pp. 41–52).
8 Morel (1981b, p. 87).
9 Ibid. (p. 88).
10 Parker (1992, pp. 16–17).
11 Morel (1981b, p. 88).
12 Pucci (1985, p. 375).
13 Among others, Dragendorff (1895) and Loeschcke (1909).
14 Hayes (1985, p. 10).
15 See discussion in Pucci (1985, p. 372).
16 Wells (1990).
17 Pucci (1985, p. 368).
18 Millett (1991, p. 20).
19 Barker (1991, p. 5).
20 See, for example, Barker & Lloyd (1991).

21 Greene (1979, pp. 75–84).
22 For example, France (Greene, 1979, pp. 13–55; Ricci, 1985, pp. 349–53) and Spain (Mayet, 1975; López Mullor, 1990).
23 Mandel (1988).
24 Hayes (1972, p. 412).
25 Hochuli-Gysel (1977).
26 Martin (1995, pp. 63, 64).
27 Greene (1979, pp. 86–105); Maccabruni (1987, pp. 72–3, bibliography).
28 Peña (1990).
29 Aguarod Otal (1991).
30 Hayes (1972, pp. 17–18); Tortorella (1985).
31 Hayes (1983, pp. 105–8).
32 Pucci (1985); Ettlinger et al (1980).
33 Paturzo (1996, pp. 71–85).
34 Ettlinger (1990).
35 Peacock (1982, p. 122).
36 Pasqui (1896, p. 455).
37 Peacock (1982, p. 121).
38 Paturzo (1996, p. 27).
39 Pucci (1985, p. 377).
40 Johnson (1936, pp. 394–6).
41 BM GR 1919.7–18.24; Johnston (1985).
42 Pucci (1985, p. 376).
43 Pucci (1992).
44 Pucci (1985, p. 369).
45 Wells (1990, p. 24).
46 Pucci (1985, p. 376).
47 Ibid.
48 Hayes (1985, p. 51).
49 Wells (1990, p. 24); Peacock (1982, p. 166).
50 Gatti & Onorati (1992, p. 229).
51 Pucci (1985, p. 369); von Schnurbein (1990).
52 Hoffmann (1995).
53 Bémont & Jacob (1986).
54 Marichal (1988).
55 Bet & Vertet (1986).
56 Garbsch (1982).
57 Marichal (1988, pp. 3–8).
58 See, for example, ibid. (pp. 114–19).
59 Ibid. (p. 106).
60 Mezquiriz (1985).
61 Hayes (1972; 1980); Carandini et al (1985).
62 Carandini (1981).
63 Mackensen (1993).
64 Peacock (1982, p. 130).
65 Hayes (1972, pp. 292–5).
66 Ibid. (pp. 323–70).
67 Ibid. (pp. 371–86).
68 Hayes (1972, pp. 387–401); Rodziewicz (1976).
69 Gempeler (1992).
70 Bailey (1990).
71 Hayes (1972, pp. 387–401).
72 See, for example, Gempeler (1992, pls 2–81).
73 Kubiak (1990, p. 74).
74 See ch. 6, p. 54, n. 58.

Chapter 30
1 Dillon (1976).
2 For information on Yuan production at Jingdezhen see, for example, Medley (1975).
3 For information on Ming production at Jingdezhen see, for example, Lion-Goldschmidt (1978).
4 For information on Qing production at Jingdezhen see Beurdeley & Raindre (1987) and Kerr (1986).
5 Liu Xinyuan in Krahl (ed., 1995, p. 11).
6 Wood (1985, pp. 74–5).
7 Clunas (1984, pp. 27–32).
8 Tichane (1983, pp. 51–128).
9 Bushell (1910).
10 Sayer (1951).
11 Sayer (1959).
12 Liu Xinyuan, 'The Kiln Sites of Jingdezhen and their Place in the History of Chinese Ceramics', in Fung Ping Shan Museum, University of Hong Kong (1992, pp. 32–53).
13 Ibid. (n. 12).
14 J. M. Addis, 'The Evolution of Techniques at Jingdezhen with particular reference to the Yuan dynasty', in Oriental Ceramic Society of Hong Kong (1984, p. 12).
15 Ibid. (n. 14).
16 M. Tregear, 'Early Jingdezhen', in Oriental Ceramic Society of Hong Kong (1984, pp. 20–22).
17 Fung Ping Shan Museum, University of Hong Kong (1992, pp. 94–5).
18 Liu Xinyuan (1980).
19 Luo Zhongzhen et al, 'Significance of the Tang Blue and white porcelain unearthed from the ruins of an Ancient city in Yangzhou', in Shanghai Institute of Ceramics, Academia Sinica (1986, pp. 117–21).
20 See-Yiu Lam (1990).
21 Scott (1992), Feng Xianming (1985).
22 Yu Pei-chin (1995).
23 Fujio Nakazawa & Shoko Hasegawa (1995, pp. 106–12).
24 Hong Kong Museum of Art & Jingdezhen Museum of Ceramic History (1989).
25 Rogers (1990, p. 67).
26 Tsui Museum of Art (1993).
27 Tokyo (1981, pp. 195–7).

28 S. Kwan, 'Chinese Porcelain of the Early Twentieth Century', in Hong Kong Museum of Art (1990, pp. 36–55).
29 Fung Ping Shan Museum, University of Hong Kong (1992, p. 47).
30 Lam (1984, p. 16).
31 Hong Kong Museum of Art & Jingdezhen Museum of Ceramic History (1989).
32 Krahl (1986).
33 Pope (1956).
34 See, for example, Sheaf & Kilburn (1988); Ball (1995).
35 Carswell (1985).
36 Pollard & Wood (1986).
37 A detailed account of Chinese glaze technology is given by Wood (1997).
38 Kingery & Vandiver (1985).

Chapter 31
1 For pottery in Staffordshire between 1660 and 1760, see Weatherill (1971; 1986).
2 Mills were very important in Staffordshire; see Copeland (1972) and Baker (1991, pp. 26–8).
3 Baker (1991, p. 15).
4 Copeland (1972, pp. 2, 9, 13–14).
5 Weatherill (1971, p. 5).
6 Baker (1991, p. 33), quoting J. Ward (The Borough of Stoke-upon-Trent, London, W. Lewis and Son, reprinted 1984, Stoke-on-Trent, Webberley, p. 43).
7 Baker (ibid., p. 36), quoting J. Ward (ibid.).
8 Nixon (1976, p. 20).
9 Baker (1991, pp. 17–22).
10 A letter of 1 May 1816, on loan to Keele University, Staffordshire, from the Trustees of the Wedgwood Museum, quoted in Nixon (1976, ch. 6), gives hours from November to February as 7.30 am to 6 pm; hours in summer would be longer, but there were many holidays.
11 John Dwight at the Fulham Pottery, London, pioneered this technique for stoneware in Britain (see ch. 18).
12 For creamwares see Towner (1978) and Lockett (ed., 1986).
13 Mountford (1975, pp. 3–8); for documents giving minimum potters' selling prices for Queen's Earthenware (i.e. creamware) and 'Egyptian ware' (i.e. black basalt), printed ware and 'Common Cream-coloured Ware' in the 1780s and 1790s, see ibid. (pp. 9–11).
14 Reilly (1989, vol. I, pp. 518–19).
15 See Halfpenny (1991, p. 12).
16 Lewis (1984) is a thorough survey of this subject.
17 Baker (1991, pp. 22–3).
18 For porcelain in Staffordshire see Lockett (ed., 1979) and Godden (ed., 1983).
19 The excavation of this factory is discussed by Bemrose (1973).
20 For Longton Hall see Watney (1957) and Tait & Cherry (1980) for the excavation of the site; Watney et al (1993) analyse some of the finds made there.
21 Documents relating to Baddeley's enterprises were published by Mallet (1966); the products are discussed by Godden in Godden (ed., 1983, pp. 32–44).
22 Holgate (1971; 1987) and Holgate in Godden (ed., 1983, pp. 58–88).
23 Copeland (1972, pp. 2–3).
24 Barker & Halfpenny (1990, pp. 7–9, passim).
25 A carved wooden model of a vase attributed to John Coward is illustrated by Reilly (1989, vol. I, fig. 383, p. 308).
26 For the history of the technique at Wedgwood and illustrations of the machinery used, see Reilly (1989, pp. 691–3).
27 See Reilly (1989, vol. I, p. 280) for names of workers; ibid. (pp. 283, 250–51) for Robinson and Rhodes; ibid. (pp. 211–13) for Sadler and Green.
28 For a discussion of printing on ceramics and enamels and a detailed account of the process published in 1799 by James Poulton see Wyman (1980; forthcoming).
29 See Drakard (1995, pp. 331–40; 1992, pp. 31–2) who illustrates the method.
30 Plot (1686).
31 Barker (1990, p. 127) quoting J. Aitkin (A Description of the Country from Twenty to Forty Miles Round Manchester, 1795).
32 Nixon (1976, p. 19).
33 Kingery & Vandiver (1986, pp. 195–207) give the results of the analysis of a jasperware body.
34 For details of English porcelain bodies see Tite & Bimson (1991); for French porcelains see Kingery & Smith (1985).
35 Longton Hall porcelains are analysed by Middleton & Cowell in Watney (ed., 1993).
36 Limehouse and Newcastle-under-Lyme (Pomona factory) porcelains analysed by Freestone (1993).

Chapter 32
1 Hitchling (1995).
2 Yeo (1992).

Bibliography

Adam, J.-P., 1994. Roman Building (trans. A. Matthews), London, Batsford
Adams, B., 1974. Ancient Hierakonpolis Supplement, Warminster
Adams, E. B., 1990. Korea's Pottery Heritage, Seoul International Publishing House
Adams, R. McC., 1965. Land Behind Baghdad: A History of Settlement on the Diyala Plains, Chicago & London
Adams, R. McC., 1981. Heartland of Cities: Surveys of ancient settlement and land use on the central floodplain of the Euphrates, Chicago & London
Adams, R. McC. & Nissen, H. J., 1972. The Uruk Countryside: The natural setting of urban societies, Chicago & London
Addison, F. A., 1949. Jebel Moya, London, New York, Toronto
Aguarod Otal, C., 1991. Cerámica Romana importada de cocina en la Tarraconense, Zaragoza, Institucion Fernando el Católico
Ahsan, M. M., 1979. Social Life under the Abbasids 170-289 AH, 786-902 AD, London & New York
Aikens, C. M. & Higuchi, T., 1982. Prehistory of Japan, New York, Academic Press
Aikens, C. M., 1995. 'First in the World: The Jomon Pottery of Early Japan', in Barnett, W. K. & Hoopes, Y. W. (eds), pp. 11–21
Akkermans, P. M. M. G., 1993. Villages in the Steppe: Late Neolithic settlement and subsistence in the Balikh Valley, northern Syria, Ann Arbor, MI
al-Bakri, 1965. Description de l'Afrique septentrionale, trans. De Slane, Paris, Adrien-Maisonneuve
al-Manūnī, 1979. La Civilisation marocaine à l'époque des Méinides, Feuillets, al-Ribat
Alden, J. R., 1978. 'Excavations at Tal-i Malyan, Part 1: A Sasanian kiln', Iran 16, pp. 79–86
Alden, J. R., 1988. 'Ceramic Ring Scrapers: An Uruk Period pottery production tool', Paléorient 14/1, pp. 143–50
Alexander, J. & Binski, P. (eds), 1987. Age of Chivalry: Art in Plantagenet England 1200-1400, London
Algaze, G., 1993. The Uruk World System: The dynamics of expansion of early Mesopotamian civilization, Chicago & London
Allan, J. W., 1973. 'Abu'l Qasim's Treatise on Ceramics', Iran 11, pp. 114–19
Allchin, B. & Allchin, R., 1982. The Rise of Civilisation in India and Pakistan, Cambridge
Allen, C. S. M., 1990. 'Thin sections of Bronze Age pottery from the East Midlands of England', in Recent Developments in Ceramic Petrology, Middleton, A. & Freestone, I. (eds), British Museum Occasional Paper 81, pp. 1–15
Ames-Lewis, F., 1988. 'Nicola da Urbino and Raphael', Burlington Magazine 130, pp. 690–92
Amiran, R. & Shenhav, D., 1984. 'Experiments with an ancient potter's wheel', in Rice, P. M. (ed.), Pots and Potters, Monograph 24, University of California, pp. 107–112
Amyx, D. A., 1988. Corinthian Vase-Painting of the Archaic Period, Berkeley, University of California Press
Andrae, W., 1925. Coloured Ceramics from Ashur, London
Anon., 1996. Ortaköy-Sapinuva Arkeoloji arastirmalari/Ortaköy-Sapinuwa archaeological research, Ankara
Arkell, A. J., 1949. Early Khartoum, Oxford
Arkell, A. J., 1953. Shaheinab, Oxford
Arnold, C., 1983. 'The Sancton-Baston Potter', Scottish Archaeological Review 2(1), pp. 17–30
Arnold, C., 1988. 'Early Anglo-Saxon pottery of the Illington-Lackford type', Oxford Journal of Archaeology 7, pp. 343–54
Arnold, D., 1976. 'Wandbild und Scherbenbefund. Zur Töpfertecknik der Alten Ägypter vom Beginn der pharaonischen Zeit bis zu den Hyksos', Mitteilungen des Deutschen Archäologischen Instituts, Abteilung Kairo 32, Wiesbaden, pp. 1–34
Arnold, D. (ed.), 1981. Studien zur Altägyptischen Keramik, Mainz
Arnold, D., 1981. 'Ägyptische Mergeltone ("Wüstentone") und die Herkunft einer Mergeltonware des Mittleren Reiches aus der Gegend von Memphis', in Arnold, D. (ed.), pp. 167–191
Arnold, D. & Bourriau, J. E. (eds), 1993. Introduction to Ancient Egyptian Pottery, Mainz
Arnold, D., 1996. Ancient Art from the Shumei Family Collection, New York
Arnold, D. E., 1985. Ceramic Theory and Cultural Process, Cambridge, Cambridge University Press
Art of the Adivasi (Indian Tribal Art), 1988. Exhibition catalogue, Japan

Baart, J. M., 1989. 'Ceramic consumption and supply in early modern Amsterdam: local production and long-distance trade', in Archeologische Dienst, Publicaties 1972–1989 2, Dienst Openbare Werken Amsterdam, pp. 609–33
Bader, N. O., 1989. Earliest Cultivators in Northern Mesopotamia: The Investigations of Soviet Archaeological Expeditions in Iraq at Settlements Tell Maghzaliya, Tell Sotto, Kül Tepe, Moscow
Bader, N. O., 1993. 'The Early Agricultural Settlement of Tell Sotto', in Yoffee, N. & Clark, J. J. (eds), Early Stages in the

Evolution of Mesopotamian Civilization: Soviet excavations in Northern Iraq, Tucson & London, pp. 41–54
Badler, V. R., McGovern, P. E. & Glusker, D. L., 1996. 'Chemical Evidence for a Wine Residue from Warka (Uruk) inside a Late Uruk Period Spouted Jar', *Baghdader Mitteilungen* 27, pp. 39–44
Bahgat Bey Ali, 1914. 'Les fouilles de Fustat', *Bulletin de l'Institut Egyptien*, 5th series, vol. VIII
Bailey, D. M., 1965. 'Lamps in the Victoria and Albert Museum', in *Opuscula Atheniensia* 6
Bailey, D. M., 1972. *Greek and Roman Pottery Lamps*, London
Bailey, D. M., 1975. *A Catalogue of the Lamps in the British Museum I: Greek, Hellenistic and Early Roman Lamps*, London, British Museum Publications
Bailey, D. M., 1976. 'Pottery Lamps', in Strong, D. & Brown, D. (eds), *Roman Crafts*, London
Bailey, D. M., 1980. *A Catalogue of the Lamps in the British Museum II: Roman Lamps made in Italy*, London, British Museum Publications
Bailey, D. M., 1985. *Excavations at Sidi Khrebish, Benghazi (Berenice) III: 2, The Lamps*, Tripoli
Bailey, D. M., 1987. 'The Roman Terracotta Lamp Industry: Another View about Exports', in Oziol, Th. & Rebuffat, R. (eds), *Les lampes de terre cuite en Méditerranée*, Lyon
Bailey, D. M., 1988. *A Catalogue of the Lamps in the British Museum III: Roman Provincial Lamps*, London, British Museum Publications
Bailey, D. M., 1990. 'The Local Late Roman Red Slip Ware of Hermopolis Magna', in Godlewski, W. (ed.), pp. 4–26
Bailey, D. M., 1995. 'The Lamps', in Peacock, D. P. S. & Maxfield, V. A., *The Roman Imperial Porphyry Quarries: Gebel Dokhan, Egypt, Interim Report, 1995*, Southampton
Bailey, D. M., 1996. *A Catalogue of the Lamps in the British Museum IV: Lamps of Metal and Stone, and Lampstands*, London, British Museum Press
Baker, D., 1991. *Potworks: The Industrial Architecture of the Staffordshire Potteries*, London, Royal Commission on the Historical Monuments of England
Balfet, H., 1965. 'Ethnographical Observations in North Africa and the Archaeological Interpretation: The Pottery of the Maghreb', in Matson, F. R. (ed.), *Ceramics and Man*, Chicago, Aldine
Balfet, H., 1984. 'Methods of Formation and the Shape of Pottery', in van der Leeuw, S. E. & Pritchard, A. C. (eds), *The Many Dimensions of Pottery: Ceramics in archaeology and anthropology*, Amsterdam, University of Amsterdam
Ball, D., 1995. *The Diana Adventure*, Groningen
Ballet, P. & Picon, M., 1987. 'Essai de classification des coupes type Maidum-Bowl du sondage nord de 'Ayn-Asil (Oasis de Dakhla). Typologie et evolution', *Cahiers de la céramique égyptienne* 1, Cairo, pp. 1–16
Balog, P., 1974. 'Sasanian and Early Islamic ornamental glass vessel-stamps', in Kouymjian, D. K. (ed.), pp. 131–40
Bammesberger, A., 1991. 'Three Old English runic inscriptions: I) The Loveden Hill Urn; 2) The Overchurch Stone; 3) The Derbyshire Bone Piece', in Bammesberger, A. (ed.), *Old English Runes*, pp. 125–36
Bankes, G., 1980. *Moche Pottery from Peru*, London, British Museum Publications
Barbier, J. P., 1962. *Altpersische Kunst*, Basel
Barker, D., 1984. '18th and 19th century ceramics excavated at the Foley Pottery, Fenton, Stoke-on-Trent', *Staffordshire Archaeological Studies* 1, pp. 63–86
Barker, D., 1986. 'North Staffordshire post-medieval ceramics – a type-series. Part one: Cistercian ware', *Staffordshire Archaeological Studies*, Museum Archaeological Society Report, new ser. 3, Stoke-on-Trent, pp. 52–7
Barker, D., 1991a. *Beneath the Six Towns*, City Museum and Art Gallery, Stoke-on-Trent
Barker, D., 1991b. *William Greatbatch, a Staffordshire Potter*, London, Jonathan Horne
Barker, D., 1991c. 'A group of Staffordshire red stonewares of the eighteenth century', *Transactions of the English Ceramic Circle* 14, part 2, pp. 177–98
Barker, D., 1993. *Slipware*, Shire Album 297, Princes Risborough
Barker, D. & Halfpenny, P., 1990. *Unearthing Staffordshire*, City Museum and Art Gallery, Stoke-on-Trent
Barker, G. & Lloyd, J. (eds), 1991. *Roman Landscapes*, London, British School at Rome Archaeological Monographs 2
Barker, G., 1991. 'Approaches to Archaeological Survey', in Barker, G. & Lloyd, J. (eds), pp. 1–9
Barley, N., 1994. *Smashing Pots: Feats of clay from Africa*, London, British Museum Press
Barnett, W. K. & Hoopes, Y. W. (eds), 1995. *The Emergence of Pottery: Technology and Innovation in Ancient Societies*, Washington, DC, Smithsonian Institution Press
Barrelet, M. Th., 1968. *Figurines et reliefs en terre cuite de la Mésopotamie antique*, Paris
Bartl, K., Schneider, G. & Böhme, S., 1995. 'Notes on "Brittle Wares" in north-eastern Syria', *Levant* 27, pp. 165–77
Barton, K. J., 1965. 'Medieval Pottery at Rouen', *Archaeological Journal* 122, pp. 73–85
Barton, K., 1992. 'Ceramic changes in the western European littoral at the end of the Middle Ages', in Gaimster, D. R. M. & Redknap, M. (eds), pp. 246–55
Baumann, M. P. (ed.), 1996. *Cosmologia y Música en los Andes*, Frankfurt & Madrid
Baumann, M. P., 1996. 'Andean Music, Symbolic Dualism and Cosmology', in Baumann, M. P. (ed.), pp. 15–66
Béart, H. & Duformier, D., 1989. 'Influence de nace sur les couleurs et la composition des pâtes ceramique calcaires au cours de leur cuisson', *Revue d'Archéométrie* 13, pp. 43–53
Beazley, J. D., 1986. *The Development of Attic Black-Figure*, rev. edn, Berkeley & Los Angeles, University of California Press
Beckmann, B., 1975. *Der Scherbenhügel in der Siegburger Aulgasse, I*, Rheinische Ausgrabungen 16, Bonn, Rheinisches Landesmuseum
Beijing shi wenwu gongzuo dui, 1964. 'Shunyi xian Liao Jingguang shilita qi qingli jian bao' (A discussion of a Liao pagoda: Jingguang, Shunyi), *Wenwu* 1964.8, pp. 49–54
Beijing, 1986. *The 2nd International Conference on Ancient Chinese Pottery and Porcelain: Its Scientific and Technical Insights (Abstracts), Beijing, China, 15-19 November 1985*
Bel, A., 1918. *Les Industries de la Céramique à Fès*, Paris, Leroux
Bellamy, C. V. & Le Patourel, H. E. J., 1970. 'Four medieval pottery kilns on Woodhouse Farm, Winksley, near Ripon, W. Riding of Yorkshire', *Medieval Archaeology* 14, pp. 104–25
Bémont, C. & Jacob, J.-P. (eds), 1986. *La terre sigillée gallo-romaine*, Paris, Maison des Sciences de l'Homme, Documents d'Archéologie Française 6
Bemrose, P., 1973. 'The Pomona Potworks, Newcastle, Staffs., Part I, Soft-paste: Its production at Lower Street 1744–54', *Transactions of the English Ceramic Circle* 9, part 1, pp. 1–18
Bemrose, P., 1975. 'The Pomona Potworks, Newcastle, Staffs., Part II, Samuel Bell: His red earthenware productions 1724–44', *Transactions of the English Ceramic Circle* 9, part 3, pp. 292–303
Bennett, W. C., 1946. 'The Archaeology of the Central Andes', in *The Handbook of South American Indians*, Bureau of American Ethnology Bulletin 143, vol. 2, Washington, DC
Benson, J. L., 1989. *Earlier Corinthian Workshops: A study of Corinthian Geometric and Protocorinthian stylistic groups*, Amsterdam
Beresford, M. & Hurst, J. (eds), 1971. *Deserted Medieval Villages*
Berman, J., 1994. 'The Ceramic Evidence for Sociopolitical Organization in 'Ubaid Southwestern Iran', in Stein, G. & Rothman, M. S. (eds), *Chiefdoms and Early States in the Near East: The organizational dynamics of complexity*, Madison, WI, pp. 23–33
Bet, P. & Vertet, H., 1986. 'Centre de Production de Lezoux', in Bémont, C. & Jacob, J.-P. (eds), pp. 138–44
Betts, I. A., Black, E. W. & Gower, J. L., 1997. 'A Corpus of Relief-Patterned Tiles in Roman Britain', *Journal of Roman Pottery Studies* 7
Beurdeley, M. & Raindre, G., 1987. *Qing Porcelain: Famille Verte, Famille Rose*, London
Beyer, D., 1993. 'Mashnaqa 1993: rapport sommaire sur les travaux de la Mission archéologique française', *Orient-Express* 1993/2, pp. 7–8
Bimson, M., 1961. 'John Dwight', *Transactions of the English Ceramic Circle* 5, part 2, pp. 95–109
Binns, C. F., Klem, M. & Mott, H., 1932. 'An Experiment in Egyptian Blue Glaze', *Journal of the American Ceramic Society* 15, pp. 271–2
Bishop, R. L. & Lange, F. W. (eds), 1991. *The Ceramic Legacy of Anna O. Shepard*
Black, E. W., 1985. 'The dating of relief-patterned flue-tiles', *Oxford Journal of Archaeology* 4, pp. 353–76
Blake, H., 1987. 'Archaeology and Maiolica', in Wilson, T., pp. 15–16
Blinkhorn, P., 1989. 'Middle Saxon Pottery from the Buttermarket kiln, Ipswich, Suffolk', *Medieval Ceramics* 13, pp. 12–16
Blurton, T. R., 1985. 'Tribal Terracotta Figurines in Gujarat: The technology of their production', *South Asian Studies* I, pp. 67–77
Boardman, J., 1974. *Athenian Black Figure Vases*, London
Boardman, J., 1975. *Athenian Red Figure Vases: The Archaic period*, London
Boardman, J., 1989. *Athenian Red Figure Vases: The Classical period*, London
Boast, R., 1995. 'Fine pots, pure pots, Beaker pots', in Kinnes, I. & Varndell, G. (eds), pp. 69–80
Bobrinsky, A. A., 1993. *The Origin of the Potter's Wheel*, Ekaterinburg
Bock, E. K. de, 1988. *Moche: Gods, warriors, priests*, Leiden
Boüard, M. de, 1974. 'Observations on the treatise of Eraclius, *De coloribus et artibus Romanorum*', in Evison, V. I., Hodges, H. & Hurst, J. G. (eds), *Medieval Pottery from Excavations: Studies presented to Gerald Clough Dunning*, pp. 67–76
Boukobza, A., 1974. *La Poterie Marocaine*, Casablanca, Éditions Alpha
Bourriau, J. E., 1981. *Umm el-Qa'ab: Pottery from the Nile valley before the Arab Conquest*, Cambridge
Bourriau, J. E. & Nicholson, P. T., 1992. 'Marl clay pottery fabrics of the New Kingdom from Memphis, Saqqara and Amarna', *Journal of Egyptian Archaeology* 78, pp. 29–91
Bowman, S. G. E. (ed.), 1991. *Science and The Past*, London, British Museum Publications
Boyce, A., 1989. 'Notes on the Manufacture and use of Faience Rings at Amarna', in Kemp, B. J. (ed.)
Braidwood, R. J. et al, 1952. 'Matarrah: A southern variant of the Hassunan assemblage, excavated in 1948', *Journal of Near Eastern Studies* 11/1, pp. 1–75
Braidwood, R. J. & Howe, B., 1960. 'The archaeological assemblages', in Braidwood, R. J. & Howe, B. (eds), *Prehistoric Investigations in Iraqi Kurdistan*, Chicago, pp. 33–62
Brandt, P., 1927. *Schaffende Arbeit und Bildende Kunst im altertum und Mittelalter*
Brears, P., 1974. *The Collector's Book of English Country Pottery*, Newton Abbot, Devon, David & Charles
Brears, P., 1989a. 'The continuing tradition', *Medieval Ceramics* 13, pp. 3–8
Brears, P., 1989b. *North Country Folk Art*, Edinburgh
Brisbane, M., 1981. 'Incipient markets for early Anglo-Saxon ceramics: Variations in levels and modes of production', in Howard, H. & Morris, E. L. (eds), *Production and Distribution: A Ceramic Viewpoint*, British Archaeological Reports, Int. Ser. 120, Oxford, pp. 229–42
Briscoe, T., 1980. 'Anglo-Saxon pot stamps', *Current Archaeology* 72, p. 15
Briscoe, T., 1981. 'Anglo-Saxon pot stamps', *Anglo-Saxon Studies in Archaeology and History* 2, pp. 1–36
Briscoe, T., 1982. 'The terminology for Anglo-Saxon stamped pottery', *Current Archaeology* 81, p. 303
Briscoe, T., 1983. 'A classification of Anglo-Saxon pot stamp motifs and proposed terminology', *Studien zur Sachsenforschung* 4, pp. 57–71
Briscoe, T., 1985. 'The use of brooches and other jewellery as dies on pagan Anglo-Saxon pottery', *Medieval Archaeology* 29, pp. 136–42
Briscoe, T., 1992. 'The history of the archive of early Saxon pottery stamps', *Medieval Ceramics* 16, p. 65
Britton, F., 1987. *London Delftware*, London
Brodribb, G., 1987. *Roman Brick and Tile*, Gloucester, Sutton
Broneer, O., 1930. *Corinth* IV, 2, Cambridge, MA
Brovarski, E., 1982. 'Chalices', in *Egypt's Golden Age: The Art of Living in the New Kingdom 1558-1085 B.C.*, Boston Museum of Fine Arts, pp. 145–8
Brown, D., 1981. 'Swastika Patterns', in Evison, V. (ed.), *Angles, Saxons and Jutes: Essays Presented to J. N. L. Myres*, pp. 227–40
Brown, S. C., 1990. 'Media in the Achaemenid period: The Late Iron Age in Central West Iran', in *Achaemenid History IV: Centre and Periphery*, Sancisi-Weerdenburg, H. & Kuhrt, A. (eds), Leiden, pp. 63–76
Brown, T. & Bruce-Mitford, R., 1960. *Evangelium Quattuor Codex Lindisfarnensis*
Bruijn, A., 1959. 'Die mittelalterliche Töpferindustrie in Brunssum', *Berichten van de Rijksdienst voor het Oudheidkundig Bodemonderzoek* 9 (1960), pp. 139–88
Bruijn, A., 1962/3. 'Die mittelalterliche keramische Industrie in Südlimburg', *Berichten van de Rijksdienst voor het Oudheidkundig Bodemonderzoek* 12/13 (1964), pp. 356–459
Brunton, G. & Caton-Thompson, G., 1928. *The Badarian Civilization and the Predynastic Remains near Badari*, London
Brunton, G., 1937. *Mostagedda and the Tasian Culture*, London
Bryant, G. F. & Steane, J. M., 1969. 'Excavations at the deserted medieval settlement at Lyveden', *Journal of Northampton Museums* 5
Bryant, G. F., 1977. 'Experimental kiln firings at Barton-on-Humber, S. Humberside, 1971', *Medieval Archaeology* 21, pp. 106–23
Buccellati, G., 1990. 'Salt at the Dawn of History: The case of the Bevelled-Rim Bowls', in Matthiae, P., Van Loon, M. & Weiss, H. (eds), *Resurrecting the Past: A joint tribute to Adnan Bounni*, Istanbul & Leiden, pp. 17–40
Buhl, M.-L., 1968. *Skatte fra det gamle Persien*, Stockholm
Bushell, S. W., 1910. *Description of Chinese Pottery and Porcelain: Being a translation of the T'ao Shuo with introduction, notes and bibliography*, Oxford
Bushnell, G., 1959. 'Some post-Columbian whistling jars from Peru', in *Actas del XXXIII Congreso Internacional de Americanistas* 2, San José
Butterworth, B., 1956. 'Limeblowing: some notes on the literature', *Transactions of the British Ceramic Society* 55, pp. 532–44
Bynon, J., 1982. 'Berber Women's Pottery: Is the Decoration Motivated?', in Picton, J. (ed.), *Earthenware in Asia and Africa*, Percival David Foundation Colloquies on Art and Archaeology in Asia 12, London, School of Oriental & African Studies, University of London

Cabello, P. & Martínez, C., 1988. *Música y Arqueologia en América Precolumbina*, British Archaeological Reports, Oxford
Caiger-Smith, A. (ed.), 1985. *Lustre Pottery*, London
Callmer, J., 1995. 'The influx of Oriental beads into Europe during the eighth century AD', in Rasmussen, M., Lund Hansen, U. & Näsman, U. (eds), *Glass Beads: Cultural history, technology, experiment and analogy*, Lejre, Denmark, pp. 49–54
Calvet, Y., 1991. 'Un niveau de la periode Uruk a Tell el 'Oueili', in Huot, J-L. et al, *'Oueili: Travaux de 1985*, Paris, pp. 159–209
Campbell, S., 1986. 'The Halaf culture pottery from the 1983 season', in Watkins, T. & Campbell, S. (eds), *Excavations at Kharabeh Shattani: Vol. 1*, Edinburgh, pp. 37–169
Caneva, I. (ed.), 1988. *El Geili: The History of a Middle Nile Environment 7000 B.C.–A.D. 1500*, BAR Int. Ser. 424, Oxford

Caneva, I. & Marks, A., 1990. 'More on the Shaqadud pottery: evidence for Saharo-Nilotic connections during the 6th–4th millennium B.C.', *Archéologie du Nil Moyen* 4, pp. 11–35
Caneva, I., 1991. 'Jebel Moya revisited: a settlement of the 5th millennium BC in the Middle Nile Basin', *Antiquity* 65, pp. 262–8
Caneva, I., 1993. 'Pre-pastoral Middle Nile: local developments and Saharan contacts', in Krzyzaniak, L., Kobusiewicz, M. & Alexander, J. (eds), *Environmental Change and Human Culture in the Nile Basin and Northern Africa until the Second Millennium B.C.*, Poznan, pp. 405–11
Capelle, T., 1987. 'Animal stamps and animal figures on Anglo-Saxon and Anglian pottery', *Medieval Archaeology* 31, pp. 94–6
Carandini, A. (ed.), 1981. *Atlante delle Forme Ceramiche II, Enciclopedia dell'Arte Antica*, Rome
Carandini, A., 1981. 'Ceramica Africana: introduzione', in Carandini, A. (ed.), pp. 11–18
Carandini, A., Tortorici, E., Tortorella, S. & Sagui, L., 1981. 'Ceramica Africana: Vasi', in Carandini, A. (ed.), pp. 19–183
Carmichael, P. H., 1989. 'Nasca Ceramic Production', in Purin, S. & Imschoot, D. J. (eds), *Les Incas: Pérou*, Gent
Carmichael, P. H., 1990. 'Nasca Pottery Construction', *Nawpa Pacha* 24, Berkeley, Institute of Andean Studies, pp. 31–48
Carr, C., 1990. 'Advances in ceramic radiography and analysis: Applications and potentials', *Journal of Archaeological Science* 17, pp. 13–34
Carr, C. & Riddick, E. B., 1990. 'Advances in ceramic radiography and analysis: Laboratory methods', *Journal of Archaeological Science* 17, pp. 35–66
Carswell, J., 1985. *Blue and White: Chinese porcelain and its impact on the western world*, David and Alfred Smart Gallery, University of Chicago
Caygill, M. & Cherry, J. (eds), 1997. *A. W. Franks: Nineteenth-century collecting and the British Museum*, London, British Museum Press
Celoria, F. & Kelly, J., 1973. 'A post-medieval site with a kiln base found off Albion Square, Hanley, Stoke-on-Trent', *City of Stoke-on-Trent Museum Archaeological Society Report* 4
Cerulli Ireli, G., 1977. 'Officina di lucerne fittili a Pompei', in Carandini, A. (ed.), *L'instrumentum domesticum di Ercolano e Pompei*, Rome
Chadli, M., 1992. 'Ceramics: Contemporary and domestic pottery in Fès', in Hedgecoe, J. & Damluji, S. (eds), *Zillij: The Art of Moroccan Ceramics*, Reading, Garnet Publishing
Chazan, M. & Lehner, M., 1990. 'An Ancient Analogy: Pot-baked bread in Ancient Egypt and Mesopotamia', *Paléorient* 16/2, pp. 21–35
Cherry, J. & Tait, H., 1980. 'Excavations at the Longton Hall Porcelain Factory, Part II', *Post-Medieval Archaeology* 14, pp. 1–22
Cherry, J., 1985. 'Sex, magic and Dr Gerald Dunning', *Medieval Ceramics* 9, pp. 5–20
Cherry, J., 1991a. 'Pottery and Tile', in Blair, J. & Ramsay, N. (eds), *English Medieval Industries: craftsmen, techniques, products*, London, Hambledon Press, pp. 189–209
Cherry, J., 1991b. *Medieval Decorative Art*, London, British Museum Publications
Cherry, J., 1992. 'The use of seals as decoration on medieval pottery and bronze vessels', in Gaimster, D. & Redknap, M. (eds), *Everyday and Exotic Pottery from Europe c. 650-1900*, pp. 59–65
Childe, V. R., 1954. 'Rotary motion', in Singer, C., Holmyard, A. J. & Hall, A. R. (eds), *A History of Technology*, Oxford, pp. 187–215
Christensen, A., 1936. *L'Iran sous les sassanides*, Copenhagen
Christie's, 1994. *Fine Antiquities, London, 7 December 1994*, London
Christie's, 1996. *Antiquities, Islamic and Oriental Works of Art, London, 17 October 1996*, London
Clark, G. & Hughto, M., 1979. *A Century of Ceramics in the United States 1878-1978*, New York, E. P. Dutton
Clark, G., 1995. *The Potter's Art*, London, Phaidon
Cleal, R., 1995. 'Pottery fabrics in Wessex in the fourth to second millennia BC', in Kinnes, I. & Varndell, G. (eds), pp. 185–94
Clifford, T. & Mallet, J., 1976. 'Battista Franco as a designer for maiolica', *Burlington Magazine* 118, pp. 387–410
Clifford, T., 1991. 'Some unpublished drawings for maiolica and Federigo Zuccaro's role in the Spanish Service', in Wilson, T. (ed.), pp. 166–76
Clunas, C., 1984. *Chinese Export Watercolours*, Victoria and Albert Museum, London, Far Eastern series
Coldstream, J. N., 1977. *Geometric Greece*, London
Coldstream, J. N., 1991. 'The Geometric Style: Birth of the picture', in Rasmussen, T. & Spivey, N. (eds), pp. 36–56
Coleman-Smith, R. & Pearson, T., 1988. *Excavations in the Donyatt Potteries*, Chichester
Colledge, M. A. R., 1976. *The Art of Palmyra*, London
Colledge, M. A. R., 1977. *Parthian Art*, London
Collins, P., 1987. 'Prints and the development of istoriato painting on Italian Renaissance maiolica', *Print Quarterly* 4, pp. 223–35
Cook, R. M., 1997. *Greek Painted Pottery*, 3rd edn, London
Cooper, E., 1988. *A History of World Pottery*, 3rd edn, London, Batsford
Copeland, R., 1972. *A Short History of Pottery Raw Materials and the Cheddleton Flint Mill*, Leek, Cheddleton Flint Mill Industrial Heritage Trust
Cort, L. A., 1970. *Shigaraki: A Potter's Village*, London & New York, Kodansha International
Cort, L. A., 1992. *Seto and Mino Ceramics in the Freer Gallery of Art*, Washington, DC, Smithsonian Institution Press
Cotter, J., 1997. *A Twelfth-century Pottery Kiln at Pound Lane, Canterbury: Evidence for an Immigrant Potter in the Late Norman Period*, Canterbury Archaeological Trust Occasional Paper 1
Courtois, L. & Velde, B., 1987. 'Analyses a la microsonde et description matérielle de quelques céramiques Obeid 0 a Obeid 3 de 'Oueili (Campagne de 1983), Larsa (10e campagne, 1983) et 'Oueili (4e campagne, 1983)', in Huot, J.-L. et al, *Rapport préliminaire*, Paris, pp. 121–40
Courtois, L. & Velde, B., 1991. 'Les peintures ceramique à chromite de l'Obeid 3 et 4', in Huot, J.-L. (ed.), *Ouelli: Travaux de 1985*, Paris, pp. 267–83
Courtright, P. B., 1985. *Ganesha: Lord of Obstacles, Lord of Beginnings*, Oxford
Crowfoot, G. M., 1932. 'Pots, Ancient and Modern', *Palestine Exploration Fund Quarterly Statement* (October), pp. 179–87, pls 1–3
Cunliffe, B., 1984. *Danebury: An Iron Age hillfort in Hampshire*, London, Council for British Archaeology
Cunliffe, B., 1987. *Hengistbury Head, Dorset, Vol.1: The prehistoric and roman settlement*, Oxford
Cunliffe, B., 1991. *Iron Age Communities in Britain*, 3rd edn, London, Routledge & Kegan Paul
Curtis, J. E., 1979. 'Loftus' Parthian cemetery at Warka', *Akten des VII Internationalen Kongresses für Iranische Kunst und Archaologie, München 7–10 September 1976, Archäologische Mittlungen aus Iran* Erganzungsband 6, pp. 309–17
Curtis, J. (ed.), 1982. *Fifty Years of Mesopotamian Discovery: The Work of the British School of Archaeology in Iraq 1932–1982*, London
Curtis, J. E. & Green, A. R., 1987. 'Preliminary report on excavations at Khirbet Khatuniyeh, 1985', in Damerji, M. (ed.), pp. 73–78
Curtis, J. E., 1989a. 'Case of the missing column', *British Museum Society Bulletin* 60 (Spring), pp. 7–9
Curtis, J. E., 1989b. *Ancient Persia*, London, British Museum Publications
Curtis, J. E., 1989c. 'A Grave-Group from Qeytariyah near Tehran (?)', in *Archaeologica et Orientalis: Miscellanea in Honorem Louis Vanden Berghe*, De Meyer, L. & Haerinck, E. (eds), Gent, vol. I, pp. 323–33
Curtis, J. E. et al, 1989. *Excavations at Qasrij Cliff and Khirbet Qasrij*, London, British Museum Publications
Curtis, J. E. & Reade, J. E. (eds), 1995. *Art and Empire: Treasures from Assyria in the British Museum*, London, British Museum Press

Dalley, S., 1984. *Mari and Karana: Two Old Babylonian Cities*, London
Damerji, M. (ed.), 1987. *Researches on the Antiquities of Saddam Dam Basin Salvage and Other Researches*, Baghdad
Dandamaev, M. A., 1989. *A Political History of the Achaemenid Empire*, Leiden
Daskiewicz, M. & Schneider, G., 1996. 'Chemical Composition of North-Mesopotamian Early Dynastic Period Ceramics from Tall Rad Shaqrah', in *Polish Archaeology in the Mediterranean VII, Reports 1995*, Warsaw, pp. 171–5
Davey, N., 1961. *A History of Building Materials*, London, Phoenix House
Davidson, T. E. & McKerrell, H., 1976. 'Pottery Analysis and Halaf Period Trade in the Khabur Headwaters Region', *Iraq* 38, pp. 45–56
Davidson, T. E. & McKerrell, H., 1980. 'The neutron activation analysis of Halaf and 'Ubaid pottery from Tell Arpachiyah and Tepe Gawra', *Iraq* 42, pp. 155–67
Davidson, T. E. & Watkins, T., 1981. 'Two seasons of excavations at Tell Aqab in the Jezirah, N.E. Syria', *Iraq* 43, pp. 1–18, pl. I
Davidson, T. E., 1981. 'Pottery Manufacture and Trade at the Prehistoric Site of Tell Aqab, Syria', *Journal of Field Archaeology* 8, pp. 65–77
Davison, A. et al, 1993. *Illington: a study of a Breckland Parish and its Anglo-Saxon Cemetery*
Dawson, G., 1979. 'Excavations at Guy's Hospital 1967', *Surrey Archaeological Society Research* 7, pp. 27–65
De Cardi, B. et al, 1975. 'Archaeological Survey in Northern Oman', *East & West* 25, pp. 9–75
Dean, D., forthcoming. 'The Design and Consumption of English Country Pottery in the Seventeenth Century', Ph.D. thesis, Royal Colleage of Art/ Victoria and Albert Museum, London
Debevoise, N. C., 1934a. 'The history of glaze and its place in the ceramic technique of ancient Seleucia on the Tigris', *Bulletin of the American Ceramic Society* 13/11, pp. 293–300
Debevoise, N. C., 1934b. *Parthian pottery from Seleucia on the Tigris*, Ann Arbor, MI
Debevoise, N. C., 1938. *A Political History of Parthia*, Chicago & London
Debono, F. & Mortensen, G., 1990. *El-Omari*, Mainz
Deer, W. A., Howie, R. A. & Zussman, J., 1962. *Rock-forming Minerals V: Non-silicates*, London, Longman
Delougaz, P., 1952. *Pottery from the Diyala Region*, Chicago
Deneauve, J., 1969. *Lampes de Carthage*, Paris
Desborough, V. R. d'A., 1972. *The Greek Dark Ages*, London
Deuchler, M., forthcoming. 'Connoisseurs and Artisans: A social view of Korean culture', in Krahl, R. (ed.), forthcoming
Dickinson, O. T. P., 1994. *The Aegean Bronze Age*, Cambridge
Dickinson, T., 1978. 'British Antiquity: Post Roman and Pagan Anglo-Saxon', *Archaeological Journal* 135, pp. 332–44
Didsbury, P., 1992. 'An Anglo-Saxon mammiform pottery vessel from Barton-on-Humber', *Medieval Ceramics* 16, pp. 66–7
Digby, A., n.d. X-ray examination of Peruvian pottery, unpublished laboratory notes dated 28/2/1939, London
Digby, A., 1948. 'Radiographic examination of Peruvian pottery techniques', in *Actes du XVIIIe Congrés des Americanistes*, Paris, pp. 605–8
Digby, A., 1951. 'The technical development of whistling vases in Peru', in *Civilizations of Ancient America* (Selected Papers of the International Congress of Americanists), Chicago, pp. 252–7
Dillon, M., 1976. 'A History of the Porcelain Industry in Jingdezhen', unpub. thesis, University of Leeds
Dingxian Museum, 1972. 'Hebei Dingxian faxian liangzuo Songdai taji' (Two Song dynasty pagoda foundations discovered in Dingxian, Hebei province), *Wenwu* 1972.8, pp. 39–51
Donnan, C. B., 1992. *Ceramics of Ancient Peru*, Los Angeles, University of California Press
Donnan, C. B., 1997. 'A Chimú-Inka Ceramic-Manufacturing Center from the North Coast of Perú', *Latin American Antiquity* 8 (1), pp. 30–54
Dormer, P., 1986. *The New Ceramics: Trends and traditions*, London, Thames & Hudson
Dornbusch, J. B., 1873. 'Die Kunstgilde der Töpfer in der abteilichen Stadt Siegburg und ihre Fabricate', *Annalen des Historischen Vereins für den Niederrhein* 25, pp. 1–130
Dragendorff, H., 1895. 'Terra Sigillata: Ein Betrag zur Geschichte der griechischen und römischen Keramik', *Bonner Jahrbucher* 96 (1895), pp. 18–155; 97 (1896), pp. 54–163
Drakard, D., 1992. *Printed English Pottery: History and humour in the reign of George III, 1760-1820*, London, Jonathan Horne
Drakard, D. (ed.), 1993. *Limehouse Ware Revealed*, London, English Ceramic Circle
Drakard, D., 1995. 'A Report on the seminar on early on-glaze transfer-printing', *Transactions of the English Ceramic Circle* 15, part 3, pp. 331–40
Dreyer, G., 1986. *Elephantine VIII: Der Tempel der Satet. Die Funde der Frühzeit und des Alten Reiches*, Mainz
Dumortier, C., 1991. 'Description d'un atelier de majoliques à Anvers au XVIieme et debut XVIIieme siècle', in Wilson, T. (ed.), pp. 241–6
Duncan-Jones, R., 1990. *Structure and Scale in the Roman Economy*, Cambridge
Dunning, G. C., 1969. 'Medieval jugs with brooches', *Antiquaries Journal* 49, pp. 388–90
Dunning, G. C., 1975. 'Some local and imported wares from Southampton', in Platt & Coleman-Smith, pp. 47–50
Dunning, G. C., 1976. 'The French Imported Jug', in Ketteringham, L. L., *Alsted: Excavation of a Thirteenth–Fourteenth Century Sub-Manor House with its Ironworks in Netherne Wood, Merstham, Surrey, Res Vol Surrey Archaeological Society* 2, pp. 45–7
Dyson, R. H., 1965. 'Problems of Protohistoric Iran as seen from Hasanlu', *Journal of Near Eastern Studies* 24, pp. 193–217, pls 31–44
Dyson, R. H., 1989. 'The Iron Age Architecture at Hasanlu: An Essay', *Expedition* 31/2–3, pp. 107–27

Eccles, H. & Rackham, B., 1922. *Analysed Specimens of English Porcelain*, London, HMSO
Edwards, I. & Jacobs, L., 1986. 'Experiments with stone "pottery wheel" bearings: notes on the use of rotation in the production of ancient pottery', *Newsletter, Department of Pottery Technology, Leiden University* 4, pp. 49–55
Egami, N., Fukai, S. & Masuda, S., 1965. *Dailaman I: The Excavations at Ghalekuti and Lasulkan 1960*, Tokyo
Egami, N., 1973. *The Beginnings of Japanese Art*, Heibonsha Survey of Japanese Art, New York & Tokyo, Weatherhill & Heibonsha
Eiwanger, J., 1984a. *Merimde-Benisalâme I. Die Funde der Urschict*, Mainz
Eiwanger, J., 1984b. *Merimde-Benisalâme III. Die Funde der jüngeren Merimdekultur*, Mainz
Eiwanger, J., 1988. *Merimde-Benisalâme II. Die Funde der Mittleren Merimdekultur*, Mainz
Elliott, G., 1977. 'Staffordshire red and black stonewares', *Transactions of the English Ceramic Circle* 10, part 2, pp. 85–6
Ellison, R., 1984a. 'The uses of pottery', *Iraq* 46, pp. 63–8
Ellison, R., 1984b. 'Methods of food preparation in Mesopotamia (*c.* 3000–600 BC)', *Journal of the Economic and Social History of the Orient* 27, pp. 89–98
Ellison, R., 1986. 'Table Manners in Mesopotamia', *Bulletin of the Institute of Archaeology London* 23, pp. 151–9
Ennabli, A., 1976. *Lampes Chrétiennes de Tunisie*, Paris
Erdmann, K., 1935. 'Partho-Sasanian Ceramics', *The Burlington Magazine* 67/389 (August), pp. 71–7

Ettinghausen, R., 1938. 'Parthian and Sasanian Pottery', in Pope, A. U. (ed.), vol. I, pp. 646–80, vol. IV, pls 179–96
Ettlinger, E., Hedinger, B., Hoffman, B., Kenrick, P., Pucci, G., Roth-Rubi, K., Schneider, G., von Schnurbein, S., Wells, C. & Zabehlicky-Scheffenegger, S., 1990. *Conspectus Formarum Terrae Sigillatae Italico Modo Confectae*, Bonn, Habelt
Ettlinger, E., 1990. 'Die italische Produktion: 1. Die klassische Zeit', in Ettlinger, E. et al, pp. 4–13
Evans, A., 1921. *The Palace of Minos I*, London
Evely, D., 1988. 'The potter's wheel in Minoan Crete', *Annual of the British School at Athens* 83
Evison, V., 1979. *A Corpus of Wheel-Thrown Pottery in Anglo-Saxon Graves*

Fairbrother, J. R., 1990. *Faccombe Netherton: Excavations of a Saxon and Medieval Manorial Complex*, 2 vols, British Museum Occasional Paper 74
Fakhry, A., 1983. *The Oases of Egypt: Bahriyah and Farafra Oases*, vol. II, Cairo, American University in Cairo Press
Falk, A., 1991. 'Herstellungsspuren an mittelalterlicher und frühneuzeitlicher Keramik aus Lübeck', in *Töpferei- und Keramikforschung* 2, Bonn, pp. 357–65
Fan Dongqing, 1991. 'Early Ding Wares in the Shanghai Museum', *Orientations*, February 1991, vol. 22, no. 2, pp. 48–53
Farley, M., 1983. 'A Mirror Burial at Dorton, Buckinghamshire', *Proceedings of the Prehistoric Society* 49, pp. 269–302
Farmer, P. G., 1979. *An introduction to Scarborough ware and a reassessment of knight jugs*
Farmer, P. G. & N. C., 1982. 'The dating of the Scarborough ware pottery industry', *Medieval Ceramics* 6, pp. 66–86
Fattovich, R., 1996. 'The Origins of the Kingdom of Kush: views from the African hinterland', *Archéologie du Nil Moyen* 7, pp. 69–78
Feng Xianming, 1959. 'Henan, Gongxian guyao zhi diaocha jiyao' (An investigation into the Gongxian kilns, Henan), *Wenwu* 1959.3, pp. 56–8
Feng Xianming, 1964. 'Henan Mixian, Fengfu Tang Song Guyao Zhidiao cha' (An investigation into the Tang and Song kiln at Fengfu, Mixain, Henan), *Wenwu* 1964.3, pp. 45, 47–55
Feng Xianming, 1985. 'Red-glazed and Underglazed-red Porcelain of the Yuan Dynasty', *Orientations* 16 (July), pp. 44–8
Feng Xianming, 1987. *Essays on Chinese Old Ceramics*, Hong Kong
Fielden, K., 1977. 'Tell Brak 1976: the pottery', *Iraq* 39, pp. 245–55
Fielden, K., 1981. 'A Late Uruk pottery group from Tell Brak, 1978', *Iraq* 43, pp. 157–66
Finke, U. Ch., 1983. 'Über Westerwälder Steinzeug', in *Salzglasiertes Steinzeug*, Höhr-Grenzhausen, Keramikmuseum Westerwald
Finster, B. & Schmidt, J., 1976. 'Sasanidische u. Frühislamische Ruinen im Iraq', *Baghdader Mitteilungen* 8, pp. 1–169, Taf. 1–79
Fiocco, C. & Gherardi, G., 1994. *La ceramica di Deruta dal XIII al XVIII secolo*, Perugia
Fischer, E. & Shah, H., 1970. *Rural Craftsmen and their Work: Equipment and techniques in the Mer village of Ratadi in Saurashtra, India*, Ahmedabad
Fisher, N. (ed.), 1993. *Mud, Mirror and Thread: Folk traditions of rural India*, Middletown, NJ, Santa Fe, NM & Ahmedabad
Fleming, D., 1989. 'Eggshell Ware Pottery in Achaemenid Mesopotamia', *Iraq* 51, pp. 165–85
Ford, D., 1995. 'Medieval pottery in Staffordshire, AD 800–1600: A Review', *Staffordshire Archaeological Studies* 7, Stoke-on-Trent
Forti, L., 1965. *La ceramica di Gnathia*, Naples
Foster, K. P., 1991. 'Ceramic imagery in ancient Near Eastern literature', in Vandiver, P. B. et al (eds), pp. 389–413
Francaviglia, V. & Palmieri, A. M., 1988. 'Ceramic Fabrics and Source Locations in the Khartoum Province', in Caneva (ed.), 1988, pp. 345–58
Frankel, D., 1979. *Archaeologists at work: Studies on Halaf pottery*, London
Franken, H. J. & Kalsbeek, J., 1984. 'Some techniques used by the potters of Tell ed-Der', in De Meyer, L. (ed.), *Tell ed-Der IV: Progress reports*, 2nd series, Leuven, pp. 81–9
Freestone, I. C. & Hughes, M. J., 1989. 'Examination of Ceramics from Qasrij Cliff and Khirbet Qasrij', in Curtis, J. E. et al, pp. 61–75, figs 47–9
Freestone, I. C. & Rigby, V., 1982. 'Class B cordoned and other imported wares from Hengistbury Head, Dorset', in Freestone, I. C., Johns, C. & Potter, T. (eds), *Current Research in Ceramics: Thin-section studies*, London, British Museum Occasional Paper 32, pp. 29–42
Freestone, I. C. & Rigby, V., 1988. 'The introduction of Roman ceramic styles and techniques into Roman Britain: a case study from the King Harry Lane cemetery, St Albans, Hertfordshire', in Sayre, E. V., Vandiver, P., Druzik, J. & Stevenson, C. (eds), *Materials Issues in Art and Archaeology*, Materials Research Society Symposium Proceedings 123, pp. 109–15
Freestone, I. C., 1991a. 'Looking into Glass', in Bowman (ed.), pp. 37–56
Freestone, I. C., 1991b. 'Technical Examination of Neo-Assyrian Glazed Wall Plaques', *Iraq* 53, pp. 55–8
Freestone, I. C., 1993. 'A technical study of Limehouse ware', in Drakard, D. (ed.), pp. 68–73
Freestone, I. C., Middleton, A. P. & Meeks, N. D., 1994. 'Significance of phosphate in ceramic bodies: discussion', *Journal of Archaeological Science* 21, pp. 425–6
Fremersdorf, F., 1922. *Römische Bildlampen*, Bonn
French, P. G., 1990. 'A Preliminary study of pottery in Lower Egypt in the Late Dynastic and Ptolemaic Periods', *Cahiers de la céramique égyptienne* 3, Cairo, pp. 83–93
Friendship-Taylor, D. E., 1983/4. 'Pottery-making and open firing at Piddington Romano-British Villa, August, 1983', *Bulletin of the Experimental Firing Group* 2, pp. 75–81
Fujii, H. (ed.), 1976. *Al-Tar I: Excavations in Iraq, 1971–1974*, Tokyo
Fujii, H. et al, 1987. 'Working report on first season of Japanese archaeological excavation in Saddam [Dam] Salvage Project', in Damerji, M. (ed.), pp. 33–61
Fujii, H., 1987. 'Working report on second season of Japanese archaeological excavation in Saddam Dam Salvage Project (Tell Jigan)', in Damerji, M. (ed.), pp. 62–7
Fujio Nakazawa & Shoko Hasegawa, 1995. *Blue and White in the Yuan and Ming Dynasties*, vol. 8 (in Japanese), Heibonsha Chinese Ceramics series, supervised by Gakuji Hasebe, Japan
Fukai, S., 1981. *Ceramics of Ancient Persia*, New York, Tokyo & Kyoto
Fulford, M. G. & Peacock, D. P. S., 1984. *Excavations at Carthage: The British Mission*, vols I, II, Sheffield
Fung Ping Shan Museum, University of Hong Kong, 1992. *Ceramic Finds from Jingdezhen Kilns (10th–17th Century): Exhibition catalogue jointly presented by the Jingdezhen Institute of Ceramic Archaeology and the Fung Ping Shan Museum, University of Hong Kong*, 8 April to 19 June 1992, Fung Ping Shan Museum, Hong Kong

Gabus, J. & Junod, R.-L., 1967. *Amlash Art*, Berne
Gadd, C. J., 1940. 'Tablets from Chagar Bazar and Tell Brak, 1937–38', *Iraq* 7, pp. 22–66
Gaimster, D. R. M., 1988. 'Pottery production in the Lower Rhineland: the Duisburg sequence *c.* 1400–1800', in Gaimster, D. R. M., Redknap, M. & Wegner, H.-H. (eds), *Medieval and later pottery from the Rhineland and its markets*, British Archaeological Reports Int. Ser. 440, pp. 151–72
Gaimster, D. R. M., 1991. 'The development of decorated earthenware in the Lower Rhineland *c.* 1550–1675: recent finds from Duisburg', in Burhenne, V., Gaimster, D. R. M., Stephan, H.-G. & Schilling, L., *Frühe dekorierte Irdenware. Malhorndekor und Kammstrichverzierung vom Niederrhein und aus dem Köln-Frechener Raum*, Führer und Schriften des Rheinischen Freilichtmuseums 43, Kommern/Cologne, pp. 45–60
Gaimster, D. R. M. & Redknap, M. (eds), 1992. *Everyday and Exotic Pottery from Europe c. 650–1900: Studies in Honour of John Hurst*, Oxbow Monograph 23, Oxford
Gaimster, D. R. M. & Verhaeghe, F., 1992. 'Handles with face-masks: a cross-Channel type of late medieval highly decorated basin', in Gaimster, D. R. M. & Redknap, M. (eds), pp. 303–23
Gaimster, D. R. M., 1993. 'Cross-Channel ceramic trade in the late Middle Ages: evidence for the spread of Hanseatic culture to Britain', in Gläser-Mührenberg, M. (ed.), *Archäologie des Mittelalters und Bauforschung in Hanseraum. Eine Festschrift für Günter Fehring*, Schriften des Kulturhistorischen Museums in Rostock 1, Rostock, pp. 251–60
Gaimster, D. R. M., 1994. 'The archaeology of post-medieval society, *c.* 1450–1750: material culture studies in Britain since the War', in *Building on the Past: Papers celebrating 150 years of the Royal Archaeological Institute*, London, Royal Archaeological Institute, pp. 283–312
Gaimster, D. R. M., 1995. 'Stoneware jug, applied in relief with scenes after Sebald Beham, 1576', in Bartrum, G., *German Renaissance Prints 1450–1550*, cat. no. 124, London, British Museum Press
Gaimster, D. R. M., 1997. *German Stoneware 1200–1900: Archaeology and Cultural History*, London, British Museum Press
Gaimster, D. R. M. & Hurst, J. G. H., forthcoming (1997). 'Werra ware in Britain, Ireland and North America', *Post-Medieval Archaeology* 31
Gaimster, D. R. M. & Nenk, B., forthcoming (1997). 'Fittings, furnishings and utensils: English households in transition 1400–1600', in Gaimster, D. R. M. & Stamper, P. (eds), *The Age of Transition: The Archaeology of English Culture 1400–1600*, Oxford, Oxbow Books
Ganjavi, S., 1975. 'Survey in Xuzestan, 1974', in *Proceedings of the Third International Symposium on Archaeological Research in Iran (Tehran 1974)*, Tehran, pp. 137–46
Garbsch, J., 1982. *Terra Sigillata*, Munich
Gardiner, M., 1989. 'A Medieval Anthropomorphic Jug from Crawley', *Sussex Archaeological Collections* 127, pp. 247–9
Gates, M-H., 1988. 'Dialogues Between Ancient Near Eastern Texts and the Archaeological Record: Test Cases from Bronze Age Syria', *Bulletin of the American Schools of Oriental Research* 270 (May), pp. 63–91
Gatti, S. & Onorati, M. T., 1992. 'Praeneste medio-Repubblicana: Gentes ed attività produttive', in *AaVv La Necropoli di Praeneste: periodi orientalizzante e medio-repubblicano*, Palestrina, Comune, pp. 189–252
Gempeler, R., 1992. *Elephantine X: Die Keramik römischer bis früharabischer Zeit*, Mainz am Rhein, von Zabern
Gentilini, A., Ravanelli Guidotti, C., & Morello, G., 1993. *L'Istoriato, libri a stampa e maioliche italiane del cinquecento*, Città del Vaticano, Biblioteca Apostolica Vaticana
Geus, F., 1984. 'Excavations at El Kadada and the Neolithic of the Central Sudan', in Krzyzaniak, L. & Kobusiewicz, M. (eds), *Origin and Early Development of Food-Producing Cultures in North-Eastern Africa*, Poznan, pp. 361–72
Ghirshman, R., 1938/9. *Fouilles de Sialk près de Kashan*, 2 vols, Paris
Ghirshman, R., 1964. *Persia from the Origins to Alexander the Great*, London
Gibson, A., 1986. 'The excavation of an experimental firing area at Stamford Hall, Leicester: 1985', *Bulletin of the Experimental Firing Group* 4, pp. 5–14
Gibson, A. & Woods, A., 1990. *Prehistoric Pottery for the Archaeologist*, Leicester, Leicester University Press
Gibson, McG., 1972. *The City and Area of Kish*, Miami, FL
Gibson, McG., 1974. 'Coins as a Tool in Archaeological Surface Survey', in Kouymjian, D. K. (ed.), pp. 9–14
Gibson, McG. & McMahon, A., 1995. 'Investigation of the Early Dynastic-Akkadian transition: Report of the 18th and 19th seasons of excavation in Area WF, Nippur', *Iraq* 57, pp. 1–39
Gilotta, F., 1985. *Gutti e askoi a rilievo italioti ed etruschi*, Rome
Glanzman, W. D., 1983. 'Xeroradiographic examination of pottery manufacturing techniques: A test case from the Baq'ah Valley, Jordan', *MASCA Journal* 2, pp. 163–9
Göbels, K., 1985. *Rheinisches Töpferhandwerk gezeigt am Beispiel der Frechener Kannen-, Duppen- und Pfeifenbäcker*, 1st edn 1971, Cologne
Godden, G. (ed.), 1983. *Staffordshire Porcelain*, London, Barrie & Jenkins
Godlewski, W. (ed.), 1990. *Coptic and Nubian Pottery, Part 1: International Workshop, Nieborów, August 29–31, 1988*, Warsaw, National Museum, Occasional Paper 1
Goethert, K., 1993. 'Die verzierten spätantiken Tonlampen des Rheinischen Landesmuseums Trier', in *Trierer Zeitschrift* 56
Goff, C., 1969. 'Excavations at Baba Jan, 1967: Second Preliminary Report', *Iran* 7, pp. 115–30, pls 1–4
Goff, C., 1970. 'Excavations at Baba Jan, 1968: Third Preliminary Report', *Iran* 8, pp. 141–56, pls 1–4
Goff, C., 1977. 'Excavations at Baba Jan: The Architecture of the East Mound, Levels II and III', *Iran* 15, pp. 103–40, pls 1–20
Goff, C., 1978. 'Excavations at Baba Jan: The Pottery and Metal from Levels III and II', *Iran* 16, pp. 29–65, pls 1–4
Goff, C., 1985. 'Excavations at Baba Jan: The Architecture and Pottery of Level I', *Iran* 23, pp. 1–20
Goldthwaite, R., 1989. 'The economic and social world of Renaissance maiolica', *Renaissance Quarterly* 42, no. 1, pp. 1–32
Golvin, L., Thiriot, J. & Zakariya, M., 1982. *Les Potiers de Fustat*, Cairo, Institut Français d'Archéologie Orientale du Caire
Gompertz, G., 1963. *Korean Celadon*, London, Faber & Faber
Goodwin, J., 1995. The First Millennium B.C. Pottery', in Baird, D., Campbell, S. & Watkins, T. (eds), *Excavations at Kharabeh Shattani*, Edinburgh, vol. 2, pp. 91–141
Gose, P., 1994. *Deathly Waters and Hungry Mountains: Agrarian Ritual and Class Formation in an Andean Town*, Toronto, University of Toronto Press
Gosselain, O. P., 1992. 'Bonfire of the enquiries: Pottery firing temperatures in archaeology: what for?', *Journal of Archaeological Science* 19, pp. 243–59
Gourdin, W. H. & Kingery, W. D., 1975. 'The Beginnings of Pyrotechnology: Neolithic and Egyptian lime plaster', *Journal of Field Archaeology* 2, pp. 133–50
Grant, A., 1983. *North Devon Pottery: The Seventeenth Century*, Exeter
Greaves, S. J., 1976. 'A post-medieval excavation in Woodbank Street, Burslem, Stoke-on-Trent, Staffs., SJ 866497', *City of Stoke-on-Trent Museum Archaeological Report* 10, Stoke-on-Trent
Green, B. et al, 1981. 'The Illington-Lackford workshop', in Evison, V. (ed.), *Angles, Saxons and Jutes: Essays Presented to J. N. L. Myres*, pp. 187–226
Greene, K., 1979. *Report on the Excavations at Usk, 1965–1976: The Pre-Flavian Fine Wares*, Cardiff, University of Wales Press
Greene, K., 1992. *Interpreting the Past: Roman Pottery*, London, British Museum Press
Grigoni, C., 1942. 'Le malattie professionali dei vasai', *Faenza* 20, pp. 51–7
Grigsby, L. B., 1993. *English Slip-decorated Earthenware at Williamsburg*, Colonial Williamsburg Foundation, Williamsburg, VA
Grimes, W. F., 1930. *Holt, Denbighshire, the Works-Depôt of the Twentieth Legion at Castle Lyons*, London
Grimm, G., 1972. 'Two Early Imperial Faience Vessels from Egypt', in *Miscellanea Wilbouriana* 1, Brooklyn, pp. 71–101
Gudea, N., 1987. 'Pannonian Glazed Pottery: a view from the East', in *Rei Cretariae Romanae Fautorum*, Acta 25–6
Güner, G., 1988. *Anadolu'da yasamakta olan ilkel çömlekçilik*, Istanbul
Gunter, A. C., 1988. 'The Art of Eating and Drinking in Ancient Iran', *Asian Art* 1/2 (Spring), pp. 3–54

Guo Yanyi, 1987. 'Raw materials for making porcelain and the characteristics of porcelain wares in north and south China', *Archaeometry* 29, pp. 3–20
Guyot, Paye & Le Tourneau, 1935. 'L'Industrie de la Poterie à Fès', *Bulletin Économique et Social du Maroc* II, pp. 268–72
Gyllensvard, B., 1971. *Chinese Gold, Silver and Porcelain: The Kempe Collection*, New York

Haaland, R., 1987. *Socio-economic differentiation in the Neolithic Sudan*, BAR Int. Ser. S–350, Oxford
Haaland, R., 1995. 'Early Holocene sites and the emergence of sedentism in the Atbara region', *Cahiers de Recherches de l'Institut de Papyrologie et d'Egyptologie de Lille* 17, pp. 97–115
Haditti, A.-M. M. A. R. al-, 1995. 'Umm Kheshm: A summary report', *Mesopotamia* 30, pp. 217–39
Haerinck, E., 1983. *La ceramique en Iran pendant la periode parthe (ca. 250 av. J.C. a ca. 225 apres J.C.): Typologie, chronologie et distribution*, Gent
Haerinck, E., 1989. 'The Achaemenid (Iron Age IV) Period in Gilan, Iran', in *Archaeologica et Orientalis: Miscellanea in Honorem Louis Vanden Berghe*, De Meyer, L. & Haerinck, E. (eds), Gent, pp. 455–74
Haggar, R. G., 1959. *Pottery through the Ages*, London, Methuen
Hähnel, E., 1992. 'Archäometrie: Siegburger Keramik und Naturwissenschaften', in Hähnel, E. (ed.), *Siegburger Steinzeug: Bestandkatalog, Bd. 2*, Cologne, Führer und Schriften des Rheinischen Freilichtmuseums und Landesmuseums für Volkskunde in Kommern, nr. 38, pp. 9–37
Hakem, A. el & Khabir, A. R. M., 1989. 'Sarourab 2: a contribution to the Early Khartoum tradition from Bauda site', in Krzyzaniak, L. & Kobusiewicz, M. (eds), *Late Prehistory of the Nile Basin and the Sahara*, Poznan, pp. 381–6
Hakemi, A., 1968. 'Kaluraz and the Civilisation of the Mardes', *Archaeologia Viva* 1 (September/November), pp. 63–81
Halfpenny, P. & Lockett, T. (eds), 1979. *Staffordshire Porcelain 1740–1851*, Hanley, Stoke-on-Trent, City Museum and Art Gallery
Halfpenny, P., 1991. *English Earthenware Figures 1740–1840*, Woodbridge, Suffolk, Antique Collectors' Club
Hall, H. R. & Woolley, C. L. et al, 1927. *Ur Excavations, Volume I: Al-'Ubaid*, London
Hamer, F., 1985. 'The science of lustre', in Caiger-Smith, A. (ed.), pp. 221–36
Hamer, F. & J., 1986. *The Potter's Dictionary of Materials and Techniques*, London, A. & C. Black
Hamerow, H., 1987. 'Anglo-Saxon settlement pottery and the spatial development at Mucking, Essex', *Berichten van de Rijksdienst vor het Oudheidugkundig Bodemonderzoek* 37, pp. 245–73
Hamerow, H., 1993. *Excavations at Mucking, vol. 2: The Anglo-Saxon Settlement*
Hamilton, S., 1985. 'Iron Age Pottery', in Bedwin, O. & Holgate, R., 'Excavations at Copse Farm, Oving, West Sussex', *Proceedings of the Prehistoric Society* 51, pp. 220–28
Hamlin, C., 1974. 'The early second millennium ceramic assemblage of Dinkha Tepe', *Iran* 12, pp. 125–53
Hannestad, L., 1983. *Ikaros: The Hellenistic Settlements, Volume 2: The Hellenistic Pottery from Failaka, with a Survey of Hellenistic Pottery in the Near East*, Aarhus
Harden, D. B., 1934. 'Excavations at Kish and Barghuthiat 1933, II: The Pottery', *Iraq* 1, pp. 124–36, pl. XVII
Harlan, J. F., 1982. 'Excavations at Locality IIc', in Hoffman, M. A. (ed.), pp. 14–25
Harper, P. O. et al, 1978. *The Royal Hunter: Art of the Sasanian empire*, New York
Harris, O., 1987. 'The Dead and the Devils among the Bolivian Laymi', in Bloch, M. & Parry, J. (eds), *Death and the Regeneration of Life*, 2nd edn, Cambridge, Cambridge University Press, pp. 45–73
Harris, W. V., 1980. 'Roman Terracotta Lamps: the organization of an industry', in *Journal of Roman Studies* 70
Harris, W. V., 1993. 'Production, Distribution, and *instrumentum domesticum*', in Harris, W. V. (ed.), *The Inscribed Economy*, Ann Arbor, MI
Hartman, L. & Oppenheim, A. L., 1950. 'On Beer and Brewing Techniques in Ancient Mesopotamia', *Journal of the American Oriental Society*, Supplement 10
Hatsushige, O. & Mitsunori, T., 1996. *Nihon Kokogaku Yogo Jiken* (Dictionary of Archaeological Terms), Tokyo, Kashiwa Shobo
Hauser, S. R., 1996. 'The Production of Pottery in Arsacid Ashur', in Bartl, K. & Hauser, S. R. (eds), *Continuity and Change in Northern Mesopotamia from the Hellenistic to the Early Islamic Period*, Berlin, pp. 55–85
Hawkes, S., 1974. 'British Antiquity', *Archaeological Journal* 131, pp. 412–14
Hayes, J. W., 1972. *Late Roman Pottery*, London, British School at Rome
Hayes, J. W., 1980. *Late Roman Pottery: Supplement*, London, British School at Rome
Hayes, J. W., 1983. 'The Villa Dionysus Excavations, Knossos: The Pottery', *Annual of the British School at Athens* 78, pp. 96–169
Hayes, J. W., 1985. 'Sigillate Orientali', *Atlante delle Forme Ceramiche II, Enciclopedia dell'Arte Antica*, Rome, pp. 1–95
Hayes, J. W., 1991. 'Fine wares in the Hellenistic world', in Rasmussen, T. & Spivey, N., pp. 183–202
Hayes, J. W., 1997. *Handbook of Mediterranean Roman Pottery*, London, British Museum Press
Hayes, W. C., 1937. *Glazed Tiles from a Palace of Ramesses II at Kantir*, New York
Hedges, R. E. M. & Moorey, P. R. S., 1975. 'Pre-Islamic glazes at Kish and Nineveh in Iraq', *Archaeometry* 17, pp. 25–43
Hedges, R. E. M., 1982. 'Early Glazed Pottery and Faience in Mesopotamia', in Wertime, T. A. & S. F. (eds), *Early Pyrotechnology: The evolution of the first fire-using industries*, Washington, DC, Smithsonian Institution Press, pp. 93–103
Heinrich, E., 1935. *Sechster vorläufiger Bericht über die von der Deutschen Forschungs Gemeinschaft in Uruk-Warka unternommenen Ausgrabungen*, Berlin
Hellebrandt, H., 1977. 'Raerener Steinzeug', *in Steinzeug aus dem Raerener und Aachener Raum*, Aachener Beiträge für Baugeschichte und Heimatkunst, Bd. 4, Aachen, Aachener Geschichtsverein, pp. 9–171
Hendrickx, S., 1996. 'The Relative Chronology of the Naqada Culture: Problems and Possibilities', in Spencer, A. J. (ed.), pp. 36–69
Henrickson, E. F., 1986. 'Ceramic Evidence for Cultural Interaction between Chalcolithic Mesopotamia and Western Iran', in Kingery, W. D. (ed.), pp. 87–132
Henrickson, R. C., 1983. 'A Reconstruction of the Painted Chamber Ceiling at Baba Jan', *Iranica Antiqua* 18, pp. 82–96
Henrickson, R. C., 1991. 'Wheelmade or wheel-finished? Interpretation of "wheelmarks" on pottery', in Vandiver, P. B., Druzik, J. & Wheeler, G. S. (eds), *Materials Issues in Art and Archaeology II*, Pittsburgh, Materials Research Society Symposium 185, pp. 523–41
Henrickson, R. C., 1992. 'Analysis of use wear on ceramic potter's tools', in Vandiver et al (eds), pp. 475–93
Herborn, W., Klinger, S. & Schainberg, H., 1987. 'Studien zur Siegburger Töpferei', in Hähnel, E. (ed.), *Siegburger Steinzeug. Bestandkatalog, Bd. 2*, Führer und Schriften des Rheinischen Landesmuseums und Landesmuseums für Volkskunde in Kommern, 31, Cologne, pp. 69–103
Herrmann, C., 1985. *Formen fur Ägyptischen Fayence*, Freiburg
Herrmann, G., 1977. *The Iranian Revival*, Oxford
Herrmann, G., Kurbansakhatov, K. & Simpson, St J. et al, 1996. 'The International Merv Project: Preliminary Report on the Fourth Season (1995)', *Iran* 34, pp. 1–22, pls I–VI
Herzfeld, E., 1930. *Die Vorgeschichtlichen töpfereien von Samarra*, Berlin
Hickmann, E., 1990. *Musik aus dem altertum der Neuen welt*, Frankfurt, Bern, New York & Paris, Peter Lang
Hickmann, E., 1996. 'The Iconography of Dualism: Pre-Columbian Instruments and Sounds as Offerings?', in Baumann, M. P. (ed.)
Higuchi, T., 1968. *Japanese Arts: Jomon Pottery*, Tokyo, Kodansha
Hijara, I., 1980. 'Three new graves at Arpachiyah', *World Archaeology* 10/2, pp. 125–8
Hijara, I. et al, 1980. 'Arpachiyah 1976', *Iraq* 42, pp. 131–54
Hillewaert, B., 1992. 'An English lady in Flanders: reflections on a head in Scarborough ware', in Gaimster, D. & Redknap, M. (eds), *Everyday and Exotic Pottery from Europe c. 650–1900*, pp. 76–82
Hills, C., 1974. 'A runic pot from Spong Hill, North Elmham', *Antiquaries Journal* 54, pp. 87–91
Hills, C., 1977. 'The Anglo-Saxon cemetery at Spong Hill, North Elmham, Part I', *East Anglian Archaeological Report* 6
Hills, C., 1979. Review of Myres (1977), *Antiquity* 53, pp. 65–7
Hills, C., 1980a. 'Anglo-Saxon cremation cemeteries with particular reference to Spong Hill, Norfolk', in Rahtz, P. et al (eds), *Anglo-Saxon Cemeteries*, British Archaeological Reports, British Series 82, pp. 197–207
Hills, C., 1980b. 'Anglo-Saxon chairperson', *Antiquity* 54, pp. 52–4
Hills, C. & Penn, K., 1981. 'The Anglo-Saxon cemetery at Spong Hill, North Elmham, Part II', *East Anglian Archaeological Report* 11
Hills, C., 1983. 'Animal stamps on Anglo-Saxon pottery in East Anglia', *Studien zur Sachsenforschung* 4, pp. 93–110
Hills, C. et al, 1984. 'The Anglo-Saxon cemetery at Spong Hill, North Elmham, Part III', *East Anglian Archaeology* 21
Hills, C., 1987. 'Spong Hill, Part IV, Catalogue of Cremations', *East Anglian Archaeology* 34
Hills, C., 1994. 'The Anglo-Saxon Cemetery at Spong Hill, North Elmham, Part V, Catalogue of Cremations', *East Anglian Archaeological Report* 67
Hilprecht, H. V., 1903. *Explorations in Bible Lands During the 19th Century*, Edinburgh
Hirst, S. & Clark, D., forthcoming. *Excavations at Mucking: Volume 3: The Anglo-Saxon Cemeteries*
Hitchling, S., 1995. 'Pottery in Ethiopia', *Ceramic Review* 151, pp. 40–42
Hobson, R. L., 1903. *Catalogue of the Collection of English Pottery in the Department of British and Medieval Antiquities and Ethnography of the British Museum*, London, British Museum
Hochuli-Gysel, A., 1977. *Kleinasiatische glasierte Reliefkeramik: Acta Bernensia* VII, Bern, Stampfli
Hoffman, M. A. (ed.), 1982a. *The Predynastic of Hierakonpolis, an Interim Report: Egyptian Studies Association* 1, Cairo
Hoffman, M. A., 1982b. 'Excavations at Locality 29', in Hoffman, M. A. (ed.), 1982a, pp. 7–13
Hoffmann, B., 1995. 'A propos des relations entre les sigillées de La Graufesenque et les sigillées d'Italie', *Annali della scuola normale superiore di Pisa* 25, pp. 1–2
Højlund, F. & Hellmuth Andersen, H. et al, 1994. *Qala'at al-Bahrain, Volume 1: The Northern City Wall and the Islamic Fortress*, Aarhus, Moesgard
Hole, F., 1984. 'Analysis of structure and design in prehistoric ceramics', *World Archaeology* 15/3, pp. 326–47
Holgate, D., 1971. *New Hall and its Imitators*, London, Faber & Faber
Holgate, D., 1987. *New Hall*, London, Faber & Faber
Hölscher, U., 1951. *The Excavation of Medinet Habu IV*, Chicago
Holthoer, R., 1977. *New Kingdom Pharaonic Sites: The Pottery*, Lund
Honey, W. B., 1946. *The Art of the Potter*, London, Faber & Faber
Hong Kong Museum of Art & Jingdezhen Museum of Ceramic History (eds), 1989. *Imperial Porcelain of the Yongle and Xuande Periods excavated from the Site of the Ming Imperial Factory at Jingdezhen*, Urban Council of Hong Kong
Hong Kong Museum of Art, 1990. *Brush and Clay: Chinese porcelain of the early 20th century*, Urban Council of Hong Kong
Hong Kong Museum of Art, 1994a. *Ancient Chinese Tea Wares*, Flagstaff House Museum of Teaware, Hong Kong
Hong Kong Museum of Art, 1994b. *Song Ceramics from the Kwan Collection*, Hong Kong
Hood, S., 1978. *The Arts in Prehistoric Greece*, London
Hoopes, J. W. & Barnett, W. K., 1995. 'The shape of early pottery studies', in Barnett, W. K. & Hoopes, J. W. (eds), *The Emergence of Pottery: Technology and innovation in ancient societies*, Washington, DC, Smithsonian Institution Press, pp. 1–7
Hope, C., 1981. 'Two ancient Egyptian potter's wheels', *Journal of the Society for the Study of Egyptian Antiquities* 11 (3), Toronto
Hope, C., 1982a. 'Concerning Egyptian potter's wheels', *Journal of the Society for the Study of Egyptian Antiquities* 12 (1), Toronto
Hope, C., 1982b. 'Blue-painted pottery', in *Egypt's Golden Age: The Art of Living in the New Kingdom 1558–1085 B.C.*, Boston Museum of Fine Arts, pp. 88–100
Hope, C., 1987a. *Egyptian Pottery*, Aylesbury
Hope, C., 1987b. 'Blue-painted and polychrome decorated pottery from Amarna: a preliminary corpus', *Cahiers de la céramique égyptienne* 2, pp. 17–92
Horschik, J., 1978. *Steinzeug 15. bis 19. Jahrhundert von Bürgel bis Muskau*, Dresden
Howard, H. & Morris, E. L. (eds), 1981. *Production and Distribution: A ceramic viewpoint*, Oxford, BAR Int. Ser. 120
Howard, H. 1981. 'In the wake of distribution: towards an integrated approach to ceramic studies in prehistoric Britain', in Howard, H. & Morris, E. L. (eds), pp. 1–30
Howard-Johnston, J., 1995. 'The Two Great Powers in Late Antiquity: a Comparison', in Cameron, A. (ed.), *The Byzantine and Early Islamic Near East III: States, Resources and Armies: Papers of the Third Workshop on Late Antiquity and Early Islam*, Princeton, NJ, pp. 157–226
Hsieh Ming-liang, 1987. *Catalogue of the Special Exhibition of Ting Ware White Porcelain*, National Palace Museum, Taipei, Taiwan
Huggett, J., 1988. 'Imported grave goods and the early Anglo-Saxon economy', *Medieval Archaeology* 32, pp. 63–96
Hurst, J., 1959. 'Middle Saxon Pottery', in Dunning, G. et al, 'Anglo-Saxon Pottery: a Symposium', *Medieval Archaeology* 3, pp. 13–31
Hurst, J. G., 1976. 'The Pottery', in Wilson, D. M. (ed), *The Archaeology of Anglo-Saxon England*, pp. 283–348
Hurst, J. G., Neal, D. S. & van Beuningen, H. J. E., 1986. *Pottery Produced and Traded in North-West Europe, 1350–1650*, Rotterdam Papers 6, Rotterdam
Hurst, J., 1991. 'Italian pottery imported into Britain', in Wilson, T. (ed.), pp. 212–31
Huyler, S. P., 1993.'Clay, Sacred and Sublime: Terracotta in India', in Fisher, N. (ed.)
Huyler, S. P., 1996. *Gifts of Earth: Terracottas and clay sculptures of India*, Middletown, NJ, Ahmedabad & New Delhi

Ibrahim, J. K., 1986. *Pre-Islamic Settlement in Jazirah*, Baghdad
Ii, H., 1988. 'Seals and seal impressions from Tell Gubba', *Al-Rafidan* 9, pp. 97–134, pls 29–38
Ii, H., 1991. '"Potters tool" in Mesopotamia during the fifth to third millennium B.C.' (in Japanese), *Al-Rafidan* 12, pp. 1–57
Ikutaro Itoh, 1992. 'Koreanization in Koryo Celadon', *Orientations*, Dec. 1992
Institut du Monde Arabe, 1994. *Couleurs de Tunisie*, Paris, Adam Biro
International Labour Office, 1984. *Small-scale Brickmaking*, Technical Memorandum 6, Geneva
Invernizzi, A., 1977. 'Trench on the South Side of the Archive Square', *Mesopotamia* 12, pp. 19–20
Ippolitoni, F., 1970/71. 'The Pottery of Tell es-Sawwan: First Season', *Mesopotamia* 5/6, pp. 105–79

Izikowitz, K. G., 1935. *Musical and Other Sound Instruments of the South American Indians*, 2nd edn, East Ardsley & Wakefield, S. R. Publishers

Jacobs, L., 1991/2. 'Causes for the pale colour of iron-containing, second millennium B.C. pottery from three archaeological sites in Mesopotamia', *Newsletter, Department of Pottery Technology, Leiden University* 9/10, pp. 7–21

James, S. et al, 1984. 'An Early Medieval Building Tradition', *Archaeological Journal* 141, pp. 182–215

Janssen, H. L. & de Paepe, P. A., 1976. 'Petrological examination of medieval pottery from South Limburg and the Rhineland', *Berichten van de Rijksdienst voor het Oudheidkundig Bodemonderzoek* 26, pp. 217–27

Janssen, W., 1987. 'Der technische Wandel der Töpferöfen von der Karolingerzeit zum Hochmittelalter, dargestellt anhand rheinischer Beispiele', in Chapelot, J., Galinié, J. & Pilet-Lemière, J. (eds), *La Céramique (V^e-XIXe s.). Fabrication – Commercialisation – Utilisation. Actes de premier colloque international d'archéologie médiévale, 4–6 Octobre 1985)*, Caen, Société d'Archéologie Médiévale, pp. 107–19

Jasim, S. A., 1985. *The Ubaid Period in Iraq: Recent excavations in the Hamrin region*, Oxford

Jayakar, P., 1980. *The Earthen Drum: An introduction to the ritual arts of rural India*, New Delhi

Jenkins, I. & Sloan, K., 1996. *Vases and Volcanoes: Sir William Hamilton and his Collection*, London, British Museum Press

Jenkins, I., 1996. '"Contemporary Minds": William Hamilton's affair with antiquity', in Jenkins, I. & Sloan, K., pp. 40–64

Jenner, A., 1985. 'The potter's wheel – a product of function or tradition', *London Archaeologist* 5, no. 5 (Winter), pp. 130–34

Jennings, S., 1992. *Medieval Pottery in the Yorkshire Museum*

Jenyns, R. S., 1971. *Japanese Pottery*, London, Faber & Faber

Jing Zhuyou, 1996. 'Santai chutude baiding guanzi yuan ciqi' (Porcelains bearing the character guan unearthed at Santai), *Sichuan Wenwu* 1996.1, pp. 57–8

Johnson, A. C., 1936. *Roman Egypt to the reign of Diocletian, Economic Survey of Ancient Rome, II*, Baltimore, Johns Hopkins Press

Johnson, G. A., 1973. *Local Exchange and Early State Development in South Western Iran*, Ann Arbor, University of Michigan Press

Johnston, A. W., 1985.'A Greek graffito from Arezzo', *Oxford Journal of Archaeology* (March), pp. 119–21

Johnston, D. & Williams, D., 1979. 'Relief-patterned tiles: a reappraisal', in McWhirr, A. (ed.), *Roman Brick and Tile*, British Archaeological Report 68, Oxford, pp. 375–93

Jomier, J., 1965. 'Al-Fustat', in *Encyclopaedia of Islam*, vol. II, 2nd edn, Leiden

Jones, M., 1975. 'Woolcomb warmers from Mucking, Essex', *Antiquaries' Journal* 55, pp. 411–13

Jones, R. E., 1986. *Greek and Cypriot Pottery: A review of scientific studies*, Athens, British School of Archaeology at Athens, Occasional Paper 1

Junker, H., 1930. 'Vorlaufiger Bericht über die zweite Grabung der Akademie der Wissenschaften in Wien auf der vorgeschichtlichen Siedlung Merimde Beni-Salâme vom 7 Februar bis 8 April 1930', Vorgelegt in der *Sitzung der phil.-hist.Klasse (Wien)*, 14 Mai 1930, Vienna

Jürgens, A., 1979. 'Ein mittelalterlicher Töpferbezirk in Langerwehe-Jüngersdorf, Kreis Düren', in *Ausgrabungen im Rheinland 1978*, Bonn, Rheinisches Landesmuseum, pp. 259–63

Jürgens, A. & Bös, B., 1983. 'Spätmittelalterliche und frühneuzeitliche Töpferöfen in Langerwehe, Kr. Düren und Frechen, Erftkreis', *Ausgrabungen in Rheinland 1981/82*, Bonn, Führer des Rheinischen Landesmuseums 112, pp. 201–7

Jürgens, A., 1985. 'Mittelalterliche und neuzeitliche Töpfereien in Frechen, Erftkreis', in *Ausgrabungen im Rheinland 1983/84*, Kunst und Altertum am Rhein 122, pp. 218–23

Jürgens, A., 1988. 'Langerwehe-Brühl-Frechen. Neue Grabungen und Erkenntnisse in Rheinischen Töpfereizentren', in Gaimster, D.R.M., Redknap, M. & Wegner, H.-H. (eds), *Zur Keramik des Mittelalters und der beginnenden Neuzeit im Rheinland/Medieval and later pottery from the Rhineland and its Markets*, Oxford, British Archaeological Reports Int. Ser. 440, pp. 125–50

Jürgens, A., 1993. 'Grabungen, Ofenbefunde und Keramikbestand des hochmittelalterlichen Töpfereibezirkes von Langerwehe–Jüngersdorf', in Jürgens, A., Mommsen, H., Beier, Th., Heimermann, D. & Hein, A., 'Untersuchungen zum hochmittelalterlichen Töpfereibezirk von Langerwehe–Jüngersdorf', *Nearchos* 1, pp. 79–92

Jürgens, A., 1995. 'Ausgrabungen und Restaurierungen von Töpferöfen in der Frechener Broichgasse', in Jürgens, A., Kleine, D. et al (eds), pp. 6–22

Jürgens, A., Kleine, D. et al (eds), 1995. *Ausgegraben. Keramik aus Frechen vom Mittelalter bis zum 19. Jahrhundert*, Keramikmuseum der Stadt Frechen, Frechen

Kaczmarczyk, A. & Hedges, R. E. M., 1983. *Ancient Egyptian Faience*, Warminster

Kaczmarczyk, A., 1986. 'The source of cobalt in ancient Egyptian pigments', in *Proceedings of the 24th International Archaeometry Symposium*, Olin, J. S. & Blackman, M. J. (eds), Washington, DC, Smithsonian Institution Press, pp. 369–76

Kaiser, W., 1957. 'Zur Inneren Chronologie der Naqadakultur', *Archaeologica Geographica* 61, pp. 67–77

Kaissy, B. al- & Mynors, S., 1987. 'Ceramic Analyses of Mesopotamian Wares in the Early Dynastic Period', in Damerji, M. (ed.), *Researches on the Antiquities of Saddam Dam Basin Salvage and Other Researches*, Baghdad, pp. 134–54

Kalsbeek, J., 1980. 'La Ceramique de Serie du Djebel 'Aruda (a l'époque d'Uruk)', *Akkadica* 20, pp. 1–11

Kamada, H. & Ohtsu, T., 1993. 'Third report on the excavations at Songor A', *Al-Rafidan* 14, pp. 183–200, pls 1–7

Kamada, H. & Ohtsu, T., 1996. 'Fifth report on the excavations at Songor A.: Details of Samarra features, stone and bone objects', *Al-Rafidan* 17, pp. 57–68, pls 1–8

Kamilli, D. C. & Steinberg, A., 1985. 'New aproaches to mineral analyses of ancient ceramics', in Rapp, G. & Gifford, J. A. (eds), *Archaeological Geology*, New Haven, Yale University Press, pp. 313–30

Kaner, S., 1990. 'The Western Language Jomon: A Review', in *Bibliographical Reviews of Far Eastern Archaeology 1990: Hoabinhian, Jomon, Yayoi, Early Korean States*, Barnes, G. L. (ed.), Oxford, Oxbow Books

Karivieri, A., 1996. *The Athenian Lamp Industry in Late Antiquity*, Helsinki

Karvonen-Kannas, K., 1995. *The Seleucid and Parthian terracotta figurines from Babylon in the Iraq Museum, the British Museum and the Louvre*, Firenze

Kawamata, M., 1981. 'Telul Hamediyat', *Al-Rafidan* 2, pp. 97–8, 194, pl. 23

Kawami, T. S., 1992. *Ancient Iranian Ceramics from the Arthur M. Sackler Collections*, New York

Keall, E. J., 1970. 'The Significance of Late Parthian Nippur', PhD thesis, University of Michigan, Ann Arbor, University Microfilms, 1990

Kelly, J. H., 1969. 'The Hill Top Site, Burslem', *City of Stoke-on-Trent Museum Archaeological Society Report* 3, Stoke-on-Trent

Kelly, J. H. & Greaves, S. J., 1974. 'The excavation of a kiln base in Old Hall Street, Hanley', *City of Stoke-on-Trent Museum Archaeological Society Report* 6

Kelly, J. H., 1975. 'Post-medieval pottery from Newcastle St., Burslem, Stoke-on-Trent, SJ 867498', *City of Stoke-on-Trent Museum Archaeological Society Report* 8, Stoke-on-Trent, pp. 11–24

Kelly-Buccellati, M. & Shelby, W. R., 1977. 'Terqa Preliminary Report No. 4: A typology of ceramic vessels of the third and second millennia from the first two seasons', *Syro-Mesopotamian Studies* 1/6 (August), pp. 1–56, pls 1–8

Kemp, B. J. (ed.), 1989. *Amarna Reports V*, London

Kemp, B. J. (ed.), 1995. *Amarna Reports VI*, London

Kenrick, D. M., 1995. *Jomon of Japan: The World's Oldest Pottery*, New York, Kegan Paul International

Kerkhoff-Hader, B., 1980. *Lebens- und Arbeitsformen der Töpfer in der Südwest Eifel. Ein Beitrag zur Steinzeugforschung im Rheinland*, Rheinisches Archiv 110, Bonn

Kerkhoff-Hader, B., 1987. 'Krugöfen in Kreis Bernkastel-Wittlich', *Jahrbuch für den Kreis Bernkastel-Wittlich*, pp. 203–23

Kerkhoff-Hader, B., 1988. 'Töpfereiforschung aus volkskundlicher Sicht. Das Beispiel Südwesteifel', in *Töpferei- und Keramikforschung* 1, Bonn, pp. 197–203

Kerkhoff-Hader, B., 1991. 'Rezente Ofenanlagen in der Rheinischen Steinzeugproduktion', in Töpferei- und Keramikforschung 2, Bonn, pp. 339–56

Kerr, R., 1986. *Chinese Ceramics: Porcelain of the Qing Dynasty 1644–1911*, Victoria and Albert Museum, London, Far Eastern series

Kidd, D., 1976. Review of Myres, J. N. L. & Southern, W. (1973), *The Anglo-Saxon Cremation Cemetery at Sancton, East Yorkshire, Medieval Archaeology* 20, pp. 202–4

Kiddell, A. J. B., 1954. 'Wrotham slipware and the Wrotham brick yard', *Transactions of the English Ceramic Circle* III, pt. 2, pp. 105–18

Kidder, J. E., 1957. *The Jomon Pottery of Japan*, Ascona, Artibus Asiae

Kidder, J. E. & Esaka, T., 1968. *Prehistoric Japanese Arts: Jomon Pottery*, Tokyo, Kodansha

Kilikoglou, V., Vekinis, G. & Maniatis, Y., 1995. 'Toughening of ceramic earthenwares by quartz inclusions: an ancient art revisited', *Acta Metall. Mater.* 43, pp. 2959–65

Killick, R. G. et al, 1988. *Tell Rubeidheh: An Uruk Village in the Jebel Hamrin*, Warminster

Kilmurry, K., 1980. 'The Pottery Industry of Stamford, Lincolnshire *c.* 850–1250', Oxford, British Archaeological Report 84

Kim Jaeyeol, 1994. 'Jade Green, Koryo Celadon', in *Korean Cultural Heritage, vol. 1: Fine Arts*, Seoul, Korea Foundation

Kingery, W. D. (ed.), 1985. *Ceramics and Civilization I: Ancient Technology to Modern Science*, Columbus, OH, American Ceramic Society

Kingery, W. D. & Smith, D., 1985. 'The development of European soft-paste (frit) porcelain', in Kingery, W. D. (ed.), pp. 273–92

Kingery, W. D. (ed.), 1986. *Ceramics and Civilization II: Technology and Style*, Columbus, OH, American Ceramic Society

Kingery, W. D. & Vandiver, P. B., 1986. 'The eighteenth century change in technology and style from the famille verte to the famille rose style', in Kingery, W. D. (ed.), pp. 363–81

Kingery, W. D. & Vandiver, P. B., 1986. *Ceramic Masterpieces*, New York, The Free Press

Kingery, W. D. (ed.), 1987. *Ceramics and Civilization III: High Technology Ceramics*, Columbus, OH, American Ceramic Society

Kingery, W. D. (ed.), 1990. *Ceramics and Civilization V: The Changing Roles of Ceramics in Society*, Columbus, OH, American Ceramic Society

Kingery, W. D. & Aronson, M., 1990. 'On the technology of Renaissance maiolica glazes', *Faenza* 76, pp. 226–34

Kingery, W. D., 1991. 'Attic pottery gloss technology', *Archaeomaterials* 5, pp. 47–54

Kingery, W. D., 1993. 'Painterly maiolica of the Italian Renaissance', *Technology and Culture*, pp. 28–48

Kinnes, I. & Varndell, G., 1995. *Unbaked Urns of Rudely Shape: Essays on British and Irish Pottery for Ian Longworth*, Oxford, Oxbow Monograph 55

Kirkbride, D., 1972. 'Umm Dabaghiyah 1971: a preliminary report', *Iraq* 34, pp. 3–15, pls 1–18

Kirkbride, D., 1973a. 'Umm Dabaghiyah 1972: a second preliminary report', *Iraq* 35, pp. 1–7, pls 1–11

Kirkbride, D., 1973b. 'Umm Dabaghiyah 1973: a third preliminary report', *Iraq* 35, pp. 205–9, pls 77–80

Kirkbride, D., 1975. 'Umm Dabaghiyah 1974: a fourth preliminary report', *Iraq* 37, pp. 3–10, pls 1–8

Kleiss, W., 1973. 'Qal'eh Zohak in Azerbaidjan', *Archäologische Mitteilungen aus Iran* (NF) 6, pp. 163–88, taf. 41–3

Knowles, K., 1990. 'The Pottery Lamps', in Peacock, D.P.S. & Maxfield, V. A., *Archaeological Reports from Mons Claudianus 1990*, Southampton

Koh Choo, C. K., 1995. 'A scientific study of traditional Korean celadons and their modern developments', *Archaeometry* 37, pp. 53–81

Köhler, E. C., 1989. 'Die Keramik', in von der Way, T., 'Tell el-Farain-Buto 4 Bericht', *Mitteilungen des Deutschen Archäologischen Instituts Abteilung Kairo* 45, pp. 289–300

Köhler, E. C., 1992a. 'The Pre- and Early Dynastic pottery of Tell el-Farain/ Buto', in van den Brink, E. C. M. (ed.), pp. 11–22

Köhler, E. C., 1992b. 'Problems and priorities in the study of Pre- and Early-Dynastic pottery', *Cahiers de la céramique égyptienne* 3, pp. 7–15

Kolb, C. C. & Lackey, L. M., 1988. *A Pot for All Reasons: ceramic ecology revisited*

Koldewey, R., 1914. *The excavations at Babylon*, London

Korte-Böger, A. (ed.), 1991. *Eine Siegburger Töpferwekstatt der Familie Knütgen*, Kunst und Altertum am Rhein 133, Cologne

Kouymjian, D. K. (ed.), 1974. *Near Eastern Numismatics: Iconography, epigraphy and history*, Beirut

Krahl, R. (ed.), with Erbahar, N. & Ayers J., 1986. *Chinese Ceramics in the Topkapi Saray Museum, Istanbul: A complete catalogue, II: Yuan and Ming dynasty porcelains*, London

Krahl, R., 1994. *Chinese Ceramics from the Meiyintang Collection*, vols 1–2, London

Krahl, R. (ed.), 1995. *The Emperor's Broken China: Reconstructing Chenghua porcelain – an exhibition of Chinese porcelains of the Chenghua period (1465–1487) recently excavated from the imperial kiln site at Jingdezhen in South China*, Sotheby's, London, 21 August–22 September 1995, Hong Kong

Krahl, R. (ed.), forthcoming. *Catalogue of the Gompertz Collection of Korean Ceramics*, Cambridge, Cambridge University Press

Kramer, C., 1977. 'Pots and People', in Levine, L. D. & Cuyler Young Jr., T. C. (eds), *Mountains and Lowlands: Essays in the Archaeology of Greater Mesopotamia*, Malibu, pp. 91–112

Kroeper, K., 1986/7. 'The Ceramics of the Pre/ Early Dynastic Cemetery of Minshat Abu Omar', *Bulletin of the Egyptological Seminar* 8, pp. 73–94

Krönig, W., 1934. 'Ägyptische Fayenceschalen des Neuen Reiches', *Mitteilungen des Deutschen Archaölogischen Instituts Abteilung Kairo* 5, pp. 144–66

Krueger, I., 1981. 'Patrizen und Matrizen. Eine neue Wandvitrine zum rheinischen Steinzeug (1)', *Berichte aus der Arbeit des Museum* 2, Bonn, Rheinisches Landesmuseum Bonn, pp. 24–9

Krzyzaniak, L., 1991. 'Early farming in the Middle Nile Basin: recent discoveries at Kadero', *Antiquity* 65, no. 248, pp. 515–32

Krzyzaniak, L., 1996. 'The Kadero Project', *Sudan Archaeological Research Society Newsletter* 10, pp. 14–18

Kubiak, W., 1990. 'Roman-type Pottery in Medieval Egypt', in Godlewski, W. (ed.), pp. 77–82

Kühne, H., 1976. *Die Keramik vom Tell Chuera und ihre beziehungen zu funden aus Syrien-Palästina, der Türkei und dem Iraq*, Berlin

Kühne, H. & Schneider, G., 1988. 'Neue Untersuchungen zur Metallischen Ware', *Damaszener Mitteilungen* 3, pp. 83–139, taf. 25

Kuper, R., 1995. 'Prehistoric Research in the Southern Libyan Desert: A brief account and some conclusions of the B.O.S. project', *Cahiers de Recherches de l'Institut de Papyrologie et d'Egyptologie de Lille* 17, pp. 123–40

Kurtz, D. C., 1975. *Athenian White Lekythoi*, Oxford

Lam, P., 1984. 'Jingdezhen Wares of the Yuan Dynasty', *Orientations* 15, no. 6 (June), pp. 14–26

Lama, M., 1939. *Il libro dei conti di un maiolicaro del Quattrocento*, Faenza

Lamm, C. J., 1941. *Oriental Glass of Medieval Date found in Sweden and the Early History of Lustre Painting*, Stockholm

Lane, P., 1980. *Studio Porcelain*, London, Pitman House

Lane, P., 1988. *Ceramic Form, Design and Decoration*, London, Collins

Lang, J. & Middleton, A. P., forthcoming. *Radiography of Cultural Materials*, Oxford, Butterworth-Heinemann

Lathrap, D. W. et al, 1975. *Ancient Ecuador: Culture, clay and creativity 3,000–300 B.C.*, Chicago, Field Museum of Natural History

Lauer, J. P., 1962. *Histoire Monumentale des pyramides de l'Egypte I*, Cairo

Le Miere, M., 1989. 'Clay Analyses of the Prehistoric Pottery: First Results', in Akkermans, P. M. M. G. (ed.), *Excavations at Tell Sabi Abyad*, Oxford, pp. 233–5

Le Patourel, H. E. J., 1966. 'Hallgate, Doncaster, and the incidence of face-jugs with beards', *Medieval Archaeology* 10, pp. 160–64

Le Patourel, H. E. J., 1968. 'Documentary Evidence and the Medieval Pottery Industry', *Medieval Archaeology* 12, pp. 101–26

Le Patourel, H. E. J., 1986. 'Potters and Pots: the Fifth Gerald Dunning Memorial Lecture', *Medieval Ceramics* 10, pp. 3–16

Leach, B., 1940. *A Potter's Book*, London, Faber & Faber

LeBlanc, S. A. & Watson, P. J., 1973. 'A Comparative Analysis of Painted Pottery from Seven Halafian Sites', *Paléorient* 1, pp. 117–33

Leibundgut, A., 1977. *Die römischen Lampen in der Schweiz*, Berne

Lévêque, P. & Morel, J.-P. (eds), 1987. *Céramiques Hellénistiques et Romaines II*, Paris, Centre National de la Recherche Scientifique

Levine, L. D., 1987. 'The Iron Age', in *The Archaeology of Western Iran: Settlement and Society from Prehistory to the Islamic Conquest*, Hole, F. (ed.), Washington, DC, pp. 229–50

Lewis, J. & G., 1984. *Pratt Ware: English and Scottish relief decorated and underglaze coloured earthenware 1780–1840*, Woodbridge, Suffolk, Antique Collectors' Club

Lewis, R. A., 1969. *Staffordshire Pottery Industry* (rev. edn 1981), Staffordshire County Council Education Committee Local History Source Book G4

Li Guozhen & Guo Yenyi, 1986. 'An investigation of Ding white porcelain of successive dynasties', in *Scientific and Technological Insights on Ancient Chinese Pottery and Porcelain*, Beijing, Science Press, pp. 134–40

Li Huibing, 1984. 'Guanyu guan xinguan kuan bai ci chan di wenti de ji' (An inquiry into the problems of the origin of the white porcelain marked *guan* or *xinguan*), *Wenwu* 1984.12, pp. 58–63

Li Huibing, 1988. 'Lue tan "zaoqi baici"' (A brief discussion of 'early white ware'), *Kaogu yu Wenwu* 1988.1, pp. 88–92, 94

Li Jiazhi & Chen Xianqiu (eds), 1989. *Proceedings of 1989 International Symposium on Ancient Ceramics*, Shanghai

Liddell, D. M., 1929. 'New Light on an Old Problem', *Antiquity* 3, pp. 283–91

Lima-de-Faria, A., 1995. 'Genetic information preserved in ceramics: a new tool for archaeological studies', *Medieval Ceramics* 19, pp. 99–100

Lion-Goldschmidt, D., 1978. *Ming Porcelain* (trans. Katherine Watson), Fribourg

Lisse, P. & Louis, A., 1956. *Les Potiers de Nabeul*, Tunis, Bascone & Muscat

Liu Liangyou, 1989. 'Ding Ware: The beauty and fine elegance of these high-fired wares', *Cultural Splendours*, vol. 3, National Palace Museum, Taipei, Taiwan, pp. 164–73

Liu Xinyuan, 1980. 'Jingdezhen Hutian tao ge qi dian xing wan lei de zao xing te zheng ji qi cheng yin kao' (A study of the shapes and manufacture of typical bowls of Hutian kilns, Jingdezhen, in various periods), *Wenwu* 1980.11, pp. 50–60

Lloyd, S., 1940. 'Iraq Government soundings at Sinjar', *Iraq* 7, pp. 13–21, pls 2–4

Lloyd, S. & Safar, F., 1943. 'Tell Uqair: Excavations by the Iraq Government Directorate of Antiquities in 1940 and 1941', *Journal of Near Eastern Studies* 2, pp. 131–58, pls 3–31

Lloyd, S. & Safar, F., 1945. 'Tell Hassuna: Excavations by the Iraq Government Directorate of Antiquities in 1943 and 1944', *Journal of Near Eastern Studies* 4/4 (October), pp. 255–89, figs 1–38, pls 1–21

Lobban, R. A., 1988. 'El Sebou': Egyptian Birth Ritual', *American Anthropologist* 90, pp. 242–3

Lockett, T. & Halfpenny, P., 1982. *Stonewares and Stone Chinas of Northern England to 1851*, Stoke-on-Trent, City Museum and Art Gallery

Lockett, T. & Halfpenny, P., 1986. *Creamware and Pearlware*, Stoke-on-Trent, City Museum and Art Gallery

Loeschcke, S., 1909. 'Keramische Funde in Haltern', *Mitteilungen der Altertumskomm: für Westfalen* 5, pp. 101–90

Loeschcke, S., 1919. *Lampen aus Vindonissa*, Zürich

Loftus, W. K., 1857. *Travels and researches in Chaldaea and Susiana*, London

Lombard, P. & Kervran, M. (eds), 1989. *Bahrain National Museum Archaeological collections, Volume 1: A selection of pre-Islamic antiquities from excavations 1954–1975*, Manama, Bahrain

López Mullor, A., 1990. *Las cerámicas Romanas de paredes finas en Cataluña*, Zaragoza, Portico

Loviconi, A. & Belfitah, D., 1991. *Regards sur la faïence de Fès*, Aix-en-Provence, Édisud

Loviconi, A. & D., 1994. *Les Faïences de Tunisie: Qallaline et Nabeul*, Paris, Édisud

Lowther, A. W. G., 1948. 'Roman relief-patterned flue-tiles found in Surrey, and others of this type found in southern England', *Research Papers of the Surrey Archaeological Society* 1, pp. 1–35

Lucas, A. & Harris, J. R. (eds), 1962. *Ancient Egyptian Materials and Industries*, 4th edn, London, Histories and Mysteries of Man Ltd

Luoyangshi wenwu gongzuodui, 1995. 'Luoyang houliang Gao jichan mu fajue jianbao' (Excavation of Guo Jichan's tomb of the later Liang dynasty in Luoyang) and 'Luoyang nanjiao hunjiao shucun Song mu' (A Song dynasty tomb in Shucun, Hunjiao, in the southern suburbs of Luoyang), *Wenwu* 1995.8, pp. 52–60, 68–72

Maccabruni, C., 1987. 'Cenno su alcuni centri di produzione nelle province transalpine', in Lévêque, P. & Morel, J.-P. (eds), pp. 172–3

Macfadyen, W. A., 1947. 'Bedyal Pottery: A Painted Ware Made in Iraqi Kurdistan', *Man* 47 (March), pp. 47–8

MacGregor, A., 1985. *Bone, Antler, Ivory and Horn: The technology of skeletal materials since the Roman period*

MacGregor, A. (ed.), 1994. *Sir Hans Sloane: Collector, Scientist, Antiquary, Founding Father of the British Museum*, London, British Museum Press

Mackensen, M., 1993. *Die spätantiken Sigillata- und Lampentopferein von El Mahrine (Nordtunisien)*, Munich, Beck

Makovicky, E. & Thuesen, I., 1990. 'Paint and paste studies on selected pottery sherds from Tell Razuk, Iraq', in Gibson, McG. (ed.), *Uch Tepe II: Technical Reports*, Chicago & Copenhagen, pp. 19–63

Mallet, J., 1966. 'John Baddeley of Shelton', *Transactions of the English Ceramic Circle* 6, part 2, pp. 124–66

Mallet, J., 1967. 'John Baddeley of Shelton', *Transactions of the English Ceramic Circle* 6, part 3, pp. 181–247

Mallet, J., 1984. 'La biografia di Francesco Xanto Avelli alla luce dei suoi sonnetti', *Faenza* 70, pp. 5–6, 398–400

Mallet, J., 1988. 'Xanto: i suoi compagni e seguaci', in *Francesco Xanto Avelli da Rovigo*, Atti del Convegno Internazionale di Studi, Rovigo, pp. 67–108

Mallowan, M. E. L. & Rose, J. C., 1935. 'Excavations at Tell Arpachiyah, 1933', *Iraq* 2, pp. 1–178

Manchester City Art Gallery, 1969. *The Incomparable Art: English Pottery from the Thomas Greg Collection*, Manchester

Mandel, U., 1988. *Kleinasiatische Reliefkeramik der mitteren Kaiserzeit: D. 'Oinophorengruppe' und Verwandtes*, Berlin, De Gruyter

Maniatis, Y. & Tite, M. S., 1981. 'Technological examination of Neolithic-Bronze Age pottery from central and south-east Europe and from the Near East', *Journal of Archaeological Science* 8, pp. 59–76

Marconi Cosentino, R. & Ricciardi, L., 1993. *Catacomba di Commodilla*, Rome

Marichal, R., 1988. *Les graffites de La Graufesenque*. Paris, Centre National de la Recherche Scientifique, Gallia supplement, no. 47

Marshak, B. I. & Raspopova, V. I., 1990. 'Wall Paintings from a House with a Granary, Panjikent, 1st Quarter of the 8th Century', *Silk Road Art and Archaeology* 1, pp. 123–76

Marti, S., 1992. *Music Before Columbus*, Mexico City

Martin, A., 1995. 'Central Italian Lead-Glazed Ware', *Rei Cretariae Romanae Fautorum Acta* 34, pp. 63–8

Martin, H. P., Moon, J. & Postgate, J. N., 1985. *Abu Salabikh Excavations, Volume 2: Graves 1 to 99*, Hertford

Martin, T., 1977. 'Fouilles de Montans, note préliminaire sur les résultats de la campagne 1975', in *Figlina* 2

Mason, R. B. & Keall, E. J., 1991. 'The Abbasid glazed ceramic wares of Siraf and the Basra connection', *Iran* 29, pp. 51–66

Mason, R. B., 1994. *Islamic Glazed Pottery: 700–1250*, PhD dissertation, Oxford University

Mason, R. B. & Tite, M. S., 1994. 'The beginnings of Islamic stonepaste technology', *Archaeometry* 36, pp. 77–92

Mason, R. B. & Tite, M. S., 1997. 'Early opaque glazes and the beginnings of tin-opacification', *Archaeometry* 27, pp. 161–78

Mason, R. B. & Tite, M. S., 1997. 'The beginnings of tin-opacification of pottery glazes', *Archaeometry* 39, pp. 41–58

Matheson, S., 1976. *Persia: An Archaeological Guide*, London

Matson, F. R., 1939. *A Technological Study of the Unglazed Pottery and Figurines from Seleucia on the Tigris*, Philadelphia

Matson, F. R., 1943. 'Technological Notes on the Pottery', in Toll, N. (ed.), *The Green Glazed Pottery*, New Haven, pp. 81–95

Matson, F. R., 1955. 'Ceramic Archaeology', *The American Ceramic Society Bulletin* 34/2 (15 February), pp. 33–44

Matson, F. R., 1960. 'Specialized ceramic studies and radio-active carbon techniques', in Braidwood, R. J. & Howe, B. (eds), *Prehistoric Investigations in Iraqi Kurdistan*, Chicago, pp. 63–70

Matson, F. R., 1963. 'Some aspects of ceramic technology', in Brothwell, D. & Higgs, E. (eds), *Science in Archaeology*, London, Thames & Hudson, pp. 489–98

Matson, F. R. (ed.), 1965. *Ceramics and Man*, London, Methuen

Matson, F. R., 1965. 'Ceramic ecology: an approach to the study of early cultures in the Near East', in Matson, F. R. (ed.), pp. 202–17

Matson, F. R., 1971. 'A Study of Temperatures Used in Firing Ancient Mesopotamian Pottery', in Brill, R. H. (ed.), *Science and Archaeology*, Cambridge, MA, pp. 65–79

Matson, F. R., 1974. 'The Archaeological Present: Near Eastern Village Potters at Work [Summary]', *American Journal of Archaeology* 78, pp. 345–7

Matson, F. R., 1975. 'Technological studies of Egyptian pottery: Modern and ancient', in Bishay, A. (ed.), *Recent Advances in Science and Technology of Materials* III, pp. 129–39

Matson, F. R., 1983. 'The Banahilk Potter', in Braidwood, L. S. et al, *Prehistoric Archaeology along the Zagros Flanks*, Chicago, pp. 615–28, figs 223–6

Matson, F. R., 1985. 'The brickmakers of Babylon', in Kingery, W. D. (ed.), pp. 61–75

Matson, F. R., 1986. 'Glazed Brick from Babylon: Historical Setting and Microprobe Analyses', in Kingery, W. D. (ed.), pp. 133–56

Matson, F. R., 1995. 'Potters and Pottery in the Ancient Near East', in Sasson, J. M. (ed.), *Civilizations of the Ancient Near East*, New York, vol. III, pp. 1553–65

Matthews, D., 1995. 'Artisans and Artists in Ancient Western Asia', in Sasson, J. M. (ed.), *Civilizations of the Ancient Near East*, New York, vol. I, pp. 455–68

Mayet, F., 1975. *Les Céramiques a parois fines dans la Peninsule Iberique*, Paris, Centre Pierre

Mazar, A., 1990. *Archaeology of the Land of the Bible 10,000–586 B.C.E.*, New York, Doubleday

Mazzoni, S., 1985. 'Frontières ceramiques et le Haut Euphrat au Bronze Ancien IV', *MARI* 4, pp. 561–77

Mazzucato, O., 1986. 'La bottega di un vasaio della fine del XVI secolo', in Nota, M. (ed.), *Archaeologia nel centro storico*, Rome, pp. 88–147

McCarthy, M. R. & Brooks, C. M., 1988. *Medieval Pottery in Britain AD 900–1600*

McEwan, C. & van de Guchte, M., 1992. 'Ancestral Time and Sacred Space in Inca State Ritual', in Townsend, R. F. (ed.), *The Ancient Americas: Art from Sacred Landscapes*, Chicago, The Art Institute of Chicago

McGovern, P. E., Fleming, S. J. & Katz, S. H. (eds), 1995. *The Origins and Ancient History of Wine*, Philadelphia

McKinley, J., 1994a. 'The Anglo-Saxon Cemetery at Spong Hill, North Elmham, Part VIII: The Cremations', *East Anglian Archaeological Report* 69

McKinley, J., 1994b. 'Bone fragment size in British cremation burials and its implications for pyre technology and ritual', *Journal of Archaeological Science* 21, pp. 339–42

McKinley, J., 1994c. 'A pyre and grave-goods in British cremation burials: Have we missed something?', *Antiquity* 68, pp. 132–4

McNaughton, P., 1988. *The Mande Blacksmiths: Knowledge, power and art in West Africa*, Bloomington, Indiana University Press

McWhirr, A. & Viner, D., 1978. 'The products and distribution of tiles in Roman Britain with particular reference to the Cirencester region', *Britannia* 9, pp. 359–76

Meaney, A., 1964. *A Gazetteer of Anglo-Saxon Burial Sites*

Mediterraneum, 1992. *Ceramica Spagnola in Italia/Cèramica Espanola en Italia*, Viterbo

Medley, M. 1975. *Korean and Chinese Ceramics*, Cambridge, Fitzwilliam Museum

Medley, M., 1975. *Yuan Porcelain and Stoneware*, London

Medley, M., 1977. 'Korea, China and Liao in Koryo Ceramics', *Oriental Art* 23, Spring 1977, pp. 80–86

Medley, M., 1980. *Illustrated Catalogue of Ting and Allied Wares*, Percival David Foundation, University of London, School of Oriental and African Studies, London

Mellaart, J., 1975. *The Neolithic of the Near East*, London

Mellor, M., 1994. *Medieval Ceramic Studies in England: A review for English Heritage*

Merpert, N. I., Munchaev, R. M. & Bader, N O., 1981. 'Investigations of the Soviet expedition in northern Iraq 1976', *Sumer* 37, pp. 22–54

Merpert, N. I. & Munchaev, R. M., 1993. 'Yarim Tepe I', in Yoffee, N. & Clark, J. J. (eds), *Early Stages in the Evolution of Mesopotamian Civilization: Soviet Excavations in Northern Iraq*, Tucson & London, pp. 73–114

Méry, S. & Schneider, G., 1996. 'Mesopotamian Pottery Wares in Eastern Arabia from the 5th to the 2nd Millennium B.C.: A Contribution of Archaeometry to the Economic History', *Proceedings of the Seminar for Arabian Studies* 26, pp. 79–102, pl. 1

Mezquiriz, M., 1985. 'Terra Sigillata Ispanica', in Carandini, A. (ed.), pp. 97–174

Middleton, A. P., 1987. 'Technological investigation of the coatings on some "haematite-coated" pottery from southern England', *Archaeometry* 29, pp. 250–61

Middleton, A. P., Cowell, M. R. & Black, E. W., 1992. 'Romano-British relief-patterned flue tiles: a study of provenance using petrography and neutron activation analysis', *Documents et Travaux*, Institut Géologique Albert-de-Lapparent 16, pp. 49–59

Middleton, A. P., Lang, J. and Davis, R., 1992. 'The application of xeroradiography to the study of museum objects', *Journal of Photographic Science* 40, pp. 34–41

Middleton, A. P. & Cowell, M. R., 1993. 'Report on the examination and analysis of some porcelains from Longton Hall and West Pans', *Post-Medieval Archaeology* 27, pp. 94–109

Middleton, A. P., forthcoming. 'Ceramics', in Lang, J. & Middleton, A. P. (eds), *Radiography of Cultural Materials*, Oxford, Butterworth Heinemann

Mikami, T., 1972. *The Art of Japanese Ceramics*, Heibonsha Survey of Japanese Art, vol. 29, New York & Tokyo, Weatherhill & Heibonsha

Millard, A. R., 1973. 'The Canaanites', in Wiseman, D. J. (ed.), *Peoples of Old Testament Times*, Oxford, pp. 29–52

Millard, A. R., 1988. 'The Bevelled-Rim Bowls: Their Purpose and Significance', *Iraq* 50, pp. 49–57

Miller, M. C., 1993. 'Adoption and Adaption of Achaemenid Metalware Forms in Attic Black-Gloss Ware of the Fifth Century', *Archäologische Mitteilungen aus Iran* 26, pp. 109–46, taf. 18–42

Miller, R. A., 1960. *Japanese Ceramics*, Tokyo, Toto Shuppan

Millett, M., 1991. 'Pottery: Population or supply patterns? The Ager Tarraconensis approach', in Barker, G. & Lloyd, J. (eds.), pp. 18–26

Milward, A. J., 1982. 'Bowls', in *Egypt's Golden Age: The Art of Living in the New Kingdom 1558–1085 B.C.*, Boston Museum of Fine Arts, pp. 141–5

Minsauer, K., 1991. 'A Note on the Date of Black Decorated Pottery from Southern Mesopotamia', *Orient-Express* 1991/2, pp. 18–19

Moon, J., 1982. 'The distribution of upright-handled jars and stemmed dishes in the Early Dynastic period', *Iraq* 44, pp. 36–69

Moon, J., 1987. *Abu Salabikh Excavations, vol. 3: Catalogue of Early Dynastic Pottery*, Hertford

Moorey, P. R. S., 1971. *Catalogue of the Ancient Persian Bronzes in the Ashmolean Museum*, Oxford

Moorey, P. R. S., 1980. *Cemeteries of the First Millennium B.C. at Deve Hüyük*, Oxford

Moorey, P. R. S., 1985. 'The Iranian Contribution to Achaemenid Material Culture', *Iran* 23, pp. 21–37

Moorey, P. R. S., 1994. *Ancient Mesopotamian Materials and Industries: The Archaeological Evidence*, Oxford

Moorhouse, S., 1978. 'Documentary evidence for the uses of medieval pottery: an interim statement', *Medieval Ceramics* 2, pp. 3–21

Moorhouse, S., 1981. 'The medieval pottery industry and its markets', in Crossley, D. W. (ed.), *Medieval Industry*, pp. 96–125

Moorhouse, S. & Roberts, I., 1992. *Wrenthorpe Potteries: Excavations of 16th- and 17th-century Potting Tenements near Wakefield, 1983–86*, Yorkshire Archaeology 2, West Yorkshire Archaeology Service

Morel, J.-P., 1969. 'L'atelier des petites estampilles', *MEFRA* 81, pp. 59–117

Morel, J.-P., 1981a. *Céramique Campanienne: les formes*, Paris, École Française de Rome

Morel, J.-P., 1981b. 'La produzione della ceramica campana: aspetti economici e sociali', in Giardina, A. & Schiavone, A. (eds), *Società Romana e Produzione Schiavistica II: Merci, Mercati e Scambi nel Mediterraneo*, Bari, Laterza

Morris, E. L., 1994. 'Production and distribution of pottery and salt in Iron Age Britain: A review', *Proceedings of the Prehistoric Society* 60, pp. 371–93

Morris, J., 1974. Review of Myres, J. & Green, B. (1973), *The Anglo-Saxon Cemeteries of Caistor-by-Norwich and Markshall, Norfolk*, in *Medieval Archaeology* 18, pp. 225–32

Morse, E. S., 1879. 'The Shell Mound of Omori', *Memoirs of the Science Department, University of Tokyo* 1/1

Mountford, A. R., 1971. *The Illustrated Guide to Salt-Glazed Stonewares*, London, Barrie & Jenkins

Mountford, A. R., 1972. 'The Whieldon Manufactory at Fenton Vivian', *Transactions of the English Ceramic Circle* 8, part 2, pp. 164–82

Mountford, A. R., 1975. 'A group of Astbury-type pottery found in Shelton', *City of Stoke-on-Trent Museum Archaeological Society Report* 7, pp. 28–38

Mountford, A. R., 1975. 'Documents relating to English ceramics of the 18th & 19th centuries', *Journal of Ceramic History* 8, pp. 3–11

Mountford, A. R., 1975. 'The Sadler Teapot Manufactory Site, Burslem, Stoke-on-Trent, SJ 868498', *City of Stoke-on-Trent Museum Archaeological Society Report* 7, Stoke-on-Trent, pp. 1–20

Munchaev, R. M. & Merpert, N., 1971. 'The Archaeological Research in the Sinjar Valley (1971)', *Sumer* 27, pp. 23–32

Munro-Hay, S., 1981. *Aksum: An African Civilisation of Late Antiquity*, Edinburgh

Muscarella, O. W., 1974. 'The Iron Age at Dinkha Tepe, Iran', *The Metropolitan Museum of Art Journal* 9, pp. 35–90

Muscarella, O. W., 1984. 'Fibulae and Chronology, Marlik and Assur', *Journal of Field Archaeology* 11, pp. 413–19

Musty, J., Algar, D. J. & Ewence, P. F., 1969. 'The Medieval Pottery Kilns at Laverstock near Salisbury, Wiltshire', in *Archaeologia* 102, pp. 83–150

Musty, J., 1974. 'Medieval pottery kilns', in Evison, V. I., Hodges, H. & Hurst, J. G. (eds), *Medieval Pottery from Excavations: studies presented to Gerald Clough Dunning*, pp. 41–65

Musty, J., 1984. 'Technology and Affinities of the Nuneaton Kilns', in Mayes, P. & Scott, K., *Pottery Kilns at Chilvers Coton, Nuneaton*, Society for Medieval Archaeology Monograph 10, pp. 26–8

Mynors, H. S., 1982. 'An examination of Mesopotamian ceramics using petrographic and neutron activation analysis', in Aspinall, A. & Warren, S. E. (eds), *Proceedings of the 22nd Symposium on Archaeometry, University of Bradford, Bradford, March 30th–April 3rd 1982*, pp. 377–87

Myres, J., 1969. *Anglo-Saxon Pottery and the Settlement of England*

Myres, J., 1977. *A Corpus of Anglo-Saxon Pottery of the Pagan Period*

Mysliwiec, K., 1996. 'In the Ptolemaic workshops of Athribis', *Egyptian Archaeology* 9, pp. 34–6

Najafi, H. M. al-, 1987/8. 'Discovering a Part of the City of Meturnat in Tell es-Sib', *Sumer* 45, pp. 64–95; *Sumer* Supplement 1996, pp. 22–39

Naville, E., 1913. *The XIth Dynasty Temple at Deir El-Bahari III*, London

Needler, W., 1984. *Predynastic and Archaic Egypt in the Brooklyn Museum*, New York

Negahban, E. O., 1996. *Marlik: The Complete Excavation Report* (2 vols), Philadelphia

Negev, A., 1974. *The Nabataean Potter's Workshop at Oboda*, Bonn

Negroni, F., 1986. 'Niccolo Pelliparío, ceramista fantasma', *Notizie di Palazzo Albani* 14, pp. 13–20

Nenk, B. & Walker, H., 1991. 'An Aquamanile and a Spouted Jug in Lyveden-Stanion Ware', *Medieval Ceramics* 15, pp. 25–8

Nenk, B., 1992. 'A medieval sgraffito-decorated jug from Mill Green', *Essex Archaeology and History* 23, pp. 51–6

Nenk, B. & Pearce, J., 1994. 'Two Stamford-type Ware Modelled Birds from London', *Medieval Ceramics* 18, pp. 77–80

Nenk, B., Margeson, S. & Hurley, M., 1996. 'Medieval Britain and Ireland in 1995', *Medieval Archaeology* 40, forthcoming

Nenna, M.-D. & Seif el-Din, M., 1993. 'La vaiselle en faience du Musée Greco-Romain d'Alexandrie', *Bulletin de Correspondance Hellénique: études, chroniques et rapports* 117 (2), Athens, pp. 565–602

Nenna, M.-D. & Seif el-Din, M., 1994. 'La petite plastique en faience du Musée Greco-Romain d'Alexandrie', *Bulletin de Correspondance Hellénique* 118, pp. 291–320

Neusner, J., 1970. *A History of the Jews in Babylonia: vol. V: Later Sasanian times*, Leiden

New English Bible, 1970. 2nd edn, Cambridge, Cambridge University Press

Newell, R. W., 1994. 'Thumbed and Sagging Bases on English Medieval Jugs: A Potter's View', *Medieval Ceramics* 18, pp. 51–8

Newell, R. W., 1995. 'Some Notes on "Splashed Glazes"', *Medieval Ceramics* 19, pp. 77–88

Newman, J., 1932. *The Agricultural Life of the Jews in Babylonia between the years 200 C.E. and 500 C.E.*, London

Newton, E. & Bibbings, E., 1960. 'Seventeenth-century pottery sites at Harlow, Essex', *Transactions of the Essex Archaeological Society* 25, pt. 3, pp. 358–77

Nezu Institute of Fine Arts, 1983. *White Porcelain of Ding Ware*, Osaka

Nezu Institute of Fine Arts, 1988. *Tang Pottery and Porcelain*, Tokyo

Nicholson, P. T. & Patterson, H. L., 1989. 'Ceramic technology in Upper Egypt: a study of pottery firing', *World Archaeology* 21/1, pp. 71–86

Nicholson, P. T., 1989. 'Report on the 1987 excavation: the evidence for pottery making at Q.48.4', in Kemp, B. J. (ed.), 1989, pp. 64ff

Nicholson, P. T., 1993a. 'The firing of pottery', in Arnold, D. & Bourriau, J. E. (eds), pp. 106–20

Nicholson, P. T., 1993b. *Egyptian Faience and Glass*, Princes Risborough

Nicholson, P. T., 1996. 'New evidence for glass and glazing at Tell el-Amarna (Egypt)', *Annales du 13e Congrès de l'Association Internationale pour l'Histoire du Verre*, Lochem, AIHV, pp. 11–19

Nissen, H. J., 1988. *The Early History of the Ancient Near East 9000–2000 BC*, Chicago & London

Nixon, M. I., 1976. *The Emergence of the Factory System in the Staffordshire Pottery Industry*, PhD thesis, University of Ashton-in-Birmingham

Noble, J. V., 1969. 'The Technique of Egyptian Faience', *American Journal of Archaeology* 73, pp. 435–9

Noble, J. V., 1988. *The Techniques of Painted Attic Pottery*, 2nd edn, London, Thames & Hudson

Noll, W., 1976. 'Mineralogie und Technik der frühen Keramiken Grossmesopotamiens', *Neues Jahrbuch für Mineralogie Abhandlungen* 127, pp. 261–88

Noll, W., 1981. 'Mineralogy and technology of the painted ceramics of ancient Egypt', in *Scientific Studies in Ancient Ceramic*, Hughes, M. J. (ed.), London, British Museum Occasional Paper 19, pp. 143–54

Nordstrom, H. A., 1986. 'Ton', in Helck, W. & Westendorf, W. (eds), *Lexikon der Ägyptologie VI*, Wiesbaden, pp. 629–34

Norman, A., 1976. *Wallace Collection, Catalogue of Ceramics I: Pottery, Maiolica, Faience, Stoneware*, London

Northedge, A., 1981. 'Selected Late Roman and Islamic coarse wares', in Matthers, J. (ed.), *The River Qoueiq, Northern Syria, and its Catchment: Studies arising from the Tell Rifa'at Survey 1977–79*, Oxford, vol. 2, pp. 459–71

Northedge, A., 1988. 'Middle Sasanian to Islamic Pottery', in Northedge, A., Bamber, A. & Roaf, M. et al, *Excavations at Qal'at 'Ana 1981–1982*, Warminster, pp. 76–114

Oates, D. & J., 1958. 'Nimrud 1957: The Hellenistic Settlement', *Iraq* 20, pp. 114–57, pls 16–30

Oates, D. & J., 1959. 'Ain Sinu: A Roman frontier post in northern Iraq', *Iraq* 21, pp. 207–42, pls 52–59

Oates, D. & J., 1976. *The Rise of Civilization*, Oxford

Oates, J., 1959. 'Late Assyrian pottery from Fort Shalmaneser', *Iraq* 21, pp. 130–46, pls 35–39

Oates, J., 1983. 'Ubaid Mesopotamia Reconsidered', in Cuyler Young Jr., T., Smith, P. E. L. & Mortensen, P.(eds), *The Hilly Flanks and Beyond: Essays on the Prehistory of Southwestern Asia*, Chicago, pp. 251–81

Ochsenschlager, E., 1974. 'Mud objects from al-Hiba: A Study in Ancient and Modern Technology', *Archaeology* 27/3 (Spring), pp. 162–74

Oriental Ceramic Society of Hong Kong, 1984. *Jingdezhen Wares, The Yuan Evolution: Catalogue of an exhibition presented by the Oriental Ceramic Society of Hong Kong and the Fung Ping Shan Museum, University of Hong Kong, 23 March–31 May 1984*, Hong Kong

Orton, C. & Pearce, J., 1984. 'The pottery', in Thompson, A., Grew, F. & Schofield, J., 'Excavations at Aldgate, 1974', *Post-Medieval Archaeology* 18, pp. 34–68

Orton, C., 1985. 'Diffusion or impedence – obstacles to innovation in medieval ceramics', *Medieval Ceramics* 9, pp. 21–34

Orton, C., Tyers, P. & Vince, A. G., 1993. *Pottery in Archaeology*, Cambridge Manuals in Archaeology, Cambridge

Owen, G., 1981. *Rites and Religions of the Anglo-Saxons*

Päffgen, B., 1995. 'Spätmittelalterliche Töpfereifunde aus Langerwehe/ Kreis Düren', in *Ein Land Macht Geschichte: Archäologie in Nordrhein-Westfalen*, Schriften zur Bodendenkmalpflege in Nordrhein-Westfalen, Römisch-Germamisches Museum der Stadt Köln, Cologne, pp. 339–43

Pagenstecher, R., 1909. *Die calenische Reliefkeramik*, Berlin, Reimer

Paleani, M. T., 1993. *Le lucerne paleocristiane*, Rome

Paoletti, M., 1995. 'Cn.Ateius a Pisa. Osservazioni preliminari all'edizione dello scarico di fornace in Via San Zeno', *Annali della scuola normale superiore di Pisa* 25 (1–2), pp. 319–31

Papathanassopoulos, G. A. (ed.), 1996. *Neolithic Culture in Greece*, Athens

Parker, A. J., 1992. *Ancient Shipwrecks of the Mediterranean and the Roman Provinces*, Oxford, Tempus Reperatum, British Archaeological Reports, Int. Series 580

Parker Pearson, M., 1990. 'The production and distribution of Bronze Age pottery in South-western Britain', *Cornish Archaeology* 29, pp. 5–32

Parker Pearson, M., 1995. 'Southwestern Bronze Age Pottery', in Kinnes, I. & Varndell, G. (eds), pp. 89–100

Parr, P. J., 1978. 'Pottery, People and Politics', in Moorey, P. R. S. & Parr, P. (eds), *Archaeology in the Levant: Essays for Kathleen Kenyon*, Warminster, pp. 202–9

Parrot, A., 1959. *Mission Archeologique de Mari II: Le Palais*, Paris

Parry, J. P. M., 1979. *Brickmaking in Developing Countries*, Watford, Building Research Establishment

Pasqui, U., 1896. 'Nuove scoperte di antiche figuline della fornace di M.Perennio', *Notizie degli Scavi* 21, pp. 453–66

Paturzo, F., 1996. *Arretina Vasa: La ceramica aretina da mensa in età romana, Arte, Storia e Tecnologia*, Cortona, Calosci

Payne, J. C., 1993. *Catalogue of the Predynastic Egyptian Collection in the Ashmolean Museum*, Oxford

Peacock, D. P. S., 1968. 'A petrological study of certain Iron Age pottery from western England', *Proceedings of the Prehistoric Society* 34, pp. 414–27

Peacock, D. P. S., 1969. 'A contribution to the study of Glastonbury ware from south-western Britain', *Antiquaries Journal* 49, pp. 41–61

Peacock, D. P. S., 1969. 'Neolithic pottery production in Cornwall', *Antiquity* 43, pp. 145–9

Peacock, D. P. S., 1970. 'The Scientific Analysis of Ancient Ceramics: a review', *World Archaeology* 1, pp. 376–89

Peacock, D. P. S. (ed.), 1977. *Pottery and Early Commerce: characterisation and trade in early ceramics*, London, Academic Press

Peacock, D. P. S., 1981. 'Archaeology, ethnology and ceramic production', in Howard, H. & Morris, E. L. (eds), pp. 187–94

Peacock, D. P. S., 1982. *Pottery in the Roman World: an ethnoarchaeological approach*, Harlow, Longman

Peacock, D. P. S. & Williams, D. F., 1986. *Amphorae and the Roman Economy: an introductory guide*, London, Longman

Pearce, J., Vince, A. & White, R. with Cunningham, C. M., 1982. 'A dated type-series of London medieval pottery, part 1: Mill Green ware', *Transactions of the London Middlesex Archaeological Society* 33, pp. 266–98

Pearce, J., Vince, A. & Jenner, M. A., 1985. *A Dated Type-Series of London Medieval Pottery, Part 2: London-type Ware*, London and Middlesex Archaeological Society Special Paper 6

Pearce, J. & Vince, A., 1988. *A Dated Type-Series of London Medieval Pottery, Part 4: Surrey Whitewares*, London and Middlesex Archaeological Society Special Paper 10

Pearson, R. J., Barnes, G. L. & Hutterer, K. L. (eds), 1986. *Windows on the Japanese Past: Studies in Archaeology and Prehistory*, Ann Arbor, Center for Japanese Studies, University of Michigan

Peltenburg, E., 1991. *The Burrell Collection: Western Asiatic Antiquities*, Edinburgh

Peña, J. T., 1990. 'Internal Red-Slip Cookware (Pompeian Red Ware) from Cetamura de Chianti, Italy: Mineralogical Composition and Provenience', *American Journal of Archaeology* 94, pp. 647–61

Peters, J. P., 1897. *Nippur, or Explorations and Adventures on the Euphrates*, 2 vols, New York & London

Petrie, W. M. F., 1886. *Naucratis I*, London, Egypt Exploration Fund

Petrie, W. M. F., 1894. *Tell el-Amarna*, London

Petrie, W. M. F. & Quibell, J. E., 1896. *Naqada and Ballas*, London

Petrie, W. M. F., 1900. *Royal Tombs of the First Dynasty*, London

Petrie, W. M. F., 1902. *Abydos II*, London

Petrie, W. M. F., 1909. *Memphis I*, London

Petrie, W. M. F., 1911. In Knobel, F. B. et al, *Historical Studies*, London

Petrie, W. M. F., 1921. *Corpus of Prehistoric Pottery and Palettes*, London

Piccolpasso, C., 1980. *The Three Books of the Potter's Art: A facsimile of the manuscript in the Victoria and Albert Museum*, Lightbown, R. & Caiger-Smith, A. (eds), 2 vols, London, Scolar Press

Pinch, G., 1993. *Votive Offerings to Hathor*, Oxford

Pinder-Wilson, R., 1991. 'The Islamic Lands and China', in Tait (ed.), pp. 112–43

Platt, C. & Coleman-Smith, R., 1975. *Excavations in Medieval Southampton, 1953–1969*

Plot, R., 1686. *The Natural History of the Countie of Staffordshire*

Polinger Foster, K., 1979. *Aegean Faience of the Bronze Age*, New Haven & London, Yale University Press

Pollard, A. M. & Hatcher, H., 1986. 'The chemical analysis of oriental ceramic body compositions, part 2: greenwares', *Journal of Archaeological Science* 13, pp. 261–87

Pollard, A. M. & Hatcher, H., 1994. 'The chemical analysis of oriental ceramic body compositions, part 1: wares from north China', *Archaeometry* 36, pp. 41–62

Pollard, A. M. & Wood, N., 1986. 'Development of Chinese porcelain technology at Jingdezhen', in Olin, J. S. & Blackman, M. J. (eds), *Proceedings of the 24th Archaeometry Symposium*, Washington, DC, Smithsonian Institution Press

Ponsford, M., 1979. 'A bearded face jug from Wedmore, Somerset and anthropomorphic Medieval vessels from Bristol', *Rescue Archaeology in the Bristol Area: 1*, City of Bristol Museum and Art Gallery Monograph 2

Pope, A. U. (ed.), 1938. *Survey of Persian Art*, 4 vols, London & New York

Pope, J. A., 1956. *Chinese Porcelains from the Ardebil Shrine*, Freer Gallery of Art, Washington, DC, Smithsonian Institution Press

Porada, E., 1965. *Ancient Iran: The Art of Pre-Islamic Times*, London

Porada, E., 1984. 'Pottery in scenes of the period of Agade?', in Rice, P. M. (ed.), pp. 21–5

Porat, N., 1986/7. 'Local industry of Egyptian pottery in southern Palestine during the early Bronze I period', *Bulletin of the Egyptological Seminar* 8, pp. 109–29

Porter, V. & Watson, O., 1987. '"Tell Minis" Wares', *Oxford Studies in Islamic Art* IV, pp. 175–220

Porter, V., 1995. *Islamic Tiles*, London, British Museum Press

Poster, A. et al, 1986. *From Indian Earth: 4,000 years of terracotta art*, Brooklyn

Postgate, J. N., 1977. 'Excavations at Abu Salabikh, 1976', *Iraq* 39, pp. 269–99

Postgate, J. N. & Moon, J., 1982. 'Excavations at Abu Salabikh, 1981', *Iraq* 44, pp. 103–36

Postgate, J. N., 1987. 'Employer, Employee, and Employment in the Neo-Assyrian Empire', in Powell, M. A. (ed.), *Labor in the Ancient Near East*, New Haven, pp. 257–70

Postgate, J. N., 1990. 'Excavations at Abu Salabikh, 1988–89', *Iraq* 52, pp. 95–106

Postgate, J. N., 1992. *Early Mesopotamia: Society and economy at the dawn of history*, London & New York

Potter, T. W. & Johns, C., 1992. *Roman Britain*, London, British Museum Press

Potts, D., 1984. 'On Salt and Salt Gathering in Ancient Mesopotamia', *Journal of the Economic and Social History of the Orient* 27/3, pp. 225–71

Powell, C., 1995. 'The nature and use of ancient Egyptian potter's wheels', in Kemp, B. J. (ed), pp. 309–35

Price, R., 1959. 'Some groups of English redware of the mid-eighteenth century', *Transactions of the English Ceramic Circle* 4, part 5, pp. 1–9

Price, R., 1962. 'Some groups of English redware of the mid-eighteenth century', *Transactions of the English Ceramic Circle* 5, part 3, pp. 153–68

Pryor, S. & Blockley, K., 1978. 'A 17th century kiln-site at Woolwich', *Post-Medieval Archaeology* 12, pp. 30–85

Pucci, G., 1985. 'Terra Sigillata Italica', in Carandini, A. (ed.), pp. 359–406

Pucci, G. (ed.), 1992. *La Fornace di Umbricio Cordo: L'officina di un ceramista romano e il territorio di Torrita di Siena nell'antichità*, Florence, All'insegna del Giglio

Qiao Wenzheng, 1991. 'Cong chutu taoci kan Tangdai zhongwai wenhua jiaoliu' (An examination of Tang China's cultural relations with foreign powers from the evidence of excavated ceramics), *Wenbo* 1991.1, pp. 74–6

Quarentelli, E. (ed.), 1985. *The Land between Two Rivers: Twenty years of Italian archaeology in the Middle East, The Treasures of Mesopotamia*, Torino

Quibell, J. E. & Firth, C. M., 1935. *The Step Pyramid II: Plates*, Cairo

Quibell, J. E. & Green, F. W., 1902. *Hierakonpolis II*, London

Rackham, B., 1940. *Victoria and Albert Museum: Catalogue of Italian Maiolica*, London

Ragg, E. R. (ed.), 1976. *Hofämterspiel. Famous Pack of Playing Cards*, Vienna

Rahtz, P., 1976. 'Buildings and settlement' and 'A gazetteer of Anglo-Saxon settlement sites', in Wilson, D. (ed.), *The Archaeology of Anglo-Saxon England*, pp. 49–98, 402–52

Rasmussen, T. & Spivey, N. (eds), 1991. *Looking at Greek Vases*, Cambridge

Rasmussen, T., 1991. 'Corinth and the Orientalising phenomenon', in Rasmussen, T. & Spivey, N. (eds), pp. 57–78

Ravaglioli, A., Keajewski, A., Tite, M. S., Burn, R. R., Simpson, P. A. & Bojani, G. C., 1996. 'A physico-chemical study on some glazes coming from Romagna's and Neaples' Maiolica', *Faenza* 82, pp. 18–29

Rawson, J., 1984. 'Song Silver and its Connexions with Ceramics', *Apollo* (July), pp. 18–23

Rawson, J., 1995. *Chinese Jade from the Neolithic to the Qing*, London, British Museum Press

Rawson, P. S., 1954. 'Palace wares from Nimrud: technical observations on selected examples', *Iraq* 16, pp. 168–72

Reade, J. E., 1968. 'Tell Taya (1967): Summary report', *Iraq* 30, pp. 234–64, pls 77–87

Reade, J. E., 1978. 'Kassites and Assyrians in Iran', *Iran* 16, pp. 137–43

Reade, J. E., 1982. 'Tell Taya', in Curtis, J. (ed.), pp. 72–8, pl. 5

Reade, J. E., 1995. 'The Symposion in Ancient Mesopotamia: Archaeological Evidence', in Murray, O. & Tecusan, M. (eds), *In Vino Veritas*, London, pp. 35–56

Rech, M., 1991. 'Zur Einführung- Töpfereigewerbe in der Siegburger Aulgasse', in Korte-Böger, A. (ed.), pp. 1–14

Reed, I., 1990. *1000 Years of Pottery. An Analysis of Pottery Trade and Use. Fortiden i Trondheim Bygrunn: Folkbibliotekstomten (the Library Site)*

Reeves, C. N. & Spurr, S., 1995. 'Ancient Egypt at Eton', *Egyptian Archaeology* 6, pp. 19–22

Reilly, R., 1989. *Wedgwood*, 2 vols, London, Macmillan

Reineking-von Bock, G., 1986. *Steinzeug, Kataloge des Kunstgewerbemuseums Köln*, Bd. IV, 3rd edn (1st edn 1971), Cologne

Reinold, J., 1985. 'Inhumations d'enfants en vase à El Kadada', in Geus, F. & Thill, F. (eds), *Melanges offerts à Jean Vercoutter*, Paris, pp. 279–90

Reisner, G. A., 1908. 'The Archaeological Survey', *The Archaeological Survey of Nubia Bulletin* 1, pp. 9–24

Reisner, G. A., 1910. *The Archaeological Survey of Nubia: Report for 1907–1908*, Cairo

Reitlinger, G., 1951. 'Unglazed relief pottery from Northern Mesopotamia', *Ars Islamica* 15, pp. 11–22, figs 1–25

Rhodes, D., 1957. *Clay and Glazes for the Potter*

Ricci, A., 1985. 'Ceramica a pareti sottili', in Carandini, A. (ed.), pp. 231–357

Rice, P. & Gowing, C., 1989. *British Studio Ceramics in the Twentieth Century*, London, Barrie & Jenkins

Rice, P. M., 1981. 'Evaluation of specialised pottery production: a trial model', *Current Anthropology* 22, pp. 219–40

Rice, P. M. (ed.), 1984. *Pots and Potters: Current approaches in ceramic archaeology*, UCLA Institute of Archaeology Monograph 24, Los Angeles, University of California Press

Rice, P. M., 1987. *Pottery Analysis: a sourcebook*, Chicago & London, University of Chicago Press

Rice, P. M., 1991. 'Specialisation, standardisation and diversity: a retrospective', in Bishop, R. L. & Lange, F. W. (eds), pp. 257–9

Richards, C.-A., 1985. 'Early Northern Whitewares of Gongxian, Xing and Ding', *Transactions of the Oriental Ceramic Society* 49 (1984/5), pp. 58–77

Richards, J., 1987. *The significance of form and decoration of Anglo-Saxon cremation urns*, British Archaeological Reports, British Series 166, Oxford

Richter, G. M. A., 1938. 'Two Roman Glazed Amphorae', *Bulletin of the Metropolitan Museum of Art* 33, pp. 240–42

Richter, J., 1989. 'Neolithic sites in the Wadi Howar (Western Sudan)', in Krzyzaniak, L. & Kobusiewicz, M. (eds), *Late Prehistory of the Nile Basin and the Sahara*, Poznan, pp. 431–42

Rickett, R., 1995. *The Anglo-Saxon Cemetery at Spong Hill, North Elmham, Part VII: Iron Age, Roman and Early Saxon*

Ricketts, C., 1918. 'Two Faience Chalices at Eton College from the Collection of the Late Major W. J. Myers', *Journal of Egyptian Archaeology* 5, pp. 145–7

Riddick, S., 1990. *Pioneer Studio Pottery: The Milner-White Collection*, London, Lund Humphries with York City Art Gallery

Riddler, I., 1986. 'Pottery stamps - a middle Saxon faunal viewpoint', *Medieval Ceramics* 10, pp. 17–22

Riddler, I., 1988. 'Pot dies from Southampton: a note', in Andrews, P. (ed.), *Southampton finds, vol. I: The coins and the pottery from Hamwic*, p. 125

Riederer, J., 1981. 'Zum gegenwärtigen Stand der naturwissenschaftlichen Untersuchung antiker Keramik', in Arnold, D. (ed.), pp. 193–202

Riefstahl, E., 1968. *Ancient Egyptian Glass and Glazes in the Brooklyn Museum*, New York

Rigby, V. & Freestone, I. C., 1985. 'The petrology and typology of the earliest identified central Gaulish imports', *Journal of Roman Pottery Studies* 1, pp. 6–21

Rigby, V., Middleton, A. P. & Freestone, I. C., 1989. 'The Prunay Workshop: technical examination of La Tène bichrome painted pottery from Champagne', *World Archaeology* 21, pp. 1–16

Rizkana, I. & Seeher, J., 1987. *Maadi I: The Pottery of the Predynastic Settlement*, Mainz

Roaf, M., 1982. 'Hamrin Sites', in Curtis, J. (ed.), pp. 40–47, pls 2–3

Roaf, M., 1983. 'A report on the work of the British Archaeological Expedition in the Eski Mosul Dam Salvage Project from November 1982 to June 1983', *Sumer* 39, pp. 68–82

Roaf, M. D. (ed.), 1984. 'Tell Madhhur, a summary report on the excavations', *Sumer* 43, pp. 108–67

Roaf, M., 1984. 'Ubaid houses and temples', *Sumer* 43, pp. 80–90

Roaf, M., 1985. 'Media and Mesopotamia: History and Architecture', in *Later Mesopotamia and Iran: Tribes and Empires 1600–539 BC*, Curtis, J. E. (ed.), London, British Museum Press, pp. 54–66

Roaf, M. & Killick, R., 1988. 'A mysterious affair of styles: The Ninevite 5 Pottery of Northern Mesopotamia', *Iraq* 49, pp. 199–230

Roaf, M., 1989. 'Social Organization and Social Activities at Tell Madhhur', in Henrickson, E. F. & Thuesen, I. (eds), *Upon this Foundation: The 'Ubaid Reconsidered, Proceedings from the 'Ubaid Symposium, Elsinore May 30th–June 1st 1988*, Copenhagen, pp. 91–146

Roaf, M., 1990. *Cultural Atlas of Mesopotamia and the Ancient Near East*, Oxford

Roaf, M. & Galbraith, J., 1994. 'Pottery and p-values: 'Seafaring merchants of Ur?' re-examined', *Antiquity* 68/261 (December), pp. 770–80

Robertson, M., 1992. *The Art of Vase-painting in Classical Athens*, Cambridge

Rodziewicz, M., 1976. *La céramique romaine tardive d'Alexandrie, Alexandrie I*, Warsaw

Rogers, M. A., 1990. 'In Praise of Errors', *Orientations* (September), pp. 62–78

Rose, M., 1970. *Artist Potters in England*, London, Faber & Faber

Rosen, A. M., 1986. *Cities of Clay: The geoarchaeology of tells*, Chicago, University of Chicago Press

Rudling, D. R., 1986. 'The excavation of a Roman tilery on Great Cansiron Farm, Hartfield, East Sussex', *Britannia* 17, pp. 191–230

Rumayidh, S. S., 1981. 'Initial Results of the Excavations at Tell Chawkah', *Sumer* 37, pp. 112–30 (Arabic section)

Ruppel, T., 1991a. 'Siegburg, Aulgasse Nr. 8 – Die Ausgrabungsergebnisse im Überblick', in Korte-Böger, A. (ed.), pp. 15–28

Ruppel, T., 1991b. 'Zur Brandschatzung der Aulgasse während des Truchsessischen Krieges- Historische Überlieferung und archäologische Spuren', in Korte-Böger, A. (ed.), pp. 59–64

Ruppel, T., 1991c. 'Zur Rekonstruktion der Töpferscheiben-Archäologischer Befund und zeitgenössische Abbildungen', in Korte-Böger, A. (ed.), pp. 73–84

Ruppel, T., 1991d. 'Zum Herstellungsverfahren der Modeln für Verzierungsauflagen von Siegburger Steinzeug', in Korte-Böger, A. (ed.), pp. 85–92

Ruppel, T., 1995. *Katalog der Modeln, Siegburg, Aulgasse 8*, Denkmalschutz in Siegburg, Band 2, Stadtarchiv/ Untere Denkmalbehörde, Siegburg

Russel, A., 1984. 'Early Anglo-Saxon Ceramics from East Anglia: A Microprovenience Study', PhD thesis, University of Southampton

Rutten, K., 1996. 'Abu Qubur: Operation J: Late Achaemenid and Early Hellenistic pottery from Ensembles III and IV', *Northern Akkad Project Reports* 9, pp. 35–49

Rutter, J. A., 1977. 'Ashton', in Davey, P. J. (ed.), *Medieval Pottery from Excavations in the North West*, pp. 70–85

Rye, O. S. & Evans, C., 1976. *Traditional Pottery Techniques of Pakistan: Field and laboratory studies*, Washington, DC

Rye, O. S., 1976. 'Keeping your temper under control: materials and the manufacture of Papuan pottery', *Archaeology and Physical Anthropology in Oceania* 11, pp. 106–37

Rye, O. S., 1977. 'Pottery manufacturing techniques: X-ray studies', *Archaeometry* 19, pp. 205–11

Rye, O. S., 1981. *Pottery Technology: principles and reconstruction*, Washington, DC, Taraxacum

Safar, F., Mustafa, M. A. & Lloyd, S., 1981. *Eridu*, Baghdad
Salonen, A., 1966. 'Die Hausgeräte des alten Mesopotamiens', *Annales Academiae Scientiarum Fennicae*, ser. B, p. 144
Sarfaraz, A. A., 1969/70. 'Le site historique de Dastova dans la region de Chouchtar', Bastan Chenassi va Honar-e, *Iran* 4, pp. 12–13 (foreign section), 72–9 (Iranian section)
Sawyer, A. R., 1966. *Ancient Peruvian Ceramics: The Nathan Cummings Collection*, New York, Metropolitan Museum of Art
Sayer, G. R., 1951. *T'ao Lu, or The Potteries of China: Being a translation with notes and an introduction*, London
Sayer, G. R., 1959. *T'ao Ya, or Pottery Refinements: Being a translation with notes and an introduction*, London
Schiller, F. N., 1926. 'The Quest of the Purple Ting', *Transactions of the Oriental Ceramic Society* (1925/6), pp. 15–20
Schmidt, M., 1929. *Kunst und Kultur von Peru*, Berlin
Schmitz (Vicaire), 1879. 'Grès Limbourgeois de Raeren. 8e Lettre', *Bulletin des Commissions Royales d'Art et d'Archéologie* (1867), Brussels, pp. 61–76
Schneider, G., 1988. 'Stoneware from 3rd Millennium B.C.: Investigation of a Metal-Imitating Pottery from North Mesopotamia', in Farquhar, R. M., Hancock, R. G. V. & Pavlish, L. A. (eds), *Proceedings of the 26th International Archaeometry Symposium held at University of Toronto, Canada, May 16th–May 20th, 1988*, Toronto, pp. 17–22
Schneider, G., 1989. 'A technological study of North-Mesopotamian Stone Ware', *World Archaeology* 21/1, pp. 30–50
Schnitzer, B. K., 1977. 'Further evidence of Rhenish influence on decorated wares of Wrotham', *Post-Medieval Archaeology* 11, pp. 103–5
Schwarz, J., 1937. 'Das rheinische Töpferhandwerk, seine Entstehungsgrundlage, sein Wesen und seine Entwicklung', *Zeitschrift für Rheinische Geschichte*, 9 Jahrg., Heft 2, pp. 208–17
Scott, R. E., 1989. *A Guide to the Collection, Percival David Foundation of Chinese Art*, School of Oriental and African Studies, University of London
Scott, R. E. (ed.), 1992. *Chinese Copper Red Wares*, Percival David Foundation Monograph 3, University of London
See-Yiu Lam, T., 1990. *Tang Ceramics Changsha Kilns*, Hong Kong
Senior, L. & Weiss, H., 1992. 'Tell Leilan "sila bowls" and the Akkadian Reorganization of Subarian Agricultural Production', *Orient-Express* 1992/2, pp. 16–23
Sethom, S., 1969. 'La tunique de la mariage en Tunisie', *Cahiers des Arts et Traditions Populaires* 3, pp. 5–20
Shah, H., 1985. *Votive Terracottas of Gujarat*, Living Traditions of India series, New York
Shanghai Institute of Ceramics, Academia Sinica, 1986. *Scientific and Technological Insights on Ancient Chinese Pottery and Porcelain: Proceedings of the International Conference on Ancient Chinese Pottery and Porcelain, Shanghai, 1–5 November 1982*, Beijing
Sheaf, C. & Kilburn, R., 1988. *The Hatcher Porcelain Cargoes: The Complete Record*, Oxford
Shepard, A. O., 1956. *Ceramics for the Archaeologist*, Washington, DC, Carnegie Institution Publication 609
Shimada, I., 1994. *Tecnología y organización de la producción cerámica prehispánica en los Andes*, Lima, Pontificia Universidad Católica del Perú, Fondo Editorial
Sidebotham, S., 1978. 'Lamps from Carthage in the Kelsey Museum', in Humphrey, J. H. (ed.), *Excavations at Carthage 1975, conducted by the University of Michigan* II, Ann Arbor
Sidebotham, S., 1982. 'Roman Lamps', in Whitcomb, D. S. & Johnson, J. H., *Quseir al Qadim 1980*, Malibu
Sijelmassi, M., 1986. *Les Arts Traditionnels au Maroc*, Paris, ACR Éditions Internationales
Sillar, W., 1994. 'Pottery's Role in the Reproduction of Andean Society', PhD thesis, Department of Anthropology and Archaeology, Cambridge University
Simpson, St J., 1990. 'Iron Age Crop Storage and Ceramic Manufacture in Rural Mesopotamia: A Review of the British Museum Excavations at Qasrij Cliff and Khirbet Qasrij in Northern Iraq', *Bulletin of the Institute of Archaeology, London*, 27, pp. 119–40
Simpson, St J., 1993. 'Mouse-traps from Mesopotamia', *Orient-Express* 1993/1, pp. 18–20
Simpson, St J., 1995. 'Wider Implications of the Achaemenid Period Ceramics', in Baird, D., Campbell, S. & Watkins, T. (eds), *Excavations at Kharabeh Shattani*, Edinburgh, vol. 2, pp. 142–6
Simpson, St J. & Watkins, T., 1995. 'Kharabeh Village', in Baird, D., Campbell, S. & Watkins, T. (eds), *Excavations at Kharabeh Shattani*, Edinburgh, vol. 2, pp. 175–84
Simpson, St J., 1996. 'From Tekrit to the Jaghjagh: Sasanian sites, settlement patterns and material culture in Northern Mesopotamia', in Bartl, K. & Hauser, S. R. (eds), *Continuity and change in northern Mesopotamia from the Hellenistic to the Early Islamic period*, Berlin
Simpson, St J., 1997a. 'Ctesiphon', in Meyers, E. M. (ed.), *The Oxford Encyclopedia of Archaeology in the Near East*, New York & Oxford, vol. 1, pp. 77–9
Simpson, St J., 1997b. 'Mesopotamia from Alexander to the Rise of Islam', in Meyers, E. M. (ed.), *The Oxford Encyclopedia of Archaeology in the Near East*, New York & Oxford, vol. 3, pp. 484–7
Sinopoli, C. & Blurton, T.R., 1986. 'Modern Pottery Production in Rural Karnataka', in *Dimensions of Indian Art: Pupul Jayakar Seventy*, Chandra, L. & Jain, J. (eds), pp. 439–56
Sireix, C., 1994. 'Officines de potiers du second Age du Fer dans le Sud-Ouest de la Gaulle: organisation, structures de cuisson et production', *Acquitania* XII, pp. 95–109
Skibo, J. M., Schiffer, M. B. & Reid, K. C., 1989. 'Organic-tempered pottery: an experimental study', *American Antiquity* 54, pp. 122–46
Smedley, N. & Owles, E., 1963. 'Some Suffolk kilns, IV: Saxon kilns in Cox Lane, Ipswich, 1961', *Proceedings of the Suffolk Institute of Archaeology* 29, pp. 304–35
Smith, C. S. & Gnudi, M. T., 1943. *The Pirotechnia of Vannuccio Biringuccio*, New York
Smith, I. F., 1965. *Windmill Hill and Avebury: Excavations by Alexander Keillar, 1925–1939*, Oxford, Clarendon Press
Smith, M. C. & Wright, H. T., 1988. 'The Ceramics from Ras Hafun in Somalia: Notes on a Classical Maritime Site', *Azania* 23, pp. 115–41
Soof, B. Abu al-, 1985. *Uruk Pottery: Origin and Distribution*, Baghdad
Sotheby's, 1996. *Antiquities and Islamic Art: New York, December 17th, 1996*, New York
Soukiassian, G., Wuttman, M., Pantalacci, L., Ballet, P. & Picon, M., 1990. *Balat III: Les Ateliers de Potiers de 'Ayn-Asil*, Cairo
Sparkes, B. A., 1991. *Greek Pottery: An introduction*, Manchester
Spencer, A. J., 1980. *Catalogue of Egyptian Antiquities in the British Museum V: Early Dynastic Objects*, London, British Museum Publications
Spencer, A. J. et al., 1984. *Ashmunein (1983)*, London, British Museum Publications
Spencer, A. J., 1993a. *Excavations at El-Ashmunein III*, London, British Museum Press
Spencer, A. J., 1993b. *Early Egypt*, London, British Museum Press
Spencer, A. J. (ed.), 1996. *Aspects of Early Egypt*, London, British Museum Press
Starr, R. F. S. et al, 1939. *Nuzi*, 2 vols, Cambridge, MA
Stead, I. M., 1967. 'A La Tène III burial at Welwyn Garden City', *Archaeologia* 101, pp. 1–62
Stead, I. M. & Rigby, V., 1989. *Verulamium: The King Harry Lane site*, London, English Heritage, pp. 264–5
Stein, D. L., 1984. 'Khabur Ware and Nuzi Ware: Their Origin, Relationship, and Significance', *Assur* 4/1 (March)
Steinberg, A. & Kamilli, D. C., 1984. 'Paint and Paste Studies of Selected Halaf Sherds from Mesopotamia', in Rice, P. M. (ed.), pp. 187–208
Stephan, H.-G., 1987. *Die Bemalte Irdenware der Renaissance in Mitteleuropa: Ausstrahlungen und Verbindungen der Produktionzentren im gesampteuropäischen Rahmen*, Forschungshefte Bayerisches Nationalmuseum 12, Munich
Steponaitis, V., 1983. *Ceramics, Chronology and Community Patterns*, New York, Academic Press
Stobart, H., 1993. 'Whistling Pots and Wailing Llamas', unpublished lecture delivered at ILAS, 4 December 1993, London
Stobart, H., 1996a. '*Tara* and *q'iwa*: Worlds of sound and meaning', in Baumann, M. P. (ed), pp. 67–81
Stobart, H., 1996b. 'The llama's flute: Musical misunderstandings in the Andes', *Early Music* (August), pp. 470–83
Stokes, M., 1984. 'Anglo-Saxon pottery and die-stamps: preliminary notes on a programme of experimental archaeology', *Medieval Ceramics* 8, pp. 27–30
Stone-Miller, R., 1995. *Art of the Andes from Chavin to Inca*, London, Thames & Hudson
Strauss, E. C., 1974. *Die Nunschale: Eine Gefässgruppe des Neuen Reiches*
Stronach, D., 1961. 'Excavations at Ras al 'Amiya', *Iraq* 23, pp. 95–137, pls 43–65
Stronach, D., 1969. 'Excavations at Tepe Nush-i Jan, 1967', *Iran* 7, pp. 1–20, pls 1–12
Stronach, D., 1974. 'Achaemenid Village I at Susa and the Persian Migration to Fars', *Iraq* 36, pp. 239–48, pls 49–55
Stronach, D., 1978. 'Excavations at Tepe Nush-i Jan, Part 2: Median Pottery from the Fallen Floor in the Fort', *Iran* 16, pp. 11–24
Stronach, D. & Roaf, M., 1978. 'Excavations at Tepe Nush-i Jan, Part 1: A Third Interim Report', *Iran* 16, pp. 1–11
Sumner, W. M., 1994. 'Archaeological measures of cultural continuity and the arrival of the Persians in Fars', in *Achaemenid History VIII: Continuity and Change*, Sancisi-Weerdenburg, H., Kuhrt, A. & Cool Root, M. (eds), Leiden, pp. 97–105
Sürenhagen, D., 1978. *Keramik-produktion in Habuba Kabira-Süd*, Berlin
Sussman, V., 1982. *Ornamented Jewish Oil-Lamps*, Warminster
Swaddling, J. (ed.), 1986. *Italian Iron Age Artefacts in the British Museum*, London

Tafazzoli, A., 1974. 'A List of Trades and Crafts in the Sassanian Period', *Archäologische Mitteilungen aus Iran* (NF) 7, pp. 191–6
Tait, G. A. D., 1963. 'The Egyptian Relief Chalice', *Journal of Egyptian Archaeology* 49, pp. 93–139
Tait, H., 1957. 'Samuel Malkin and the "SM" slipware dishes', *Apollo* 65, pp. 3–6, 48–51
Tait, H., 1963. 'Blocks for spouts', *British Museum Quarterly* 26 (3/4), pp. 103–10
Tait, H. & Cherry, J., 1978. 'Excavations at the Longton Hall Porcelain Factory', *Post-Medieval Archaeology* 12, pp. 1–29
Tait, H. (ed.), 1991. *Five Thousand Years of Glass*, London, British Museum Publications
Taylor, J. P., 1977. 'The origin and use of cobalt compounds as blue pigments', *Science and Archaeology* 19, pp. 3–15
Tenri Sankokan Museum, 1983. *Pottery of Ancient Persia*, Tokyo
Thompson, F. H., 1953. 'A medieval pottery figure from Nottingham', *Transactions of the Thoroton Society of Nottinghamshire* 57, pp. 1–5
Thompson, R. C., 1923. 'Some Notes on Modern Babylonia', *Journal of the Royal Asiatic Society*, pp. 233–42, pls 2–4
Thuesen, I., Heydorn, K. & Gwozdz, R., 1982. 'Investigation of 5000-year-old pottery from Mesopotamia by instrumental neutron activation analysis', *PACT* 7, Second Nordic Conference on the Application of Scientific Methods in Archaeology, Elsinore, Denmark, 17–19 August 1981, part 2, pp. 375–81
Thuesen, I. 1990. 'Introduction to the Scientific Analysis of Early Dynastic Pottery from Tell Razuk and the Diyala Region', in Gibson, McG. (ed.), pp. 9–18
Thuesen, I. & Heydorn, K., 1990. 'Instrumental Neutron Activation Analysis of ED I-II Pottery from the Diyala Region and Farukhabad', in Gibson, McG. (ed.), pp. 65–89
Tichane, R., 1983. *Ching-te-chen: Views of a porcelain city*, New York
Timby, J. et al, 1993. 'Sancton I: Anglo-Saxon cemetery excavations carried out between 1976 and 1980', *Archaeological Journal* 150, pp. 243–365
Tite, M. S., 1969. 'Determination of the Firing Temperature of Ancient Ceramics by Measurement of Thermal Expansion: A Reassessment', *Archaeometry* 11, pp. 131–43
Tite, M. S., Bimson, M. & Freestone, I. C., 1982. 'An examination of the high gloss surface finishes on Greek Attic and Roman Samian wares', *Archaeometry* 24, pp. 117–26
Tite, M. S., Maniatis, Y., Meeks, N. D., Bimson, M., Hughes, M. J. & Leppard, S. C., 1982. 'Technological studies of ancient ceramics from the Near East, Aegean and southeast Europe', in Wertime, T. A. & S. F. (eds), *Early Pyrotechnology*, Washington, DC, Smithsonian Institution Press, pp. 61–71
Tite, M. S., Freestone, I. C. & Bimson, M., 1983. 'Egyptian faience: An investigation into the methods of production', *Archaeometry* 25, pp. 7–27
Tite, M. S., Freestone, I. C. & Bimson, M., 1984. 'A technological study of Chinese porcelain of the Yuan dynasty', *Archaeometry* 26, pp. 139–54
Tite, M. S., 1986. 'Egyptian Blue, Faience and Related Materials: Technological Investigations', in Jones, R. E. & Catling, H. W. (eds), *Science in Archaeology: Fitch Laboratory Occasional Paper* 2, Athens, pp. 39–41
Tite, M. S & Bimson, M., 1986. 'Faience: An investigation of the microstructures associated with the different methods of glazing', *Archaeometry* 28, pp. 69–78
Tite, M. S. & Bimson, M., 1991. 'A technological study of English Porcelains', *Archaeometry* 33, pp. 3–27
Tite, M. S., 1991. 'Technological investigations of Italian Renaissance ceramics', in Wilson, T. (ed.), 1991, pp. 280–85
Tite, M. S., Middleton, A. P. & Postgate, J. N., 1994/5. 'Scientific investigation of fire installations at Abu Salabikh', *Sumer* 47, pp. 46–51
Tobert, N., 1984. 'Ethno-archaeology of pottery firing in Darfur, Sudan: Implications for ceramic technology studies', *Oxford Journal of Archaeology* 3, pp. 141–56
Tobler, A. J., 1950. *Excavations at Tepe Gawra*, vol. II, Philadelphia
Toker, A., 1992. *Museum of Anatolian Civilizations: Metal Vessels*, Ankara
Tokyo, 1981a. *Chugoku Toji Zenshu: 9 Ding yaki* (Chinese Ceramics Collected Works, vol. 9: Ding wares), Tokyo
Tokyo, 1981b. *Chugoku Toji Zenshu: 21* (Chinese Ceramics Collected Works, vol. 21: Jingdezhen polychrome porcelains), Tokyo
Toll, N., 1943. 'The Excavations At Dura-Europos ... Final Report IV', Rostovtzeff, M. I. et al, part I, fasc. 1, *The Green Glazed Pottery*, New Haven
Tortorella, S., 1985. 'Ceramica Africana: Ceramica da Cucina', in Carandini, A. (ed.), pp. 208–27
Towner, D. C., 1978. *Creamware*, London, Faber & Faber
Tregear, M., 1982. *Song Ceramics*, Fribourg & London
Trendall, A. D., 1989. *Red Figure Vases of South Italy and Sicily*, London
Treptow, O., 1991. 'Miscellen zu verschiedenen Persönlichkeiten der Siegburger Ulnerzunft im späten 16. und zu Beginn des 17. Jahrhunderts', in Korte-Böger, A. (ed.), pp. 103–12
Triki, H. & Ouazzani, T., 1993. *La Colline des Potiers: histoire d'une ville et de sa poterie*, Casablanca, Lak International

Trokay, M., 1989. 'Les deux documents complémentaires en basalte du Tell Kannas: Base de tournette ou meule?' in Lebeau, M. & Talon, P. (eds), *Reflets des deux fleuves: Volume de Mélanges offerts a André Finet*, Leuven, pp. 169–75

Trokay, M., 1990. 'Upper part of a tournette', in Bunnens, G. (ed.), *Tell Ahmar: 1988 Season*, Leuven, pp. 123–5

Tsuboi, K. (ed.), 1987. *Recent Archaeological Discoveries in Japan* (trans. G. L. Barnes), Tokyo & Paris, Toyo Bunko & UNESCO

Tsui Museum of Art, 1993. *A Legacy of Chenghua: Imperial porcelain of the Chenghua reign excavated from Zhushan, Jingdezhen, jointly presented by the Jingdezhen Institute of Ceramic Archaeology and the Tsui Museum of Art*, Hong Kong

Tufnell, O., 1953. *Lachish III: The Iron Age*, Oxford, Oxford University Press

Tufnell, O., 1958. *Lachish IV: The Bronze Age*, Oxford, Oxford University Press

Turino, T., 1993. *Moving Away from Silence*, Chicago & London

Turner-Rugg, A., 1995. 'Medieval pottery from St Albans', *Medieval Ceramics* 19, pp. 45–65

Tusa, S., 1980. 'Notes on the Tell Abu Husaini Excavation', *Paléorient* 6, pp. 225–7

Tzschoppe, J., 1995. 'Technologische Entwicklung am Frechener Kannenofen', in Jürgens, A., Kleine, D. et al (eds), pp. 63–71

Ussishkin, D., 1985. 'Levels VII and VI at Tel Lachish and the end of the Late Bronze Age in Canaan', in Tubb, J. N. (ed.), *Palestine in the Bronze and Iron Ages*, Occasional Paper 11, Institute of Archaeology, University of London, pp. 213–30

Vainker, S. J., 1991. *Chinese Pottery and Porcelain: From Prehistory to the Present*, London, British Museum Press

Valenstein, S. G., 1989. *A Handbook of Chinese Ceramics*, rev. edn, New York & London

Valtz, E., 1984. 'Pottery from Seleucia on the Tigris', in Boucharlat, R. & Salles, J.-F. (eds), *Arabie Orientale, Mesopotamie et Iran meridional de l'age de fer au debut de la periode islamique*, Paris, pp. 41–8

Valtz, E., 1991. 'New observations on the Hellenistic pottery from Seleucia-on-the-Tigris', in Schippmann, K., Herling, A. & Salles, J.-F. (eds), *Golf-Archäologie. Mesopotamien, Iran, Kuwait, Bahrain, Vereinigte Arabische Emirate und Oman*, Buch am Erlbach, pp. 45–56

Van As, A. & Jacobs, L., 1985. 'Technological research of Palaeo- and Meso-Babylonian pottery from Tell ed-Der (Iraq) – a report', *Newsletter*, Department of Pottery Technology, Leiden University 3, pp. 15–26

Van As, A. & Jacobs, L., 1986. 'Technological research of Palaeo- and Meso-Babylonian pottery – a report on the 1986 season at Tell ed-Deir (Iraq) and some preliminary results', *Newsletter*, Department of Pottery Technology, Leiden University 4, pp. 21–8

Van As, A. & Jacobs, L., 1987. 'Second millennium B.C. goblet bases from Tell ed-Deir – the relationship between form and technique', *Newsletter*, Department of Pottery Technology, Leiden University 5, pp. 39–53

Van As, A. & Jacobs, L., 1989. 'Technological Aspects of the Prehistoric Pottery', in Akkermans, P. M. M. G. (ed.), *Excavations at Tell Sabi Abyad*, Oxford, pp. 215–32

Van As, A. & Jacobs, L., 1991/2. 'Causes for the pale colour of iron-containing, second millennium B.C. pottery from three archaeological sites in Mesopotamia', *Newsletter*, Department of Pottery Technology, Leiden University 9/10, pp. 7–21

Van As, A. & Jacobs, L., 1992. 'The work of the potter in ancient Mesopotamia in the second millennium B.C.', in Vandiver, P. B. et al (eds), pp. 529–44

van den Brink, E. C. M. (ed.), 1992. *The Nile Delta in Transition, 4th–3rd millennium BC: Proceedings of the Seminar held in Cairo, 21–24 October 1990, at the Netherlands Institute of Archaeology and Arabic Studies*, Tel Aviv

van Gennep, A., 1918. 'Recherches sur les poteries peintes de l'Afrique du Nord', *Harvard African Studies* II, Cambridge, MA, pp. 235–97

van Ingen, W., 1939. *Figurines from Seleucia on the Tigris*, Ann Arbor, MI

Vanden Berghe, L., 1964. *La Nécropole de Khurvin*, Leiden

Vandiver, P., 1982. 'Faience Vessels', in *Egypt's Golden Age: The Art of Living in the New Kingdom 1558–1085 B.C.*, Boston Museum of Fine Arts, pp. 140–41

Vandiver, P., 1983. 'Egyptian faience manufacture', in Kaczmarczyk, A. & Hedges, R. E. M., *Ancient Egyptian Faience*, Warminster, Aris & Phillips

Vandiver, P. & Lacovara, P., 1985/6. 'An outline of technological changes in Egyptian pottery manufacture', *Bulletin of the Egyptological Seminar* 7, New York, pp. 53–85

Vandiver, P. B., 1987. 'Sequential Slab Construction: A conservative Southwest Asiatic ceramic tradition ca. 7000–3000 BC', *Paléorient* 13/2, pp. 9–36

Vandiver, P. & Kingery, W. D., 1987a. 'Manufacture of an Eighteenth Dynasty faience chalice', in Bimson, M. & Freestone, I. C. (eds), *Early Vitreous Materials*, London, British Museum Occasional Paper 56, pp. 79–90

Vandiver, P. & Kingery, W. D., 1987b. 'Egyptian faience: the first high-tech ceramic', in Kingery, W. D. (ed.), pp. 19–34

Vandiver, P. B., Cort, L. A. & Handwerker, C. A., 1989. 'Variations in the practise of ceramic technology in different cultures: a comparison of Korean and Chinese celadon glazes', in Notis, M. D. (ed.), *Ceramics and Civilization IV*, Columbus, OH, American Ceramic Society, pp. 347–88

Vandiver, P. B., Soffer, O., Klima, B. & Svoboda, J., 1989. 'The origins of ceramic technology at Dolni Vestonice, Czechoslovakia', *Science* 246, pp. 1002–8

Vandiver, P. B., Soffer, O. & Klima, B., 1990. 'Venuses and wolverines: the origins of ceramic technology, ca. 26,000 years B.P.', in Kingery, W. D. (ed.), pp. 13–81

Vandiver, P. B., 1991. 'The technology of Korean celadons', in Ikutaro Itoh & Yukata Mino (eds), *The Radiance of Jade and the Clarity of Water*, pp. 151–8

Vandiver, P. B., 1992. 'Preliminary study of the technology of selected Seto and Mino ceramics', appendix in Cort, L. A., pp. 219–29

Vandiver, P. B., Druzik, J. R., Wheeler, G. S. & Freestone, I. C. (eds), 1992. *Materials Issues in Art and Archaeology III: Symposium held April 27–May 1, 1992, San Francisco*, Pittsburgh, PA

Vannini, G. (ed.), 1977. *La maiolica di Montelupo: Scavo di uno scarico di fornace*, Montelupo

Vaughan, J., 1970. 'Caste Systems in the Western Sudan', in Tuden, A. (ed.), *Social Stratification in Africa*, New York, Free Press

Velde, B. & Courtois, L., 1987. 'Observations Techniques sur les Ceramiques Obeid 0 et Obeid 1–3 de Tell el 'Oueili (Campagne de 1983)', in Huot, J.-L. (ed.), *Préhistoire de la Mésopotamie*, Paris, pp. 153–62

Venco Ricciardi, R., 1967. 'Pottery from Choche', *Mesopotamia* 2, pp. 93–104, figs 131–91

Venco Ricciardi, R., 1970/71. 'Sasanian Pottery from Tell Mahuz (North Mesopotamia)', *Mesopotamia* 5/6, pp. 427–82, figs 87–96

Venco Ricciardi, R., 1982. 'La Ceramica Partica', in Pecorella, P. E. & Salvini, M. (eds), *Tell Barri/Kahat 1*, Roma, pp. 55–75, pls 7–8

Venco Ricciardi, R., 1984. 'Sasanian Pottery from Choche (Artisans' Quarter) and Tell Baruda', in Boucharlat, R. & Salles, J.-F., (eds), *Arabie Orientale, Mesopotamie et Iran meridional de l'age de fer au debut de la periode islamique*, Paris, pp. 49–57

Verbanck-Pierard, A. & Viviers, D. (eds), 1995. *Culture et Cité: L'avènement d'Athènes à l'époque archaïque*, Brussels

Verhaeghe, F., 1991. 'An aquamanile and some thoughts about ceramic competition with quality metal goods in the Middle Ages', in Lewis, E. (ed), *Custom and Ceramics: Essays presented to Kenneth Barton*, pp. 25–61

Vermeule, E., 1966. 'Graffito on a Steatite Jewelry Mold from Mycenae', *Kadmos* 5

Vertet, H., 1983. *Les techniques de fabrication des lampes en terre cuite du centre de la Gaule*, Avignon

Vickers, M., 1986. 'Silver, Copper and Ceramics in Ancient Athens', in Vickers, M. (ed.), *Pots and Pans: A Colloquium on Precious Metals and Ceramics in the Muslim, Chinese and Graeco-Roman Worlds, Oxford, 1985*, Oxford, pp. 137–51

Victoria and Albert Museum, 1982. *The Indian Heritage: Court life and arts under Mughal rule*, London

Vidler, L. A., 1933. 'Mediaeval pottery and kilns found at Rye', *Sussex Archaeological Collections* 74, pp. 44–64

Vidler, L. A., 1936. 'Mediaeval pottery, tiles and kilns found at Rye: Final Report', *Sussex Archaeological Collections* 77, pp. 107–18

Vince, A., 1981. 'Recent research on post-medieval pottery from the City of London', *London Archaeologist* 4, no. 3, pp. 74–80

Vince, A. & Young, J., 1991. 'The East Midlands Anglo-Saxon pottery project (First Report)', *City of Lincoln Archaeological Unit Report* 119

Vince, A. & Young, J., 1992. 'The East Midlands Anglo-Saxon pottery project (Second Report)', *City of Lincoln Archaeological Unit Report* 4

Vince, A. & Young, J., 1993. 'The East Midlands Anglo-Saxon pottery project (Third Report)', *City of Lincoln Archaeological Unit Report* 70

Vince, A. & Young, J., 1994. 'The East Midlands Anglo-Saxon pottery project (Fourth Report)', *City of Lincoln Archaeological Unit Report* 86

Von Bissing, F. W., 1902. *Fayancegefässe, Catalogue Générale des Antiquités Egyptiennes du Musée du Caire, Nos. 3618–4000; 18001–18037; 18600; 18603*, Vienna

von Falke, O., 1899. 'Kölnisches Steinzeug', *Jahrbuch der Königlich-Preussischen Kunstsammlungen* 20, Heft I, pp. 30–53

von Falke, O., 1908. *Das Rheinische Steinzeug*, 2 vols, Berlin, reprinted 1977, Osnabrück

von Schnurbein, S., 1990. 'Die ausseritalische Produktion', in Ettlinger, E. et al, pp. 17–22

Wang Qingzheng, 1993. *Underglaze Blue and Red: Elegant Decoration of Porcelain of Yuan, Ming, Qing*, Hong Kong

Warburton, R. C. & D.A., 1991. 'Ein Achamenidischer Topferstampel von Abu Qubur und einige vergleichsstucke aus Mesopotamien', *Northern Akkad Project Reports* 5, pp. 41–6

Watney, B. M., 1957. *Longton Hall Porcelain*, London, Faber & Faber

Watney, B. M., Middleton, A. P. & Cowell, M. R., 1993. 'Excavations at the Longton Hall porcelain manufactory, Part III: The porcelain and other ceramic finds', *Post-Medieval Archaeology* 27, pp. 57–109

Watson, O., 1985. *Persian Lustreware*, London

Watson, O., 1990. *British Studio Pottery: The Victoria and Albert Museum Collection*, London, Phaidon and Christie's, Oxford, with Victoria and Albert Museum

Watson, P. J., 1983. 'The Halafian culture: a review and synthesis', in Cuyler Young Jr., T., Smith, P. E. L. & Mortensen, P. (eds), *The Hilly Flanks and Beyond: Essays on the Prehistory of Southwestern Asia*, Chicago, pp. 231–50

Watson, P. J. & LeBlanc, S. A., 1990. *Girikihaciyan: A Halafian site in southeastern Turkey*, Los Angeles

Watson, W., 1986. *Italian Renaissance Maiolica from the William A. Clark Collection*, Washington, DC & London, Corcoran Gallery of Art

Weatherill, L., 1971. *The Pottery Trade and North Staffordshire 1660–1760*, Manchester, Manchester University Press

Weatherill, L., 1986. *The Growth of the Pottery Industry in England 1660–1815*, New York & London, Garland Publishing

Wehgartner, I., 1983. *Attisch weissgrundige Keramik*, Mainz

Weisberg, D. B., 1967. *Guild Structure and Political Allegiance In Early Achaemenid Mesopotamia*, New Haven & London

Weiss, H. (ed.), 1985. *Ebla to Damascus: Art & Archaeology of Ancient Syria*, Washington, DC

Welch, M., 1992. *Anglo-Saxon England*

Wells, C. M., 1990. '"Imitations" and the spread of Sigillata manufacture', in Ettlinger, E. et al, pp. 24–5

Wenke, R. J., 1975/6. 'Imperial Investments and Agricultural Developments in Parthian and Sasanian Khuzestan: 150 BC to AD 640', *Mesopotamia* 10/11, pp. 31–221

West, S., 1963. 'Excavations at Cox Lane, Ipswich (1958)', *Proceedings of the Suffolk Institute of Archaeology* 29, pp. 223–63

West, S., 1985. *West Stow: The Anglo-Saxon Village*

Westermarck, E., 1926. *Ritual and Belief in Morocco*, London, Macmillan

Westfälisches Museum für Archäologie, Münster, 1987. *Vergessene Städte am Indus: Frühe Kulturen in Pakistan vom 8. bis 2. Jahrtausend*, Mainz

Wheeler, R. E. M., 1954. *Rome beyond the Imperial Frontiers*, London

Whitcomb, D. S., 1985. *Before the Roses and Nightingales: Excavations at Qasr-i Abu Nasr, Old Shiraz*, New York

Whitfield, R. (ed.), 1984. *Treasures from Korea*, London, British Museum Publications

Whybrow, M., 1996. *The Leach Legacy: St Ives Pottery and its influence*, Bristol, Sansom

Wilkinson, T. J. & Tucker, D. J., 1995. *Settlement Development in the North Jazira, Iraq: A study of the Archaeological landscape*, Warminster

Williams, D. F., 1977. 'The Romano-British black-burnished industry: An essay in characterisation by heavy mineral analysis', in Peacock, D. P. S. (ed.), *Pottery and Early Commerce*, London, Academic Press

Williams, D., 1985. *Greek Vases*, London, British Museum Publications

Williams, D., 1986. 'Greek potters and their descendants in Campania and Southern Etruria, c. 720–630 BC', in Swaddling, J. (ed.), pp. 295–304

Williams, D., 1991. 'The invention of the red-figure technique and the race between vase-painting and free painting', in Rasmussen, T. & Spivey, N., pp. 103–18

Williams, D., 1995. 'Potter, Painter and Purchaser', in Verbanck-Pierard, A. & Viviers, D. (eds), pp. 139–160

Wilson, D. M., 1984. *The Forgotten Collector: Augustus Wollaston Franks of the British Museum*, London, British Museum Publications

Wilson, T., 1987a. 'Maiolica in Renaissance Venice', *Apollo* 125, pp. 184–9

Wilson, T., 1987b. *Ceramic Art of the Renaissance*, London, British Museum Publications

Wilson, T., 1989. *Maiolica: Italian Renaissance Ceramics in the Ashmolean Museum*, Oxford

Wilson, T. (ed.), 1991. *Italian Renaissance Pottery: Papers written in association with a Colloquium at the British Museum*, London, British Museum Publications

Wilson, T., 1993. 'Il pittore di maioliche "Lu Ur", compagno e seguace di Francesco Xanto Avelli', *Fimantiquari* 2, pp. 19–31

Wilson, T., 1996. 'The beginnings of lustreware in Renaissance Italy', in *Handbook of the International Ceramics Fair and Seminar*, London, pp. 35–43

Winlock, H. E., 1941. 'Materials used at the embalming of King Tut-ankh-Amun', in *The Metropolitan Museum of Art Papers* 10, New York, pp. 10–11

Wirgin, J., 1970. *Sung Ceramic Designs*, Stockholm

Wood, D. A., Tanaka, T. & Chance, F., 1994. *Eight Hundred Years of Japanese Stoneware*, University of Washington Press

Wood, F., 1985. *Chinese Illustration*, London, British Library Publishing

Wood, N., 1994. 'Parallels between Yue wares and Koryo celadons', in *Papers of the British Association for Korean Studies*, vol. 5

Wood, N., forthcoming (1997). *Chinese Glazes: Their origins, chemistry and recreation*, London

Wood, N., Freestone, I. & Stapleton, C., 1995. 'Some technological parallels between Chinese Yue wares and Korean Koryo celadons', in Vincenzini, P. (ed.), *The Ceramics Cultural Heritage*, Faenza, Techna, pp. 175–82

Woods, A. J., 1986. 'Form, Fabric, and Function: Some observations on the cooking pot in antiquity', in Kingery, W. D. (ed.), pp. 157–72

Woods, A. J., 1993. 'Smoke gets in your eyes: patterns, variables and temperature measurement in open firings', *Bulletin of the Experimental Firing Group* 1, pp. 11–25

Woolley, C. L., 1934. 'The Prehistoric Pottery of Carchemish', *Iraq* 1, pp. 146–62

Woolley, C. L., 1956. *Ur Excavations Vol. IV: The Early Periods*, London

Woolley, C. L. & Mallowan, M., 1976. *Ur Excavations Vol. VII: The Old Babylonian Period*, London

Woolley, C. L., 1982. *Ur 'of the Chaldees'*, rev. edn, London

Wright, H. T., 1981. 'The Southern Margins of Sumer: Archaeological Survey of the Area of Eridu and Ur', in Adams, R. McC., pp. 295–345

Wright, R. P., 1986. 'The boundaries between technology and stylistic change', in Kingery, W. D. (ed.), pp. 1–20

Wulff, H. E., Wulff, H. S. & Koch, L., 1986. 'Egyptian faience: a possible survival in Iran'. *Archaeology* 21, pp. 98–107

Wyman, C., 1980. 'The early techniques of transfer printing', *Transactions of the English Ceramic Circle* 10, part 4, pp. 187–99

Xia Nai & Feng Xianming (eds), 1991. *Zhongguo meishu quanji: gongyi meishu bian 2 taoci: zhong* (An encyclopaedia of Chinese art: decorative arts), Shanghai

Yanagi, S., 1972. *The Unknown Craftsman*, Tokyo, Kodansha International

Yap, C. T. & Hua Younan, 1994. 'A study of Chinese porcelain raw materials for Ding, Xing, Gongxian and Dehua wares', *Archaeometry* 36, pp. 63–76

Yaseen, G. T., 1995. *Old Babylonian Pottery from the Hamrin: Tell Halawa*, London

Ye Zhimin, 1995. 'A Discussion of the Ding Ware Kilns', *Transactions of the Oriental Ceramic Society* 59 (1994/5), pp. 63–9

Yeivin, S., 1933. 'The Tombs Found at Seleucia (Seasons 1929–30 and 1931–32)', in Waterman, L., *Second Preliminary Report upon the Excavations at Tel Umar, Iraq*, Ann Arbor, MI, pp. 33–64, pls 14–23

Yelon, A., Saucier, A., Larocque, J.-P., Smith, P. E. L. & Vandiver, P., 1992. 'Thermal analysis of early neolithic pottery from Tepe Ganj Dareh, Iran', in Vandiver, P. B. et al (eds), pp. 591–608

Yeo, R., 1992. 'Nicaragua: a production potter's paradise', *Ceramic Review* 138, pp. 13–14

Young, T. C., 1965. 'A Comparative Ceramic Chronology for Western Iran, 1500–500 B.C.', *Iran* 3, pp. 53–85

Young, T. C., 1967. 'The Iranian migration into the Zagros', *Iran* 5, pp. 11–34

Young, T. C., 1985. 'Early Iron Age Iran revisited: preliminary suggestions for the re-analysis of old constructs', in *L'Indus aux Balkans: Recueil a la mémoire de Jean Deshayes*, Huot, J.-L., Yon, M. & Calvet, Y. (eds), Paris, pp. 361–78

Yu Jingxiu, 1993. *Huaxia wuqian nian yishu buneng buzhidao congshu: taoci ji* (A compendium of indispensible facts regarding five thousand years of Chinese art: ceramics), Tianjin

Yu Pei-chin, 1995. 'The Manufacture of Imperial Porcelains at Civilian Kilns and the Stylistic Impact on Late Ming Period Wares', *Orientations* 26, no. 9 (October), pp. 78–9

Yuan Nanzheng, 1988. 'Hefei chutu de ziding jincai ping' (A gold-decorated purple Ding bottle excavated in Hebei), *Wenwu* 1988.6, pp. 86–7

Yutaka Mino & K. Tsiang, 1980. *Freedom of Clay and Brush through Seven Centuries in Northern China: Tz'u chou Type Wares, 960–1600 AD*, Indianapolis

Zaccagnini, C., 1977. 'The merchant at Nuzi', *Iraq* 39, pp. 171–89

Zhang Fukang, 1985. 'The origin and development of traditional Chinese glazes and decorative ceramic colours', in Kingery, W. D. (ed.)

Zuidema, R. T., 1989. 'Lugares Sagrados e Irrigación: Tradicion Historica, Mitos y Rituales en el Cusco', in *Reyes y Guerreros: Ensayos de Cultura Andina*, Grandes Estudios Andinos, Lima

Zwalf, W. (ed.), 1985. *Buddhism*, London, British Museum Publications

Illustration References

British Museum inventory numbers are prefaced by the initials of the Department in whose collections the objects can be found: EA (Egyptian). Ethno (Ethnography). GR (Greek and Roman), JA (Japanese). MLA (Medieval & Later), OA (Oriental), PRB (Prehistoric & Romano-British), WA (Western Asiatic); illustrations including micrographs, radiographs and computer artwork have also been provided by SR (Scientific Research) and DO (Design Office). Photography by the British Museum Photographic Service (PS) unless otherwise noted.

Introduction

1 John & Andrew Van Rymsdyck, *Museum Britannicum*, 1778, pls XXVI. XXII
2 GR 1772.3-20.F284
3 MLA 1856,7-1,1566 B40
4 From series OA 1946.7-13.01 (1–24) (donated by Miss R. W. M. Giles)

Chapter 1

1 Illustration by Jim Thorn (MLA), based on sherd JA 1964.4-23,3c
2 JA 1964.4-23,5a; 8d; 4b; 3c; 6a (given by Tokyo National Museum)
3 JA 1956,7-16,1; OA+20
4 JA OA+686 (Siebold collection); OA+675; OA+633; OA+19; OA+654 (Siebold collection)
5 JA OA+668 (Siebold collection); OA+651 (Dr J. Anderson collection); OA+639 (Dr J. Anderson collection); OA+653 (Dr J. Anderson collection); OA+670 (Siebold collection)
6 JA F2238 (Gowland collection)

Chapter 2

1 Illustration by Claire Thorne (EA)
2 Illustration by Claire Thorne (EA), centre after Krzyzaniak (1996)
3 Photo D. A. Welsby
4 Sudan National Museum SNM.26.899. photo Jean-François Gout
5 Illustration by Claire Thorne (EA)
6 Illustration by Claire Thorne (EA)
7 Photo D. A. Welsby

Chapter 3

1 PRB 1892.9-1.232; 1892.9-1.240; 1958.5-6.556; WG 2285; 1893.4-26.8; P1982.1-1.86
2 PRB 1892.9-1.232
3 PRB 1921.3-15.1
4 After Howard (1981) and Smith (1965)

Chapter 4

1 WA 1932-12-12,378,423 K-L; 1924-4-16.8; 250; 251
2 Photo St John Simpson (WA)
3 WA 127615
4 WA 1924-4-16,24; 146; 68; 29; 124826A; 124109; 124103; 124101; 1924-9-20,43B; 436; 135314; 135315; 1924-9-20.417; 115327; 1934-2-10,229; 190; 247; 212; 258; 118; 1920-12-11.157
5 WA 122883; 1855-12-5,368; 1930-12-13,350; 1919-10-11.4615

Chapter 5

1 EA 62201
2 EA 27754; 58222; 30934; 49022
3 EA 62414
4 EA 30898; 49045
5 EA 47996; 26636
6 EA 30891; 30883; 30886

Chapter 6

1 WA 123545
2 WA 139451; 134525; 1935-12-7.20; 1930-12-13,299; 1919-11-11,526; 535; 536; 117973; 1932-12-10,106; 1937-12-11,225; 121923; 1932-12-10,133; 145; 143
3 WA 1992-3-2,29; 137294; 138319; 1992-3-2,14; 92494; 1992-3-2,134; 167; 1994-11-5,149; 116377; 123250; 1992-3-2,178; 1984-5-12,25; 26; 27; 32; 34; 36; 37; 52; 56; 58; 61
4 WA 92902; 1923-11-10,85; 139111; 120902; 126429; 126421; 141471; 129764
5 Photo J. E. Curtis (WA)

Chapter 7

1 Illustration by Tony Simpson (SR)
2 Illustration by Karen Hughes (PRB)
3 Photo by I. C. Freestone (SR)
4 Illustration by Karen Hughes (PRB)
5 PRB 1976.5-1.270; 603
6 PRB 1976.5-1.89; 919; 835; 603; 1883.12-13.228

Chapter 8

1 After Simpson (1993)
2 EA 22194; 22220
3 After Soukiassian et al (1990)
4 EA 58275; 50748
5 EA 58038; 58032
6 EA 5275

Chapter 9

1 WA 1980.12-14.2259; 2261; 2260; 2262; 2253; 2254; 2250; 2249; 2248; 2252; 2251; 2255
2 Lachish Archive (WA)
3 Lachish Archive (WA)
4 WA 1980.12-14.2066; 2068; 2072; 3230; 2077; 2076; 2078
5 WA 1980.12-14.2277; 2084; 2299g; 1803
6 WA 1980.12-14.2429; 2068; 2078; 2076; 2077

Chapter 10

1 WA 92004
2 WA E.37452
3 WA 92394B; 92386; N.1677; 120451; 118373; 92094
4 WA 92008; E.62979; 141463; 56-9-3,1346; 1337; 92105
5 WA N.1806

Chapter 11

1 JA 1958,10-23,103 (given by R. S. Jenyns); 1987,6-2,1; OA+806
2 JA F2227 (Gowland collection)
3 JA 1958,10-21,1 (given by Mrs Walter Sedgwick)
4 JA F1889 (given by Sir A. W. Franks)
5 JA 1992,4-7,1

Chapter 12

1 GR 1921.5-15.32 (Vase A425)
2 GR 1912.5-22.1
3 GR 1847.11-25.18 (Vase B432)
4 GR 1873.8-20.277 (Vase E784)
5 GR 1892.7-18.9 (Vase D15)
6 GR 1842.7-28.848 (Vase G98)

Chapter 13

1 MLA 1853,3-15,1; 1874.11-1,1 (Hobson B86)
2 MLA 1910,5-5,4; 1915,12-8,192; 191; 1856,7-1,1566 (Hobson B40)
3 MLA 1985,11-1,411; 1855,10-29,11 (Hobson B119); 1868,3-18,10 (Hobson B30)
4 MLA 1926,4-28,251
5 MLA 1867,3-20,38 (Hobson B76); 37 (Hobson B75); 35 (Hobson B73); 36 (Hobson B74)
6 Illustration by Jim Farrant (MLA)

Chapter 14

1 After Adams (1990)
2 OA 1936.10-12.202
3 OA 1973.7-26.391
4 OA 1931.6-18.1
5 OA 1938.5-24.763
6 OA 1974.10-31.1; 1936.10-12.19

Chapter 15

1 EA 35028
2 EA 67970
3 EA 22818; 65359; 26226
4 GR 1860.4-4.75; 94
5 GR 1875.11-10.2 (Vase K1); 1856.12-26.192 (Vase K76)
6 GR 1980.10-17.1; 1908.10-15.66

Chapter 16

1 OA 1951.10-9.1
2 OA 1923.7-26.6, OA+6223
3 OA 1920.3-26.1
4 OA G.1983.395 (Godman bequest)
5 OA 1992.8-6.1
6 OA G.1983.197 (Godman bequest); OA 1978.12-30.574-5 (Henderson bequest)

Chapter 17

1 Victoria and Albert Museum, London, 1717-1855
2 National Art Library, London; facsimile (p.35) courtesy Scolar Press
3 National Art Library, London; facsimile (p.197) courtesy Scolar Press
4 MLA 1855,12-1,74; 1895,12-20,2 (given by A. W. Franks)
5 MLA 1878,12-30,426; 1898,10-19,37; 1953,2-3,22; 1898,10-19,18; 1898,10-19,38
6 MLA 1970,12-11,1; 1855,3-13,12 (given by A. W. Franks)
7 MLA 1855,12-1,69; 1851,12-1,20

235

Chapter 18
1 Illustration by Jim Thorn (MLA)
2 Kunstkammer, Kunsthistorisches Museum, Vienna, KK5105
3 MLA 1887,6-17,43; 1855,12-1,211; 138; 1894,3-9,31; 1855,12-1,145; 179; 1887,2-11,10; 1865,12-20,122
4 MLA 1994,6-2,1
5 Rheinisches Amt für Bodendenkmalplege, Bonn
6 Photos K. Heinz-Fischer

Chapter 19
1 Illustration by Jim Thorn (MLA) after Grigsby (1993, figs 5–13)
2 MLA 1925,4-10,1; D24; D36
3 MLA D1
4 MLA 1996,11-2,1 (purchased by BM Society)
5 MLA D51; 1973,6-11
6 MLA 1914,4-1,1

Chapter 20
1 Photo J. Hudson (Ethno)
2 Photo J. Hudson (Ethno)
3 Ethno 1992,Af.1.8
4 Ethno 1973,Af.28.13
5 Ethno 1979,Af.1.1
6 Photo N. Barley (Ethno)

Chapter 21
1 Photo MM039808 (PS)
2 Photo MM039809/B (PS)
3 Photo MM039809/A (PS)
4 Photo N. Barley (Ethno)
5 Photo N. Barley (Ethno)
6 Photo N. Barley (Ethno)

Chapter 22
1 MLA OA233; 1937,11-11,9; 1891,6-24,27
2 MLA 1964,7-2,370; 1873,3-10,14; 1893,7-16,26; 1930,5-11,45
3 Illustration by Jim Thorn (MLA) after Hamerow (1993)
4 © Field Archaeology Division, Norfolk Museums Service, 1012ELN/839
5 Photo Pete Stringer (PS)
6 Illustration by Jim Thorn (MLA)

Chapter 23
1 Illustration by Paul Goodhead (DO)
2 WA 1995-6-22.6 (presented by Mr E. Litthauer); 134874; 131441; 1995-6-22.8 (presented by Mr E. Litthauer)
3 WA 131079; 131118; 136184; 131077; 136162; 136093
4 WA 132973
5 WA 136794
6 WA 135291; 131062; 131068; 131022; 123308; 128603; 131063; 131092
7 WA 135947; 135948; 135950; 135952

Chapter 24
1 Photos by Kate Warren
2 PRB 1861.3-1.2; 1861.3-1.3; 1852.4-19.1; P1973.4-3.190; 71
3 Illustration by I. C. Freestone (SR)
4 Photo I. C. Freestone (SR)
5 Illustration by Tony Simpson (SR)

Chapter 25
1 GR 1772.3-6.64 (Bailey 1980, Q757, Hamilton collection); 1856.12-26.484 (Bailey 1980, Q1206, bequeathed by Sir William Temple); 1814.7-4.178 (Bailey 1980, Q1169, Townley collection); 1927.7-12.1 (Bailey 1988, Q2284, given by Mrs T. Stevenson); 1980.10-1.85 (Bailey 1988, Q2483); PRB 1856.7-1.358 (Bailey 1988, Q1605, Roach Smith collection)
2 GR 1868.8-4.2 (Bailey 1988, Q3252, given by J. Henderson); 1842.7-28.902 (Bailey 1988, Q3268, Burgon collection); MLA Sl. 591 (Bailey 1988, Q1816, Sloane collection); GR 1756.1-1.1046 (Bailey 1980, Q1261, Sloane collection); 1756.1-1.1057 (Bailey 1980, Q1266, Sloane collection); 1970.12-28.1 (Bailey 1980, Q1264, given by D. E. Strong)
3 GR 1859.12-26.592 (Bailey 1988, Q2983); 1963.7-15.54 (Bailey 1975, Q105, bequeathed by F. W. Robins)
4 GR 1975.1-29.1 (Bailey 1988, Q1753); 1987.4-2.6 (Bailey 1996, Q1958 bis)
5 GR 1867.11-22.333 (Bailey 1975, Q181); 1886.4-1.1366 (Bailey 1988, Q2102, given by the Egypt Exploration Fund); 1850.5-30.1 (Bailey 1988, Q3262)
6 GR 1926.2-16.127 (Bailey 1988, Q3039); 1971.4-26.54 (Bailey 1988, Q3038)

Chapter 26
1 Photo T. Richard Blurton (OA)
2 Ethno 1985.As.15.12; 1984.As.23.10; 2
3 Photo T. Richard Blurton (OA)
4 Ethno 1985.As.15.3
5 Photo T. Richard Blurton (OA)
6 Photo T. Richard Blurton (OA)

Chapter 27
1 Illustration by Jude Simmons (DO)
2 Ethno 1938-20
3 Ethno 1970.Am.8.1
4 Illustration by Hans Rashbrook (Ethno) after Donnan (1992, fig. 22)
5 Ethno 1921.10-27.28
6 Ethno 1938.5-7.2, illustration by Hans Rashbrook (Ethno)
7 Ethno 1971.Am.6.1
8 Ethno 82.110-14.17
9 Ethno 1938.5-7.2, illustration by Hans Rashbrook (Ethno)
10 Ethno 1909.12-18.30

Chapter 28
1 OA 1936.10-12.245; 1926.4-21.1
2 OA 1947.7-12.62 (Oppenheim Bequest)
3 OA 1936.10-12.266
4 OA 1937.7-16.52
5 OA 1936.10-12.26 (bought with the help of public subscription from the Eumorfopoulos collection)
6 OA 1926.3-19.13; 1947.7-12.61 (Oppenheim Bequest)

Chapter 29
1 Illustration by Sue Bird (GR)
2 GR 1931.5-14.1; 1873.8-20.332; 1849.6-20.8 (Vase G186); 1904.2-4.758 (Vase M137); 1856.12-26.584 (Vase K25)
3 GR 1756.5-9.507; 1928.1-17.71
4 GR 1869.2-5.4 (Vase L54)
5 GR 1896.12-17.10 (Vase L91); 1900.7-26.1 (Vase L95); 1857.8-4.22 (Vase E46); 1814.7-4.1100 (Vase L154); 1919.7-18.24
6 GR 1973.6-14.15 (Vase M100); 1869.2-5.5 (Vase M4); 1888.9-30.1 (Vase M62)
7 GR 1994.7-20.6; 1920.11-18.25; 1994.5-19.1; MLA 1928.4-13.8

Chapter 30
1 OA 1936.10-12.153 (bought with the help of public subscription from the Eumorfopoulos collection)
2 OA 1968.4-22.26 (bequeathed by Mrs Walter Sedgwick)
3 OA 1968.4-22.41 (bequeathed by Mrs Walter Sedgwick)
4 OA 1936.4-13.9.10 (bequeathed by Reginald R. Cory)
5 OA 1936.4-13.26 (bequeathed by Reginald R. Cory)
6 OA 1991.5-29.1

Chapter 31
1 MLA Porc. Cat. V.12; 1981,1-1,271; Porc. Cat. XIV.24; 1959,11-2.78; Porc. Cat. X.10; 1959,11-2,108; on loan from Newcastle-under-Lyme Museum
2 Illustration by Jim Farrant (MLA)
3 MLA Pot. Cat. S.7a; 1891,5-16,1; 1919,5-3,114
4 MLA Pot. Cat. G.30; Pot. Cat. O.5; 1981,1-1,48
5 MLA 1909,12-1,118; Pot. Cat. K.29; 1909,12-1,440; 1909,12-1,41; Pot. Cat. K.14; Pot. Cat. G.40
6 MLA 1919,5-3,61; 1957,12-1,11; 1919,5-3,71; 1919,5-3,10; 1919,5-30,30; 1938,3-14,92
7 MLA 1923,1-22,59; 1909,12-1,453; Pot. Cat. H.41; 1909,12-1,481; Pot. Cat. K.4; 1909,12-1,446

Chapter 32
1 Courtesy *Ceramic Review*
2 Courtesy *Ceramic Review*
3 Courtesy *Ceramic Review*
4 Courtesy *Ceramic Review*
5 Photo Simon Birkett
6 Courtesy *Ceramic Review*
7 Courtesy *Ceramic Review*

Orientation Map
Illustration by Tony Simpson (SR)

Index

References to figures and to text within boxes are indicated by page numbers in *italics*.